THE 3-D BOOK OF Dinosaurs

INDEX

This edition published 1998 for
Index Direct Book Supplies
Henson Way
Kettering
Northants NN16 8PX

ISBN 0-7489-5301-9

Packaged by De Agostini Rights/DP-MEB

Printed in the Czech Republic

TYRANNOSAURUS REX

***Tyrannosaurus rex* was the biggest meat-eating dinosaur that ever lived on Earth and was probably one of the fiercest.**

T *rex* was about as long as four cars, as tall as the tallest giraffe, and weighed about the same as an African elephant. The head of a tall man would have come half way up its thigh. No one knows exactly the sort of noises *T rex* made, but it may have roared or squealed to call its young and to keep in touch with other members of its group.

HUGE FEET

Each of its back feet would have covered four of these pages and had three long claws at the front and one at the back. Its front legs were quite small and high up on its body. They ended in what looked like small 'hands' with two thin, clawed fingers. No one knows for certain what these front legs were used for, but they may have been used to grip prey. They were not even long enough to reach its mouth to push food in. Some experts, though, have suggested that *T rex* used its front legs to heave itself up on to its back legs after it had been resting or sleeping on the ground.

18 CM THE LENGTH OF ONE T REX TOOTH

Thick, powerful neck, to move heavy head when twisting and tearing the flesh of its victim

Strong, thick skull, to take the strain when *T rex's* massive jaws bit into prey

Teeth slightly curved backwards, to grip prey

Saw-like teeth, 18cm long

1.2m

BIG HEAD

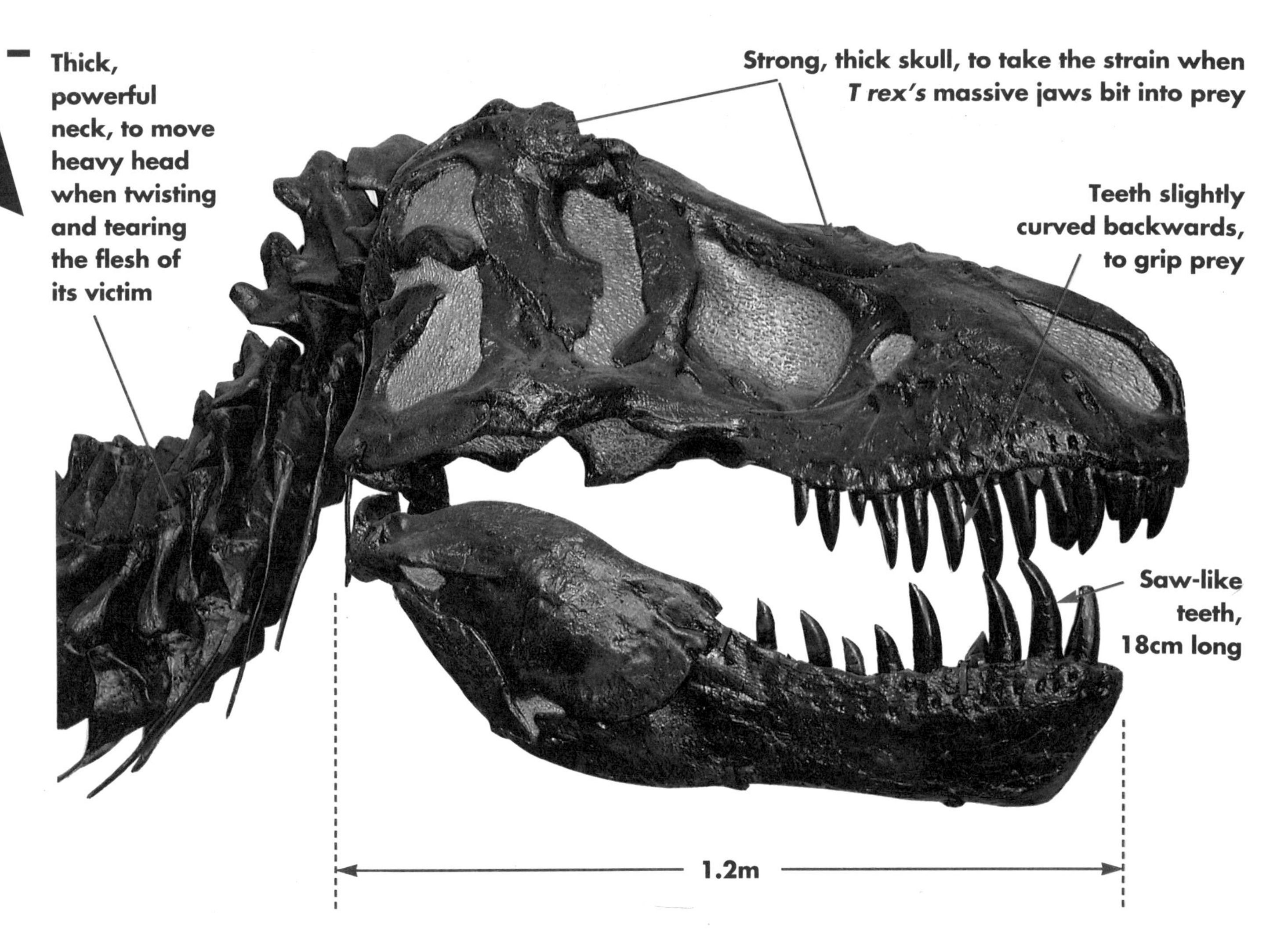

Its heavy head was about 1.2m long, held up by a short, strong neck. *Tyrannosaurus* also had huge jaws, big enough to swallow a human being whole. Its rows of sharp teeth were slightly curved to get a better grip on its prey. Like a shark, once *Tyrannosaurus* had bitten into its prey, the victim had no chance of sliding out of its mouth and getting away. If any teeth were broken off in a fight, they may have grown again.

MONSTER FACTS

- **NAME:** *Tyrannosaurus rex* (ty-ran-oh-saw-rus-reks) means 'king of the tyrant reptiles'
- **SIZE:** 14m long and 5.6m high
- **FOOD:** meat, especially other dinosaurs
- **LIVED:** about 67 million years ago in the Cretaceous Period in North America, China and possibly South America and India

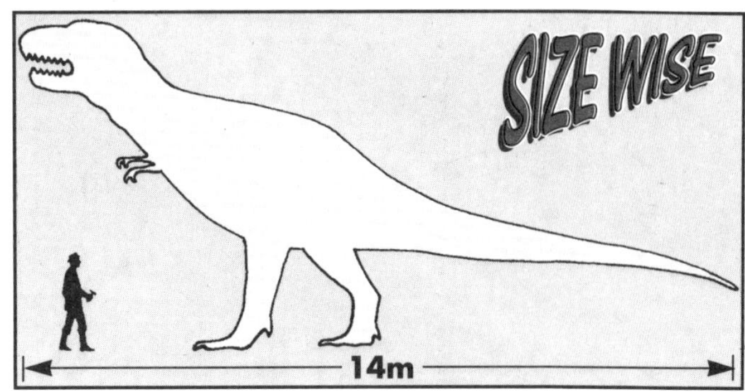

WALKING TALL

Walking upright on its powerful back legs, *Tyrannosaurus* balanced its huge body with its long, thick tail. With its enormous legs, it could run very fast, but it was probably too big and heavy to move quickly for a long time, like hunting dogs do today. Instead, *T rex* may have relied on ambushing its prey in the thick trees and ferns. Some experts think that *Tyrannosaurus* may have hunted in packs, surrounding other dinosaurs, such as a herd of plant-eating *Triceratops* or *Edmontosaurus*, so that they could not escape. Scientists think that it may also have eaten carrion (dead dinosaurs), and perhaps any dying or helpless young dinosaurs that it came across.

IT'S A FACT

T REX DISCOVERED

In 1902, part of a huge skeleton was uncovered in Montana, USA. Later, another was found in Wyoming, also in the USA. From these bones the American palaeontologist Henry Fairfield Osborn drew up the first picture of this giant creature. He named it *Tyrannosaurus rex* (meaning 'king of the tyrant reptiles') because it was the biggest meat-eating dinosaur then known to have lived on Earth.

POWERFUL FIGHTERS

Many dinosaurs were very large, but they had trouble defending themselves against *Tyrannosaurus*. They did not have the teeth or claws to put up a real fight, but some were protected by tough, armour-plated skins, thick bony plates around their necks or long, sharp horns on their heads. Others were small and light, and could run fast enough to escape.

AVACERATOPS

***Avaceratops* was about as long as a mini car and sturdily built, like a miniature tank.**

This dinosaur had a bony frill, like a collar, around its neck and a short horn on its nose. The horn was probably used to protect it from much larger meat-eating dinosaurs.

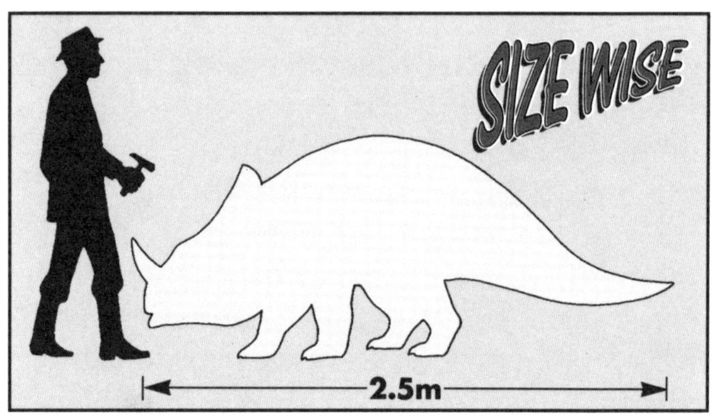

MONSTER FACTS

- **NAME:** *Avaceratops* (a-va-serra-tops), 'ceratops' means 'horned face'
- **SIZE:** about 2.5m long and 1m high
- **FOOD:** low-growing plants
- **LIVED:** between about 100 – 66 million years ago in the late Cretaceous Period, in North America

BEAK LIKE A PARROT

Avaceratops was a plant-eater. It chopped off the stems with its special mouth, which was rather like a parrot's beak. *Avaceratops* then sliced up the woody parts of the plants with rows of sharp teeth at the back of its jaws.

STRONG LEGS

It is possible that *Avaceratops* could run quite fast on its four well-muscled legs. As it ran, it balanced itself with its heavy tail which it held off the ground.

JUST ONE SKELETON

So far, only part of one skeleton of *Avaceratops* has been discovered. It was found in 1981 in Montana USA. It was not named until 1988.

LIVING IN HERDS

Some scientists think that these animals may have lived in large herds, roaming the North American plains.

DICRAEOSAURUS

Dicraeosaurus was a peaceful plant-eater as big as a medium-sized truck.

Deep in the thick forests of tree-ferns, conifers (trees that have cones) and palms, *Dicraeosaurus* wandered about eating plants and seeds. This tall dinosaur had a long thin neck, a thin, whippy tail and long, pencil-like teeth at the front of its jaws.

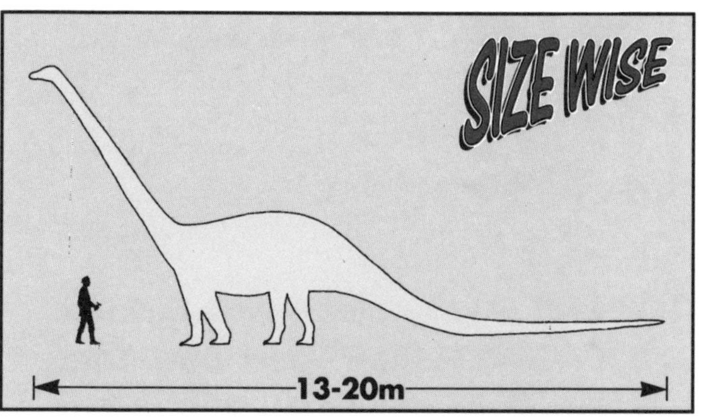

MONSTER FACTS

- **NAME:** *Dicraeosaurus* (die-cray-oh-saw-rus), called 'forked lizard' because of the forked spines in each of its backbones
- **SIZE:** up to 6m tall and 13 – 20m long
- **FOOD:** plants
- **LIVED:** about 195 – 141 million years ago, in the Jurassic Period, in East Africa

SMALL HEAD

Dicraeosaurus had a small head for its size. Its eyes and nostrils were also small. As a plant-eater, it must have been attacked by the large meat-eating dinosaurs. It had no armour or sharp claws to defend itself, but it may have used its tail as a whip lash. Scientists think *Dicraeosaurus* may also have been able to move fast enough to run away from its enemies when threatened by them.

DISCOVERING DICRAEOSAURUS

A huge discovery of dinosaur bones was made in 1907 in Tanzania, East Africa. It seems that many dinosaurs died near the mouth of a river and their bodies were washed on to mud banks. Some of the bones that were dug up belonged to dinosaurs that had not been discovered before. Among them was *Dicraeosaurus,* although it was not called this until 1935.

When did dinosaurs live?

The Earth is very old. It was formed about 4,500 million years ago. The first dinosaurs appeared 220 million years ago. But how long ago is that?

It is hard to imagine such huge amounts of time. It seems as if the dinosaurs lived at the very beginning of time, but, in fact, the Earth existed for billions of years before the Age of the Dinosaurs.

HOW LONG DID DINOSAURS RULE THE EARTH?

Dinosaurs lived on Earth for about 160 million years. That is an extremely long time. Humans have only existed for 3 million years, so we have a long way to go before we are as successful as dinosaurs.

THE CHANGING EARTH

Since the Earth was formed it has changed a great deal. The land masses, seas and climate changed, so did the animals and plants. Even the dinosaurs changed (evolved). Many different kinds of dinosaurs evolved during the time that they lived on Earth.

The skyscraper of time

If you imagine that the time since the world began is like this towering skyscraper, it will help you to understand when the dinosaurs lived. Start at the bottom and work your way to the top. The Earth was formed on the ground floor of this skyscraper. Look how near the top of the block the dinosaurs appear. Humans are so recent that they only just manage to get on to the flag on the very top of the building.

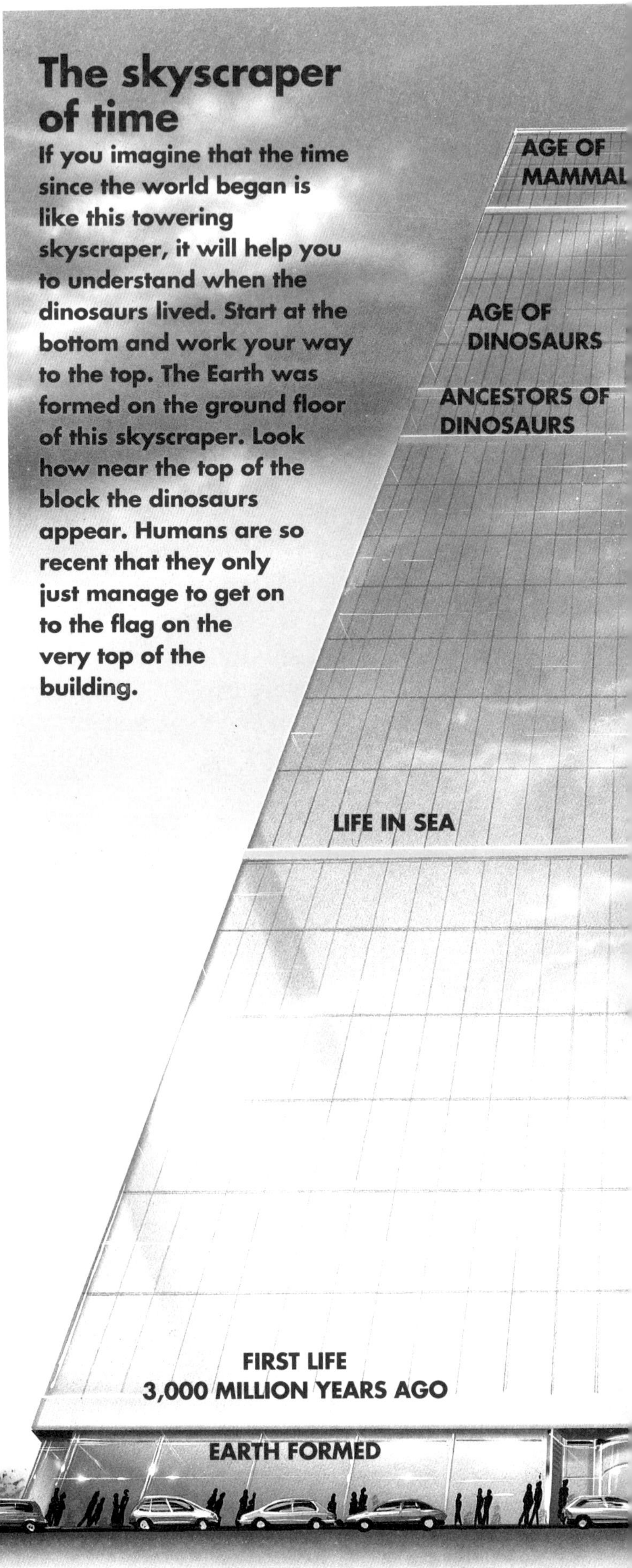

HUMANS
3 MILLION YEARS AGO

Woolly mammoth

OM
MYA

Allosaurus

220 - 66
MYA

245 MILLION
YEARS AGO

Thecodont

Dinichthys

Jellyfish and shellfish

Worms

600 MILLION YEARS AGO

Blue-greens and algae

Single-cell creatures

FIRST LIFE
3,000 MILLION YEARS AGO

4,500 MILLION YEARS AGO

IT'S A FACT

DINOSAUR EGGS

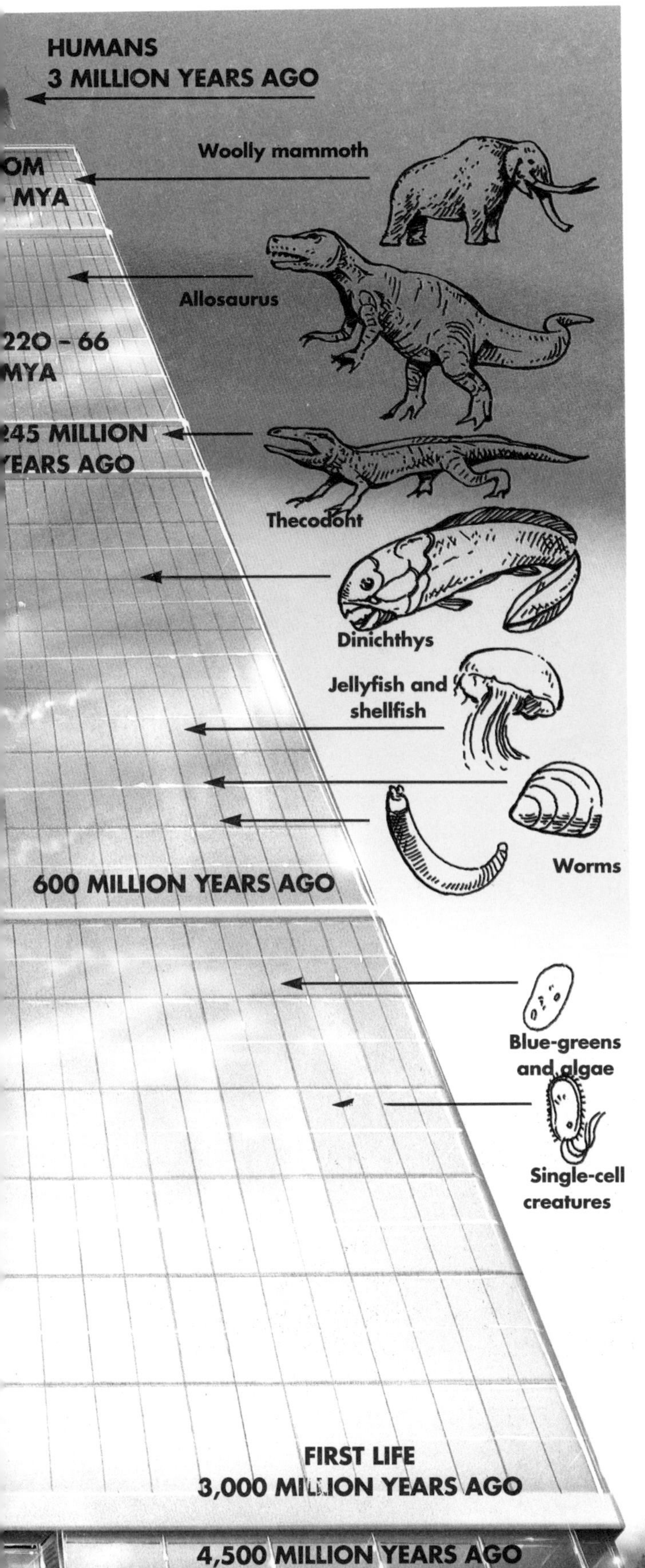

Dinosaurs laid eggs with hard shells. The shell protected the baby dinosaur inside and contained its own private pond where the young could grow in safety.

THE SECRETS OF DINOSAUR SUCCESS

Dinosaurs were a great success of the animal kingdom, they lasted for about 160 million years because:

- They adapted to the world around them.
- They had scaly, waterproof skin. The overlapping scales kept the dinosaur dry and protected it.
- They laid hard-shelled eggs which helped many young to survive.
- Dinosaurs could walk on land more easily than many of the other animals of the time, so they could find food and escape from enemies quickly.
- Some dinosaurs ate plants and some ate meat. This meant that there was usually enough food to go round.

Life before dinosaurs

Dinosaurs were not the first living things. Life began billions of years before them with the simplest living thing – the single cell. Gradually animals with many cells, such as reptiles and mammals, evolved.

1 FIRST LIFE 3,000 MYA [MILLION YEARS AGO]

The first living things on Earth were very simple, single-celled forms of life. There were bacteria and a type of algae called blue-greens. Fossils of blue-greens and bacteria have been found in rocks 3,000 million years old. These hot springs in Yellowstone Park, North America (right), contain bacteria and simple algae. Perhaps this scene is similar to 3,000 million years ago when life began.

1

2 LIFE IN THE SEA 600 – 530 MYA

Before fish, the seas were home to other creatures. Many of them were like sea animals that live today. There were jellyfish, shellfish called brachiopods and many sorts of sea worms. One type of animal that hasn't survived is the trilobite. Trilobites were sea creatures with hard bodies like armour, which were jointed so that they could move. They had legs like those of shrimps. To protect themselves some could curl up into a ball, rather like a woodlouse.

3 LEAFLESS PLANTS & INSECTS 410 – 380 MYA

The first plants were leafless and flowerless and no more than 4 or 5cm tall. They lived on boggy ground. Through this miniature jungle, scorpions hunted millipedes that fed on the plants.

9 THE AGE OF THE DINOSAURS BEGINS 220 MYA

8 DINOSAUR ANCESTOR 245 MYA

Archosaur reptiles, some of which were rather like modern crocodiles, were among the animals on Earth. Some, such as *Euparkeria*, may have have been the ancestors of the dinosaurs.

7 FLYING INSECTS, TOWERING FORESTS 300 MYA

Through huge forests flew the first flying insects such as dragonflies. Some of these had vast wingspans up to 70cm across. They were the largest flying insects ever to exist.

6 REPTILES RULE 310 MYA

There were more reptiles on land than amphibians. Scientists think that one group of reptiles were the ancestors of mammals. *Dimetrodon* belonged to this group.

5 AMPHIBIANS RULE 370 – 280 MYA

Amphibians live on land and in water, where they lay their eggs. Amphibians evolved from fish. At this time in history amphibians were very successful. Some amphibians were quite big. *Ichthyostega* was about 1m long. It looked a bit like a fish and had scales and a fin, but it had legs and could walk on land, although it spent most of its time in water.

4 FISH TEEM IN THE SEA 390 MYA

The first animals with backbones were fish. It is thought that sometime during this period *Eusthenopteron,* a fish that used its front fins to help it 'walk', crawled out of the water to live on land. It was the ancestor of land animals.

3-D Gallery

CERATOSAURUS

- A horned dinosaur
- Lived 150 - 135 million years ago in North America
- Measured 6m from head to tail
- Ate meat

3-D Gallery 2

STEGOSAURUS

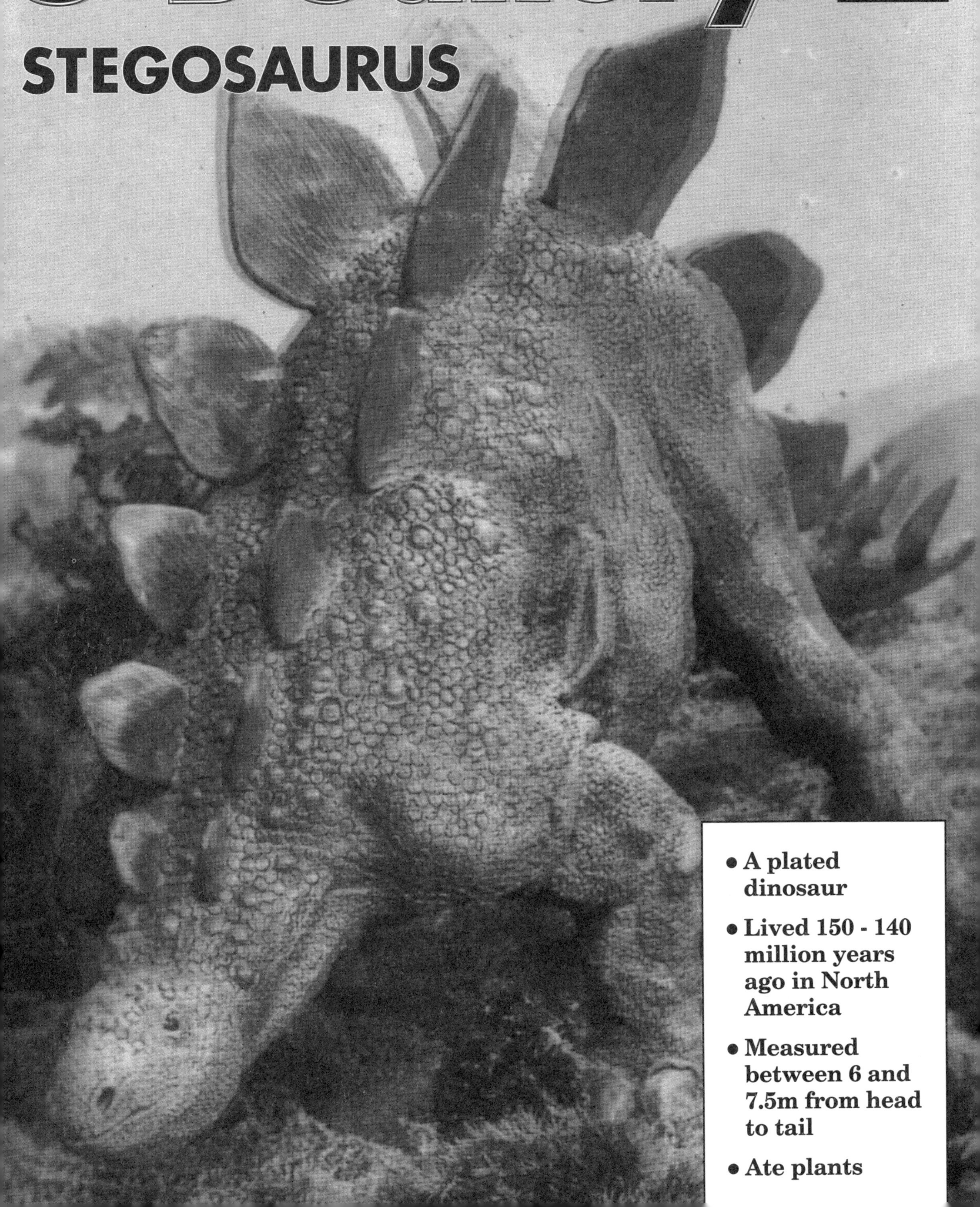

- A plated dinosaur
- Lived 150 - 140 million years ago in North America
- Measured between 6 and 7.5m from head to tail
- Ate plants

GIANTS OF THE PAST

A battle to the death rages on the plains. *T rex* bares its teeth and prepares to pounce on its prey, *Ankylosaurus*. Although it is much smaller, the heavily-armoured plant-eater may have a chance of beating *Tyrannosaurus*. One well-aimed swipe with its tail club could cripple *T rex*, perhaps breaking a leg and bringing the huge king of the tyrant replies crashing to the ground.

TYRANNOSAURUS REX

How to spot a dinosaur

Millions of years ago, long before humans walked on this planet, one of the most extraordinary animals ever ruled the Earth – the dinosaur.

Dinosaurs are among the most successful animals that have ever lived. Some dinosaurs were harmless and ate plants. Others were ruthless hunters with vicious teeth who caught their prey then slashed into their bodies with razor-sharp teeth before eating their flesh.

SPECIAL REPTILES

All dinosaurs were reptiles. They lived on land, and most laid eggs with hard shells. They had tough scaly skin and claws of some sort. Reptiles cannot make their own body heat, they have to rely on the air around them to make them warm or to cool them down. Some scientists now think that some dinosaurs were 'warm-blooded' – that they could make their own heat inside their bodies, just as mammals do.

So what made dinosaurs different from other reptiles? Their legs were tucked straight under their bodies, not sticking out to the side like the legs of other reptiles. They could walk and move about much more easily than other reptiles who had to drag their bodies along the ground as they walked, which made movement more difficult. Dinosaurs walked in a more upright way, either on two or on four legs and although some moved quite slowly, other dinosaurs could run very fast indeed.

A dinosaur's legs were straight and upright like this:

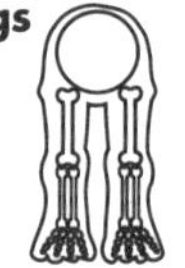

Other reptiles' legs stick out at the side, like this:

A REPTILE

Today's reptiles include lizards, crocodiles, alligators, snakes, tortoises and turtles.

Reptiles do not have a 'central heating system'. They cannot control the heat inside their bodies as mammals, such as humans, can. If the air is cold, their blood is cold, but if the air is warm, their blood is warm.

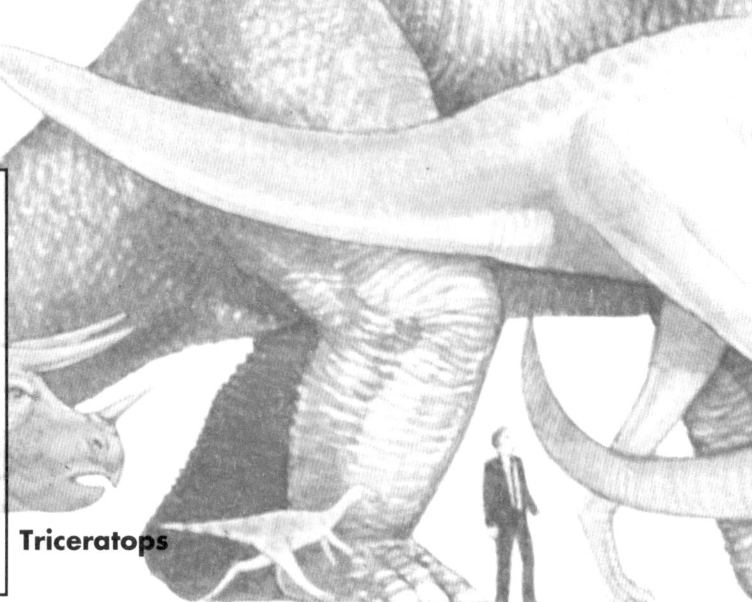

Triceratops

Ornitholestes

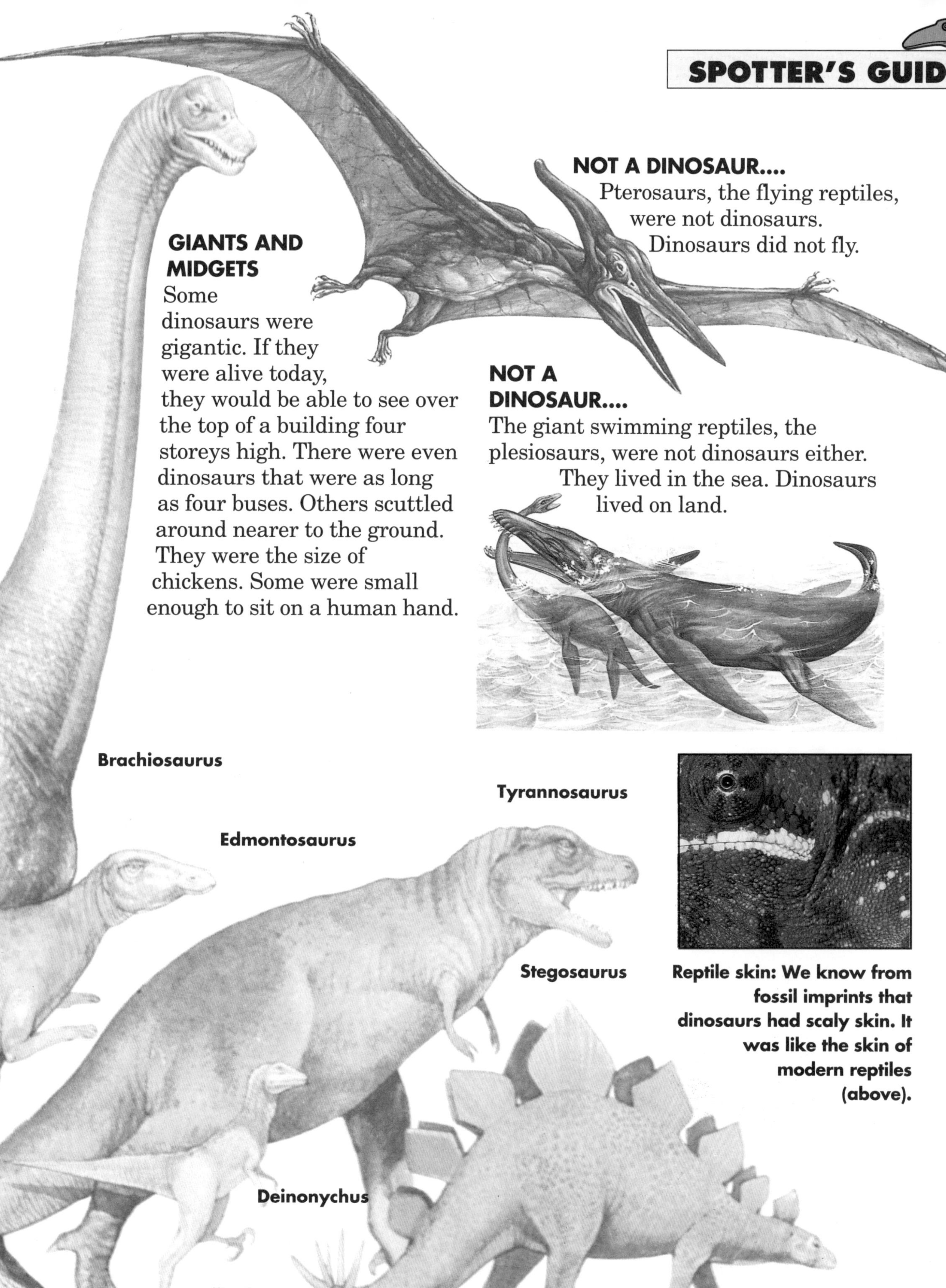

NOT A DINOSAUR....
Pterosaurs, the flying reptiles, were not dinosaurs. Dinosaurs did not fly.

GIANTS AND MIDGETS
Some dinosaurs were gigantic. If they were alive today, they would be able to see over the top of a building four storeys high. There were even dinosaurs that were as long as four buses. Others scuttled around nearer to the ground. They were the size of chickens. Some were small enough to sit on a human hand.

NOT A DINOSAUR....
The giant swimming reptiles, the plesiosaurs, were not dinosaurs either. They lived in the sea. Dinosaurs lived on land.

Reptile skin: We know from fossil imprints that dinosaurs had scaly skin. It was like the skin of modern reptiles (above).

The world's biggest detective story

Dinosaurs died out millions of years before the first humans appeared on Earth. So how do we know that these incredible reptiles ever existed?

We know about dinosaurs because about 160 years ago several people who studied rocks and fossils found some clues and began to piece together the evidence, just as detectives do. The first clue they found is on this page. Follow this and the other clues and try your hand at being a dinosaur detective.

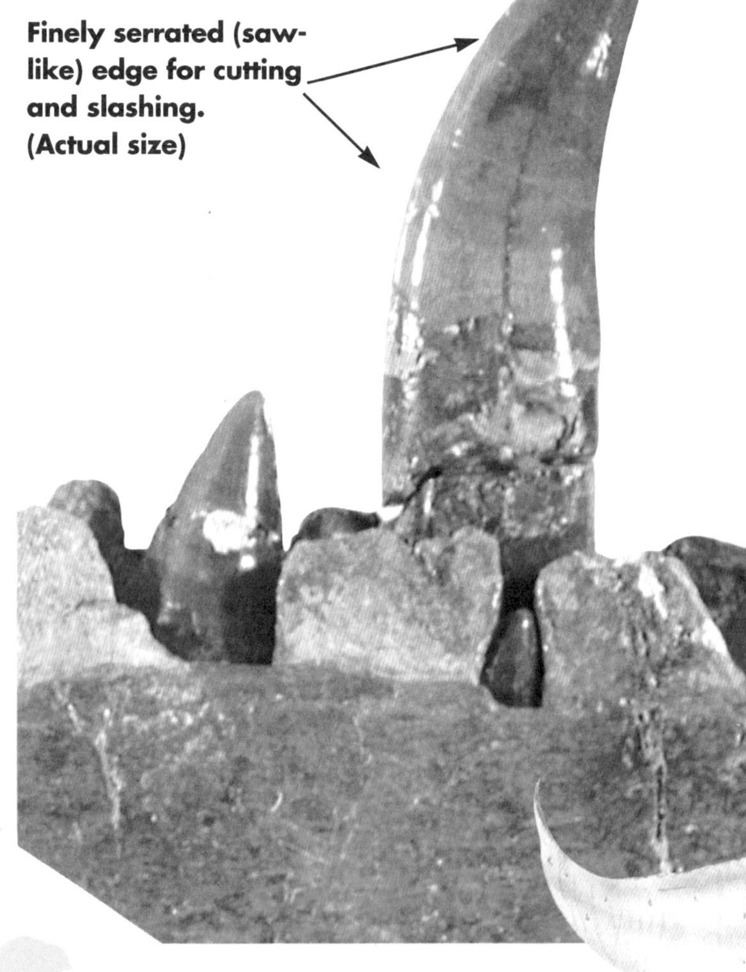

Finely serrated (saw-like) edge for cutting and slashing. (Actual size)

CLUE 1 If you found this large, pointed object (right) amongst some rocks what would you think it was? This is its actual size. It is curved, it has a serrated (saw-like) edge, it feels like a piece of rock but it looks more like part of an animal – a claw, or maybe a tooth. Yes, that's what it is, an enormous tooth.

CLUE 2 The tooth is so large that it must have belonged to an enormous animal. The biggest land animal is an elephant. Could it have belonged to an elephant? The answer is no, because this tooth is designed for cutting and tearing flesh – and elephants don't eat meat.

Is it true that a tooth was the first clue to the existence of dinosaurs?

Yes, it is true that the first clue that dinosaurs had existed was a tooth. In 1824 William Buckland, a professor of Geology (the study of rocks), carried out the detective work on a large tooth that was found in a slate quarry in Oxfordshire. It was Buckland who gave the name *Megalosaurus* to the dinosaur that once owned the giant tooth. *Megalosaurus* was the first dinosaur to be named. When the teeth were found, they were still firmly fixed into the animal's jaw-bone.

CLUE 3

Question: What's big and eats meat? Answer: Tigers are the largest meat-eaters. So did the tooth belong to a tiger? Possibly. But wait a bit, here's another clue. This tooth is not the same shape as a tiger's. This tooth is the right shape for cutting and slashing.

A tiger's tooth has a smooth edge and is designed for stabbing. Our tooth didn't belong to a tiger, or a lion. So what did it belong to?

CLUE 4

In fact, this tooth is very like the teeth of meat-eating reptiles. The largest one alive today is the Komodo dragon, a 3m long monitor lizard that lives in Indonesia. Therefore the tooth must have belonged to a meat-eating reptile, but it is too big to belong to a modern lizard. So it must have belonged to a very large reptile, probably at least 9m long.

GOT IT!

But no such creature exists today. However, the tooth was found in rocks millions of years old and is, itself, a fossil. So it must have belonged to a huge meat-eating reptile that lived and died millions of years ago. It did. It belonged to a dinosaur called *Megalosaurus,* which means 'giant reptile'.

Megalosaurus

What is a fossil?

Fossils are often the only clues to animals and plants that lived millions of years ago. But how were they made?

Fossils are the remains or prints of animals and plants that have been preserved in rocks. Quite often, only the hard parts of an animal, such as the teeth or bones, are left. The rest has rotted away. But even when nothing remains of an animal, it may have left a hollow, the exact shape of its body, in the rock. Sometimes an animal left a footprint when it walked in soft sand or mud. A single footprint may be all that remains of an animal that was as big as four cars. Fossils can take millions of years to form.

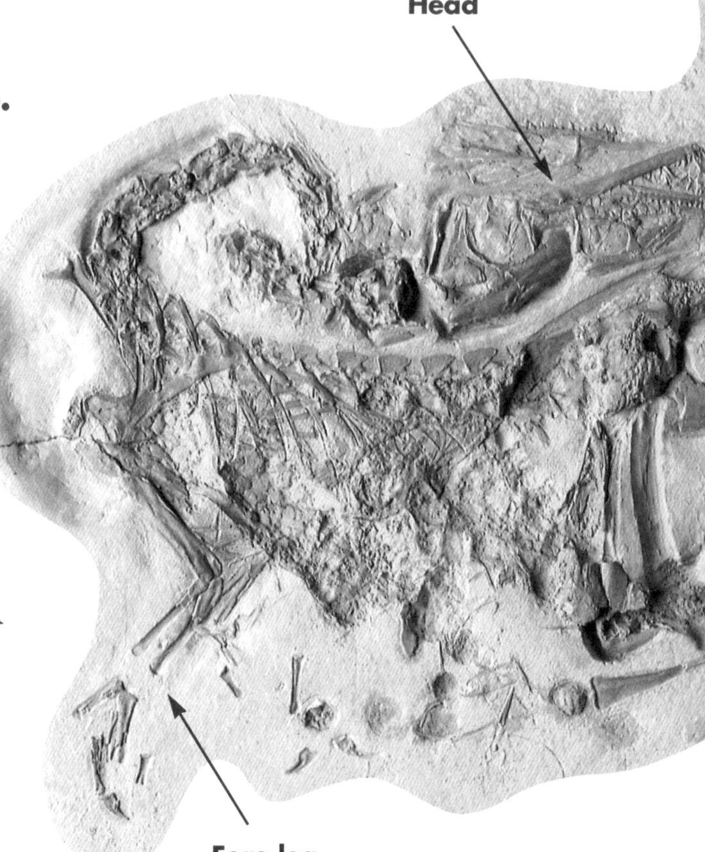

HOW A DINOSAUR BECAME A FOSSIL

1 When a dinosaur died, its body may have fallen, or been washed, into a river.

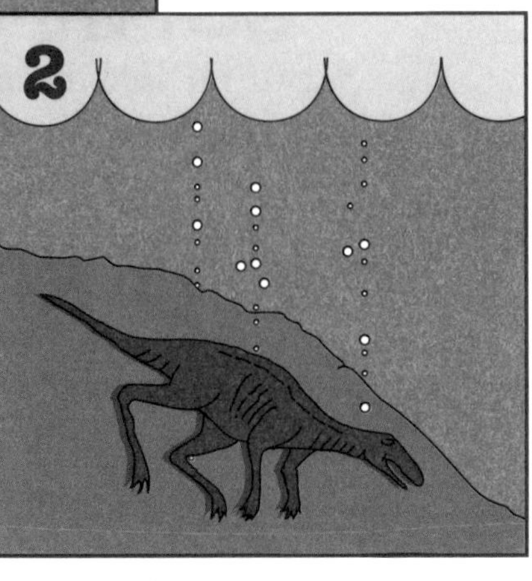

2 The dead body lay on the bottom of the river and the flesh rotted away.

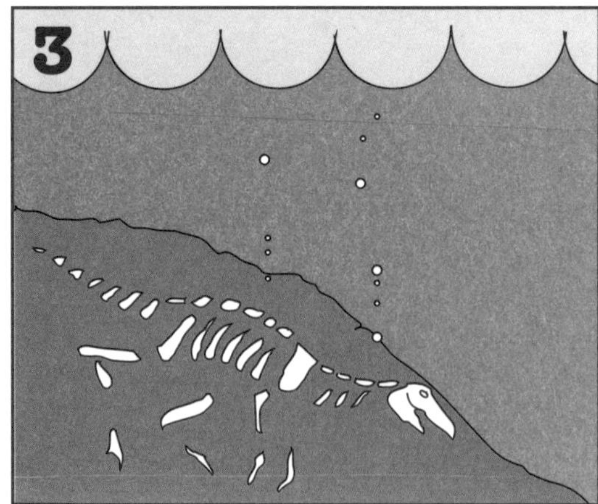

3 The skeleton was gradually buried under mud, and minerals from the water seeped into the bones and preserved them. Over millions of years, the mud turned into layers of rock and the dinosaur skeleton become a fossil.

THE FOSSIL DETECTIVES

The scientists who do all the detective work on fossils are called palaeontologists (pay-lee-on-toll-o-jists). They have found fossils all over the world. Their job can be very difficult because the fossil bones are often scattered in pieces. Only very rarely is a whole skeleton preserved in the rocks. Palaeontologists identify the fossil bones, remove them from the ground, put them together, like a jigsaw, and decide how old they are. You can see the results of their work in natural history museums where dinosaur fossils are mounted and put on display.

Fossils like this footprint are called trace fossils, because they are not part of an actual animal.

DINOSAUR DROPPINGS

Fossil bones and teeth are not the only clues that these giants of the past left behind them. Dinosaur footprints and the imprint of scaly skin, made in soft mud millions of years ago have also been found. Some of the most remarkable fossils found are dinosaur droppings.

nd leg

Still in the rock where it died millions of years ago: the fossil of *Compsognathus*, a little dinosaur the size of a chicken.

Scientists grind up dinosaur droppings, or coprolites, into fine dust to find out what dinosaurs ate.

▲4 Millions of years later, the sea level dropped. The wind and rain wear away the rock revealing the fossil: proof that dinosaurs once lived.

IT'S A FACT

WHAT'S IN A NAME ?

The word 'dinosaur' was first used in 1842. It was invented by Professor Richard Owen who studied British fossil reptiles. Owen realised that some of the large fossils belonged to a special group of animals that did not have a name. So he called them dinosaur which means 'terrible lizard'.

3-D Gallery 30

CETIOSAURUS

- A large sauropod
- Lived about 160 million years ago in Europe and northern Africa
- Measured 59ft (18m) long
- Ate plants

Dr. David Norman of Cambridge University answers your dinosaur questions
ASK THE EXPERT

How long did a dinosaur live?

It is almost impossible to work out exactly how old individual dinosaurs were when they died. However, scientists are trying to find out the rate of bone growth in dinosaurs, which is a bit like using tree rings to age trees. They think that a smallish dinosaur, *Massospondylus* (mass-oh-spond-il-lus), lived for between 30 and 70 years, much the same as a human being.

Which was the biggest dinosaur?

Seismosaurus (size-mo-saw-rus) may have been the biggest dinosaur that ever lived. Part of its skeleton is still being dug out from the ground in the USA. This monster may have been 36.5m long, which is as long as one and a half tennis courts. It probably weighed about 51 tonnes, so it was heavier than nine African elephants.

Did dinosaurs live in the sea?

Dinosaurs did not live in the sea all the time in the way that dolphins and whales do today. Of course, they may have waded into shallow water or even swum out to sea for short distances, just as horses can. But none lived in the sea all the time, so creatures such as plesiosaurs, which lived in water, were not dinosaurs.

Did different sized dinosaurs live to different ages?

Experts cannot be certain but they think that large dinosaurs probably lived longer than smaller ones. This is because smaller dinosaurs grew up quicker and lived life at a faster rate.

DINOSAURS!
DISCOVER THE GIANTS OF THE PREHISTORIC WORLD

TRICERATOPS

***Triceratops* was a horned dinosaur. It was as long as two cars and weighed as much as five rhinoceroses.**

Triceratops was a large, powerful dinosaur. It had one horn on its nose, which was small and stumpy, and one above each eye, which were up to 1m long. *Triceratops* probably used these long horns as weapons. *Triceratops* walked on all fours and had sturdy pillar-like legs. Its front legs were especially strong because they had to support the weight of its extremely heavy head.

BONY FRILL

Around *Triceratops'* neck was a huge, bony frill which protected its shoulders and could withstand shattering blows from other dinosaurs. Although nobody really knows what colour dinosaurs were, some scientists think that *Triceratops'* neck frill was brightly coloured. They believe that *Triceratops* was so well armed, it didn't need to be a green or brown colour for camouflage, but had a brightly coloured frill to attract females.

18 CM THE LENGTH OF TRICERATOPS' NOSE HORN

1m long eyebrow horns
Bony neck frill
Eye socket
Nose horn
Parrot-like beak
2m

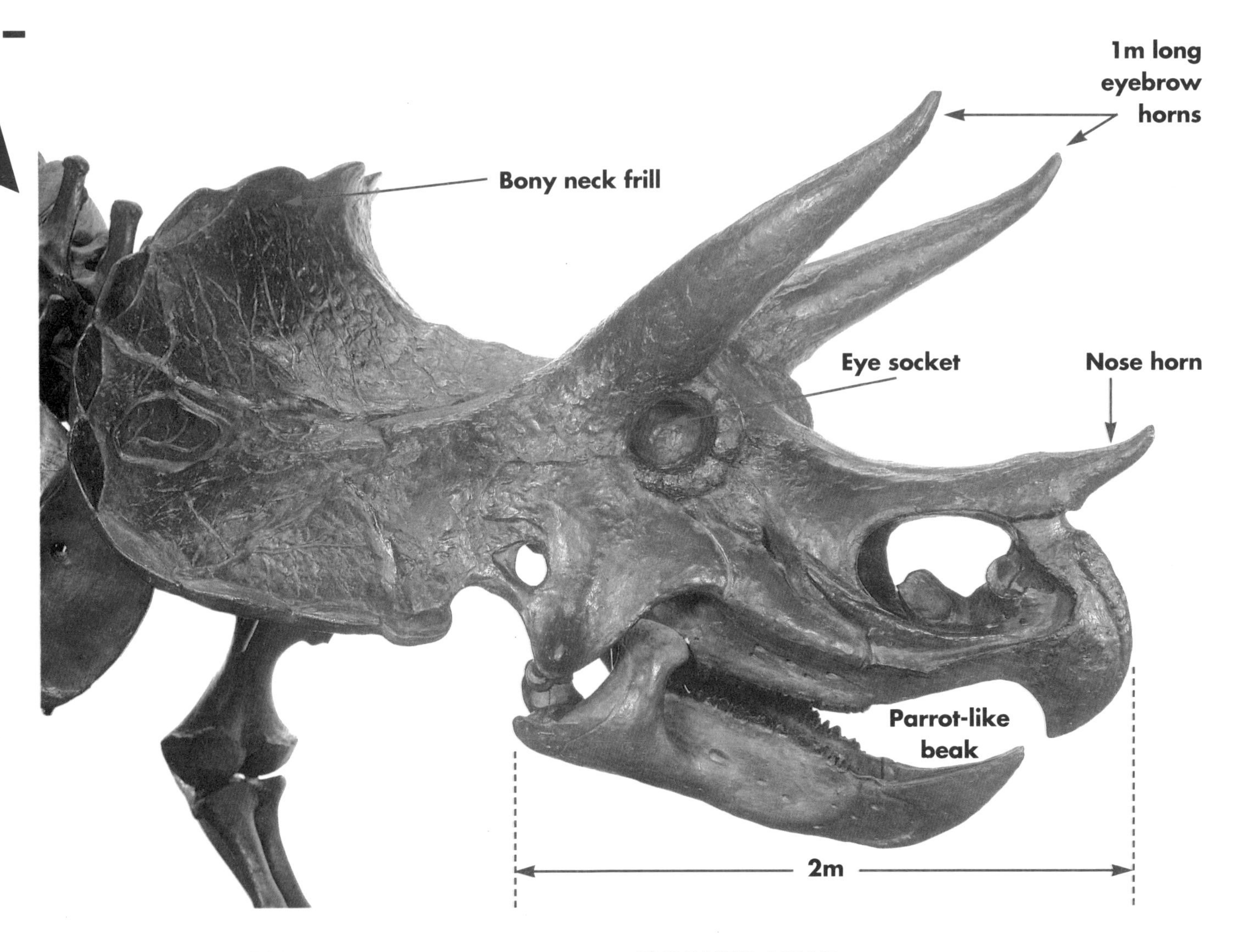

BEAKS AND TEETH

Triceratops was a herbivore. It nipped off shoots and leaves with its bony parrot-like beak. It ground them up with rows of teeth at the back of its mouth. As the teeth wore down, new ones grew in their place.

HORNED HEAD

On its massive head, *Triceratops* had three horns: one above each eye and another on the end of its nose. It used the horns to defend itself from hunting dinosaurs, such as *Tyrannosaurus rex.* It also used the horns to fight other male *Triceratops* for the females, before mating.

MONSTER FACTS

- **NAME:** *Triceratops* (try-serra-tops) means 'three-horned face'
- **SIZE:** up to 9m long and 3m high
- **FOOD:** all types of plants
- **LIVED:** 70 – 66 million years ago in the Late Cretaceous in North America

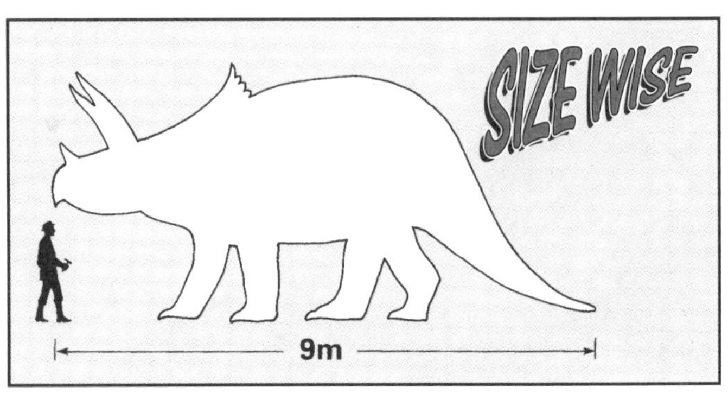

What is? A HERBIVORE

A herbivore is an animal that eats only plants. Herbivores eat many different kinds of plants, from grass to flowers and trees. They eat different parts of plants: leaves, shoots, roots and stalks. Cows are herbivores, so are elephants, rhinoceroses and giraffes. A herbivore's teeth are different shapes from those of a meat-eating animal. Many dinosaurs were herbivores, including *Iguanodon* and *Stegosaurus*.

BRUISING BATTLE

The males probably fought each other to become leader of a herd and to attract females. They did not use their horns to wound. Instead, two males shoved and butted each other with their massive heads, locking horns in a bruising battle to prove which was the strongest.

A *Triceratops'* neck frill would protect its shoulders and body from a head-on attack by another male. Scientists have found damaged neck frills, which show that these fights between males were fierce enough to cause injuries.

A charging rhino is very dangerous. Imagine what a charge from giant *Triceratops* was like.

A FIERCE ENEMY

Even dinosaurs as large as *Tyrannosaurus rex* would have thought twice about attacking *Triceratops*, because it could cause serious wounds by stabbing the enemy with its sharp horns. *Triceratops* was well protected against attacking dinosaurs. Its bony neck frill was a good defence against sharp teeth and claws and it had tough skin with occasional hard knobs along its back.

Triceratops could charge at its enemies by sprinting at a top speed of 35 km/h. A charge from this rhinoceros-like dinosaur would probably have been enough to scare off many predators.

STRUTHIOMIMUS

With its long neck, small head, beak and long legs, *Struthiomimus* looked rather like an ostrich.

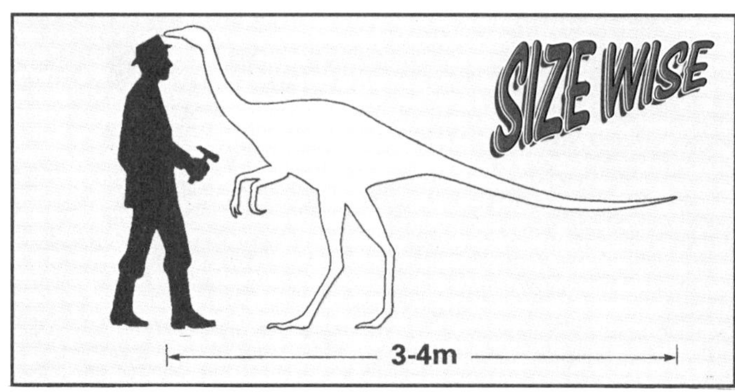

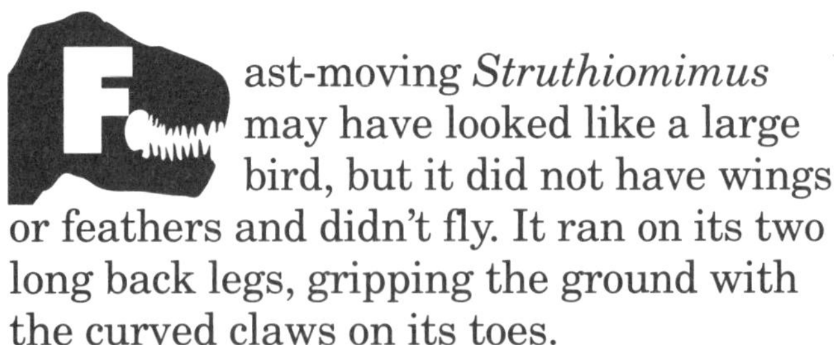

Fast-moving *Struthiomimus* may have looked like a large bird, but it did not have wings or feathers and didn't fly. It ran on its two long back legs, gripping the ground with the curved claws on its toes.

Struthiomimus used its long thin, stiff tail to balance itself. It had two short, slim arms and long, three-fingered hands, which it probably used for reaching and picking up food.

MONSTER FACTS

- **NAME:** *Struthiomimus* (strooth–ee-oh-mime-us) means 'ostrich mimic' because it looked, and probably moved, like an ostrich
- **SIZE:** 3 – 4m long and 2m high
- **FOOD:** plants, seeds, fruits, eggs and lizards
- **LIVED:** 80 – 66 million years ago in the Cretaceous Period in western North America

A VARIED DIET

Struthiomimus ate many things, including plants, seeds, nuts and fruits. It snapped at flying insects with its toothless, horny beak and gobbled up small ground creatures, such as lizards. It may even have raided the nests of other dinosaurs, to eat eggs and even the newly hatched young.

FAST SPRINTER

These fast-running dinosaurs had no weapons to defend themselves, so they travelled in groups for safety. If *Struthiomimus* was attacked by other dinosaurs, it ran away. It was a very fast runner and could sprint at speeds of up to 40 km/h, over short distances, so could probably outrun most large predators (hunting animals).

CAMPTOSAURUS

***Camptosaurus* was as tall as a camel and weighed as much as a pony.**

A peaceful, plant-eating dinosaur, *Camptosaurus* usually walked on its two back legs. However, it also had small hooves on its fingers and probably walked on all fours some of the time, especially when feeding on low-growing plants and on the lower leaves of trees.

MONSTER FACTS

- **NAME:** *Camptosaurus* (camp-toe-saw-rus) means 'bent lizard' because of its curved thigh bones
- **SIZE:** 7m long and up to 6m tall
- **FOOD:** plants
- **LIVED:** 155 – 140 million years ago, in the Late Jurassic and Early Cretaceous Periods in western Europe and North America

CHEEKS TO CHEW

Camptosaurus had a long, broad head with rows of ridged teeth. The tips of its jaws were covered by a horny beak, which it probably used to chop off the tough fern and palm leaves. Scientists think that *Camptosaurus* had a tongue, which it wrapped around the leaves, and used to drag them into its mouth. It also had stretchy cheeks, which could expand to take large amounts of food as it chewed.

CURVED THIGHS

The curved thigh bones of this dinosaur enabled it to run quite fast on its powerful hind legs. As it ran, *Camptosaurus* balanced its bulky body with its heavy tail. This peaceful dinosaur had no weapons, such as horns or sharp claws, and the only way it could escape larger meat-eating dinosaurs was to run away.

Dinosaur time

Dinosaurs existed through three huge chunks of the Earth's history.

Scientists think that the Earth has existed for about 4,500 million years. To understand such a vast amount of time they divide it into Periods. The dinosaurs lived through three Periods: the **Triassic** (try-ass-ic), the **Jurassic** (joo-rass-ic) and the **Cretaceous** (cret-ay-shus). Dinosaurs first appeared near the end of the Triassic and finally died out at the end of the Cretaceous. Different kinds of dinosaurs lived during the three Periods.

CHANGING LANDSCAPES

During the 179 million years from the beginning of the Triassic to the end of the Cretaceous, the world changed greatly. Dinosaurs of the Triassic and Jurassic wandered through ferns, seed ferns, conifers and horsetails. The landscape was very different from our world today: there was no grass at all, instead, ferns covered the ground. During the Cretaceous new types of vegetation grew and dinosaurs lived among, and fed on, plants that we know today, such as willow, rose, magnolia, oak and grape vine.

DINOSAUR CLIMATE

The climate in the Triassic, Jurassic and Cretaceous was warmer and wetter than it is now. There were no extremes of heat and cold, and not much difference between winter and summer. Nor were areas of the Earth covered in ice and snow, as our polar regions are.

The dinosaurs arrive

THE TRIASSIC: 245 – 204 MYA

At the end of the Triassic, when dinosaurs first appeared, there were vast areas of hot, dry desert. But near rivers and coasts there were lush forests of tree ferns. In drier areas there were thinner forests of conifers (cone-bearing trees), rather like the monkey-puzzle trees of today, and cycads, a palm-like plant. In these Triassic forests lived dinosaurs such as *Anchisaurus, Coelophysis* and *Saltopus*.

Is it true that there were no flowers in the Triassic?

Yes, it is true that there were no flowers at all during the Triassic. Nor were there any flowers in the Jurassic. Flowering plants did not appear on Earth until the middle of the Cretaceous Period.

Plateosaurus **was the first large dinosaur. It was about 8m long and was tall enough to reach and eat leaves on trees.**

The flying reptile *Kuehneosaurus* could glide from branch to branch searching for insects to eat.

Glevosaurus **was not a dinosaur, but an early lizard-like animal.**

Procompsognathus **was a fast-running meat-eater that preyed on insects, small mammals and reptiles.**

Horsetails were plants that flourished near water.

The time of the giants

THE JURASSIC: 204 – 140 MYA

The weather was warm and wet in the Jurassic, which meant that many plants flourished. The world was greener, with many thick forests. In these conditions, giant sauropod dinosaurs, such as *Apatosaurus* and *Brachiosaurus,* evolved. There was plenty of vegetation for these huge plant-eaters to live on. Birds first appeared in the Jurassic.

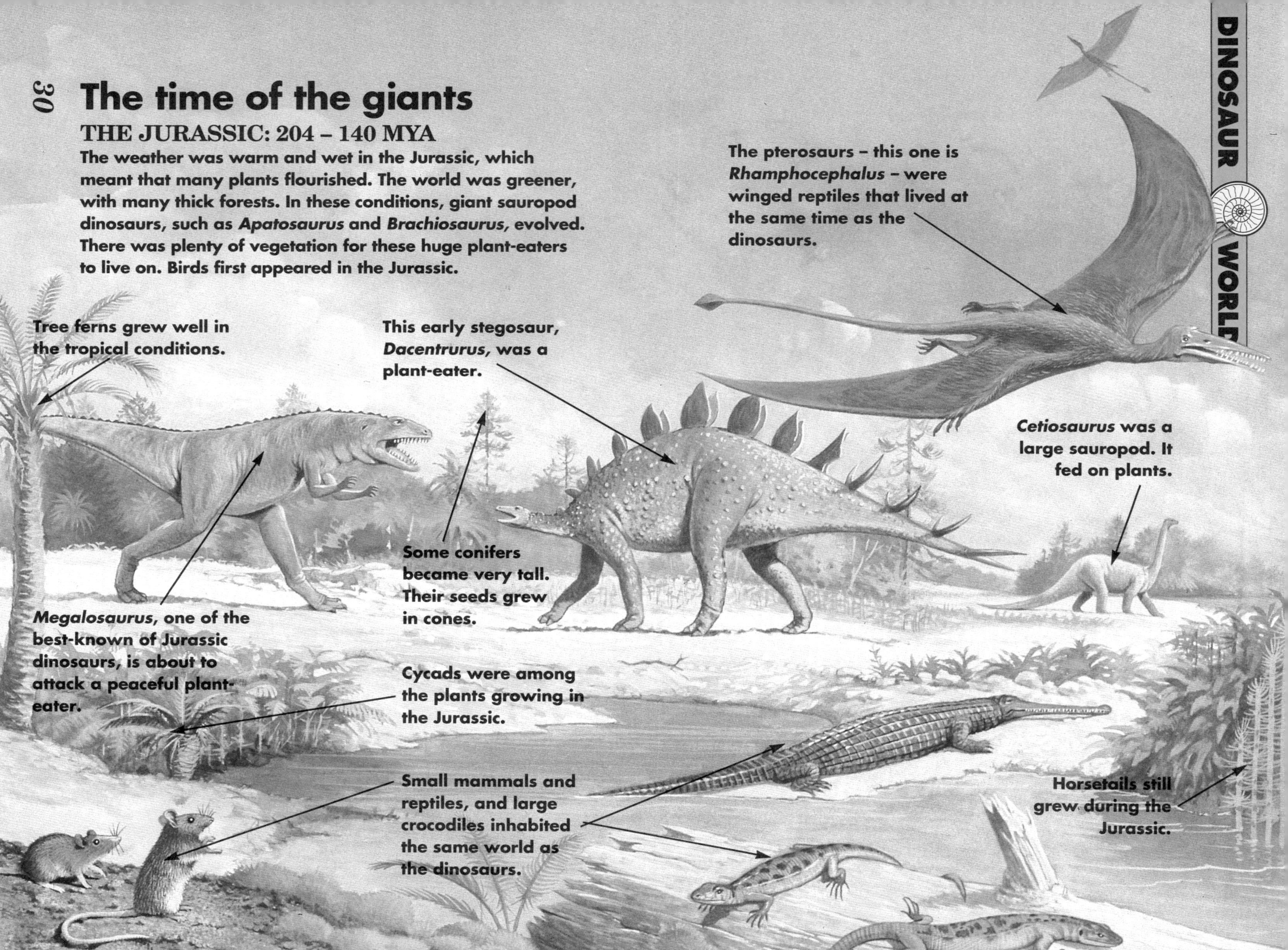

The pterosaurs – this one is *Rhamphocephalus* – were winged reptiles that lived at the same time as the dinosaurs.

Tree ferns grew well in the tropical conditions.

This early stegosaur, *Dacentrurus,* was a plant-eater.

Cetiosaurus was a large sauropod. It fed on plants.

Some conifers became very tall. Their seeds grew in cones.

Megalosaurus, one of the best-known of Jurassic dinosaurs, is about to attack a peaceful plant-eater.

Cycads were among the plants growing in the Jurassic.

Small mammals and reptiles, and large crocodiles inhabited the same world as the dinosaurs.

Horsetails still grew during the Jurassic.

Monsters and flowers

THE CRETACEOUS: 140 – 66 MYA

The first flowering plants, such as magnolia and rose, appeared towards the end of the Cretaceous. Ferns, horsetails, conifers and cycads continued to grow too. The massive sauropod dinosaurs gave way to faster-moving meat-eaters, such as *Tyrannosaurus* and *Albertosaurus*, and plant-eaters such as *Iguanodon.*

Many birds, such as waders, cormorants and owls, evolved during the Cretaceous.

Large pterosaurs (flying reptiles) shared the skies with feathered birds.

Triceratops, one of the best-known dinosaurs, lived during the Cretaceous Period.

Broad-leaved flowering trees, such as oaks, gradually formed forests during this period.

Parasaurolophus were dinosaurs with long tube-like crests on their heads.

During the middle of the Cretaceous, flowering plants appeared on Earth for the first time.

Corythosaurus was a duck-billed dinosaur that ate plants.

Mammals existed, but they were still small animals at this time.

Ostrich-like *Stenonychosaurus* was a fast-running meat-eater.

GIANTS OF THE PAST

TRICERATOPS

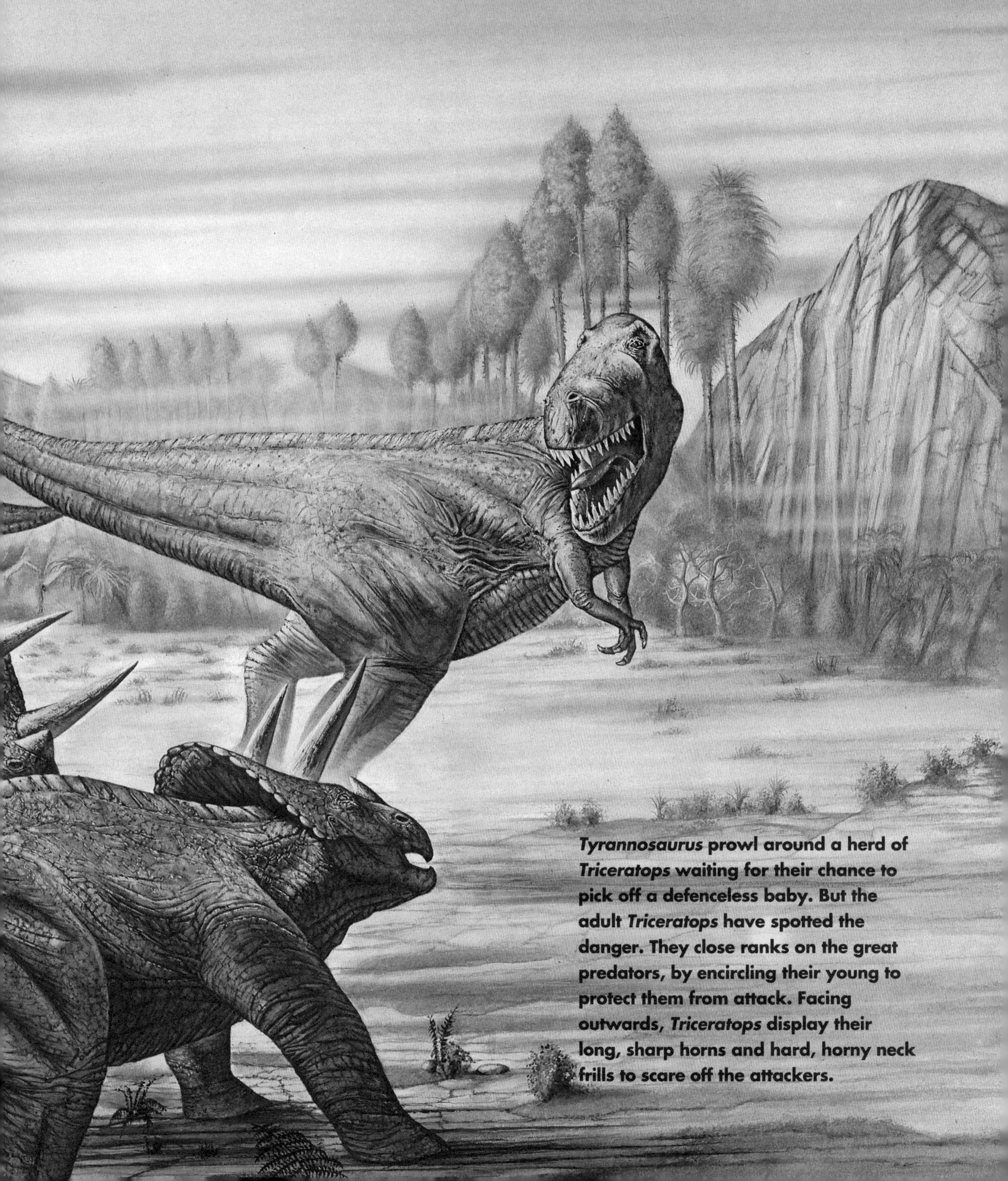

Tyrannosaurus prowl around a herd of *Triceratops* waiting for their chance to pick off a defenceless baby. But the adult *Triceratops* have spotted the danger. They close ranks on the great predators, by encircling their young to protect them from attack. Facing outwards, *Triceratops* display their long, sharp horns and hard, horny neck frills to scare off the attackers.

3-D Gallery 3

MEGALOSAURUS

- A theropod
- Lived 145 - 135 million years ago in western Europe
- Measured about 9m long from head to tail
- Ate meat

3-D Gallery 4

BRACHIOSAURUS

- A sauropod
- Lived 150 - 130 million years ago in America and Africa
- Measured 23m long and 12m high
- Ate plants

All shapes and sizes

There is an amazing array of dinosaur shapes and sizes. Spot how each animal was suited to its lifestyle.

The different shapes and sizes of dinosaurs evolved to suit the way in which the animals lived. Tiny, agile *Compsognathus* lived on small animals and could move fast enough to catch them. *Allosaurus* was a huge, fierce and muscular dinosaur; while long-necked *Diplodocus* could reach the leaves that most other dinosaurs could not reach.

GIGANTIC AND SLOW

Diplodocus (di-plod-o-cus) had a very long neck and tail and reached 27m in length. It had a slender body and a tiny head for its size. *Diplodocus* needed to eat vast amounts of food to survive and had a huge stomach to digest all the leaves.

TINY AND FAST

Compsognathus (comp-sog-nay-thus) is one of the smallest dinosaurs to be discovered so far. It was a meat-eater, but it was light and could run very fast. It was a clever predator, which chased after, and fed on, lizards and insects.

LARGE AND MUSCULAR

Dragon-like *Allosaurus* (al-oh-saw-rus) was a fierce meat-eater. It was strongly built so that it could attack and kill. It could not run fast for long distances, but probably caught smaller, younger or slow dinosaurs, or ate carrion (animals that are already dead).

TINY AND FAST
Compsognathus
- **Size of a chicken**
- **Walked upright on two legs**

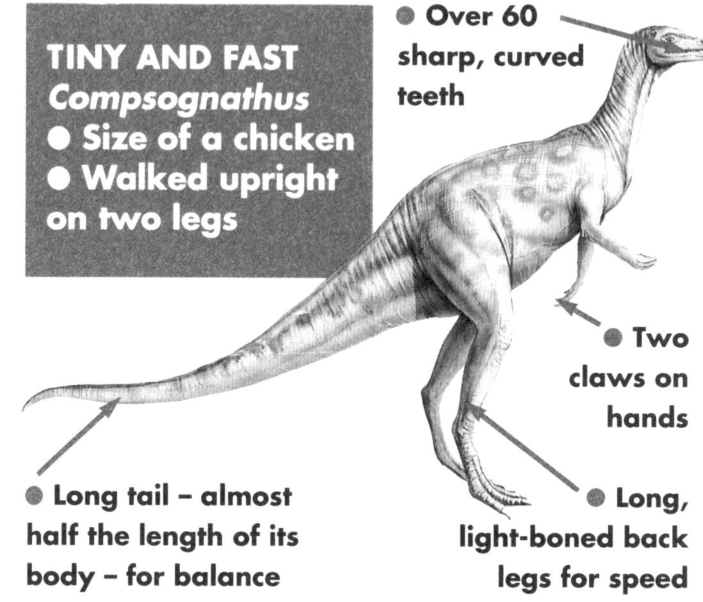

What is? A SAUROPOD

Sauropods, such as *Diplodocus, Apatosaurus* and *Ultrasaurus,* were among the longest, tallest and heaviest animals that have ever lived. Only the blue whale is bigger. Sauropods were plant-eating giants that had extremely long necks and tails, slim bodies and small heads. They were peaceful giants that lumbered through the forests feeding on the leaves. The word sauropod means 'reptile feet'.

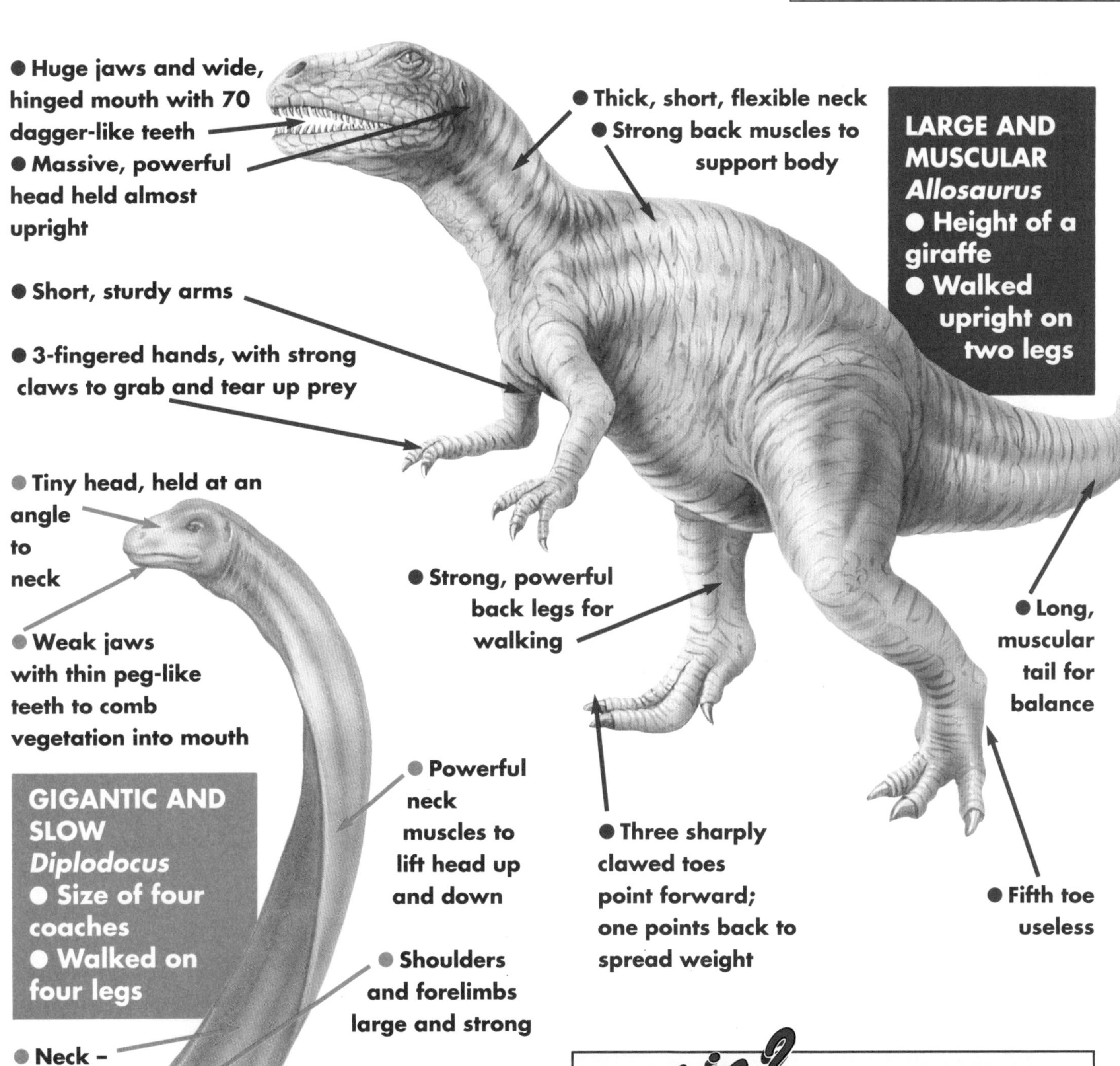

What is? A THEROPOD

Theropods were all meat-eating bipedal (walking on two legs) dinosaurs. They were called theropods, which means 'beast foot', because of their sharply clawed toes. Large theropods, such as *Allosaurus*, *Tyrannosaurus rex* and *Megalosaurus*, had massive heads, powerful hind limbs, slender arms and long, muscular tails. Smaller theropods, such as *Compsognathus* and *Oviraptor*, were much more lightly built.

Discovering

Discovering a complete dinosaur skeleton is very rare, but once one has been found experts are needed to dig it up.

Finding a fossil dinosaur can be difficult detective work. First you must search for special sorts of rocks, such as sandstone or mudstone, 66 to 204 million years old. Experts look for traces of fossils, such as broken fragments of bone at the foot of cliffs, in hills or quarries, or down mines.

FREEING THE GIANT

A whole team of experts is needed to dig the fossil bones carefully out of the rock so that the giant skeleton can be pieced together like a jigsaw at the museum laboratory. Soon the site, or 'dig' as it is known, is busy with people.

WHERE TO SEARCH

Fossil skeletons of dinosaurs are generally found in rocks that were being formed from mud and sand when dinosaurs were still alive. The dinosaur fossils are buried deep down in the lowest layers of the rock.

Palaeontologists do not dig holes all over the place in the hope of finding a fossil. First they look for the right kind of rock, then they let the wind and rain do their work for them. The best places to look for fossils are where the rock has been worn right down to its lower layers by the action of the wind and rain or waves. Sometimes large parts of a hill or cliff crumble away and reveal part of a fossil.

a dinosaur

BEWARE, DANGER!
The places where fossils are most frequently found are often dangerous. Never go fossil hunting unless you are with an adult. And always get the owner's permission before you search on private land.

STRIKING IT LUCKY
Palaeontologists often go to quite remote parts of the world, such as Mongolia or China, to search for dinosaurs. But fossils can also be found by accident, by workmen making roads, quarry workers blasting for stone, or miners digging underground.

SPOT THE DINOSAURS
There are five more dinosaurs hidden in the picture. Can you spot them?

IT'S A FACT

CLAWS
In 1983, a huge, sickle-shaped claw was found by accident, buried in a quarry in Surrey, England. It led to one of the most exciting recent dinosaur finds. Experts from the British Museum discovered the giant skeleton to which the claw belonged buried nearby. It was identified as a completely new dinosaur. They named it *Baryonyx walkeri* after Mr Walker who discovered the claw. *Baryonyx* was a meat-eater, as long as a bus.

Digging up a dinosaur

Most dinosaur fossils are embedded in rock. It can take many people several months to dig a large dinosaur out of the rock.

Everything we know about dinosaurs, from what they looked like, to what they ate, has come from what the experts have discovered through their 'digs'. Follow the footprints to find out how a dinosaur is dug up.

1 BLAST OFF

Many tonnes of rock may have to be blown up, or bulldozed to reach the fossil.

Only the top layers of rock are blasted away, otherwise the fossil skeleton may be damaged.

2 SLOW BUT SURE

Great care must be taken to dig out the fossils without damaging them. Hammers, chisels and even dentist's drills are used to chip away the rock that encases the bones.

7 HANDLE WITH CARE

Once they are out of the ground, the bones are wrapped in tissue paper, then plaster-soaked bandages, or special foam jackets, that set hard to protect them on their journey to the laboratory.

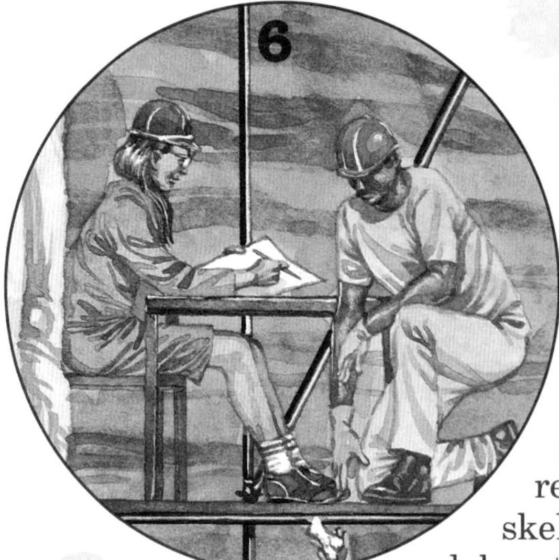

6 PIECING TOGETHER THE JIGSAW

Every fossil piece must be numbered and recorded to help the scientists reconstruct the skeleton in the laboratory. It is slow and very painstaking work, but it is important.

Rocks from different periods of time build up in layers – the oldest at the bottom. Fossils are buried deep in each layer: the lower the layer, the older the fossils. Fast-flowing rivers can wear rock down and expose the layers with fossils buried deep inside. At the Grand Canyon (left), in the United States of America, the different rock layers are revealed in spectacular multi-coloured bands.

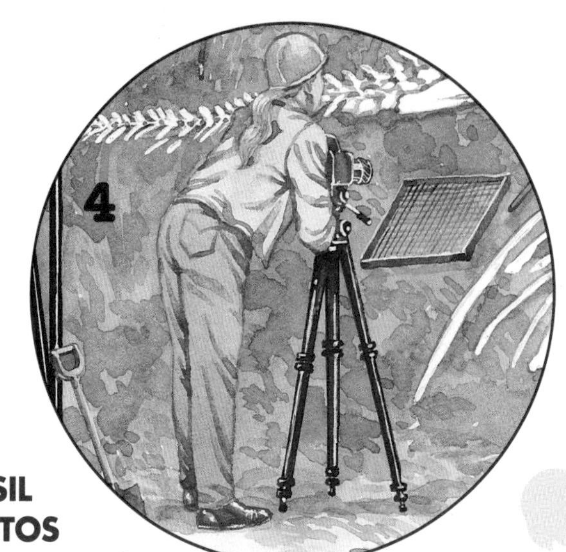

4 FOSSIL PHOTOS

The bones must be photographed in position before being moved, to show where they were found. Scientists can learn much about how the animal died and where it lived, from studying how it was lying, and by looking closely at the ground around it for clues.

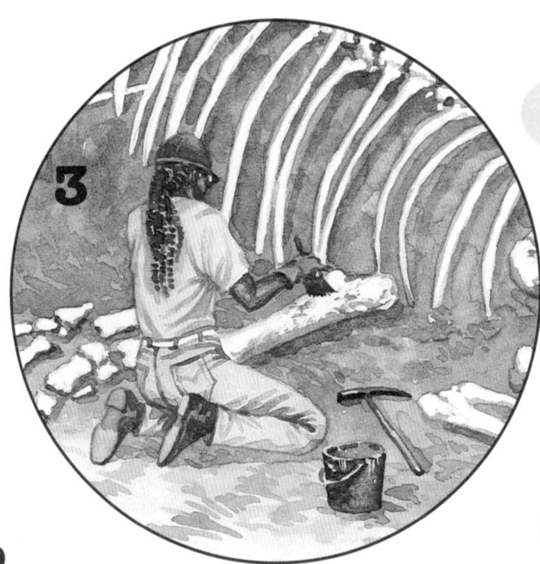

3 BRUSHWORK

Soft brushes are used to clear away earth and stones. Brushes do not damage the ancient bones. Crumbly bones can be painted with special glues to harden them.

5 SEARCHING FOR CLUES

The surrounding rocks are searched for signs of bones that might have broken away from the main skeleton – or maybe another fossil dinosaur buried nearby.

5

IT'S A FACT

IMPORTANT DINOSAUR FINDS

Dinosaur	Named
Megalosaurus	1824
Iguanodon	1825
Hadrosaurus	1858
Stegosaurus	1877
Diplodocus	1878
Triceratops	1889
Brachiosaurus	1903
Tyrannosaurus rex	1905
Ankylosaurus	1908
Pachycephalosaurus	1943
Baryonyx	1986

3-D Gallery 31

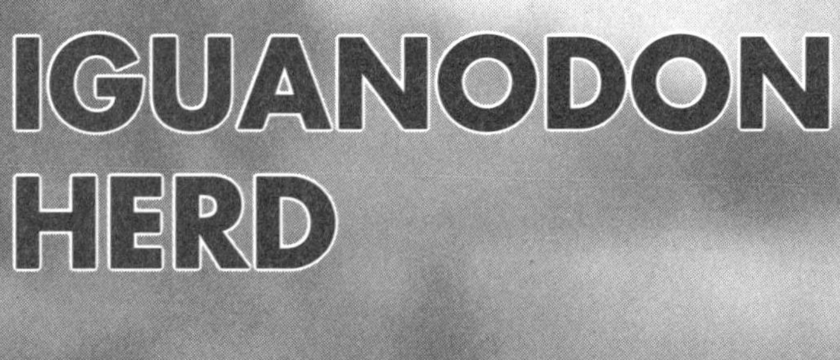

IGUANODON HERD

- A group of ornithopod dinosaurs
- Lived about 130 – 110 million years ago in Europe, North America and Asia
- Measured 33ft (10m) long
- Ate plants

Dr. David Norman of Cambridge University answers your dinosaur questions
ASK THE EXPERT

Could dinosaurs fly?

Dinosaurs could not fly or glide. They were all land animals and had no wings. But there was a creature called *Archaeopteryx* (ark-ee-op-ter-ix) which lived 150 MYA. It was not a dinosaur, but experts are not sure whether it was a bird or a reptile. It had feathers and wings and looked like a bird, but it also had the tail, claws and teeth of the early reptiles.

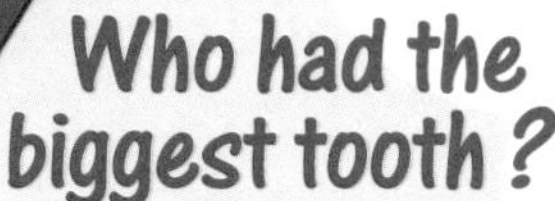

Who had the biggest tooth?

One of the biggest dinosaur teeth known belongs to *T rex*. The teeth at the side of the mouth, near the front, may be 30cm long from the root to the tip of the crown. The tooth could grow 18cm above the gum.

Which was the fastest dinosaur?

Nobody will ever know which dinosaur was the fastest. But some dinosaurs, such as *Struthiomimus* and *Gallimimus* (gal-ih-mime-us), had legs the same length as the modern ostrich. Scientists think that they could have run at about 40 km/h.

Which dinosaur had the longest neck?

The dinosaur with the longest neck discovered so far is *Mamenchisaurus* (ma-men-chih-saw-rus), which lived in China 150 MYA. Its neck was 14m long – it could have seen over a three storey house. Scientists are still digging up the bones of *Seismosaurus* (size-mo-saw-rus), which may have a longer neck than any other dinosaur.

DINOSAURS!
DISCOVER THE GIANTS OF THE PREHISTORIC WORLD

STEGOSAURUS

One swipe of its spiked tail and *Stegosaurus* could cripple any predator that threatened it.

Stegosaurus had a small head, a thick, clumsy body and a spiky tail. Along its back were two rows of bony, diamond-shaped plates. Some of these were about three times the height of this page. Although it looked fierce, *Stegosaurus* ate mainly low-growing ferns and other plants. It lived in herds that grazed together.

BIG-BODIED

This dinosaur was about as long as two cars and weighed about the same. Its tail was long and used for balance.

STUMPING ALONG

It moved on all four legs, stumping heavily along. It could not walk or run very fast and was preyed on by fast-running, meat-eating dinosaurs, such as *Allosaurus*.

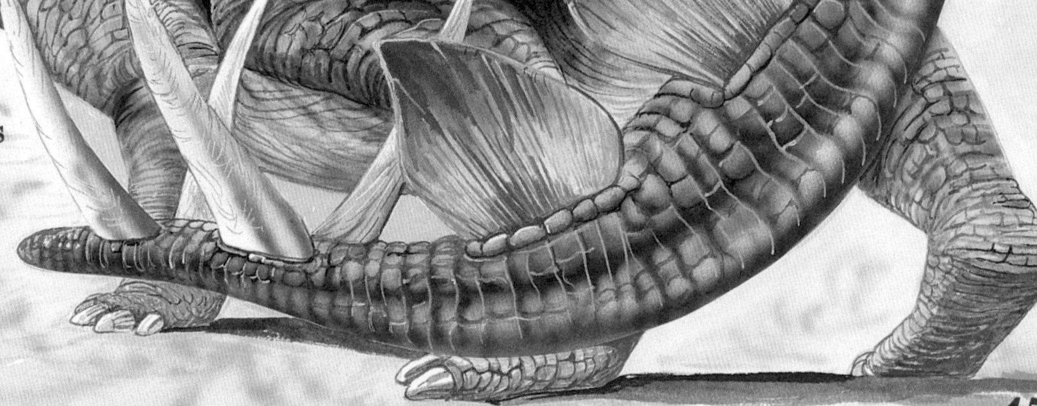

Stegosaurus had very short front legs and much longer back ones to support the weight of its body.

Stegosaurus had a very small skull and its jaws were weak

Case surrounding a brain about the size of a walnut

Eye socket

Nostril for breathing

Horny beak for slicing plants

Serrated teeth for cutting plants

35cm

TINY HEAD

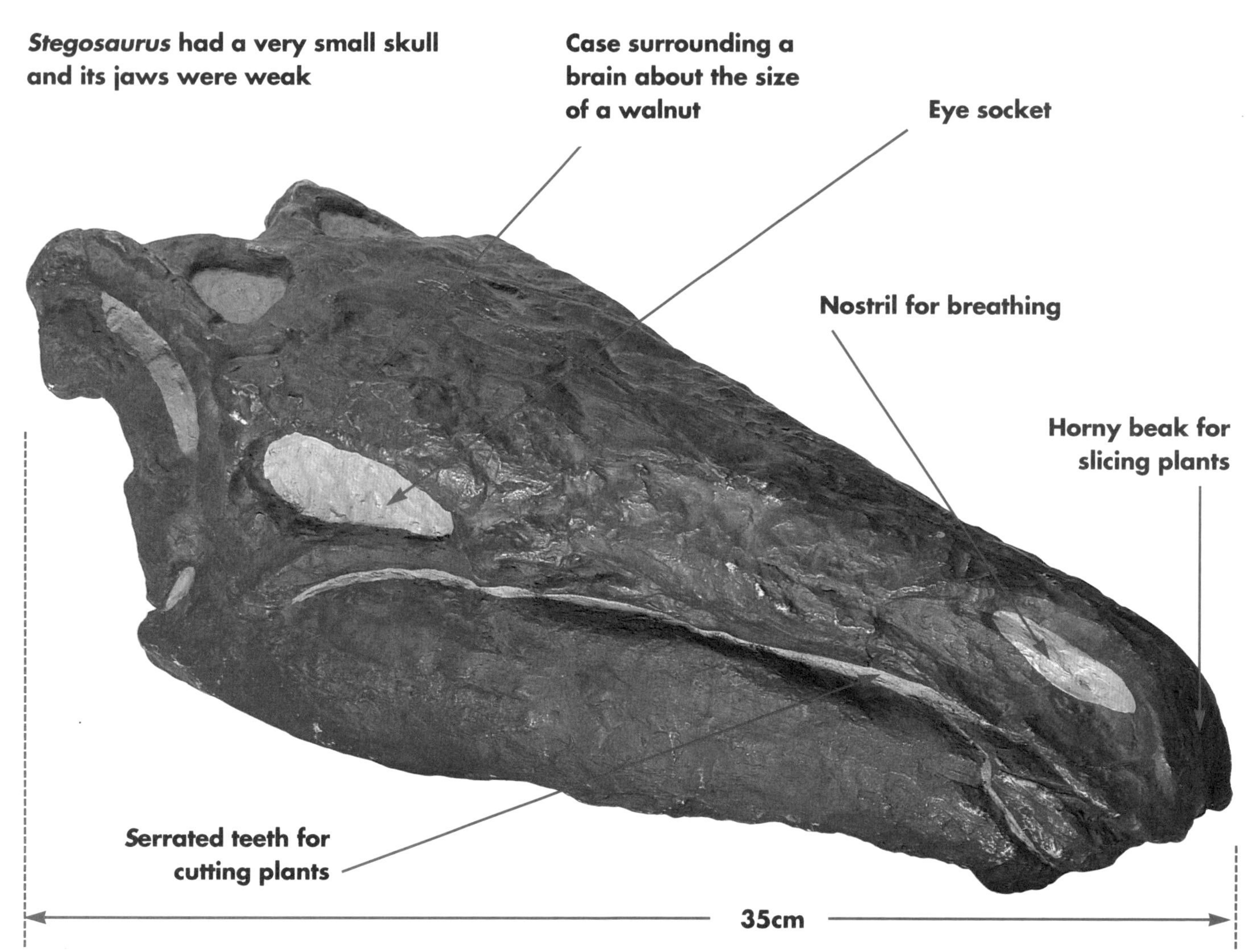

Its small head, which was about the size of a large dog's, was close to the ground so *Stegosaurus* grazed mainly on low-growing plants. It had a weak jaw, and could chew only soft, leafy food. Its brain was tiny, about the size of a walnut. This means it had the smallest brain of any animal, compared to its size, that ever lived.

SPIKY TAIL

Stegosaurus also had a tail that was very thick and powerful, with bony plates all the way down. At the tip of the tail were four spikes, each one up to 1m long. *Stegosaurus* may have used its tail to defend itself, and its young, against any meat-eating dinosaur which came within range.

MONSTER FACTS

- **NAME:** *Stegosaurus* (steg-oh-saw-rus) means 'roofed lizard'
- **SIZE:** up to 7.5m long and 4m high
- **FOOD:** low-growing ferns and other plants
- **LIVED:** about 140 million years ago in the Late Jurassic Period in North America

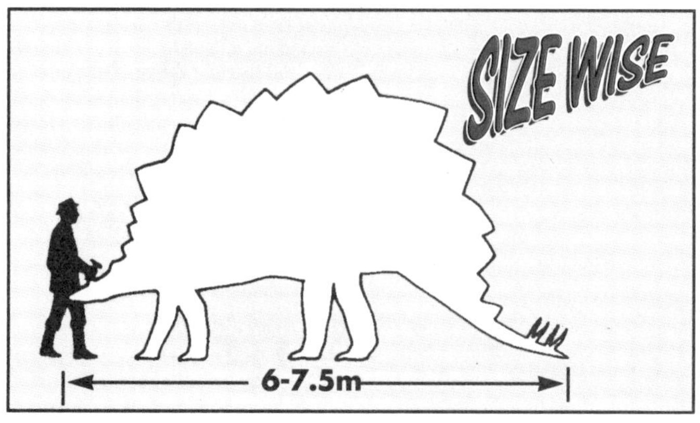

The plates on *Stegosaurus'* back may have been a prehistoric version of solar heating panels, like those in the photograph. These panels work by soaking up the sun's rays and provide heat for homes, offices and factories today.

ARMOUR PLATING

On its back, *Stegosaurus* had a row of bony plates. These grew out of the dinosaur's skin, and could easily be torn off by a large predator. Some experts think that the plates were a special sort of solar-heating and air-conditioning system which *Stegosaurus* used to warm or cool its body. *Stegosaurus* turned its body so that its plates faced the sun, collecting as much heat as possible in the cool early mornings. Once it was warm enough, it could start moving about and feeding.

COLOURFUL CREATURES

Scientists have also suggested that the plates on *Stegosaurus'* back may have been very brightly coloured. So the males probably used the plates to warn off other males in the herd and to attract the females at the start of the mating season.

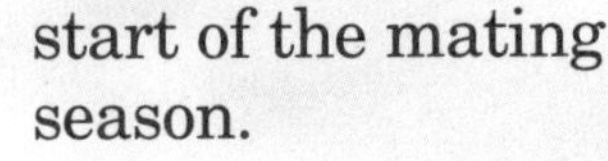

STYGIMOLOCH

Stygimoloch's tough, bony skull protected its brain during its amazing head-butting fights.

Stygimoloch lived in herds and grazed in woodland areas. It had short front legs, but far longer back legs. It also had a lengthy tail which it held level with its body when running. On its head were prominent horns. These were for show and not used as weapons.

MONSTER FACTS

- **NAME:** *Stygimoloch* (stij-ee-mol-ok) means 'thorny devil'
- **SIZE:** 3m long
- **FOOD:** plants
- **LIVED:** about 70 million years ago during the Cretaceous Period in North America

BUTTING CONTESTS

Like some types of sheep and deer alive today, *Stygimoloch* males probably had frequent head-butting contests. The strongest then became leader of the herd. *Stygimoloch* males took up their positions, with their necks stretched out and their heads held down. Then they charged, crashing their heads, but not their horns, together. The thick bone on the top of its head was probably used to protect its brain. The contest went on until one animal gave up, and limped away.

VELOCIRAPTOR

Not as big as *Tyrannosaurus rex*, *Velociraptor* was still one of the most vicious killers that roamed the dinosaur world.

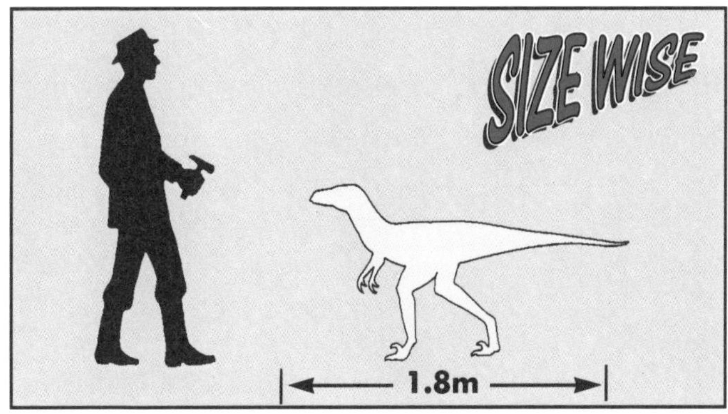

elociraptor was a feared predator and could run very fast on its long back legs. It chased through the Cretaceous forests after small mammals or small plant-eating dinosaurs which it killed and then ate.

MONSTER FACTS

- **NAME:** *Velociraptor* (vel-o-si-rap-tor) means 'speedy predator'
- **SIZE:** about 1.8m long and 1m high
- **FOOD:** meat, especially other dinosaurs
- **LIVED:** about 90 million years ago during the Cretaceous Period in Mongolia, near China

FIERCE KILLER

Creatures that it chased were terrified of it and had little chance of escape. *Velociraptor* stood on one back leg, attacked with the other, and used its tail for balance. It also had a long, sharp claw on one toe of each foot. This faced inwards and was used to stab and slash at its helpless prey.

SHARP TEETH

Velociraptor had a long head and a flat snout, with rows of sharp teeth for tearing at its victims.

FAST AND INTELLIGENT

Before the discovery of *Velociraptor* in Mongolia in 1924, scientists had thought of dinosaurs as slow and stupid creatures. But *Velociraptor* was built for speed. It was also perhaps one of the most intelligent of all dinosaurs.

Earth on the move

Our planet has not always looked the way it does today. Hundreds of millions of years ago, the world was just one continent, surrounded by sea.

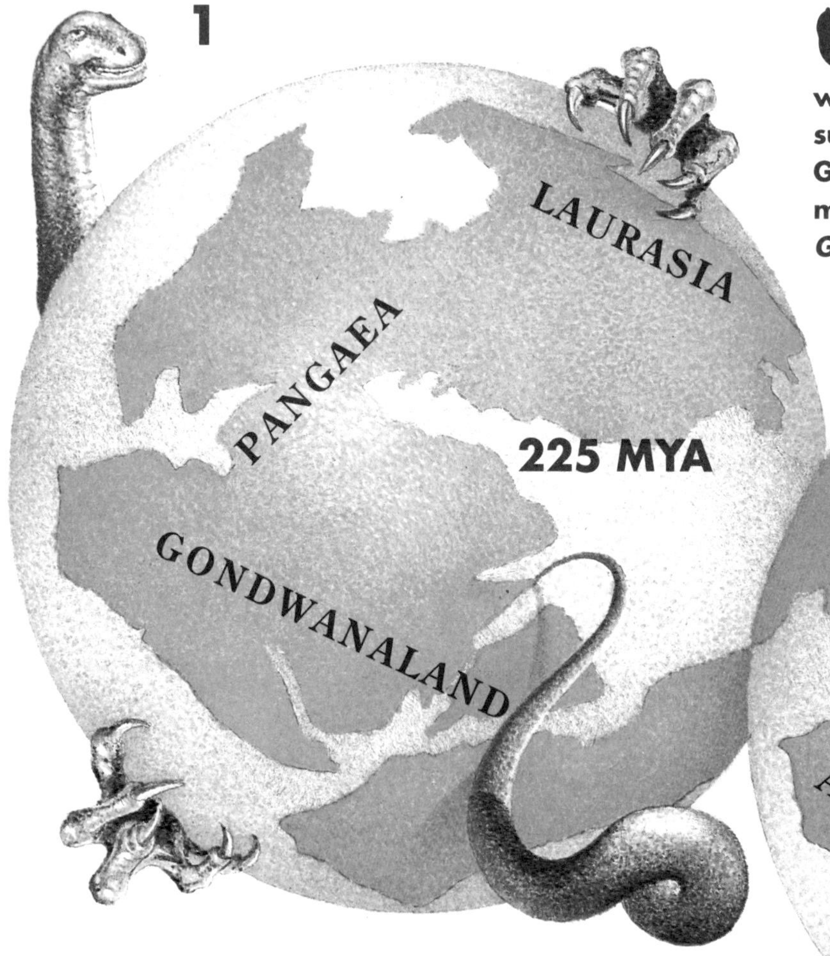

1

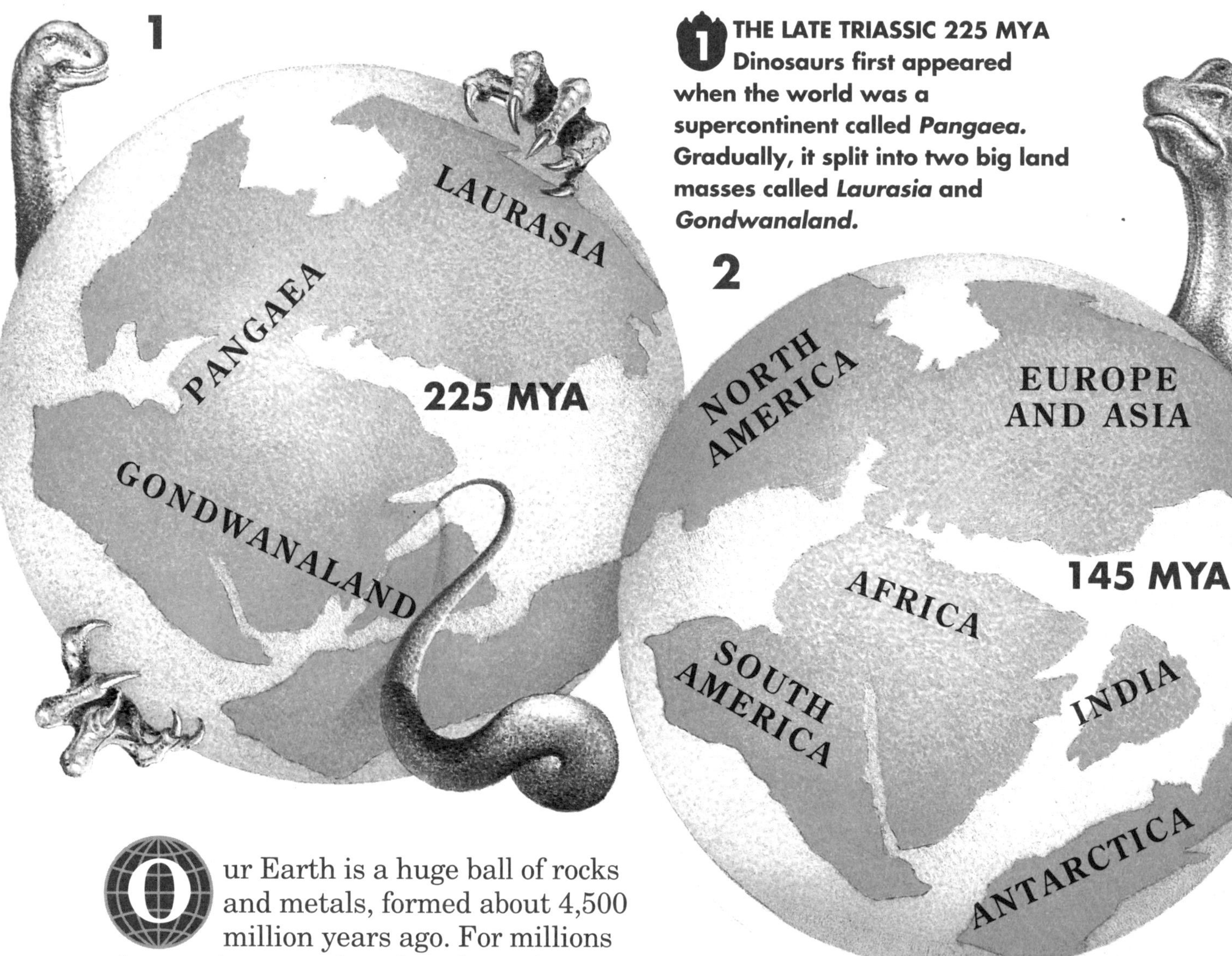

1 THE LATE TRIASSIC 225 MYA
Dinosaurs first appeared when the world was a supercontinent called *Pangaea.* Gradually, it split into two big land masses called *Laurasia* and *Gondwanaland.*

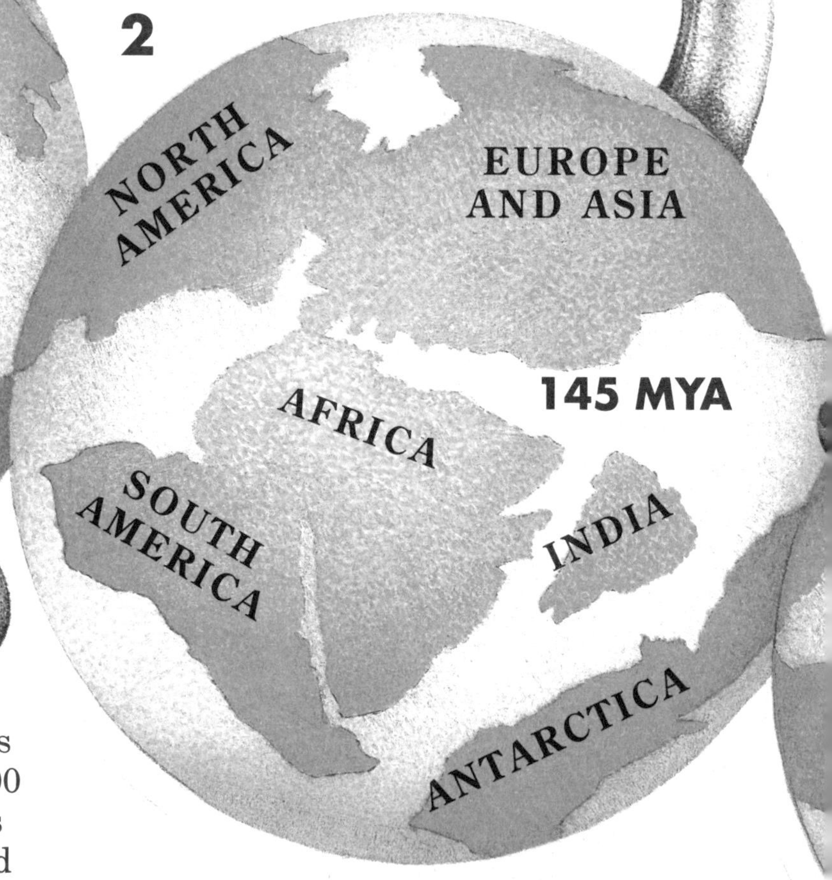

2

Our Earth is a huge ball of rocks and metals, formed about 4,500 million years ago. For millions of years, it was so hot that the rocks and metals were liquid. Then, very slowly, the surface cooled down.

PLATES OF ROCK

The Earth's surface may look solid but it is cracked into enormous pieces called plates. These float on the hot rocks which lie under the crust. Over millions of years, some plates have bumped into each other.

2 THE LATE JURASSIC 145 MYA
By this time the land masses had drifted further apart. The northern land mass included Asia and Europe which was joined to North America. This land mass was drifting northwards. What are now the separate continents of Africa and South America were joined together in one land mass that was drifting south.

ONE CONTINENT
About 200 million years ago, all the land was joined up into one huge continent, called *Pangaea* (Pan-jee-a). So dinosaurs could roam right round the Earth without crossing water.

SHIFTING PLATES
Slowly, over millions of years, the shifting plates began to pull this continent apart into two great land masses called *Laurasia* (Law-race-ia) and *Gondwanaland* (Gon-dwan-a-land).

IT'S A FACT

STILL CHANGING
The map of the world will look very different millions of years in the future as the continents continue to move. North America and Russia are drifting towards each other and could even bump in about 50 million years time. The Atlantic Ocean is also growing wider by about 4cm a year.

3 THE LATE CRETACEOUS 66 MYA
Gaps between the continents had become far wider. The sea filled them and formed vast oceans, including the Atlantic.

4 TWENTIETH-CENTURY EARTH
This is the world as we know it today, with wide stretches of ocean between the continents.

3
EUROPE AND ASIA
AFRICA
INDIA
ATLANTIC OCEAN
SOUTH AMERICA
66 MYA
ANTARCTICA AND AUSTRALIA

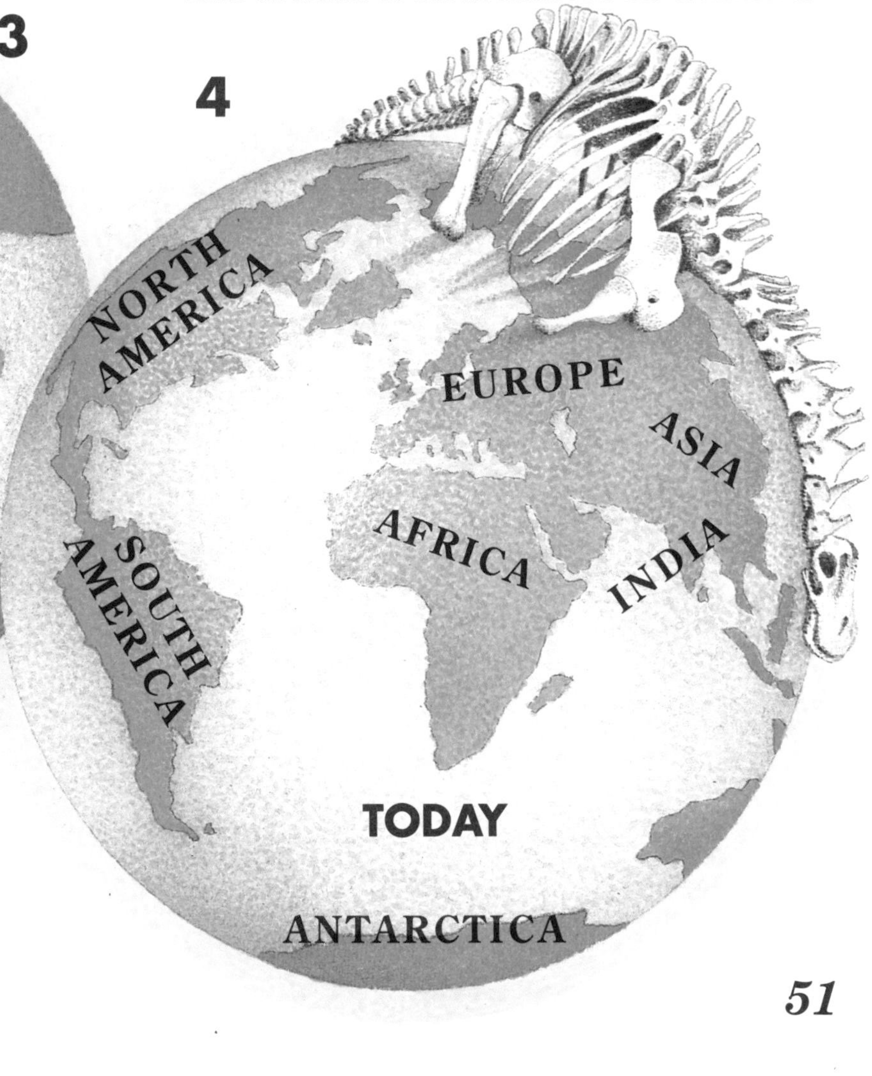

4
NORTH AMERICA
EUROPE
ASIA
AFRICA
INDIA
SOUTH AMERICA
TODAY
ANTARCTICA

Dinosaur discoveries

Dinosaur remains have been found all over the world – usually by scientists on expeditions, but sometimes just by chance.

The map on these two pages shows where some of the hundreds of dinosaurs we know about were found.

Some have been dug up in places that are very far apart. *Brachiosaurus,* for example, has been discovered in North America, Tanzania (Africa) and Portugal (Europe). Dinosaurs, remember, could roam the whole world when the Earth was one great land mass.

Triceratops
Brachiosaurus
NORTH AMERICA
Iguanodon
Tyrannosaurus rex
Stegosaurus
Iguanodo
Hypsilophodon
Hypsilophodon
Brachiosaurus
SOUTH AMERICA
Herrerasaurus
Mussaurus
Hypsilophodon
ANTARCTICA

NORTH AMERICA

- Hundreds of dinosaurs have been found in the USA and Canada.
- Early palaeontologists even fought over who had made the most finds here.
- So far, *Triceratops* and *Tyrannosaurus rex* have only been dug up in North America. *Iguanodon,* however, has also been discovered in England and Belgium (Europe) and in Mongolia (Asia).

SOUTH AMERICA

- Fossilized remains have been dug up in most South American countries, particularly Argentina and Brazil.

EUROPE

- Some of the first ever dinosaur finds were made in England. In 1824, the first dinosaur teeth were found in Oxfordshire.
- Dinosaurs continue to be discovered in England and France, either in quarries or by the sea.

AFRICA

- Many finds have been made in Africa. One of the tallest dinosaurs was dug up in Tanzania. It was a *Brachiosaurus* and is now on display in Berlin, Germany.

ASIA

- Expeditions to remote parts of China have resulted in lots of very exciting finds.
- Many skeletons have also been dug up in Mongolia and a few in India.

AUSTRALIA

- Not many dinosaur skeletons have been found here so far.
- Scientists have found hundreds of fascinating footprints, however. This leads them to think that important remains will be dug up in the future.

ANTARCTICA

- No one knows how many skeletons lie under this ice-covered region.
- Only two types have been found so far. Scientists think that one is related to *Hypsilophodon,* which has been found in Great Britain and Portugal.

The symbol by each dinosaur on the map provides a clue to how long ago it lived.

GIANTS OF THE PAST

Stegosaurus **turns its back on** ***Allosaurus*** **and defends itself with one mighty swipe of its tail.** ***Stegosaurus*** **could make good use of the four spikes in its tail. A blow on the leg with one of these and** ***Allosaurus*** **probably decided that its next meal was not going to be a** ***Stegosaurus*** **after all.**

STEGOSAURUS

3-D Gallery
5
CORYTHOSAURUS
• A duck-billed dinosaur
• Lived 140 - 66 million years ago in North America
• Measured 10m long from head to tail
• Ate plants

3-D Gallery 6

BRACHYCERATOPS

- A small horned dinosaur
- Lived 140 - 66 million years ago in North America
- Measured 1.8m from head to tail
- Ate plants

More shapes and sizes

Many dinosaurs were remarkably different in how they looked and also how they behaved.

Some dinosaurs – *Styracosaurus,* for example – looked a bit like a rhinoceros. *Psittacosaurus* had a beak rather like a parrot's. *Pachycephalosaurus* fought head to head like today's mountain sheep, but had a thick skull instead of horns.

FOUR-FINGERED AND BEAKED

Psittacosaurus (si-tak-oh-saw-rus) was given a name that means 'parrot-reptile' because it had a sharp, horny beak at the front of its mouth for slicing through plants. This dinosaur had long back legs but shorter arms, with four long fingers. It may have walked on all-fours at times.

FOUR-FINGERED AND BEAKED
Psittacosaurus
- Almost as tall as a man
- Long, clawed fingers
- A ceratopian

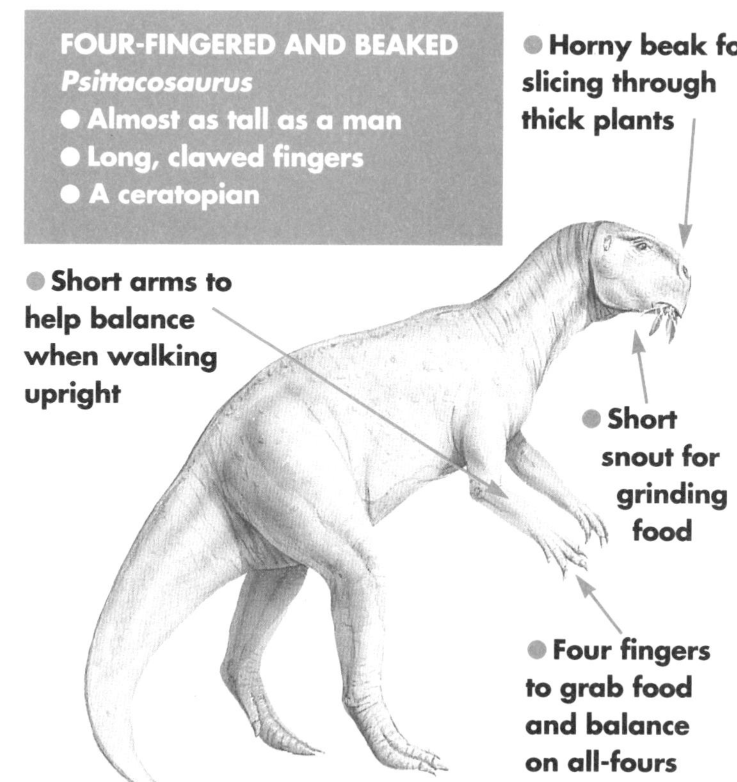

LARGE AND THICK-HEADED
Pachycephalosaurus
- Height of an elephant
- A head-butter

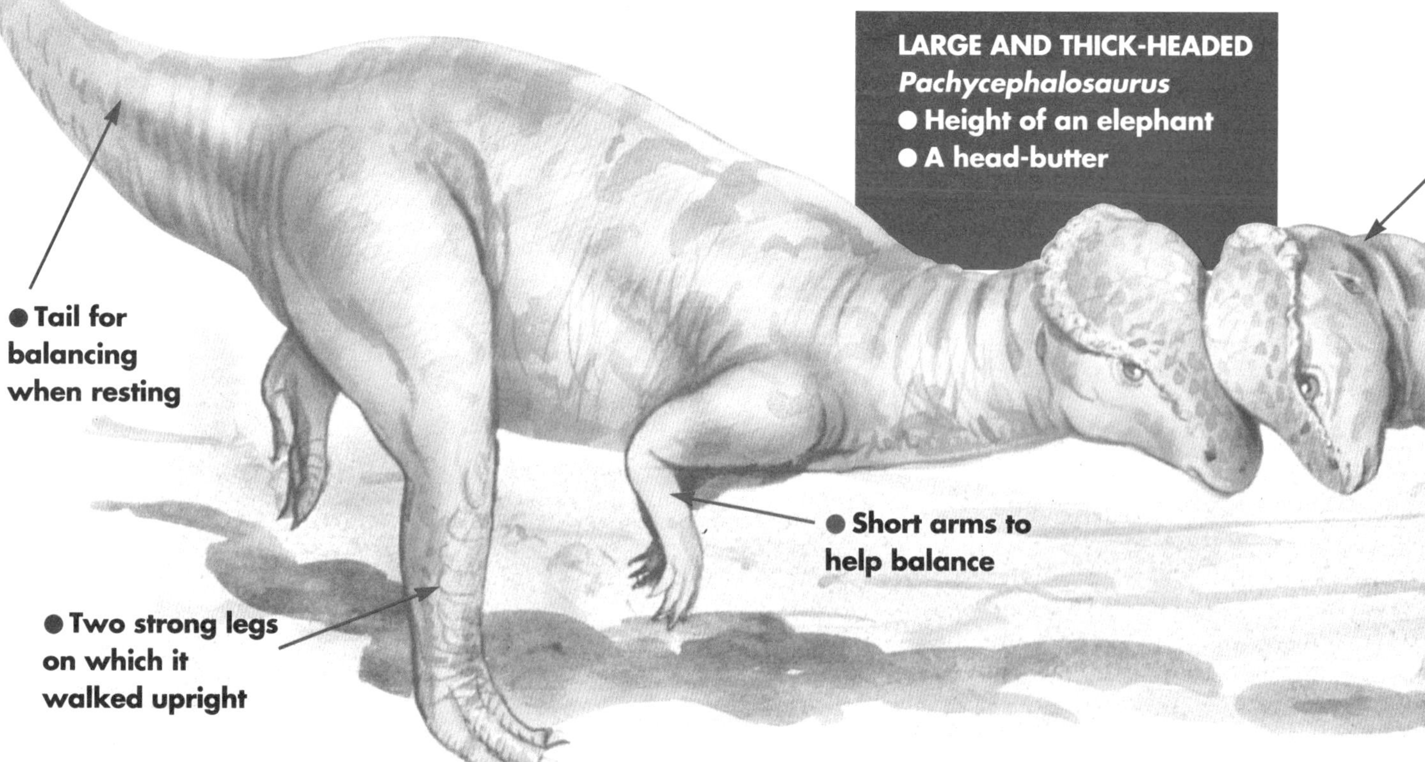

What is? A CERATOPIAN

Ceratopians were herbivores. Many looked like rhinoceroses, with sturdy bodies and horned faces. However, ceratopians had curved beaks at the front of their jaws. They lived in the Cretaceous Period, and have been found in North America and Asia. They included *Triceratops, Styracosaurus* and *Psittacosaurus.*

HORNED AND SPIKED
Styracosaurus
● Taller than a man
● Walked on all-fours
● Nose horn for defence
● Long spikes on frill to attract mate and frighten off rivals
● Four sturdy legs for galloping

LARGE AND THICK-HEADED
Pachycephalosaurus (pak-ee-kef-al-oh-saw-rus) had a skull with a very thick top, decorated with knobs and spikes. It may have used these as weapons for head-butting fights with other members of its species. It walked upright, and used its tail to balance on when resting.

HORNED AND SPIKED
Styracosaurus (sty-rak-oh-saw-rus) had a large horn on its nose, and a spiky frill around its neck. These were probably used to warn off enemies and rivals, and to attract mates. This plant-eating dinosaur was a ceratopian and was related to *Triceratops.* Its name means 'spiked reptile'.

● Skull with thick top to protect head while fighting

What is? HEAD-BUTTING

Some dinosaurs clashed in head-to-head battles like today's mountain sheep. This head-butting took place among males. It was a test of strength to see which would lead the herd or win a mate. The brains of dinosaurs like *Pachycephalosaurus* were quite small and were protected from head blows by very thick bone on the top of the skull.

Back to the lab

1

Before a dinosaur skeleton can be built, the bones must be carefully cleaned in the lab.

After the bones of a dinosaur have been dug up, they will be sent to a scientific laboratory. Here, scientists can set about the task of cleaning and preserving the bones. They have been buried beneath the ground for millions of years, and need a lot of looking after.

1 The bone that the scientist is holding comes from a *Camptosaurus*. It was found in Peterborough, England, and is about 140 million years old. The bone comes from the dinosaur's thigh, and is called a femur. When bones are dug up, they are wrapped in bandages before being transported. The first thing the scientist does is fill out a Condition Report. This records whether bones are damaged.

2 Most of the scientist's work is done whilst looking through a microscope at the bone. He uses a pneumatic pen, which acts like a mini road-drill and breaks away the rock from around the bone. The rock around the bone is called the matrix. A lot of it may have become stuck to the bone over many millions of years.

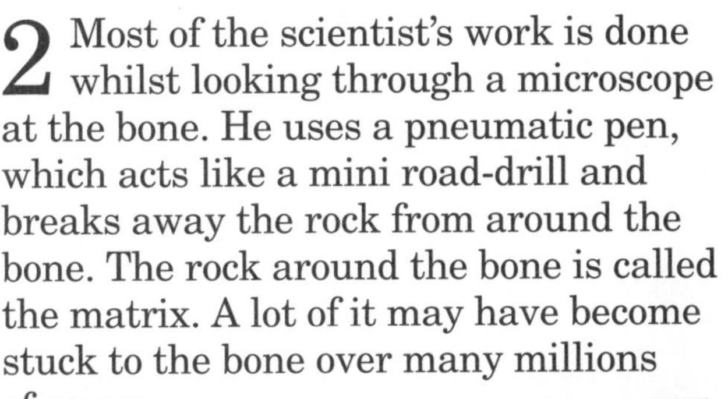

What is? FOSSILIZED BONE

Bone is hard material that makes up an animal's skeleton. It is also a living substance that begins to grow when a baby animal is still developing inside an egg. When an animal dies in the wild, its flesh is eaten or rots away, but the bones remain. This happened with dinosaur bones, too. Over millions of years, they turned into a kind of rock.

It is these remains that are dug up by palaeontologists and then taken back to the laboratory to be cleaned.

3 The scientist injects a special glue into the rock to stop it breaking. Any gaps in the rock will also be filled to make sure the fossil does not fall apart.

femur

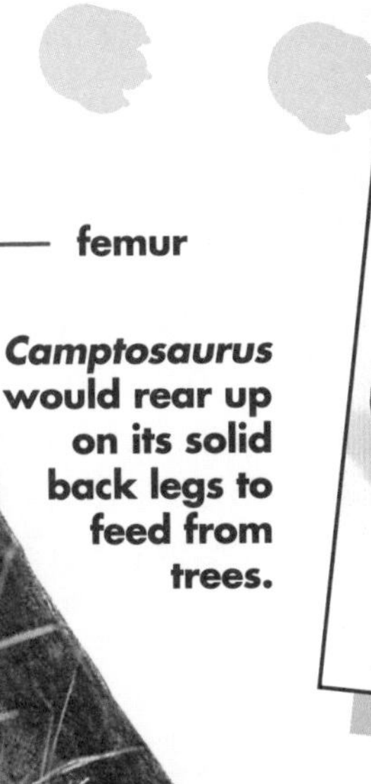

Camptosaurus **would rear up on its solid back legs to feed from trees.**

4 An acid preparation sink, or acid bath, may also sometimes be used for stripping off layers of matrix that are hard to remove in any other way. The scientist wears protective gloves to save his hands being burned by acid.

5

5 Taking care of a dinosaur bone is a very delicate job. The scientist brushes away pieces of dust from the surface. For very dirty bones, the scientist may dip the brush in water or use a mild detergent.

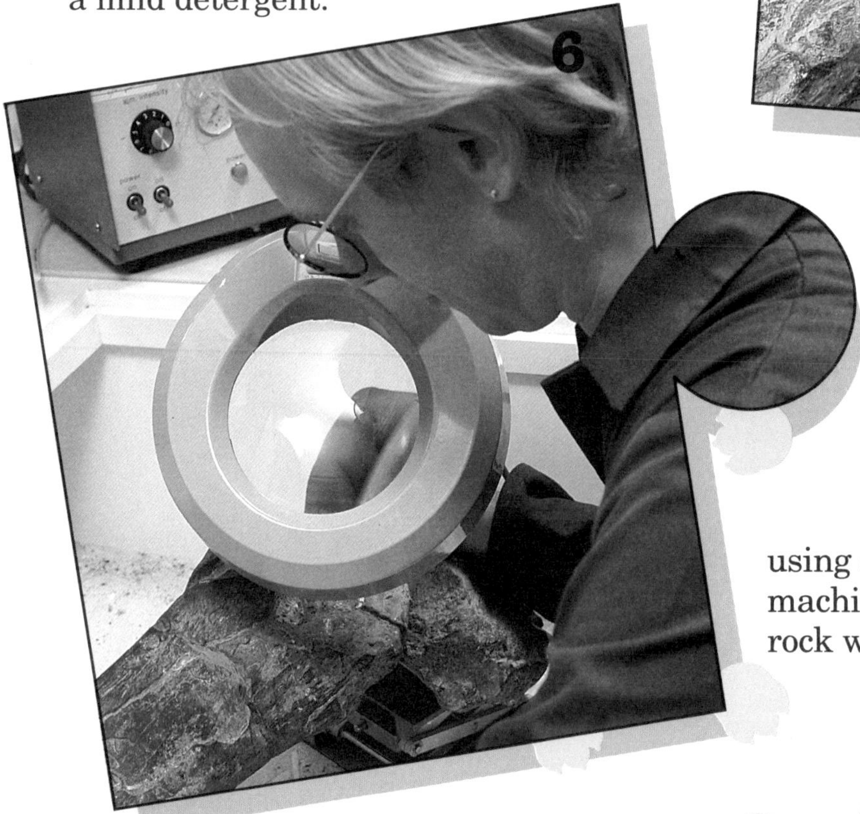

6

6 The next stage in the cleaning and preparing process involves using an air abrasive machine. This machine takes off very tiny amounts of rock without damaging the bone beneath.

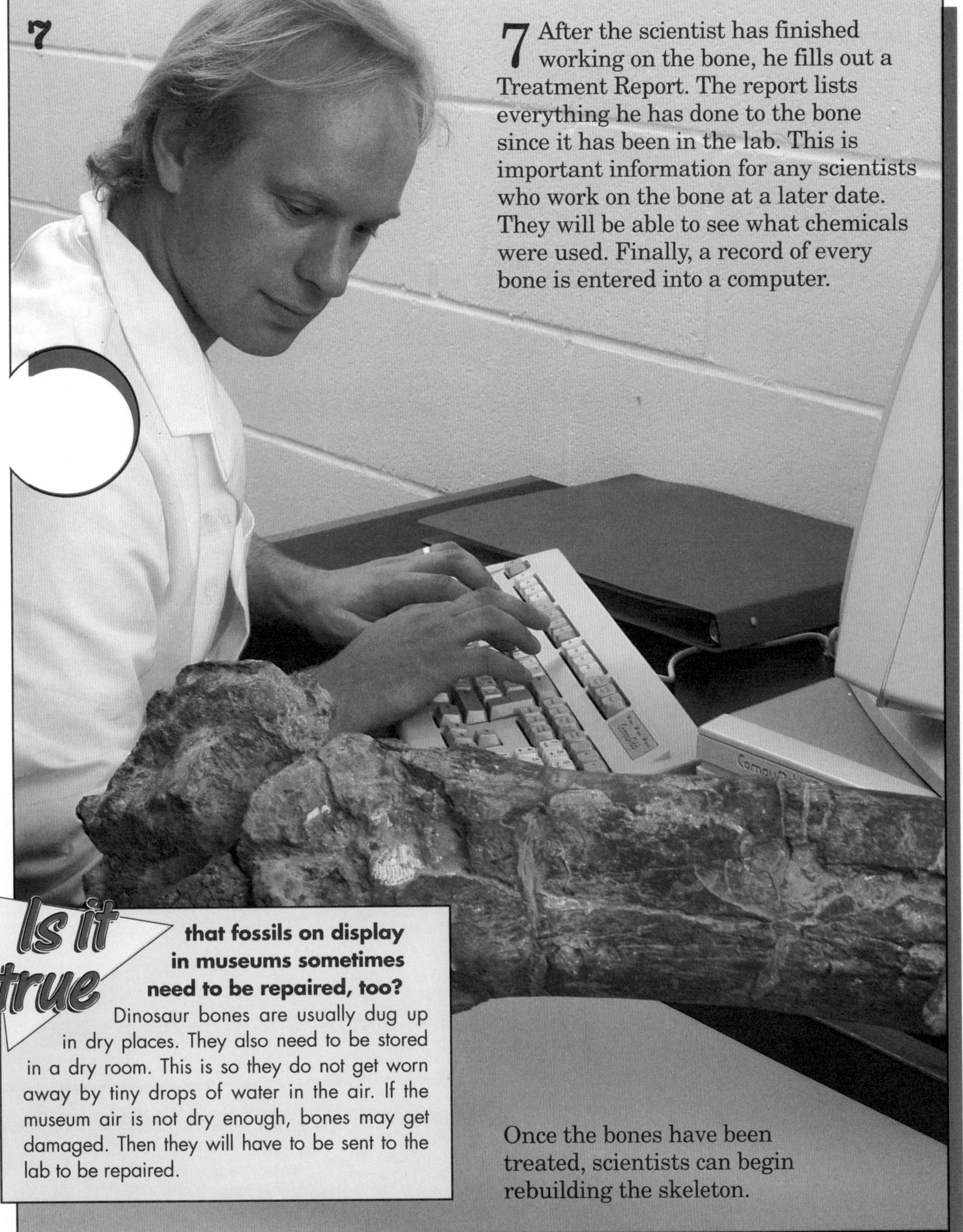

7 After the scientist has finished working on the bone, he fills out a Treatment Report. The report lists everything he has done to the bone since it has been in the lab. This is important information for any scientists who work on the bone at a later date. They will be able to see what chemicals were used. Finally, a record of every bone is entered into a computer.

Is it true that fossils on display in museums sometimes need to be repaired, too?

Dinosaur bones are usually dug up in dry places. They also need to be stored in a dry room. This is so they do not get worn away by tiny drops of water in the air. If the museum air is not dry enough, bones may get damaged. Then they will have to be sent to the lab to be repaired.

Once the bones have been treated, scientists can begin rebuilding the skeleton.

3-D Gallery 32

MUTTABURRASAURUS

• Duckbilled dinosaur
• Lived 107 – 99 million years ago in the Mid Cretaceous Period in Australia
• Measured 23ft (7m) long
• Ate plants

ASK THE EXPERT
Dr. David Norman of Cambridge University answers your dinosaur questions

Did dinosaurs hibernate?

It seems very unlikely that any dinosaurs hibernated. Animals such as tortoises and bears hibernate today because the weather becomes too cold for them and food is scarce. But the climate in dinosaur times was warmer than it is now.

How big was a dinosaur egg?

Dinosaur eggs vary quite a lot in size. Some, such as those found near a *Mussaurus* skeleton, were just 2-3cm long. But others, such as some eggs from a *Hypselosaurus* found in southern France, measured about 20cm long by 16cm wide – that's twice as large as an ostrich egg.

Did dinosaurs have ears?

Dinosaurs had tiny bones to conduct sounds from the eardrum to those parts of the brain where sounds are detected. But they did not have ears like ours. Dinosaur 'ears' would have been small holes in the sides of their heads, near where the head joins on to the neck. This is the same as in birds (whose ear holes are covered by fine feathers) and lizards.

Which dinosaur had the most teeth?

The hadrosaurs (duck-billed dinosaurs) had the most teeth: 480 teeth in the lower jaw and 480 in the upper jaw. That's a grand total of 960 teeth. An adult human has only 32 teeth. Throughout its lifetime, a hadrosaur may have grown as many as 10,000 teeth.

Did dinosaurs have fur?

So far, there is no evidence that dinosaurs had fur. However, it is hard to find out the truth as fur is a soft material, which is unlikely to fossilize.

DINOSAURS!
DISCOVER THE GIANTS OF THE PREHISTORIC WORLD

BRACHIOSAURUS

Brachiosaurus was as long as a tennis court, as high as a three-storey house and weighed as much as 10 large elephants.

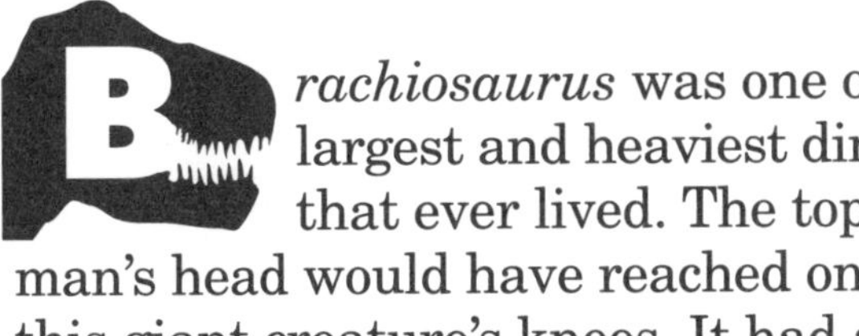

B*rachiosaurus* was one of the largest and heaviest dinosaurs that ever lived. The top of a man's head would have reached only to this giant creature's knees. It had a huge body, a very long neck, a small head and a long tail.

POWERFUL HEART

A large, powerful heart pumped blood all the way up *Brachiosaurus'* neck to its small brain. Some scientists believe it may even have had several hearts to pump the blood around its massive body. Strong muscles along the neck bones helped to hold up its head. Unlike most dinosaurs, *Brachiosaurus'* front legs were longer than its back legs. These helped to support the weight of its long neck.

LONG NECK

Brachiosaurus browsed among the tree tops that were out of reach for other plant-eaters. Using its long neck, it could pluck the highest leaves, in the same way that giraffes feed today. *Brachiosaurus* had strong jaws with teeth shaped rather like sharp-edged spoons for nipping off shoots and twigs.

STRAIGHT LEGS

Brachiosaurus' legs ended in short, thick toes. Underneath the bones of each foot was a pad which cushioned the legs against the jarring shock of its weight. *Brachiosaurus* held its legs straight underneath its body. This helped to support its enormous body weight. Elephants also hold their legs very straight beneath their bodies.

BIG APPETITE

Brachiosaurus needed to eat an enormous amount to supply enough energy for its huge body to grow and move about. An elephant eats about 150kg of food a day. *Brachiosaurus* may have eaten as much as 1,500kg of food a day – 10 times as much as today's giant! It probably travelled in herds and roamed over large areas of land each day to find fresh trees.

MONSTER FACTS

- **NAME:** *Brachiosaurus* (brak-ee-oh-saw-rus) means 'arm lizard'
- **SIZE:** up to 23m long and 12m high
- **FOOD:** leaves and shoots of trees
- **LIVED:** about 152 – 145 million years ago in the Late Jurassic Period in Tanzania and Algeria (Africa) and western North America

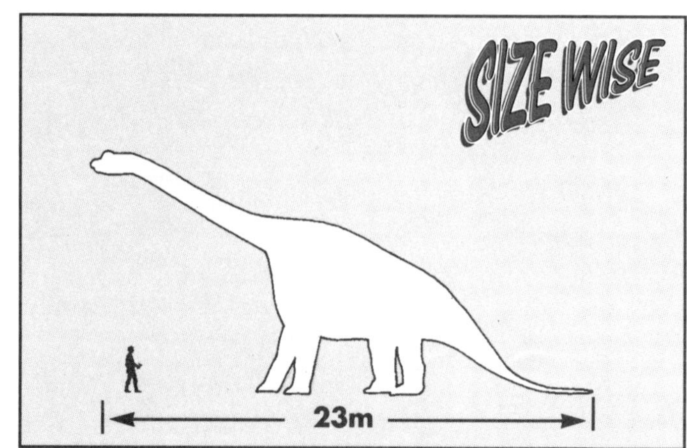

IT'S A FACT

AFRICAN DISCOVERY

A nearly complete skeleton of *Brachiosaurus* was found in Tanzania, Africa, in 1907. It was chipped out of the rock, using only hammers and chisels. Hundreds of workers carried the bones to the nearest port, from where they were sent to Germany. There the skeleton was put together and it now stands in the Natural History Museum in Berlin.

SAFE FROM ATTACK

Because *Brachiosaurus* was so heavy, scientists once thought that it lived in lakes and rivers, where the water would support its massive weight. They thought that its legs would sink deep into the ground as it walked on land. Its nostrils were on the top of its head so it could probably keep its head above the water to breathe. In the water, *Brachiosaurus* would be safe from attack by fierce meat-eaters.

LIVING ON LAND

Nowadays, however, scientists believe that *Brachiosaurus* lived only on the land. The pressure of water would have crushed its ribs, squashing its lungs. We now know, too, that its legs were strong enough to carry the weight of its body as it lumbered through forests, along rivers and around lakes.

LESOTHOSAURUS

Lesothosaurus was one of the tiniest dinosaurs that ever lived, and a natural victim for predators.

Lesothosaurus was only about 1m long, which is no bigger than a Labrador dog. This little dinosaur looked very much like a lizard with a long tail. It had a small head with a tough, beak-like mouth which it used to nip off leaves and plants for food. Inside its mouth, along its cheeks, were small teeth shaped like arrow heads. *Lesothosaurus* used these to chew up the tough and woody parts of plants before swallowing them.

MONSTER FACTS

- **NAME:** *Lesothosaurus* (le-soo-too-saw-rus) means 'reptile from Lesotho'
- **SIZE:** up to 1m long
- **FOOD:** low-lying plants
- **LIVED:** about 190 million years ago in the Early Jurassic Period in Lesotho, southern Africa

BUILT FOR SPEED

Lesothosaurus had a body that was built for speed. It was light and nimble with long, slender back legs. Always on the alert for danger, it could run very fast to escape from meat-eating dinosaurs which tried to catch and kill it.

WARNING SIGNALS

It had no weapons with which to defend itself. But scientists think it may have had a way of warning another *Lesothosaurus,* by a noise or a signal, when a predator was on the prowl.

ALBERTOSAURUS

Small dinosaurs in the forests of North America had to watch out for the frightening form of *Albertosaurus*.

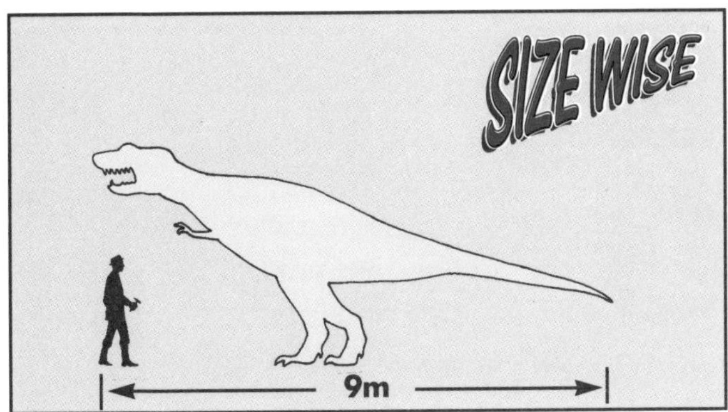

Albertosaurus was a fierce meat-eating dinosaur related to *Tyrannosaurus rex.* Although it was smaller than *T rex, Albertosaurus* probably ran faster on its long, powerful back legs. It chased after plant-eating dinosaurs or may have pounced on them while they grazed.

MONSTER FACTS

- **NAME:** *Albertosaurus* (al-bert-oh-saw-rus) means 'reptile from Alberta', in Canada
- **SIZE:** 9m long
- **FOOD:** meat, especially other dinosaurs
- **LIVED:** about 75 million years ago in the Cretaceous Period in North America

KNIFE-LIKE TEETH

Albertosaurus had rows of backward-pointing, knife-like teeth in its huge mouth for tearing and chewing up meat. On each of its two feet there were three long, sharp claws and another smaller one. At the end of each of its short arms were two small claws. With these, *Albertosaurus* could grab and hold on to its prey – dinosaurs such as *Anatosaurus, Lambeosaurus* and *Chasmosaurus.*

NO ESCAPE

When *Albertosaurus* attacked another dinosaur, its victim had little chance of escaping. Bitten and clawed, the victim was quickly overpowered and killed.

Rise of the dinosaurs

Dinosaurs first appeared on Earth in the Late Triassic Period. Follow the frames of the film and watch their story unfold.

The very first dinosaurs lived during the last part of the Late Triassic Period, about 225 to 204 million years ago. The climate was not the same as it is today. Near the seas and rivers, it was warm and damp. But away from the coasts, inland, it was much drier. The plants then were mostly ferns, horsetails (similar to bamboo) and cycads, which looked like stumpy palm trees. The dinosaurs were not alone in this strange landscape. Many other kinds of animals lived alongside them. They included the earliest turtles, crocodiles and pterosaurs.

1 Alongside the dinosaurs

One animal that shared the dinosaurs' world was the rhynchosaur. It looked like a pig, but had a strange beak made of bone. It also had jaws with plates of tiny, pimple-like teeth for crushing plants. Another creature was *Protosuchus*, the first true crocodile, which you can see here climbing on to the river bank. Its skin was just as knobbly as a crocodile's is today.

2 Creatures that flew

One of the earliest dinosaur-like creatures was *Lagosuchus*, seen running after a dragonfly. In the foreground is a gliding lizard, *Kuehneosaurus*. Above them flies a pterosaur – not a bird, but a flying reptile.

3 Chasing its prey

Herrerasaurus was an early meat-eating dinosaur. Here, it is chasing a thecodont, a reptile with pointed teeth.

What is? A CANNIBAL

When an adult animal eats others of its own species it is called a cannibal. This sometimes happens among present-day meat-eaters, such as male lions and crocodiles. They usually do this through hunger, and also to kill off possible rivals. The best-known cannibal dinosaur was *Coelophysis* of the Late Triassic Period.

5 Speedy and small

The three tiny dinosaurs walking together are *Saltopus* – the smallest flesh-eating dinosaurs that ever lived. They were just 60cm long – the length of a cat. Beside them is *Staurikosaurus.* Its long legs were built for fast running. Beyond, runs speedy, 1m-long *Procompsognathus*.

4 Cannibal dinosaur

A fully grown *Coelophysis* is eating a young of its own species here. It was a vicious cannibal dinosaur. We know this from the bones of babies found in the stomachs of adults. *Coelophysis* was one of the smaller meat-eating dinosaurs. It was very slim and measured up to 3m long – about the length of a dolphin. It also ate other small creatures, such as lizards.

6 A peaceful leaf-eater

Plateosaurus was a large and heavy plant-eating dinosaur that measured 8m in length – which is about the length of a double-decker bus. It was able to stand on its hind legs, and with its long neck reached up to eat the leaves on fairly tall trees. It chopped up the vegetation with its leaf-shaped teeth that were spaced out along its long jaws. Palaeontologists believe that *Plateosaurus* usually went about in herds, like the one in the background, in order to protect itself and its young from meat-eating dinosaurs.

When dinosaurs ruled

Ferocious predators and quiet leaf-eaters – the dinosaurs of the Early Jurassic evolved into a dazzling variety of species.

In the Early Jurassic Period – which lasted from 204 to 184 million years ago – the world began to change. As the continents started to split apart, the climate altered. It rained more and the world became a lot greener. This was the age when dinosaurs really began to rule the Earth.

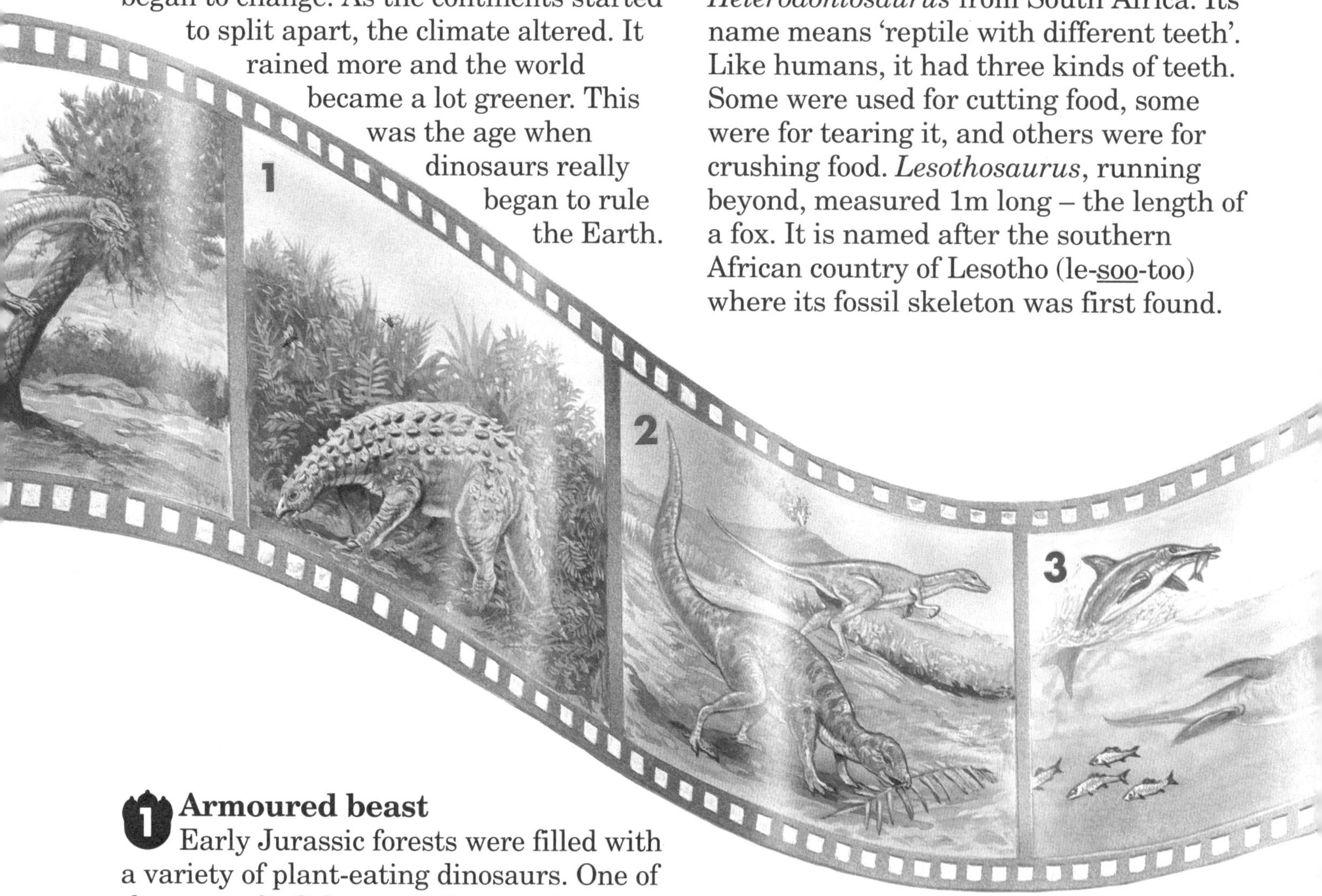

2 Two African plant-eaters

Among the smaller plant-eating dinosaurs of the Early Jurassic Period was *Heterodontosaurus* from South Africa. Its name means 'reptile with different teeth'. Like humans, it had three kinds of teeth. Some were used for cutting food, some were for tearing it, and others were for crushing food. *Lesothosaurus*, running beyond, measured 1m long – the length of a fox. It is named after the southern African country of Lesotho (le-soo-too) where its fossil skeleton was first found.

1

2

3

1 Armoured beast

Early Jurassic forests were filled with a variety of plant-eating dinosaurs. One of them was *Scelidosaurus*. It was a beast with heavy armour that protected it from fierce enemies. It had strong legs like pillars to support its heavy body, and four toes on each foot. *Scelidosaurus* also had a small head, and a horny beak which was filled with tiny, ridged teeth.

3 Life in the water

Creatures swam in the Early Jurassic seas. These were reptiles, not dinosaurs. One was the dolphin-like ichthyosaur, seen leaping in the air. Swimming alongside is a plesiosaur, *Elasmosaurus*.

5 A dinosaur attack

Large, plant-eating dinosaurs (sauropods) were often attacked by smaller predators. Here, a 6.5m-long *Vulcanodon* is threatened by a smaller, meat-eating dinosaur, *Syntarsus*. *Vulcanodon* rears up to defend itself with its large claws. It uses its long tail to help keep its balance. The remains of both these dinosaurs were discovered in Zimbabwe, in southern Africa. *Vulcanodon* is one of the earliest sauropods yet found.

4 Dinosaur from China

Lufengosaurus was about 6m long and nibbled the tops of tall plants by standing on its two powerful back legs. Its name comes from Lu-feng, the place in China where its remains were found. A pair of pterosaurs – flying reptiles – called *Dimorphodon* fly overhead. They had large skulls and deep snouts. Like modern birds, they also had very light, hollow bones, which were rather like drinking straws, so they were light enough to fly.

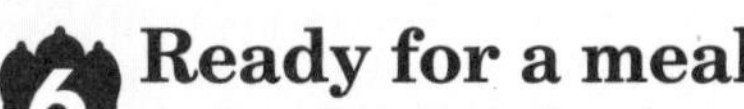

6 Ready for a meal

A 6m-long *Dilophosaurus* is about to devour its meal under the shadow of an erupting volcano. *Dilophosaurus*' jaws were not strong enough to catch live prey, so it was probably a scavenger, eating animals that were already dead. The crest on its head was made of two thin ridges of bone set side by side.

What is? A PLESIOSAUR

Plesiosaurs were long-necked members of a group of marine reptiles. They lived throughout the Age of the Dinosaurs. They had small heads and very long necks. One scientist described the plesiosaur as a 'snake threaded through a turtle'. The neck of the plesiosaur *Elasmosaurus* was over half the length of its 13m-long body.

GIANTS OF THE PAST

Huge and long-necked, *Brachiosaurus* spent its days browsing peacefully among tall trees. It had such a large appetite that it may have eaten up to 1,500kg of food each day! For safety, these gentle giants lived in herds.

BRACHIOSAURUS

3-D Gallery
7
CENTROSAURUS
• A large-horned dinosaur
• Lived 85 – 75 million years ago in North America
• Measured 6m from head to tail
• Ate plants

3-D Gallery 8

IGUANODON

- A huge, thumb-spiked dinosaur
- Lived 130 – 110 million years ago in Europe, North America and Asia
- Measured 10m long
- Ate plants

Spot the difference

Although these dinosaurs appear similar, look hard and you will see the differences between them.

Bony plates and spikes were features of all these dinosaurs. But they looked different on each of them. *Dacentrurus,* for instance, had pairs of spines right along its back. *Kentrosaurus* had an extra spine over each hip. And as well as bony plates on its back, *Ankylosaurus* had a club at the end of its tail.

PLATES AND SPINES
Kentrosaurus
- **Small plates on neck area**
- **About 2.5m long**
- **One extra spine over each hip**

What is? AN ANKYLOSAUR

Ankylosaurs were a family of plant-eating dinosaurs that moved a bit like gigantic rhinos. They had knobs and spines along their backs. These formed a sort of bony armour to protect them from meat-eating predators. Some ankylosaurs, such as *Ankylosaurus* and *Pinacosaurus,* also had clubs at the end of their tails that could be swung against enemies with great force.

TANK-SIZED AND CLUB-TAILED
Ankylosaurus
- **Bony plates on armoured body**
- **Up to 19m long**
- **Large club at the end of its tail**

LARGE AND SPINY
Dacentrurus
- **An early stegosaur**
- **Paired spines along its back**
- **About 7m long**

What is? A STEGOSAUR

Stegosaurs were medium-sized, four-footed dinosaurs, with rows of spikes or plates along the middle of their backs, and sometimes on their hips and tails. Skeletons have been found in North America, Asia, Europe and Africa. Examples of these dinosaurs include *Dacentrurus*, *Kentrosaurus* and *Stegosaurus*.

- **Robust forearms for grabbing at branches**
- **Spines extending right along the back**
- **Small, pointed head**
- **Spines on tail had sharp edges for extra protection**
- **Back legs longer than front legs – for rearing up when feeding**

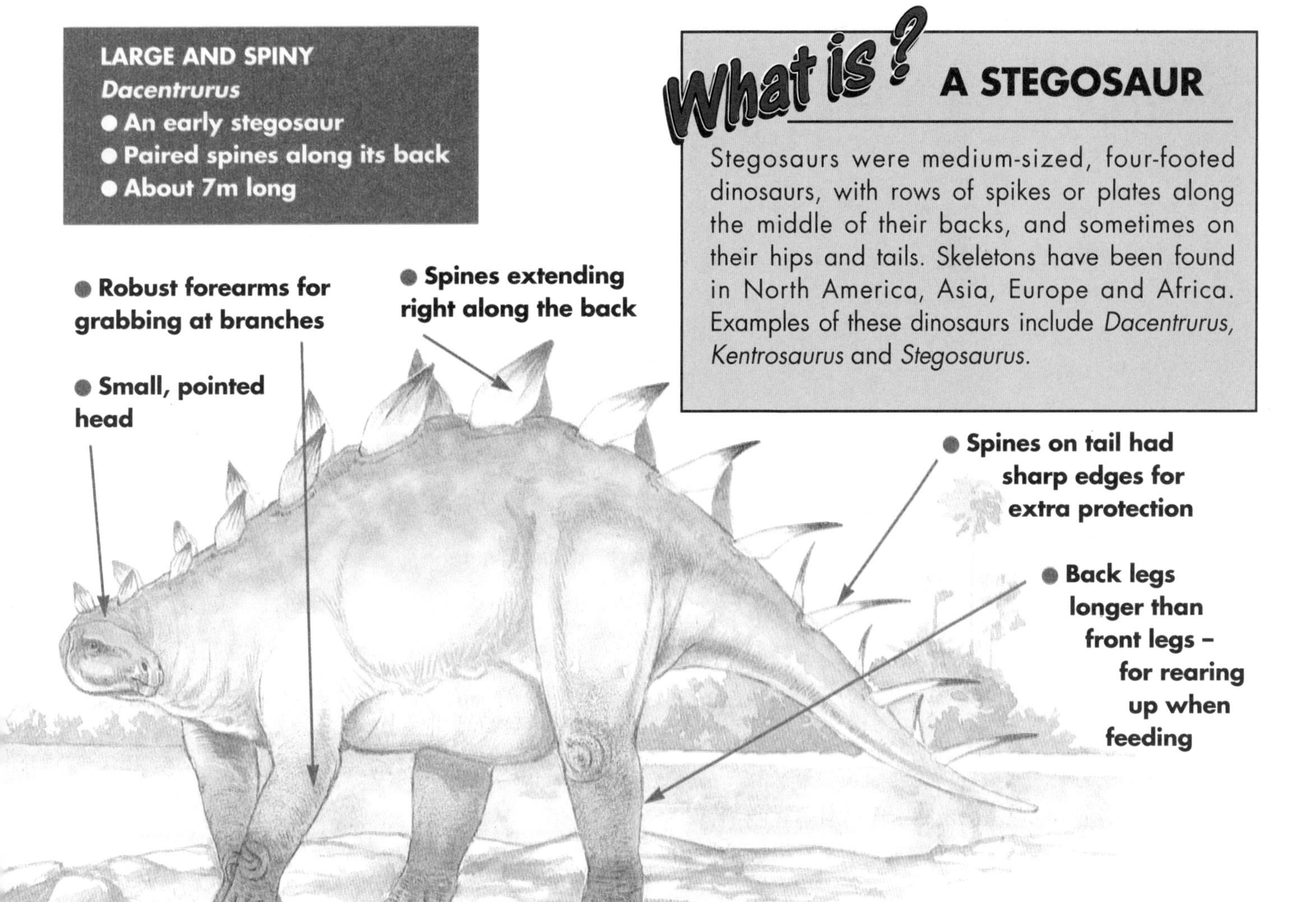

TANK-SIZED AND CLUB-TAILED
Ankylosaurus (an-ky-loh-saw-rus) grew up to 19m long and was about the height of a man. It was built like a tank, and its powerful body was protected by spines and bony plates. At the end of its long tail was a bony club which it used to defend itself.

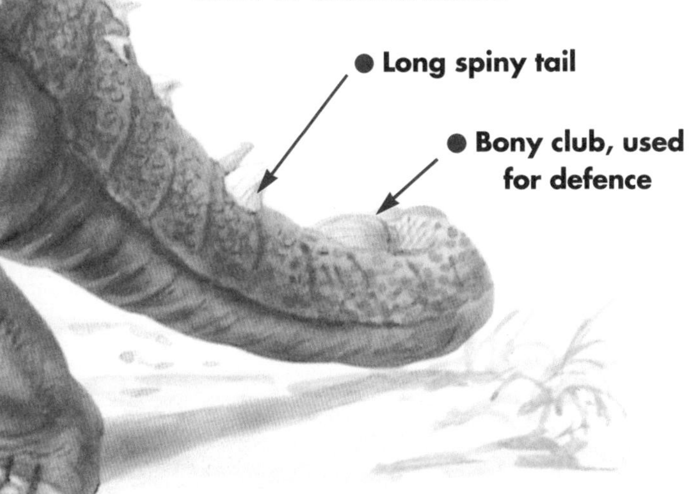

LARGE AND SPINY
Dacentrurus (da-sen-troo-rus) was a herbivore and walked on all-fours. It had spines on its back, and on its tail. The spines had sharper edges than those of other stegosaurs such as *Stegosaurus* and *Kentrosaurus*. Skeletons of *Dacentrurus* have been found in England, France and Portugal.

PLATES AND SPIKES
Kentrosaurus (ken-tro-saw-rus) was a stegosaur about half the height of a man and 2.5m long. Small, triangular plates led down its neck and shoulders. Pairs of spines ran down its back and tail. On both sides of its body, at the hip, there was an extra spine that stuck out sideways.

Rebuilding a dinosaur

Scientists spend hours rebuilding dinosaur skeletons so that they can see more clearly what the animals were like when they were alive.

Studying and rebuilding a dinosaur's skeleton is an exciting piece of detective work. From the skeleton, scientists can tell how the animal moved – whether it walked on two or four legs – and what it ate – whether it was a plant-eater or a meat-eater. They can also tell what the animal's body looked like.

BODY BUILDING
There are marks on some of the bones where muscles were attached which give the experts clues as to how big the muscles were and how much flesh was on the body. With this information, artists can build up a picture of what the dinosaur looked like by adding muscles, flesh and skin to the skeleton either in a drawing or by making a model.

REPLACEMENT BONES
Dinosaur skeletons are not usually complete. If any bones are missing or badly damaged, replacements are made from fibreglass and these are used to complete the skeleton.

LIFE-LIKE
Scientists go to great trouble to rebuild a dinosaur's skeleton in a natural position so that it will look as it did millions of years ago.

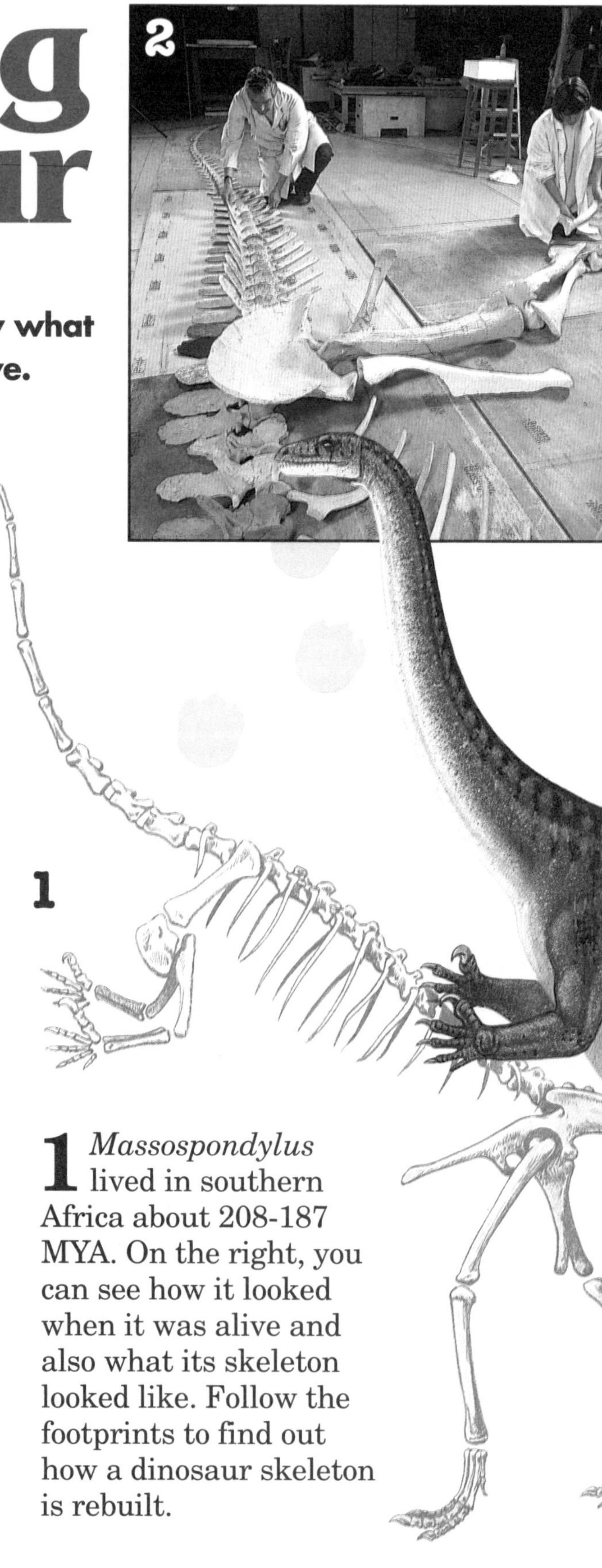

1 *Massospondylus* lived in southern Africa about 208-187 MYA. On the right, you can see how it looked when it was alive and also what its skeleton looked like. Follow the footprints to find out how a dinosaur skeleton is rebuilt.

2 All the bones, including fibreglass replacements, are laid out in their correct order. Scientists study the bones of other animals, including dinosaurs, to see how the bones of the skeleton fit together.

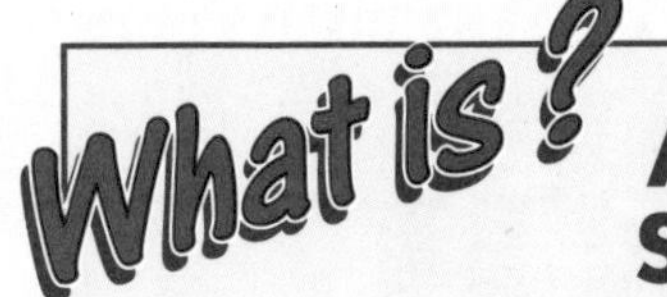

What is? A SUSPENDED SKELETON

Some dinosaur skeletons are now being put together in a new way. Instead of fitting the bones together and resting the final skeleton on a stand, scientists suspend the bones from the museum's ceiling, using steel wires. The bones look as if they are joined, but are really hanging from the ceiling, like a giant puppet.

3 To hold the bones in place, an engineer makes an armature. This is a steel framework to support the bones. The leg bones are put on the armature first, then the spine and ribs are added. The dinosaur is beginning to take shape.

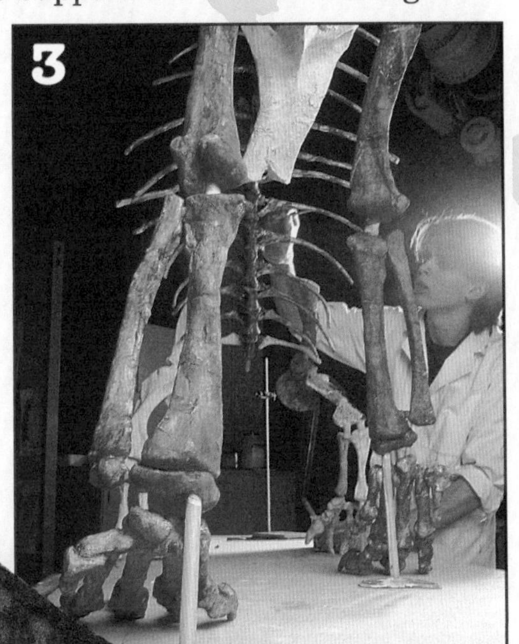

3

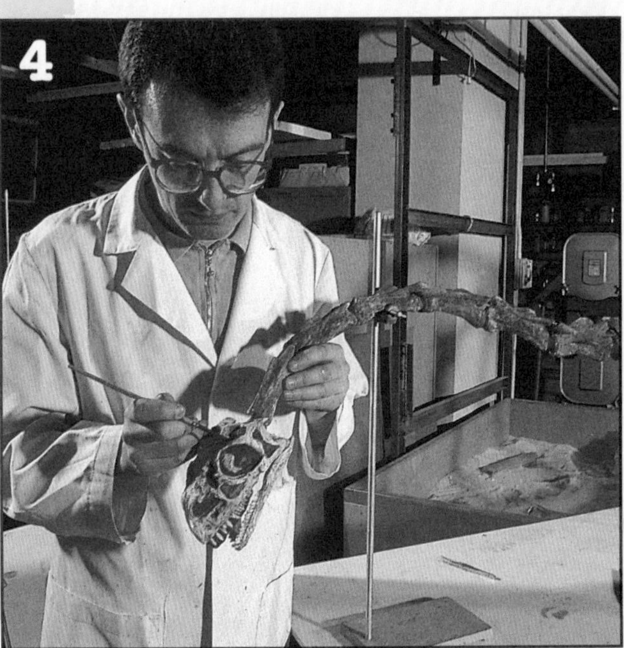

4

4 Once the legs, spine and ribs of the skeleton are mounted on the armature, the tail and skull are added. Here, fibreglass replacement bones are being painted to match the true bone colouring. The skeleton is now complete and ready to display in a museum.

Robot dinosaurs

Computer experts, designers, engineers and palaeontologists combine their skills to produce robotic dinosaur models that move, fight – and even roar.

We cannot bring dinosaurs back to life, but robots in museums give an idea of how these creatures moved.

1 Inside a robot *Triceratops,* the metal skeleton contains the working parts. Air, pushed through cylinders makes the robot move. A computer controls it.

2 The body of a robot dinosaur is sculpted from polyurethane foam, which is light and easy to carve and mould.

Is it true that air operates the robot dinosaurs?

Yes. Air is used to make the dinosaur robots move. Its flow is controlled by a computer. The air is compressed (put under pressure). Inside the robot, the force of the air operates the dinosaur's joints and makes the robots move silently.

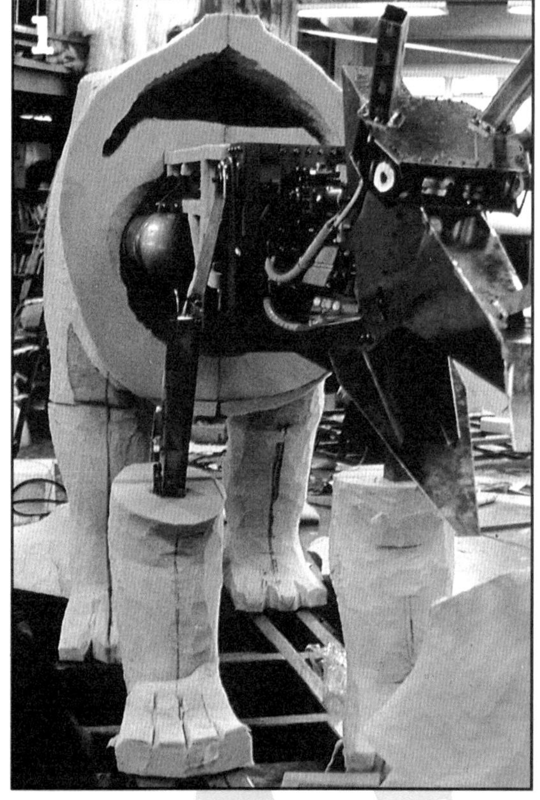

1

3

2

3 *T rex* snarls and bares its teeth, it is almost possible to feel its hot breath. But it is only a robot. However, model makers and engineers do a lot of research by reading, talking to scientists and visiting museums, so that the robot dinosaurs they create are as realistic and accurate as possible.

4 The dinosaur robots are correct in every detail. Here, an artist recreates the animal's rough skin by melting the surface of the polyurethane body to create scales and bony plates. The skin is also painted.

5 In the workshops, the final touches are made to a very realistic *Triceratops* robot. A soundtrack of dinosaur noises is added to the computer programme that controls the robot. Soon, thousands of visitors will hear its ferocious bellow echoing round the museum.

3-D Gallery 33

TYRANNOSAURUS REX AND TRICERATOPS

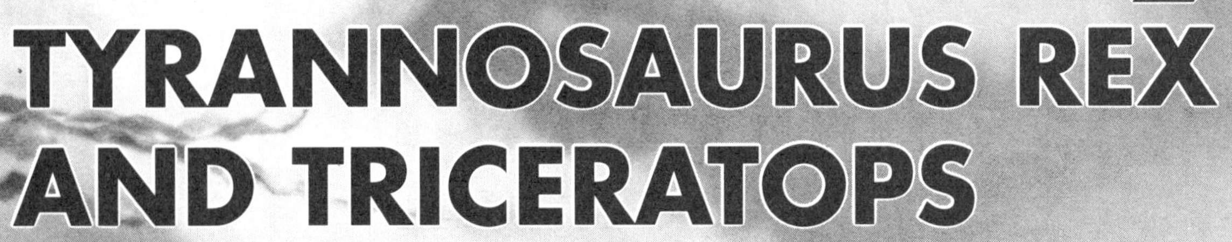

- Two ceratopians come face-to-face with a carnosaur
- This meeting may have taken place 67 million years ago in the Late Cretaceous in North America
- *T rex* was 46ft (14m) long, *Triceratops* was 30ft (9m) long
- *T rex* ate meat, *Triceratops* ate plants

ASK THE EXPERT
Dr. David Norman of Cambridge University answers your dinosaur questions

Did dinosaurs climb trees?

Some of the smaller dinosaurs were very light and agile, and may well have scampered among the trees. The great majority of dinosaurs, however, were far too big to have been comfortable in trees. Many of the giant plant-eaters may even have pushed over trees to get at juicy leaves growing near the top.

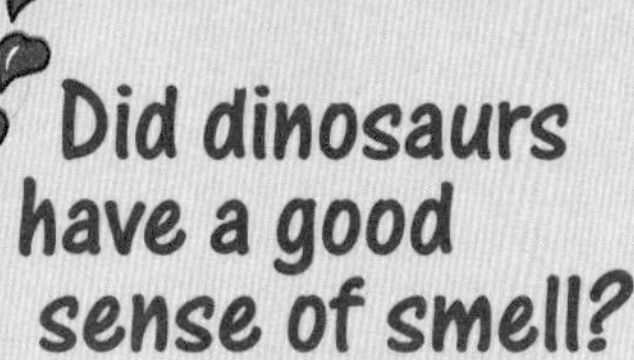

Did dinosaurs have a good sense of smell?

Several dinosaurs had quite large nostrils. The part of the brain (near the front) associated with a sense of smell was also large. So it seems likely that many had a reasonable sense of smell.

Did dinosaurs swallow stones?

Yes, some dinosaurs probably did swallow stones. These were useful for grinding up tough leaves, twigs and shoots in the stomach. In much the same way, canaries swallow grit to help them digest seed.

Is there such a creature as a Brontosaurus?

A few years ago, there was a great deal of fuss about a new set of American stamps. One of the stamps was incorrectly labelled *Brontosaurus.* This wonderful name means ‘thunder lizard’ and was invented by Professor O.C. Marsh in 1879. But a similar skeleton had been named *Apatosaurus* two years earlier. So the name *Apatosaurus* is now correct, and the name *Brontosaurus* is no longer used.

DINOSAURS!
DISCOVER THE GIANTS OF THE PREHISTORIC WORLD

PROTOCERATOPS

When scientists found *Protoceratops'* nests in the Mongolian desert, it was proof that dinosaurs laid eggs and that some lived in family groups or herds.

Protoceratops was a small dinosaur, only about the size of a large dog. Although it looked fierce, with its heavy head, sharp, beak-like mouth and large bony frill around its neck, *Protoceratops* ate only plants. It had a heavy, squat body, with a long, thick tail. *Protoceratops* walked on its four stumpy legs, but moved quite quickly when it was in danger.

BONY FRILL

There was a bony frill or shield around its neck, which grew bigger and broader as the dinosaur grew older. The frill protected the neck of *Protoceratops* from attack by meat-eating dinosaurs. Males also used their frills for display to attract females at the beginning of the mating season. Their frills made them look big and powerful, which warded off rival males.

POWERFUL JAW MUSCLES

Protoceratops had large, strong muscles around its jaws. These helped it bite off tough leaves and woody plants with its hooked beak. It then sliced up the plants with its scissor-like teeth.

Eye socket

Parrot-like beak for cutting vegetation

Strong muscles were linked to the jaw here to help with chewing of plants

Rows of strong teeth in cheek for slicing up food

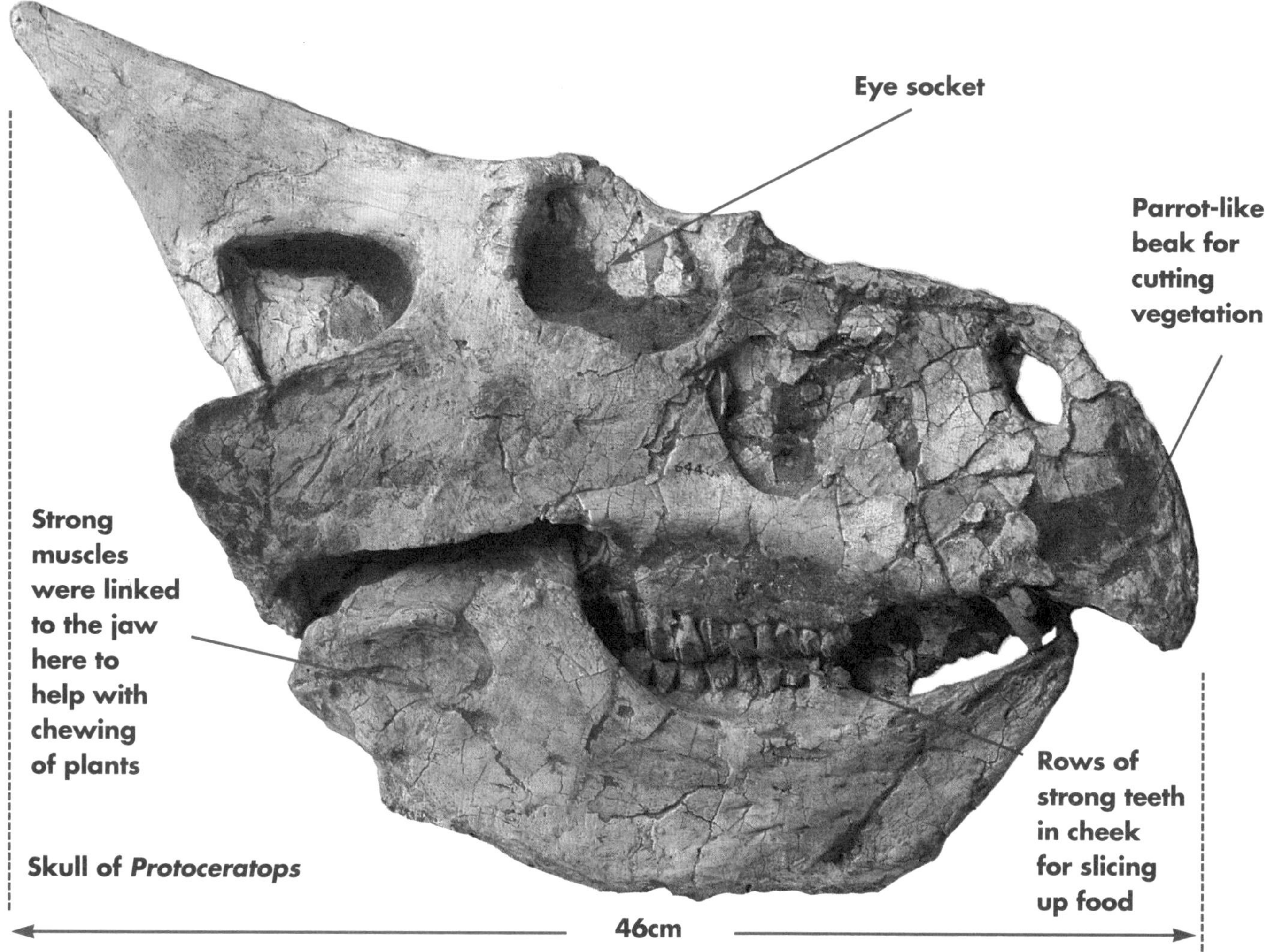

Skull of *Protoceratops*

46cm

Some herbivore dinosaurs, such as *Protoceratops,* had sharp, pointed beaks like the parrot, shown left. These were used to cut through tough plants, which they then ate.

EGGS IN THE DESERT

In 1922, a scientific expedition to the Gobi Desert, in Mongolia, unearthed nests of *Protoceratops'* eggs. These contained the first dinosaur eggs ever found. The discovery proved for the first time that dinosaurs laid eggs. Until then, no one knew if they laid eggs, like crocodiles or lizards, or gave birth to live young, like mammals. As many as 30 eggs were found in one nest. It is unlikely that one female laid so many eggs at once, so scientists think that two or more *Protoceratops* females may have shared the same nest.

MONSTER FACTS

- **NAME:** *Protoceratops* (pro-toe-ser-a-tops) means 'first horned face'
- **SIZE:** about 1.8m long and 1m high
- **FOOD:** tough leaves and plants
- **LIVED:** about 110 – 66 million years ago in Mongolia in the Late Cretaceous Period

IT'S A FACT

EGG-STEALERS

Protoceratops had to guard its nests against predators such as *Oviraptor*, whose name means 'egg-stealer'. Dinosaur eggs would have made an ideal meal for it. A fossilized *Oviraptor* skeleton, with its skull smashed in, was found above a nest of *Protoceratops'* eggs. Perhaps an angry parent had killed it when it tried to rob the nest.

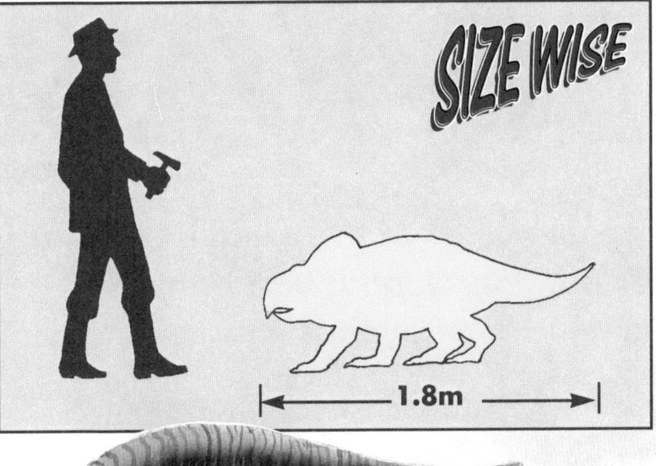

FAMILY GROUPS

Several nests have been found close together. This seems to show that *Protoceratops* lived in family groups or small herds. Once the eggs had hatched safely, the babies which broke out of the shells were about 30cm long. The adult females brought food to the nests until their young had grown big enough to find it for themselves.

DIFFERENT SIZES

Skeletons of *Protoceratops* found in Mongolia range from tiny ones still inside the eggs to small babies and fully grown adults. Some of the adults vary slightly. They have differently shaped frills, for example. Scientists think that this may be because the males were bigger with larger heads, frills and crests than the females.

SAUROLOPHUS

Despite rows of teeth and its crested head, *Saurolophus* was unable to defend itself against attack.

aurolophus is one of the duckbilled dinosaurs, known as hadrosaurs. It used its toothless beak to nip off twigs, tough leaves and pine needles, which it ground up between its many rows of teeth.

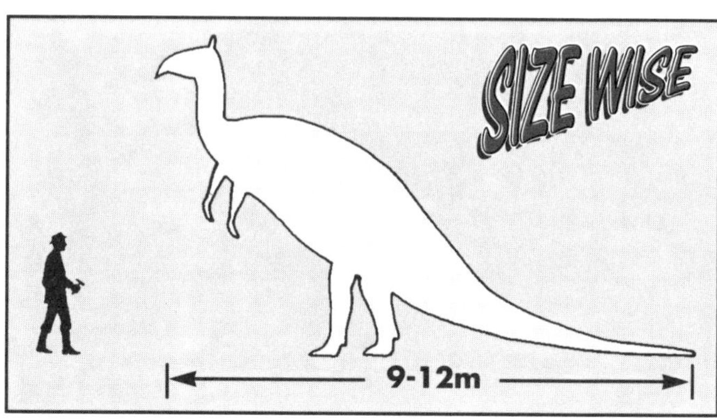

DEFENCELESS DINOSAUR

About as long as a bus, *Saurolophus* walked on its back legs, but supported its body on its shorter front legs when feeding. It had no claws on its toes and no way of defending itself against meat-eating dinosaurs.

MONSTER FACTS

- **NAME:** *Saurolophus* (sore-oh-loh-fuss) means 'ridged lizard'
- **SIZE:** 9 – 12m long and about 3m high
- **FOOD:** tough plants and leaves, seeds, fruit
- **LIVED:** about 80 – 66 million years ago in western North America and eastern Asia in the Late Cretaceous Period

WARNING SIGNALS

Scientists think that *Saurolophus* had a pouch of skin on its face. It blew this up like a balloon to send warning signals to the herd or to attract a mate. It may also have used this pouch to increase the noises it made, just as frogs blow out their throats when croaking.

SYNTARSUS

***Syntarsus* was a speedy, small dinosaur. Some scientists think it might have been covered in feathers.**

Syntarsus was about the length of a small car, and had a long neck and tail. It fed on lizards, small mammals and flying insects. *Syntarsus* ran quickly on its long back legs, like a huge bird, to chase its prey. It also needed to dart about to escape from large meat-eating dinosaurs.

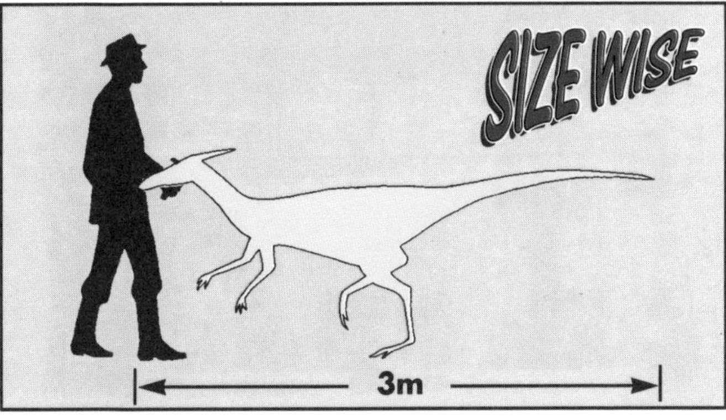

MONSTER FACTS

- **NAME:** *Syntarsus* (sin-tar-sus) means 'fused tarsus'; the 'tarsus' is a bone in the ankle
- **SIZE:** 3m long
- **FOOD:** lizards, mammals and flying insects
- **LIVED:** about 205 – 195 million years ago in Zimbabwe, Africa, in the Late Triassic Period

CURIOUS CREST

On top of its wedge-shaped head was a curious crest. *Syntarsus* could probably turn its head quickly to snatch at its food and to watch for danger.

Syntarsus had long arms ending in large hands with curved claws. Its tail was long and it held it up level with its body when moving at speed.

FEATHERED DINOSAUR?

Some scientists believe that *Syntarsus* had feathers on its head and body. They think that it lifted them away from its body to let the air cool it down during the heat of the day. It could also lower the feathers close to its body to keep in the warmth during the cool evenings and night, using them like a blanket. Other palaeontologists argue, however, that there is no proof for this and that *Syntarsus* had no feathers at all.

A wealth of dinosaurs

Gigantic, plant-eating sauropods and fierce meat-eaters – these were among the many types of dinosaurs roaming the Middle Jurassic landscape.

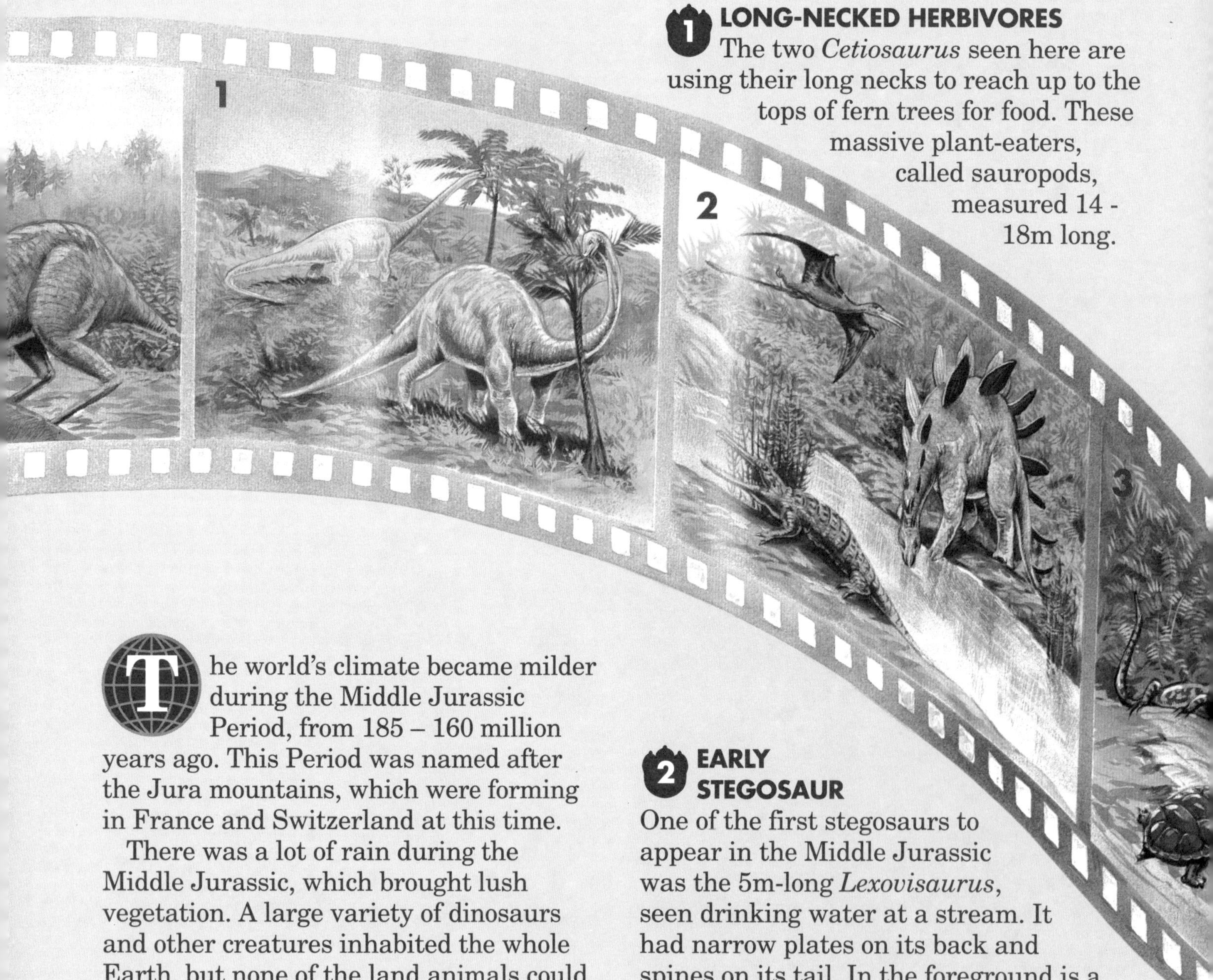

1 LONG-NECKED HERBIVORES
The two *Cetiosaurus* seen here are using their long necks to reach up to the tops of fern trees for food. These massive plant-eaters, called sauropods, measured 14 - 18m long.

The world's climate became milder during the Middle Jurassic Period, from 185 – 160 million years ago. This Period was named after the Jura mountains, which were forming in France and Switzerland at this time.

There was a lot of rain during the Middle Jurassic, which brought lush vegetation. A large variety of dinosaurs and other creatures inhabited the whole Earth, but none of the land animals could rival the dinosaurs for size. The huge carnosaurs and heavyweight armour-plated stegosaurs were all alive in the Middle Jurassic.

2 EARLY STEGOSAUR
One of the first stegosaurs to appear in the Middle Jurassic was the 5m-long *Lexovisaurus*, seen drinking water at a stream. It had narrow plates on its back and spines on its tail. In the foreground is a crocodile of this period. A pterosaur, *Rhamphocephalus*, flies overhead. This creature had a furry body and a long, beaked jaw for catching insects.

4 FEARED PREDATOR

On wings 2m across, a pterosaur, *Rhamphocephalus*, flies above two large dinosaurs. One is a *Cetiosaurus*. The other, to the right, is a *Megalosaurus*. This was perhaps the most feared predator of the Middle Jurassic.

5 OCEAN ODDITY

Metriorhynchus, seen with a fish it has just caught, was a strange, sea-going ancestor of crocodiles. Measuring 2m long – the length of today's common seal – *Metriorhynchus* had a face like a crocodile, but grew a fish-like tail.

Is it true that crocodiles have lived on Earth for 200 million years?

Yes, it is true that crocodiles have inhabited this planet for about 200 million years. The ancestors of the crocodiles first appeared in the Jurassic Period. By the Cretaceous Period, they had become very similar to the crocodiles that live on Earth today.

6 HUGE HUNTER

In this scene, a *Megalosaurus* tears the flesh from its prey. *Megalosaurus* was designed to be a hunter and meat-eater. It had a mouth full of sharp teeth with long roots that were firmly fixed into the jaw bone. The edges of each tooth were serrated, like the blade of a saw, to make it easier to slice through the flesh of its victim.

3 RIVER-BANK CREATURES

Frogs, lizards and turtles, seen along a river-bank, now shared the dinosaurs' world. The first true frogs appeared in the Middle Jurassic. Lizards and turtles, however, had evolved far earlier.

Age of the giants

In the Late Jurassic, the Earth shuddered under the footsteps of the largest dinosaurs that ever lived – sauropods such as *Brachiosaurus*.

One hundred and sixty million years ago, much of the world was covered with large forests. But shallow seas also lay over parts of what is present-day North America and Europe. The climate was generally warm and damp. Dinosaurs ranged from small, fast predators that fed on lizards to gigantic plant-eaters, weighing up to 80 tonnes.

1 UNDER ATTACK

In this scene, two meat-eating *Allosaurus* threaten a *Diplodocus*, which rears up above them. *Diplodocus* was the longest of all dinosaurs. It measured 27m from head to tail – equal to three buses. It was risky for the *Allosaurus* to tackle a *Diplodocus,* because of the danger of being trampled, or struck by its tail.

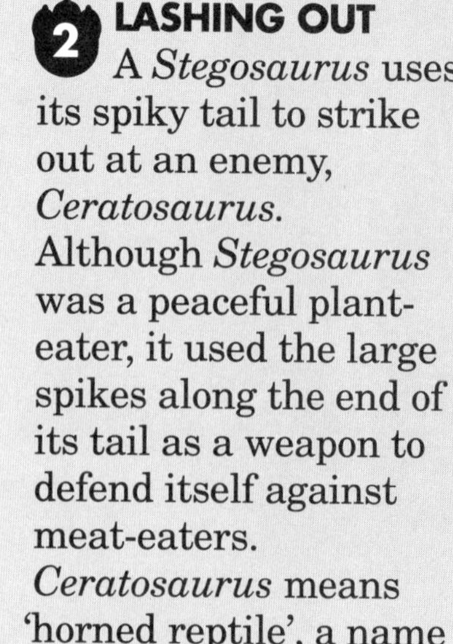

2 LASHING OUT

A *Stegosaurus* uses its spiky tail to strike out at an enemy, *Ceratosaurus.* Although *Stegosaurus* was a peaceful plant-eater, it used the large spikes along the end of its tail as a weapon to defend itself against meat-eaters. *Ceratosaurus* means 'horned reptile', a name that refers to the stumpy horn growing on the end of the animal's snout.

4

5

6

5 A DINOSAUR BATTLE

Amid a jungle of ferns, two *Elaphrosaurus* fight. These dinosaurs had short arms and long, slender legs for fast running. In the foreground, *Archaeopteryx* – a primitive bird – chases after an insect.

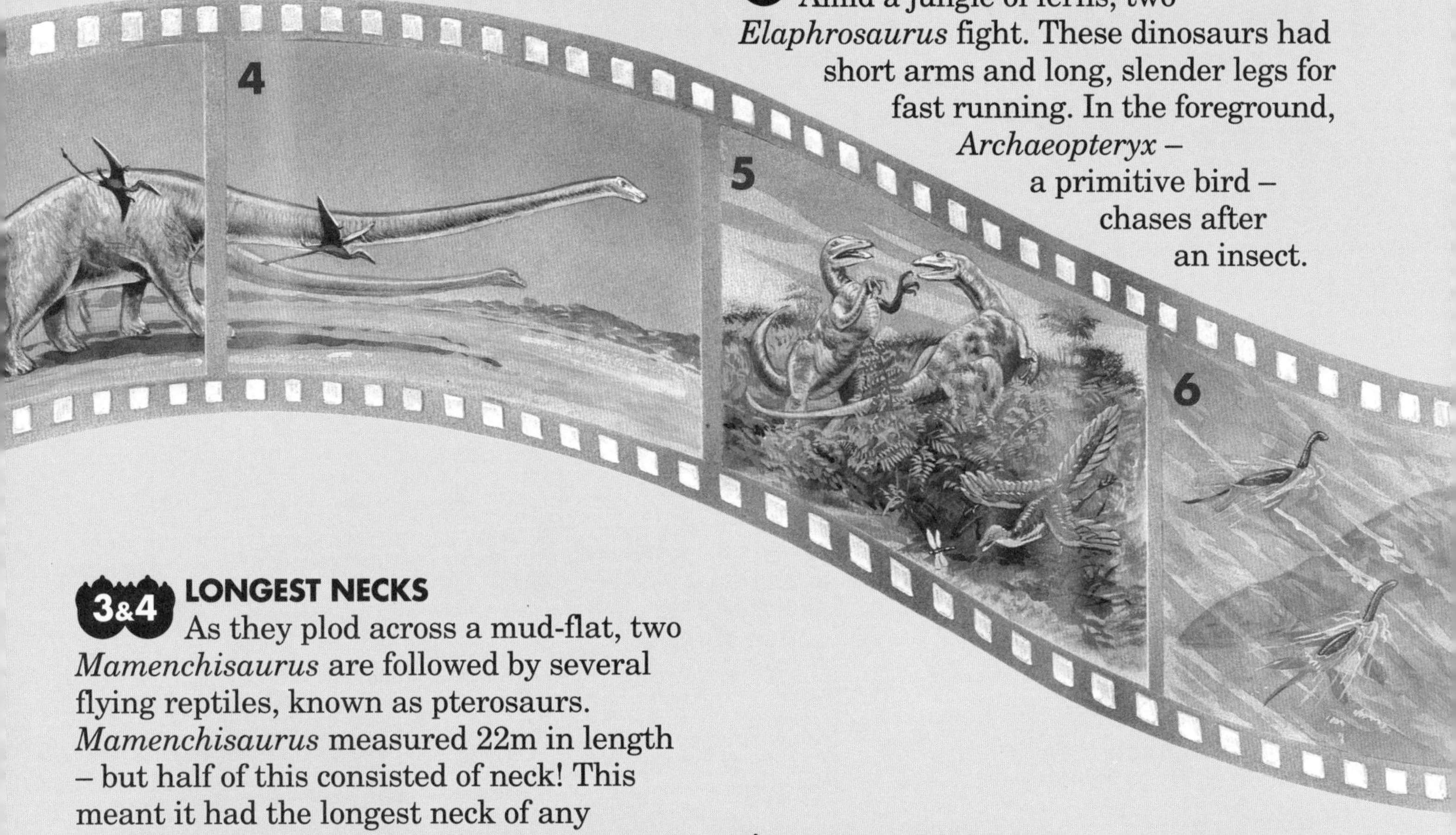

3&4 LONGEST NECKS

As they plod across a mud-flat, two *Mamenchisaurus* are followed by several flying reptiles, known as pterosaurs. *Mamenchisaurus* measured 22m in length – but half of this consisted of neck! This meant it had the longest neck of any animal that ever lived. The neck contained 19 vertebrae (bone segments) – more than any other dinosaur. *Mamenchisaurus* weighed about 30 tonnes, and so needed to eat a vast amount every day.

Is it true that birds are descended from dinosaurs?

Palaeontologists are still not certain that birds are descended from dinosaurs. But most think it is very likely. They have looked at an early bird called *Archaeopteryx*, which lived 150 million years ago. It had feathers like a modern bird, but also some very different features. These included teeth, for instance, and bones in its tail – which link it with the dinosaurs.

6 OCEAN CREATURES

In a Late Jurassic sea, two plesiosaurs, *Cryptocleidus,* swim side by side. These fish-eaters propelled themselves along in the water using their long, broad flippers, which were shaped like paddles. *Cryptocleidus* did not 'row' through the water though. It moved through the sea by flapping its front flippers like penguins do today and steered with its back fins.

Below the *Cryptocleidus* is another sea reptile – a huge pliosaur, *Stretosaurus*. Pliosaurs had short necks and large heads; their relatives the plesiosaurs had long necks and small heads.

Both plesiosaurs and pliosaurs breathed air so they had to surface in order to fill their lungs.

GIANTS OF THE PAST

PROTOCERATOPS

Two *Protoceratops* face each other, ready for a head-to-head battle over leadership of their herd. *Protoceratops* were small dinosaurs and lived in herds to help them survive attacks from large predators. But within the herds, males fought to decide who would be leader.

3-D Gallery 9

HYPSILOPHODON

- A fast runner
- Lived 120 - 110 million years ago in England
- Measured 2m from head to tail
- Ate low-lying plants

3-D Gallery 10

STYRACOSAURUS

- A horned dinosaur
- Lived 85 - 75 million years ago in North America
- Measured 5.5m from head to tail
- Ate plants

Dinosaur portraits

Study this gallery of dinosaur heads and discover how different their faces were in size and shape.

Some dinosaurs had huge, spined heads. Others were horned, duckbilled or had snouts like beaks.

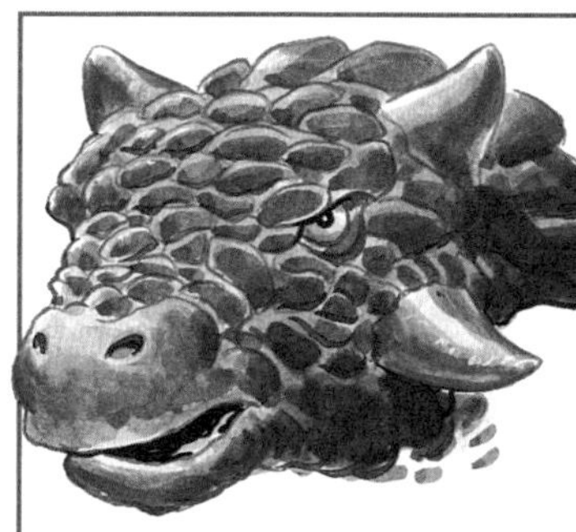

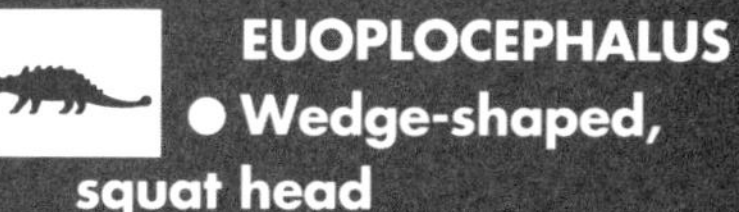

EUOPLOCEPHALUS

- Wedge-shaped, squat head
- Protected by spikes
- Short, wide mouth
- 40cm from tip of snout to back of bony neck

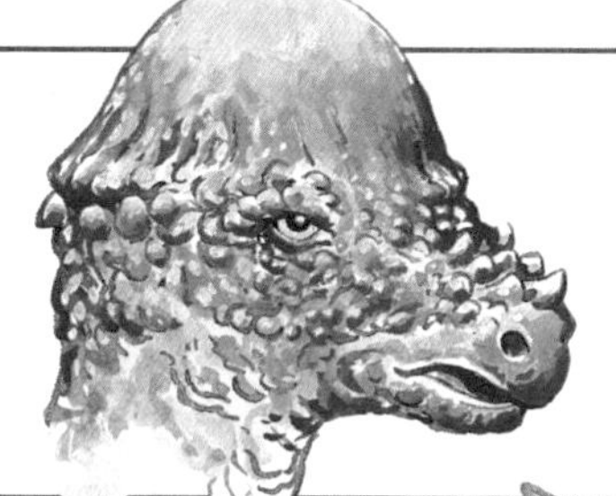

PRENOCEPHALE

- Domed head used in head-butting fights
- Large, forward-facing eyes
- Plant-eater with sharp front teeth for cutting food
- 26cm from tip of snout to back of head

TROODON

- Carnivore (meat-eater) with a slight, slender jaw for snapping at its prey
- Large, forward-facing eyes
- Sharp cutting, stabbing teeth
- 24cm from tip of snout to back of head

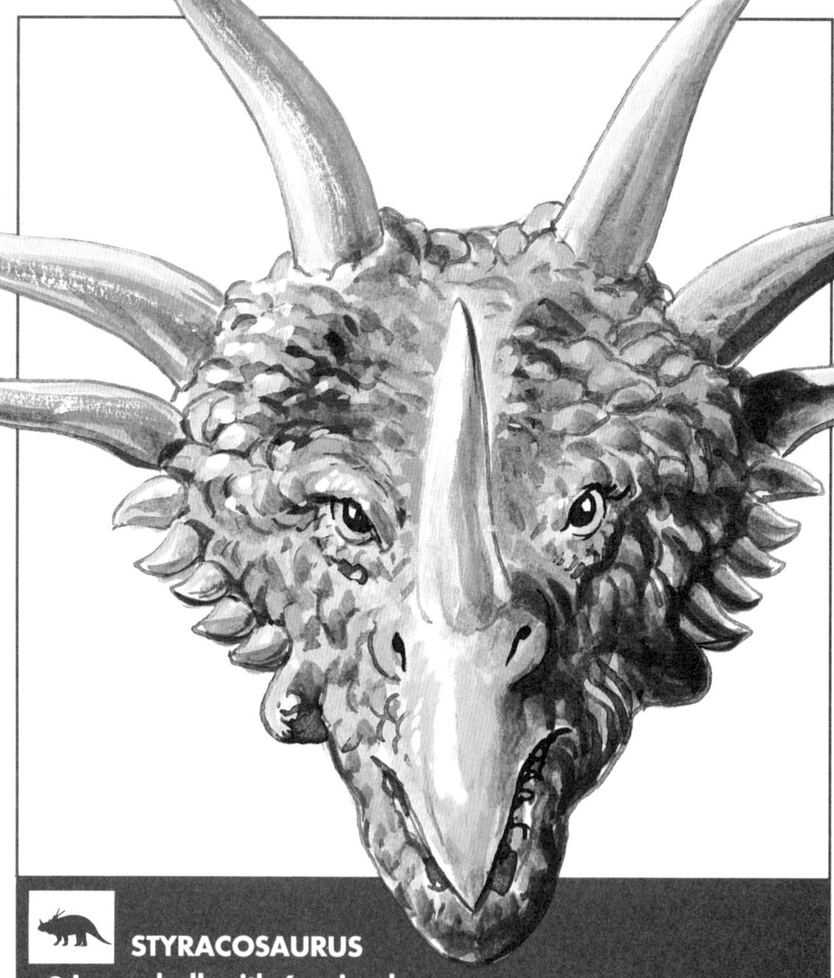

STYRACOSAURUS

- Long skull with 6-spined frill for display and defence
- Tall horn over nose for stabbing at predators
- Parrot-like beak for slicing vegetation
- 2m from tip of snout to tip of longest spike

CORYTHOSAURUS

- Duckbilled dinosaur
- Crest on top of head for mating display
- Also used hollow crest for making calling sounds
- 55cm from tip of snout to back of head

OURANOSAURUS

- No frills or crests
- Flattened beak, but not a true hadrosaur
- Large cheeks for holding in food while chewing
- 55cm from tip of snout to back of head

A HADROSAUR

Hadrosaurs were broad-beaked dinosaurs that lived in the Late Cretaceous Period. These animals are also called 'duckbills', because their wide, toothless beaks looked like those of ducks. Unlike ducks, however, they had rows of teeth near the back of their mouths for grinding food. Hadrosaurs varied in size. Some were only about the height of a man, while others were about the height of a two-storey house.

PARASAUROLOPHUS

- Duckbilled dinosaur
- Long, hollow crest used for making loud calling sounds
- Large cheeks for holding in food while chewing
- 1.25m from tip of snout to end of crest

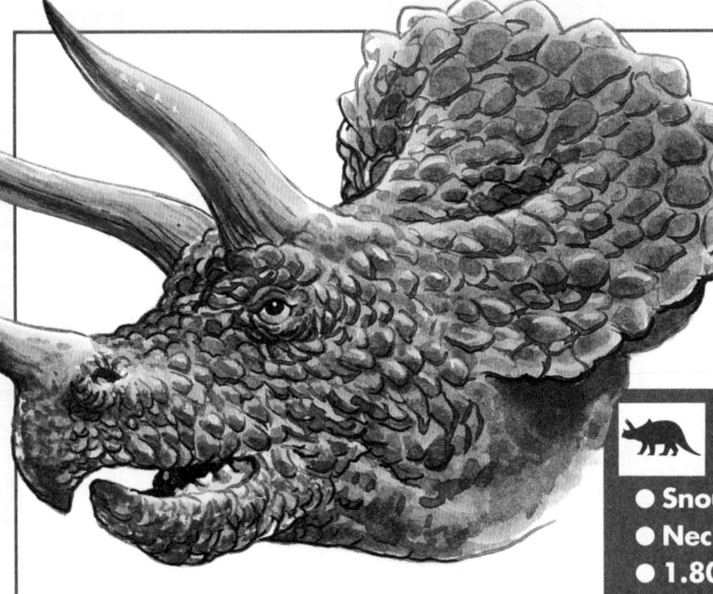

TRICERATOPS

- One horn on nose, and two above the eyes
- Snout like a parrot's beak for slicing up vegetation
- Neck frill surrounded by knobs of bone for protection
- 1.80m from tip of snout to back of frill

Match the head to the outline of the dinosaur.

Introducing the bird feet

Scientists divide dinosaurs into different groups. Each dinosaur in a group has something that makes it like the others. Grouping dinosaurs in this way can help scientists to study them more easily.

Some of the dinosaurs shown here were as small as dogs; others were the size of giraffes. They may look very different from each other, but they all have some things in common. They are all members of a group called the ornithopods.

BIRD FEET

Ornithopod means 'bird feet' and scientists have placed these dinosaurs together in the same group. Can you spot why? They walked and ran on their two strong back legs like large birds. Ornithopods were also all plant-eaters. Many of them had no teeth at the front of their jaws, their teeth were further back.

LIVING THROUGH THE AGES

The ornithopods did not all live at the same time but they were a very successful group. The Triassic, Jurassic and Cretaceous periods each had its own ornithopods. *Heterodontosaurus* (het-er-oh-dont-oh-saw-rus) lived at the beginning of the Age of Dinosaurs, about 220 million years ago. Others, such as *Anatosaurus* (an-at-oh-saw-rus), lived at the end of the Age of Dinosaurs, about 66 million years ago. There were many others in the millions of years in between.

BIG GROUP
There were between 60 and 70 different kinds of dinosaur in the ornithopod group. Some, such as *Parasaurolophus* (pa-ra-saw-oh-loaf-us), had curious crests, which curved back from their snouts. The crest had tubes inside it and was probably used to make loud bellowing noises.

WORLD WIDE
Ornithopods lived in many parts of the world. Skeletons have been dug up in North America, Asia, Europe and Africa. *Ouranosaurus* (oo-ran-oh-saw-rus) was discovered in North Africa. Like all ornithopods, it had strong back legs.

IT'S A FACT

CHANGING ORNITHOPODS
Ornithopods existed for millions of years, and over this time they evolved (changed). Most of the ornithopods that lived at the end of the Age of Dinosaurs were much bigger than those that lived at the beginning. By the end of the dinosaur age, ornithopods' mouths had also changed. Some, such as *Iguanodon* and *Hypsilophodon* (hip-see-loaf-oh-don), had horny beaks instead of front teeth.

ORNITHOPOD CHECK LIST
- Could walk upright on two legs
- Ate plants

Anatosaurus

Iguanodon

Ouranosaurus

Meet the horned eyes

Horns, frills and curved bony beaks are the clues to look for when you identify a dinosaur that belongs to the group called the ceratopians.

One of the best known of dinosaurs, *Triceratops*, belongs to the ceratopian group. Ceratopian means 'horned eye' and the magnificent horns that most of these dinosaurs had above their eyes gave the group its name. *Triceratops* was the largest of this group and its brow horns were up to one metre long.

LIFE-SAVING FRILLS

Most ceratopians had a huge neck frill. The frill was made of bone, covered with skin. It protected the dinosaur's neck from being bitten or clawed by meat-eaters. In some dinosaurs, such as huge *Torosaurus* (to-roh-saw-rus), the frill grew half way down the animal's back.

PARROT BEAKS

Psittacosaurus did not have an obvious neck frill, but it did have another feature of the group, a parrot-like beak. Ceratopians ate plants and their beaks helped them chop tough plant stems.

Triceratops

Psittacosaurus

Styracosaurus

CHANGING FACES

The horned eyes included many different kinds of dinosaur. The group lived towards the end of the Age of Dinosaurs in the Cretaceous Period. Like the ornithopods, the ceratopians evolved (changed) during their time on Earth. Some of the first ceratopians, such as *Protoceratops*, did not have horns, instead they had thick, bony areas over their snouts and eyes. But in time, ceratopians developed horns. *Pentaceratops* (pent-a-ser-a-tops) was a later dinosaur than *Protoceratops*. It had the most horns of all the horned dinosaurs. Its name means 'five horned face'.

CERATOPIAN CHECK LIST
- **Horns on face**
- **Neck frill**
- **Parrot-like beak**
- **Walked on four legs**
- **Ate plants**

Is it true that some ceratopians had holes in their frills?

The neck frills of these animals were made of bone. Some of them were so large that they must have been extremely heavy. To make them lighter, some of them had large holes in them. The skin covering the frill stretched over the holes so that they could not be seen.

FOUR FOOTED

Like today's rhinoceroses, the ceratopians walked on all fours. *Styracosaurus* had strong, muscular legs to support its huge head. Its feet ended in toes which were spread out to help carry the weight of its large body. *Psittacosaurus* usually walked on two legs, but it walked on all fours sometimes. The ceratopians lived only in North America and Asia, which are the only places where their fossils have been found so far.

Pentaceratops

Protoceratops

Torosaurus

3-D Gallery 34

DIPLODOCUS FAMILY

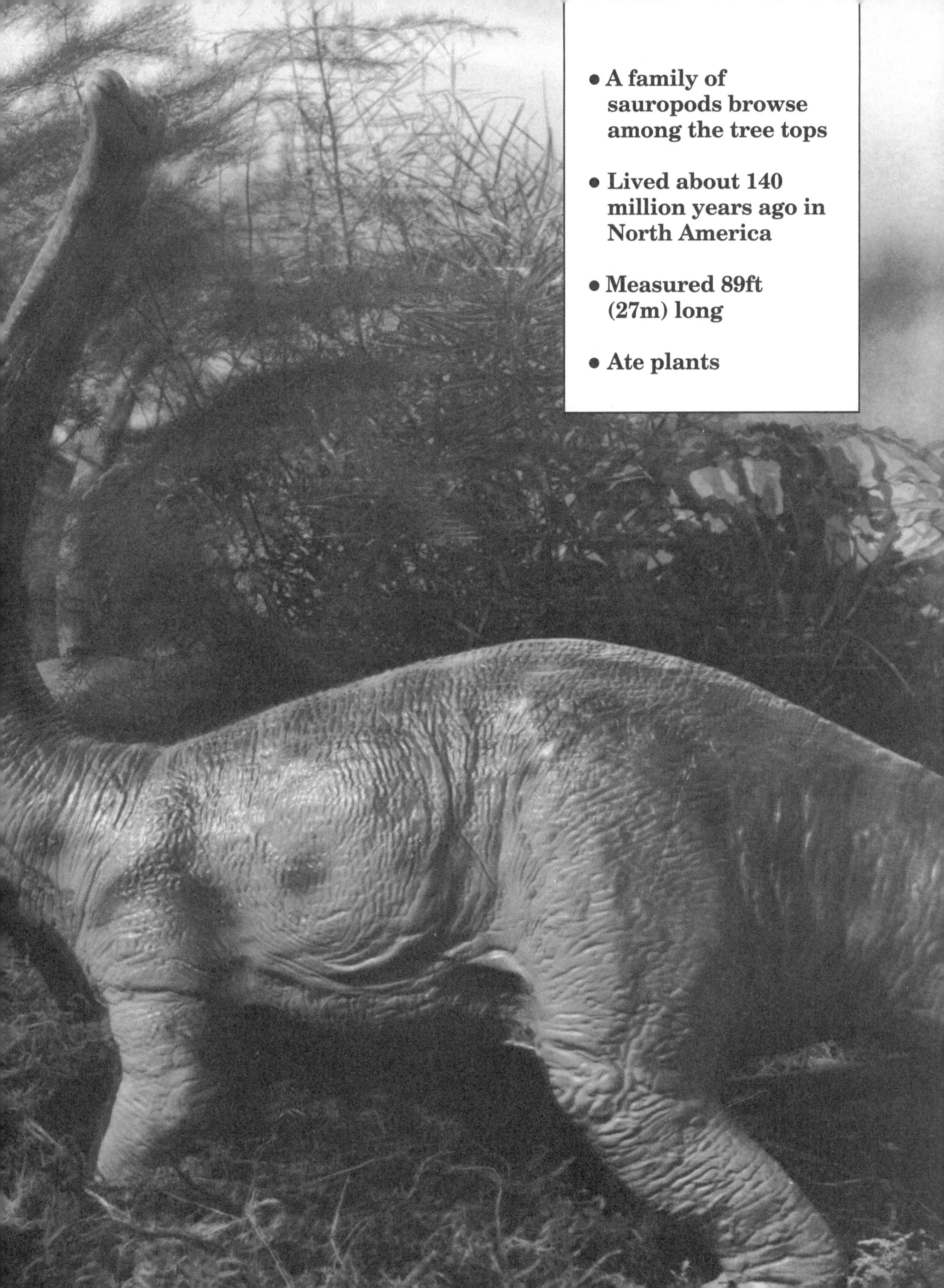

- A family of sauropods browse among the tree tops
- Lived about 140 million years ago in North America
- Measured 89ft (27m) long
- Ate plants

Dr. David Norman of Cambridge University answers your dinosaur questions
ASK THE EXPERT

How did dinosaurs use their claws?

Dinosaur claws were used for a variety of purposes. Sharp, narrow claws were probably used for ripping at prey. Broad, flat claws were used as hooves for walking on. Other types of claws were more suitable for digging, scratching, or for defence against enemies.

Did dinosaurs migrate?

Dinosaurs migrated over huge distances, looking for new hunting grounds, fresh pastures or nesting sites. Scientists now know from fossils they have found that some dinosaurs also crossed whole continents. Today, some birds fly thousands of miles to migrate to warmer countries.

Did dinosaurs live in herds?

There is a lot of evidence that certain species of dinosaur lived in herds. Thousands of bones from one type of dinosaur have been found together. These bone piles were probably made when herds of dinosaurs were killed by sudden floods.

Did humans ever meet dinosaurs?

The last of the dinosaurs trod the Earth about 66 million years ago at the end of the Cretaceous Period. The first human beings that looked as we do today did not appear much before 150,000 years ago. This means that they missed dinosaurs by 65,850,000 years. So they could not possibly have seen a live dinosaur.

How clever were dinosaurs?

Dinosaurs were not at all stupid, even though many had small brains. Some were highly intelligent and had surprisingly large brains for reptiles.

DINOSAURS!
DISCOVER THE GIANTS OF THE PREHISTORIC WORLD

IGUANODON

One of the first dinosaurs to be found, *Iguanodon* had strong back legs with three-toed feet and hoof-like nails.

Iguanodon usually walked on all-fours but sometimes got about on just its hind legs. It weighed as much as an elephant.

FAST ON ITS FEET

Scientists think that *Iguanodon* probably walked on its toes, like a cat or dog. When chased by a predator, it could run like the wind at about 35 km/h. *Iguanodon's* tail was stiff and flat, and this helped it to keep its balance.

LIVED IN HERDS

Lots of skeletons of *Iguanodon* have been found close together. This is a clue to the fact that they lived in groups or herds. *Iguanodon* was the second dinosaur to be named, in 1825.

19 CM THE LENGTH OF IGUANODON'S THUMB SPIKE

***Iguanodon* could use its hands for many different things, such as defence and for grasping food. They also served as feet when *Iguanodon* walked on all-fours.**

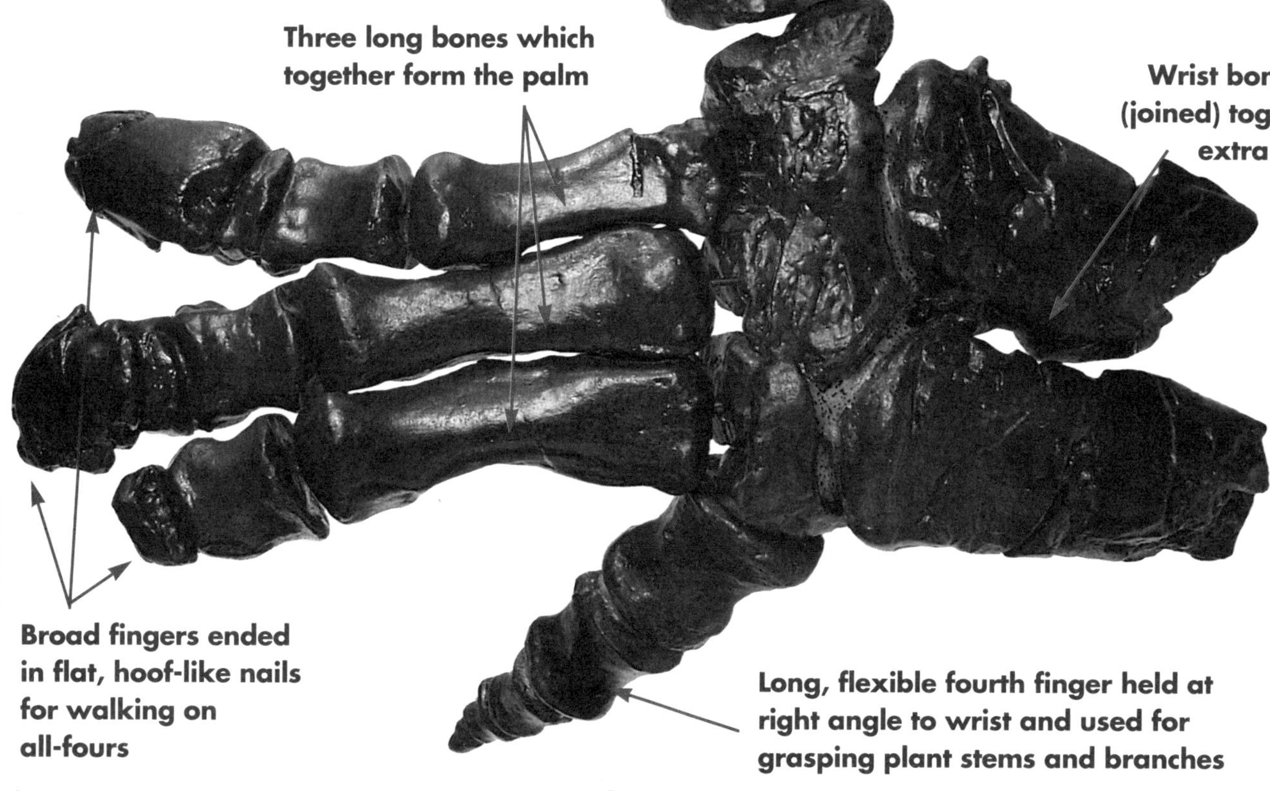

SPIKED THUMB

Iguanodon had very strange hands. These had four fingers and a pointed thumb that was like a spike. *Iguanodon* could only move the spike from side to side and used it as a weapon to defend itself. *Iguanodon* was a plant-eater and used its fourth finger to hook down branches for food.

SIZE WISE

10m

MONSTER FACTS

- **NAME:** *Iguanodon* (ig-wa-no-don) means 'iguana tooth'
- **SIZE:** up to 10m long and 5m high
- **FOOD:** plants and leaves
- **LIVED:** about 120 – 110 million years ago in the Early Cretaceous Period in Europe, Mongolia, North Africa and North America

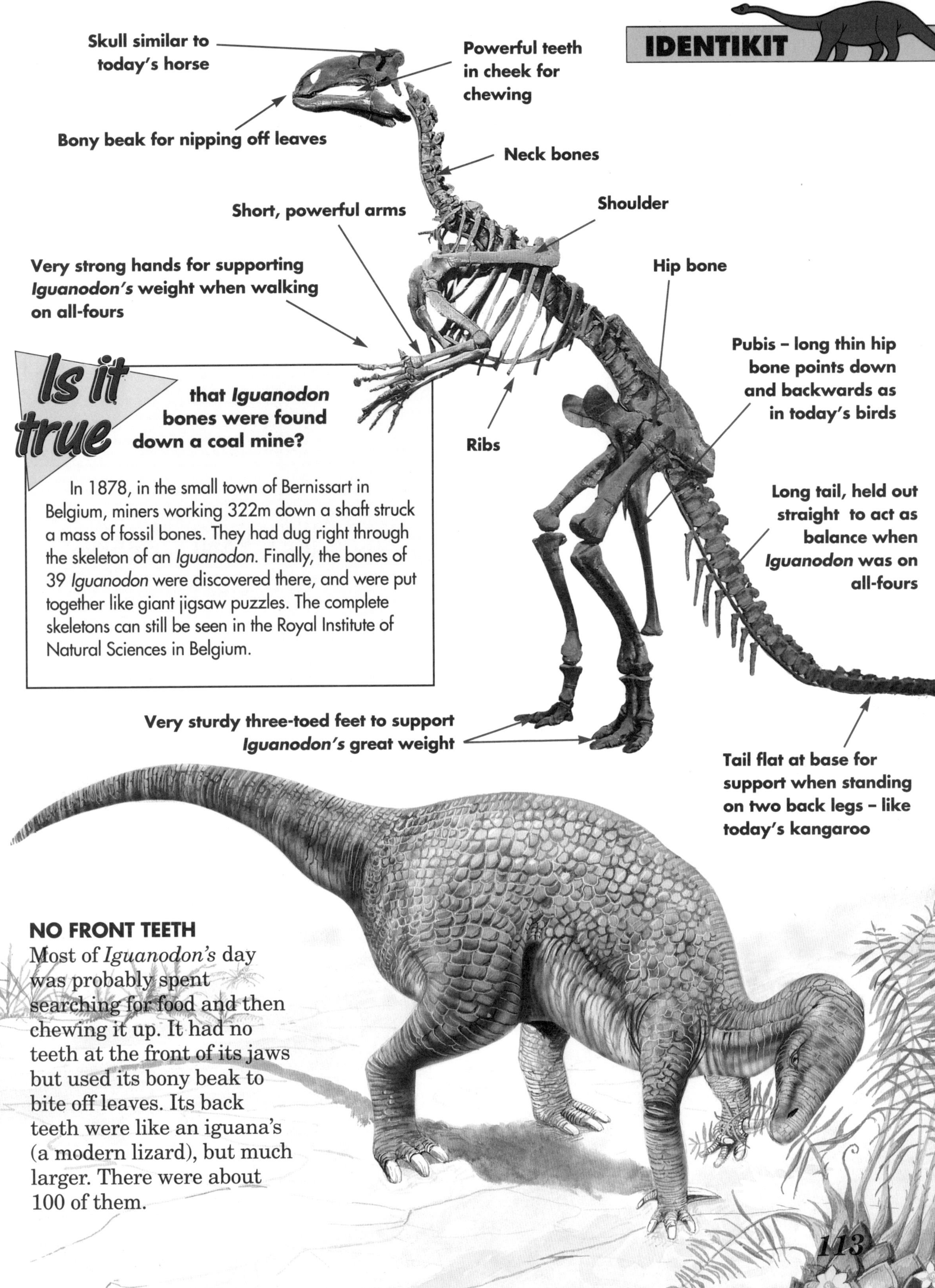

Is it true that *Iguanodon* bones were found down a coal mine?

In 1878, in the small town of Bernissart in Belgium, miners working 322m down a shaft struck a mass of fossil bones. They had dug right through the skeleton of an *Iguanodon*. Finally, the bones of 39 *Iguanodon* were discovered there, and were put together like giant jigsaw puzzles. The complete skeletons can still be seen in the Royal Institute of Natural Sciences in Belgium.

NO FRONT TEETH

Most of *Iguanodon's* day was probably spent searching for food and then chewing it up. It had no teeth at the front of its jaws but used its bony beak to bite off leaves. Its back teeth were like an iguana's (a modern lizard), but much larger. There were about 100 of them.

BAROSAURUS

***Barosaurus* had a very long neck and often fed on leaves on the top of trees, just as giraffes do today.**

uge and long-necked, *Barosaurus* also had a lengthy tail which it wielded as a weapon against enemies. It lived in herds, which was also useful for defence against predators. Like all members of the sauropod family, it had one large, curved claw on the inner toe of its front foot.

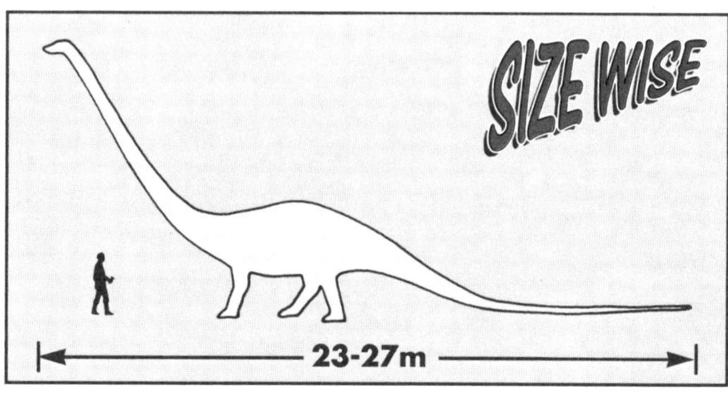

MONSTER FACTS

- **NAME:** *Barosaurus* (bar-oh-saw-rus) means 'heavy reptile'
- **SIZE:** up to 27m long
- **FOOD:** plants and leaves
- **LIVED:** about 150 – 140 million years ago in the Jurassic Period in western North America and Tanzania, East Africa

HOLLOW NECK BONES

The bones in *Barosaurus'* long neck were hollow and light, which meant it could lift its head to feed quite easily. If its neck bones had been solid, it would have been too heavy to lift.

BRAIN DRAIN

Some scientists say that *Barosaurus* probably only lifted its head for a short while at a time. Otherwise the blood might have stopped flowing to its brain, because its heart was so far away from its head. Other scientists think that *Barosaurus* may have had several hearts to help pump the blood around its massive body.

GALLIMIMUS

Gallimimus was built for speed. It could run fast enough to break the speed limit in most of today's cities.

With a short, light body and long back legs, *Gallimimus* was a fast-running dinosaur. It took very long strides and could outrun most predators. It looked like a large ostrich with its long neck and toothless beak, but it had no feathers and no wings. Its stiff tail helped it to balance when running.

MONSTER FACTS

- **NAME:** *Gallimimus* (gal-ih-mime-us) means 'hen mimic'
- **SIZE:** up to 4m long and 3m high
- **FOOD:** plants, eggs, insects and lizards
- **LIVED:** about 70 million years ago in the Cretaceous Period in Mongolia

THREE-CLAWED HAND

Gallimimus had short arms with three claws on its hands. The claws were sharp, but *Gallimimus* could not grasp things very well and did not eat meat because it could not tear it up.

DIGGING UP EGGS

Gallimimus' claws came in very useful, however, because it used them to scrape away at the soil to dig up eggs for food. It ate mostly plants, but it also fed on small insects, which it grabbed in its beak, and even chased lizards.

Reign of the plant-eaters

Plant-eaters became the most important dinosaurs 140 – 100 million years ago. Some were small and speedy. Others were large and slow.

More kinds of dinosaurs lived during the Early Cretaceous than at any other time. Most were plant-eaters but there were also some vicious meat-eaters.

1 SPIKES AND PLATES

Some of the plant-eaters of this period were armoured for defence. *Polacanthus*, seen in the background, was protected by sharp spines and bony plates on its back. *Hylaeosaurus*, pictured in the foreground, measured about 6m long – the length of an African elephant. It also had plated armour with spines. These stuck out along the lower back and tail.

2 RUSHING AFTER PREY

Megalosaurus – a fierce meat-eater – chases a group of *Hypsilophodon*. But it has to be quick as these smaller dinosaurs can run as fast as a car moves in a city. *Hypsilophodon* were 2.3m-long plant-eaters that lived in Europe. As they ran along at speed, they used their long, stiff tails to keep their balance.

3 STRANGE FISH-EATER

Baryonyx used its 30cm-long curved claws, which were as big as carving knives, to catch fish. *Baryonyx* means 'heavy claw'. Here, it has just caught a fish by hooking its huge claw through its body. *Baryonyx* also had an unusual crocodile-like head.

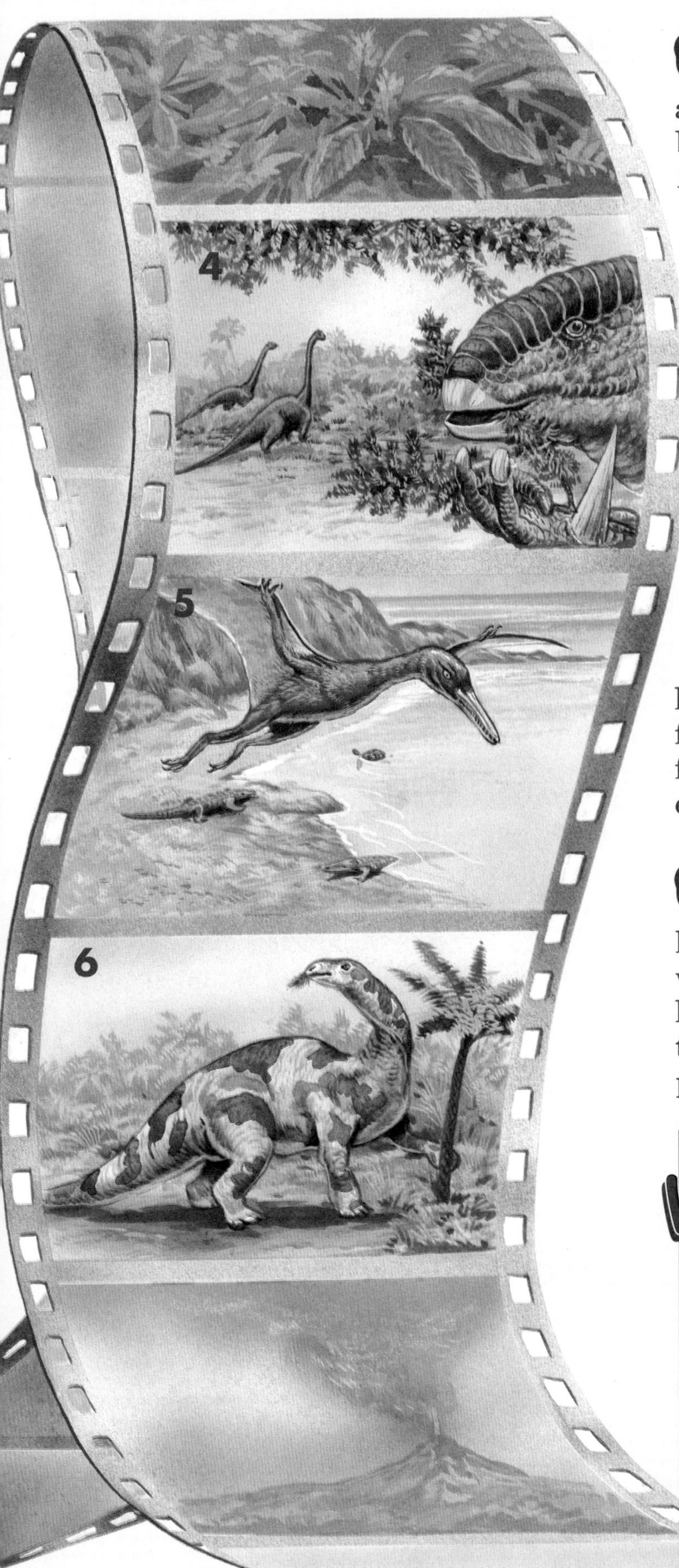

4 ENORMOUS PLANT-EATERS

Mighty *Iguanodon*, seen here chewing a branch, was common in Early Cretaceous Europe. It measured 10m in length – longer than a double-decker bus – and stood 5m high. *Iguanodon's* fingers were very useful. Its fourth finger could be bent to grab hold of branches and its spiked thumb was a fearsome weapon for stabbing. In the distance, *Pelorosaurus* feed on tall trees. These great dinosaurs became less common during the Early Cretaceous Period.

5 BRAZILIAN PTEROSAUR

The huge wings of flying reptile *Cearadactylus* darkened Early Cretaceous skies. They measured 4m from tip to tip – about the width of a hang-glider. The pterosaur had long jaws filled with teeth, and it hunted the seas for fish. Far below the pterosaur lurk some early crocodiles.

6 BIG-TAILED DINOSAUR

Tenontosaurus, seen here munching on leaves, was a heavy plant-eater that weighed up to a tonne. It was 4.5m long. It had a huge and powerful tail, which it used to protect itself from attacks by fierce predators, such as *Deinonychus*.

What is? A PTEROSAUR

Pterosaurs – it means 'winged lizard' – were very light, flying reptiles, not dinosaurs. Their wings were made of skin stretched tightly between their extremely long fourth finger bones and their tails. Pterosaur fossils show that some of these flying reptiles were the size of sparrows, while others had wing-spans of about 10m – the same size as that of a small aeroplane. There were many sizes of pterosaur in between.

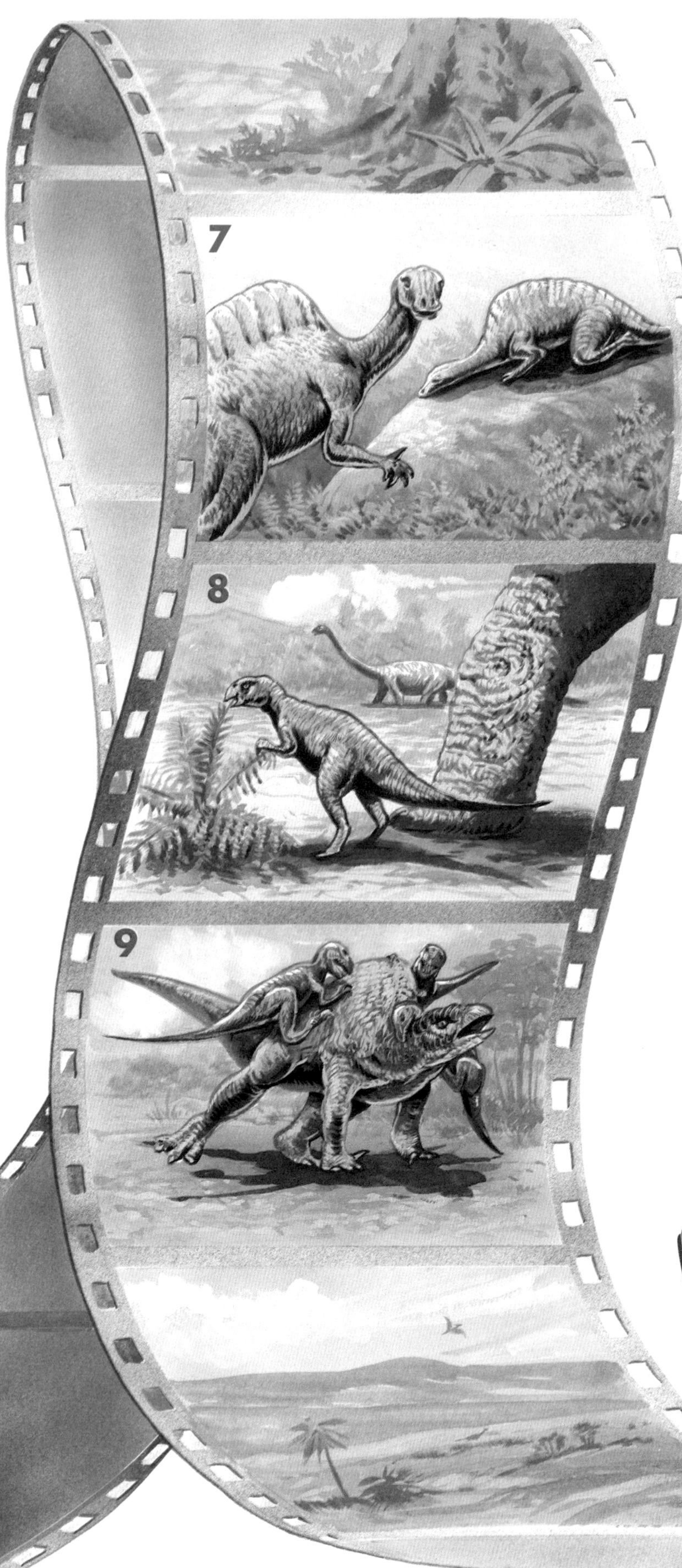

7 WARMING UP

The sun is up, and two *Ouranosaurus* are ready to start a new day. *Ouranosaurus* had a remarkable 'sail' on its back. This was made of skin stretched over long spines growing from the backbone. The skin of the sail was filled with blood vessels. These helped the dinosaur to take up heat from the sun. Once *Ouranosaurus* had warmed up, it could move more quickly.

8 PARROT BEAK

Psittacosaurus stands up on its back legs to nibble at leaves. This dinosaur had a parrot-like beak, which it used to bite tough vegetation. *Psittacosaurus* was a smallish dinosaur, measuring about 2m long. Sauropods – such as *Euhelopus* – towered over it.

9 SAVAGE ATTACK

Three hungry *Deinonychus* leap on top of an *Iguanodon*. *Deinonychus* was a very fierce meat-eater that hunted in packs, like wolves. Its main weapon was the huge claw on each foot. This claw was shaped like a new moon and measured 31cm long. When several *Deinonychus* attacked their victim, some slowed it down by clinging to its tail or back. Others used their claws to slash open its belly or to rip its flesh.

What is? A PREDATOR

A predator is an animal that hunts and kills other animals for food. Predators of the Early Cretaceous Period included *Megalosaurus, Baryonyx,* and *Deinonychus*. They were, of course, all meat-eating dinosaurs. Predators of today include the big cats such as lions and tigers, sharks, dragonflies and spiders.

10 TOOTHLESS PTERANODON

As it swoops over the sea, a *Pteranodon* catches a fish in its long, toothless beak. The *Pteranodon* was one of the largest of the pterosaurs (flying reptiles). It had a wing span of more than 5m – as long as a two small cars. At the back of its head was a long, bony crest. *Pteranodon* might have used this as a rudder to guide and balance it while it flew.

11 SMALL TANK

Silvisaurus, seen here peacefully eating plants in a lush forest, was built like a tank. Its 2.5m-long body was protected with flat, shield-like pieces of bone plates. Sharp spines also stuck out from its tail and parts of the body. This armour made it more difficult for predators to attack the plant-eater.

12 RARE AUSTRALIAN DINOSAUR

Muttaburrasaurus, a relative of *Iguanodon*, takes a refreshing drink at a waterhole. *Muttaburrasaurus* measured 7m long and had a broad head. It also had a strange, bony bump on its snout. *Muttaburrasaurus* is one of the few dinosaurs dug up in Australia so far.

IT'S A FACT

ENERGY FROM THE SUN

Modern day reptiles, such as iguanas (a kind of lizard), use the sun to help them warm their blood in a way similar to that used by *Ouranosaurus*, millions of years ago. In the morning, after a cold night, iguanas can be seen lying in the sun, absorbing its warmth. Once they are warm, iguanas have far more energy to scurry about in search of food.

GIANTS OF THE PAST

IGUANODON

The terrifying predator *Baryonyx* has attacked *Iguanodon*. But the huge plant-eater defends itself by jabbing its powerful thumb spikes into *Baryonyx's* neck. Some other *Iguanodon* from the herd are making a hasty retreat.

3-D Gallery
11
TRICERATOPS
• A horned dinosaur
• Lived 70 - 65 million years ago in North America
• Measured 9m long and 3m high
• Ate plants

3-D Gallery 12

POLACANTHUS

- An armoured dinosaur
- Lived 120 - 110 million years ago in southern England
- Measured 4m long
- Ate plants

Fantastic tails

Spiked, whip-like, clubbed, muscular or stiff, dinosaurs used their incredible tails as weapons, balancing poles or rudders.

Most plant-eating dinosaurs used their tails to protect themselves against fierce predators. *Diplodocus*, for example, had a very long tail which it used like a whip if it was threatened by an enemy. *Stegosaurus* had a spiked tail which could give a hunting dinosaur a nasty wound, and the clubbed tail of *Euplocephalus* was dangerous to meat-eaters too. Carnivores, however, did not need to use their tails to defend themselves. They used their tails to help them keep their balance as they ran.

SPIKED TAIL

Stegosaurus

Near the tip of *Stegosaurus'* tail were two pairs of spikes. These were large, made of bone and had very sharp points. They were *Stegosaurus'* weapons; it used them to defend itself against prowling predators. If attacked, *Stegosaurus* swung its tail and the spikes cut deeply into its enemy's flesh.

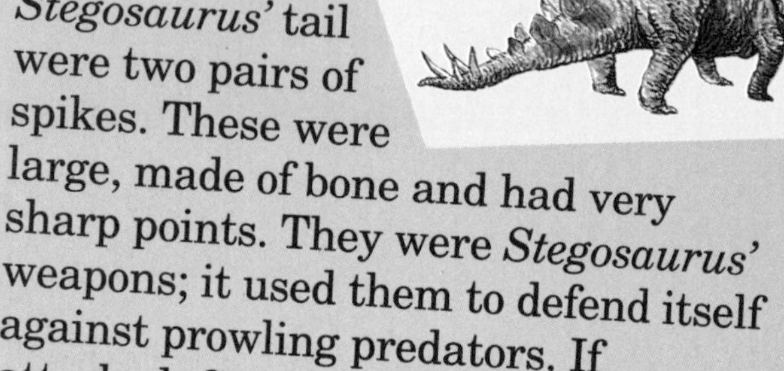

MUSCULAR TAIL

Iguanodon

Iguanodon had no clubs or spikes on its tail to defend itself. Its weapons were its two deadly thumb spikes. Its 4m-long tail was used to help it keep its balance when it reared up and walked on two legs. Because the tail was strong, some experts think that *Iguanodon* rested back on its tail sometimes, rather as today's kangaroos do.

IT'S A FACT

END OF THE TAIL

Although *Tyrannosaurus rex* is one of the most famous dinosaurs, no complete fossils of its tail have ever been found. It is mostly the end bones that are missing, so nobody knows exactly how long the tail was. Many scientists think that the tail was so long that *T rex* dragged it behind itself on the ground when it walked. *T rex* did not need to use its tail as a weapon because it attacked its enemies with its teeth and claws.

STIFFENED TAIL **Deinonychus**

A fearsome meat-eater, this dinosaur did not need to attack with its tail. It used the large, terrible, curved claws on its feet to do that. *Deinonychus* used its tail to help it keep its balance. It ran with its tail held stiff and straight behind it. The tail was stiffened by rods of bone. Some palaeontologists think that *Deinonychus* used its tail like a rudder to steer round objects when it was running flat out.

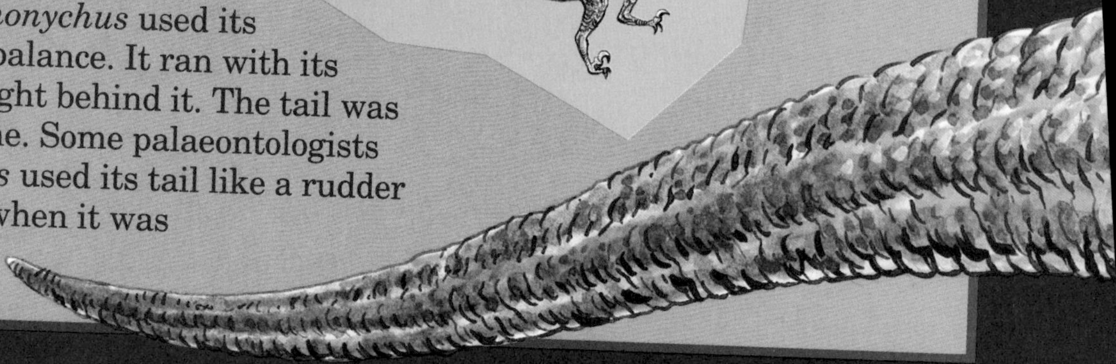

WHIPLASH TAIL **Diplodocus**

Even the biggest dinosaurs were not safe from attack. *Diplodocus* was enormous, but it had to use its tail, which was as long as the rest of its body, as a whip to lash out at meat-eating hunters such as *Ceratosaurus*. A well-aimed blow from one of these tails must have delivered a terrible lash to an enemy. *Diplodocus'* tail also helped it to balance when it reared up on its hind legs to feed on leaves in the treetops. The tail, which got thin towards its end, had 73 bones in it.

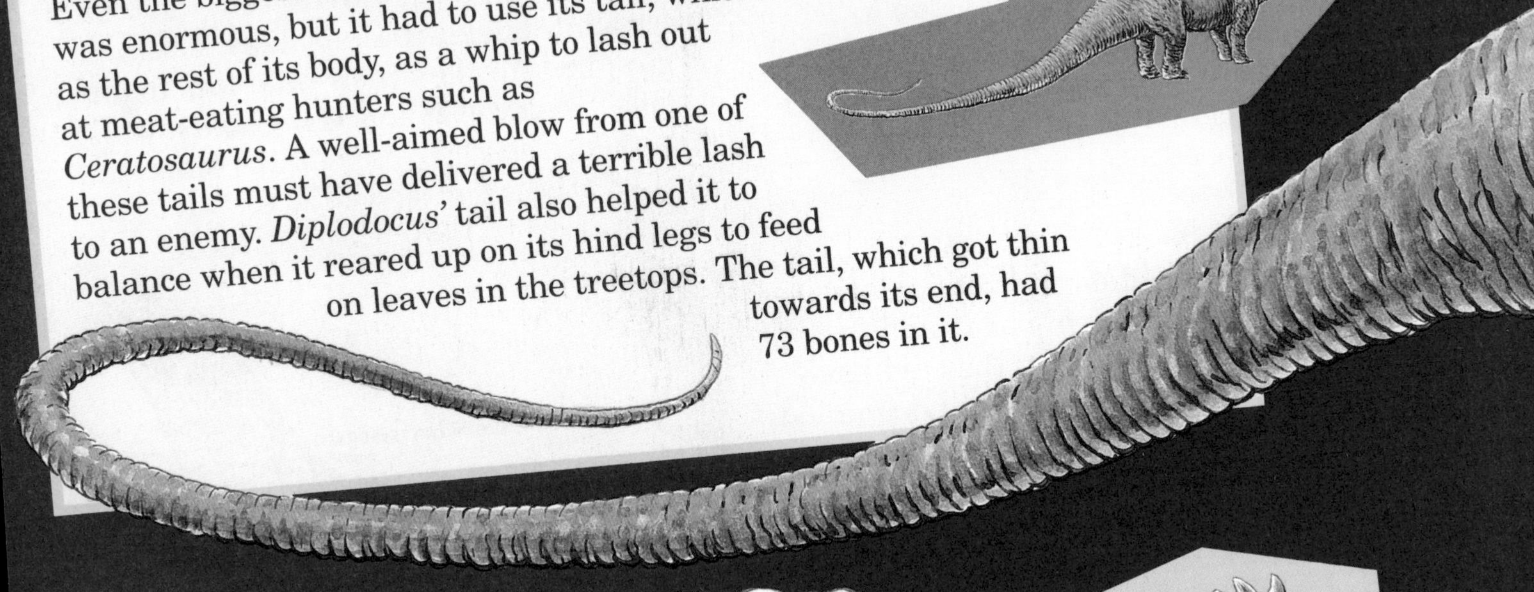

CLUBBED TAIL
Euoplocephalus

The huge club at the end of *Euoplocephalus'* tail was made of bone. When *Euoplocephalus* was attacked, it used the powerful muscles in its tail to swing the heavy club at its enemy. The club could smash a dinosaur's leg. These clubs sometimes grew to a metre wide. Being hit by one of these large clubs must have felt like being swiped sideways by a fast-moving fridge!

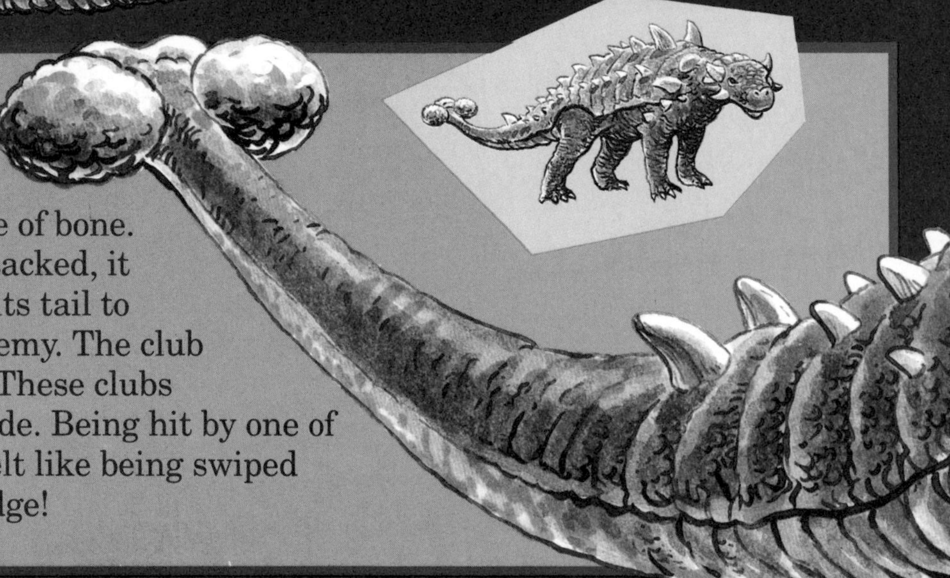

Walking with the reptile feet

The sauropods are one of the easiest dinosaur groups to identify. They were the largest dinosaurs to roam the land. They had huge bodies, four sturdy legs with clawed feet, long necks and tails, and small heads.

The biggest ever dinosaurs belong to the sauropod group. *Brachiosaurus* is a good example of what a sauropod looked like. It was a huge animal, measuring up to 23 metres long and 12 metres high. It used all four legs for support and its front feet had reptile-like claws. Its long neck was topped with a tiny head.

LONG NECKS

One of the most common features of the sauropods was their long, slim necks. They browsed (fed) on the leaves from the tops of trees a bit like giraffes do today. They sometimes stood on their hind legs to make themselves even taller. *Mamenchisaurus* (ma-mench-ih-saw-rus) had the longest neck of all the sauropods.

CLAWED FEET

The name sauropod means 'reptile feet' and, although most sauropods had heavy, elephant-like legs and feet, they did have reptile-like claws on their toes. Long tailed sauropods like *Camarasaurus* (kam-ar-a-saw-rus) could raise themselves up on their hind legs and use their clawed front feet to attack an enemy. They also used their long, whip-like tails to protect themselves.

Camarasaurus

Cetiosaurus

Opisthocoelicaudia

WATER OR LAND?

Scientists used to believe that sauropods lived in shallow swamps where water would support their great bulk. However, there are now many clues that point to them living on land. Their fossils are mostly found on land, their skeletons were light but very strong and their feet were the right shape for walking on land. If they had tried to walk on the bottom of lakes they would have sunk into the mud.

SPOON-SHAPED TEETH

All sauropods had weak, spoon-shaped teeth. At first, scientists believed that they could only eat soft weeds from lakes and swamps, but they now know sauropods like *Diplodocus* (dip-lod-oh-kus) probably used their teeth to rake leaves from tree tops.

IT'S A FACT

SWIMMING SAUROPODS?

In Texas, USA, in the late 1930s, footprints were uncovered that showed sauropods walking only on their front legs! Because of their size and shape it would have been impossible for sauropods to balance this way on land. Scientists believe that sauropods sometimes 'swam' in shallow water. They used their front legs to pull themselves along and their floating hind legs to steer and so left footprints with their front feet only.

SAUROPOD CHECK LIST

- Walked on all four feet
- Long necks
- Clawed feet

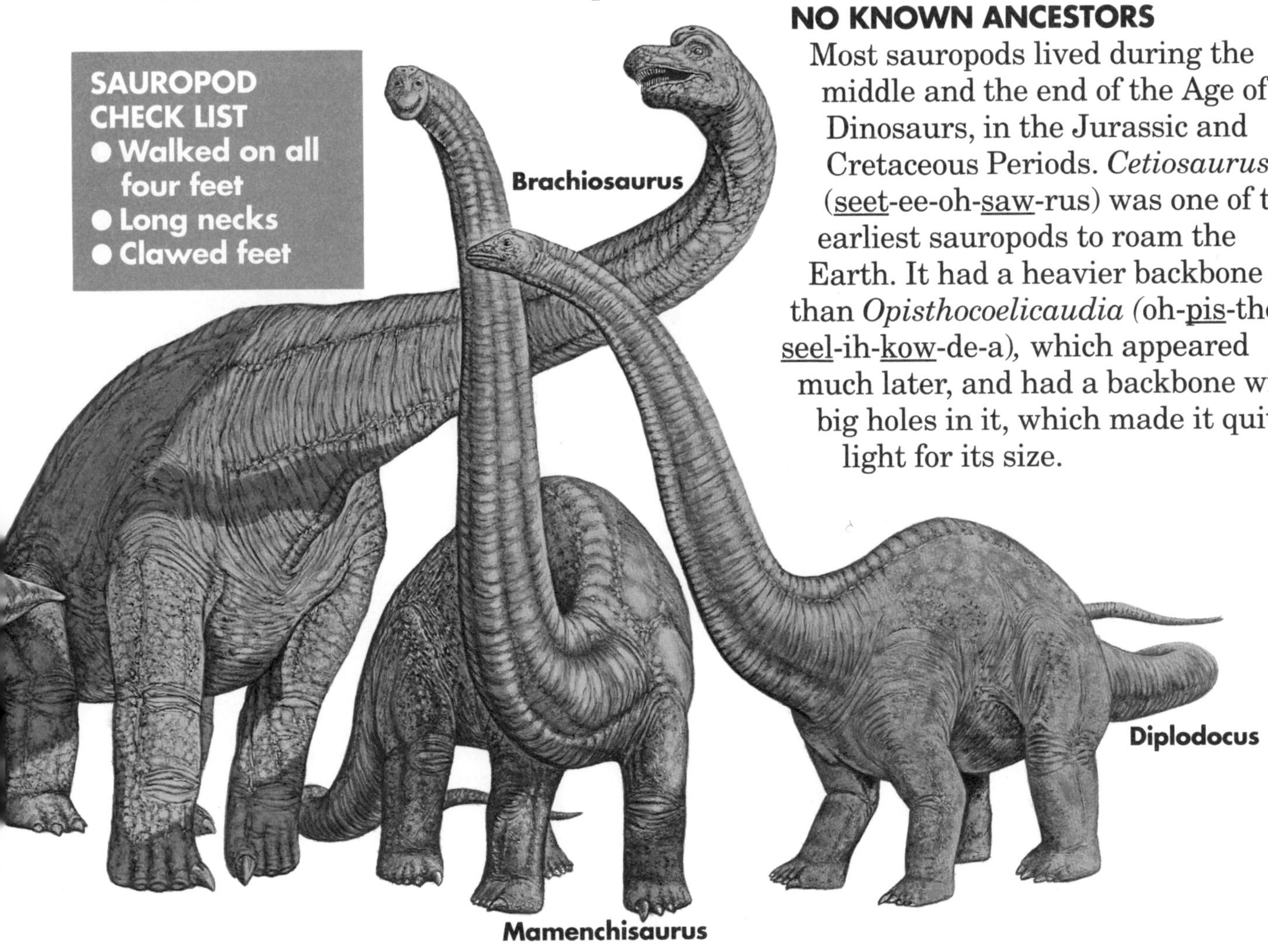

NO KNOWN ANCESTORS

Most sauropods lived during the middle and the end of the Age of Dinosaurs, in the Jurassic and Cretaceous Periods. *Cetiosaurus* (seet-ee-oh-saw-rus) was one of the earliest sauropods to roam the Earth. It had a heavier backbone than *Opisthocoelicaudia* (oh-pis-thoe-seel-ih-kow-de-a), which appeared much later, and had a backbone with big holes in it, which made it quite light for its size.

Brachiosaurus

Mamenchisaurus

Diplodocus

The ferocious beast feet

All the meat-eating dinosaurs, from the huge, fierce *Tyrannosaurus rex* to the tiny, fast-running *Compsognathus*, belonged to one group – the theropods.

Tyrannosaurus rex was one of the largest and fiercest dinosaurs ever to live. It could rip the flesh off its prey with one bite. *Compsognathus* was a tiny, chicken-like dinosaur, which could run very fast and fed on insects and lizards.

THEROPOD CHECK LIST

- **Ate meat**
- **Walked on two legs**
- **Sharp teeth and claws**

GROUPED TOGETHER

Despite the great difference in their size, *T rex* and *Compsognathus* had two very important things in common: they both ate meat and walked on two legs. This made them members of the theropod group.

A MIXED BAG

The theropods are a large group that contains meat-eating dinosaurs of all sizes.

Tyrannosaurus rex

Ornithomimus

Ceratosaurus

BEAST FOOT
All theropods had two long, strong back legs for walking and long, muscular tails to balance themselves. The name theropod means 'beast foot'. Most of the dinosaurs in the group had three forward-pointing toes with very sharp claws and a fourth clawed toe which pointed backwards. They had short arms with sharp claws. Their long jaws were lined with dagger-like teeth to tear up their prey. Theropods lived throughout the Age of the Dinosaurs.

FROM FIRST TO LAST
Early theropods, such as *Coelophysis*, were mostly small and light. They could run very quickly on their long, strong back legs and could chase lizards and other insects. *Ornithomimus* (or-nith-oh-mime-us) is different from the other theropods because it didn't have teeth. It had a horny beak and ate nuts and berries as well as lizards.

IT'S A FACT

TERRIBLE CLAW
When *Deinonychus* was found in 1964, it was put into the theropod group because it ran on its two back legs and ate meat. However, it is quite different from most of the others. It was small, but it had a very large head and unusually long arms. Its feet were also very different because they had only two forward-facing toes. Its second toe was a huge, upright, curved claw, with which it kicked its prey.

THE LARGEST OF THEM ALL
The first theropods were much smaller in size than the later ones. *T rex*, which appeared about 88 million years ago and lasted right through to the end of the Age of the Dinosaurs, was the largest of them all.

FEARSOME PREDATORS
These large theropods were very heavy and powerful. They had strong, pillar-like back legs, small arms and massive heads on short, powerful necks. They couldn't run very fast for long because they were so heavy. But they were fierce hunters and could kill slow moving dinosaurs with their claws and teeth.

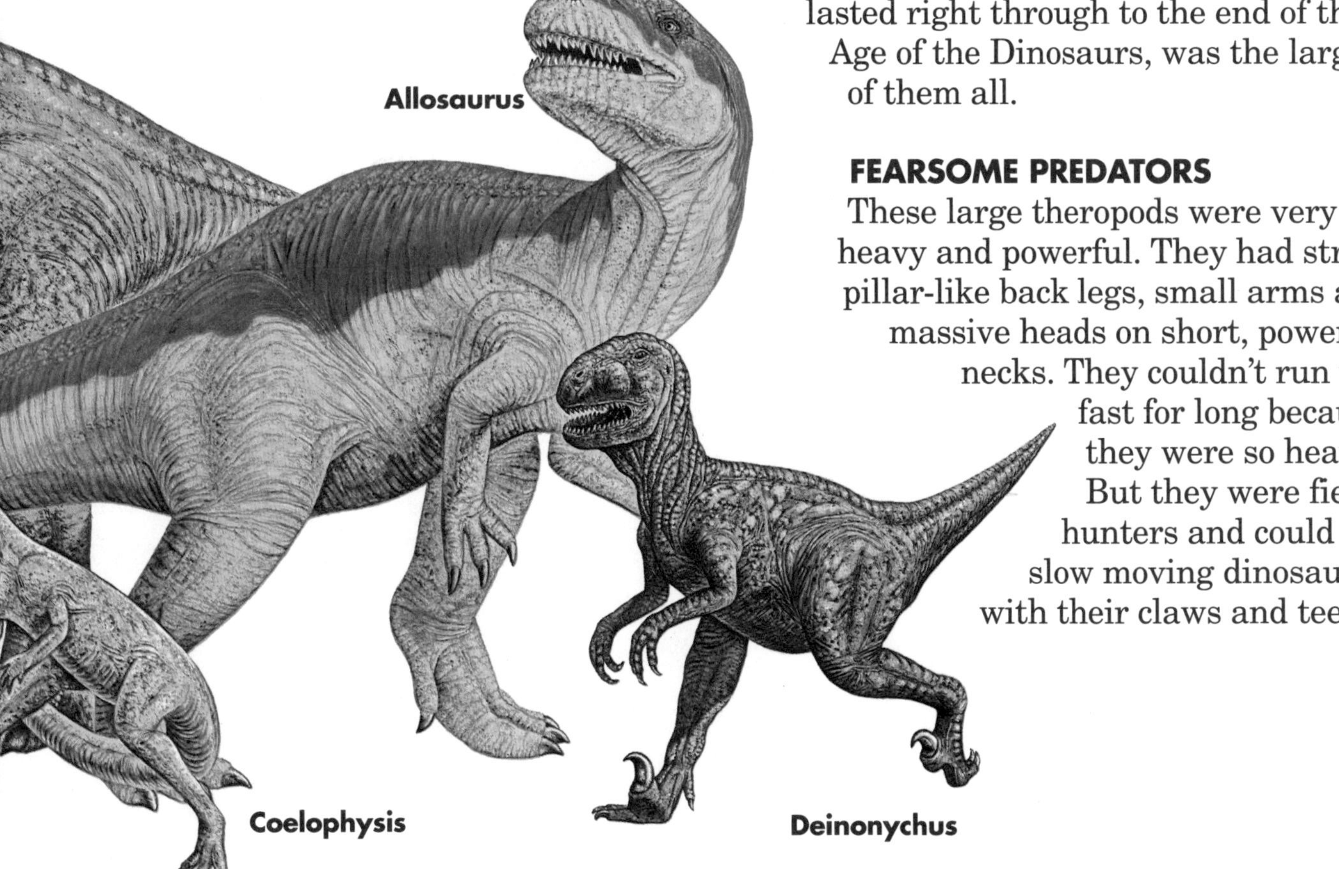

3-D Gallery 35

SPINOSAURUS

- A theropod with a back sail
- Lived about 110 million years ago in northern Africa
- Measured 49ft (15m) long
- Ate meat

ASK THE EXPERT

Dr. David Norman of Cambridge University answers your dinosaur questions

Did dinosaurs use camouflage?

Just like today's animals, it is very likely that some dinosaurs hid from predators by blending into the surroundings. Those that lived in forests may have had green skin with blotchy patterning so that they could not easily be seen among all the leaves.

Did dinosaurs have good eyesight?

As far as we can tell, dinosaurs probably had very good eyesight. Most dinosaur skulls have big eye sockets which means that their eyes were large. The part of the brain that helped with vision (seeing) was also well developed.

How do palaeontologists tell dinosaur footprints apart?

Even for experts, it is often very difficult to tell which dinosaur left which footprints, but palaeontologists look first at the shape of the feet and toes. Then they study the age of the rocks in which the footprints were found – they only consider dinosaurs that lived at the time that the rocks were formed.

Did dinosaurs ever get ill?

Dinosaurs probably became ill in much the same way as animals do today. We know that they sometimes broke bones and that these fractures healed up. The mended bones can clearly be seen in fossils. Some fossilized bones also show evidence that dinosaurs had cancer, and arthritis in their joints, as well.

DINOSAURS!
DISCOVER THE GIANTS OF THE PREHISTORIC WORLD

ALLOSAURUS

Allosaurus was as tall as a giraffe, but, unlike this gentle plant-eater, it was a lethal killer that may have hunted its prey in packs.

Allosaurus was one of the fiercest dinosaurs that stalked the plains of North America, Africa, Australia and China about 150 million years ago. It was a theropod and it could grow up to 12m long. Although it was not as big as the largest meat-eater, *Tyrannosaurus rex*, it was just as vicious. *Allosaurus* was armed with enormous jaws, full of sharp, jagged teeth. It also had curved claws and a powerful tail to lash out at any animal brave enough to attack it.

TEETH THAT CURVED

If a tall man could have stood on another's shoulders when *Allosaurus* was alive, he would have been at just the right height to peer into its mouth. He would have seen rows of about 70 saw-edged teeth, each as sharp as a steak-knife. All its teeth curved backwards, perfect for biting the flesh of its prey and preventing it from escaping. If any of its teeth fell out or were wrenched out in a fight, each was replaced by a new one that quickly grew to fill in the gap.

IDENTIKIT

Bony lumps above each eye

Strong neck, to bear weight of heavy head

Holes, or windows, in skull made it strong but light

Bony ridge from eyes to nostril

Eye socket

12 CM DIAMETER OF ALLOSAURUS' EYE SOCKET

70 sharp, backward-pointing teeth, to rip out mouthfuls of flesh

90 cm

A FAST MOVER

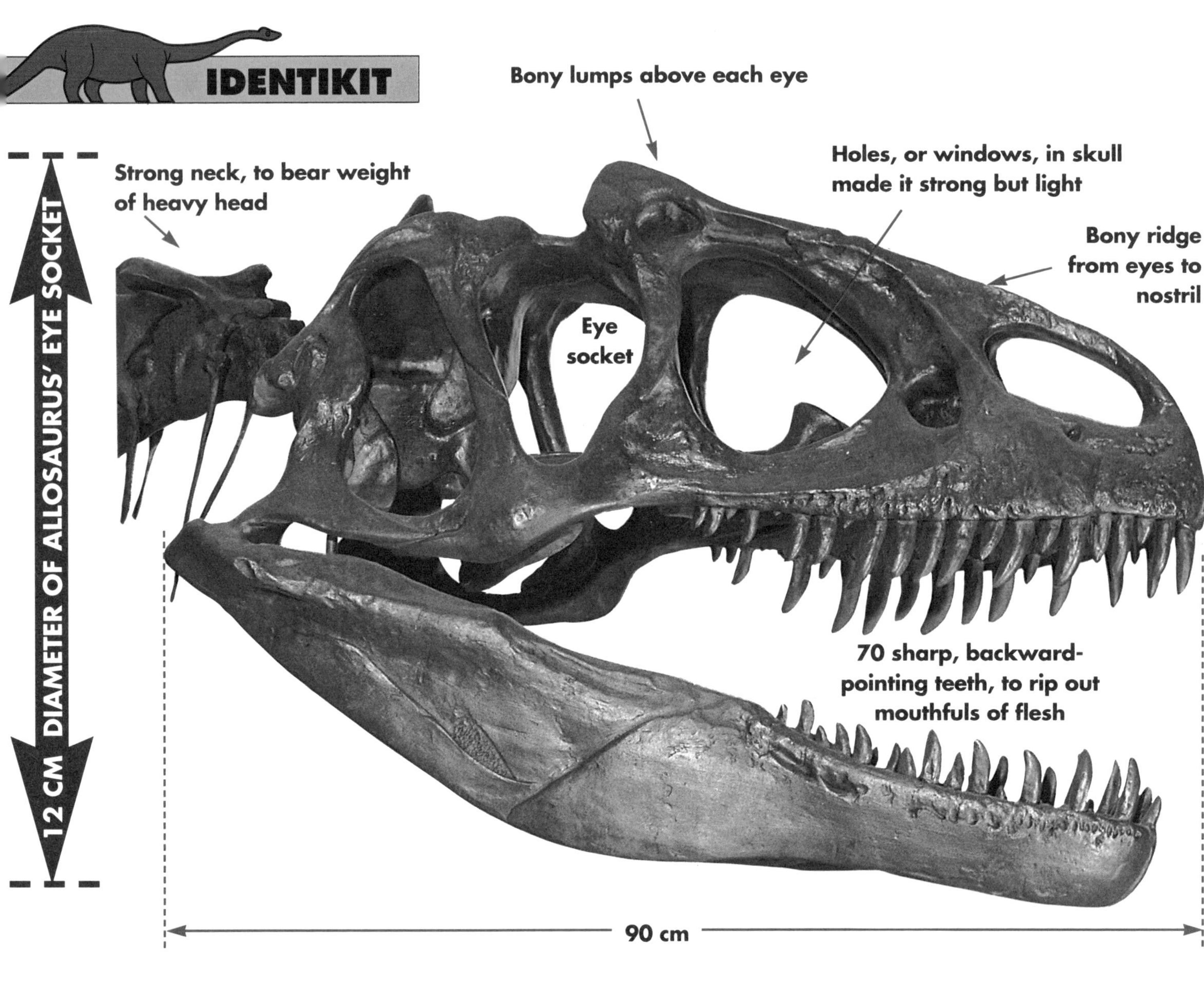

Scientists think that *Allosaurus* moved at about 8 km/h. A jogger could have just about kept up with it as it strode along on its back legs, like an enormous bird. Experts can also tell from fossil footprints that each step *Allosaurus* took was about as long as a car.

MONSTER FACTS

- **NAME:** *Allosaurus* (al-oh-saw-rus) means 'strange lizard'
- **SIZE:** about 12m long
- **FOOD:** meat, especially other dinosaurs
- **LIVED:** about 150 million years ago in the Late Jurassic in North America, Africa and China

CLAWS

The four toes on both feet ended in sharp, bird-like claws. Three of them pointed forwards and one backwards. Each claw was strong and sharp enough to tear open the soft underbelly of any other dinosaur. *Allosaurus* also had a claw on each of the three fingers of both hands. It used them to attack and hold on to prey.

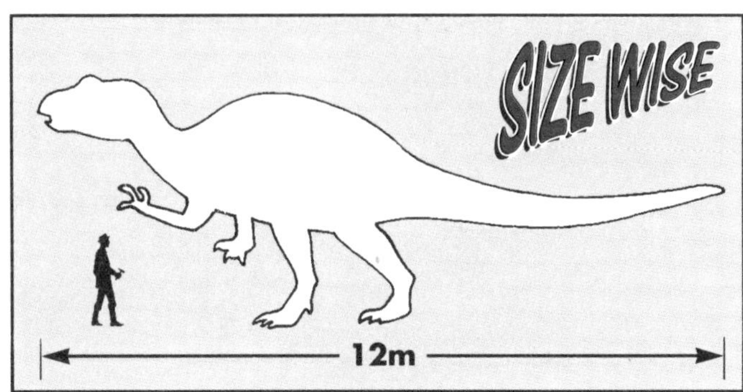

Modern jackals (left) bite into a carcass they have found. *Allosaurus* was probably a scavenger feeding on dead bodies, too.

KILLING YOUNG

Several members of the *Allosaurus* pack charged in to attack, biting and clawing at defenceless *Diplodocus* until it slumped to the ground to be ripped apart by the rest of the pack. *Allosaurus* would have had no hesitation in attacking the young of these large dinosaurs.

WELL BALANCED

Allosaurus probably held up its long, powerful tail when walking or running, to balance the weight of its body. Its tail had about 50 bones in it and was useful for lashing out at a rival during the mating season – when male fought male for the attentions of a female. Small, meat-eating dinosaurs which attacked *Allosaurus'* young were probably seen off with one mighty sweep of the tail.

SCAVENGER ON THE PROWL

Catching fresh meat was a hit and miss business, so *Allosaurus* probably also fed on the left-overs of animals killed by other meat-eaters. Animals that do this are called scavengers.

GOOD HUNTERS

Allosaurus was so large that it must have needed lots of meat to fill its ever-hungry belly. It preyed on the plant-eating dinosaurs that lived in the same area.

TOOTH MARKS

Allosaurus' toothmarks have been found on the tail bones of *Apatosaurus*, a North American plant-eater. Some of the really huge plant-eaters, such as *Diplodocus,* were far too big for *Allosaurus* to attack on its own, so *Allosaurus* may have grouped together and hunted in packs.

MAMENCHISAURUS

Half of *Mamenchisaurus'* total length was made up of its slender neck, which was longer than three cars parked bumper to bumper.

From the tip of its tail to the end of its snout, *Mamenchisaurus* was 22m long. Eleven metres of that was its neck. It had the longest neck of any animal that has ever lived. *Mamenchisaurus* could easily have stood on the ground and peered into the windows of a three-storey house.

STIFF-NECKED

Mamenchisaurus' long neck was supported by long, overlapping bones, which must have made the neck quite stiff and slow to turn. The neck also had strong muscles which supported its small, snake-like head. *Mamenchisaurus* was as long as a tennis court, but its body was slim. Its backbone was hollowed out in places, which made it very light for its size.

FOREST DWELLER

145 million years ago, the area where this dinosaur lived was covered with vast, dense forests of redwood and sequoia trees. Herds of *Mamenchisaurus* lumbered along, using their small, peg-like teeth to nip off leaves and small shoots on the tree tops that were out of the reach of other dinosaurs.

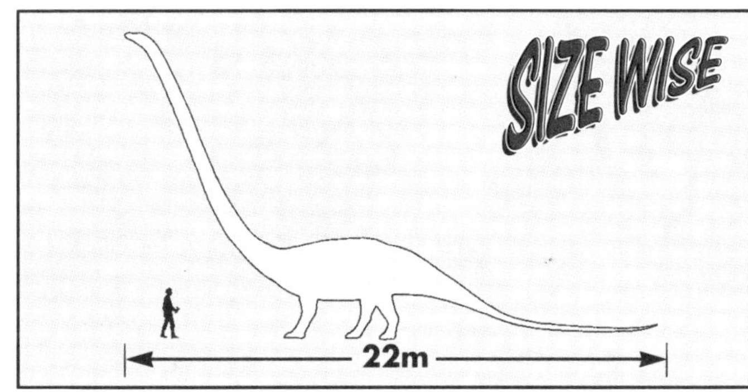

MONSTER FACTS

- **NAME:** *Mamenchisaurus* (ma-mench-ih-saw-rus) means 'lizard from Mamenchi' (the place in China where its fossil remains were first found)
- **SIZE:** 22m long and 5m high
- **FOOD:** plants
- **LIVED:** 145 million years ago in China during the Late Jurassic Period

ON FOUR LEGS

Mamenchisaurus walked on four legs, dragging its long, thin tail along the ground behind it. During the mating season, male *Mamenchisaurus* may have used their tails to lash each other in vicious fights for the females of the herd.

COELURUS

Coelurus would eat anything it came across – even the rotting carcasses of animals killed by other dinosaurs.

Coelurus was a nippy little dinosaur, with a small head about the same size as a man's hand. Its teeth were razor-sharp and curved. Once they had sunk into another animal, it was almost impossible for the prey to wrench itself free. *Coelurus* also used its powerful teeth and jaws to rip flesh from the rotting carcasses of prey killed by other meat-eaters.

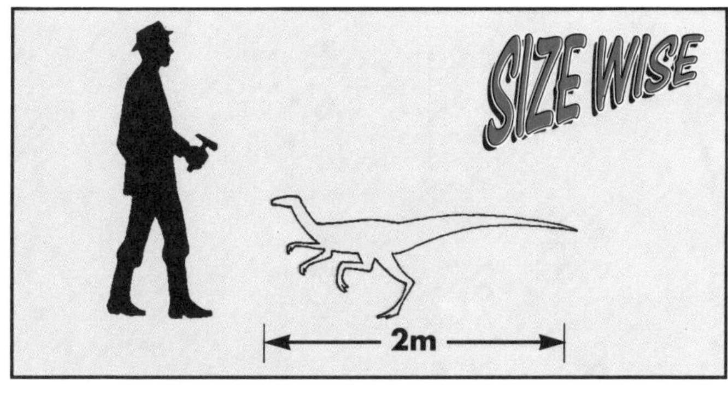

MONSTER FACTS

- **NAME:** *Coelurus* (seel-oo-rus) means 'hollow tail'. It was called this because its tail was made up of hollow bones
- **SIZE:** 2m long and 1.8m high
- **FOOD:** meat, usually dead dinosaurs it found
- **LIVED:** about 140 million years ago during the Late Jurassic Period in North America

A LIGHT, STIFF TAIL

Coelurus had very light bones and a stiff tail with hollow bones in it. Its front legs were short and slim. Its hands were small and weak, with three curved claws. *Coelurus* had similar, slightly blunter claws on the toes of both back feet. It used its hands to snatch at its prey and to keep it in its grasp, while ripping it to death with the claws on its feet.

End of an era

Dinosaurs still ruled the world during the Late Cretaceous Period, but their reign was slowly coming to an end.

1

2

3

4

1 CHANGES AFOOT

The Late Cretaceous Period, which lasted from about 100 to 66 million years ago, was a time of great change. The continents that we know today were gradually taking shape. The seasons as we know them were unfolding. Among the dinosaurs that lived at this time was *Parasaurolophus*, one of the oddest-looking of all prehistoric animals. Its long, tubular crest was as long as a hockey stick. It may have used it to bellow warnings to others of its kind. Danger was always just around the corner for peaceful plant-eaters millions of years ago, just as it is for herds of some grazing animals today.

2 BURSTING INTO BLOOM

During this time, many flowering plants burst into bloom. Roses, primroses and primula turned their heads to the sun. Heathers began to grow. Dazzling water lilies floated on the surface of lakes.

3 CHANGING LANDSCAPE

Tree-like plants had first taken root more than 300 million years ago. By the Early Cretaceous Period ferns, horsetails, cycads, ginkos and conifers were growing all over the land, adding splashes of green to the prehistoric landscape. During the Late Cretaceous Period, evergreen pines were shooting upwards. Trees that shed their leaves appeared, growing alongside breadfruit, fig and palm trees that now only grow in warm parts of the world.

4 THE BUZZING BEGINS

Insects, such as bees and butterflies, took to the air, carrying pollen from flower to flower. On and under the ground, termites began to build their extraordinary hills that looked as if they belonged on the Moon rather than on Earth.

5 SOMETHING FISHY

The first bony fish had appeared in the water during the Devonian Period which lasted from 395 to 345 million years ago. By the Late Cretaceous, the seas were teeming with fishes of all shapes and sizes. Shoals of herring-like fishes swam in the seas along with large, predatory ones for whom they provided food. It was not just swimming reptiles and larger fish that threatened the shoals of these small fishes. Seabirds that skimmed across the sea surface, and those that bobbed along in the waves, were always ready to swoop or dive down to catch a mouthful of slippery prey.

6

7

5

6 MIGHTY MOSASAURS

Even the largest fish would keep a watchful eye out for the menacing mosasaurs. These sleek killers were perfectly adapted for life underwater. Their long, powerful jaws, some as long as a man's arm, were lined with sharp teeth. They swam stealthily through the water, their deadly jaws always ready to kill.

7 THE BIRD MIMIC

One of the most curious of the Late Cretaceous dinosaurs was *Avimimus.* It was given its name, which means 'bird mimic', because it strutted across the plains of China and Mongolia like a modern-day ostrich. At the end of its arms were sharp claws which it used to slash out at predators. Its arms were covered with feathers which it could fold, like wings. But flap these 'wings' as it may, *Avimimus'* feet stayed firmly on the ground.

8 LIFE ON THE OCEAN WAVE

Ichthyornis was one of the fast-flying birds that took to the skies during the Late Cretaceous Period. It may have looked like a modern tern as it flew along, just above the surface of the water, ready to swoop down and take a passing fish into its toothed bill. *Baptornis* had wings, but it couldn't fly. It swam the lakes and seas of North America, its head splashing into the water, like someone bobbing for apples on Hallowe'en, looking for a fish to eat.

9 SNAKES ALIVE

Snakes first slithered into the animal kingdom about 100 million years ago. They evolved from an Early Cretaceous creature called *Pachyrhachis,* which had a snake-like body and the head of a lizard. Most snakes take no interest in their eggs or their young, although one exception is the female python. She carefully coils her body around her eggs to incubate them.

14 THE END OF AN ERA

Dinosaurs didn't die out overnight. But given that they dominated the prehistoric world for 160 million years, they vanished surprisingly quickly. Experts have puzzled over this for years. Some scientists believe that a gigantic rock crashed into the Earth with such force that a cloud of dust and steam rose and blocked out the Sun for months, even years. The dinosaurs froze to death in numbing snow-drifts. The fur-clad mammals lived on to rule the world.

10 MEET THE MAMMALS

Mammals, such as *Zalambdalestes*, *Purgatorius* and *Protungulatum,* scurried around the Late Cretaceous lands keeping out of sight of the meat-eaters.

11 THE HELMET LIZARDS

Herds of *Corythosaurs* roamed the plains of North America, rearing up on their powerful back legs. They nipped leaves off the trees and chewed their food between rows of grinding teeth. Young *Corythosaurs* had almost no crest at all. But by the time they were adults, the crest had grown until it stretched from the front of the head to the back of the skull, standing up to look like a very tall hat.

13 CRETACEOUS KILLER

Even *Spinosaurus* would not have been safe from Mongolian menace *Tarbosaurus*.

12 KEEPING ITS COOL

Spinosaurus had a tall sail on its back made of skin, held up by bits of bone. It may have used this sail to signal warnings to others whenever danger threatened – which it often did.

GIANTS OF THE PAST

Allosaurus **appears, as if from nowhere, and bares its massive teeth. Taken by surprise, two *Dryosaurus* rush for safety. The small plant-eaters feel the predator's breath on their necks. They hear its huge body crashing through the undergrowth, and know that they are about to be gripped by *Allosaurus'* huge claws.**

ALLOSAURUS

3-D Gallery 13

DIPLODOCUS

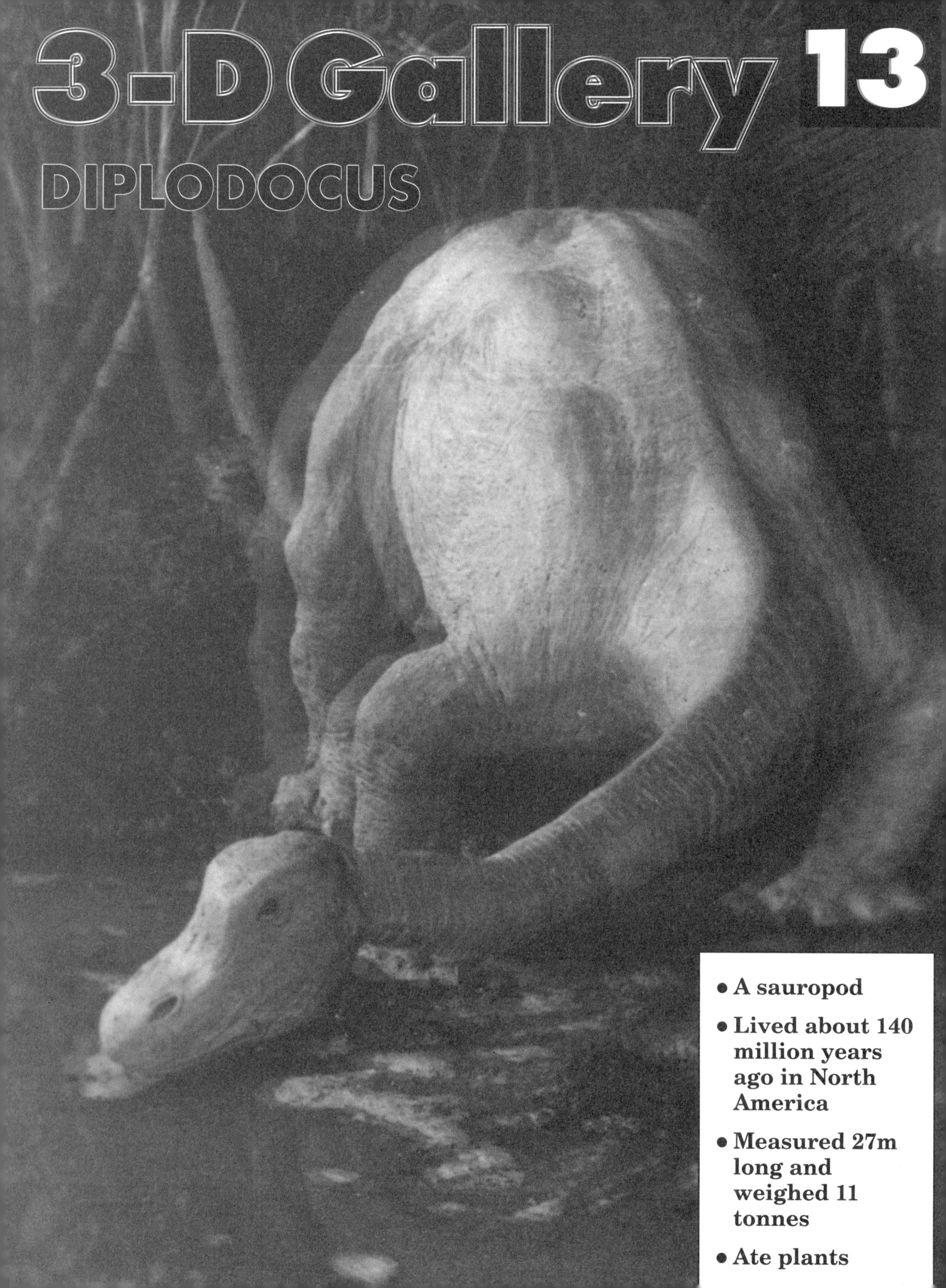

- A sauropod
- Lived about 140 million years ago in North America
- Measured 27m long and weighed 11 tonnes
- Ate plants

3-D Gallery 14

T REX

- A theropod
- Lived 67-70 million years ago in North America and China
- Measured 14m long and 5.6m high
- Ate meat

CLAWS

Sharp and deadly or broad and gripping, dinosaurs used their claws to attack prey or to defend themselves.

THE SPIKE!
Plant-eating *Iguanodon* had a very deadly thumb spike, shaped like a horn, sticking out at right angles at the side of its hand. Woe betide an attacker when *Iguanodon* jabbed at it. The needle-sharp point pierced the skin and soft flesh until the broad base stopped it going further. The spike was this shape so that it could be pulled out and stabbed back in again very quickly.

Many dinosaurs had claws of one sort or another. Some plant-eaters, like *Iguanodon* or *Apatosaurus,* used their claws to fend off attackers. Their fearsome claws flew into action whenever they sensed danger to themselves or their young. Many meat-eaters had razor-sharp claws, which they used to kill prey. One, *Baryonyx*, may have used its claws to scoop fish out of water.

A FISHING HOOK
Baryonyx had claws as long as a man's forearm. They curved from the base to a spear-sharp point. These fearful claws could cut through flesh in an instant. When tugged free, they tore shreds of skin and muscle from the prey's body. The shallow spoon shape of the inside curve allowed *Baryonyx* to catch fish, just like bears do today.

GET YOUR CLAWS INTO THIS!

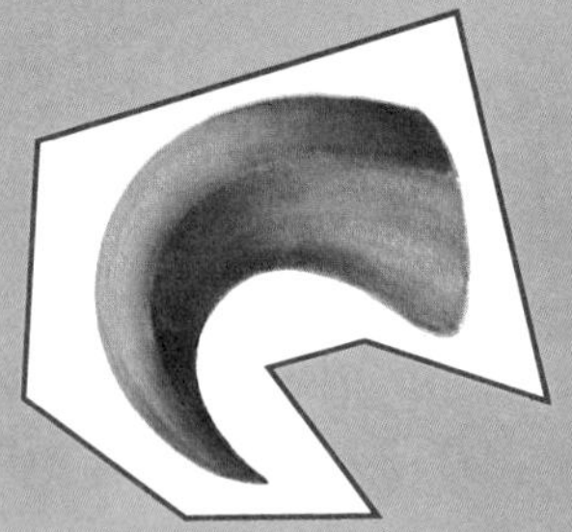

1 Vicious, sickle-shaped weapon

2 Long, curved claw for spearing prey

3 Big, heavy claw to strike the enemy

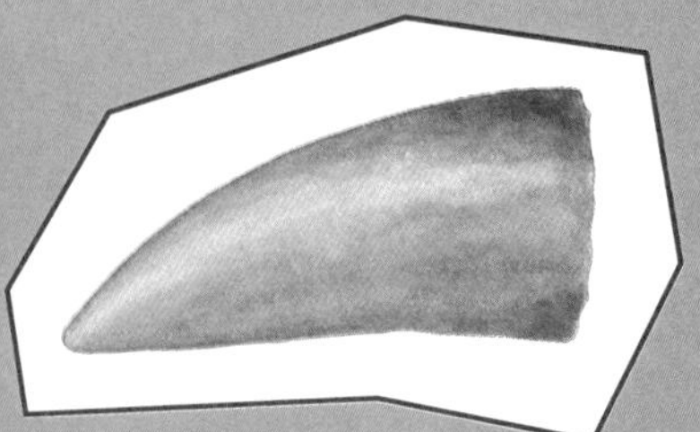

4 Sharp spike for spearing attackers

KICKING KILLER

A sharp claw on the inside of each front leg swung into action whenever *Apatosaurus* was attacked by a pack of hungry predators. Even the strongest armour offered little defence from a heavy and piercing punch from this almost clumsy-looking claw. It was designed to stun an attacker as well as cut into its body. A fierce, well-aimed kick from one of these claws, with all the strength of *Apatosaurus'* battleship bulk behind it, must have sent an attacker reeling backwards to lick its wounds.

IT'S A FACT

FIGHTING FOSSILS

Millions of years ago, a *Velociraptor* had attacked and killed a *Protoceratops*, gripping its neck with its front claws, and kicking it in the belly with its huge foot claw. *Protoceratops* must have fought back furiously. 80 million years later, their fossilized remains were unearthed in the Gobi Desert, in Mongolia. They lay as they had died – locked together in their fight to the death.

SICKLE-SHAPED

This fleet-footed killer had claws on its feet that looked like upward sweeping scythes: and they could cut through a victim's flesh as easily as a well-swung scythe harvests hay. Once *Velociraptor* got its curved claws into its prey, it was impossible for the animal to tear itself free. With the prey hooked in one claw, *Velociraptor* would gouge chunks of meat off its body with the other.

Which claw goes with which hand or foot? Match each claw to a hand or foot and the hand or foot to one of the dinosaurs on these pages. Answers at the bottom of the page.

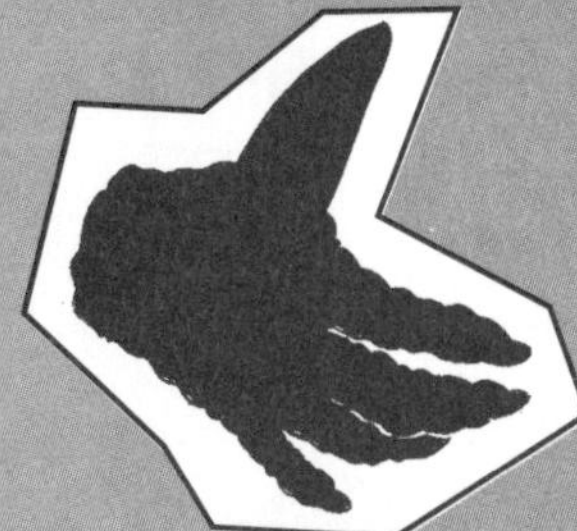

A Four fingers – and a very special thumb

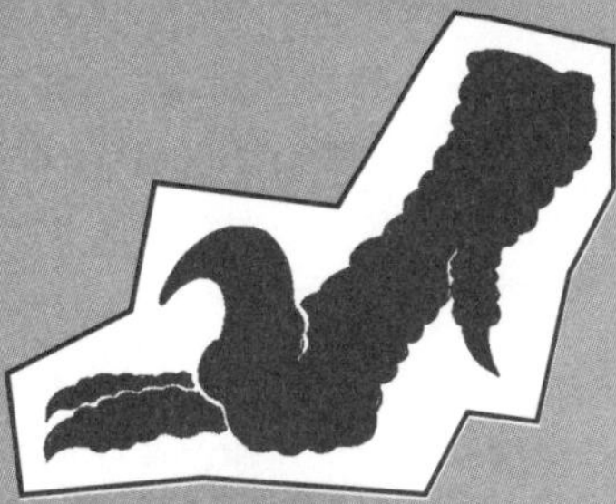

B Strong, slender leg for a fast mover

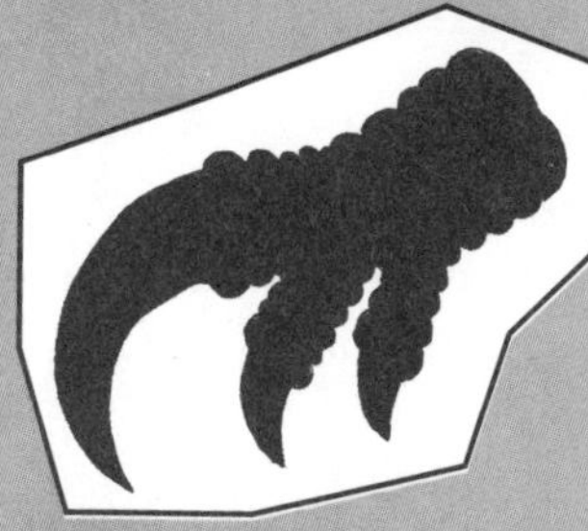

C Hand to hook and hold food

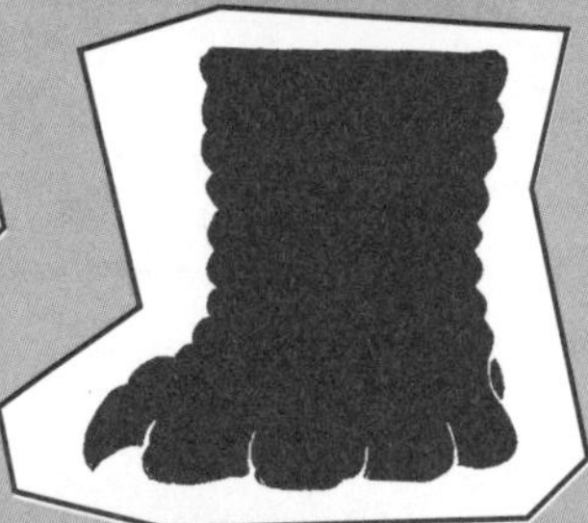

D Large and lumbering foot

ANSWERS: Iguanodon 4,A; Baryonyx 2,C; Apatosaurus 3,D; Velociraptor 1,B

Showing off

Before he could mate, a male dinosaur had to attract a female. But how could he do this, and how did the female decide which male to choose?

We only know about dinosaurs from fossils, so it's hard to tell exactly how they behaved. To learn more about dinosaurs, scientists look for clues in the modern animal kingdom. They study today's animals and use what they discover to find out how dinosaurs might have lived. Some of the clues to dinosaur behaviour are on these pages. If you put your thinking cap on you can follow the footsteps and work out how some male dinosaurs might have attracted a mate.

CLUE 1 When the peacock fans out its tail, the beautiful pattern created by the coloured feathers can be clearly seen. Why do you think it does this?

CLUE 2 The male frigate bird doesn't have a colourful tail like the peacock. But at certain times of the year he puffs out his neck and makes it stand out brightly. But why do you think he needs to do this?

Right: When experts pieced together early *Pentaceratops* fossil finds they realised that this dinosaur had neck frills. These large frills may have been for defence, but some scientists think that they had another purpose.

CLUE 3

It's not just the males of the animal kingdom that send out signals. This female baboon is displaying herself on purpose. Can you think why?

HERE'S WHY!

All these creatures are showing off because it's the time of year when animals mate. They do this in order to produce their young. Hopefully, the young will live long enough to mate. This will help to ensure that the species survives.

ATTRACTING A MATE

The peacock and the male frigate bird are showing off in order to attract female birds. The baboon is telling the males of her troop that she is ready to mate.

BRIGHTENING UP ITS FRILL

Experts believe that some dinosaurs may have behaved like the peacock, frigate bird and baboon during the mating season. Dinosaurs had to attract a mate. The male *Pentaceratops* in this picture is making his frill stand out. He has also brightened it up by making it more colourful. A female has shown that she is ready to mate by trimming her fringe with a little colour.

LAYING EGGS

The male mates with the female, who then lays the eggs. Some time later, the eggs hatch. The young *Pentaceratops* will grow up and when they are adults they will do what their parents did when the mating season comes round.

Fighting for the future

Not all male animals attract mates by brightening themselves up. Some are prepared to fight great battles in order to continue their family line.

The animal kingdom can be a very violent one. Some animals hunt and kill others for food. Animal mothers fight to protect their young. Some other animals attack out of fear. But there is another reason why, at certain times of the year, males, who usually live peacefully side by side in the same herd, square up to each other in 'winner takes all' struggles.

STANDING TALL

Bull elephant seals confront each other in Antarctica. They are both standing up on their tails. Why should they be facing each other like this?

LOCKED IN COMBAT

Look at these two deer. Why do you think they have locked their antlers together? Why do you think they will pull and shove until one of them gives up the struggle and skulks off? Here's a clue. The two seals and the two deer are males.

THE REASON IS...

The bull seals and the deer stags are fighting for the right to mate with a female. Experts believe that dinosaur males may have fought each other in the same way as these modern-day animals.

Right: These two male elephants are fighting it out for a female. They grab each other's trunks, rear up on their hind legs and cross tusks, grappling until one gives in. Their behaviour is probably like that of *Triceratops* (above), even though *Triceratops* lived 72 million years ago.

HEAD TO HEAD

The two *Triceratops* (the name means 'three-horned face') at the top of the page are doing exactly the same thing as the stags. Their horns will stay locked like this until one of them finally gives in and shakes himself free. The winner then mates with a willing female. The loser will lumber off to lick his wounds until he is strong enough to battle it out again for a female, this time with a different male.

DANGER TO THE SPECIES!

It was extremely important that enough dinosaurs should live to fight for females again. Dead dinosaurs would not be able to breed. If too many males had died out because of these vicious battles of strength, the future of the whole species would have been endangered.

IT'S A FACT

MAKING SOUND SIGNALS

Experts think that dinosaurs had a good sense of hearing. The middle parts of their ears were thin and delicate. They were well suited to picking up the sounds of other animals. It is thought that some dinosaurs may have sent out mating calls to each other – just like croaking frogs do in spring, today.

3-D Gallery 36

MAMENCHISAURUS

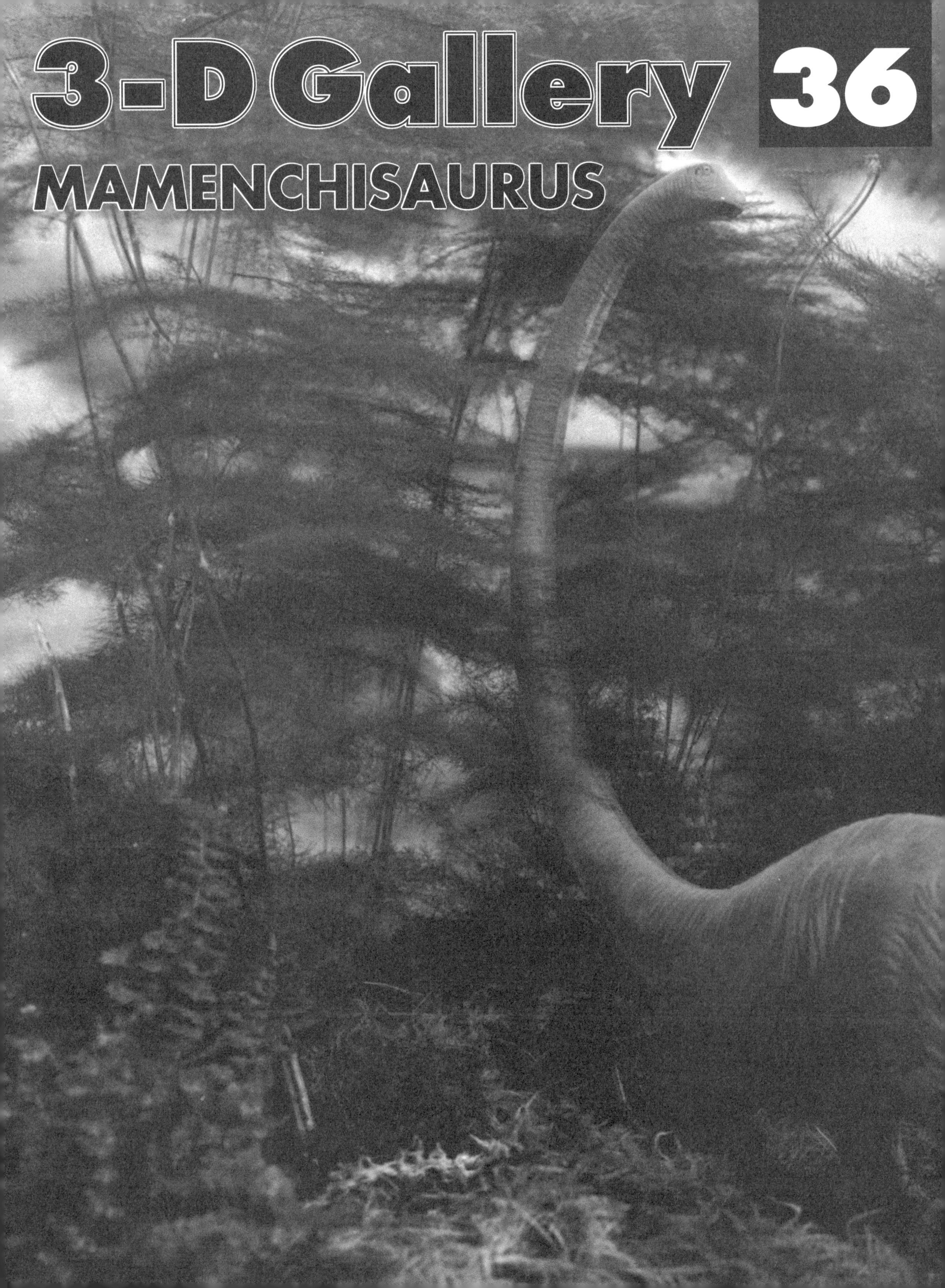

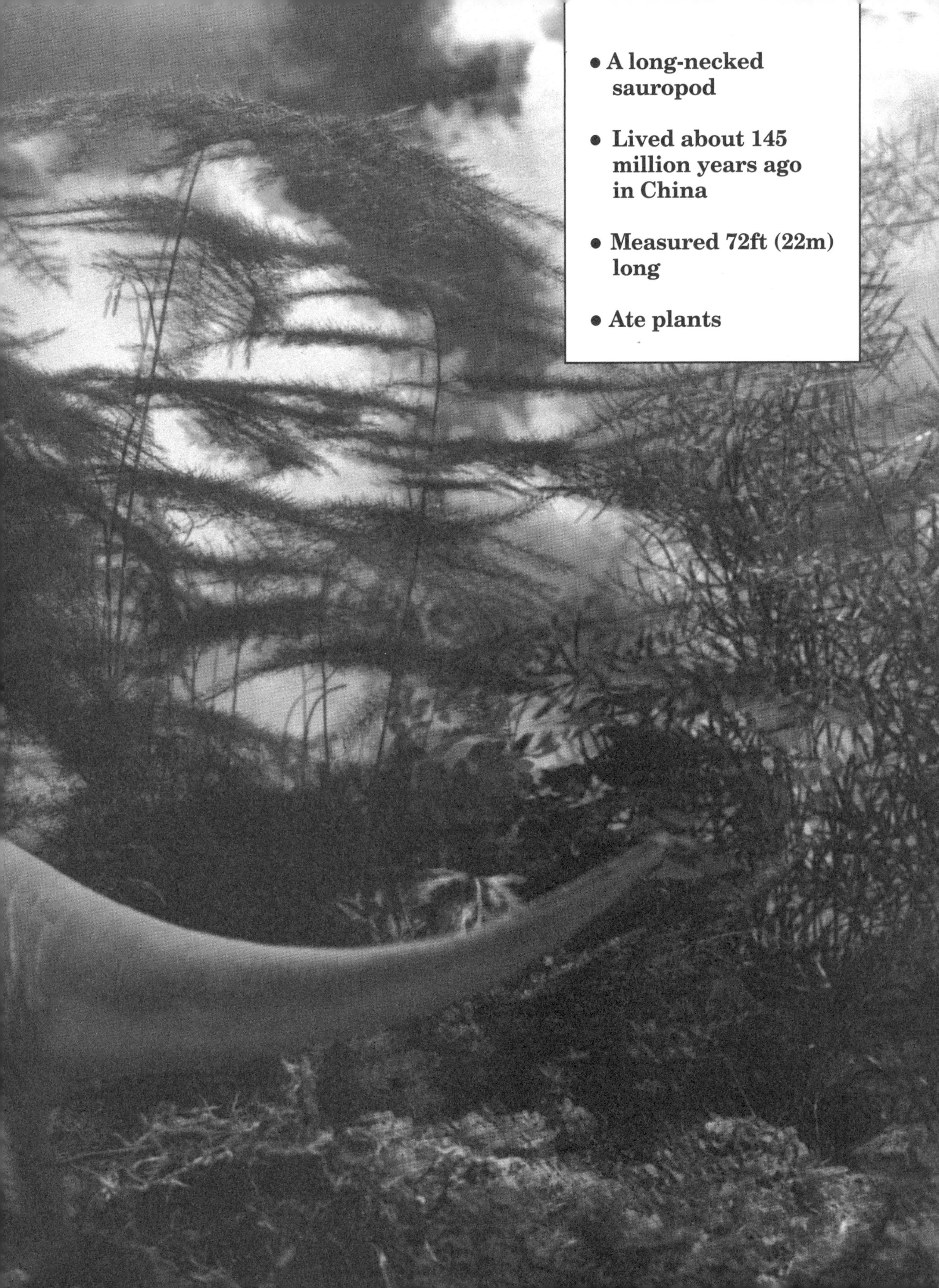

- A long-necked sauropod
- Lived about 145 million years ago in China
- Measured 72ft (22m) long
- Ate plants

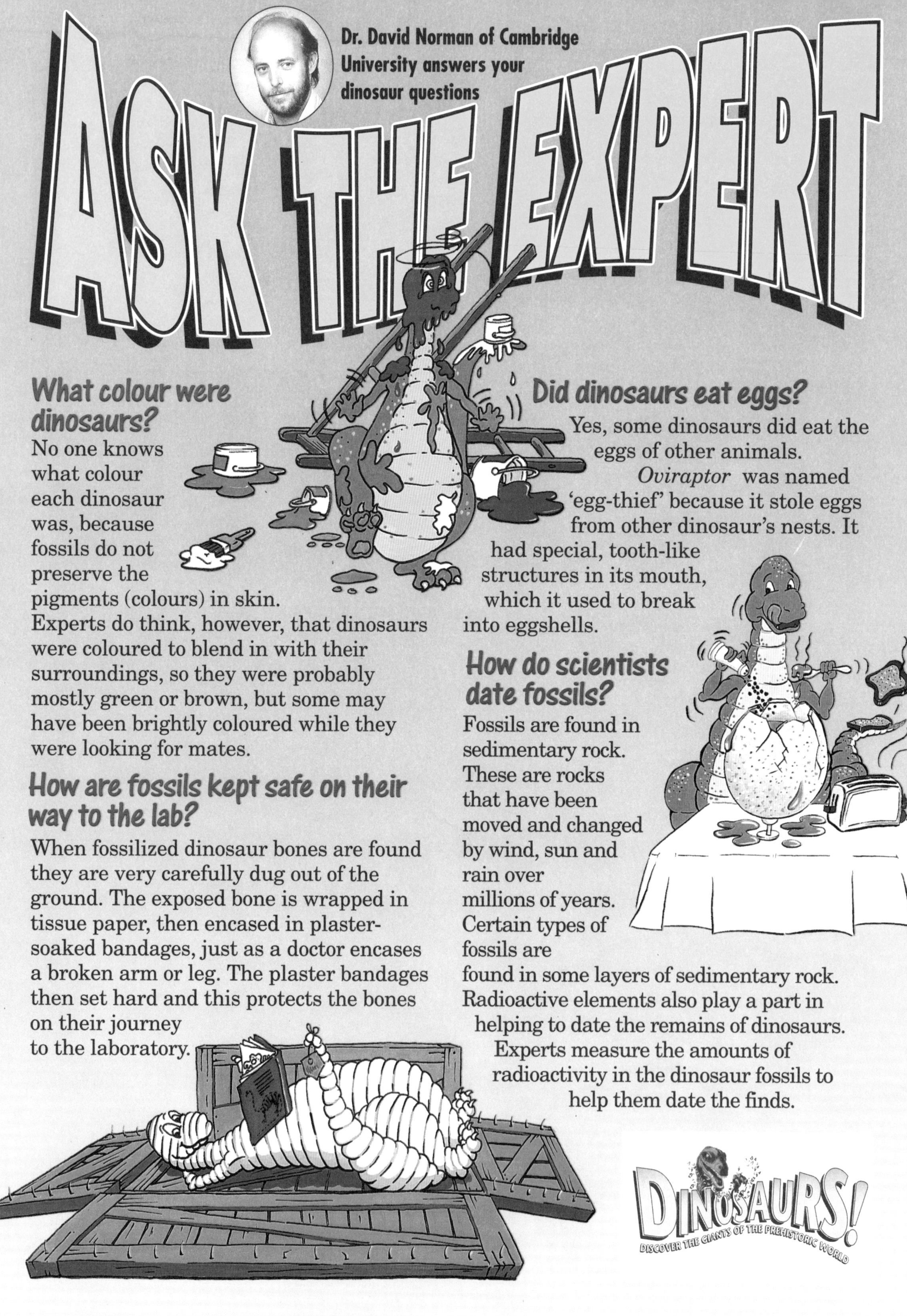

ASK THE EXPERT

Dr. David Norman of Cambridge University answers your dinosaur questions

What colour were dinosaurs?

No one knows what colour each dinosaur was, because fossils do not preserve the pigments (colours) in skin. Experts do think, however, that dinosaurs were coloured to blend in with their surroundings, so they were probably mostly green or brown, but some may have been brightly coloured while they were looking for mates.

How are fossils kept safe on their way to the lab?

When fossilized dinosaur bones are found they are very carefully dug out of the ground. The exposed bone is wrapped in tissue paper, then encased in plaster-soaked bandages, just as a doctor encases a broken arm or leg. The plaster bandages then set hard and this protects the bones on their journey to the laboratory.

Did dinosaurs eat eggs?

Yes, some dinosaurs did eat the eggs of other animals. *Oviraptor* was named 'egg-thief' because it stole eggs from other dinosaur's nests. It had special, tooth-like structures in its mouth, which it used to break into eggshells.

How do scientists date fossils?

Fossils are found in sedimentary rock. These are rocks that have been moved and changed by wind, sun and rain over millions of years. Certain types of fossils are found in some layers of sedimentary rock. Radioactive elements also play a part in helping to date the remains of dinosaurs. Experts measure the amounts of radioactivity in the dinosaur fossils to help them date the finds.

DINOSAURS!
DISCOVER THE GIANTS OF THE PREHISTORIC WORLD

DEINONYCHUS

Deinonychus was far from being one of the largest dinosaurs, but it was one of the most skilful hunters.

Deinonychus was one of the thugs of the dinosaur world. It always walked on its back legs and was armed with sharp claws and teeth that could rip into prey with alarming ease.

SECOND THOUGHTS

Until 1964, experts thought there were two separate types of theropod – big and heavy like *Tyrannosaurus rex* or small and slim like *Velociraptor*. Then, in southern Montana, USA, fossils of a theropod were found that made the experts think again.

SMALL AND FAST

The fossils they found were of an animal that had features of both types of theropod. Like all bipeds, it always walked on its back legs. It was small and fleet-footed with very special weapons – two huge, wickedly curved and pointed claws. *Deinonychus* carried these awesome weapons on the second toe of each foot. They were as long as carving knives and just as sharp. The other toes had much smaller claws.

Powerful leg muscles

Very strong ankle joint

Extremely sharp, hooked claw for slashing prey

Toe arched upwards to prevent damage to sharp tip while walking

Second toe

First toe quite small and backward pointing

Blunter, walking claws

Fourth toe

Third toe

ON THE MOVE

When *Deinonychus* was running, either chasing its prey or escaping from a larger predator, it used the strong muscles in its feet to pull its special, massive, hooked claws up, away from the ground. This protected them from damage. Its other claws were smaller and blunter and were used for gripping the ground and balance.

MONSTER FACTS

- **NAME:** *Deinonychus* (die-no-nike-us) means 'terrible claw'
- **SIZE:** 3m long and 2m high
- **FOOD:** meat, especially the flesh of plant-eating dinosaurs
- **LIVED:** around 115 million years ago in the Cretaceous Period in North America

A CHAMPION SPRINTER

Deinonychus was built for speed. It had a slim body supported by strong, slender legs. Its very strong ankle joints could absorb enormous amounts of pressure when it ran flat out. *Deinonychus'* skull had holes in the bone and scientists think that its head was quite light. A solid bone skull would have been very heavy. They think it could run at 40km/h when it had to – that's faster than an Olympic sprinter.

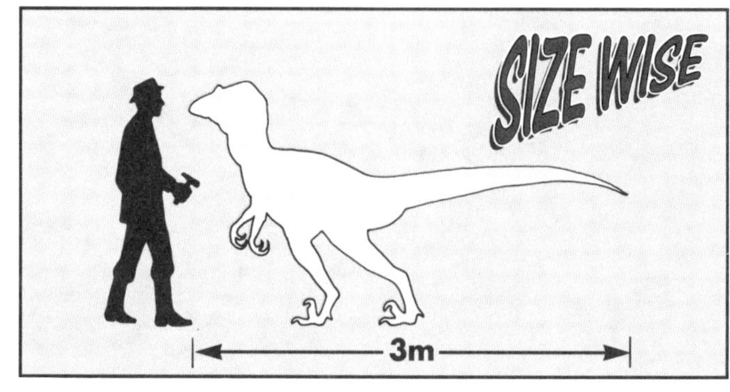

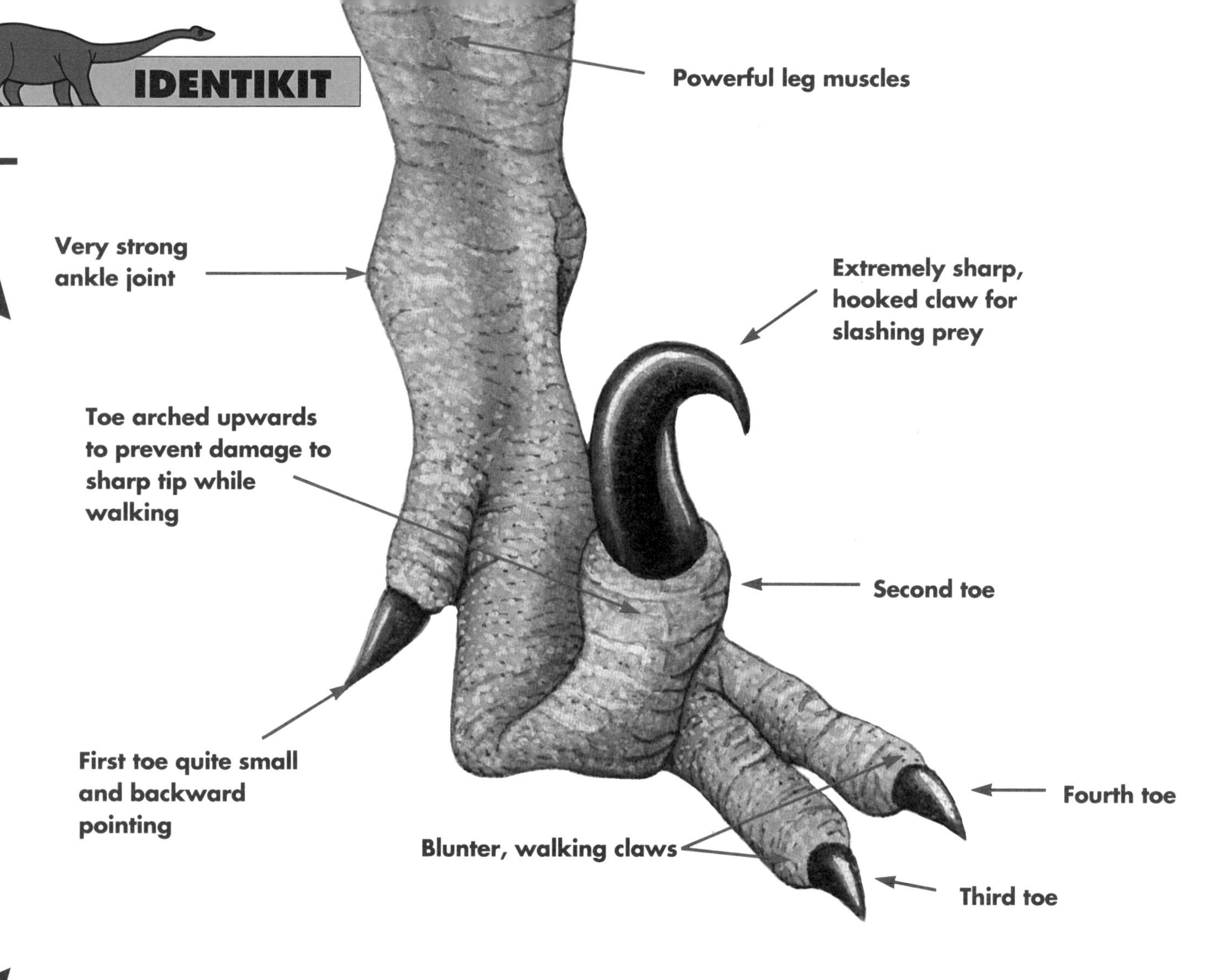

These Cape hunting dogs run in packs, just as *Deinonychus* did millions of years ago.

A BONE-BREAKING KICK

Deinonychus' kick was so strong that it could break its own toe. We know this because a fossil bone has been found that had been fractured and then healed. Scientists think that the dinosaur may have crippled itself as it kicked out at its prey.

A PACK OF KILLERS

Deinonychus hunted in packs, just like the wild dogs that hunt prey on the African plains do today. It probably prowled around herds of *Tenontosaurus* and other giant plant-eaters. It kept a watchful eye out for young or infirm members of the herd that strayed close to where it was waiting. Then *Deinonychus* attacked. It used one claw to cling on to the victim, and ripped into its soft underbelly with the other. Next, *Deinonychus'* teeth went into action. They were sharp and curved backwards, making it impossible for the victim to wrench itself free.

A SPECIAL TAIL

Deinonychus had bony rods in its tail. These made it quite stiff. When the tail was held outstretched, it helped *Deinonychus* to balance itself as it sprinted across the land. It may also have used its tail as a sort of rudder, to help it zig-zag through the rocky landscape at top speed.

SHARP SIGHTED

When experts studied *Deinonychus'* skull, they found it had large eye sockets. This made them think that the animal had eagle-sharp eyesight – perfect for spotting a likely victim from some distance away.

HYLAEOSAURUS

One swing from *Hylaeosaurus'* spiked tail was enough to stun all but the mightiest dinosaurs.

H*ylaeosaurus* was one of the armoured tanks of the prehistoric world. It belongs to a group of dinosaurs known as the ankylosaurs. It was 4m long from the tip of its nose to the end of its tail. That's as long as two cars parked bumper to bumper.

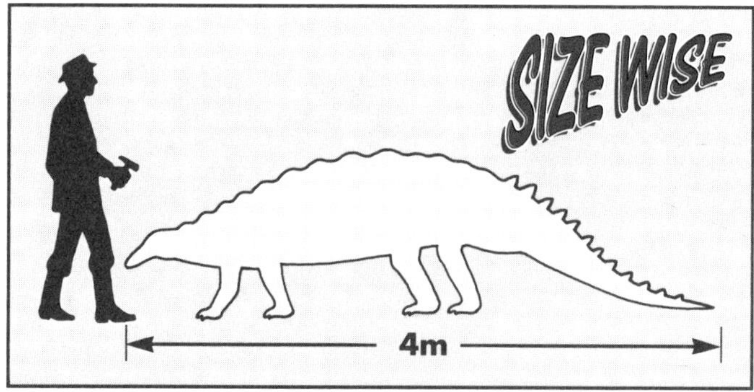

MONSTER FACTS

- **NAME:** *Hylaeosaurus* (hi-lee-oh-saw-rus) means 'woodland reptile'
- **SIZE:** 4m long and 1.8m high
- **FOOD:** plants
- **LIVED:** about 130 million years ago in the Early Cretaceous Period in southern England

DR MANTELL'S DISCOVERY

The first *Hylaeosaurus* remains to be found were dug up by Gideon Mantell in 1832. The fossils are entombed in a slab of limestone that can still be seen in London's British Museum.

A GOOD GUESS

Only the front part of the dinosaur was found. Scientists had to guess how the legs and body armour looked, but they are pretty certain that it looked like a long lizard with a cloak of sharply spiked armour running from its neck right down to the tip of its tail.

ARMOUR PLATING

Hylaeosaurus was a slow-moving plant-eater that nibbled ferns and other green plants for its food. If it was attacked, *Hylaeosaurus* was protected by its heavy armour and terrifying spikes.

TENONTOSAURUS

Tenontosaurus was a bulky, powerful plant-eater that weighed about the same as a large car.

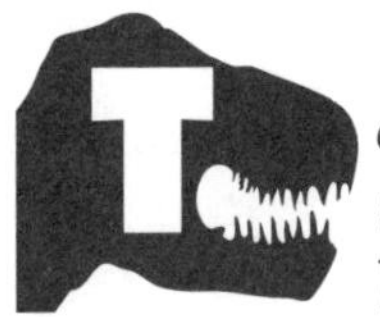

enontosaurus was about the same size as a double-decker bus. It had long, powerful limbs and a parrot-like beaked mouth.

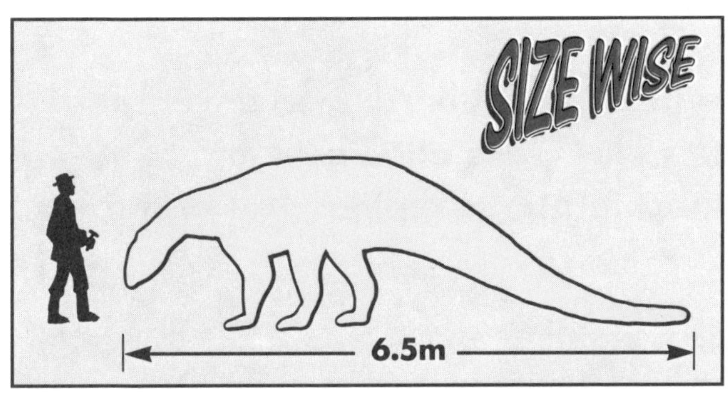

MONSTER FACTS

- **NAME:** *Tenontosaurus* (ten-on-tow-saw-rus) means 'sinew lizard'
- **SIZE:** 6.5m long
- **FOOD:** plants
- **LIVED:** 110 million years ago in the Middle Cretaceous Period in North America

TEN FINGERS, EIGHT TOES

A bulky dinosaur, *Tenontosaurus* could walk on all-fours or pick its way across the landscape on its hind legs. At the end of its front limbs were stocky hands with five fingers on each. *Tenontosaurus* balanced on the four long toes on each back foot when it stretched into the tree tops for a mouthful of leaves or twigs. When it ran, it gripped the ground with its toes, and raised its long, wide tail to balance the weight of its heavy chest and bulging belly.

A BEAKED MOUTH

Tenontosaurus' beak had no teeth, but it had ridged teeth running along the side of its beaked mouth. It used these to chew leaves it nipped off trees. When it was attacked, it would lash out with its tail.

Rulers of the waves

While dinosaurs roamed the Earth, the seas were ruled by some of the most ferocious reptiles that ever lived.

There was life in the sea hundreds of millions of years before dinosaurs roamed the Earth. Jellyfish and starfish appeared 600 million years ago. Millions of years later, the first fish appeared along with animals that could live both on land and in water. Animals that can do this today are called amphibians.

BREATHING AIR

Scientists think that reptiles evolved from these amphibians. One of the earliest reptiles was *Hylonomus,* which took to life on the land. Others took to the sea. All reptiles must breathe air. Sea reptiles had to come to the surface to take in air. Some came ashore to lay eggs.

A WIDE VARIETY

A huge number of different underwater reptiles evolved from the first early marine reptiles. They included *Placodus,* which looked a bit like a seal.

Placodus 215 MYA

An ichthyosaur 210 MYA

LAST MEALS

The ichthyosaurs appeared during the Late Triassic Period. Although ichthyosaurs looked rather like today's dolphins, they were reptiles, not mammals. We know they ate fish and cuttle fish because the remains of the last meals some of them ate have been found inside their fossils.

SEA-GOING HUNTER

In the Middle Cretaceous Period, *Champsosaurus* appeared. It looked very much like a modern-day crocodile and was just as deadly and dangerous a predator.

Champsosaurus 100 MYA

A DIET OF FISH

At the same time as the first ichthyosaurs appeared, *Nothosaurus* was among the rulers of the seas. It was well adapted to its watery world, weaving through the waves and living on a diet of fish, which it chewed between its sharply pointed, curved teeth. Scientists think that nothosaurs were the ancestors of a group of reptiles that dominated the Jurassic seas as early as 170 million years ago – the plesiosaurs and pliosaurs.

Nothosaurus
220 MYA

POWERFUL JAWS

A much later descendant of the early amphibians was *Mosasaurus.* It appeared after the ichthyosaurs had died out, during the Cretaceous Period. It swam in the prehistoric seas around 100 million years ago. Its huge, powerful jaws were as long as a broomstick and filled with wickedly sharp teeth.

Mosasaurus used its teeth to pierce the shells of the ammonites on which it fed. These were shellfish that were quite common at the time. Ammonites are one of the most commonly found of all prehistoric fossils.

Mosasaurus
100 MYA

AS BIG AS A BUS

Mosasaurus had a long, slender body that could grow to be as long as a bus. It had a deep, flat-sided tail that it used to power itself through the water. It used its front and back paddles to steer itself through the water. *Mosasaurus* may have looked like a ferocious fish, but it was, in fact, a lizard.

Paddling along

Plesiosaurs and pliosaurs were once described as 'snakes strung through the body of a turtle'. Among the creatures they shared the seas with was *Geosaurus*, an early ancestor of today's crocodiles.

Plesiosaurs were skilled swimmers that first appeared in the seas around 170 million years ago. Early on in their evolution they split into two groups, one we call plesiosaurs and the other we call pliosaurs. Plesiosaurs looked like fat dolphins with long necks and snake-like heads. Pliosaurs had plump bodies, short necks and heads that were similar to a crocodile.

LONG IN THE NECK

The largest of the plesiosaurs was *Elasmosaurus*. It measured 15m from its head to tail. That's about as long as a railway engine. Half of its total length was made up by its neck, which had over 70 small bones in it. With a quick flick of this long, snake-like neck, *Elasmosaurus* could catch a passing fish. It may even have stretched its neck out of the water to snap at an unsuspecting pterosaur gliding just above the waves.

Cryptoclidus was another long-necked plesiosaur. It was only 3m in length but was as agile as an otter and just as skilled and dangerous a hunter.

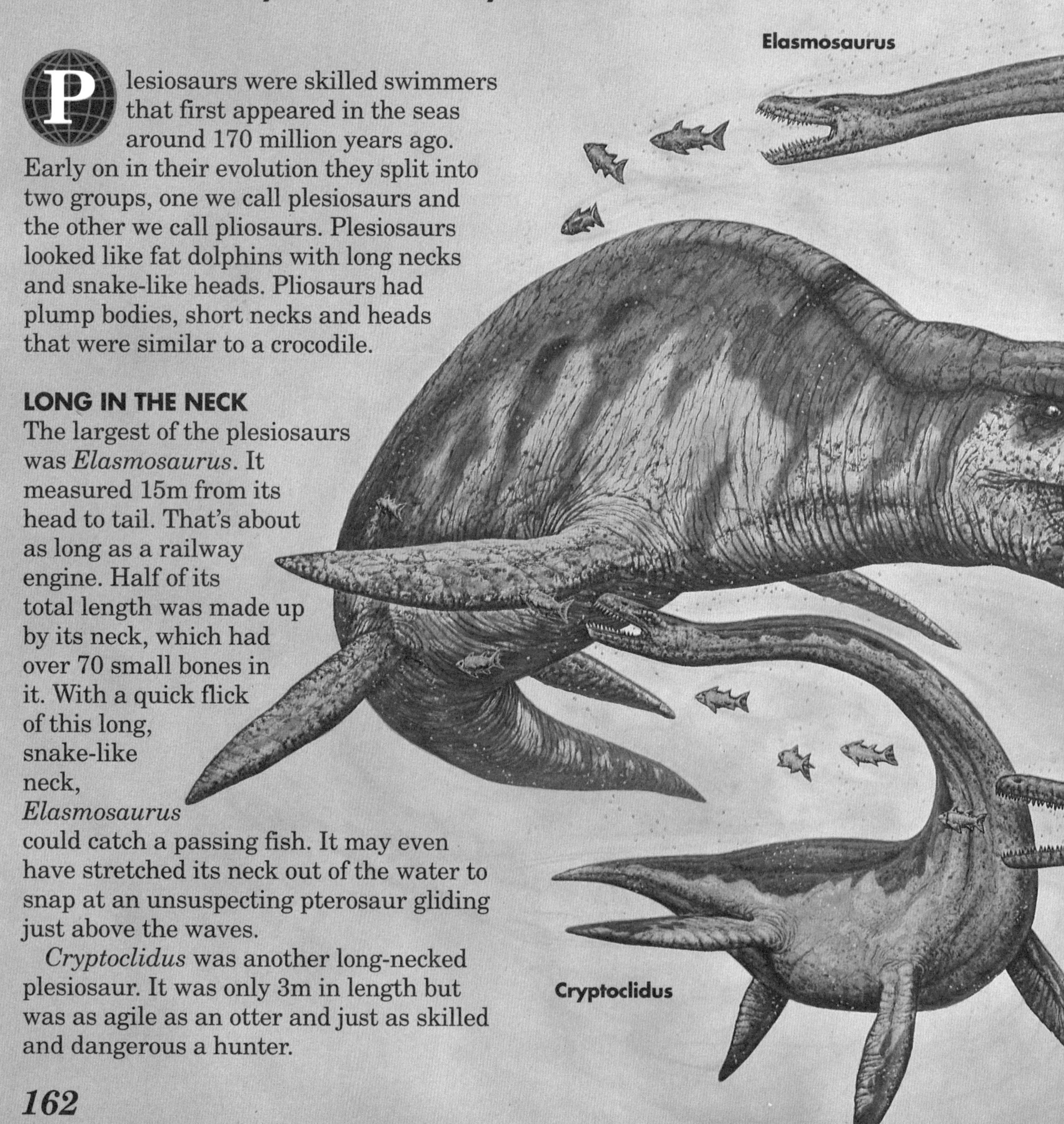

Elasmosaurus

Cryptoclidus

KILLING COUSINS

Pliosaurs had shorter necks than the plesiosaurs. They looked like whales with gigantic jaws armed with deadly teeth. They fed on big fish and probably didn't hesitate to go for smaller sea reptiles that came within their range. They were perfectly suited to living in the water. Some pliosaurs could dive down to depths of up to 300m in search of their prey.

IT'S A FACT

FOSSILIZED FORTUNE

The first fossilized plesiosaurs were found in England more than 170 years ago. Between 1800 and 1820, Mary Anning, one of the first great fossil hunters, found some plesiosaur skeletons. These fossils were so well-preserved she was able to sell them for a fortune to the British Museum in London where they can still be seen.

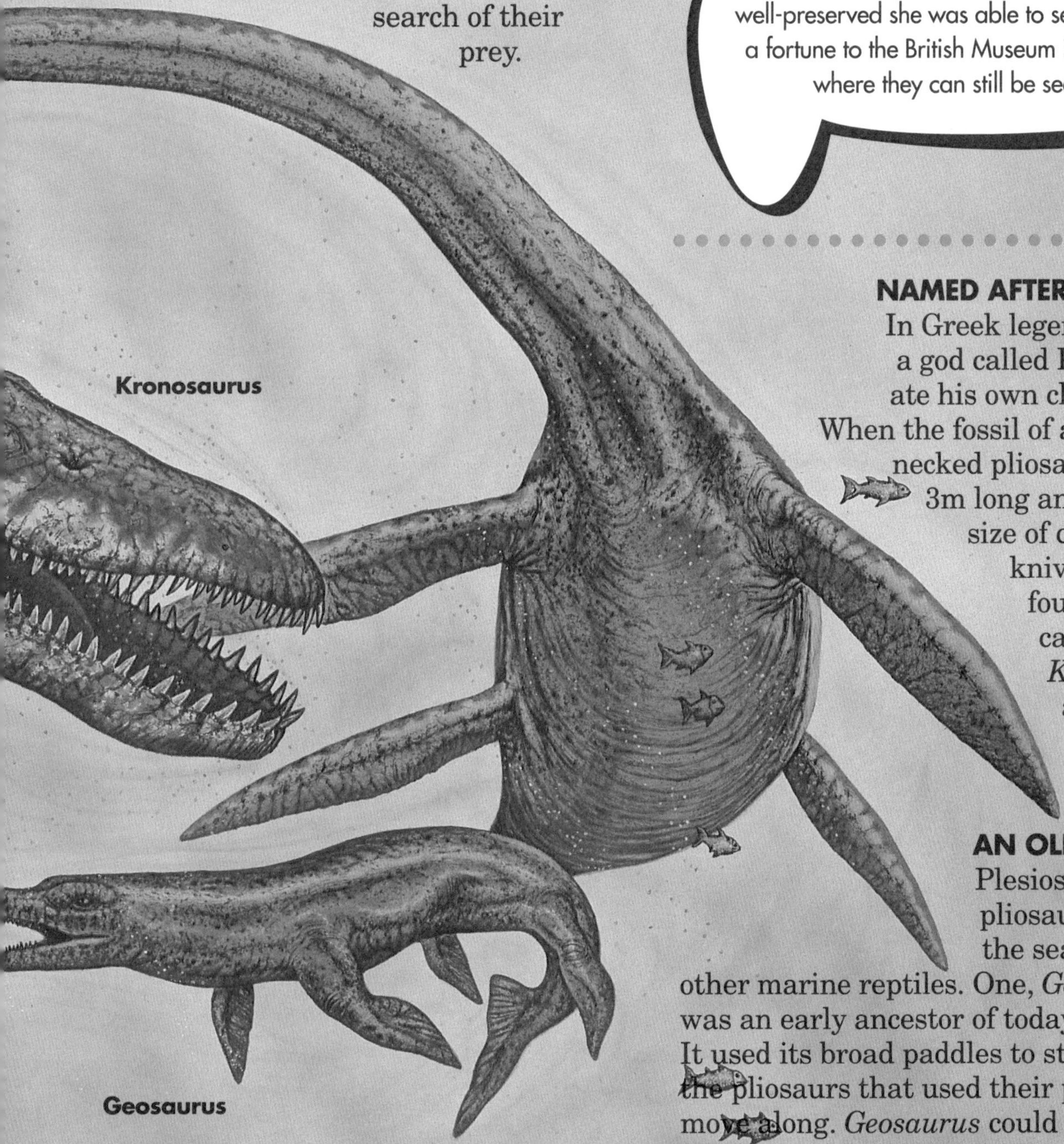

NAMED AFTER A GOD

In Greek legend there was a god called Kronos who ate his own children. When the fossil of a short-necked pliosaur with jaws 3m long and teeth the size of carving knives was found, scientists called it *Kronosaurus* after the bloodthirsty Greek god.

Kronosaurus

AN OLD CROC

Plesiosaurs and pliosaurs shared the seas with many other marine reptiles. One, *Geosaurus,* was an early ancestor of today's crocodiles. It used its broad paddles to steer, unlike the pliosaurs that used their paddles to move along. *Geosaurus* could bend its body from side to side, like an eel, and it weaved through the water on the look out for fish.

Geosaurus

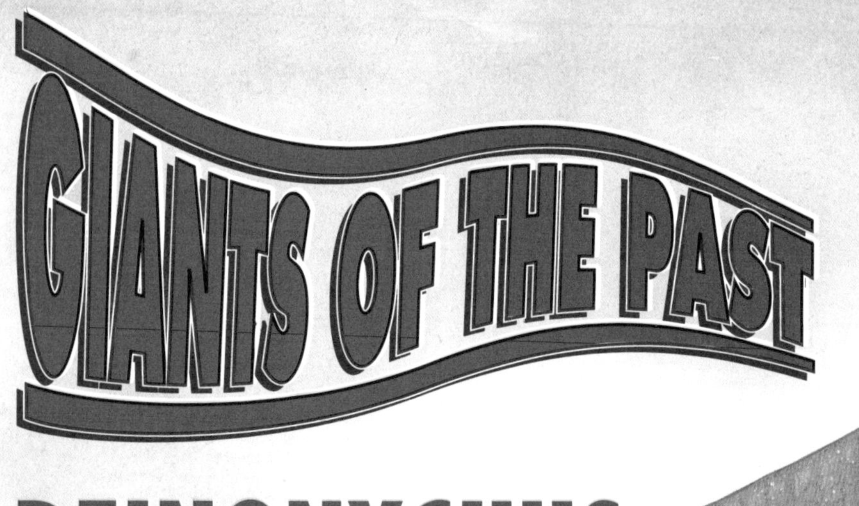

DEINONYCHUS

Despite its enormous size, *Iguanodon* stands little chance against the pack of deadly *Deinonychus* savaging the plant-eater with their curved, killing claws. The overpowered beast spills some of its attackers' blood with its thumb spike, but it is not able to withstand the attack for long. *Deinonychus* will soon be gorging themselves on hunks of flesh ripped from *Iguanodon's* still-warm corpse.

3-D Gallery

APATOSAURUS

- A huge, long-necked dinosaur
- Lived about 145 million years ago in North America
- Measured 21m from head to tail
- Ate plants

3-D Gallery 16

EUOPLOCEPHALUS

- **An armoured dinosaur**
- **Lived 80-72 million years ago in North America and China**
- **Measured 7m from head to tail**
- **Ate plants**

Feet first

Some dinosaurs had such big feet that their fossilized footprints were the size of paddling pools. Others had small feet armed with deadly claws.

Dinosaurs' feet were suited to their size and way of life. The large, plodding plant-eaters had to have feet that were broad and flat enough to support the enormous bulk of their bodies. Dinosaurs that were hunted by predators needed feet that were adapted for speed to make a fast get away.

ON THE HOOF

Corythosaurus was a duckbilled dinosaur that lived in North America. It did not have sharp claws to fend off meat-eating predators. It protected itself from its enemies in a much less obvious way: it used its feet and ran. *Corythosaurus* relied on its speed to race away when it saw signs of danger. Fortunately, its feet were perfectly adapted for beating a hasty retreat. Instead of sharp claws, each of its strong, stubby toes ended in a broad bone hoof. These special hooves helped it to balance and grip the ground as it raced away from predators to safety.

Corythosaurus

LONG TOES

When scientists looked at the first fossils of *Hypsilophodon*, they thought they were the remains of a prehistoric bird. Its toes were so long that some experts thought their owner used them to perch in trees. Now, they think that *Hypsilophodon's* feet were perfectly adapted for zooming away from predators. Each foot had four toes which it could splay out to cover a wide area. This made it less likely that it would topple over as it ran.

Is it true that some dinosaurs had webbed feet?

Today's experts think that this is unlikely. Early palaeontologists found imprints of skin between the fossil paws of hadrosaurs. They thought this proved that these dinosaurs had webbed feet like ducks today. But scientists now think that the skin formed a padded cushion under the foot, rather than a web.

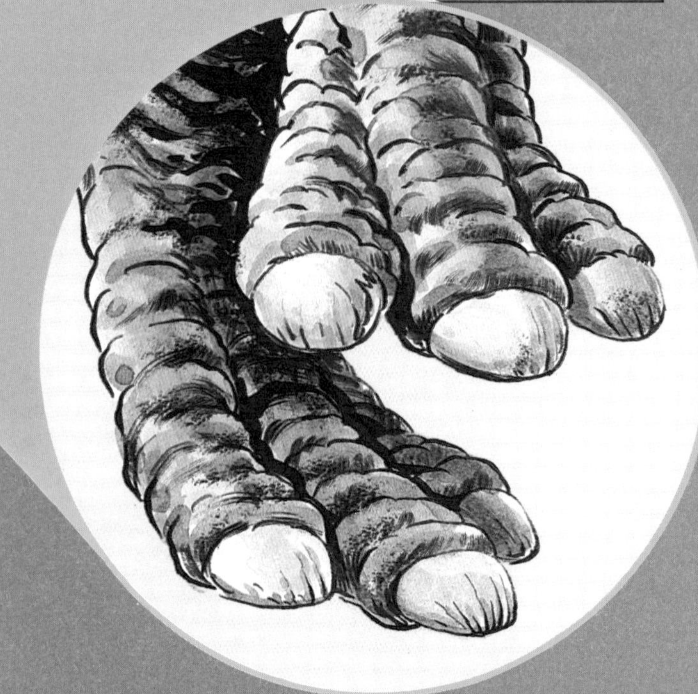

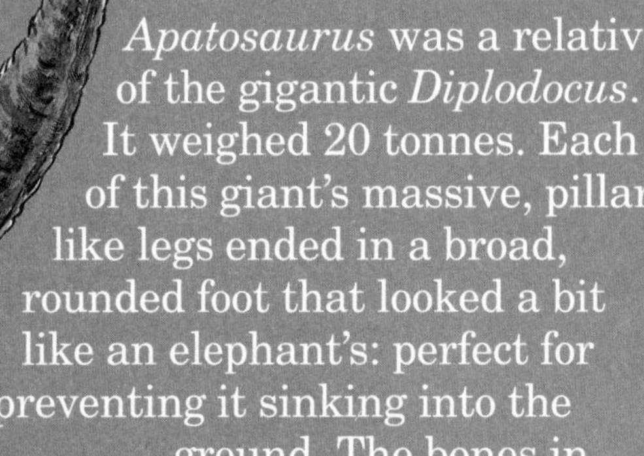

FEET LIKE AN ELEPHANT

Apatosaurus was a relative of the gigantic *Diplodocus*. It weighed 20 tonnes. Each of this giant's massive, pillar-like legs ended in a broad, rounded foot that looked a bit like an elephant's: perfect for preventing it sinking into the ground. The bones in *Apatosaurus'* feet were very strong and splayed out to support the weight of its enormous body.

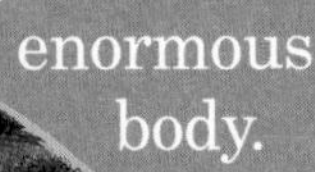

Allosaurus

THE FOUR-TOED TERROR

Allosaurus didn't need to sprint away from danger. Usually, it was the danger! Most other dinosaurs did not stand a chance against *Allosaurus'* sharply clawed feet. It had four toes on each foot. One was clawed and pointed backwards, perfect for back-slashing a savage blow into the vulnerable underbelly of its prey. The three other toes were also clawed, but they pointed forwards. It used them to rip its unfortunate victims to pieces.

A mystery solved

One of the great mysteries about dinosaurs was how their young came into the world. And then, one day in the Gobi Desert...

Almost a century after scientists discovered dinosaurs, the experts still did not know how they had their young. In 1922, an expedition to the Gobi Desert, led by Roy Chapman Andrews, made an astonishing discovery. Follow the clues to find out how he solved a great mystery.

Roy Chapman Andrews found the fossil on the right. It looks like a stone. But is it?

CLUE 2

The surface of the fossil is covered in tiny bumps. In each bump is a minute hole called a pore. The pores allowed air into the object. Whatever had been inside the fossil needed air, so it must have been alive. Question: What is oval in shape and contains something that is alive? Answer: An egg.

CLUE 3

What sort of animal laid this egg? Birds lay eggs. But this fossil is far too old to belong to a bird. It dates from a time long before birds were common. Reptiles also lay eggs. On the left, a turtle has laid a whole clutch of smooth eggs. Reptiles have existed for millions of years. Perhaps this egg belonged to a reptile.

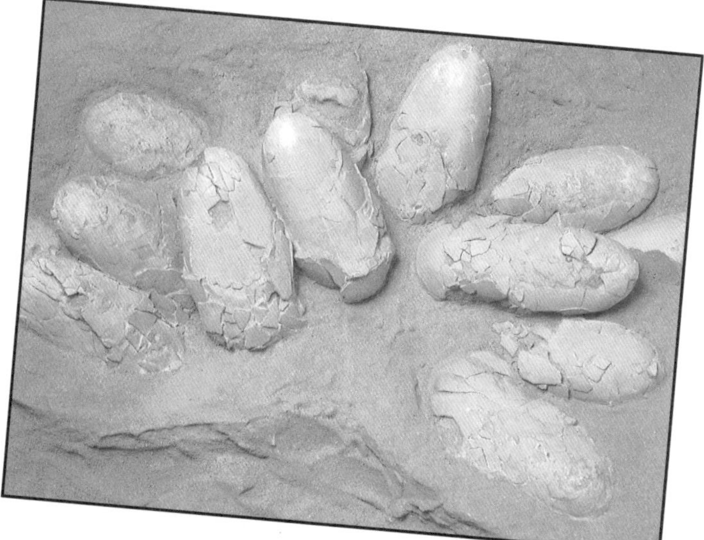

CLUE 4

As well as the fossilized egg and fragments of fossilized eggshell, Roy Chapman Andrews found a number of eggs laid in nests, like the clutch above. This was evidence that the eggs were deliberately laid by a species of animal that always built nests and laid eggs to have its young.

CLUE 5

So what kind of animal laid the eggs, and what tiny creatures hatched out of them? The final clue came when the fossilized bones of small, frilled dinosaurs and their young were found around the nests of the fossilized eggs. The dinosaur was from the Cretaceous Period. The eggs were from the same time.

IT'S A FACT

ROY CHAPMAN ANDREWS WAS THE COMPANY COOK

Before he set out on one of his early expeditions to the Gobi Desert, Dr Andrews put himself in charge of skinning, cutting up and cooking all the animals the expedition caught to eat. His wife travelled with him. Number one on their list of plans was: 'To have a thoroughly good time!'

CRACKED IT!

The eggs were laid by *Protoceratops*. So, after 100 years of wondering how dinosaurs gave birth to their young, scientists at last had scientific evidence that baby dinosaurs hatched from eggs laid by their mother.

Protoceratops

The story of an egg

What happened to the dinosaurs' eggs from the time they were laid by their mothers to the time they cracked open?

Reptiles, such as the dinosaurs, lay eggs and the young grow inside them. When they are ready, the young hatch.

This *Protoceratops* scooped a hollow in the sand then laid her eggs in neat circles.

LAYING EGGS
Dinosaurs evolved from animals that could live in water and on land: we call such animals amphibians. Some amphibians lay their eggs in water where the young develop like tadpoles do when they hatch from the eggs in frogs spawn. Reptiles can lay their eggs on land because their eggs have tough shells. Some scientists think that several females may have laid their eggs in the same nest.

THE INSIDE STORY
Inside the egg, the baby dinosaur grew from the moment the egg was fertilized. Scientists call the baby at this stage an embryo. The embryo dinosaur fed off the egg's yoke. At first, it looked nothing like a dinosaur, but by the time it hatched, it looked like a small version of its parents.

A model of an *Orodromeus* embryo neatly folded inside its egg. Scientists have scanned fossil eggs and found embryo bones inside them.

Is it true that some dinosaurs stole other dinosaurs' eggs?

Yes! What better food for a toothless dinosaur than an egg? Once it had cracked the shell, it could suck out the runny insides for a good, filling meal. Scientists have given the name *Oviraptor* to one dinosaur. It means 'egg thief' and that's exactly what it was. It grabbed eggs from nests and ran off.

Oviraptor

***Maiasaura* mothers laid their eggs in nests. They sat on their nests to keep the eggs warm and help them hatch safely just as today's birds do.**

SAFETY IN NUMBERS

At least one dinosaur, *Maiasaura,* built raised nests that looked like the rim of a tiny volcano. Fossil nests have been found so close to each other that scientists believe that *Maiasaura* mothers stayed together, as a hungry predator was less likely to attack a group of dinosaurs than one on her own.

BACK TO THE SAME SITE

Some nests and fossil remains of hadrosaurs found in the USA show signs that the nests have been used more than once. Experts believe that after they had mated, the mother dinosaurs went back to a nesting site they had used before. They now think that *Maiasaura* sat on their nests in order to keep the eggs warm and hatch them safely. They may even have cared for their young until they were old enough to fend for themselves and survive in the world in which they lived.

3-D Gallery 37

MAIASAURA

- A large hadrosaur
- Lived 90 – 66 million years ago in Montana, USA
- Measured 30ft (9m) long
- Ate plants, fruits and seeds

Dr. David Norman of Cambridge University answers your dinosaur questions
ASK THE EXPERT

Which dinosaur had the largest eyes?

Dromiceiomimus – the 'emu mimic' had huge eyes. Fossils of its skull show that it had the largest eye sockets of any dinosaur found to date, so it probably had the largest eyes. There was one on each side of its head, which gave it the good, all-round vision essential when keeping a watch out for deadly predators.

Did dinosaurs sweat?

No – dinosaurs did not sweat. Humans sweat. The moisture comes through holes in our skin called pores, but dinosaurs were reptiles and reptiles have scaly skin that makes it difficult for moisture to come to the surface. When it was too hot, dinosaurs probably stayed in the shade until it was cool enough for them to go out again.

What does the word 'reptile' mean?

The word reptile comes from the Latin word *repere*, which means to creep or crawl. The people who first used the word to describe animals like snakes and crocodiles had no idea that dinosaurs had ever existed. We know that dinosaurs were reptiles, but we don't think that any of them was a creeping crawler.

What was the first dinosaur to appear in the world?

Two creatures from Argentina compete for the honour of being the first dinosaur. *Herrerasaurus* and *Eoraptor* were both two-legged meat-eaters. They lived about 230 – 225 million years ago in the Middle Triassic. *Herrerasaurus* was the larger at 3m long. *Eoraptor* was 1m in length and was only found in 1992. The search for fossils goes on, so older dinosaurs may be discovered.

DINOSAURS!
DISCOVER THE GIANTS OF THE PREHISTORIC WORLD

MAIASAURA

***Maiasaura* was named 'good mother lizard' because scientists believe it cared for its young after they hatched.**

In 1979, in Montana, USA, scientists found some dinosaur nests with the skeletons of baby dinosaurs in them – they named the creatures *Maiasaura*. A year before, a single dinosaur nest had been found in the same place.

MUDDY NESTS

The nests were hollows, scooped out of muddy ground, and were about the size of a big, round dining room table. The parents may have lined the nest with soft plants, before the female laid between 18 and 30 hard-shelled eggs in it.

GOOD MOTHERS

Scientists think that *Maiasaura* mothers, and perhaps fathers as well, guarded the eggs in the nest, protecting them from any dinosaur that tried to steal them. The mothers may have sat on the eggs to keep them warm, going off to feed while other adults watched over them.

FEEDING BABY

When the babies hatched out, the parents looked after them and brought them food. The young dinosaurs ate all sorts of plants as well as fruit and seeds. *Maiasaura* parents may have chewed up tough plants before giving them to the babies. Experts think that parents fed the young until they were old enough to leave the nest and find their own food.

ALL ALONE

Before these babies were found, scientists thought that female dinosaurs left their babies to hatch out and take care of themselves alone.

Maiasaura leans down towards its young in their nest. The fossil display was made to show how this dinosaur may have looked after its young. Jack Horner, the palaeontologist who discovered the *Maiasaura* young in their nest, looks on.

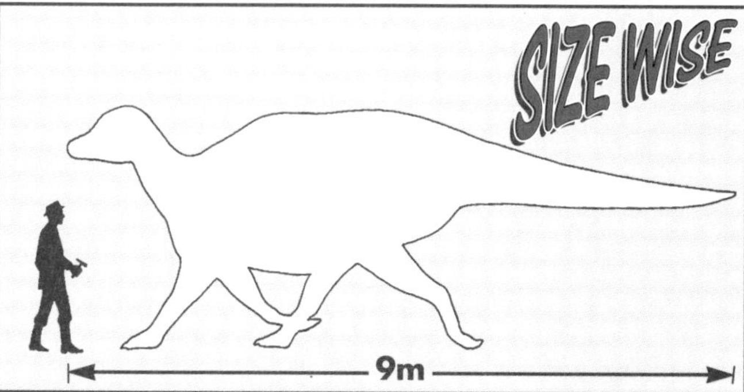

MONSTER FACTS

- **NAME:** *Maiasaura* (my-a-saw-ra) means 'good mother lizard'
- **SIZE:** about 9m long and 3m high
- **FOOD:** plants, leaves, fruit and seeds
- **LIVED:** between about 90 – 66 million years ago in the Late Cretaceous in Montana, USA

HUGE HERDS

So many nests with skeletons and pieces of eggshell have been found in one place in the USA that some palaeontologists have suggested huge herds of *Maiasaura* lived in North America. They roamed through the forests, but returned to the same nesting site each year. They probably used the same nests again and again. When the young had grown enough to look after themselves, they stayed with the herd. Eventually, the herd moved on in search of fresh plants to eat.

DUCK'S BILL

Maiasaura was a big dinosaur, about as long as a double-decker bus. It usually walked on its long back legs and had a big, flat tail, which it held out straight. When feeding on the ground it may have rested on its front legs then reared up on its back legs to reach the leaves of trees. The front of its mouth was shaped like a duck's bill. Further back in its mouth were rows of teeth which ground up the plants it cut off with its beak. On top of its head, above its eyes, was a short bony knob.

IT'S A FACT

EGG MOUNTAIN

When palaeontologists discovered a single fossilized nest of *Maiasaura* in Montana, USA, they decided to excavate the site further. The following year they returned to their dig and found so many nests, packed closely together, that they named the place 'Egg Mountain'.

ESCAPING FROM DANGER

With no way of defending itself, *Maiasaura* probably escaped from the big meat-eating dinosaurs by running away and hiding in thick forests. It probably had good eyesight and hearing, which warned it of danger.

If *Maiasaura* was very frightened, it may have plunged into the lakes or rivers. It swam along by waggling its tail and paddling with its front legs.

HERRERASAURUS

Herrerasaurus was one of the first dinosaurs to roam the Earth.

About as long as a small car, this dinosaur held its tail high off the ground when it walked. It stood upright, moving about on its long, strong back legs and probably ran very fast to catch its prey.

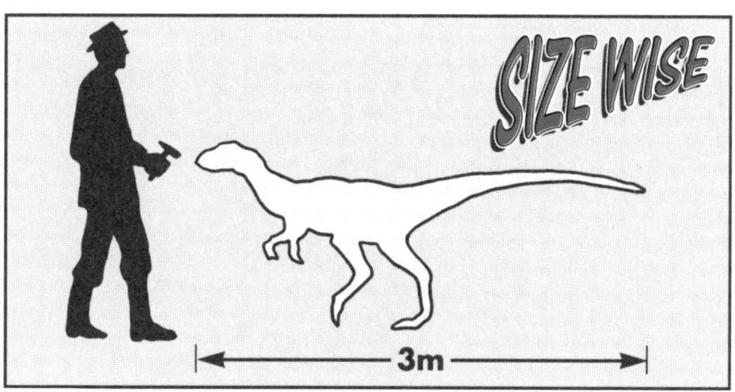

MONSTER FACTS

- **NAME:** *Herrerasaurus* (herra-ra-saw-rus) means 'Herrera lizard' after the place in Argentina where it was discovered
- **SIZE:** about 3m long and 1m high
- **FOOD:** mammals, lizards and other dinosaurs
- **LIVED:** about 230 – 215 million years ago in the Late Triassic in the north of Argentina

FIERCE KILLER

Herrerasaurus killed and ate mammals, lizards and, perhaps, other small meat-eating dinosaurs. It attacked with its front and back feet, and tore its victim with its long claws. *Herrerasaurus* held its prey in its short, strong front legs.

SHARP TEETH

Herrerasaurus had a large head with very long jaws. Like all meat-eating dinosaurs, its jaws were filled with many curved, sharp teeth. *Herrerasaurus* used these teeth to bite and tear up its food.

ONE LAND

Several skeletons of this dinosaur have been discovered in northwest Argentina in recent years. *Herrerasaurus* lived at a time when South America was still joined to the other continents. Members of its dinosaur family have been found as far away as China.

HUAYANGOSAURUS

Experts are still studying complete skeletons to find out more about this armour-plated Chinese dinosaur.

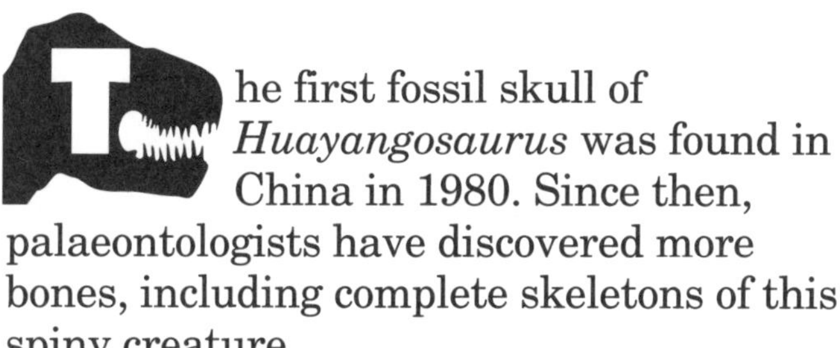

The first fossil skull of *Huayangosaurus* was found in China in 1980. Since then, palaeontologists have discovered more bones, including complete skeletons of this spiny creature.

MONSTER FACTS

- **NAME:** *Huayangosaurus* (hu-ay-ang-o-saw-rus) means 'Huayang lizard' after the place in China where it was found
- **SIZE:** about 4m long and 1.5m high
- **FOOD:** soft, juicy plants
- **LIVED:** 162 – 148 million years ago in the Middle Jurassic in China

UNUSUAL TEETH

Huayangosaurus had a square-shaped head and a short snout. It had small teeth at the front of its upper jaw, which it may have used to bite off ferns and other juicy plants. Its jaws were not built for chewing so it probably swallowed the plants whole.

SLOW AND HEAVY

Experts believe that this dinosaur was a slow, lumbering creature. It may have walked on all four stumpy legs, holding its small head and heavy tail quite close to the ground.

PLATES AND SPIKES

Along its back, *Huayangosaurus* may have had two rows of bony upright plates. At the end of its tail were four sharp spikes, which were probably for defence against other dinosaurs. It had extra spikes on its shoulders, which would have been very off-putting to an enemy.

Reptiles of the air

At the same time that the dinosaurs were leaving their footprints on the Earth, flying reptiles were soaring through the skies.

These distant relatives of the dinosaurs, called pterosaurs (tare-oh-saws), were many different shapes and sizes. Some pterosaurs were as small as sparrows, while others were so large that each wing was as long as a bus. The name pterosaur means 'winged lizard'.

EARLY IDEAS

Long before birds existed, the pterosaurs were the only animals with backbones that could fly. It took a while for the experts to work this out.

When the remains of the first pterosaur were found, scientists could not decide what sort of creature the bones belonged to. Some experts thought the skeletons belonged to a sea creature. Others disagreed – they thought the bones belonged to a flying animal.

LIGHT BONES

After a closer look at some of the bones, scientists agreed that the animals must have been flyers. The experts noticed that the bones were thin and hollow, like drinking straws. The empty spaces in their bones were filled with air, making the pterosaurs' bodies quite light. This helped them to get off the ground and to soar through the air.

***Quetzalcoatlus* had a wing-span of up to 15m, as wide as a small aircraft. Despite its huge size, this animal could soar up on gusts of warm air and may have swooped down to feed on dead animals such as dinosaurs.**

THE WINGED MONSTER

The biggest pterosaur ever found was *Quetzalcoatlus* (kwet-zal-coat-lus). This huge winged beast was discovered in Texas in the USA, and named after an American Indian god called 'feathered serpent'. This name was not a very good choice, because although some pterosaurs may have had soft fur, they never had feathers on their bodies or wings.

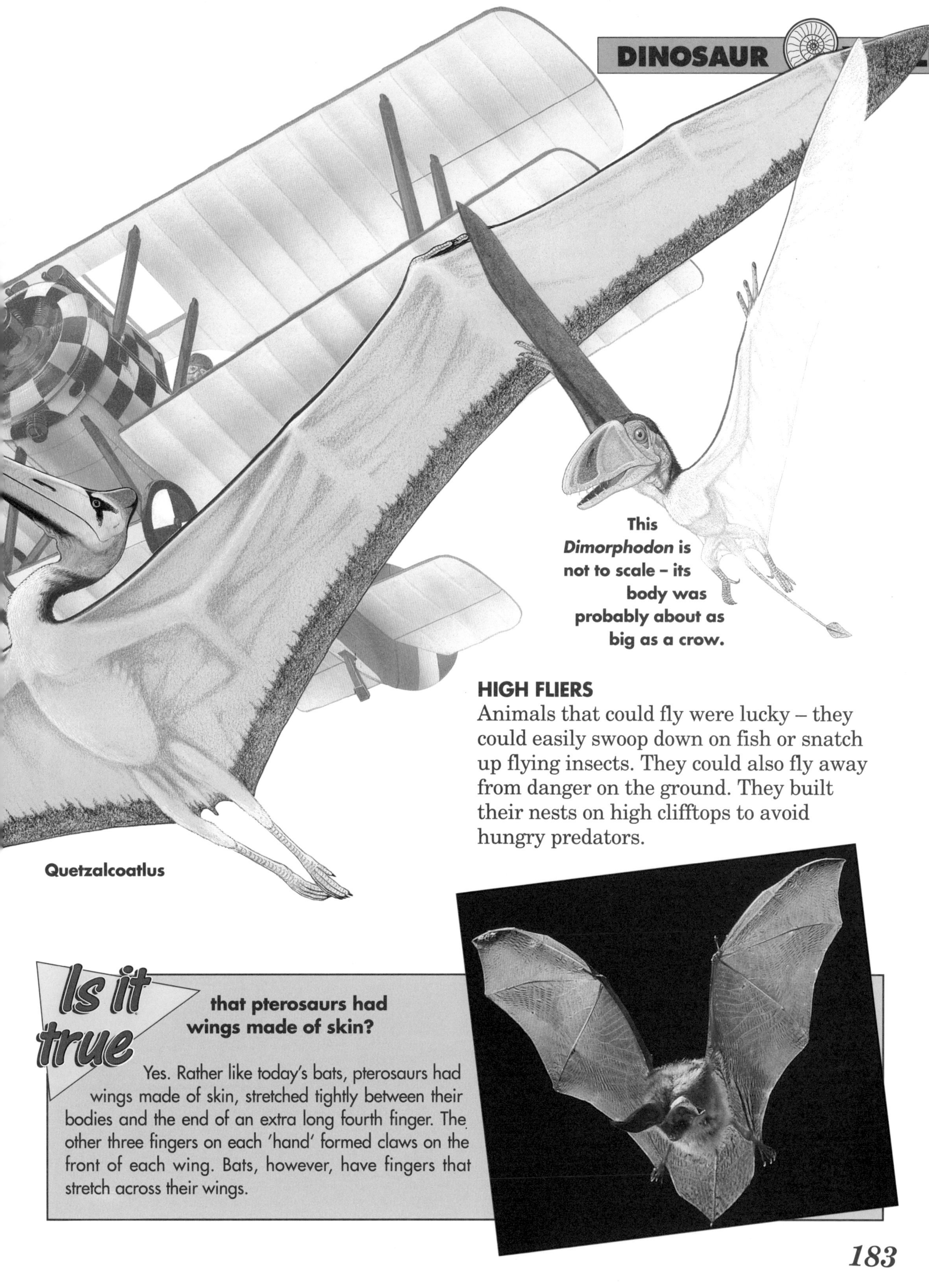

This *Dimorphodon* is not to scale – its body was probably about as big as a crow.

Quetzalcoatlus

HIGH FLIERS

Animals that could fly were lucky – they could easily swoop down on fish or snatch up flying insects. They could also fly away from danger on the ground. They built their nests on high clifftops to avoid hungry predators.

Is it true that pterosaurs had wings made of skin?

Yes. Rather like today's bats, pterosaurs had wings made of skin, stretched tightly between their bodies and the end of an extra long fourth finger. The other three fingers on each 'hand' formed claws on the front of each wing. Bats, however, have fingers that stretch across their wings.

Family differences

As time went by, pterosaurs evolved into quite different creatures and became better flyers. See if you can spot any other differences.

About 100 different types of pterosaur have been found so far. Scientists have divided them into two groups. The earlier group is called rhamphorhynchoid (ram-for-hin-koyd), meaning 'the type with narrow beaks'. They all had teeth and long tails. The later group is named pterodactyloid (tare-oh-dak-til-oid), which means 'the type with wing fingers'.

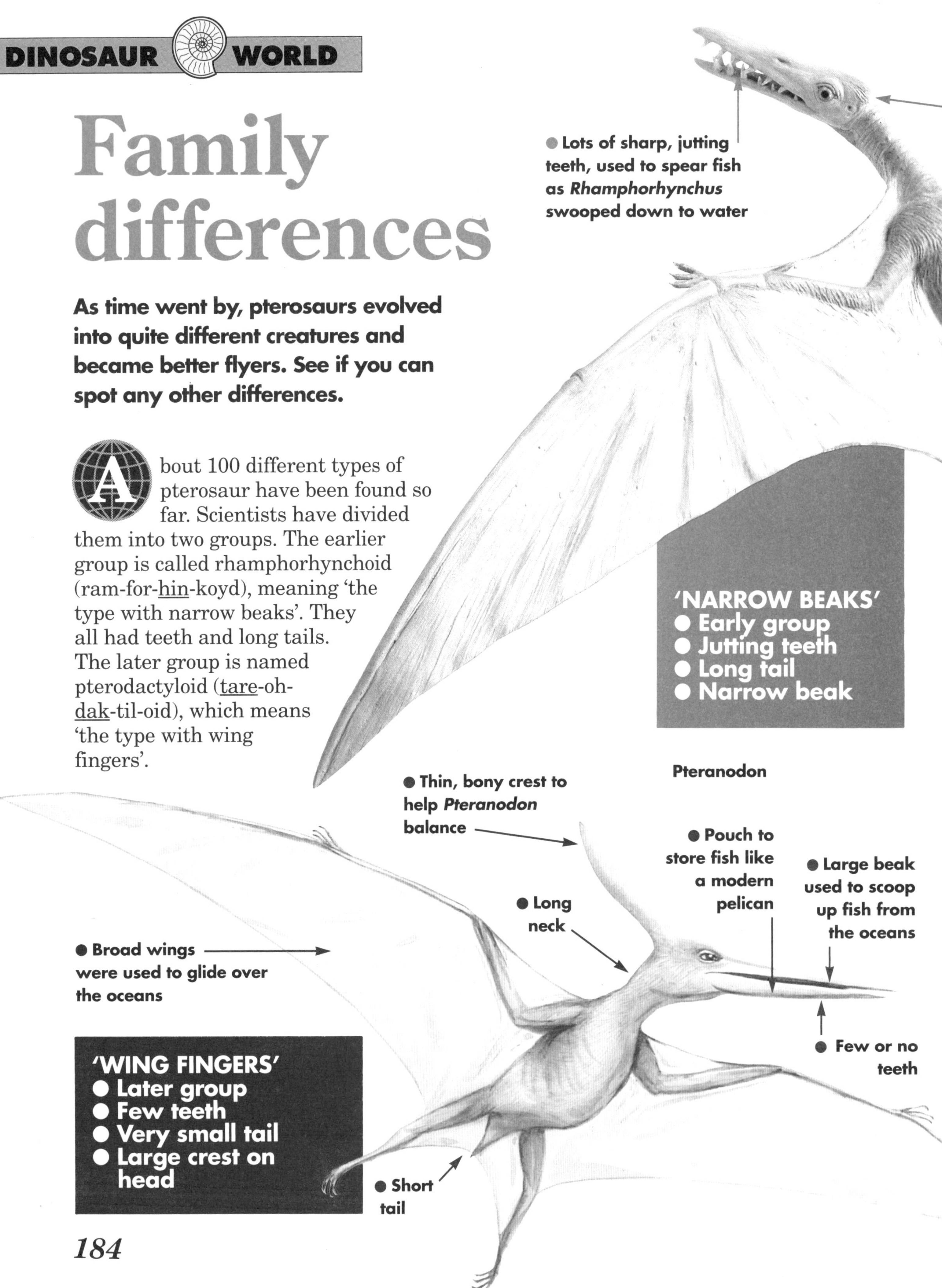

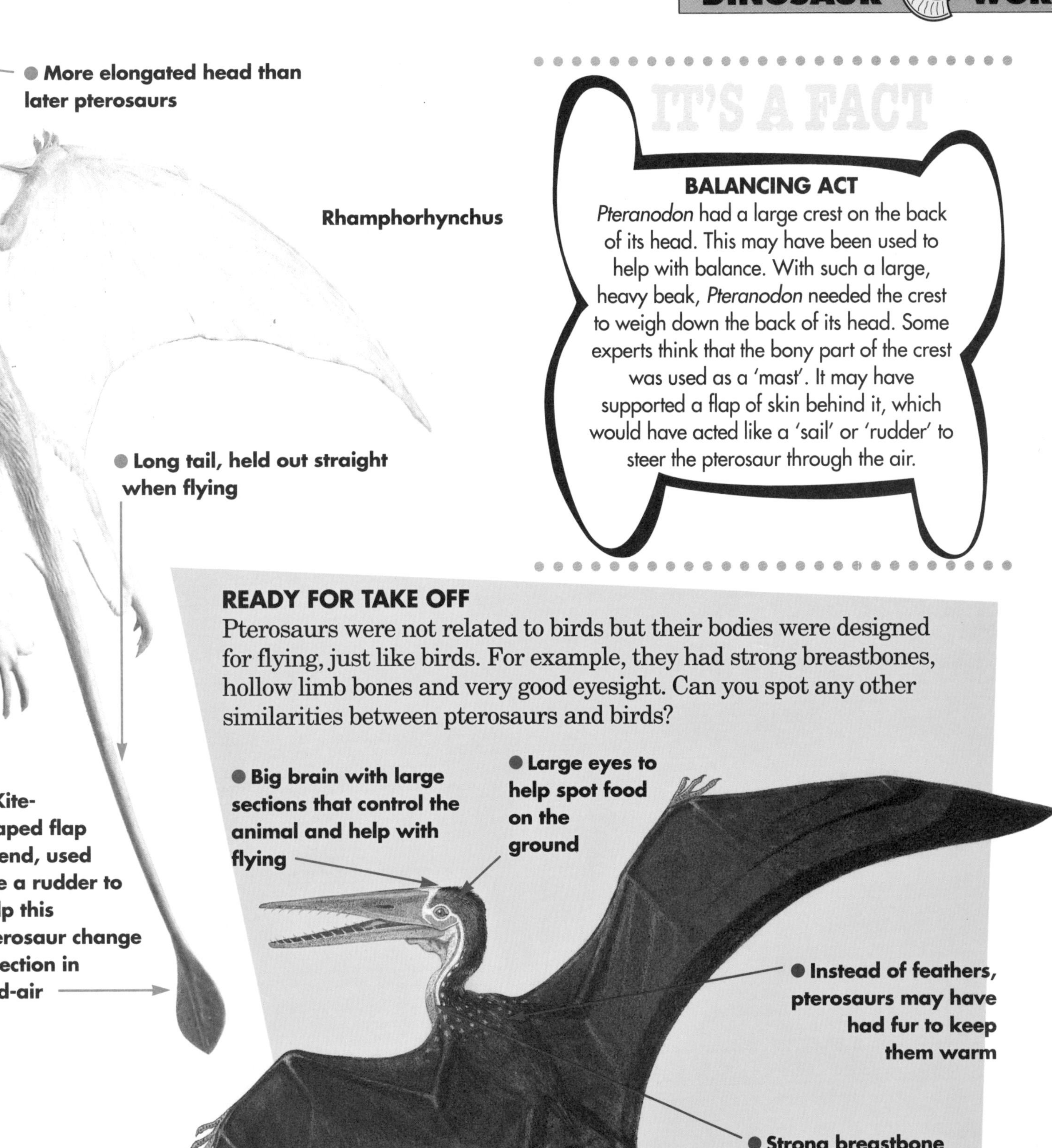
More elongated head than later pterosaurs
Rhamphorhynchus
Long tail, held out straight when flying
Kite-shaped flap at end, used like a rudder to help this pterosaur change direction in mid-air
Pterodactylus
Big brain with large sections that control the animal and help with flying
Large eyes to help spot food on the ground
Instead of feathers, pterosaurs may have had fur to keep them warm
Strong breastbone to anchor muscles that control the wing muscles. Some pterosaurs could flap their wings; others glided
Light bones with air holes to reduce weight of pterosaur's body

IT'S A FACT

BALANCING ACT

Pteranodon had a large crest on the back of its head. This may have been used to help with balance. With such a large, heavy beak, *Pteranodon* needed the crest to weigh down the back of its head. Some experts think that the bony part of the crest was used as a 'mast'. It may have supported a flap of skin behind it, which would have acted like a 'sail' or 'rudder' to steer the pterosaur through the air.

READY FOR TAKE OFF

Pterosaurs were not related to birds but their bodies were designed for flying, just like birds. For example, they had strong breastbones, hollow limb bones and very good eyesight. Can you spot any other similarities between pterosaurs and birds?

GIANTS OF THE PAST

MAIASAURA

Four baby *Maiasaura* hatch from their eggs and take a first look at the world. They will stay near to the nest until they are old enough to look for their own food. One parent keeps an eye out for danger, while the other looks around for some food to feed the newly-hatched dinosaurs. *Maiasaura* had large families, there may be as many as 30 eggs in this nest.

3-D Gallery 17

DEINONYCHUS FAMILY

- Well-armed hunter
- Lived 115 million years ago in North America
- Adults measured 3m long and 2m tall
- Ate other dinosaurs

3-D Gallery 18

STRUTHIOMIMUS

- Ostrich-like predator
- Lived 80 – 60 million years ago in Western North America
- Measured 3 – 4m long
- Ate insects, lizards and plants

Open wide

Sharp as razors, serrated like saws, or leaf shaped, dinosaur teeth can tell us a lot about how dinosaurs lived.

If a jaw, studded with pointed fangs is uncovered by scientists on a dig, they can tell that these teeth did not belong to a peaceful vegetarian – but a blood-thirsty carnivore.

LOOK SHARP!

Unlike humans, who have to look after their teeth to avoid a trip to the dentist, meat-eating dinosaurs, such as *Allosaurus*, could afford to ignore their teeth. As one tooth broke or fell out another automatically grew in its place.

DEINONYCHUS

- **Sharp teeth pointing backwards**
- **New teeth ready to replace old or damaged ones**
- **Strong jaws**

PIERCING FANGS

If you were to look at a flesh-eater's tooth under a microscope, the edge of it would look like the sharp side of a saw. A carnosaur's teeth also pointed backwards, which helped the animal to grip its struggling prey. Once the teeth had entered the victim's flesh there was no hope of survival. Carnosaurs did not have the right teeth to chew their food, they swallowed it whole.

The teeth below, although not to scale, show the huge variety of tooth shapes. The three vicious-looking teeth on the left belong to meat-eaters. All the others belong to plant-eaters, each of which had very different ways of eating.

T rex

Megalosaurus

Troodon

Iguanodon

a sauropod

Plateosaurus

Piercers

PEACEFUL PLANT EATERS

The vegetarians of the dinosaur world had very efficient teeth to cope with their leafy diet. Like today's sheep and horses, herbivorous dinosaurs had teeth that were designed for stripping branches, chopping, and grinding tough plants.

RAKING UP LEAVES

Some dinosaurs, such as *Diplodocus* and *Shunosaurus*, did not have any chewing teeth. Instead, they simply raked leaves from twigs using pencil-shaped teeth and swallowed the leaves whole. All the hard work was done by the stomach, where the vegetation was broken down.

A SLICING EDGE

Inside *Triceratops'* mouth were hundreds of teeth. They were anchored to the jaw by interlocking, 'V'-shaped roots. As *Triceratops* closed its mouth, the upper and lower teeth moved like a pair of garden shears – slicing the food into pieces that were small enough to swallow.

CHOPPERS

Ornithopods, such as *Heterodontosaurus,* were able to chop their food up. Their lower jaws rotated in and out as they opened and closed their mouth. Later ornithopods could also chew. Behind *Iguanodon's* horny beak and muscley cheeks were rows of sharp teeth. These met at an angle, interlocking tightly to help *Iguanodon* chew its food.

Is it true that some dinosaurs had as many as 1000 teeth?

Edmontosaurus was a duckbilled dinosaur. It had about 1000 strong teeth, which were used to grind vegetation into a pulp. The teeth were cemented together to form solid walls on the top and bottom jaws (right). As the dinosaur chewed, the walls met and crushed the vegetation.

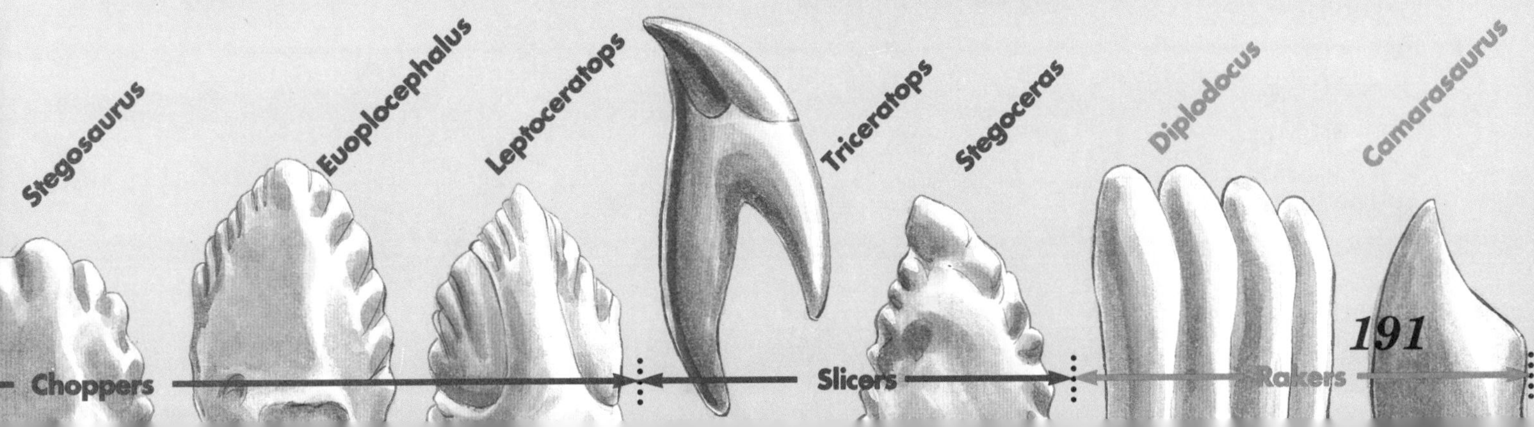

Bringing up baby

What happened to baby dinosaurs once they had hatched out of their eggs? Did they fend for themselves, or did their parents look after them? Follow the clues to find out.

In 1978, a whole nest of baby dinosaurs and their eggshells were discovered in Montana in the USA. The fossils of such young dinosaurs are rare and these little hadrosaurs were even more unusual because their skeletons, together with their nest and eggshells, gave the experts the first ever clues to how some young dinosaurs were looked after.

CLUE 1 The skeletons of the young hadrosaurs, found in the bowl-shaped mud nest, were just under 1m long. The eggs from which they hatched were only 20cm long, so the young dinosaurs were too big to have just hatched out of the eggs. They had hatched and then stayed in, or near, the nest long enough to grow from a 35cm hatchling, just out of the egg, to a baby, 1m long. Why did they stay in the nest? Experts think that they stayed to be looked after by their parents.

CLUE 2 The eggshells in the nest were all in little pieces. Why? The experts believe that the baby dinosaurs trampled their eggshells into fragments as they moved around and slept in the nest. Yet another piece of evidence that they lived in the nest for quite a while after they hatched.

CLUE 4 The young dinosaurs had died in their nests. It seems that their parents must have died or been killed and did not return to the nest to feed them. The little dinosaurs' instinct was to stay in the nest whatever happened. Even though they were very hungry, they stayed in the nest waiting for their parents to return. When their parents did not come back to feed them they eventually died of starvation. The palaeontologists saw this as clear evidence that some dinosaurs cared for their young and even looked after them so well that they collected food and returned to the nest to feed them.

CLUE 3 When the palaeontologists studied the skulls of the little dinosaurs they discovered that the teeth were worn down by grinding food. It seems that the young hadrosaurs had been brought food in the nest by their parents, just as today's birds do.

CLUE 5 The palaeontologists discovered many other nests around the first nest. The whole area was a hadrosaur nesting site. The experts believe that these dinosaurs nested close together for protection against predators. By nesting near each other, there was always an adult dinosaur around to keep an eye open for egg thieves or ferocious meat-eating dinosaurs.

ALL IN A NAME
Experts named the dinosaur *Maiasaura,* or 'good mother lizard', because it took care of its young.

HELPLESS BABIES

Although some dinosaurs were very large animals, they did not lay large eggs. The biggest eggs found so far are only about 30cm long. This means that when some baby dinosaurs hatched they must have been very small and defenceless creatures. The hatchlings of certain dinosaur species were so helpless that they were unable to look after themselves. They had to rely on their parents until they had grown enough to have some chance of survival.

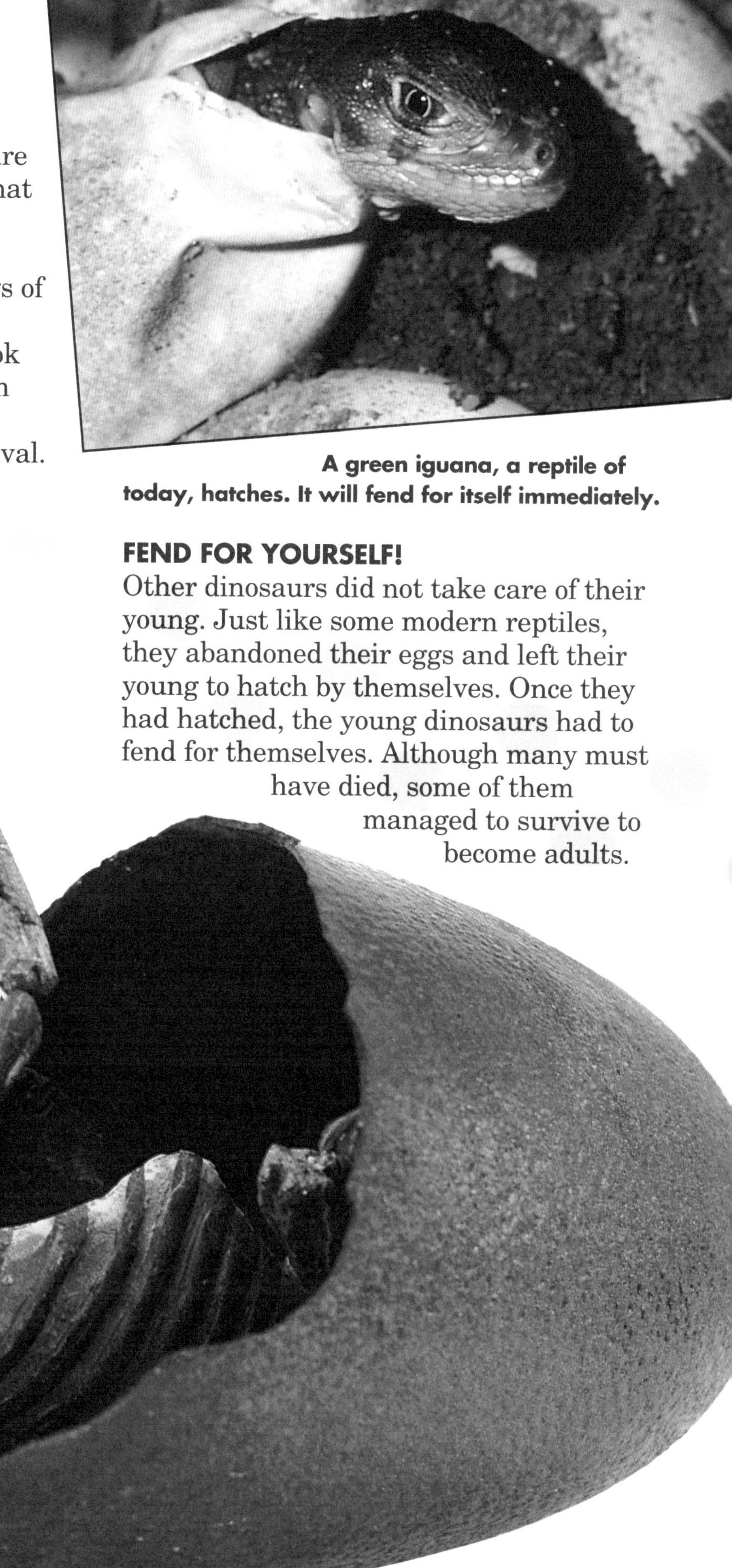

A green iguana, a reptile of today, hatches. It will fend for itself immediately.

A tiny hadrosaur emerges from its egg. This fossil model shows how helpless some hatchlings were.

FEND FOR YOURSELF!

Other dinosaurs did not take care of their young. Just like some modern reptiles, they abandoned their eggs and left their young to hatch by themselves. Once they had hatched, the young dinosaurs had to fend for themselves. Although many must have died, some of them managed to survive to become adults.

***Protoceratops* adults protected young members of their herd. Here, newly hatched, juvenile and adult *Protoceratops* live together.**

PART OF THE CROWD

Some dinosaurs, however, looked after their young as soon as they hatched. Palaeontologists have found many skeletons of adult, young and hatchling *Protoceratops* together proving that they lived together in mixed age groups. The adult dinosaurs scared predators away and protected the younger ones.

IT'S A FACT

BIG EGGS

Dinosaur eggs were not that big. Large eggs would have needed thick shells to prevent them from collapsing. The eggs of small dinosaurs were about the size of chickens' eggs. The largest dinosaur eggs known so far were laid by *Hypselosaurus*. They were up to 30cm long. An ostrich egg, which is the largest egg of any living animal, is about 15 – 20cm.

GENTLE AS AN ALLIGATOR

Some experts are not sure that a creature as huge as a dinosaur could have looked after something as small as one of its own young without trampling it to death. But, the alligator, one of today's biggest reptiles and a distant relative of the dinosaurs, looks after its tiny young very carefully.

When the young hatch they call their mother with high-pitched grunts and she comes to help them. She digs them out of the nest and carries them to a special nursery pool that she has made for them. She can bite through a human leg with her huge jaws and razor sharp teeth, but her own young are perfectly safe in her care. So it seems likely that dinosaurs were able to look after their young, too.

An American alligator hatchling perches on its mother's head, just above her eyes. It is only a few centimetres away from her fearsome teeth, but it is perfectly safe. American alligators may care for their young for up to two years.

3-D Gallery 38

PARASAUROLOPHUS

- A crested hadrosaur
- Lived about 80 – 66 million years ago in North America
- Measured 33ft (10m) long
- Ate plants and fruit

Who gave dinosaurs their names?

Since the 1820s, dinosaur names have been invented by palaeontologists. Every time a new dinosaur is discovered it is described in detail in a scientific journal. To show that this is a brand new specimen, experts choose a name that has never been used before and that gives a clue to how, or where, the fossils were found.

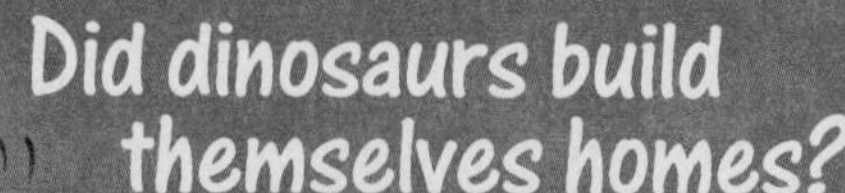

Did dinosaurs build themselves homes?

Most dinosaurs would have been too big to build homes. However, some dinosaurs did build nests. At the beginning of their lives, these nests would have been 'home' for baby dinosaurs.

Would dinosaurs have smelt of anything?

Many dinosaurs had extremely sensitive noses. A keen sense of smell would have been important for sniffing out predators, prey and choosing mates. It seems likely that dinosaurs gave off scents as signals, just as animals do today.

Is there any part of the world where dinosaurs didn't live?

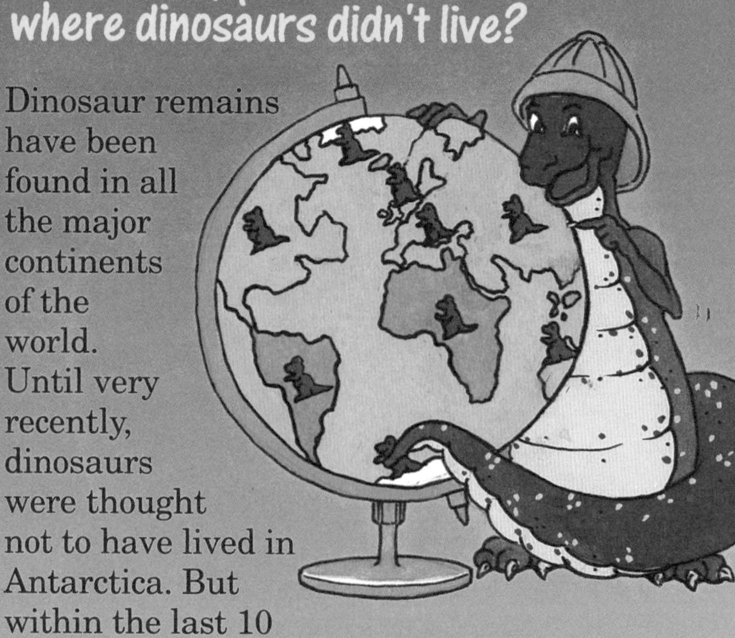

Dinosaur remains have been found in all the major continents of the world. Until very recently, dinosaurs were thought not to have lived in Antarctica. But within the last 10 years, fossils belonging to an armoured dinosaur and a small two-footed plant-eating dinosaur have been found on the rocky outskirts of this frozen continent.

STEGOCERAS

An adult male *Stegoceras* would have fought fiercely with another for control of the herd.

Although quite small, *Stegoceras* was a tough creature. A two-legged plant-eater, *Stegoceras* was a member of an unusual group called pachycephalosaurs (pack-ee-sef-a-loh-saws), meaning 'thick-headed reptiles'.

BUMPY HEAD

Pachycephalosaurs had one special feature in common – a thick, rounded skull. On *Stegoceras'* head was a semi-circle of small bony lumps. These bumps ran above its eyes and around the back of its neck. Experts are not certain what the lumps were for but they could have been for decoration. The skull was not very thick when *Stegoceras* was born, but it became thicker as the dinosaur got older.

HIS AND HERS

Some experts believe that they have discovered examples of both male and female *Stegoceras*. They have found that some skulls are thicker than others and believe that these thick skulls may have belonged to the males. A male *Stegoceras* could have a skull up to 6cm thick – which is half as thick as a brick.

6 CM THICKNESS OF SKULL

High, bony dome

Eye socket

Skull gently slopes to meet front of beak

Beaked mouth

Slightly curved, serrated teeth; used to shred plants

25cm

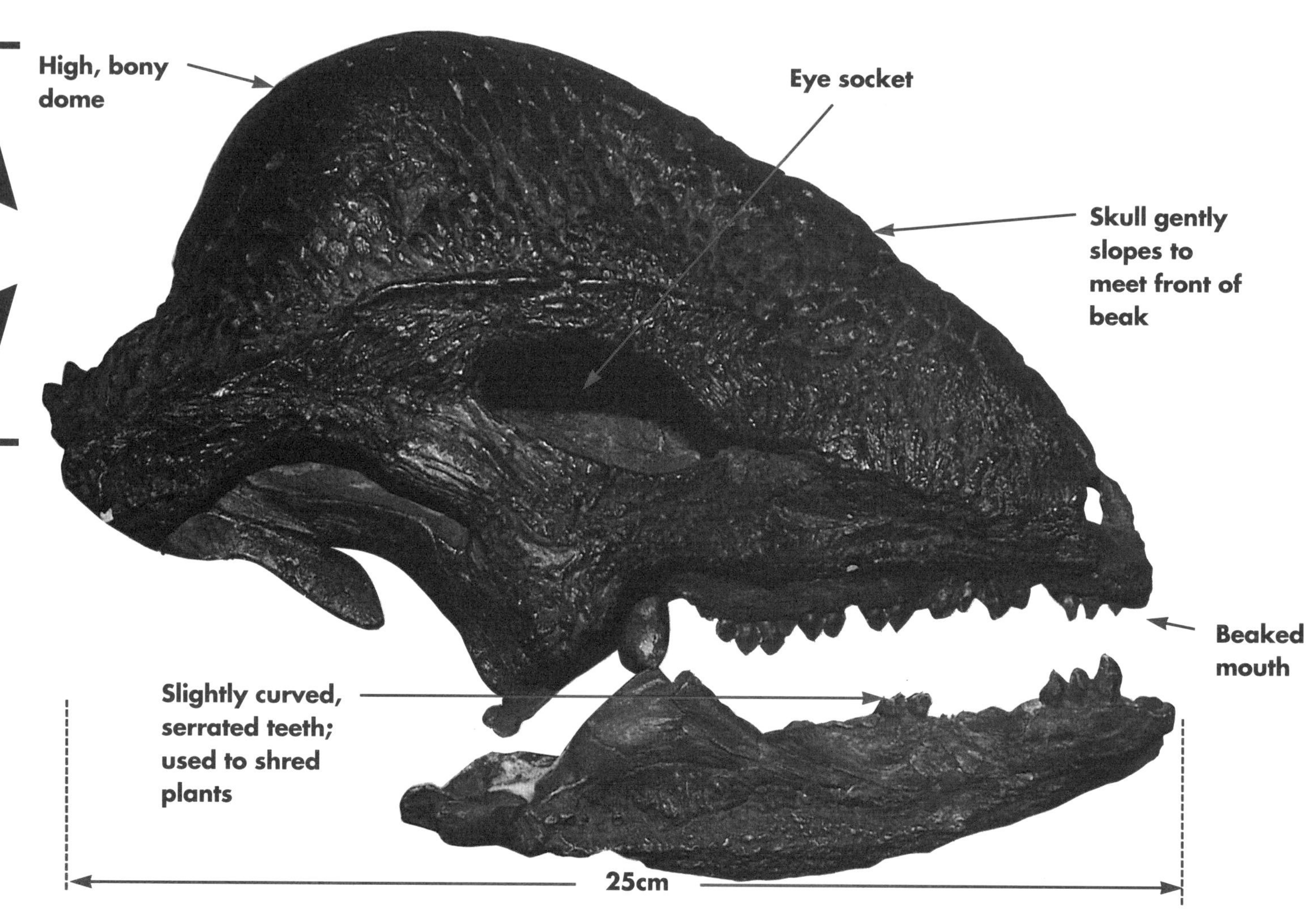

MONSTER FACTS

- **NAME:** *Stegoceras* (steg-oh-ser-as) means 'horny roof'
- **SIZE:** 2.5m long and 1.5m high
- **FOOD:** plants and ferns
- **LIVED:** 75 million years ago in the Late Cretaceous Period in North America

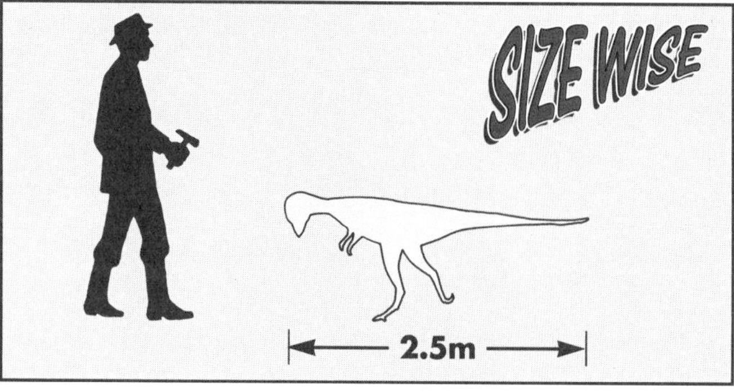

HEAD TO HEAD

Scientists believe that *Stegoceras* used its tough, heavy skull to fight against other males for control of the herd and the right to mate with the females. They think that *Stegoceras* behaved in much the same way as Bighorn rams from North America do today. The Bighorns, a kind of goat, charge at each other head-on, using their strengthened skulls as battering rams.

CRASH HELMETS

At the beginning of a fight, the two rival dinosaurs may have faced each other head-on. Then they charged at each other, colliding heads at great speed. They would not have been seriously harmed by this violent blow, as their brains, which were only the size of a chicken's egg, were protected by the extra thick skull.

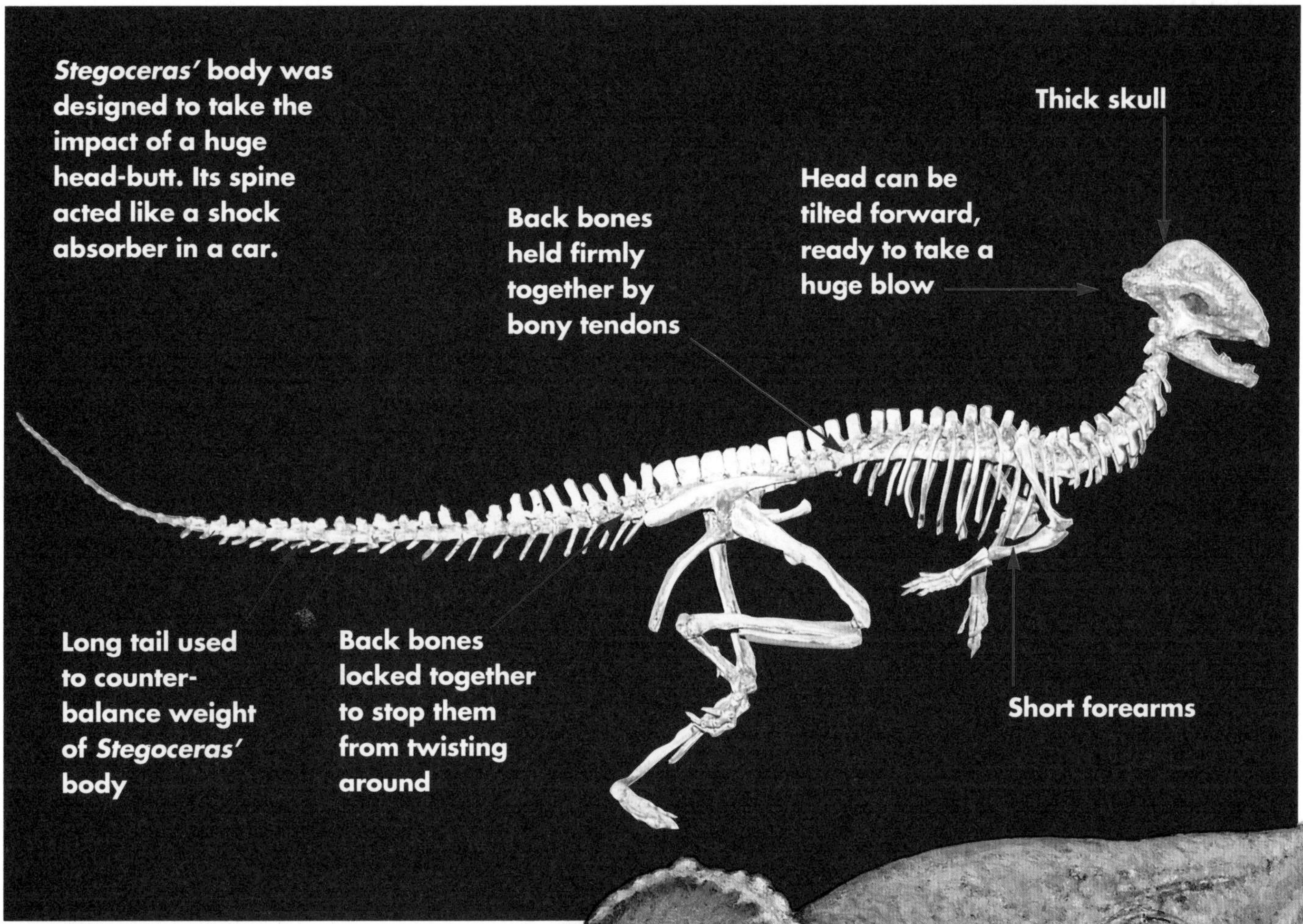

BONE CRUSHER

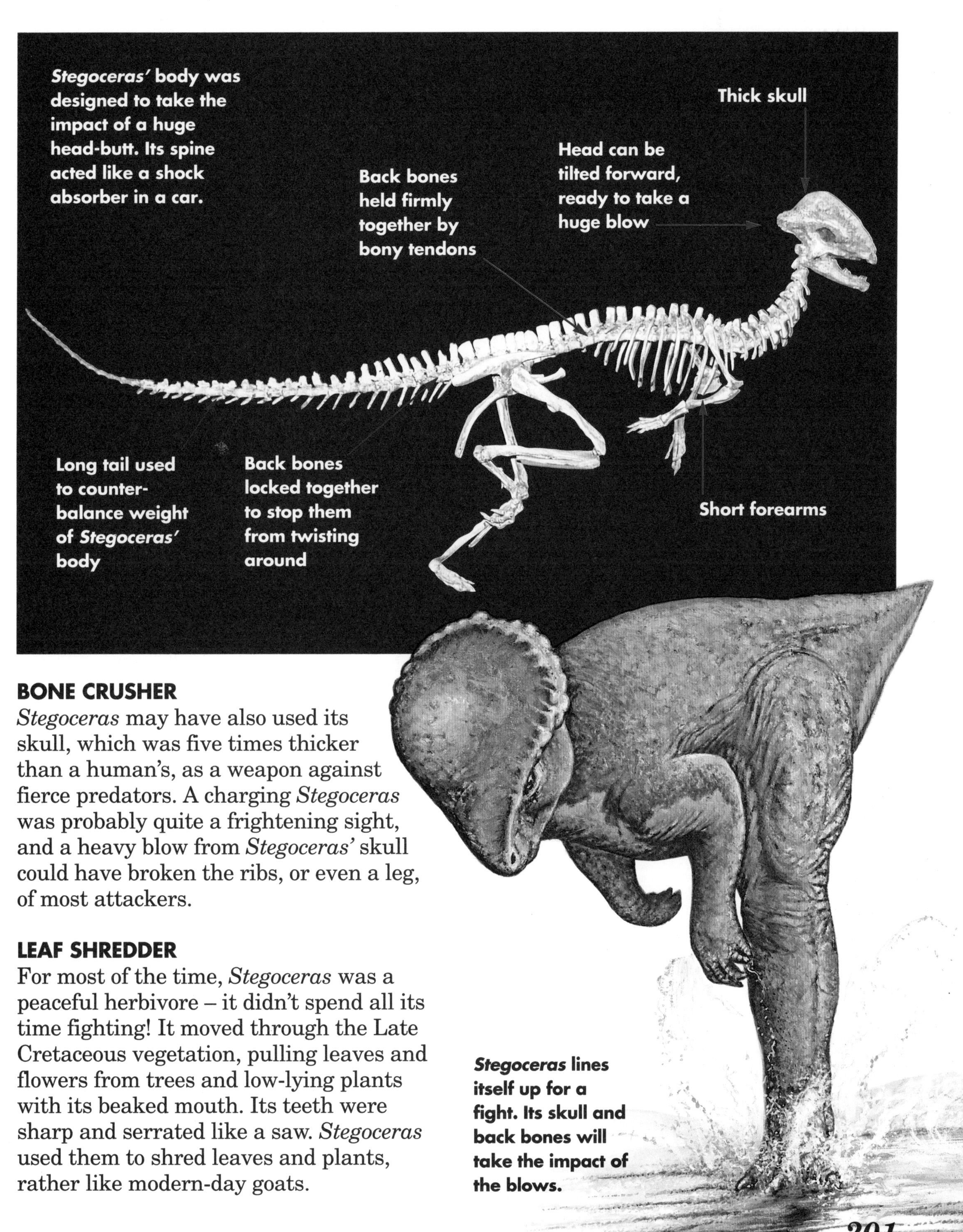

Stegoceras may have also used its skull, which was five times thicker than a human's, as a weapon against fierce predators. A charging *Stegoceras* was probably quite a frightening sight, and a heavy blow from *Stegoceras'* skull could have broken the ribs, or even a leg, of most attackers.

LEAF SHREDDER

For most of the time, *Stegoceras* was a peaceful herbivore – it didn't spend all its time fighting! It moved through the Late Cretaceous vegetation, pulling leaves and flowers from trees and low-lying plants with its beaked mouth. Its teeth were sharp and serrated like a saw. *Stegoceras* used them to shred leaves and plants, rather like modern-day goats.

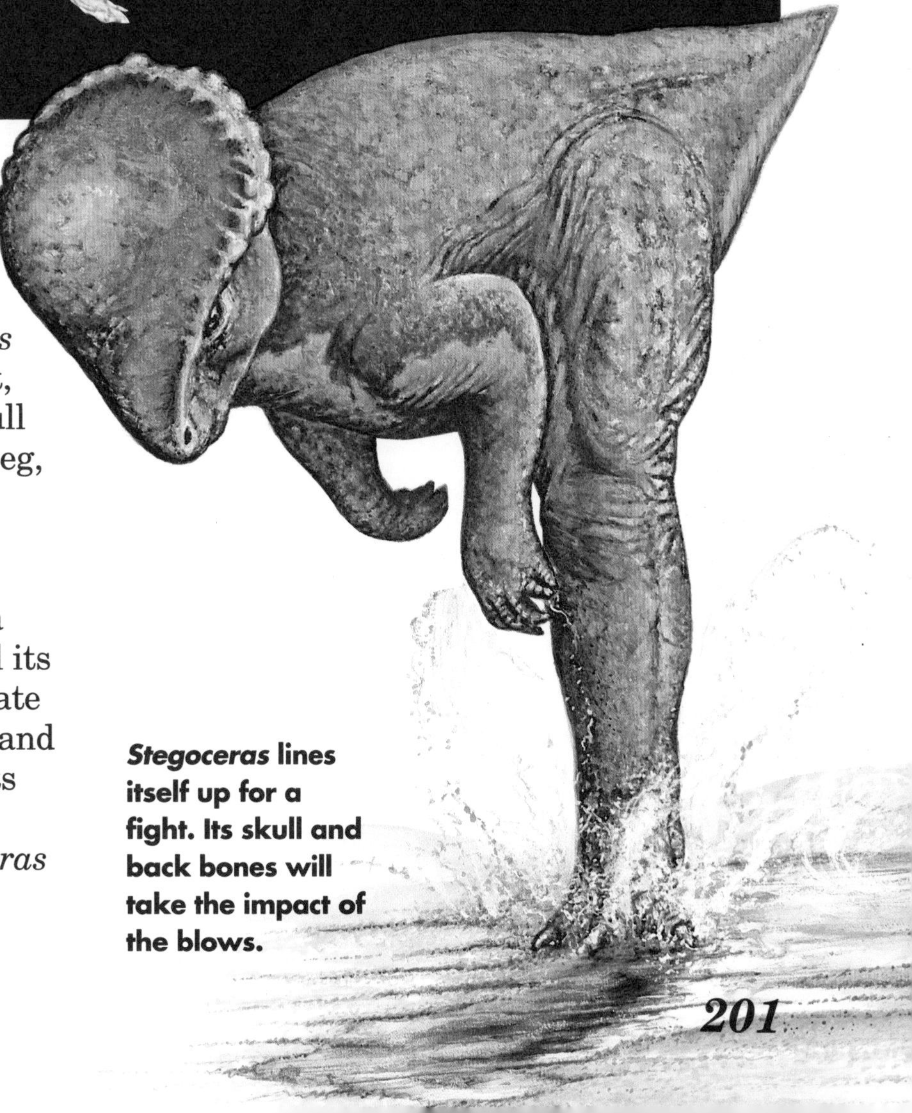

***Stegoceras* lines itself up for a fight. Its skull and back bones will take the impact of the blows.**

APATOSAURUS

Apatosaurus was a sturdy beast. It had a long, whiplash tail, which had about 80 bones in it.

patosaurus was a huge, four-legged sauropod, which was as long as a tennis court. It fed on leaves that it snipped from plants and trees with its weak, peg-like teeth. Its very long neck, which had 15 huge bones in it, was held up by strong muscles that ran along the neck bones.

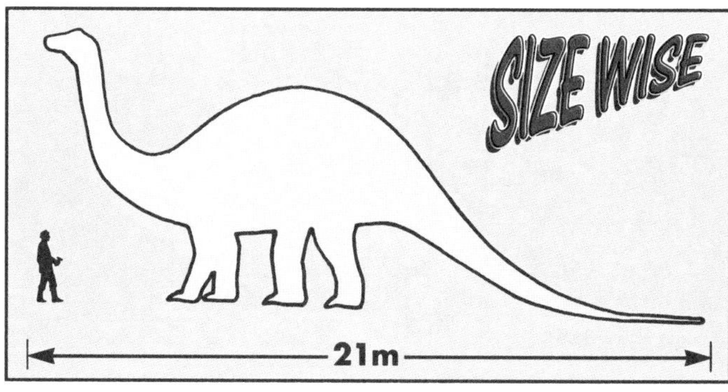

MONSTER FACTS

- **NAME:** *Apatosaurus* (a-pat-oh-saw-rus) means 'deceptive reptile'
- **SIZE:** 21m long and 8.3m high
- **FOOD:** leaves and shoots of trees and shrubs
- **LIVED:** about 150 million years ago in the Late Jurassic Period in North America

LASHING OUT

Apatosaurus had an extremely long tail, almost half of which was thin and whip-like. It probably used its tail to lash out at the hungry meat-eaters that preyed on the weakest members of the herd, such as the young and the very old dinosaurs.

LIKE AN ELEPHANT

To support its great weight, *Apatosaurus'* pillar-like legs ended in broad feet, rather like those of an elephant. Its front feet had a claw on the inside toe, which it used to kick out at attackers.

MISTAKEN IDENTITY

The first *Apatosaurus* was discovered in 1877. A few years later, the man who named it, O. C. Marsh, found a dinosaur, which he called *Brontosaurus.* But Marsh had made a mistake; *Brontosaurus* was, in fact, the same animal as *Apatosaurus.*

SEGNOSAURUS

Experts have had to piece together this dinosaur from only a few bones.

Segnosaurus was a two-legged dinosaur that was longer than a car. It had quite a small head for its size. Its arms were short with three fingers, each ending in a sharp claw.

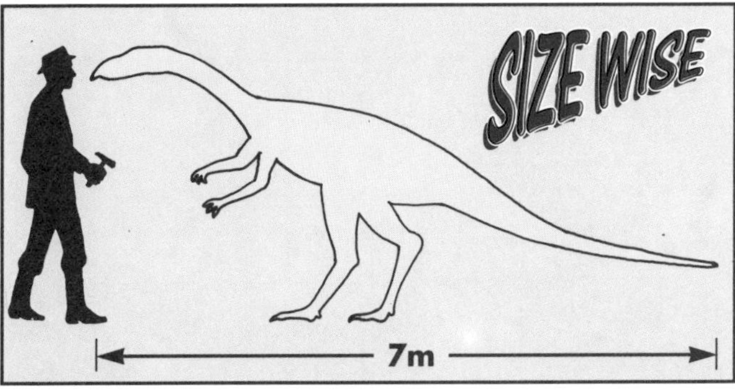

MONSTER FACTS

- **NAME:** *Segnosaurus* (seg-no-saw-rus) means 'slow reptile'
- **SIZE:** 7m long
- **FOOD:** probably plants, but some experts have suggested meat and fish
- **LIVED:** 75 million years ago in the Late Cretaceous Period in Mongolia

UNUSUAL MOUTH

Experts are not sure what sort of food *Segnosaurus* ate. It had teeth at the back of its jaw to cut up food – like the two-legged meat-eaters. But at the front of its mouth was a toothless beak – like some of the plant-eaters.

BROAD FEET

Segnosaurus also had feet quite unlike those of ordinary meat-eaters. It had sturdy legs and short, broad feet which ended in four toes. Some experts think that the feet may have been webbed.

FISH EATER

The scientist who named *Segnosaurus* in 1979 suggested that it waded, or even swam, catching fish with its claws or in its toothless beak. But scientists are still unsure; it is possible that it was a plant-eater and used its beak to nip off leaves.

Enter the mammals

Mammals rule our world today, but throughout most of the Age of the Dinosaurs mammals were tiny creatures descended from mammal-like reptiles.

Dimetrodon

When the world was one big continent called Pangaea, early mammal-like reptiles called pelycosaurs roamed across it. Pelycosaurs had huge fan-shaped sails on their backs and so they were called 'sail reptiles'. One of the most unusual pelycosaurs was *Dimetrodon*. Fossils of its jaw suggest that *Dimetrodon* may have had a permanent grin. But this friendly looking beast preyed on harmless herbivores.

Below: Two therapsids share a rock and the shade of some trees. The meat-eating *Sauroctorus* chases a lizard, while *Moschops* the plant-eater looks on.

GOOD RUNNERS

Pelycosaurs were overtaken by animals called therapsids. Some therapsids, such as *Moschops*, were plant-eaters. Others, like *Sauroctorus*, were meat-eaters. They had longer legs and shorter tails than pelycosaurs, which meant that they could run faster. They looked like a cross between a lizard and a dog. *Lycaenops*, for example, had a face rather like a German shepherd dog and a stocky mammal-like body.

Two *Cynognathus* feed on the carcass of *Lystrosaurus*.

LAST, BUT FAST

The last group of mammal-like reptiles were the cynodonts, which means 'dog teeth'. They were fast-moving animals that lived about 220 million years ago. *Cynognathus* was a hairy cynodont that had strong jaws and teeth that were excellent for chewing meat.

Fierce *Lycaenops*, a therapsid, probably hunted for food in packs.

REAL MAMMALS

At the end of the Triassic, the last mammal-like reptiles vanished from the face of the Earth. The dinosaurs were well on their way to becoming the rulers of the prehistoric world. Scampering around the feet of the mighty dinosaurs, the sound of giant footsteps thundering in their ears, was a timid group of new animals that were direct descendants of cynodonts. They did not seem important, but they were because they were the true mammals from which all mammals, even humans, came.

What is? A MAMMAL-LIKE REPTILE

As their name suggests, mammal-like reptiles were somewhere in between reptiles and mammals. They were the relatives of early reptiles, but unlike reptiles, their legs were tucked underneath their bodies. Their skulls and teeth remind us of today's mammals.

Mammal family tree

The earliest real mammals were direct descendants of the mammal-like reptiles. They were like today's shrews and ate insects.

Horse

Bat

Chimpanzee

Kangaroo

Shrew

We know what early mammals were like from their fossils. Mammals have soft skin covered in hair, they give birth to live young, feed their babies milk, produce their own body heat and have interesting teeth.

Skin and hair can tell experts a lot about an animal, but these parts do not show up in fossils, so experts concentrate on fossil teeth instead.

VALUABLE TEETH

Mammals get their energy from food. They need to eat quite a lot because mammals are usually very active creatures. Because they were more active than the prehistoric reptiles, the early mammals had different kinds of teeth to help them chew their food more thoroughly, and so get more energy from it. Scientists look carefully at teeth to tell mammal and reptile fossils apart.

THE FIRST MAMMALS

Three different groups of mammals lived during the Age of the Dinosaurs. The first group, called trichonodonts, had teeth like our back teeth. They were good for crushing insects and had three points on top of them. *Megazostrodon* was a trichonodont that lived during the Late Triassic Period.

At the end of the Cretaceous Period, the dinosaurs and great reptiles died out. At last the mammals had a chance to expand. They went on to take their place as rulers of the animal kingdom.

Megazostrodon (trichonodont)

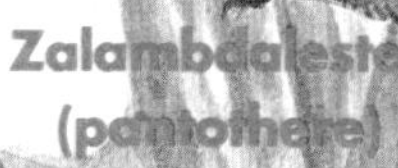

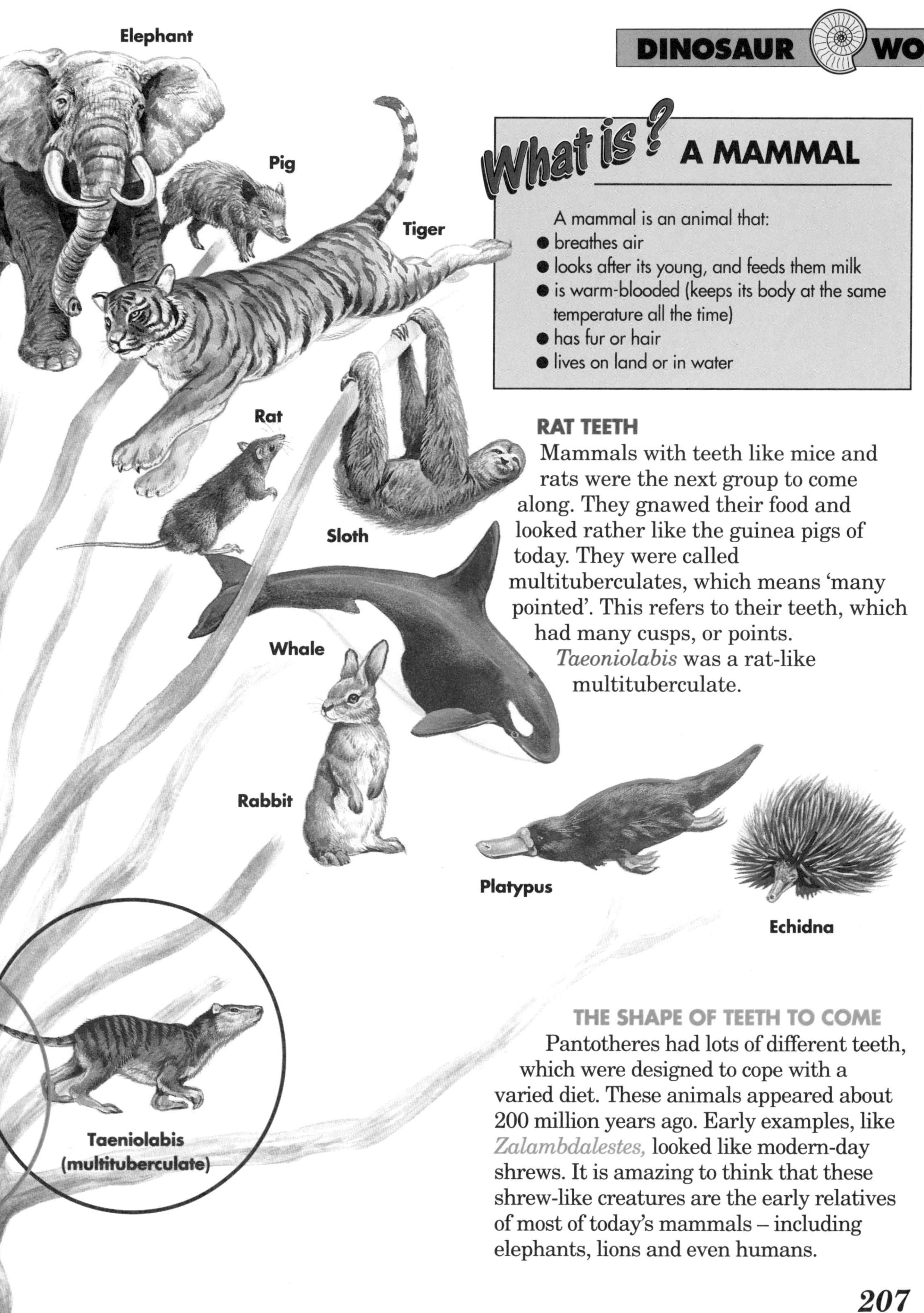

What is? A MAMMAL

A mammal is an animal that:

- breathes air
- looks after its young, and feeds them milk
- is warm-blooded (keeps its body at the same temperature all the time)
- has fur or hair
- lives on land or in water

RAT TEETH

Mammals with teeth like mice and rats were the next group to come along. They gnawed their food and looked rather like the guinea pigs of today. They were called multituberculates, which means 'many pointed'. This refers to their teeth, which had many cusps, or points. *Taeoniolabis* was a rat-like multituberculate.

THE SHAPE OF TEETH TO COME

Pantotheres had lots of different teeth, which were designed to cope with a varied diet. These animals appeared about 200 million years ago. Early examples, like *Zalambdalestes,* looked like modern-day shrews. It is amazing to think that these shrew-like creatures are the early relatives of most of today's mammals – including elephants, lions and even humans.

GIANTS OF THE PAST

STEGOCERAS

Stegoceras was not the most vicious dinosaur of its time, but when the mating season came round, males rammed into each other like two cars crashing at speed. The reward for the victorious head-butter was the chance to mate with an available female. The beaten animal was left stunned but not badly hurt, and went to look for another male to butt.

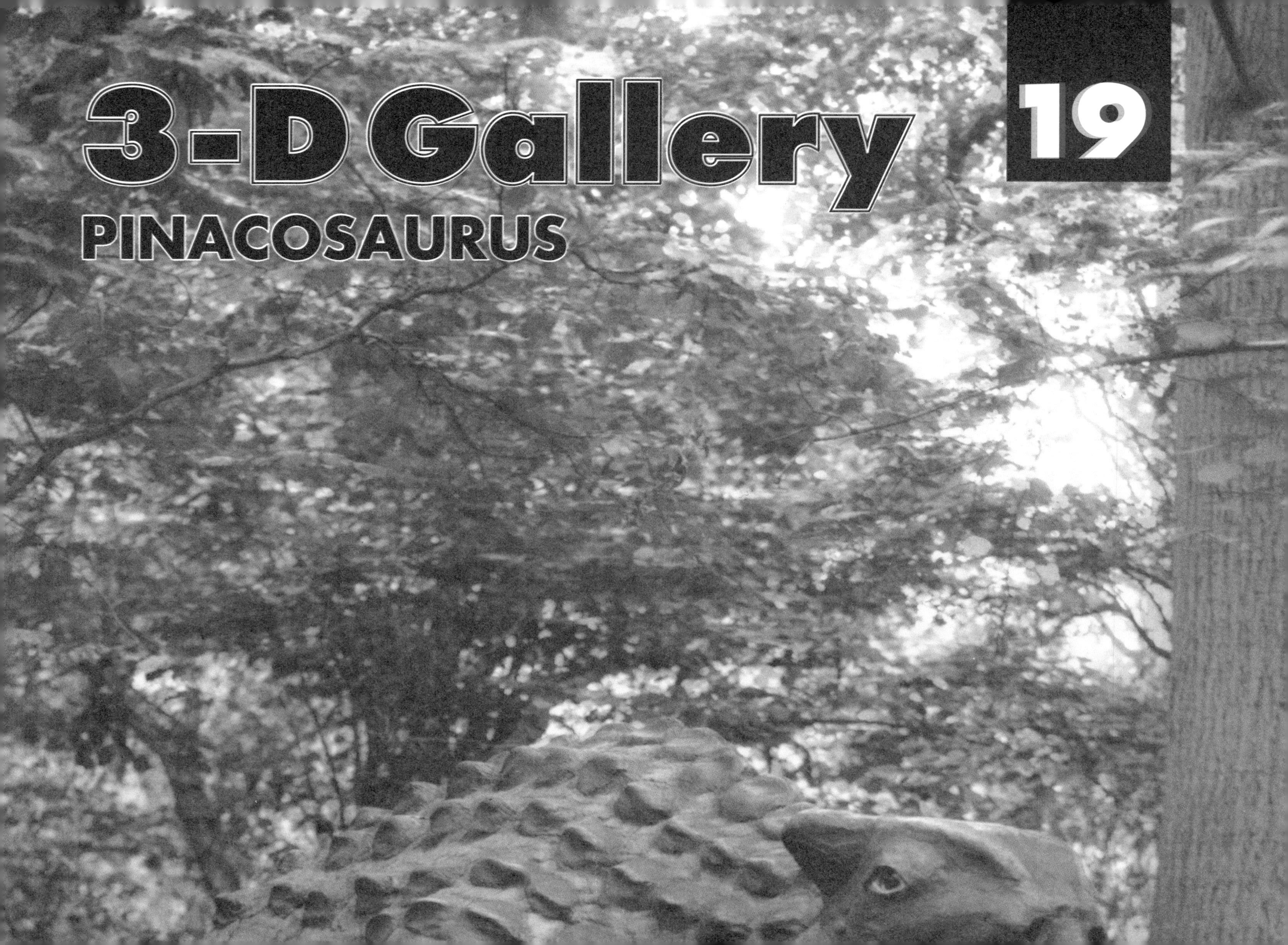

3-D Gallery

PINACOSAURUS

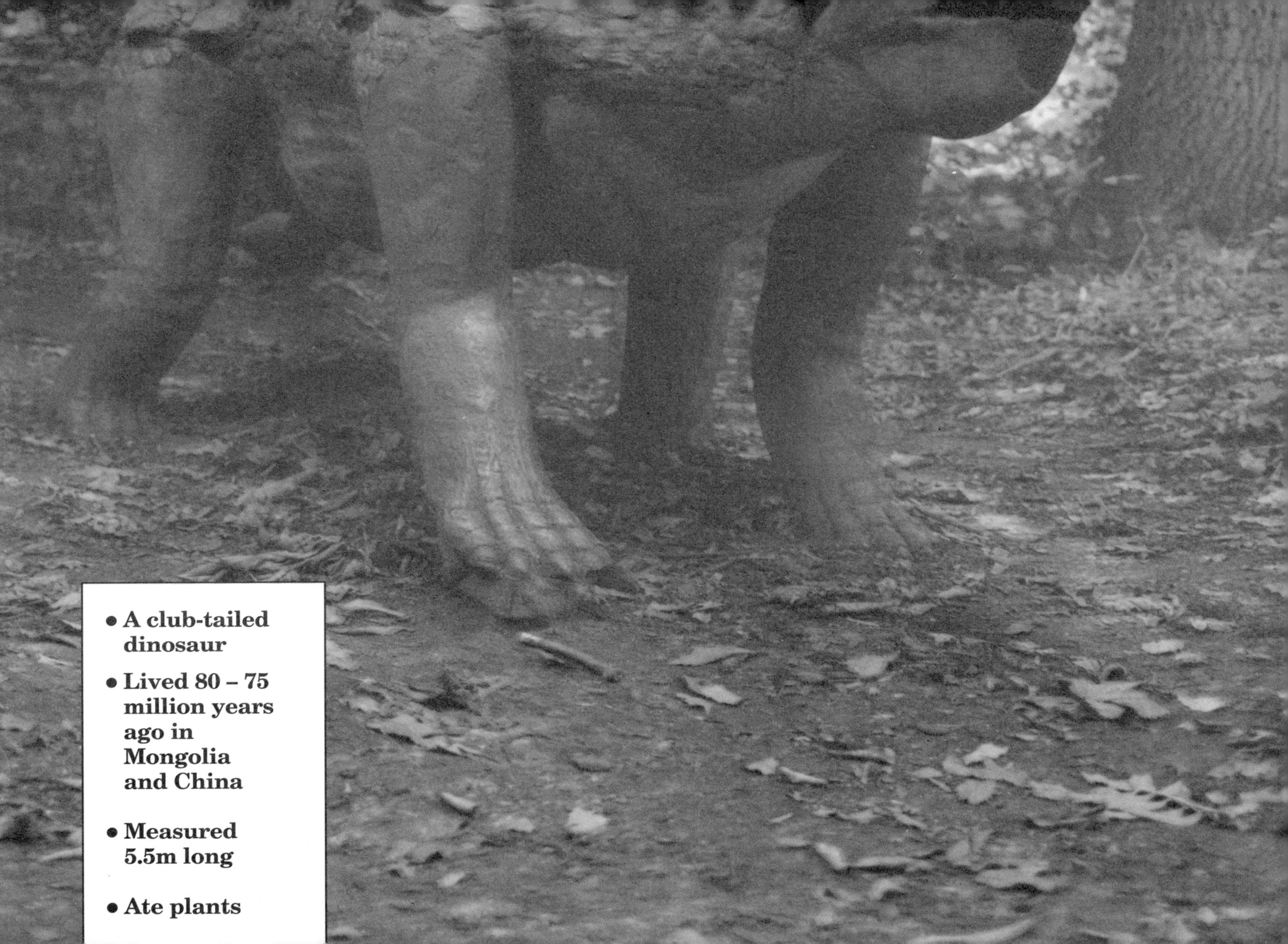

- A club-tailed dinosaur
- Lived 80 – 75 million years ago in Mongolia and China
- Measured 5.5m long
- Ate plants

Spikes

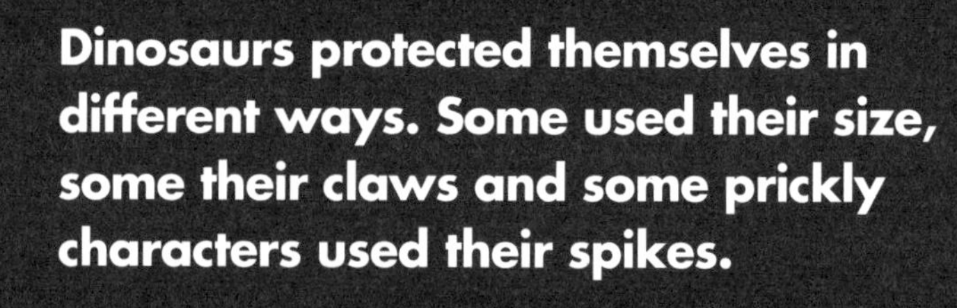

Dinosaurs protected themselves in different ways. Some used their size, some their claws and some prickly characters used their spikes.

Many of today's animals have evolved with horns and claws, but few have spikes. Animals such as hedgehogs and porcupines rely on their spikes for defence. But only a few modern reptiles have retained their spikes. The gecko, a type of lizard, for example, raises the spikes on its back to frighten off rivals. However, the gecko's moveable, fleshy spines are nothing like the solid, vicious ones that dinosaurs wore on their bodies and heads.

SPIKED COLLAR ***Styracosaurus***

Among the most impressive of dinosaurs with spikes was *Styracosaurus*. It was given its name, which means 'spiked lizard', because it had six long spikes that jutted out from its short, bony neck frill. It had many small spikes, too. The spikes protected *Styracosaurus* from predators – they made this dinosaur's neck difficult to bite. Some attackers were scared off at the sight of the spikes. Male *Styracosaurus* may have tried to attract a mate by raising their spikes in showy display.

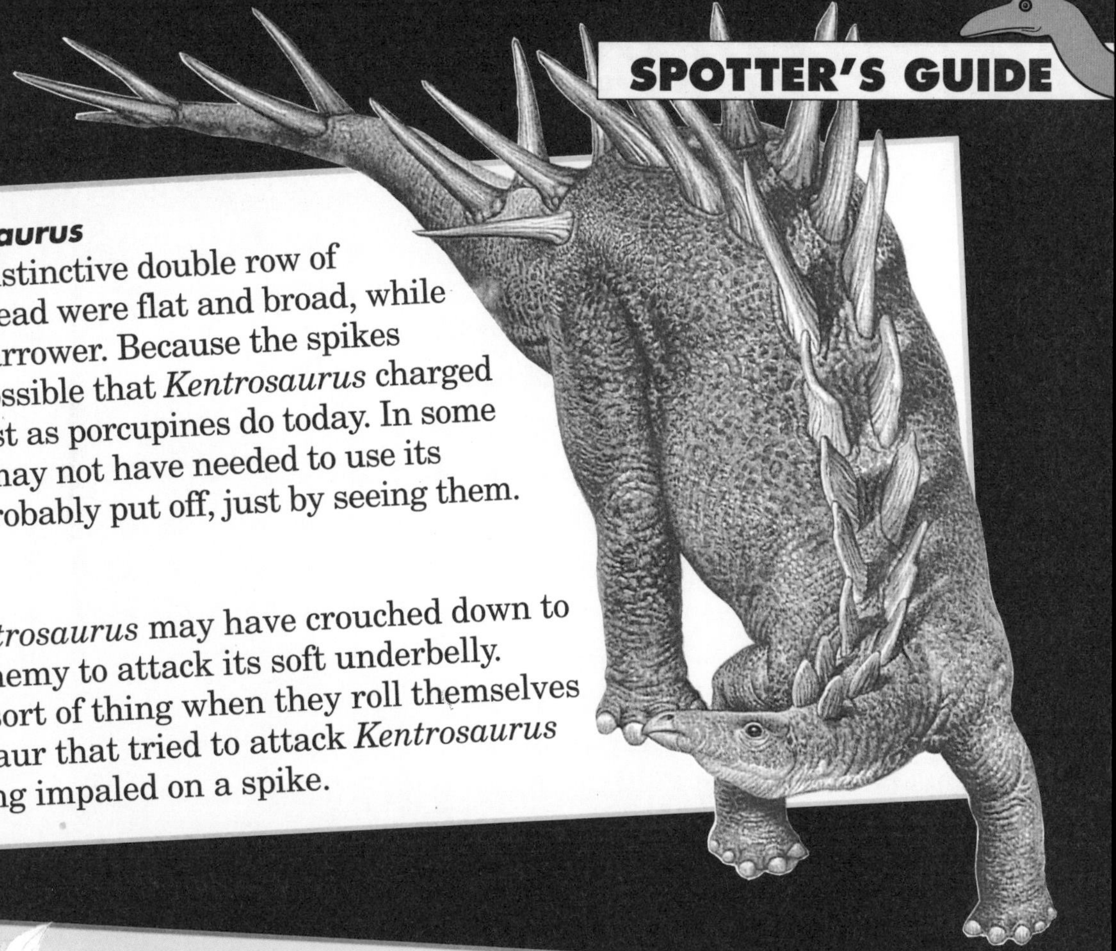

DOUBLE SPIKES ***Kentrosaurus***

Kentrosaurus had a very distinctive double row of spikes. The ones near its head were flat and broad, while the ones on its tail were narrower. Because the spikes pointed backwards, it is possible that *Kentrosaurus* charged backwards at its rivals, just as porcupines do today. In some situations, *Kentrosaurus* may not have needed to use its spikes – predators were probably put off, just by seeing them.

A BALL OF SPIKES

If it was threatened, *Kentrosaurus* may have crouched down to make it difficult for an enemy to attack its soft underbelly. Hedgehogs do the same sort of thing when they roll themselves up into a ball. Any dinosaur that tried to attack *Kentrosaurus* was in danger of becoming impaled on a spike.

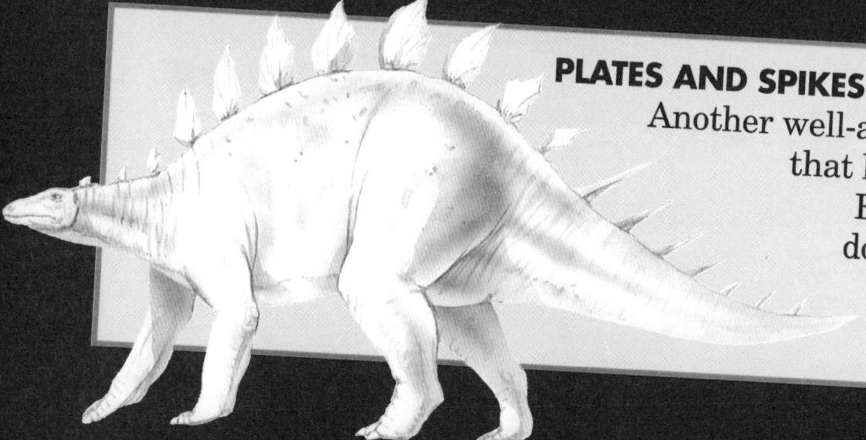

PLATES AND SPIKES ***Lexovisaurus***

Another well-armed dinosaur was *Lexovisaurus* that lived in England and northern France. It had rigid plates running down its back. They gave way to a row of sharp spikes when they reached the top of the tail.

A STING IN THE TAIL ***Stegosaurus***

Stegosaurus, a plant-eating plated dinosaur that lived about 150 million years ago, was the largest of the plated dinosaurs. The back of this curious looking creature was lined with one or perhaps two rows of huge plates. On the end of its tail, *Stegosaurus* had four sharp spikes. These spikes were broader at the base so that once they had entered the victim's flesh, they could easily be pulled out again. *Stegosaurus* was then ready to strike again with its lethal weapon.

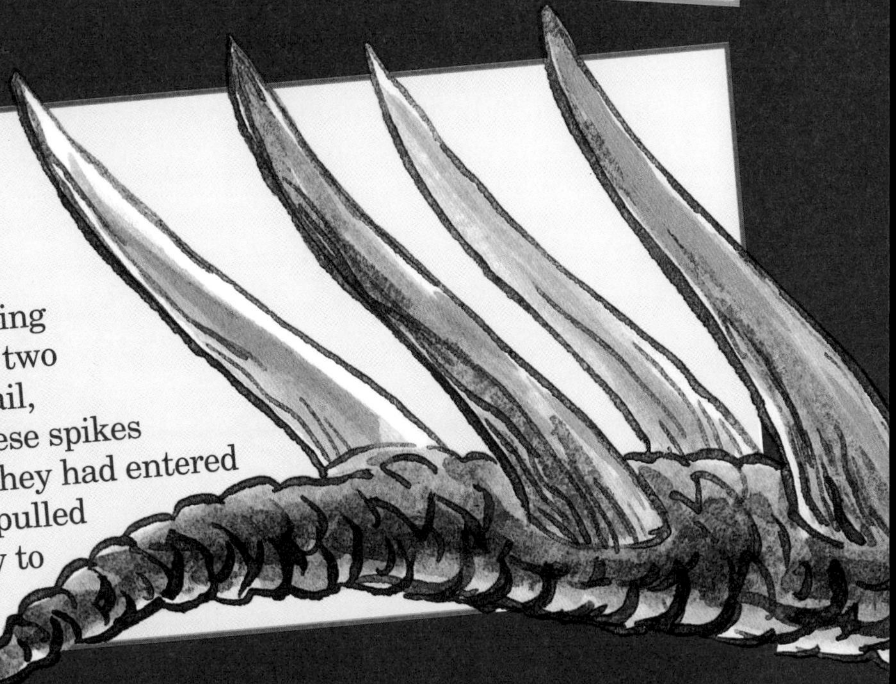

Take one dinosaur

No one has ever seen a dinosaur. When *Iguanodon* was first found, scientists had only a pile of bones to decide how it must have looked.

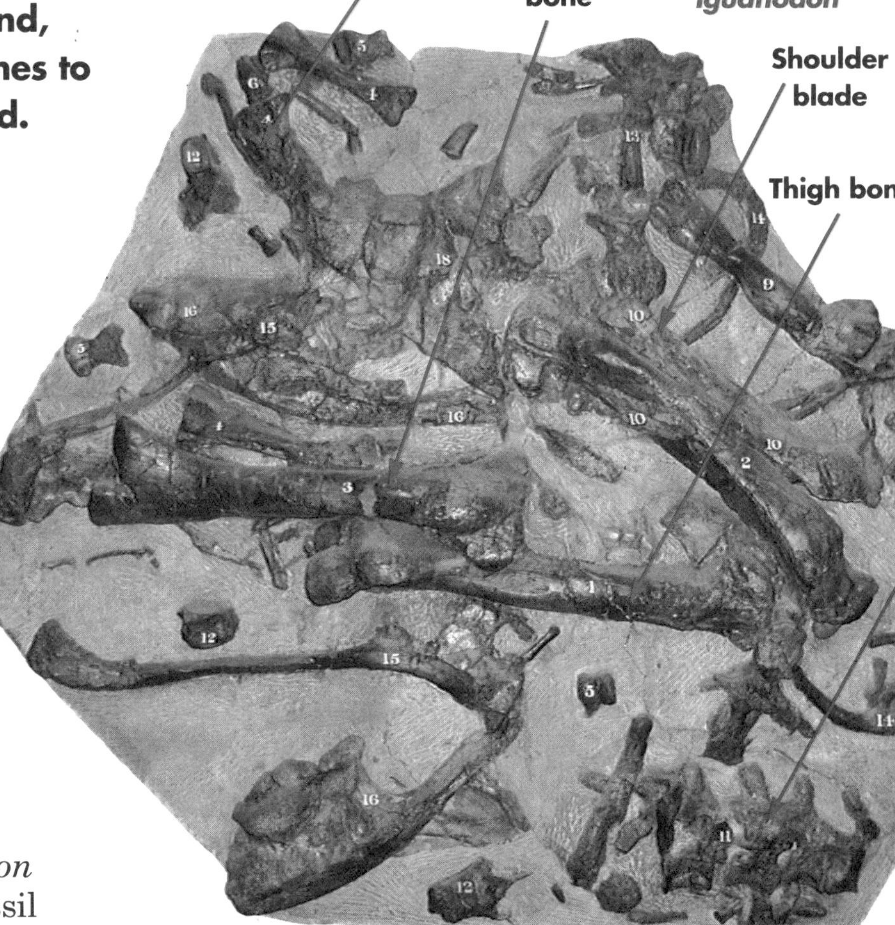

The first fossils of *Iguanodon* were discovered before anyone even knew that dinosaurs had existed. The scientists of the time had to decide what kind of animal it was and what it might have looked like, but they had a difficult task. There were no books about dinosaurs, and no pictures of them. These scientists were working in the dark. No wonder their ideas seem strange to us.

LIZARD-LIKE IGUANODON

To get some idea of how *Iguanodon* looked, scientists compared its fossil remains with living animals. Gideon Mantell, the doctor who discovered *Iguanodon*, thought it must have been like the modern lizard called an iguana, but a gigantic version of it.

THE IMPOSSIBLE TASK

In 1834, Mantell was given part of an *Iguanodon's* skeleton still in the rock. After studying the fossil (above), Mantell drew a picture of his idea of *Iguanodon*. As you can see (left), the task of creating an accurate drawing from a pile of bones was almost impossible and Mantell made many mistakes.

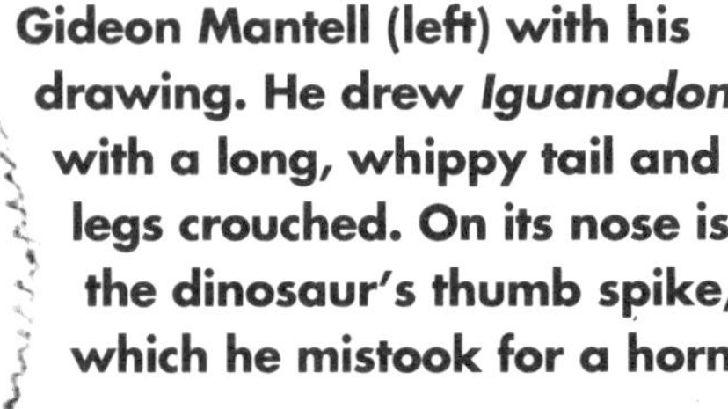

Gideon Mantell (left) with his drawing. He drew *Iguanodon* with a long, whippy tail and legs crouched. On its nose is the dinosaur's thumb spike, which he mistook for a horn.

One of the Crystal Palace *Iguanodon* peers through the undergrowth in the park. You can still see the thumb spike, which both Mantell and Owen mistook for a horn, on the end of its nose.

ANIMALS IN THE ZOO

Richard Owen, the man who gave dinosaurs their name, knew a lot about animals. His job at the Royal College of Surgeons was to dissect (cut up) and describe animals from London Zoo that died. Owen used this knowledge to help him work out what dinosaurs looked like when they were alive.

ack bones

ANIMAL MIXTURE

In 1841, Owen gave his famous lecture in which he described dinosaurs as a type of animal previously unknown. In it he described *Iguanodon* and some other dinosaurs. His ideas were different from Mantell's. Owen's *Iguanodon* had some parts taken from a crocodile, and some rather like an elephant or a hippopotamus. But the thumb spike was still firmly on the end of its nose.

CRYSTAL PALACE

Owen eventually got a chance to see his ideas made into life-size models. In 1854, the sculptor Benjamin Waterhouse Hawkins began to create dinosaur models for Crystal Palace Park in south London and Owen directed the work. They can still be seen today, but *Iguanodon* looks more like a scaly rhinoceros than a dinosaur.

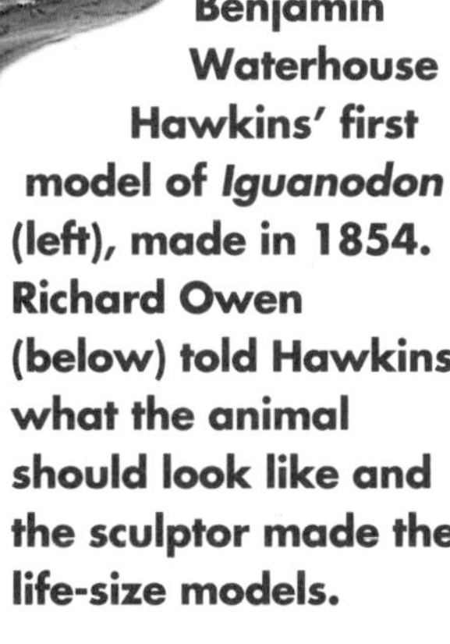

Benjamin Waterhouse Hawkins' first model of *Iguanodon* (left), made in 1854. Richard Owen (below) told Hawkins what the animal should look like and the sculptor made the life-size models.

DOWN THE MINE

Deep underground in a coal mine in Belgium, in 1878, a group of miners were digging. But coal was not the treasure they found. They dug out something far more exciting: a fossil of *Iguanodon*. In fact, it was the first of many skeletons.

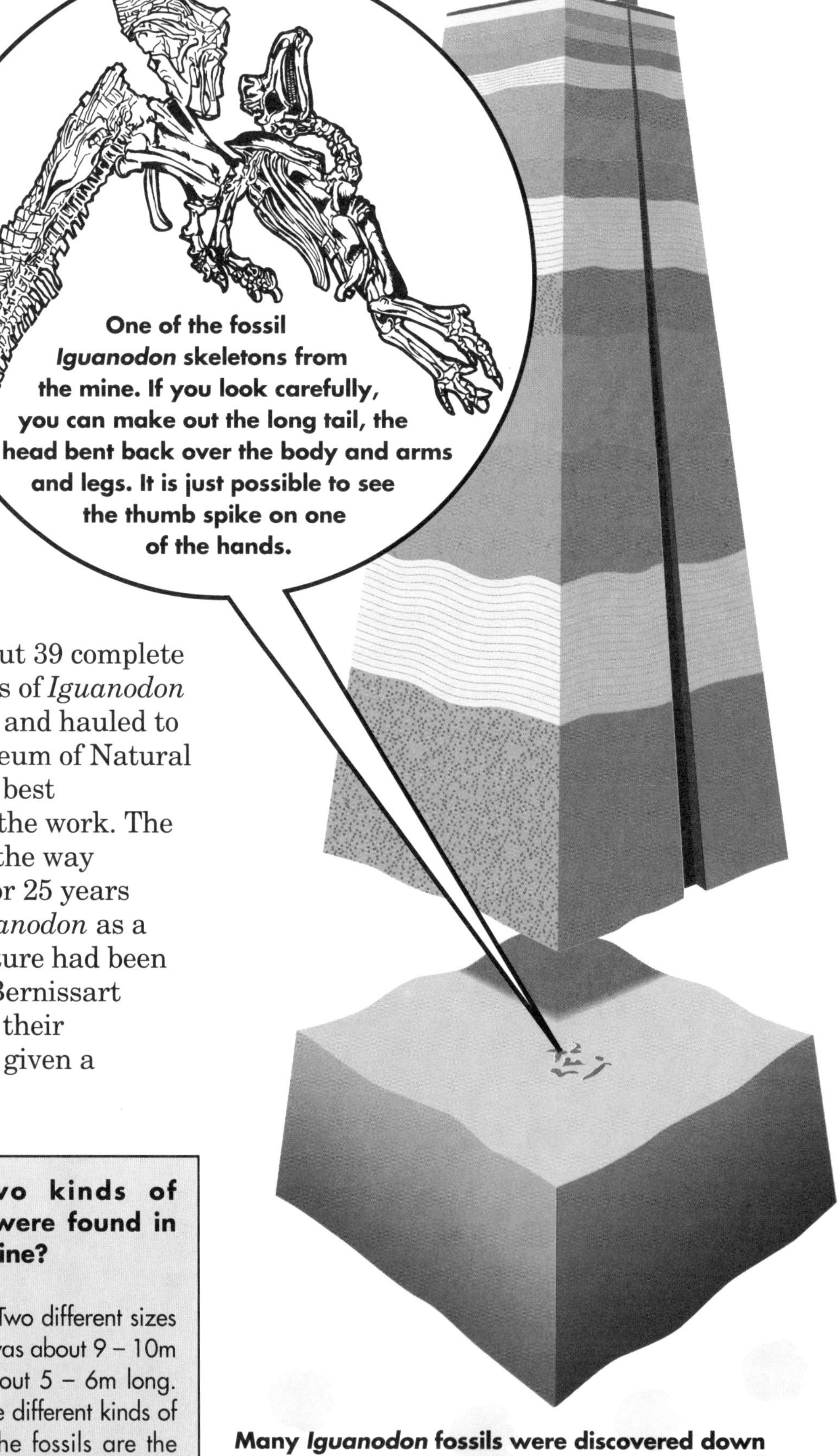

One of the fossil *Iguanodon* skeletons from the mine. If you look carefully, you can make out the long tail, the head bent back over the body and arms and legs. It is just possible to see the thumb spike on one of the hands.

FOSSIL REVOLUTION

The find at Bernissart was remarkable. Altogether about 39 complete or nearly complete skeletons of *Iguanodon* were painstakingly dug out and hauled to the surface. The Royal Museum of Natural History in Brussels sent its best palaeontologist to organise the work. The find caused a revolution in the way *Iguanodon* was pictured. For 25 years Richard Owen's view of *Iguanodon* as a stocky, rhinoceros-like creature had been popular, but the miners of Bernissart changed all that. Following their discoveries, *Iguanodon* was given a completely new look.

Is it true that two kinds of *Iguanodon* were found in the Bernissart mine?

Scientists are not certain. Two different sizes of *Iguanodon* were found. One was about 9 – 10m long. The other was smaller, about 5 – 6m long. Some scientists think that they are different kinds of *Iguanodon*. Others think that the fossils are the same kind of *Iguanodon*, but the larger dinosaurs were male and the smaller ones were female. Scientists are still debating the problem.

Many *Iguanodon* fossils were discovered down the coal mine at Bernissart, Belgium, in April 1878. They were in a deep pit of clay that ran through the coal seams 322m down. The dinosaurs had not all died at the same time.

DANGEROUS WORK

It took three years to dig all the skeletons out of the ground. The team had to work in extremely difficult conditions – it was cramped, dark and dangerous work. When all the remains were safely back in Brussels, the mammoth task of preserving and mounting the fossils began.

SOLVING THE PUZZLES

Never had so many skeletons of one kind of dinosaur been found together. It gave the museum in Brussels a unique chance study and reconstruct *Iguanodon.* Louis Dollo was the palaeontologist in charge. As he studied the fossils, Dollo was able to clear up many of the mysteries about *Iguanodon,* including where the 'nose horn' really belonged.

Strung from the ceiling of a Brussels chapel is the first *Iguanodon* reconstruction, in about 1882. The team that reassembled the fossil stands by.

NEW-LOOK IGUANODON

The work was slow and painstaking. It took place in an ancient chapel that was used as the museum's laboratory. Eventually, the new-look *Iguanodon* emerged. It was totally different from all the former ideas. It did not look like a lizard or a rhinoceros. Dollo's dinosaur was a huge, upright animal that walked on two legs. And its 'nose horn' turned out to be a large thumb spike.

A model based on the Bernissart skeletons looks like a real animal. But studies of the dinosaur continue and ideas of how it looked are still changing.

3-D Gallery 39

ALLOSAURUS AND APATOSAURUS

- A carnosaur sinks its teeth into a sauropod
- Both *Apatosaurus* and *Allosaurus* roamed North America in the Late Jurassic
- *Allosaurus* measured 39ft (12m) long, *Apatosaurus* measured 69ft (21m) long
- *Apatosaurus* ate plants, *Allosaurus* ate other dinosaurs

Dr. David Norman of Cambridge University answers your dinosaur questions
ASK THE EXPERT

Why have so many dinosaur fossils been found in Alberta in Canada?

Hundreds of millions of years ago, the part of the world now called the Alberta Badlands was like a busy crossroads for dinosaurs. This area of Canada lay on the route the dinosaurs took as they moved north towards what is now the Arctic, or south to cross the land that once joined Asia to America. Fossils of hundreds of dinosaurs have been dug up in Alberta's National Dinosaur Park. In one huge dinosaur grave, the bones of more than 50 dinosaurs have been found.

Did dinosaurs sleep?

Yes! All animals, including humans, need to rest and sleep. Today's reptiles, in particular, spend a great deal of their time dozing. There is no reason to believe that dinosaurs behaved any differently.

Were all dinosaurs ferocious?

No, many dinosaurs, such as *Diplodocus*, were gentle plant-eaters that spent most of their time munching plants. They depended on their huge size to put off attackers. Some of the smaller meat-eaters like *Compsognathus* killed small reptiles and tiny mammals, but they were not in the same league as the real killers of the prehistoric world – the carnosaurs, such as *Tyrannosaurus rex*.

Did dinosaurs pair for life?

Experts don't think dinosaurs mated for life. There are few animals that stay with the same mate for most of their adult lives. Although some dinosaurs nested in groups and may have cared for their young, it is unlikely in the world in which they lived that a male and a female dinosaur would stay together for long after they had mated.

DINOSAURS!
DISCOVER THE GIANTS OF THE PREHISTORIC WORLD

CARNOTAURUS

This large predatory (hunting) dinosaur had a thick, powerful neck, a bull-shaped head and very short forearms for its size.

C*arnotaurus* is a member of the group of dinosaurs known as carnosaurs. This group includes some of the most fearsome and well-known of all dinosaurs such as mighty *Tyrannosaurus rex* and *Allosaurus*. These dinosaurs look alike in many ways with their huge, powerful heads and teeth as sharp as steak knives. But *Carnotaurus,* a relatively new discovery, had a shorter and deeper skull than *T rex* and hornlets over its eyes.

TINY ARMS

Compared to its body, which was as long as three small cars, *Carnotaurus'* forearms were tiny. Its long, muscular hind legs may have made *Carnotaurus* much more agile than some other carnosaurs. It would have been able to rush up on its prey and take it by surprise. It probably used its sharp claws to slash and grip, while its powerful jaws took out chunks of flesh.

LIGHT HEADED

Although *Carnotaurus* had a very strong skull, it also needed to be light enough to move easily. There were spaces in the sides of the skull to help make it lighter. By jerking its head back, *Carnotaurus* could tear its prey apart. The teeth in the upper jaw could slice through the flesh, which was held by the lower jaw. *Carnotaurus* had teeth about 4cm long which curved backwards to help it keep hold of its victim.

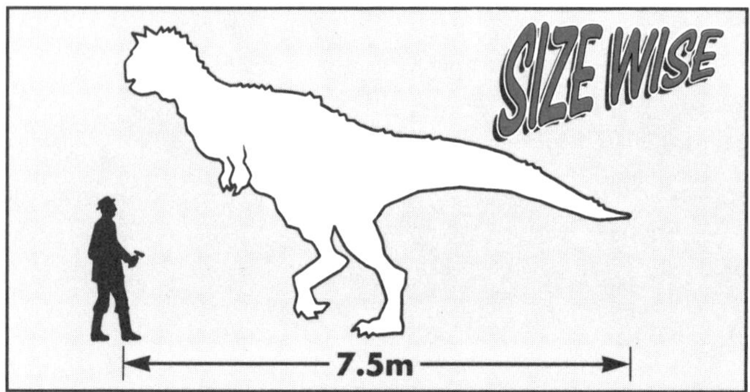

MONSTER FACTS

- **NAME:** *Carnotaurus* (carn-oh-taw-rus) means 'meat-eating bull'
- **SIZE:** 7.5m long and 3.5m high
- **FOOD:** meat – mainly other dinosaurs
- **LIVED:** 100 – 90 million years ago in the Middle to Late Cretaceous in South America

BUMPY SKIN

Carnotaurus was found in a vast area of grassland and semi-desert called Patagonia in Argentina in 1985. It was an exciting find because the remains gave scientists a very good idea of what this dinosaur's skin looked like. Along the surface of its body, from head to tail, there were rows of cone-shaped bumps. Rows of big, raised scales stood out from the smaller bumps on *Carnotaurus'* head, making a pattern around the eyes and on the upper part of its snout.

WELL BALANCED

Carnotaurus was as heavy as a car, almost as tall as an elephant and ran on two legs. Its long backbone was like a big girder supporting the weight beneath. Long rib bones from shoulder to hip gave *Carnotaurus* extra protection and support.

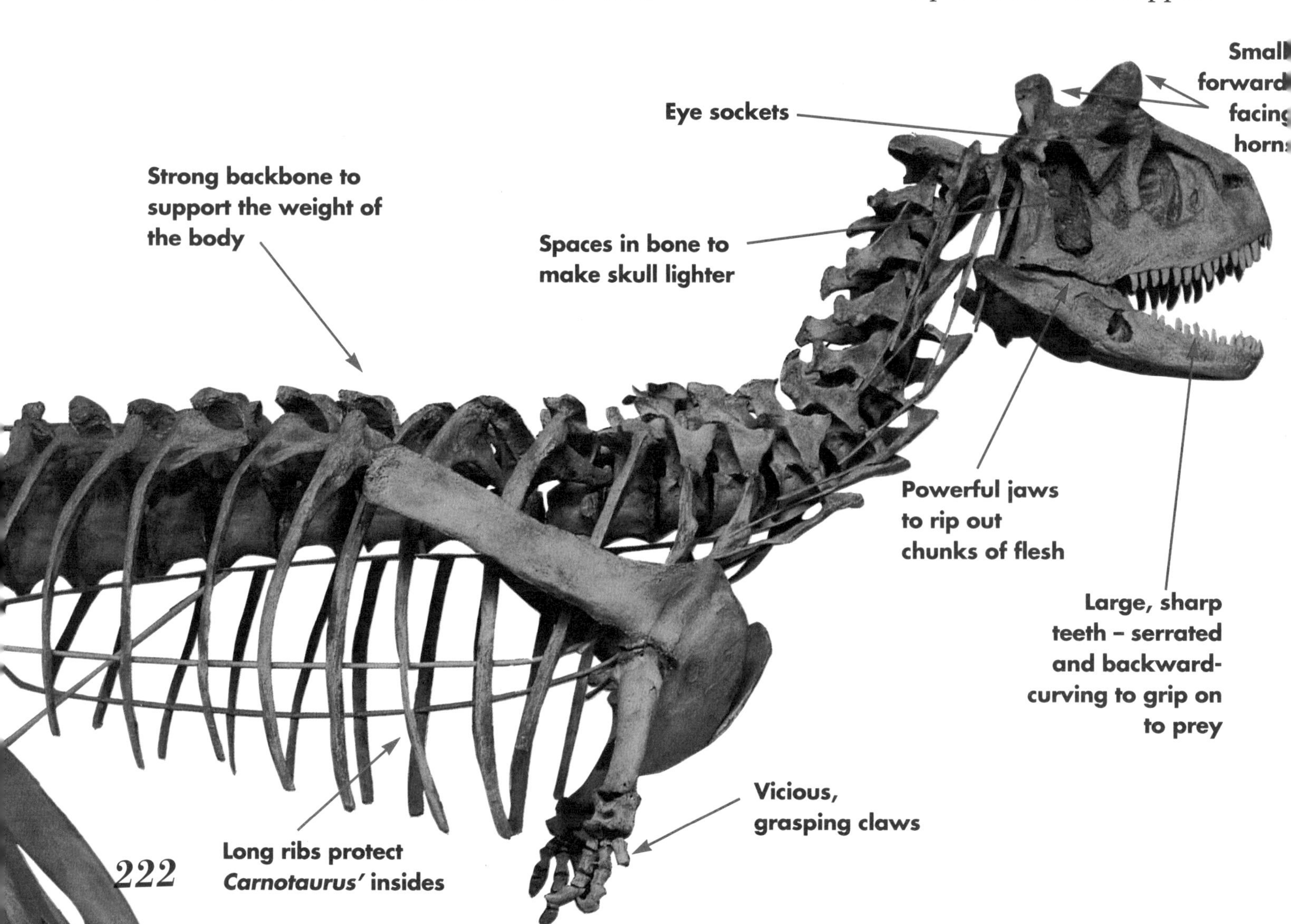

Smal forward facin horn

Eye sockets

Strong backbone to support the weight of the body

Spaces in bone to make skull lighter

Powerful jaws to rip out chunks of flesh

Large, sharp teeth – serrated and backward-curving to grip on to prey

Vicious, grasping claws

Long ribs protect *Carnotaurus'* insides

TAIL END

When *Carnotaurus* was moving at top speed it would have been unstable without its tail. *Carnotaurus* used its long, muscular tail to help to keep its balance. This enabled it to push its head forward to seize hold of its struggling prey.

What is? A CARNOSAUR

A carnosaur is the name given to several groups of meat-eating dinosaurs. This includes the large theropods which walked on two legs and had sharply clawed toes. They usually had large bodies with powerful heads and necks. Their hind legs were strong and stout, although their forelimbs were much shorter. Carnosaurs had strong jaws with sharp, dagger-like teeth which enabled them to feed on large herbivores. Dinosaurs such as *Tyrannosaurus rex, Albertosaurus, Megalosaurus and Allosaurus* can all be described as carnosaurs.

***Carnotaurus* thrusts his head forward and opens his lethal jaws to snap up a passing pterosaur. *Carnotaurus'* strength and speed made it a threat to smaller, or plant-eating, dinosaurs as well.**

LITTLE HORNS

At the top of its short, deep head *Carnotaurus* had a pair of small, flat horns. These jutted forward over its eyes rather like little wings.

Unlike the horned dinosaurs, such as *Triceratops*, *Carnotaurus'* horns were too small to have been used for defence. Experts think that they may have been coated in extra layers of horn, which would have made them longer. Like stag deer, it is also possible that the male *Carnotaurus* had larger horns than the females.

MASSOSPONDYLUS

Standing on its back legs, an adult *Massospondylus* could reach about as high as the top of a double-decker bus.

Massospondylus was one of the first plant-eating dinosaurs to appear on land. It had a small head and a long neck and tail. By tilting back on its hind legs it could reach shoots and leaves at the top of tall trees.

STOMACH STONES

Massospondylus had small teeth which could shred leaves, but they were not so good for chewing. When this dinosaur was discovered, small pebbles were found by its rib cage. Experts think *Massospondylus* may have swallowed these stones to help it digest its food. When food was swallowed, it was ground down by the stones. They worked like the blades of a food mixer to mash the leaves into a thick, mushy soup so that the dinosaur was able to absorb all the good things its large body needed.

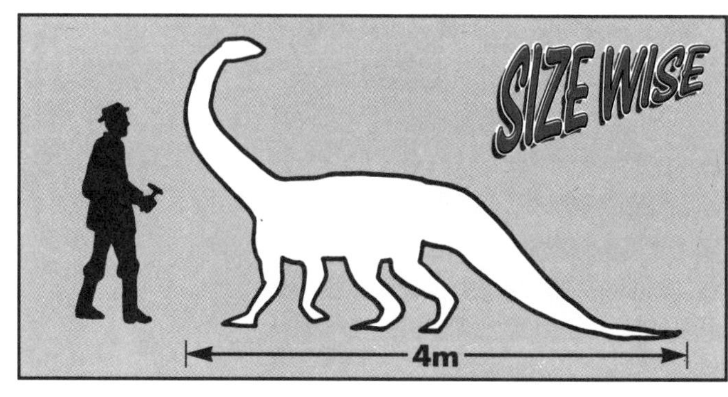

MONSTER FACTS

- **NAME:** *Massospondylus* (mass-oh-spond-ih-lus) means 'massive vertebrae' (backbone)
- **SIZE:** 4m long
- **FOOD:** plants and leaves from trees
- **LIVED:** about 200 – 180 million years ago in the Early Jurassic Period in southern Africa and North America

BIG THUMB

To defend itself, *Massospondylus* had a huge thumb with a long, curved claw. Together with the second and third fingers, the thumb may also have been used for grasping things. The other two fingers were small and weak.

LAMBEOSAURUS

***Lambeosaurus* had a toothless beak and a strange-looking crest on its head.**

This plant-eating dinosaur had pebbly skin with scales that fitted together like a mosaic. *Lambeosaurus* usually walked on four feet, but when scared it ran off on its powerful hind legs. It relied on its sharp eyes and good hearing to sense danger.

MYSTERY CREST

Lambeosaurus had a crest shaped like a mitten with a bony spike as the thumb. As males had larger crests, it may have been a way to tell them apart from females. Some experts think the crest was used as a 'snorkel' if *Lambeosaurus* went under water. It is more likely that it was used to make sounds. One scientist discovered that, as air moved through the crest of a similar dinosaur, it sounded like a medieval horn. So, *Lambeosaurus* could have had its own distinctive call.

WALL OF TEETH

Inside its huge 2m-long skull, *Lambeosaurus* had hundreds of small, sharp teeth for crunching pine needles, woody twigs or seeds. When the teeth wore down, new ones grew to replace them.

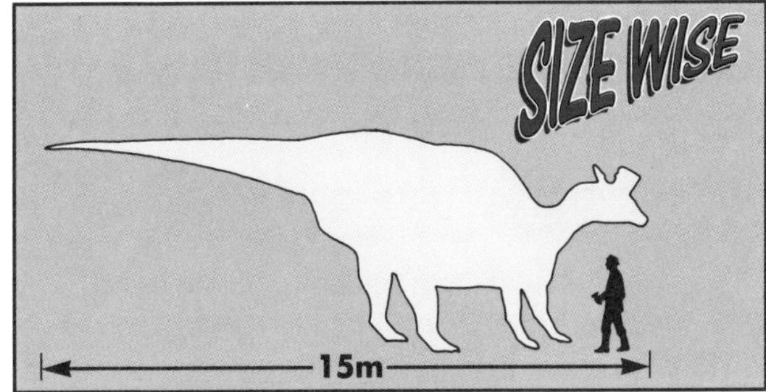

MONSTER FACTS

- **NAME:** *Lambeosaurus* (lam-bee-oh-saw-rus) means 'Lambe's dinosaur' after the Canadian palaeontologist, Lawrence Lambe
- **SIZE:** 15m long
- **FOOD:** leaves and other parts of plants
- **LIVED:** 70 – 66 million years ago in the Late Cretaceous Period in Alberta, Canada. Also in the USA and Mexico

Reptiles of the sea

Ichthyosaurs were superbly designed for a life at sea. These dolphin look-alikes cruised through the water, making the land-bound dinosaurs look quite clumsy.

The first ichthyosaurs appeared in the Late Triassic. For the next 150 million years they dominated the seas, while the dinosaurs ruled the land. They mysteriously died out at the same time as the dinosaurs.

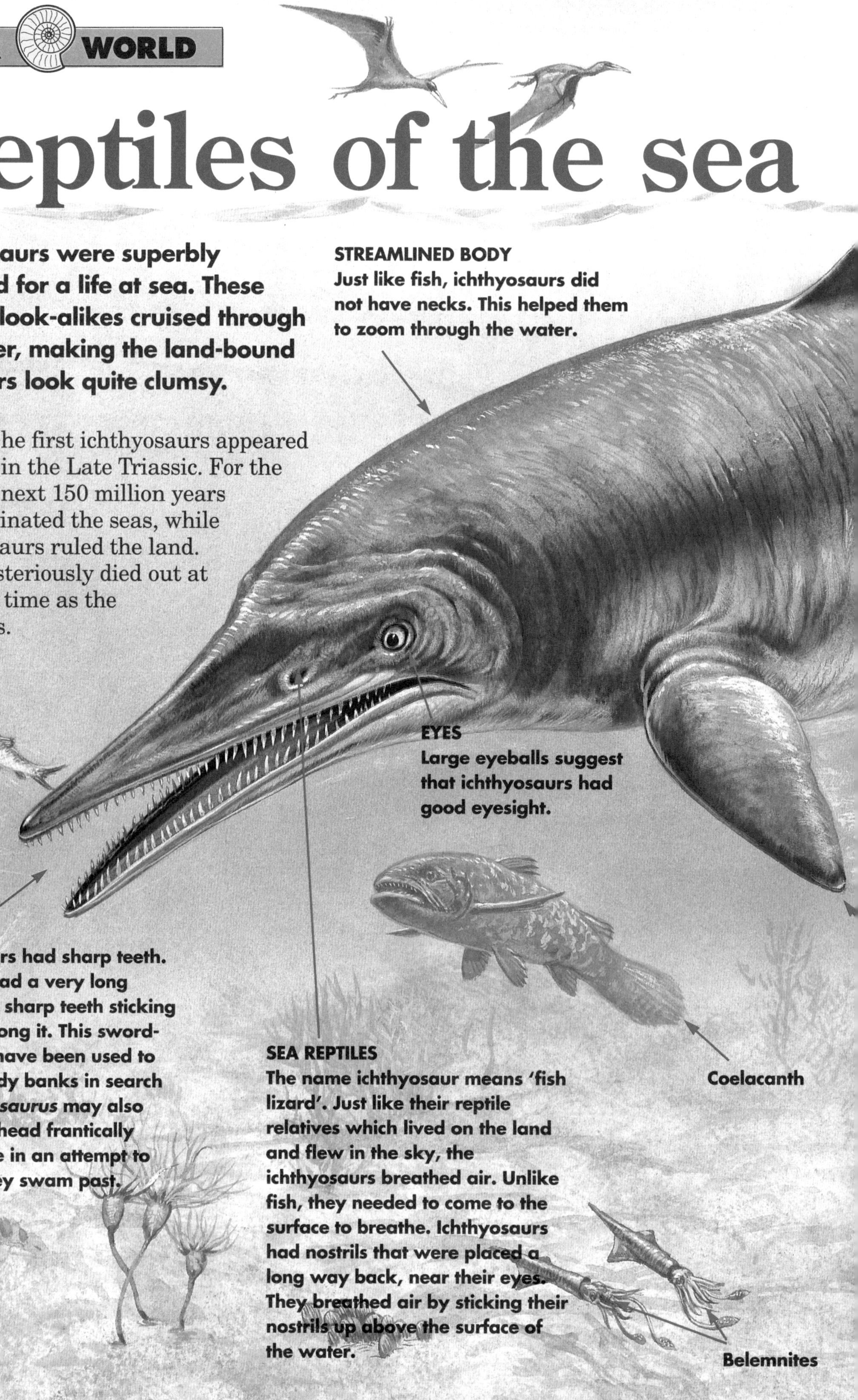

STREAMLINED BODY
Just like fish, ichthyosaurs did not have necks. This helped them to zoom through the water.

EYES
Large eyeballs suggest that ichthyosaurs had good eyesight.

SHARP TEETH
Most ichthyosaurs had sharp teeth. *Eurhinosaurus* had a very long upper jaw, with sharp teeth sticking out sideways along it. This sword-like snout may have been used to tunnel into muddy banks in search of food. *Eurhinosaurus* may also have swung its head frantically from side to side in an attempt to spear fish as they swam past.

SEA REPTILES
The name ichthyosaur means 'fish lizard'. Just like their reptile relatives which lived on the land and flew in the sky, the ichthyosaurs breathed air. Unlike fish, they needed to come to the surface to breathe. Ichthyosaurs had nostrils that were placed a long way back, near their eyes. They breathed air by sticking their nostrils up above the surface of the water.

Coelacanth

Belemnites

FINS
The dorsal fin was used to stop the ichthyosaur's body rocking from side to side.

Ichthyosaurus

SMOOTH SKIN
One fossil of an ichthyosaur from Germany clearly shows the outline of the body. The fossil shows that its skin was fleshy, plump and smooth. The smoothness of its skin was important for streamlining.

THE LAST SUPPER
Scientists can tell what sort of food ichthyosaurs enjoyed by studying fossils. They look at the fossil remains in the stomachs of these creatures. The best fossils show that ichthyosaurs had a diet of fish, shrimps, shellfish, relatives of today's squids and cuttlefish and occasionally a pterosaur.

TAIL
Broad tail moved from side to side, rather like a shark's tail.

Archelon

PADDLES
An ichthyosaur steered through the water using its paddles, rather as a turtle does today.

SUPER ICHTHYOSAUR
This *Ichthyosaurus* was about 2m long, but some ichthyosaurs were much bigger. *Shonisaurus* was a huge beast, found in Nevada, USA. At about 15m long, this was the longest known ichthyosaur. Its vast body was the same size as today's humpback whale.

Ammonite

EARLY SWIMMING

The only clue we have to early ichthyosaurs is a skull of an animal called *Grippia*. Just five million years after *Grippia*, an animal called *Mixosaurus* evolved. This early ichthyosaur had a slender body, small paddles and a narrow tail.

GETTING ABOUT

Ichthyosaurs swam by moving their tails from side to side, like sharks or tuna fish. They used their paddles to steer through the water. These sea reptiles may have reached speeds of 40 km/h or more.

Ichthyosaurs used the fin on their backs (dorsal fin) to keep their bodies straight. Without this fin, they would have been unstable in the water. Surfboards and sailing boats have similar fins underneath them to stop them rocking from side to side.

What is? STREAMLINING

Boats are a sleek and pointed shape to help them cut through the water. This is called streamlining. Boat designers make sure that the part of the boat in the water is smooth. This lets the boat move as fast as possible. In the same way, the water flows easily around the streamlined shape of these bottlenose dolphins (below) as they speed through the water.

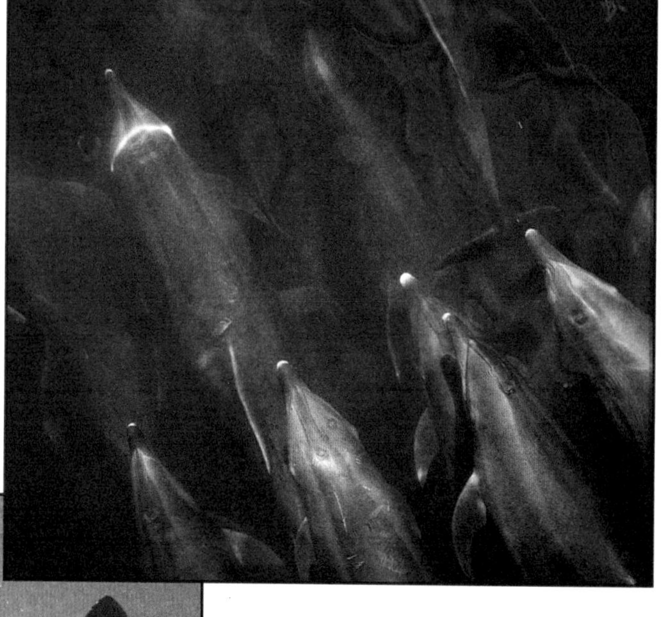

Modern dolphins (above) and porpoises speed through the water in groups.

***Mixosaurus* (bottom) had a slender tail. Later ichthyosaurs had broader tails, rather like those of today's sharks (below).**

***Ophthalmosaurus* ('eye reptile') also swam around in groups (right). It measured 3.5m long, which was larger than other Triassic ichthyosaurs, such as *Mixosaurus* or *Grippia*. *Ophthalmosaurus* had unusually large eyes.**

Mixosaurus

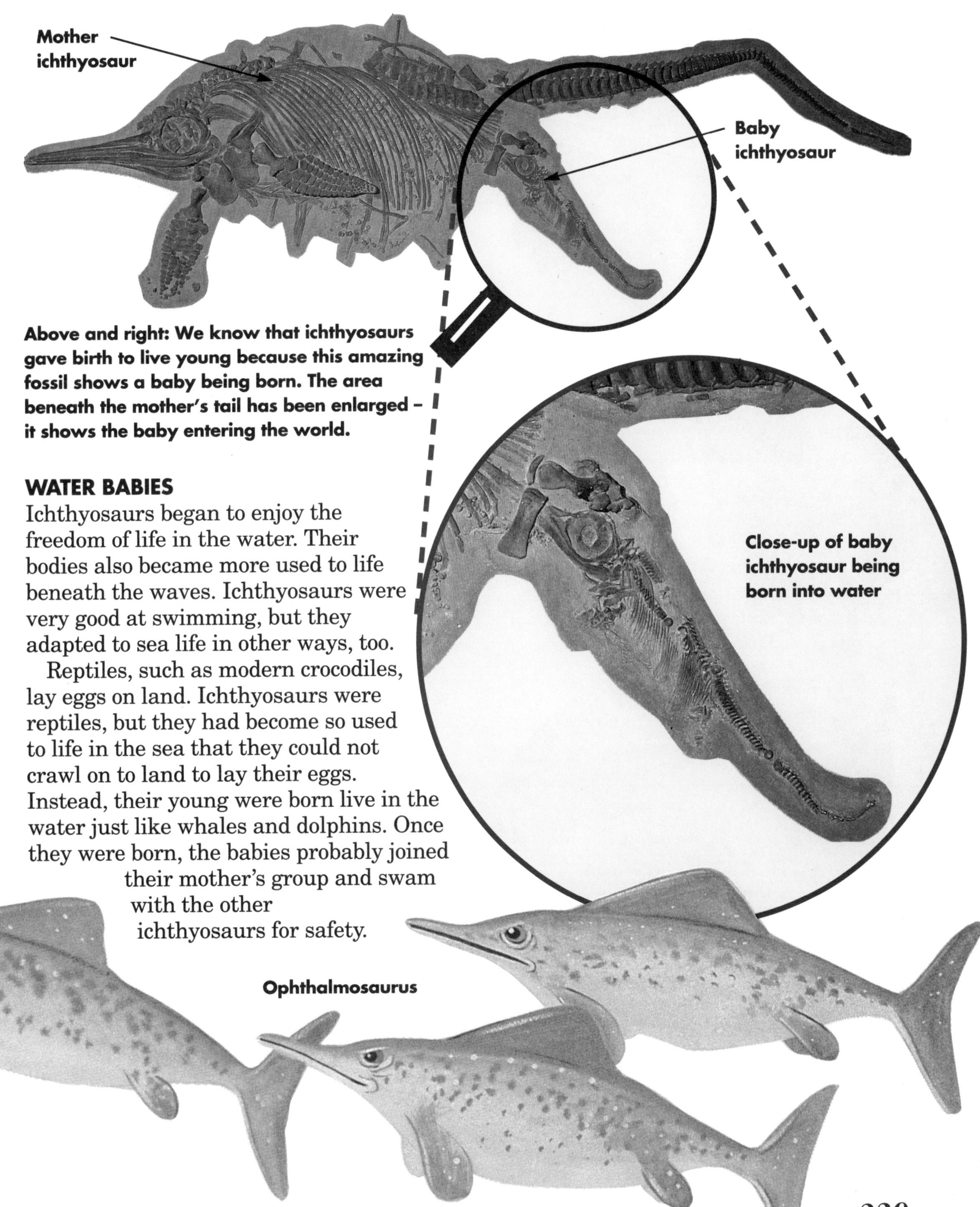

Above and right: We know that ichthyosaurs gave birth to live young because this amazing fossil shows a baby being born. The area beneath the mother's tail has been enlarged – it shows the baby entering the world.

WATER BABIES

Ichthyosaurs began to enjoy the freedom of life in the water. Their bodies also became more used to life beneath the waves. Ichthyosaurs were very good at swimming, but they adapted to sea life in other ways, too.

Reptiles, such as modern crocodiles, lay eggs on land. Ichthyosaurs were reptiles, but they had become so used to life in the sea that they could not crawl on to land to lay their eggs. Instead, their young were born live in the water just like whales and dolphins. Once they were born, the babies probably joined their mother's group and swam with the other ichthyosaurs for safety.

GIANTS OF THE PAST

CARNOTAURUS

Carnotaurus kicks up a cloud of dust as it launches a surprise attack on a harmless sauropod. The long-necked plant-eater looks round in surprise, but it will be very lucky to escape from this ferocious carnosaur. *Carnotaurus* already has his jaws open, ready to sink its knife-like teeth into the gentle giant's flesh.

3-D Gallery

KRITOSAURUS

20

- Duckbilled herbivore
- Lived 78 – 68 million years ago in North and South America
- Measured 9m long
- Ate plants

Legs

Dinosaur legs had to support some of the largest animals that ever walked the Earth. Some legs were as thick as tree trunks, while others were long, shapely and muscular.

Dinosaurs were different from any other prehistoric animal. They were the first animals to move about with their legs held straight beneath their bodies. Despite this link between all dinosaurs, their legs came in many different shapes and sizes, to suit their different ways of life.

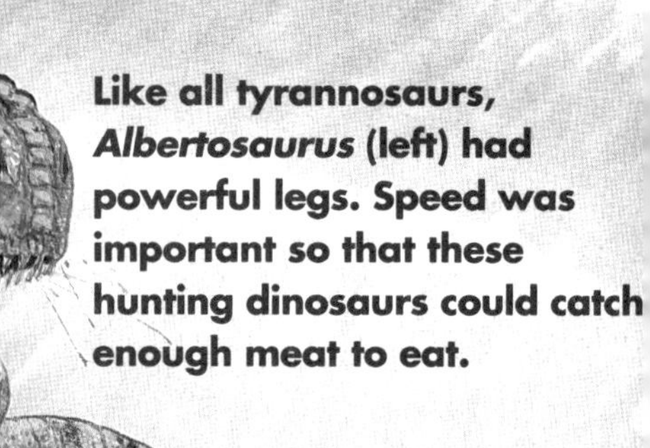

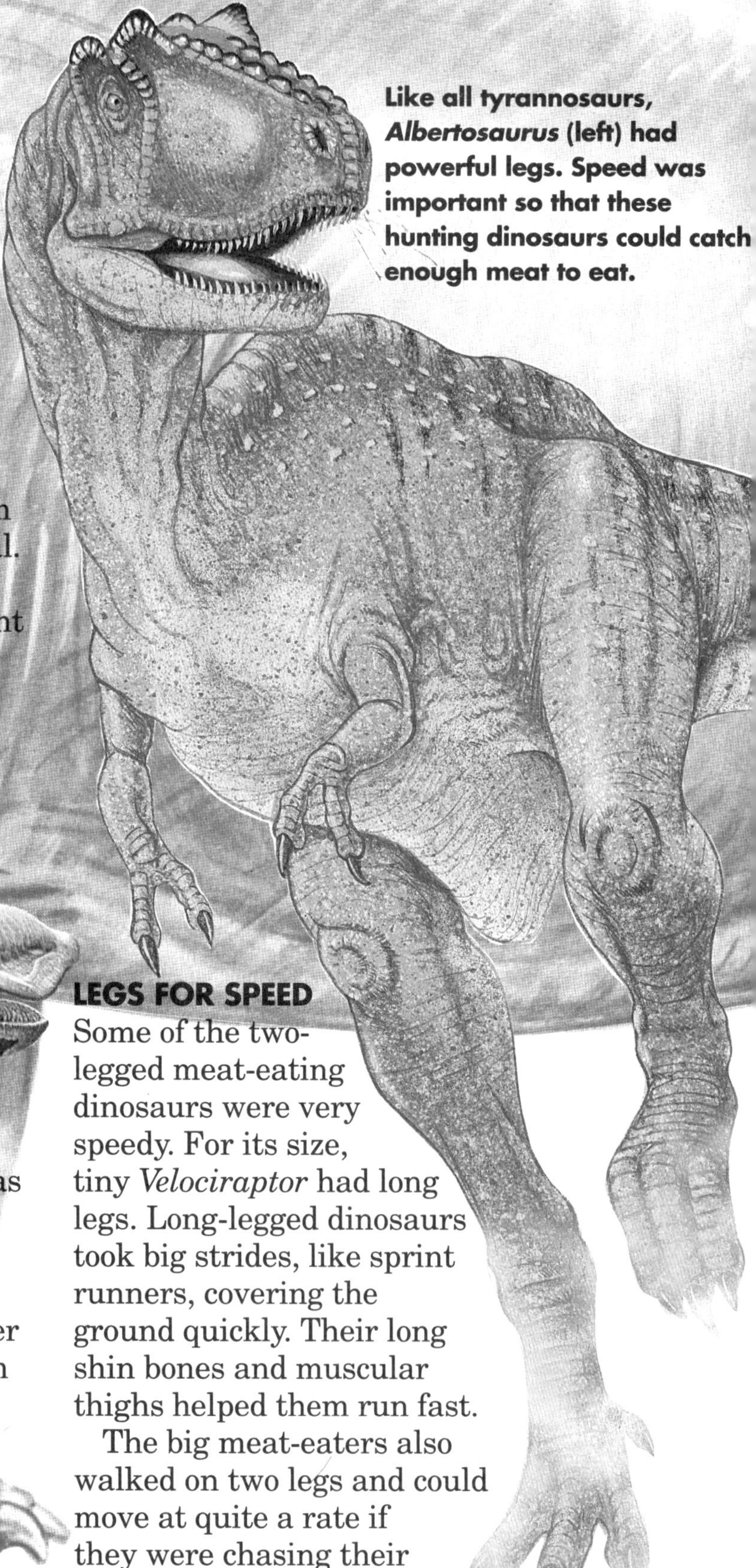

Like all tyrannosaurs, *Albertosaurus* (left) had powerful legs. Speed was important so that these hunting dinosaurs could catch enough meat to eat.

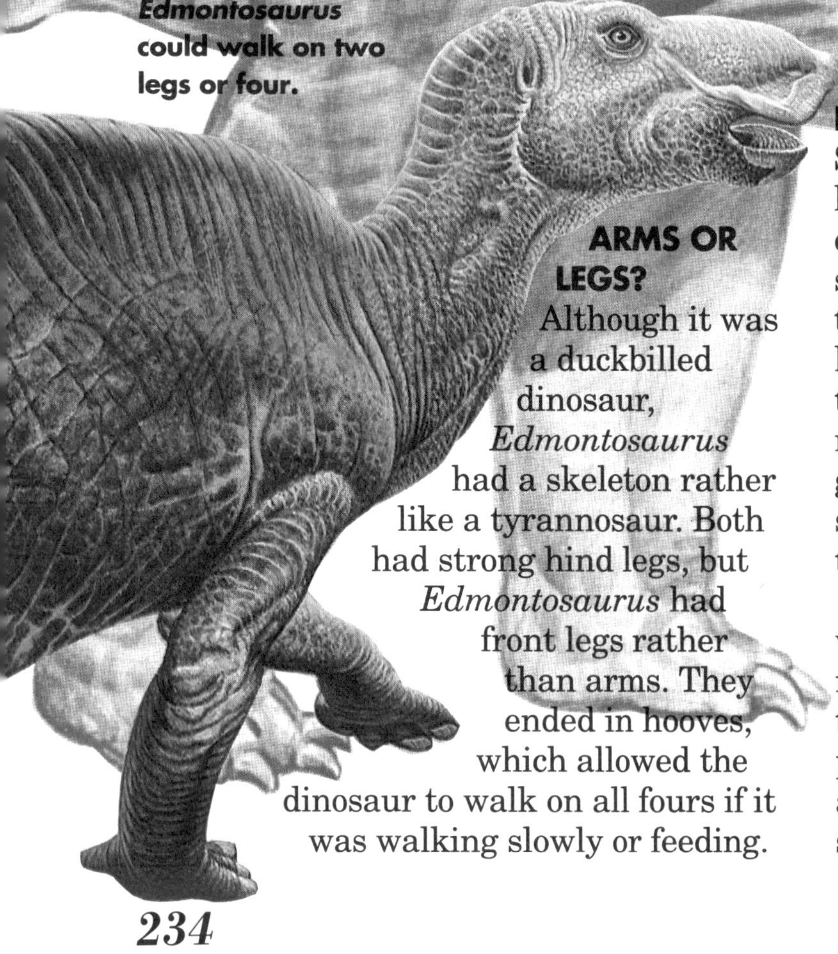

***Edmontosaurus* could walk on two legs or four.**

ARMS OR LEGS?

Although it was a duckbilled dinosaur, *Edmontosaurus* had a skeleton rather like a tyrannosaur. Both had strong hind legs, but *Edmontosaurus* had front legs rather than arms. They ended in hooves, which allowed the dinosaur to walk on all fours if it was walking slowly or feeding.

LEGS FOR SPEED

Some of the two-legged meat-eating dinosaurs were very speedy. For its size, tiny *Velociraptor* had long legs. Long-legged dinosaurs took big strides, like sprint runners, covering the ground quickly. Their long shin bones and muscular thighs helped them run fast.

The big meat-eaters also walked on two legs and could move at quite a rate if they were chasing their prey. Tyrannosaurs, such as *Albertosaurus,* had powerful legs to support their bodies and pound after prey.

Is it true that some of the huge sauropods could stand on their back legs?

Yes. Despite the fact that some sauropods weighed as much as 38 family cars, their back legs were used to support their weight as the dinosaur reared up to feed from the tree-tops. The femur (thigh bone) in the back leg was very straight in sauropods; just a slight curve in it would have made the leg quite weak.

***Diplodocus* (in the background) needed huge legs to carry its weight.**

SUPPORTING ROLE

Just as a cathedral needs large pillars to hold up a heavy ceiling, the sauropods needed pillar-like legs to carry their weight.

BIG BONED

The shoulder blades were an important part of a sauropod's skeleton. They joined the front legs to the body, and supported its huge barrel-shaped bulk. Each of *Camarasaurus'* shoulder blades was as big as a human adult. Its legs were also one of the sauropods' only means of defence; sometimes they would stamp on smaller, meat-eating animals.

***Velociraptor* had long and muscular legs built for speed.**

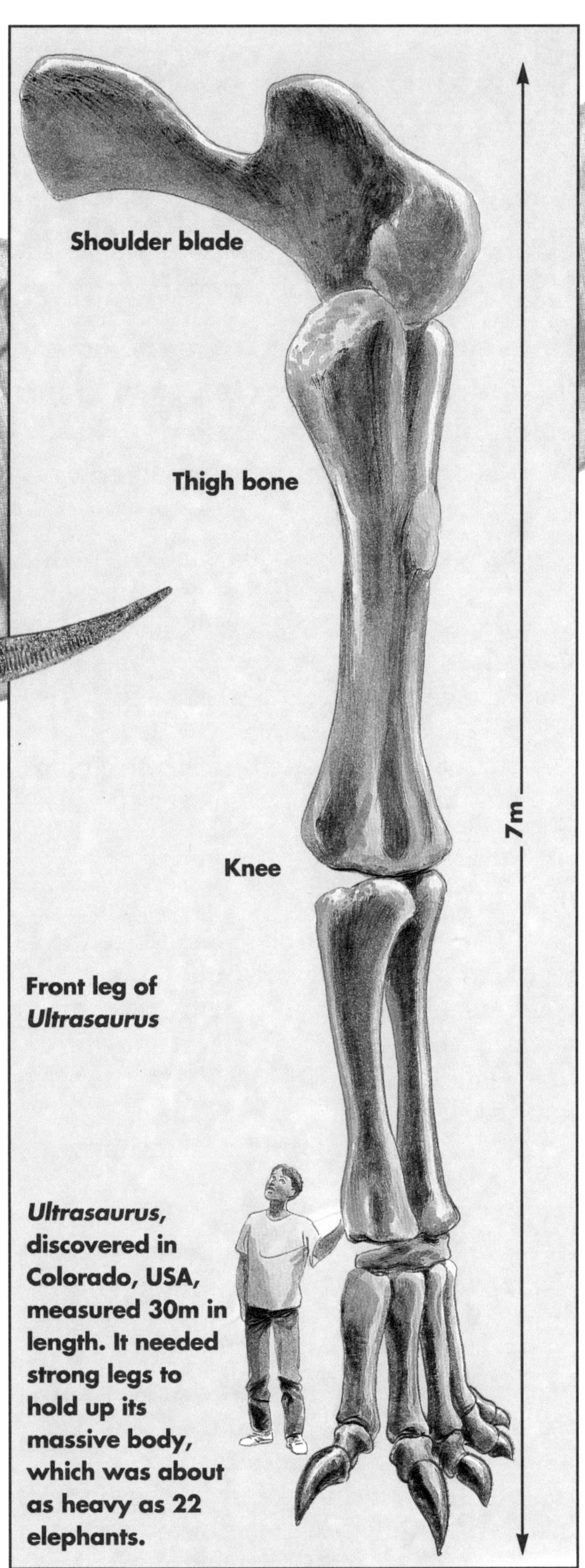

Front leg of *Ultrasaurus*

***Ultrasaurus*, discovered in Colorado, USA, measured 30m in length. It needed strong legs to hold up its massive body, which was about as heavy as 22 elephants.**

Dollo's discoveries

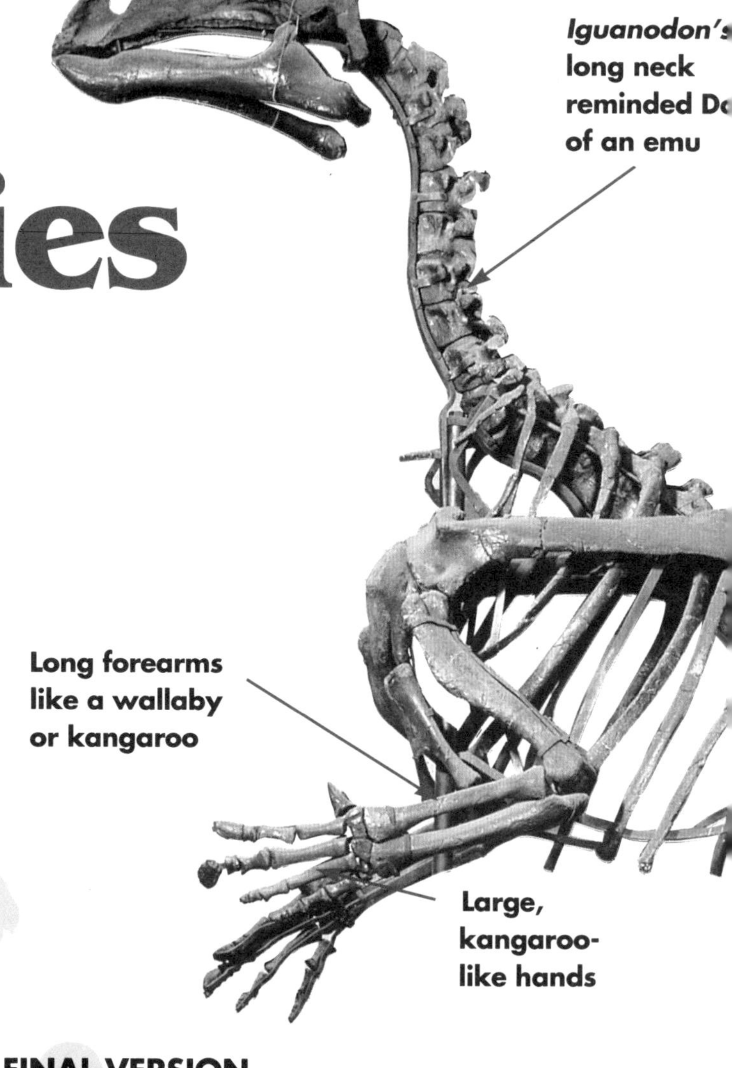

One man's study of *Iguanodon* gave the first real picture of the giant plant-eater and for the first time described how a dinosaur might have lived.

Louis Dollo was able to do something most dinosaur experts only dream about. As the palaeontologist in charge of the fossil finds in the Bernissart coal mine in 1878, he could study the complete skeletons of no less than 39 *Iguanodon*. It was the chance of a lifetime and he devoted over 40 years – most of his working life – to it.

IN WITH THE NEW

Scientists were starting to challenge the idea that dinosaurs were lumbering, elephant-like creatures. Some experts believed they were livelier and more bird-like. Dollo agreed with these new theories and reconstructed the skeletons of *Iguanodon* showing the dinosaur upright.

LIVING ANIMALS

In his efforts to give a life-like picture of *Iguanodon,* Dollo studied certain living animals. He dissected (cut open and studied) birds that do not fly, such as the emu. Dollo did this to try to discover how the dinosaur might have moved. He also made careful drawings of modern-day reptiles such as chameleons (a type of lizard) and alligators in order to find out how *Iguanodon* may have fed.

FINAL VERSION

Dollo's final version of *Iguanodon* had the same upright pose as a wallaby and a hint of emu in its bird-like neck.

DINOSAUR LIFESTYLE

Dollo believed *Iguanodon* used its long neck to graze giraffe-like, pulling the leaves from the tops of tall trees. He thought it used its tail as a support when it reared up to feed from high branches. His attempts to describe not only the dinosaur but also its way of life started a new scientific trend.

Today, scientists continue Dollo's work. In addition to studying the fossil skeleton, they find out how a dinosaur lived – what it ate, the habitat in which it lived and whether it lived in herds or alone.

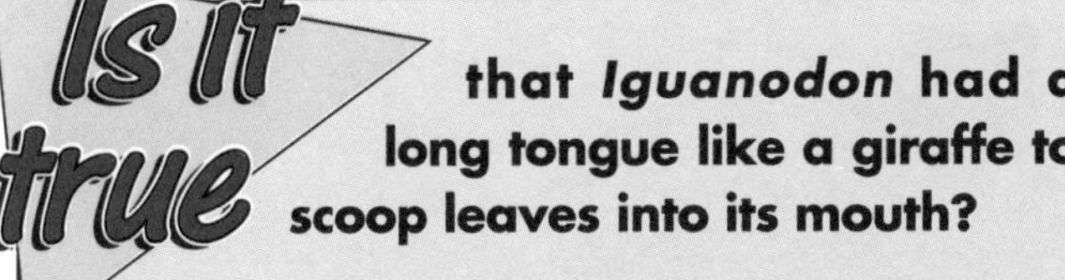

that *Iguanodon* had a long tongue like a giraffe to scoop leaves into its mouth?

Dollo believed that the dinosaur did because he spotted a round hole at the bottom of the dinosaur's lower jaw. Scientists now know that he was wrong about the extra-long tongue. They have discovered that the hole Dollo saw was simply broken bone.

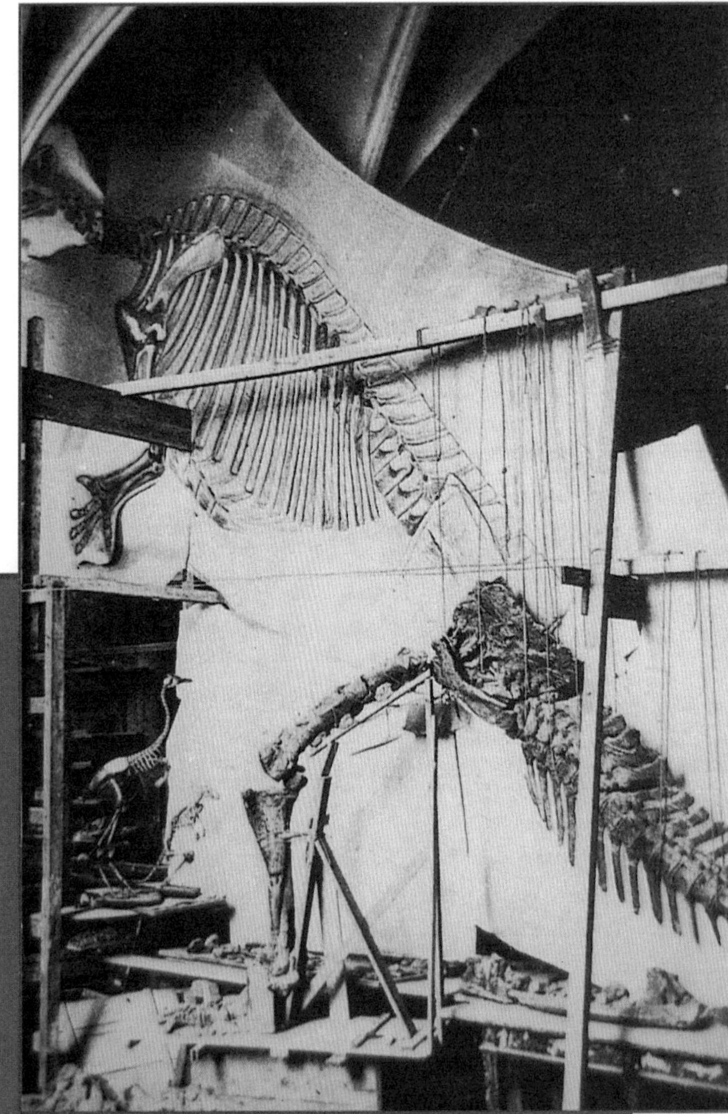

Dollo reconstructed *Iguanodon* to look like a large wallaby with a hint of emu

Hip bones like a bird's: Dollo likened this dinosaur to a large, flightless bird

Large tail like a wallaby or kangaroo

Dollo's team broke *Iguanodon's* tail here to give the dinosaur an upright stance, like a wallaby

Long, bird-like legs

When Dollo first reconstructed *Iguanodon* (above), he used the skeletons of an emu and a wallaby as a guide. You can just see their skeletons in the background.

The upright pose of a wallaby (right) helped Dollo to reconstruct *Iguanodon*.

Iguanodon reborn

Discoveries made about *Iguanodon* today have led to a very different idea of how it looked and moved. What were the clues that led to a new look for *Iguanodon*?

David Norman was the first modern palaeontologist to re-examine all the facts about *Iguanodon* in detail. He studied its skeleton, and looked again at all Dollo's evidence. His careful detective work led to a major discovery: the dinosaur was not, as Dollo had thought, an animal that always walked upright on two legs, but one that moved about on all fours most of the time.

IT'S A FACT

ARTIST'S COLOURS

Thanks to the scientists who have studied *Iguanodon*, we have a good idea what it looked like and how it moved. But we still do not know what colour the dinosaur's skin was. We will probably never know as no trace of the colour of *Iguanodon's* skin has ever been found. Each artist who draws *Iguanodon* may colour it differently.

CLUE 1

The tail was held out straight from the body. This would have tilted *Iguanodon's* body forward and downward. It was a very different position from the upright pose that Dollo gave to his reconstructions. Close study of Dollo's skeletons show that the tails had been broken by the reconstruction team to give the dinosaurs a more upright, wallaby-like appearance.

CLUE 2

The 'hands' were made for walking. With the body tilted forward, the 'hands' could touch the ground more easily. The middle three fingers have joints which allow them to be bent backwards in the same way as the toes of the foot. They also end in very broad, flattened claws, shaped like hooves. So *Iguanodon* must have put them to the ground and walked on all fours.

CLUE 3

The wrists were strong enough to carry *Iguanodon's* weight. In an ordinary wrist, the bones move freely to make movement easy. In *Iguanodon's* wrist, the bones are locked tight to make them strong enough for running or walking on.

CLUE 4

There is an extra bone in the centre of the chest. The most obvious explanation for this mystery is that it was there to strengthen the weak area of the chest between the shoulders. This area would have been under heavy strain when *Iguanodon* moved about on all fours, so the strengthening bone was very helpful.

TWO OR FOUR FEET?

So these are the main clues that led modern palaeontologists to decide that *Iguanodon* walked about with its body tilted forward, not upright as Dollo thought. Young *Iguanodon* probably moved around on their hind legs most of the time. But once they had grown up and become adults, they walked either on two hind legs or on all fours. The dinosaurs were surprisingly agile and could run at speeds of about 30 km/h.

Adult *Iguanodon* walked on four legs, its young on two.

3-D Gallery
40
LATE JURASSIC PERIOD

1. These *Camptosaurus* are always on the lookout for danger.
2. *Diplodocus* looks on, unable to help.
3. *Allosaurus* has just killed a hadrosaur and is warning other dinosaurs to keep away.
4. A group of horned *Ceratosaurus* are ready to steal any leftovers from *Allosaurus'* meal.
5. A pack of *Ornitholestes* run about excitedly.
6. Pterosaurs circle overhead.

ASK THE EXPERT
Dr. David Norman of Cambridge University answers your dinosaur questions

How long did it take for a dinosaur egg to hatch?

We can only guess the answer to this question. Some dinosaurs, such as *Maiasaura*, spent their lives travelling, but they probably laid their eggs in the same place every year. It may have taken *Maiasaura* only a few weeks to hatch. This gave the young plenty of time to mature enough in time to join the herd before it migrated to a new feeding ground.

Which dinosaur had the longest tail?

Diplodocus had the longest tail of all dinosaurs – it was 11m long. The end of the tail was quite thin, and *Diplodocus* may have used it like a whip to scare off or attack predators. The longest tail among reptiles today belongs to the salt-water crocodile. But its tail, at 4m, is only as long as a big car.

Did dinosaurs live in caves?

Most dinosaurs were probably too big to have lived in caves. One dinosaur expert thinks that some small dinosaurs retreated to burrows during the dry season, but the evidence to prove this is not very strong.

Did dinosaurs lie down when they went to sleep?

Nobody knows the answer to this question. The smaller dinosaurs lay down quite easily, but the larger ones may have found it more difficult.

However, *T rex* had large, curved bones at the bottom of its pelvis and a long row of bones beneath its ribs. These bones were there to protect its inner organs when the dinosaur lay down.

DINOSAURS!
DISCOVER THE GIANTS OF THE PREHISTORIC WORLD

DIPLODOCUS

Longer than a tennis court and as heavy as two elephants, *Diplodocus* ate shoots from the tops of the tallest trees.

Take about 20 children, all aged around 10 years, lie them down head to foot and together they would match the length of *Diplodocus.* This dinosaur had a long, thin neck, a whip-like tail and four pillar-like legs. Its back legs were slightly longer than the front pair so that the body sloped down from hip to shoulder.

ELEPHANT FEET

When we walk, the movement of our ankles makes our bodies move up and down. For sauropods like *Diplodocus,* any movement of their heavy bodies used up a lot of energy. Fossilized footprints show that sauropods had broad, round feet like an elephant's with short, stubby toes.

WELL-HEELED

A sort of wedge may have raised *Diplodocus*' toes from the ground, just like the heel of a shoe. This meant that muscles did not have to work so hard to support the dinosaur's body as it walked.

TAIL UP

From its tiny head to the tip of its enormous tail, *Diplodocus* had a long line of bones called vertebrae. Its neck had 15 vertebrae, its back 10 and its tail about 70. In spite of its size, *Diplodocus* could stand with both neck and tail raised above the ground.

BRIDGE BUILT

Diplodocus was built rather like a suspension bridge, with its front and back legs acting like twin towers. On an actual bridge, cables support the road that runs between the towers. *Diplodocus'* long backbone was supported by muscles. So that the neck and tail could move easily, a tendon probably ran along the length of its backbone.

Is it true that the giant sauropods stood upright?

Some scientists once thought that sauropods crept along like lizards with legs sprawled on each side of their body and chest close to the ground. However, footprints found in Texas, USA, in the 1930s proved that these dinosaurs must have walked with their legs held straight.

STICKING ITS NECK OUT

Diplodocus' neck was not as long as that of its Chinese cousin, *Mamenchisaurus.* At 11m, *Mamenchisaurus'* neck was just a bit longer than a bus. *Diplodocus'* neck was only 7.5m long and its enormous weight was balanced by a long tail, which stopped the giant from tipping over.

DUAL DEFENCE

Diplodocus could fight off predators with its powerful whiplash tail, or rear up on its back legs using its tail as support. This freed the dinosaur's massive front legs for defence. A large, curved claw on the inner toe could be used as a sharp weapon.

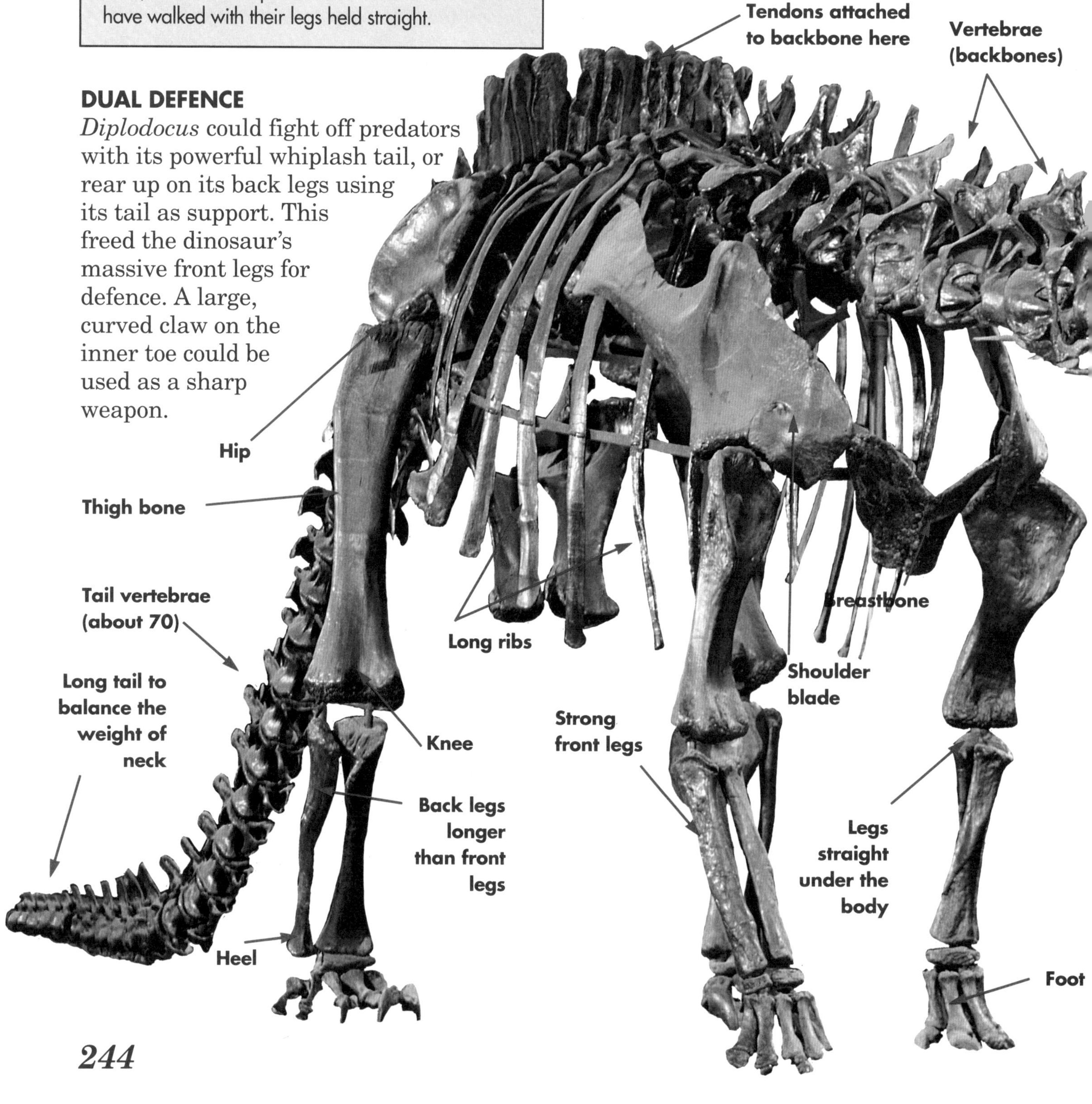

Tendons attached to backbone here

Vertebrae (backbones)

Hip

Thigh bone

Tail vertebrae (about 70)

Long tail to balance the weight of neck

Long ribs

Breastbone

Shoulder blade

Knee

Strong front legs

Back legs longer than front legs

Legs straight under the body

Heel

Foot

What is? A TENDON

Tendons are strong cords that join a muscle to a bone. Each of *Diplodocus'* backbones was attached to a muscle by a tendon. Without these small, but important tendons this gigantic animal would not have been able to stand up or support its great weight, let alone move about.

The bones that were hidden beneath *Diplodocus'* skin and muscle were designed for strength and support, rather than speed.

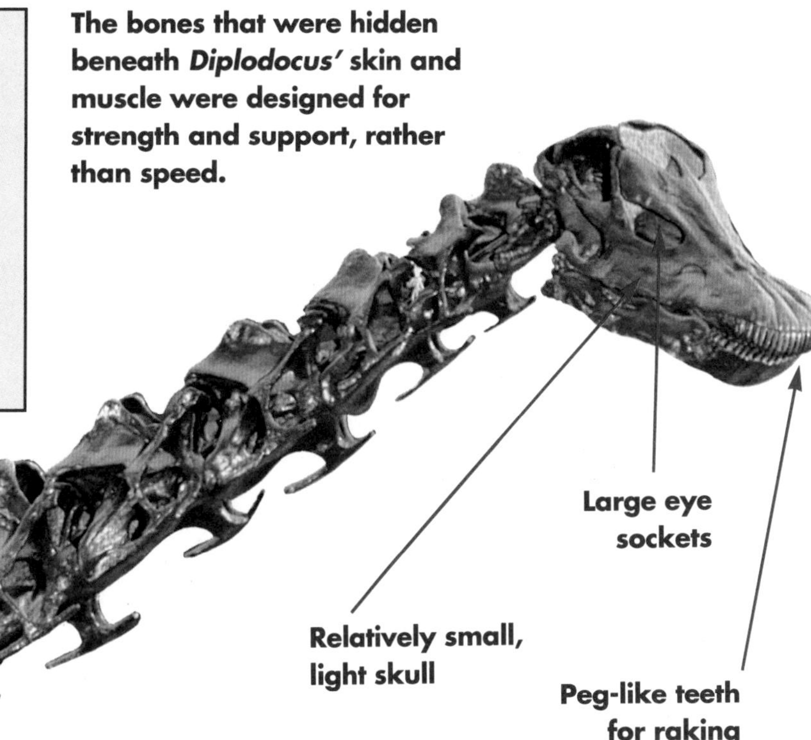

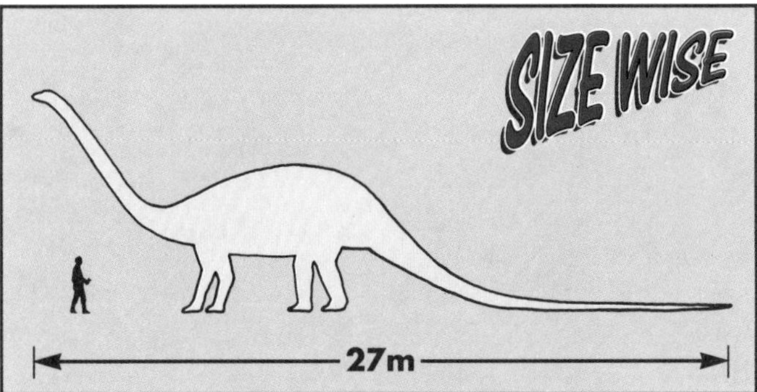

MONSTER FACTS

- **NAME:** *Diplodocus* (dip-lod-oh-kus) means 'double beam'
- **SIZE:** 27m long and 3.6m high
- **FOOD:** plants and leaves from trees
- **LIVED:** 150 – 138 million years ago in the Late Jurassic Period in North America

BIG FIND

At the end of the last century, a Scottish-American millionaire, Andrew Carnegie, was determined to have a giant dinosaur in his museum in Pittsburgh, USA. To his delight, a team of fossil collectors working for him at Sheep Creek, Wyoming, found two *Diplodocus.* A massive skeleton was made from the remains and called *Diplodocus carnegiei.*

ROYAL REPLICA

When the King of England, Edward VII, saw a painting of *Diplodocus* in Carnegie's Scottish home, he asked if a copy of the skeleton could be made for Britain. A cast of the skeleton took two years to complete and in 1905 the replica was finally put together at the Natural History Museum in London, England.

KENTROSAURUS

A sharp spike on each shoulder of this dinosaur gave it extra protection from large predators.

Kentrosaurus grazed on low-growing plants with its small head close to the ground. It walked on four chunky legs that carried its heavy body. *Kentrosaurus* lived at the same time as *Stegosaurus,* but was only about a quarter of that dinosaur's size.

MONSTER FACTS

- **NAME:** *Kentrosaurus* (ken-tro-saw-rus) means 'spiky lizard'
- **SIZE:** 2.5m long and about 1m high
- **FOOD:** low-growing plants
- **LIVED:** 150 – 140 million years ago in the Late Jurassic Period in Tanzania, East Africa

SPECIAL SPIKES

All along its back and tail, *Kentrosaurus* had a double row of armour. Near the front of its back, the spikes were quite flat. They became more narrow and pointed from its middle to the end of its tail. An extra spike pointed out and downwards on each of the dinosaur's shoulders. *Kentrosaurus* may have used its sharp spikes to defend itself rather like today's porcupines do.

FOSSIL FINDS

Fossils of all these dinosaurs were found between 1908 and 1912 by a German expedition.

TALL NEIGHBOURS

Kentrosaurus lived among some of the biggest dinosaurs, the gigantic *Brachiosaurus* and *Dicraeosaurus*, in what is now Tanzania, East Africa.

HYPSILOPHODON

It was once thought that this small, speedy dinosaur lived in trees.

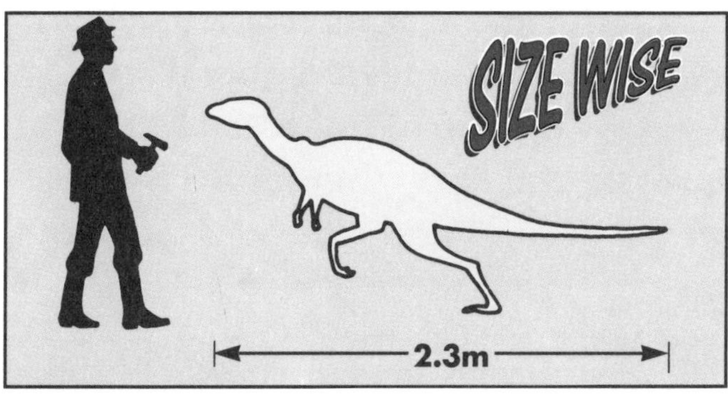

Hypsilophodon had sharp eyes set in a sheep-like head. It roamed the forests of Europe and North America during the Early Cretaceous Period, using its horny beak to nip off shoots and the short teeth at the sides of its mouth to chew them up.

MONSTER FACTS

- **NAME:** *Hypsilophodon* (hip-see-loaf-oh-don) means 'high ridged tooth'
- **SIZE:** between 1.4 and 2.3m long
- **FOOD:** plants
- **LIVED:** 115 – 110 million years ago in the Early Cretaceous in North America and Europe

LIVING IN TREES?

Scientists once thought that *Hypsilophodon* had feet like a bird's so that it could grasp branches. They believed that the first toe pointed backwards and the other three toes pointed forwards, like a bird's. Now, experts think that all the toes pointed forwards, which means that the dinosaur could not have held on to a branch. The dinosaur had a stiff tail which helped it to balance as it ran, but was useless for climbing.

FAST FOOTED

This dinosaur's shape was similar in many ways to the speedy antelopes of today. *Hypsilophodon* comes from a family of dinosaurs which has been given the nickname 'dinosaur gazelles'. Its long hind legs could swing backwards and forwards very quickly, controlled by strong muscles at the top of the leg. *Hypsilophodon* had short arms with five fingers tipped with sharp claws.

Pterosaur success

Successful in the skies for 166 million years, pterosaurs were good fliers. But how did the pterosaurs of the Late Jurassic and Early Cretaceous move on the ground and what did they eat?

Although all pterosaurs flew well, scientists are not sure how they got about on the ground. For years, pterosaurs were thought to be like bats or birds, but scientists now realise that they were not built like any other known group of animals. This makes it difficult to understand how they moved because there is nothing to compare their bones with. By studying how bones fit together, scientists are able to see how the animal might have used them.

WADDLING AND WALKING

Rhamphorhyncus (ram-for-hin-kus) could not move its legs as we do. Instead, they were splayed out like a lizard's, so when the animal was on the ground it probably crawled along.

ARMS AND LEGS

Gnathosaurus (na-tho-saw-rus) had a very large head, so it would have tipped over head-first if it had tried to walked on two legs. It could not have crawled like a bat either because it fed in water and would have drowned. Instead, it probably waddled along on its feet and hands, its long wing bones tucked up out of the way.

Small pterosaurs like *Batrachognathus* (ba-tra-cog-nay-thus), which was about the size of a crow, could perch on branches using feet and hands.

IT'S A FACT

RIDING THE CRESTS OF THE WAVES

Pterosaurs sometimes landed on the sea. They used the waves and strong, frog-like kicks with their feet to give them the lift they needed to get back into the air. Some pterosaurs had webbed feet, rather like a duck, and these helped them swim. Some scientists believe that pterosaurs with tails may have used them as rudders to help them steer in the water.

Germanodactylus had very strong finger claws, which it used to grip the trunks of trees as it climbed up. It also used its claws to hang upside-down from branches.

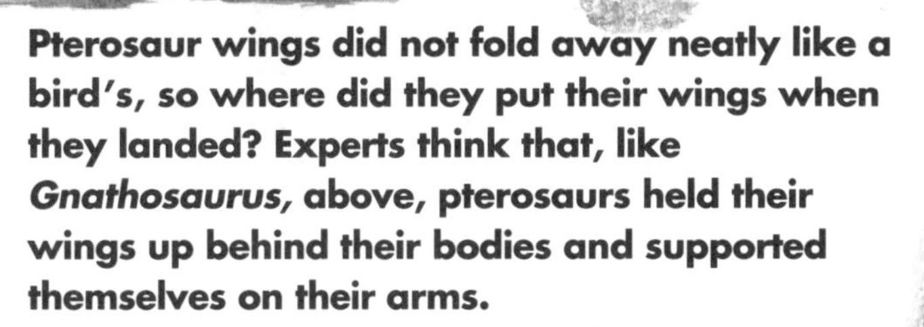

Pterosaur wings did not fold away neatly like a bird's, so where did they put their wings when they landed? Experts think that, like _Gnathosaurus,_ above, pterosaurs held their wings up behind their bodies and supported themselves on their arms.

TRAPEZE ARTIST

Not all pterosaurs lived on the ground. Some species, like *Germanodactylus*, (ger-man-oh-dak-til-us) probably lived in trees and moved about like modern fruit bats, hanging upside-down and using their claws to grip on to branches.

UP, UP AND AWAY

Pterosaurs used a variety of ways to take off. Some probably ran along the ground on their back legs then flapped their wings and jumped into the air. *Germanodactylus* probably let go of the branch it was clinging to and swooped down, before flapping its wings to stay in the air. Those with very large wings, such as *Gnathosaurus,* just spread their wings and let the wind and air currents carry them upwards.

Scaphognathus

WHAT DID PTEROSAURS EAT?

Scientists can usually work out what a pterosaur ate by comparing its jaws, teeth and size of its body with those of living animals. They can also tell whether the pterosaur was an expert flyer by looking at the strength of its wings and muscles. Good flyers probably caught prey in the air.

INSECT-EATERS?

Anurognathus (an-ur-og-nay-thus) had peg-like teeth, a small body and strong wing muscles. It was a fast flyer and probably caught large flying insects, just as modern-day bats do. *Scaphognathus* (skaf-og-nay-thus) was one of the best flyers of all the pterosaurs. With its long jaws, sharp fangs and long, balancing tail, it swept out of the sky, probably catching insects. However, experts are not sure exactly what *Scaphognathus* ate.

Experts think that insects were *Anurognathus'* prey. *Scaphognathus* may have eaten either insects or fish. Some experts believe that it may have devoured other pterosaurs, such as the young of *Anurognathus*.

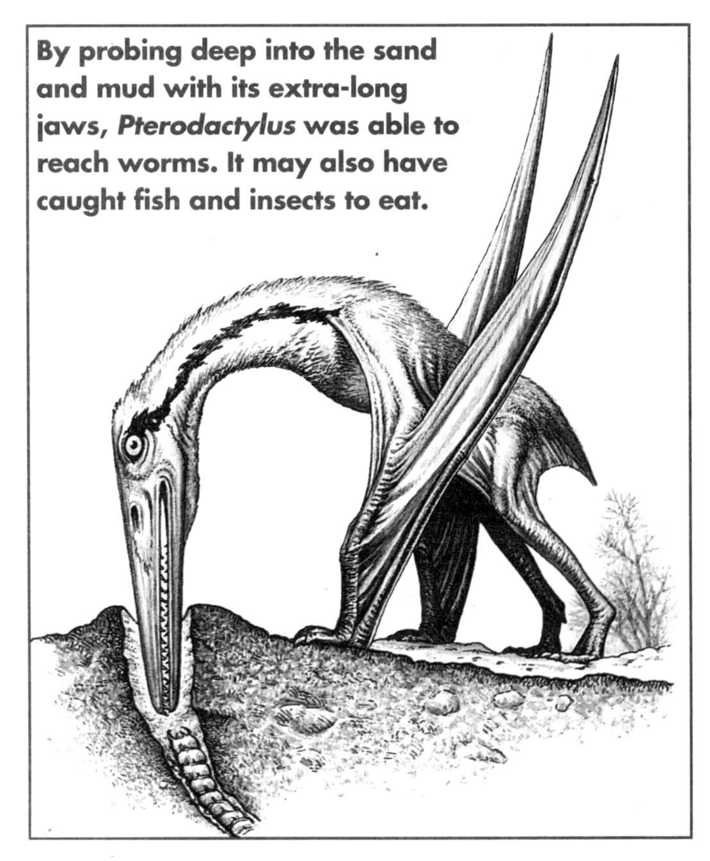

By probing deep into the sand and mud with its extra-long jaws, *Pterodactylus* was able to reach worms. It may also have caught fish and insects to eat.

PROBING THE SAND

Small flocks of *Pterodactylus* (tare-oh-dak-til-us) may have scampered along the beaches, like today's shore birds. They poked their long, narrow jaws into the sand to find worms and shellfish. They used their sharp teeth to grasp slippery worms, dragging them out to swallow them.

Is it true that pterosaurs that ate fish produced pellets of undigested food?

Yes. Most pterosaurs swallowed their food as quickly as they could, because other animals always tried to steal their prey. Bolting food meant that they ate many things that they couldn't digest, such as bones, fish scales and tough skin. After the pterosaur had digested most of its meal, it brought these parts back up in a pellet, just as owls do.

Anurognathus

CATCHING FISH

The fish-eating *Gallodactylus* (gal-oh-dak-til-us) had forward-pointing teeth to catch and keep hold of slithery fish. Experts think that some pterosaurs dived straight into the water to catch fish, while others flew low over the surface of the water, scooping up fish in their open jaws. Most fish-eating pterosaurs had pouches at the back of their throats. They may have stored extra food there to take back to their nests for a snack, rather like pelicans do today.

THE BIG SIEVE

Pterodaustro (tare-oh-daws-tro) had a bottom jaw packed with about 1000 bristles, which it used as a sieve to strain microscopic animals out of the water. The pterosaur's thin top jaw had much shorter teeth, which it used to chop up its food.

In the Early Cretaceous, *Pterodaustro* fed in shallow water, resting on its front legs while it sieved the water for food. The pterosaur was about the same size as a very large seagull.

GIANTS OF THE PAST

A young *Diplodocus* flicks back its whip-like tail and prepares to lash out at bloodthirsty [illegible]. The giant's peg-like teeth and weak jaws were designed for eating plants – they are useless to [illegible] now. The rest of the herd look on helplessly and hope that there is safety in numbers.

DIPLODOCUS

21
3-D Gallery
ALLOSAURUS

- Large predator of the Late Jurassic
- Lived 152 – 145 million years ago in North America
- Measured 12m long
- Ate meat

Skin

Dinosaur skin was well suited to life on land. Tough and scaly, it was designed to take the rough and tumble of prehistoric life.

This fossil of *Euoplocephalus* skin shows how tough and leathery armour-plated skin was.

Some of the world's greatest fossil spotters have been unable to find evidence of dinosaur skin. This is because skin does not fossilize easily.

THE FIRST TO GO

Often the skin is destroyed before it has a chance to fossilize. When an animal dies in the wild, the skin and flesh are the first part of the body to rot. Also, hungry scavengers come and eat the carcass before it has a chance to decay.

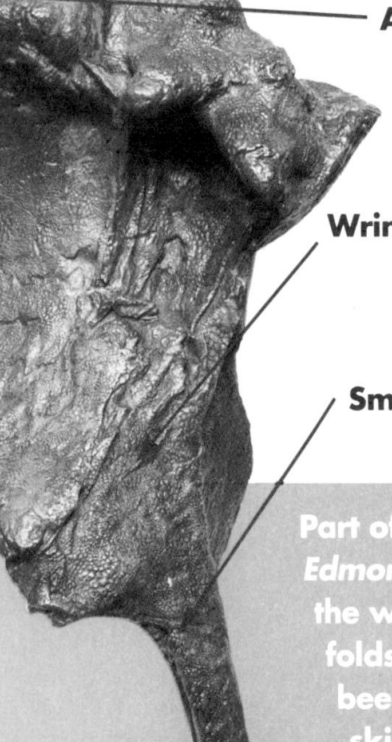

Part of a fossilized *Edmontosaurus*. Even the wrinkles and folds in the skin have been preserved. This skin is 67 million years old.

AN EXCEPTION TO THE RULE

Amazingly, fossilized prints of duckbilled dinosaurs' skin have been found in Canada. Experts think that the dry places in which these dinosaurs lived meant that when they died their skin became hard and leathery very quickly. Sand blew over the carcasses, and the hadrosaurs' skin was preserved as prints in the sand.

PROTECTIVE SKIN

Dinosaur skin was not moist like that of newts and frogs – it was dry. Like our skin, it kept out the rain and damp. It was perfectly suited to life on dry land and protected the dinosaur from injury.

BENDY SKIN

Sauropods, such as *Apatosaurus*, had scaly skin. So that dinosaurs could move, the scales were joined by bendy skin. Parts of the body that had to bend a lot had smaller scales.

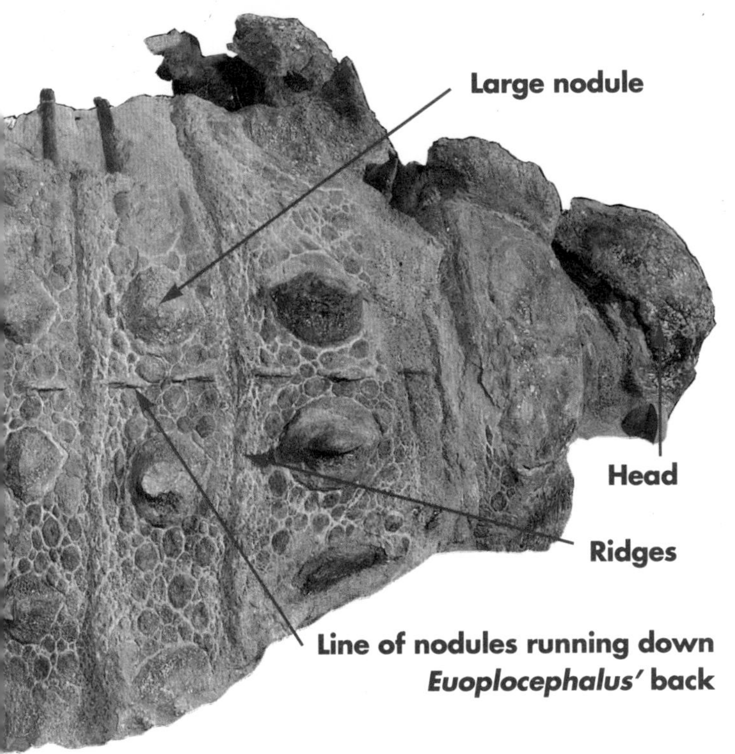

What is? CAMOUFLAGE

Animals that blend in well with their surroundings are said to be camouflaged. Just as soldiers smear their faces with dark paint and wear clothes that match the land around them, dinosaur skin was probably patterned and coloured to make it easier for dinosaurs to hide from their enemies.

LUMPS AND BUMPS

Armour-plated dinosaurs fossilized relatively easily. *Euoplocephalus* had bony lumps and nodules (bumps) for protection. Today's crocodiles have similar nodules.

SCALY SKIN

Some living reptiles, like the sungazer lizard, have scales that overlap, like tiles on a roof. Others, such as the gila monster, have scales that join neatly together, like tiles in a bathroom. Dinosaurs also had two different types of skin, depending on whether their skin was armoured or flexible.

MULTI-COLOURED COAT

When artists paint dinosaurs they often make them camouflaged, but no one knows what colour they were. Some living reptiles are brightly coloured. Skin colour helps them hide, attract a mate and control body temperature. For all we know, dinosaur skin was as colourful, scaly and bumpy as that of the modern lizards below.

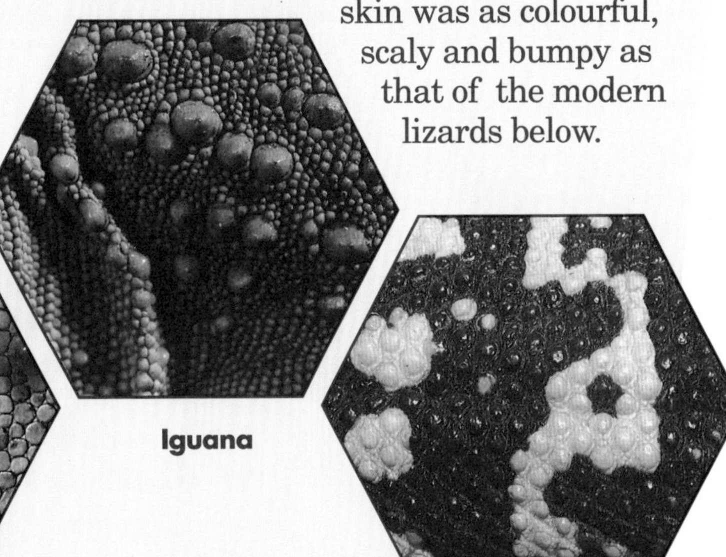

Tough scales on a sauropod's skin (left) join together, but do not overlap.

The sungazer lizard's scales overlap.

Meet the roof lizards

Their spiked backs and tails make the stegosaurs an easy group to spot.

Stegosaurs are named after one of the best known dinosaurs, *Stegosaurus*. The group contains two families. The first has only one member, called *Huayangosaurus*. The second contains not only *Stegosaurus*, but about 14 others as well.

LONG AND SHORT

Huayangosaurus is the earliest known stegosaur. It was about 4m long and shorter than a man. *Stegosaurus* was much bigger. It was more than twice as tall and measured up to 7.5m long.

PIN HEADS

All the stegosaurs had small heads and big bodies. Two rows of tall, pointed plates of bony skin ran down their backs and they had strong, spiky tails. Stegosaurs looked fierce, but they were harmless plant-eaters and probably moved around in herds eating ferns and other low-growing plants.

***Huayangosaurus*, with its off-putting display of spikes, was about as big as a Shetland pony.**

STING IN THE TAIL

Slow-moving stegosaurs were easy prey for fast-running meat-eating dinosaurs. But they had one powerful weapon to lash out with – a mighty tail armed with long, extremely sharp spikes.

ROOF LIZARD

The name *Stegosaurus* means 'roof lizard'. Stegosaurs all had bony plates on their backs. Scientists originally thought the dinosaurs' bony plates lay flat on their backs, like tiles on a roof.

Stegosaurs were named after *Stegosaurus*. It lived 140 million years ago. *Stegosaurus* was found by Othniel Marsh and named in 1877.

STEGOSAUR CHECK LIST
- Ate plants
- Spiky back and tail
- Walked on all fours

HOT AND COLD

Scientists now believe the plates stood upright, more like a spiky fence. They also think they could have been used to help control the stegosaur's body temperature. Tests have shown that the diamond-shaped plates on *Stegosaurus* were just the right shape to absorb and hold the heat from the sun to keep the dinosaur warm, or to help cool it down quickly in a breeze.

Is it true that *Stegosaurus* had two brains?

Some people believe that the hollow in part of *Stegosaurus'* spine near its hind legs could have been a space for an extra brain. However, scientists now think this is unlikely. They believe it was where all the nerves of the hind legs and tail met and that it was really a kind of relay station to send messages to and from the brain.

ALL SORTS

Every stegosaur had back plates but the shapes and sizes were often very different. *Kentrosaurus* had more than one plate shape – they were broad at the shoulder and spiky further down.

The plates were not fixed to the skeleton. They were embedded in the stegosaur's thick skin. Apart from its plates, *Stegosaurus* had smaller hard knobs and bumps all over its body.

TINY BRAINS

Stegosaurs had very small brains compared with their body size. For example, *Stegosaurus* had a tiny brain that was no bigger than a walnut. Their brains may have been small but they did the job – stegosaurs survived for more than 100 million years throughout the world.

LIVING THROUGH THE AGES

Huayangosaurus, Lexovisaurus and *Dacentrurus* were some of the earliest stegosaurs. They lived in Middle Jurassic times about 170 million years ago.

Most stegosaurs, including *Stegosaurus*, *Kentrosaurus* and *Tuojiangosaurus* lived in the Late Jurassic Period. *Wuerhosaurus,* a Chinese dinosaur, was one of the few stegosaurs from the Early Cretaceous Period, 110 million years ago.

Not all the stegosaurs below lived at the same time, but this family group shows what all stegosaurs had in common – their defensive spikes and plates.

STEGOSAUR CHECK LIST
- **Small heads**
- **Short front legs**
- **Long back legs**

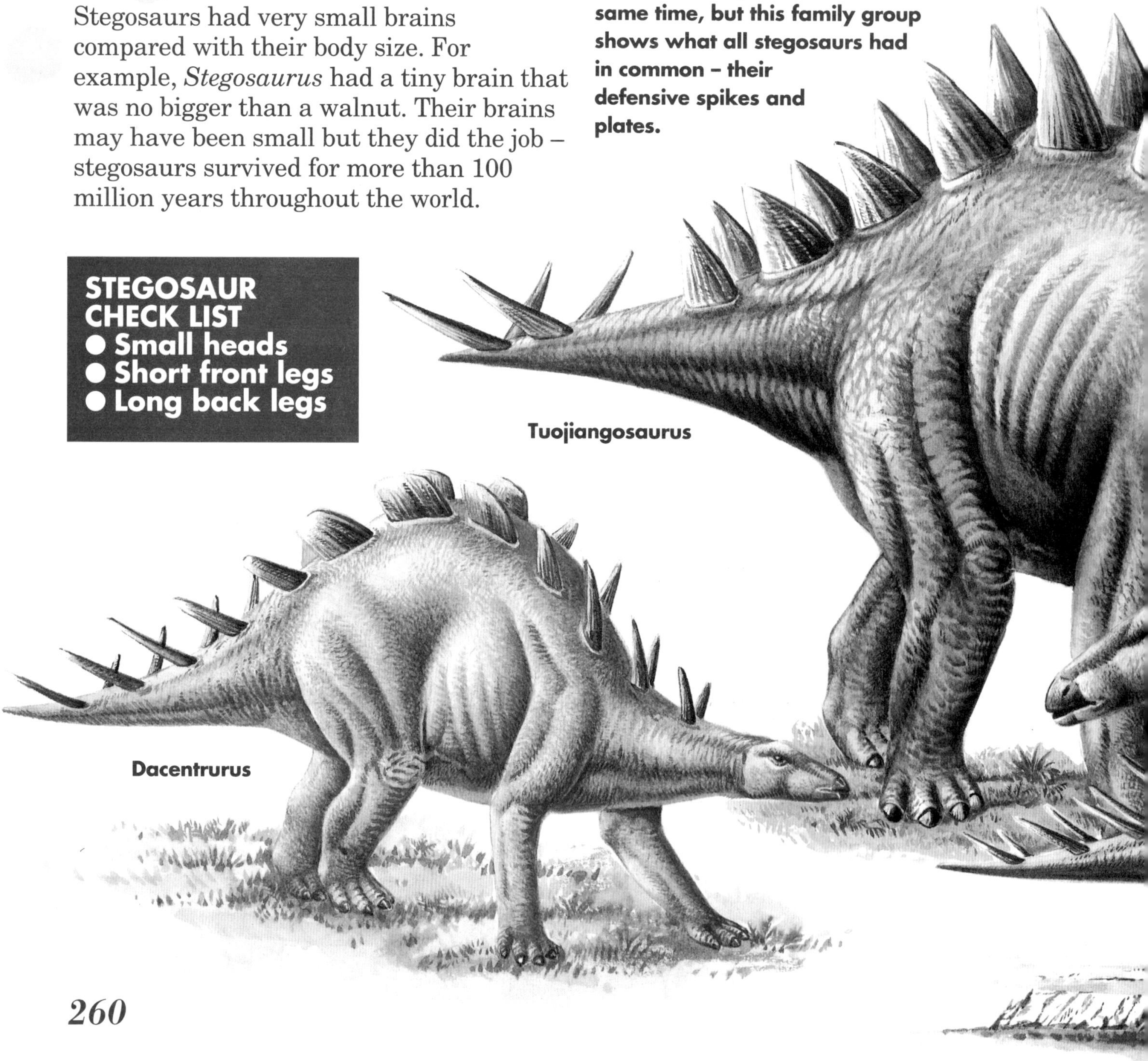

Tuojiangosaurus

Dacentrurus

WORLD WIDE

Stegosaurs lived all over the world. *Lexovisaurus* and *Dacentrurus* came from Europe. *Kentrosaurus* lived in Africa. *Stegosaurus* roamed North America, and *Huayangosaurus, Tuojiangosaurus* and *Wuerhosaurus* lived in China.

CHINESE PUZZLE

How stegosaurs spread from China is a bit of a mystery because Asia was cut off from the rest of the world by sea for most of the Age of the Dinosaurs. Dinosaur experts now think Asia and Europe must have been linked for a short time.

IT'S A FACT

SWALLOWING STONES

Stegosaurus needed to eat a lot to survive, but it was not much good at chewing. To help digest its food, the dinosaur swallowed stones and kept them in its stomach to grind down tough plants. Modern birds don't have any teeth, so they reduce their food to a pulp in a sack near their stomach, called a gizzard. To help speed up this process birds sometimes swallow pebbles, just like *Stegosaurus*.

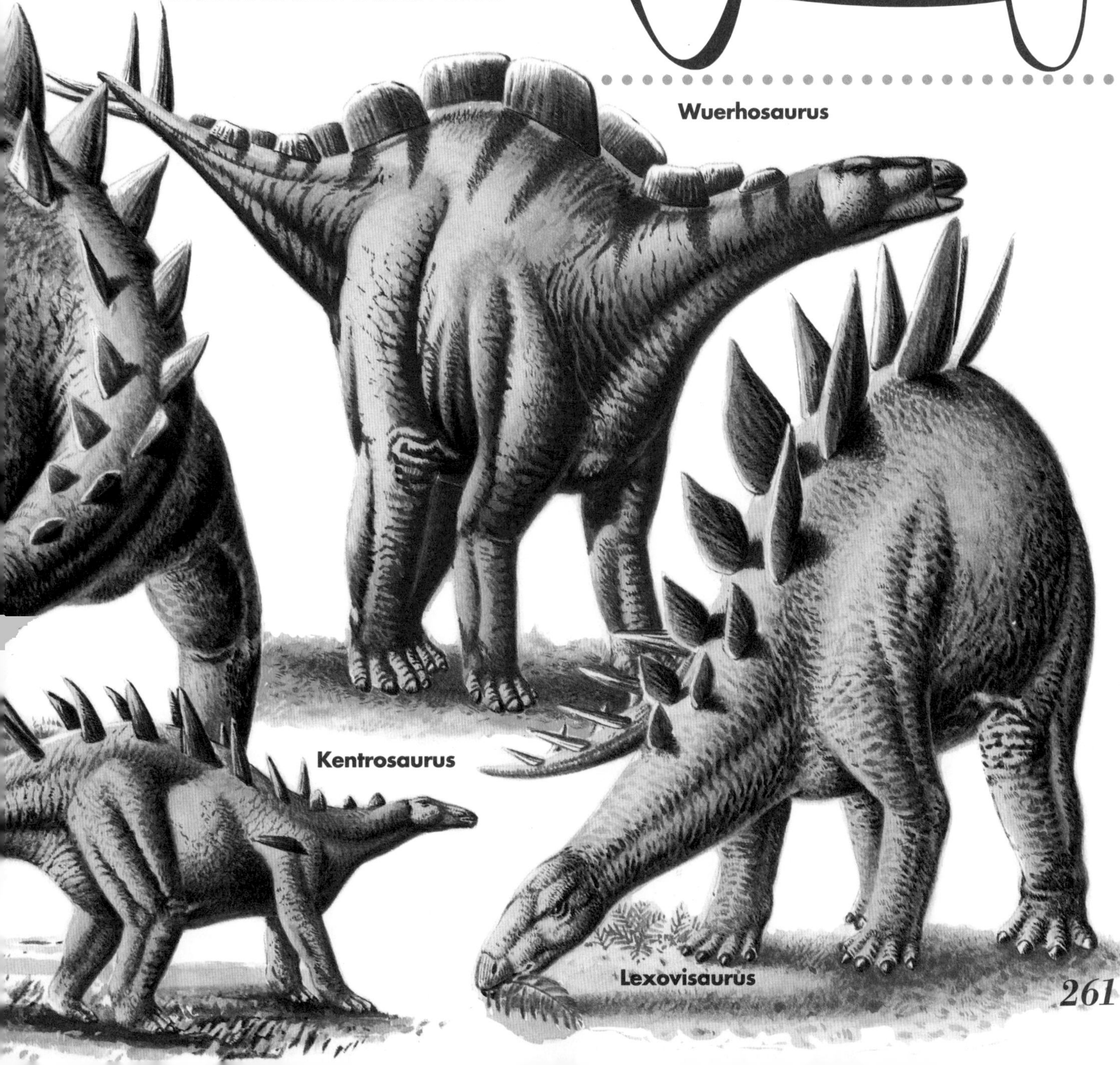

Wuerhosaurus

Kentrosaurus

Lexovisaurus

3-D Gallery 41

T REX v EUOPLOCEPHALUS

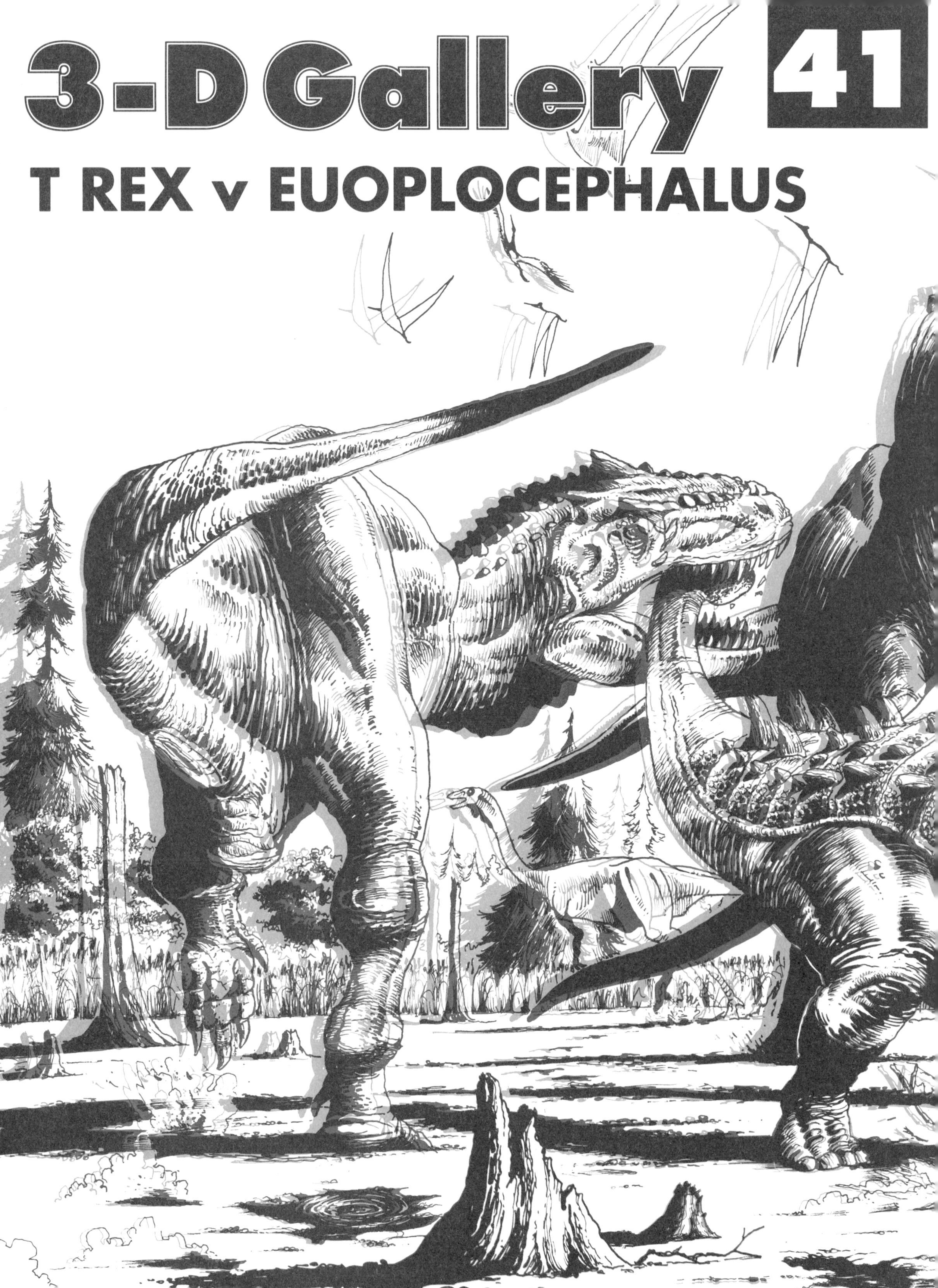

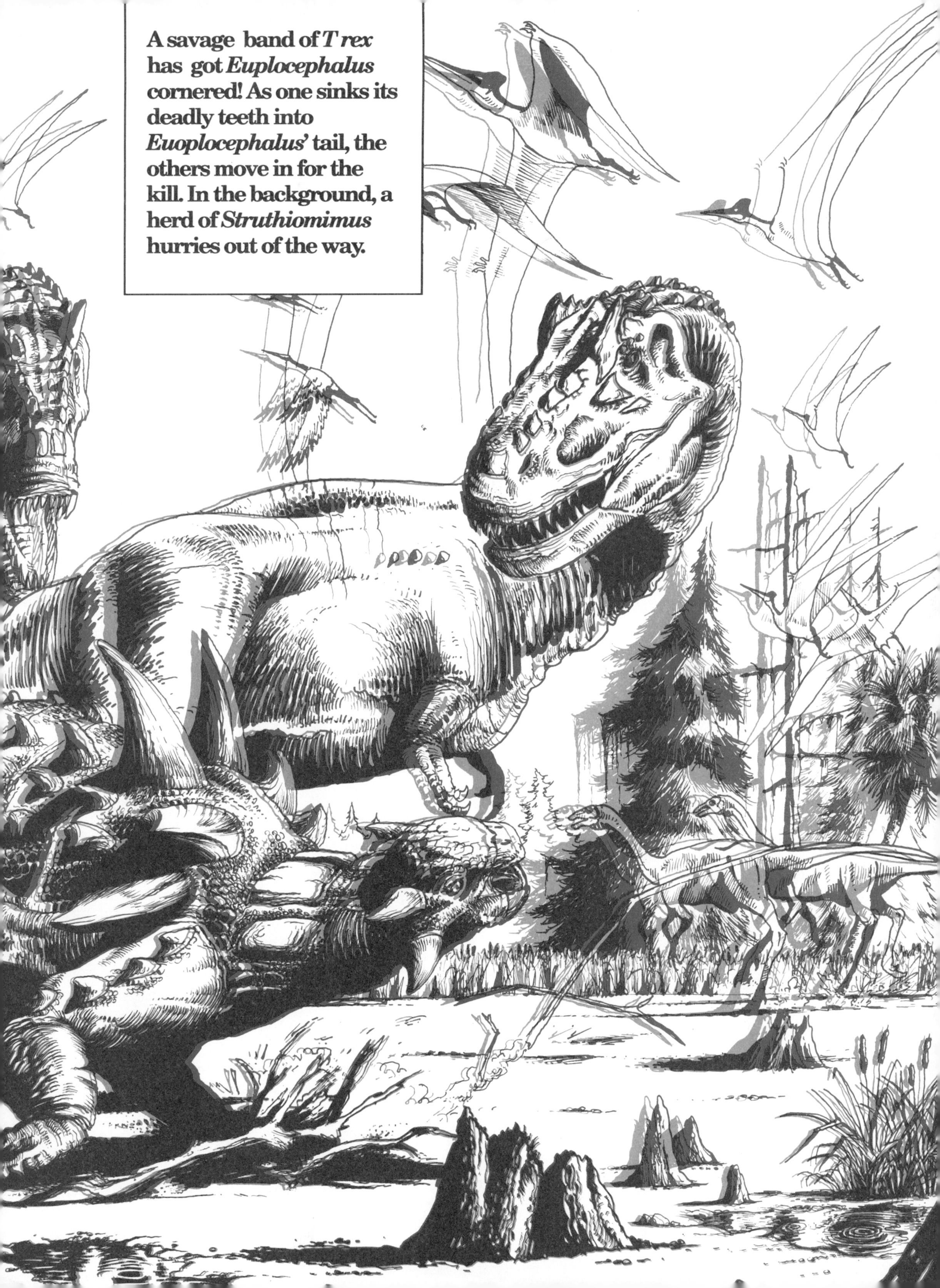

A savage band of *T rex* has got *Euplocephalus* cornered! As one sinks its deadly teeth into *Euoplocephalus'* tail, the others move in for the kill. In the background, a herd of *Struthiomimus* hurries out of the way.

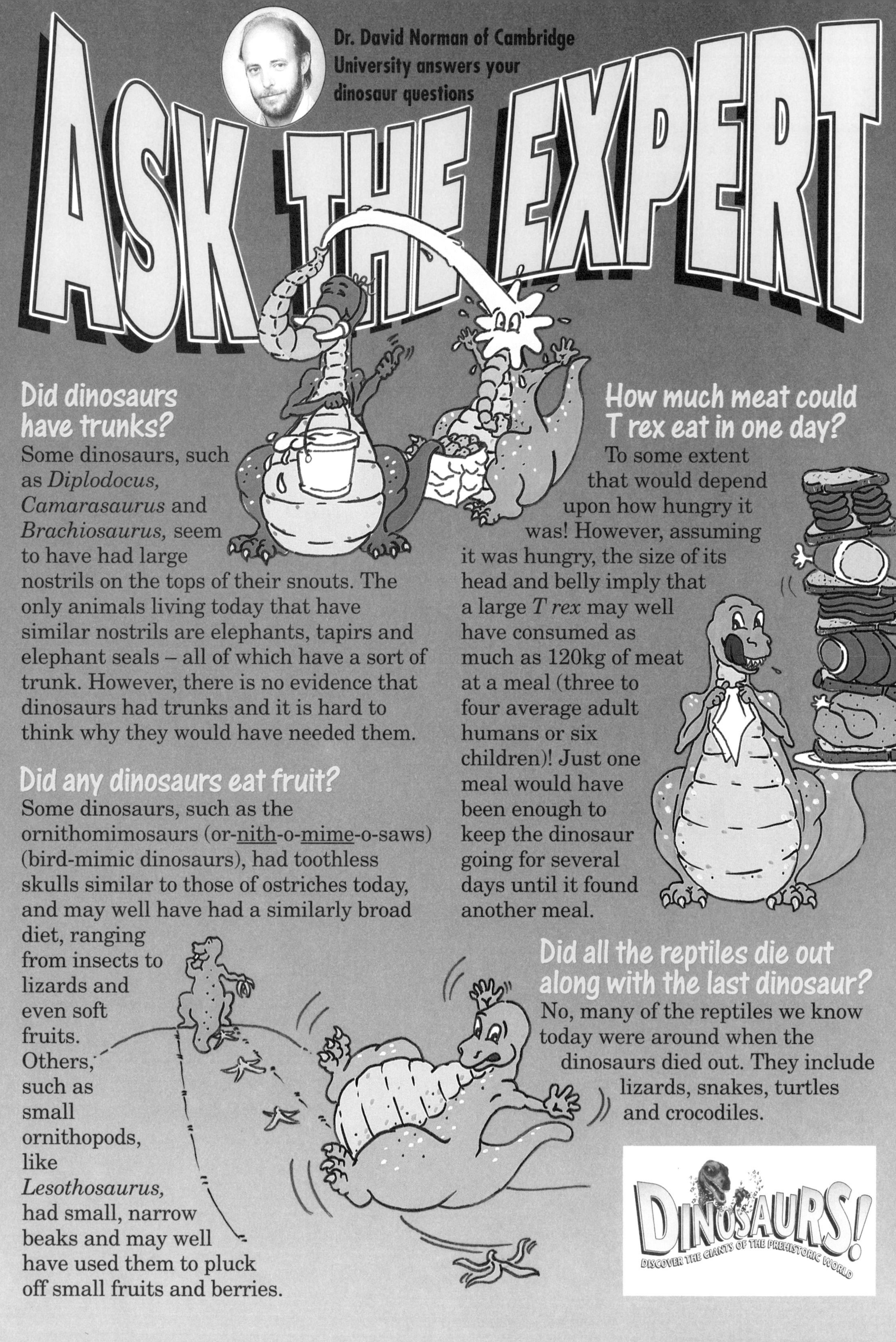

ASK THE EXPERT

Dr. David Norman of Cambridge University answers your dinosaur questions

Did dinosaurs have trunks?

Some dinosaurs, such as *Diplodocus, Camarasaurus* and *Brachiosaurus,* seem to have had large nostrils on the tops of their snouts. The only animals living today that have similar nostrils are elephants, tapirs and elephant seals – all of which have a sort of trunk. However, there is no evidence that dinosaurs had trunks and it is hard to think why they would have needed them.

Did any dinosaurs eat fruit?

Some dinosaurs, such as the ornithomimosaurs (or-nith-o-mime-o-saws) (bird-mimic dinosaurs), had toothless skulls similar to those of ostriches today, and may well have had a similarly broad diet, ranging from insects to lizards and even soft fruits. Others, such as small ornithopods, like *Lesothosaurus,* had small, narrow beaks and may well have used them to pluck off small fruits and berries.

How much meat could T rex eat in one day?

To some extent that would depend upon how hungry it was! However, assuming it was hungry, the size of its head and belly imply that a large *T rex* may well have consumed as much as 120kg of meat at a meal (three to four average adult humans or six children)! Just one meal would have been enough to keep the dinosaur going for several days until it found another meal.

Did all the reptiles die out along with the last dinosaur?

No, many of the reptiles we know today were around when the dinosaurs died out. They include lizards, snakes, turtles and crocodiles.

DINOSAURS!
DISCOVER THE GIANTS OF THE PREHISTORIC WORLD

Strange noises echoed around the hills of Alberta, Canada, 75 million years ago – these were the calls of *Parasaurolophus*.

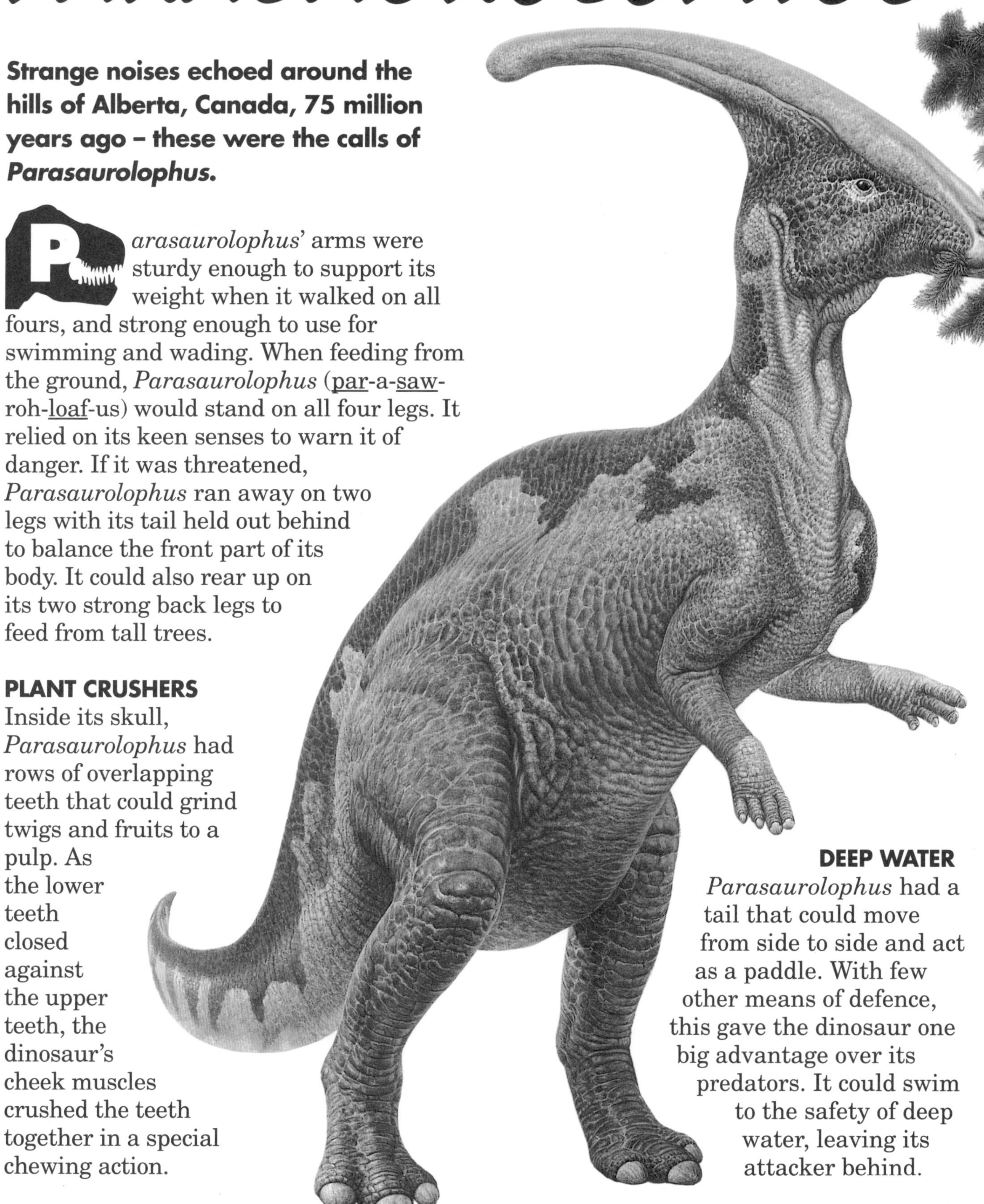

P*arasaurolophus*' arms were sturdy enough to support its weight when it walked on all fours, and strong enough to use for swimming and wading. When feeding from the ground, *Parasaurolophus* (par-a-saw-roh-loaf-us) would stand on all four legs. It relied on its keen senses to warn it of danger. If it was threatened, *Parasaurolophus* ran away on two legs with its tail held out behind to balance the front part of its body. It could also rear up on its two strong back legs to feed from tall trees.

PLANT CRUSHERS

Inside its skull, *Parasaurolophus* had rows of overlapping teeth that could grind twigs and fruits to a pulp. As the lower teeth closed against the upper teeth, the dinosaur's cheek muscles crushed the teeth together in a special chewing action.

DEEP WATER

Parasaurolophus had a tail that could move from side to side and act as a paddle. With few other means of defence, this gave the dinosaur one big advantage over its predators. It could swim to the safety of deep water, leaving its attacker behind.

TUBE-SHAPED CREST

Like many other hadrosaurs, *Parasaurolophus* had an extraordinary head. A long, tube-shaped crest stuck out of the male's skull for up to 1.8m. Set beside an adult human, the crest would have been about as tall. Scientists have had various ideas about what this enormous tube could have been used for.

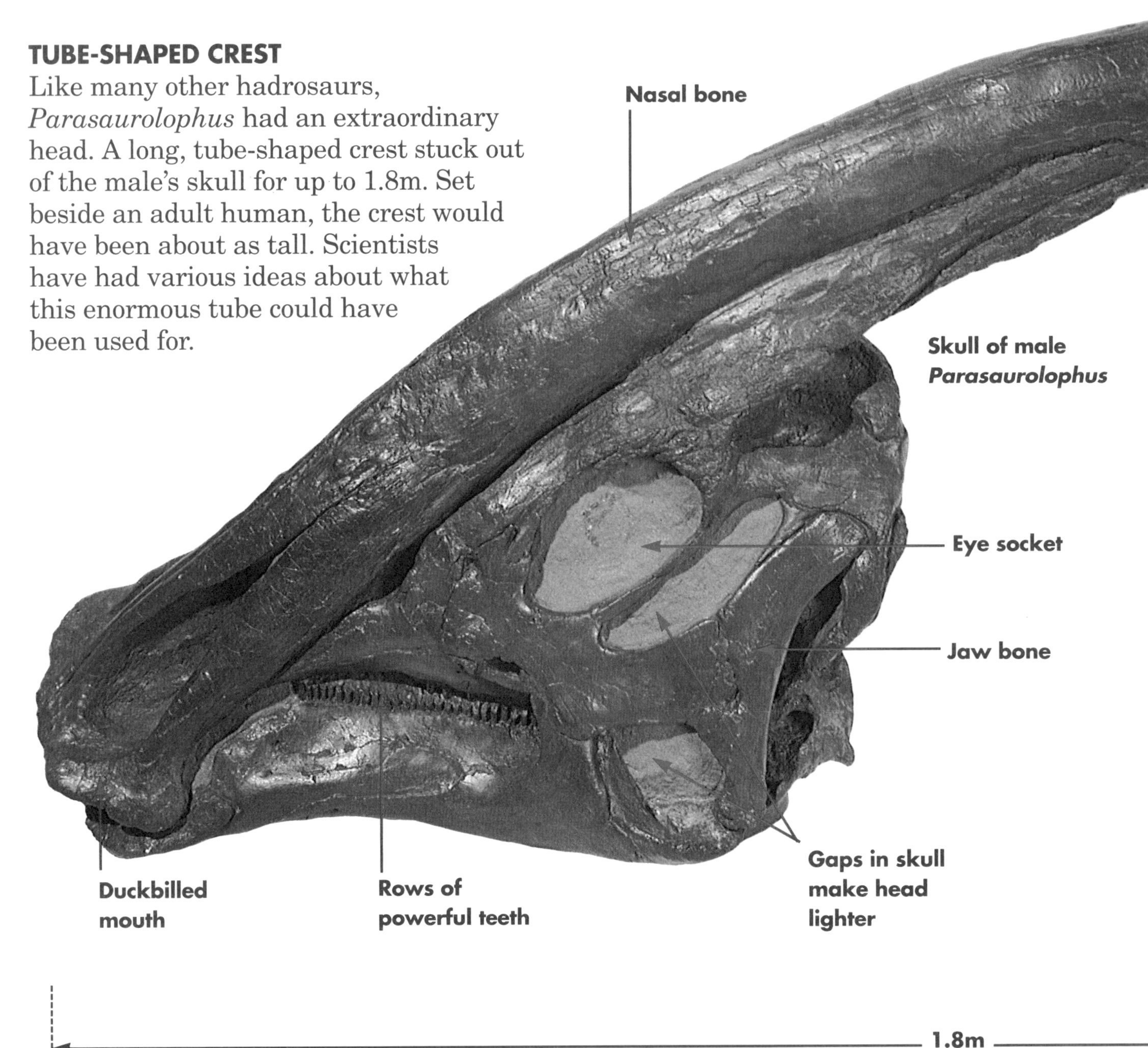

Nasal bone

Skull of male *Parasaurolophus*

Eye socket

Jaw bone

Duckbilled mouth

Rows of powerful teeth

Gaps in skull make head lighter

1.8m

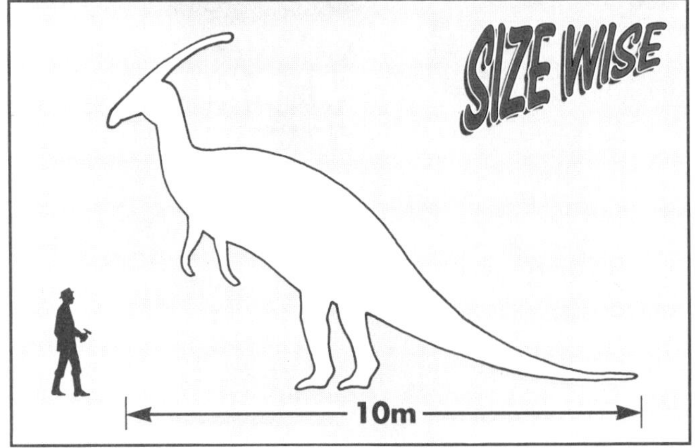

MONSTER FACTS

- **NAME:** *Parasaurolophus* (par-a-saw-roh-loaf-us) means 'reptile with parallel-sided crest'
- **SIZE:** 10m long
- **FOOD:** plants, fruit and leaves from trees
- **LIVED:** 80 – 66 million years ago in the Late Cretaceous in Alberta, Canada, and the USA

SUPER SNORKEL?

It was once thought that the crest helped *Parasaurolophus* to breathe under water, while it was feeding on waterplants, by acting as a sort of snorkel. The tip of the tube would stick up out of the water while the rest of the dinosaur's head was submerged. For this to be possible, the tip of the tube would have had an airhole, but it did not. So experts have to agree that *Parasaurolophus* was not a prehistoric snorkeller.

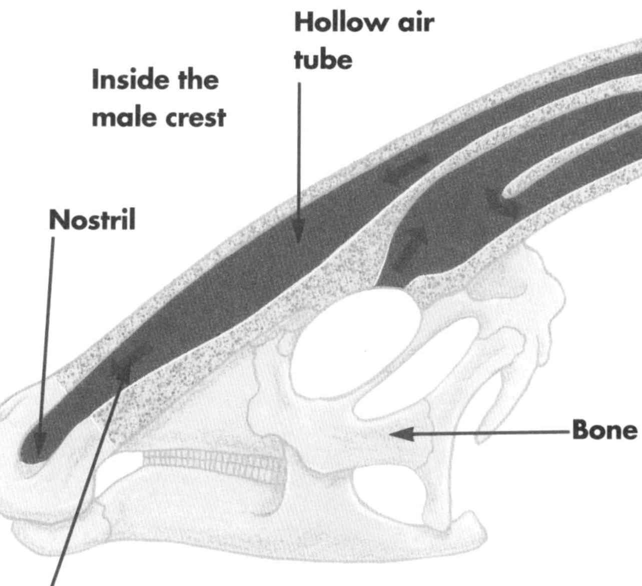

Arrows show air rushing through crest as *Parasaurolophus* breathed out

Here's how *Parasaurolophus* made a racket. As it breathed out, air rushed through its crest. This made the air vibrate, which produced a bellowing sound. Musical wind instruments work in the same way.

LOUD HOOTER

Just as humans use megaphones to make their voices louder, *Parasaurolophus* used its crest to make itself heard. The dinosaur could make the air in the tube vibrate, which produced a bellowing sound. The sound was recognized by other dinosaurs quite a distance away. These noises not only helped *Parasaurolophus* to find each other, but also warned of danger.

STRONG SIGNALS

Some scientists think that the crest was used for knocking leaves out of the way or as a sort of air tank. But the huge crest was probably to help these dinosaurs recognise each other. The crest may have signalled the sex or age of another *Parasaurolophus*. Fossils of their skulls show that fully grown males had larger crests than females and younger members of the herd.

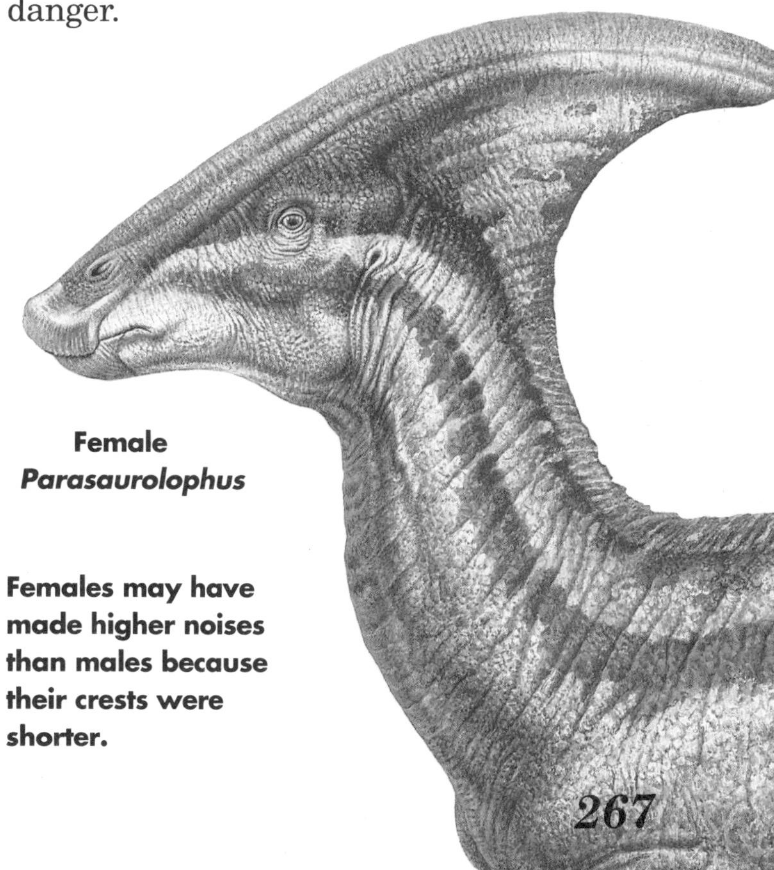
Female *Parasaurolophus*

Females may have made higher noises than males because their crests were shorter.

COMPSOGNATHUS

Compsognathus, one of the smallest dinosaurs, was the size of a chicken.

ompsognathus was a good hunter with keen eyesight. It ran fast on strong, slender back legs and could accelerate quickly to catch the speediest of small animals.

DAINTY DINOSAUR

Compsognathus was more delicate than most dinosaurs. At the end of its long, flexible neck, it had a lightly built skull with lots of space between the bones. Even its 68 sharp teeth were small and dainty, although their sharp, curved edges could do a lot of damage to a smaller creature.

LIGHT FINGERED

With only two jointed fingers, it is hard to guess how *Compsognathus* grasped hold of anything. Its third finger was made of just one bone, so it could not have been very flexible or useful.

LAST LUNCH

The remains of a reptile called *Bravarisaurus* were found inside the ribcage of one *Compsognathus* fossil. It is likely that this lizard was the dinosaur's last meal.

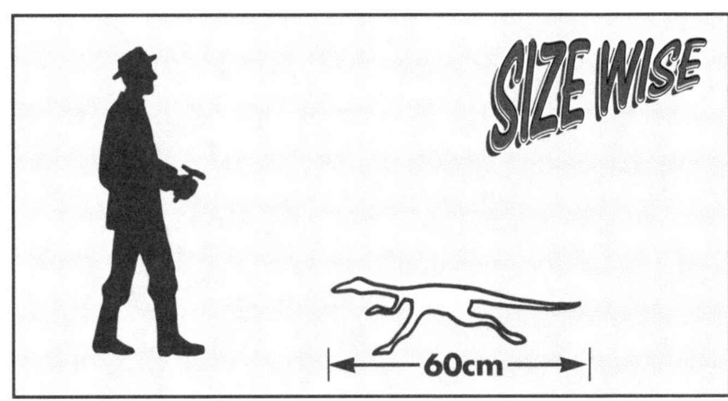

MONSTER FACTS

- **NAME:** *Compsognathus* (komp-sog-nay-thus) means 'pretty jaw'
- **SIZE:** 60cm long
- **FOOD:** flesh of smaller animals
- **LIVED:** 145 million years ago in the Jurassic Period in southern Germany and southern France

EDMONTONIA

Built like an armoured tank, *Edmontonia* was as long as an elephant and could have looked an adult human straight in the eye.

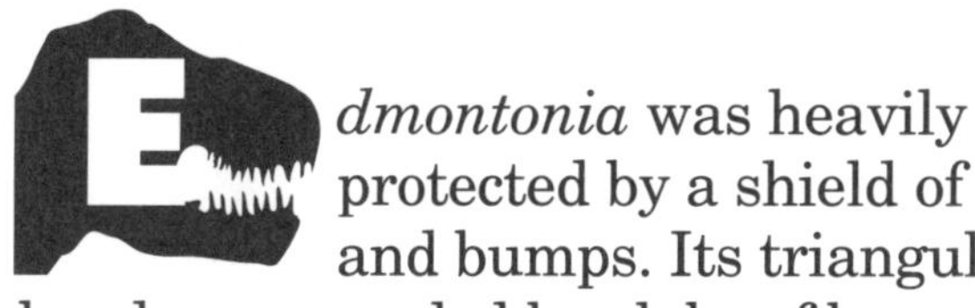

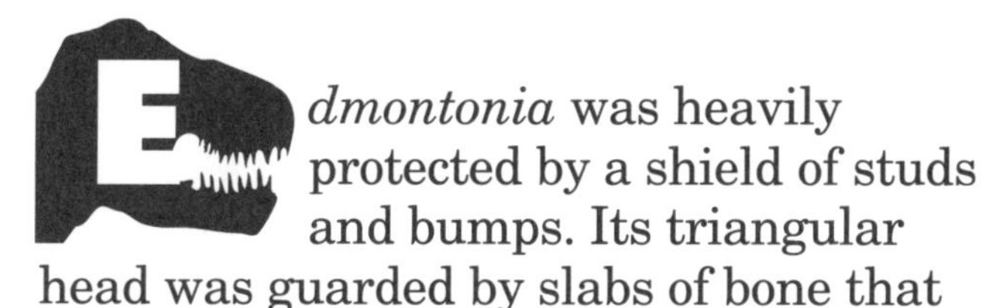

Edmontonia was heavily protected by a shield of studs and bumps. Its triangular head was guarded by slabs of bone that fitted together like a jigsaw.

As well as this thick, bumpy armour, *Edmontonia* had another way of defending itself. On each side of its body, it had a row of sharp, bony spikes. These stuck out sideways like a prickly fringe along its body. When attacked, *Edmontonia* probably crouched down on the ground to protect its soft, defenceless belly.

LEAF TEETH

As it browsed amongst low-growing plants, this dinosaur tore off shoots with its sharp, toothless beak. Further back inside its massive jaws, a row of leaf-shaped teeth helped it chew up its food.

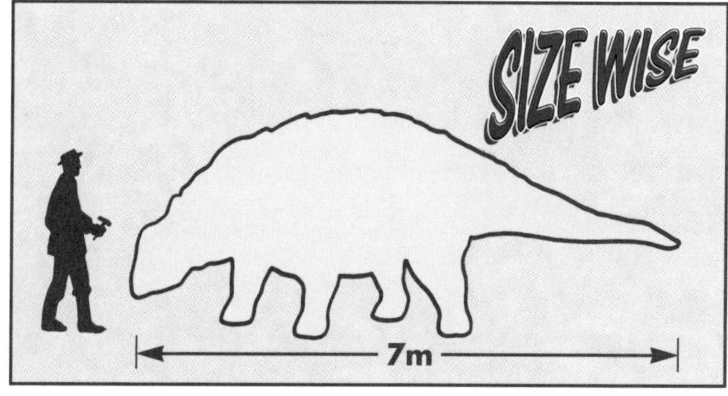

MONSTER FACTS

- **NAME:** *Edmontonia* (ed-mon-tone-ia) means 'of Edmonton'
- **SIZE:** 7m long and about 1.6m high
- **FOOD:** low-growing plants
- **LIVED:** 80 million years ago in the Late Cretaceous Period in Canada and the USA

WELL SUPPORTED

Edmontonia walked on four sturdy legs that were strong enough to support its broad, flat body. It had a short neck and a tail that was tapered at the end.

Ancient and modern lizards

The first lizards appeared when the dinosaurs were alive and there are still lizards living on Earth today.

Lizards are good at being lizards. They have lived on Earth for about 250 million years and there are over 3,700 species alive today. The lizards are one of the successes of the animal kingdom.

THE SECRETS OF SUCCESS

Lizards are reptiles, so were dinosaurs, but why did lizards manage to survive when dinosaurs died out? No one knows for certain, but it seems that lizards adapted well to life on Earth. Their shape suited their lifestyle and their skull bones gradually changed to become more successful at catching food.

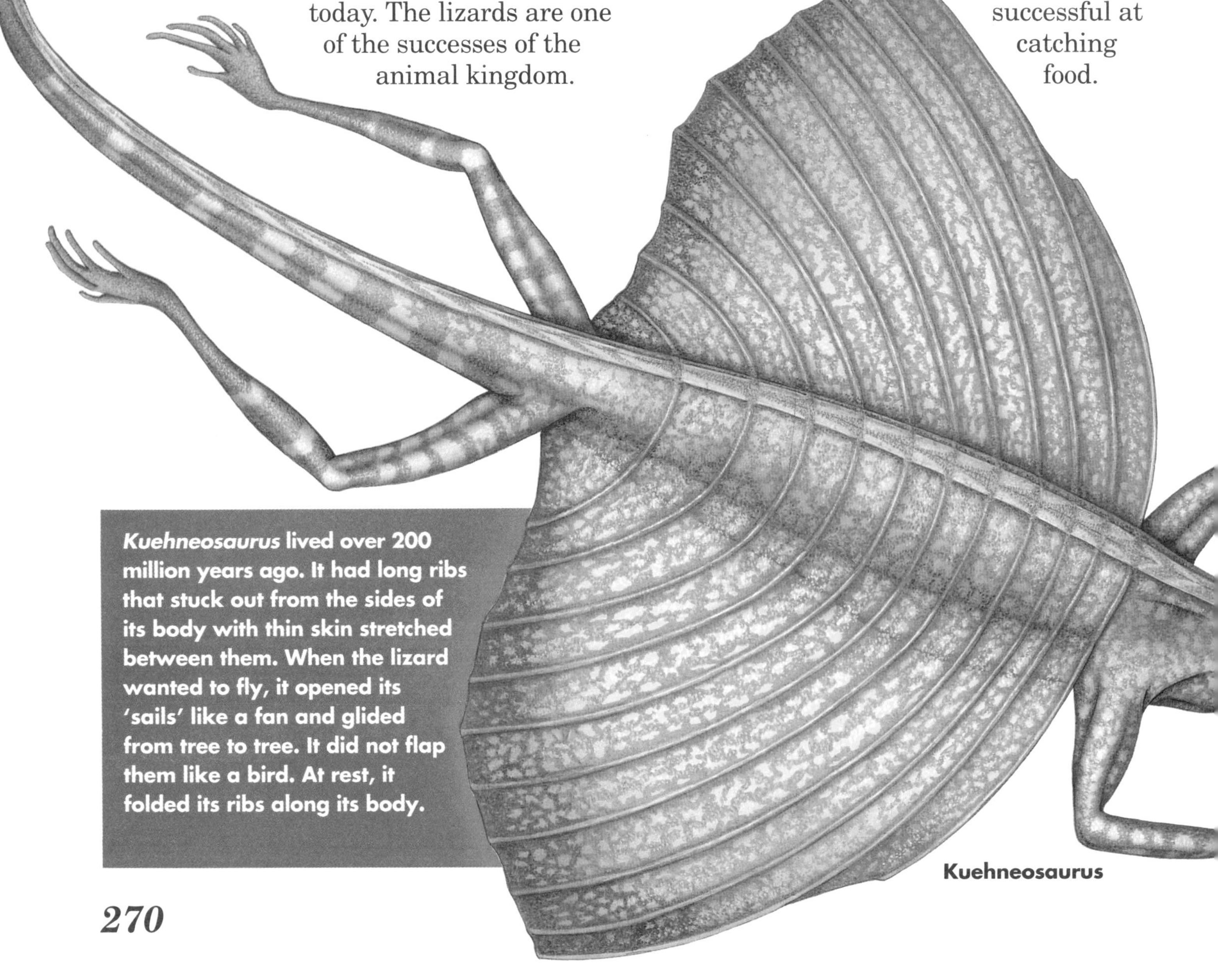

***Kuehneosaurus* lived over 200 million years ago. It had long ribs that stuck out from the sides of its body with thin skin stretched between them. When the lizard wanted to fly, it opened its 'sails' like a fan and glided from tree to tree. It did not flap them like a bird. At rest, it folded its ribs along its body.**

Kuehneosaurus

Draco volans

***Draco volans*, a modern lizard, looks very similar to *Kuehneosaurus*. It also has 'sails' of very fine skin, but they stretch between its fore- and hind-limbs. *Draco volans* uses them to glide from tree to tree in the forests of south-east Asia. Its name means 'flying dragon' and its record glide is 15m. That is about as far as 15 adult human paces.**

GLIDING LIZARDS

But some fossils survived. One of them is *Kuehneosaurus* (koo-nee-oh-saw-rus), a lizard that lived over 200 million years ago in the Early Jurassic. It used its sails of skin to glide from tree-top to tree-top searching for insects to eat. Today, there are many gliding lizards in warm countries that look very like *Kuehneosaurus*. One of them is *Draco volans*, a lizard that lives in the tropical forests of south-east Asia.

FRAGILE FOSSILS

Although lizards were alive at the same time as the dinosaurs, they have not left many fossils behind. Most of these prehistoric lizards had fragile skeletons. When they died, the bones broke up or were scattered long before they had a chance to fossilize. Some scientists also think that these lizards of ancient times lived mostly in dry, hilly and rocky places where fossils did not form very easily.

A fossil of an ancient lizard-like reptile.

LIVING LIZARDS

Geckos, iguanas and monitor lizards all shared the Earth with the dinosaurs. But they have succeeded where the dinosaurs failed. When the dinosaurs died out, these kinds of lizard were among the species that survived and they can be found in different parts of the world today.

MODERN MONSTERS

On a small island in Indonesia, a country in south-east Asia, lives Earth's largest lizard, the Komodo dragon. It is a type of monitor lizard that grows up to 3m in length and feeds on animals like monkeys, goats and deer. A giant lizard, very similar to the Komodo dragon, but much larger, stalked through what is now Australia about 2 million years ago. It was called *Megalania priscia.*

Ancient *Megalania priscia* (below) was a terrifying 8m-long lizard – much bigger than the largest lizards alive today. It lived 2 million years ago.

Geckos like this one (above) have been around since the Age of Dinosaurs. They cling to smooth surfaces using hooks on the soles of their feet.

The 3m-long Komodo dragon (below) is the largest lizard alive on Earth today. It has a mouth full of shark-like teeth and can move about quickly.

Megalania priscia

Komodo dragon

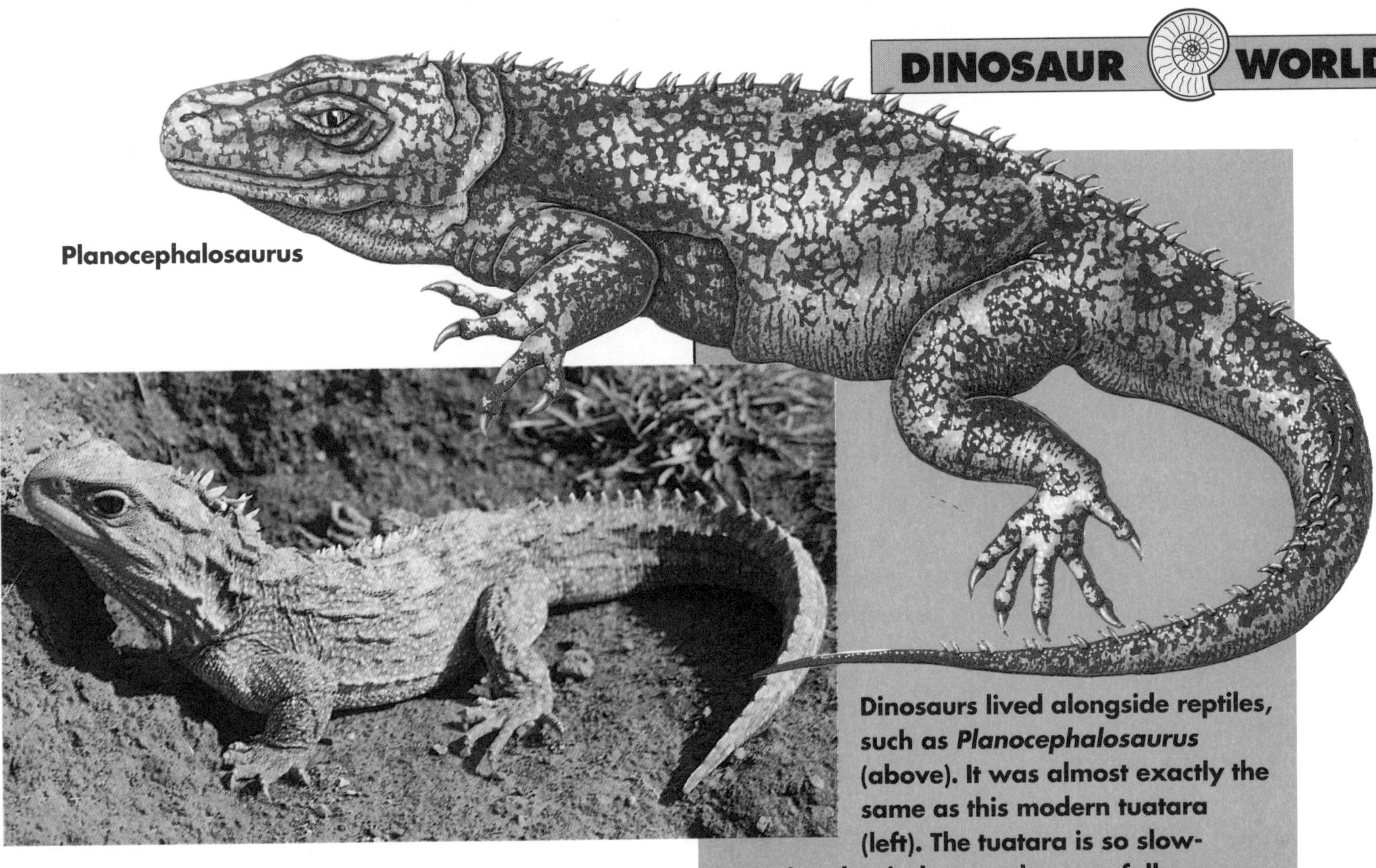

Dinosaurs lived alongside reptiles, such as *Planocephalosaurus* (above). It was almost exactly the same as this modern tuatara (left). The tuatara is so slow-growing that it does not become fully grown until it is about 50 years old and it lives until about 100. It lives life so slowly that it can fall asleep in the middle of a mouthful of food.

LIZARD RELATIVES

The first true lizards appeared on Earth about 250 million years ago – millions of years before the arrival of the dinosaurs. Lizards have some very interesting relatives that belonged to a different branch of the family tree and lived at the same time. They were the lizard-like reptiles and they also lived through the Age of the Dinosaurs.

What is? A LIVING FOSSIL

A living fossil is an animal species that has survived unchanged for millions of years. Its ancestors were alive millions of years ago and its descendants, which are almost identical, are alive today. The tuatara is a living fossil and so is a large fish called a coelacanth. Most other animal species change over long periods of time.

A LIVING FOSSIL

There is still a lizard-like reptile alive today. The tuatara is so rare that it lives only on a few islands off the north coast of New Zealand. Its ancestors, called *Planocephalosaurus* (plan-oh-sef-al-oh-saw-rus), were alive at the time of the dinosaurs. The tuatara has not changed for 200 million years – it is a special type of animal known as a living fossil.

LYING LOW

While dinosaurs ruled, lizards kept a low profile and learned to adapt. Some lizards ruled the seas. These were the mosasaurs, the gigantic lizards that lived in the oceans of the world. But like the dinosaurs, the mosasaurs died out and the lizards that lived on land were left to survive to the present day.

GIANTS OF THE PAST

PARASAUROLOPHUS

A male *Parasaurolophus* lifts its head and huge crest and prepares to raise the alarm. This will warn the other hadrosaurs that their peace is about to be shattered. *Albertosaurus* has appeared on a distant river bank, and any one of these plant-eaters will make an excellent meal for the meat-eater.

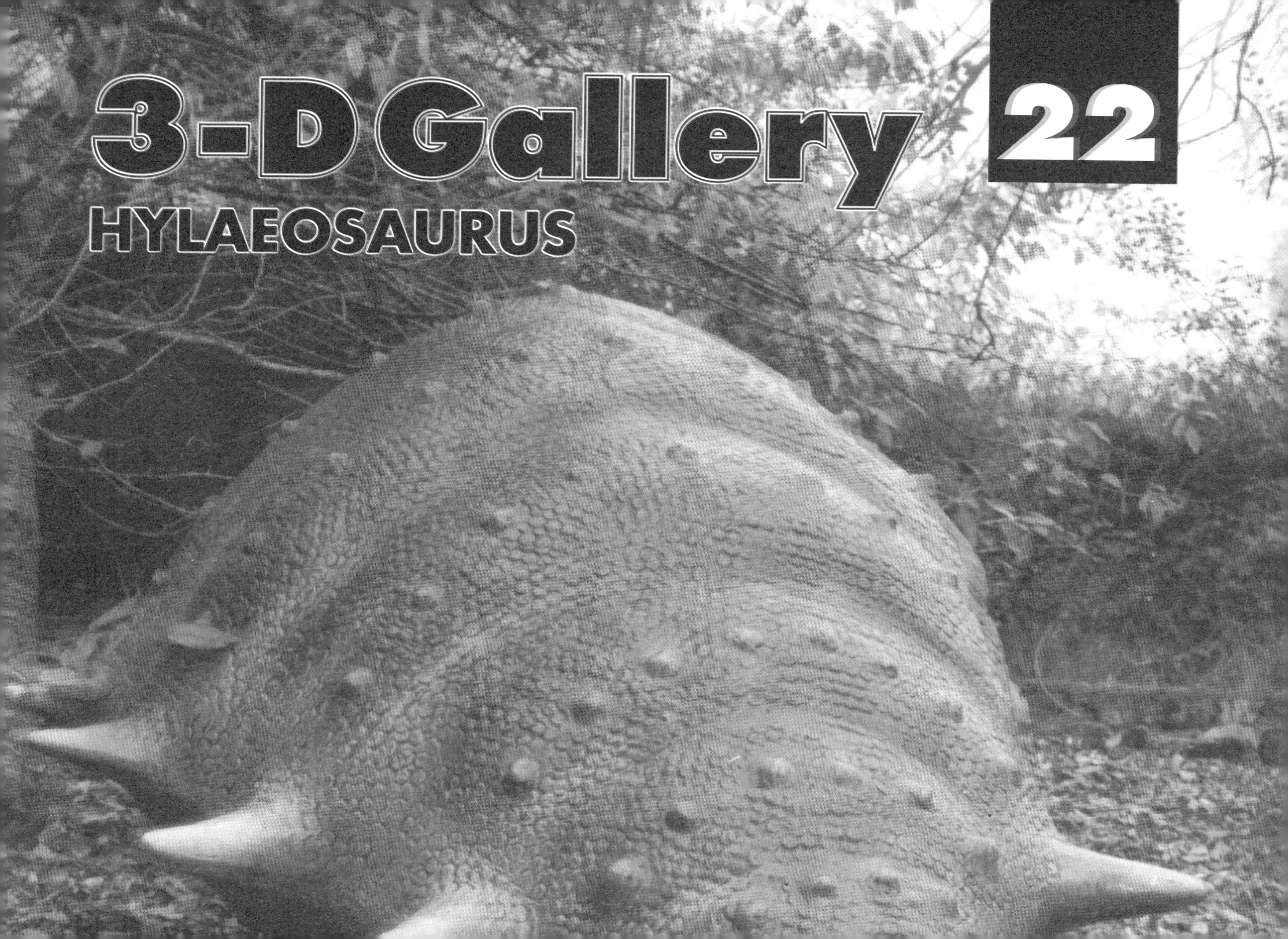

3-D Gallery 22

HYLAEOSAURUS

• Armoured dinosaur with spiked tail
• Lived about 130 million years ago in southern England
• Measured 4m long
• Ate plants

Horns

Whether they were long and threatening or just for show, dinosaurs' horns came in many shapes and sizes.

Armed with an unfriendly display of horns, the ceratopians (horned dinosaurs) looked like prehistoric warriors, but they were not the only dinosaurs with horns, nor were they always looking for a fight.

RHINO DINOS

At a glance, some ceratopians looked like rhinoceroses. They had large horns on their noses and smaller ones on their brows. This group includes *Centrosaurus*, *Monoclonius* and *Styracosaurus*. The upward-pointing nose horns were perfectly placed for spearing the soft underbelly of a tall meat-eater, such as *Tyrannosaurus rex*.

BROW HORNS

Its massive horns and huge bulk made *Triceratops* one of the most powerful plant-eaters. If you were to put one hippopotamus and two cows on the scales, they would weigh as much as one *Triceratops*. The dinosaur belonged to a group that all had horns on their brows. The horns pointed forwards and upwards, protecting the animal from attacks, particularly to its neck or face. *Triceratops* also had nose and cheek horns, but these were much smaller.

Triceratops

Dinosaur horns were made of bone and covered in a layer of horn to protect them. When you look at the fossil skull of a horned dinosaur, you see only the bony part of the horn – the covering of horn has rotted away.

Reconstruction of a *Triceratops'* horn

Centrosaurus had a big nose horn that it used to threaten any predators.

AVOIDING A FIGHT

Most horned dinosaurs were plant-eaters and usually lived a peaceful life in a herd. Although *Triceratops* had horns that were twice as long as a squash racket (1.2m), it probably tried to avoid a fight with an enemy rather than attacking and risking a deadly wound. Like a bull preparing to charge, *Triceratops* would have tucked its head down and waved its horns from side to side, hoping to scare away a predator. *Centrosaurus* may have simply stood sideways on to its opponent, showing off its massive nose horn in the hope that this would frighten off its attacker. Large horns may also have attracted a female.

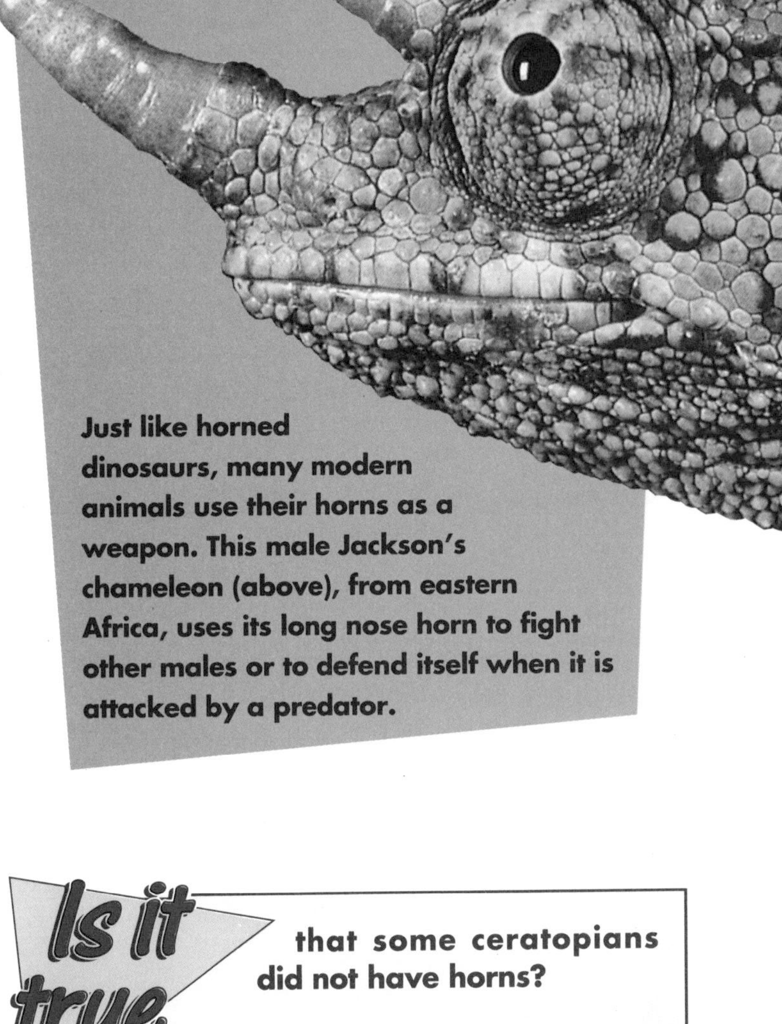

Just like horned dinosaurs, many modern animals use their horns as a weapon. This male Jackson's chameleon (above), from eastern Africa, uses its long nose horn to fight other males or to defend itself when it is attacked by a predator.

FORCED TO FIGHT

Ceratopians probably only got into a fight if they were forced to defend themselves or their herd. Rivals within one herd fought for leadership or for a mate, clashing heads and horns, just like rams do today.

HORNED MEAT-EATER

Ceratopians were not the only dinosaurs with horns. *Carnotaurus*, a meat-eater, had hornlets over its eyes. The male *Carnotaurus* probably had longer horns than the females. Horns of different lengths helped male and female dinosaurs to recognise each other.

Is it true that some ceratopians did not have horns?

Some of the horned dinosaur family (ceratopians) did not have large nose or brow horns. *Pachyrhinosaurus* ('thick-nosed reptile'), which lived in North America, had a thick lump of bone on its enormous head (its skull alone was 1.4m long). The bump was shaped like a moon crater and was probably used to butt rivals.

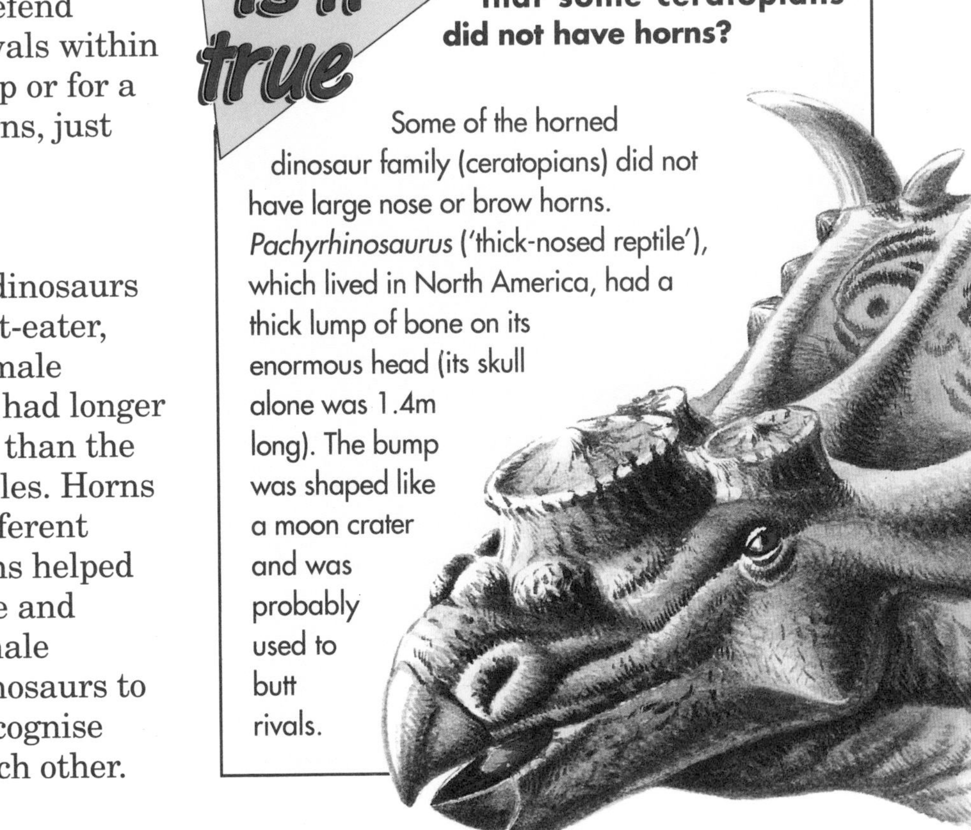

Introducing the thick-heads

With big heads and strong bodies, the pachycephalosaurs ('thick-headed lizards') were built for battering.

For almost 50 years, a tooth was the only evidence that pachycephalosaurs (pack-ee-sef-a-loh-saws) had once walked on Earth. Scientists have now found other parts of pachycephalosaurs. These include skulls or bits of skulls. The experts were amazed at how thick the bone was on the top of the skulls, and gave the dinosaurs their name, which means 'thick-headed lizards'. From the fragments, scientists have discovered much more about these animals.

PACHYCEPHALOSAUR CHECK LIST
- Ate plants
- Extra-thick skull
- Walked on two legs

LITTLE AND LARGE

The giant of the thick-heads was *Pachycephalosaurus* (pack-ee-sef-a-loh-saw-rus). Experts believe it could have grown up to 8m long – about the same length as a 24-seater bus. It was a bit taller than an elephant. Other members of the group were much smaller. *Homalocephale* (hom-al-oh-sef-a-lee) was probably less than 3m long and not much taller than a man. *Stegoceras* (steg-oh-ser-as) was just 2.5m long and about the same height as a horse.

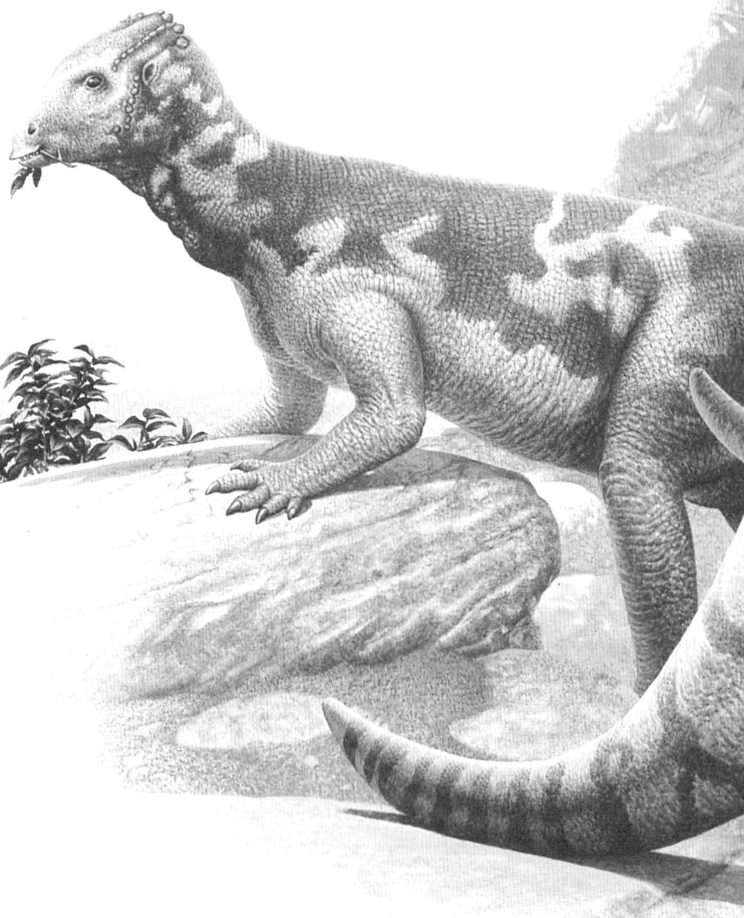

The thick-heads came in many different shapes and sizes. *Pachycephalosaurus*, the giant of the family, was almost three times as tall as *Homalocephale*.

BONE-HEADS

All the thick-heads had big, odd-looking heads. Scientists think that this was because the dinosaurs used their heads like battering rams to attack others or defend themselves.

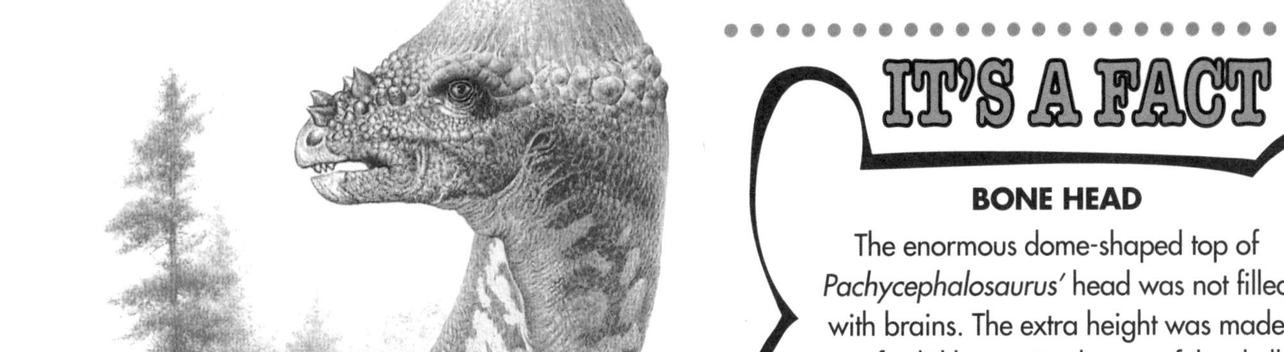

IT'S A FACT

BONE HEAD

The enormous dome-shaped top of *Pachycephalosaurus'* head was not filled with brains. The extra height was made up of solid bone. On the top of the skull, the bone was up to 25cm thick. That is almost as thick as this page is long.

BUILT TO BATTER

The thick-heads were built to batter. Unlike other dinosaurs, their heads were held at an angle to the backbone. The backbone itself was especially strong. When these animals clashed their heads together, the shock of each blow was cleverly absorbed by their bodies, like shock absorbers in a car.

LIFESTYLE

The thick-heads were slow-moving herbivores. Their only protection against meat-eating dinosaurs was their tough skulls. Pachycephalosaurs probably moved around in herds, like modern sheep and goats. Very few fossils have been found. This might be because they lived in rocky hills where it was hard for their skeletons to become fossils.

25CM THICKNESS OF PACHYCEPHALOSAURUS' SKULL

HIGH AND LOW

Pachycephalosaurus had a high, dome-shaped skull, but *Homalocephale's* head had a much lower dome. Other thick-heads are also divided into high- or low-domed types. Because of this, some experts think there may have been two separate groups of thick-heads. But other experts think that all pachycephalosaurs belonged to the same group.

NORTH AND SOUTH

Most pachycephalosaurs roamed North America and Asia. But one has been discovered much further south. *Majungatholus* was discovered on Madagascar, an island off Africa.

OUT OF THE ROCK

Prenocephale was one of the high-domed thick-heads. The bulging shape of its skull was seen sticking out of a rock in the Gobi Desert, in Mongolia, in 1970. The palaeontologists who found it could also see the row of bony knobs around its skull and its steep, narrow face.

A *Prenocephale* skull sticks out of a rock in the Gobi Desert, Mongolia, where it was discovered in 1970. The skull is facing away from the man and the photograph is taken from the top of the skull.

***Prenocephale's* smooth, high-domed skull, sloping forehead and bony frill can also be seen.**

LATE ARRIVALS

The thick-heads lived at the end of the Age of the Dinosaurs. *Stegoceras* was one of the earliest members of the group. It roamed North America about 80 million years ago. *Homalocephale* lived in southern and central Asia 70 million years ago. *Pachycephalosaurus* was not only the biggest thick-head, it was also the last. It was the only member of its group living when dinosaurs became extinct 66 million years ago.

PACHYCEPHALOSAUR CHECK LIST

- Short arms
- Long, stiff tail
- Strong legs

HEAD-TO-HEAD

The thick-heads all used their heads as weapons, but they probably used them in different ways. Scientists believe the high-domed types head-butted each other in tests of strength, just as mountain sheep and goats do today. The skulls of the low-domed types were weaker. They probably pushed their attackers aside with their heads like the modern marine iguanas (lizards that live on land and in the sea) of the Galapagos Islands, off the coast of South America.

WINNER TAKES ALL

Most of the head-to-head fights were probably with other thick-heads. When two males of the same size met during the mating season, they battled against each other to see which was the strongest. The winner then became leader of the herd and owner of all the females.

Is it true that a very early thick-head has been found?

A tiny piece of skull from a dinosaur called *Yaverlandia* was found on the Isle of Wight, in Britain. It lived in the Early Cretaceous Period and had a slightly thicker skull than most other dinosaurs. This small fragment is the only evidence that scientists have, so they cannot prove that *Yaverlandia* was definitely a pachycephalosaur.

Two marine iguanas challenge each other to a shoving match (above). These animals push each other using the fronts of their heads, just like low-domed thick-heads (inset).

Bighorn sheep are more violent (left). During the mating season, they crash skulls. High-domed thick-heads probably clashed heads, too (inset).

3-D Gallery 42

TRICERATOPS V DASPLETOSAURUS

Terror of Cretaceous times *Daspletosaurus* has snatched a baby *Triceratops* from its herd. The furious mother leads the others in a charge against the greedy predator. As the *Triceratops* mother smashes into *Daspletosaurus*, the baby flies out of its jaws.

Dr. David Norman of Cambridge University answers your dinosaur questions
ASK THE EXPERT

Did dinosaurs blink?

Dinosaurs had eyelids that would have allowed them to blink just as humans do. The best evidence to prove this are fossils of some of the heavily armoured ankylosaurs. They show that these dinosaurs had bony eyelids. When they closed their eyes they were protected behind hard, shutter-like lids.

Did dinosaurs shed their skin like lizards do?

Lizards shed complete layers of skin from time to time. Dinosaurs are not close relatives of lizards and probably did not grow their skin in the same way. Outer layers of their skin would have been shed in bits and pieces like crocodile skin.

Did any dinosaurs give birth to live young?

So far, we do not have any evidence that dinosaurs bore live young. I think it is likely that all dinosaurs laid shelled eggs, in the same way that birds lay eggs.

How did dinosaurs keep clean?

Dinosaurs did not have the sort of skin that needed to be kept especially clean. Neither did they have fur nor feathers, so they did not need to groom or preen themselves as mammals and birds do today. Dinosaur skin was tough and scaly. As with modern-day reptiles, any dirt would simply have stuck to the dinosaur's body until it rubbed off, or was shed along with skin scales. Dinosaurs would have shed their scales all the time as new ones grew to replace them.

DINOSAURS!
DISCOVER THE GIANTS OF THE PREHISTORIC WORLD

COELOPHYSIS

Nimble *Coelophysis,* an early dinosaur, may have been a cannibal.

Although *Coelophysis* was almost as tall as a man, it was lightly built for speed and agility. Lizards, amphibians and flying insects all fell victim to this dinosaur.

DINOSAUR GRAVEYARD

In 1947, an expedition to New Mexico, USA, made an amazing discovery. On a property called Ghost Ranch, hundreds of skeletons of *Coelophysis* were found lying across one another.

SUDDEN DEATH

The find was particularly exciting because it included *Coelophysis* of different ages and sizes. For the experts, it proved that this dinosaur lived in large groups. The whole herd seemed to have died at the same time. This suggests that their deaths were caused by a sudden calamity, such as a flash flood that overpowered them.

SPEEDY SPRINTER

Almost as tall as an adult human, *Coelophysis* moved quickly on two slim legs. Rather like a modern-day cat, this agile dinosaur chased after anything small that moved. *Coelophysis* had hollow bones – and its name means 'hollow form'. Its skull was lightly built with holes in the sides.

Each of *Coelophysis'* two short arms, which were about half the length of its legs, ended in clawed fingers. Its prey would have had to struggle hard to escape its clutches.

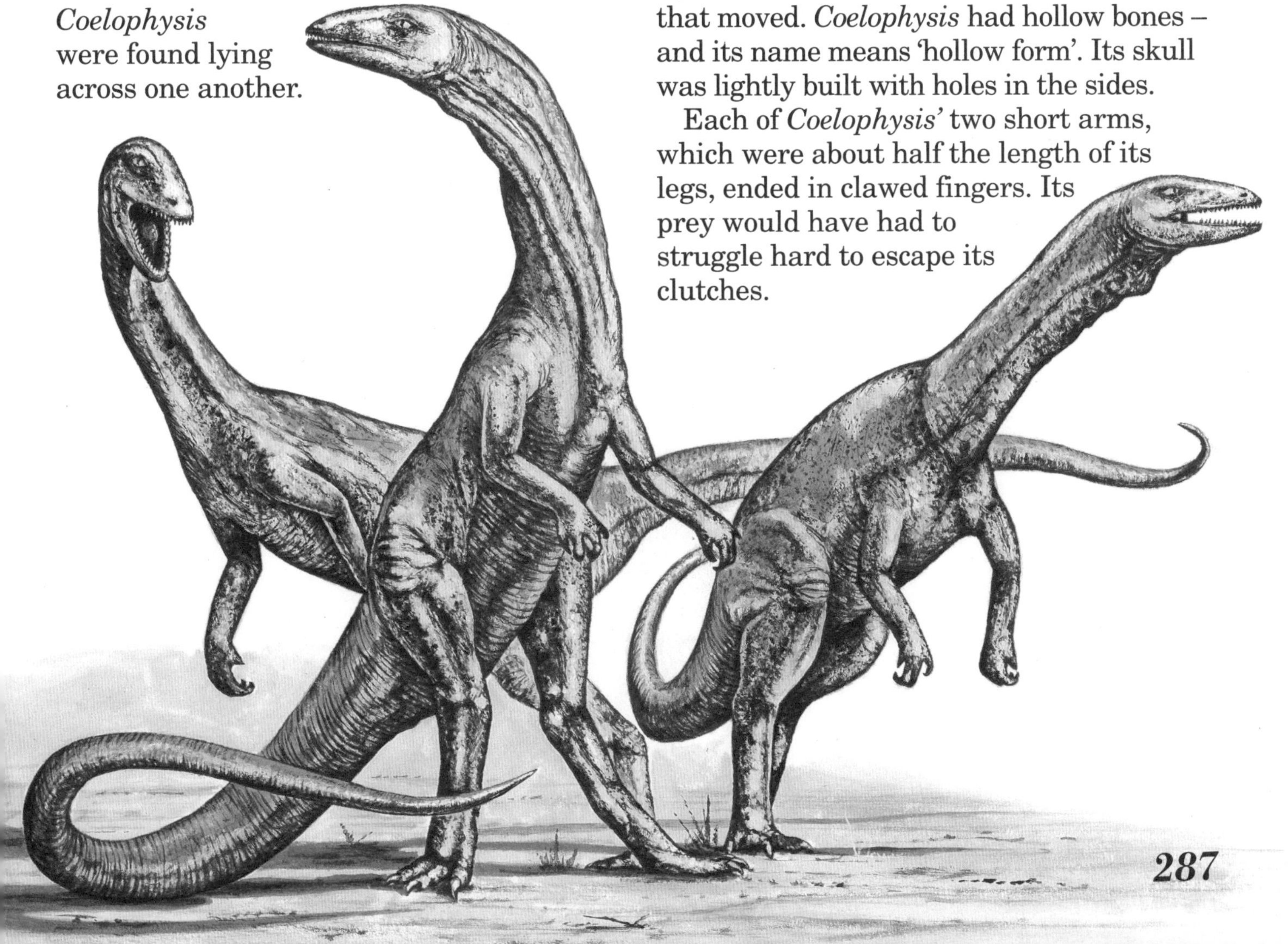

CANNIBAL CLUES

Inside the rib-cages of some of the adults were skeletons of young *Coelophysis.* At first, scientists thought they were babies that were almost ready to be born. However, as dinosaurs laid eggs rather than bearing live young, these skeletons may have been the remains of the dinosaurs' last meal! The skeletons were certainly too big to have come from inside an egg. Although it seems strange, there is a good chance that *Coelophysis* ate not only small lizards, reptiles and mammals, but its own young as well.

Nobody really knows why *Coelophysis* ate its offspring (below). It is possible that there was a sudden shortage of food and the rest of the herd needed to eat the young to stay alive. Some creatures in the modern animal world eat their young, but only if they have to.

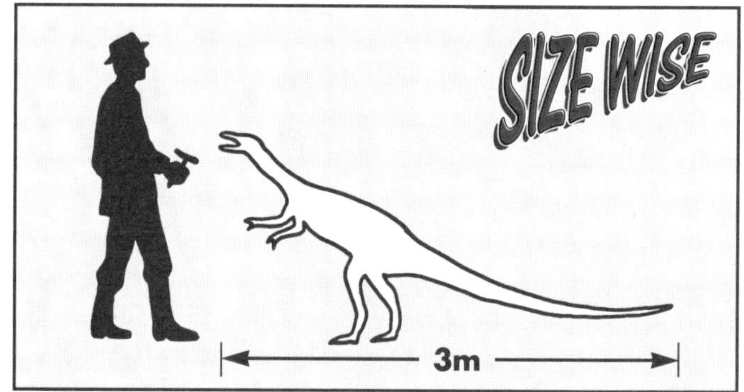

MONSTER FACTS

- **NAME:** *Coelophysis* (seel-oh-fy-sis) means 'hollow form'
- **SIZE:** up to 3m long and about 1.5m high
- **FOOD:** meat – small reptiles and insects. Also possibly its own young
- **LIVED:** 210 million years ago in the Late Triassic in south-western and eastern USA

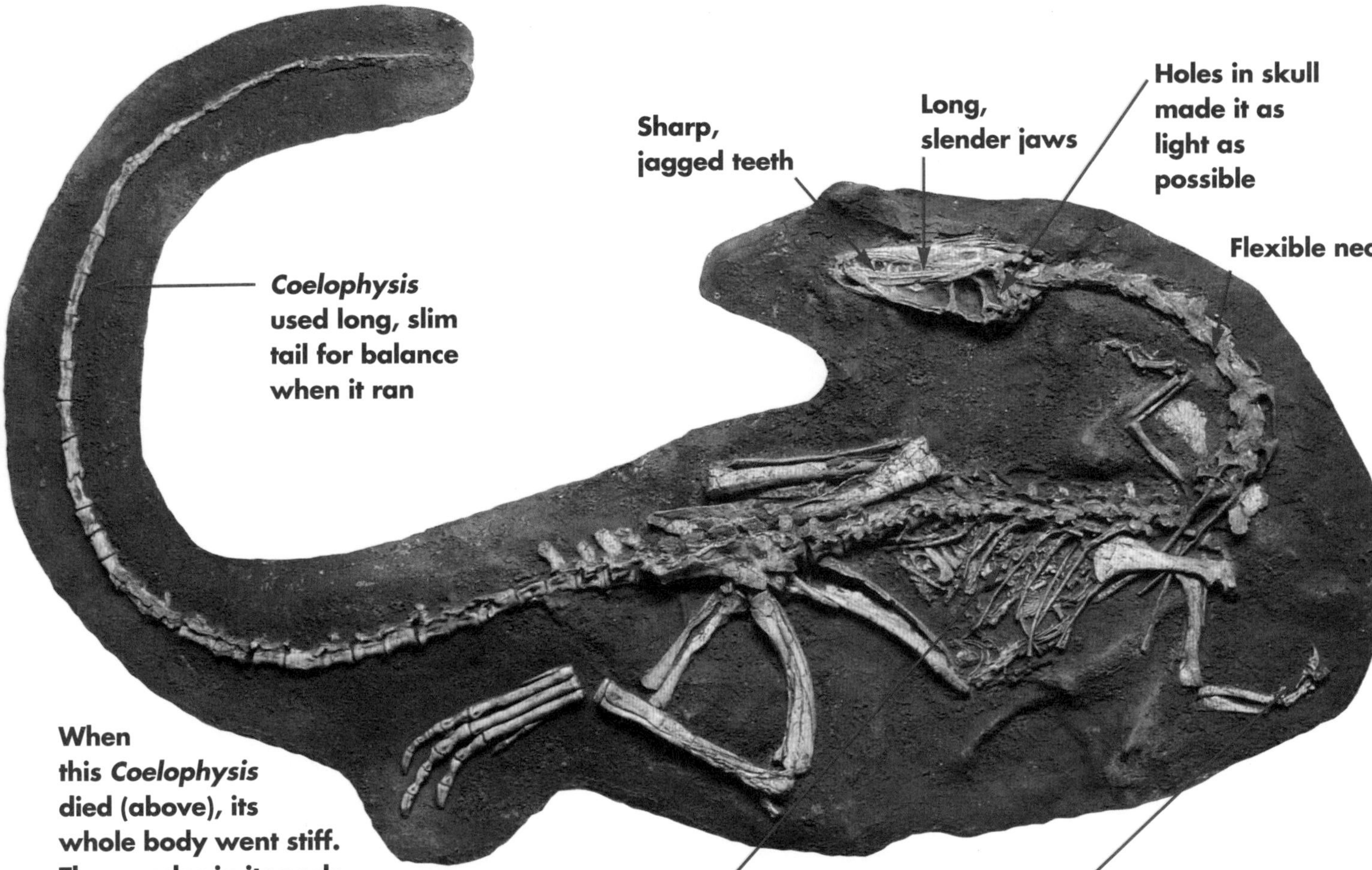

Holes in skull made it as light as possible

Long, slender jaws

Sharp, jagged teeth

Flexible neck

***Coelophysis* used long, slim tail for balance when it ran**

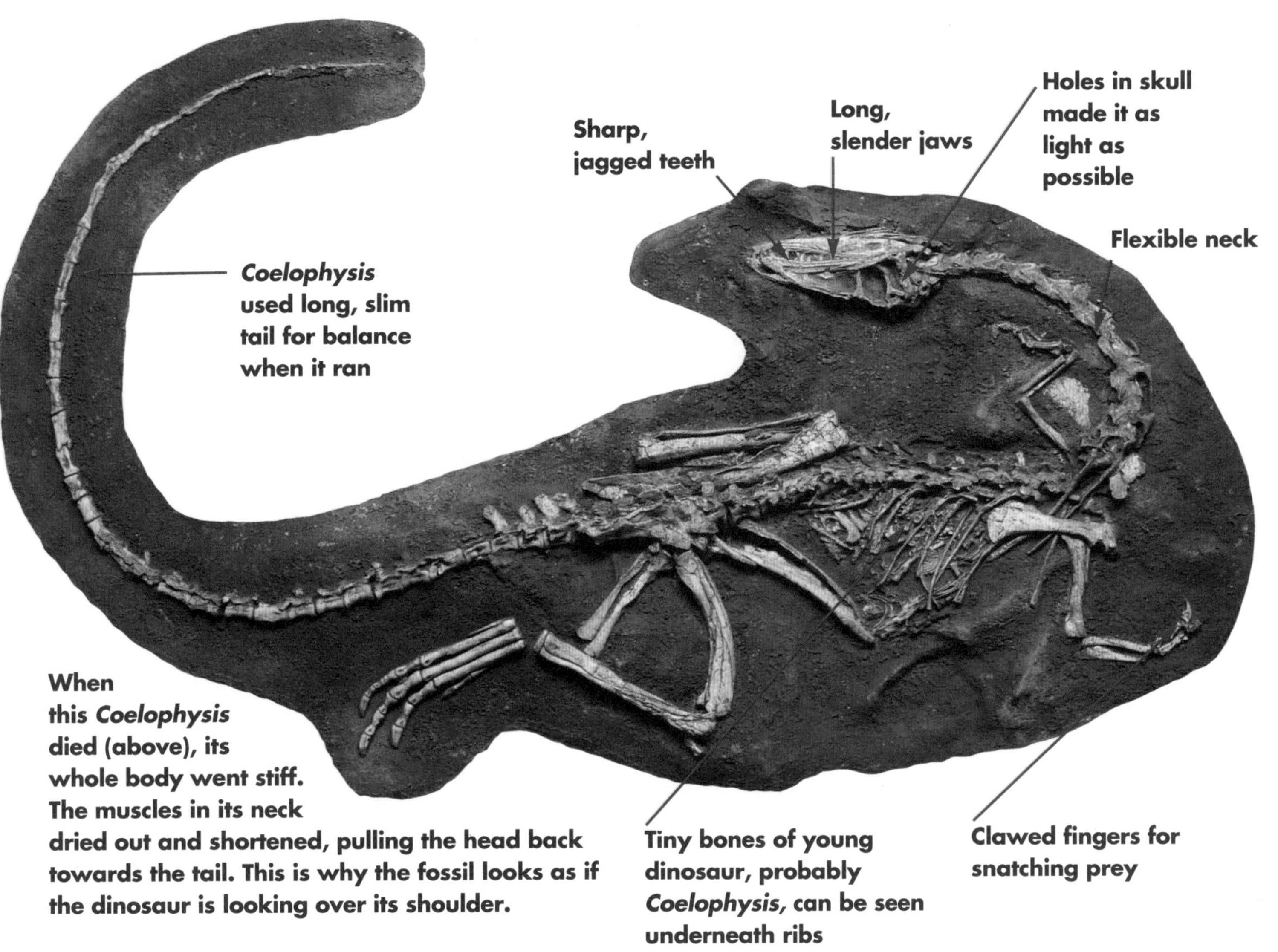

When this *Coelophysis* died (above), its whole body went stiff. The muscles in its neck dried out and shortened, pulling the head back towards the tail. This is why the fossil looks as if the dinosaur is looking over its shoulder.

Tiny bones of young dinosaur, probably *Coelophysis*, can be seen underneath ribs

Clawed fingers for snatching prey

SNAKE NECK

So that it could spot prey, *Coelophysis* had large eyes and a long, snake-like neck, which was flexible enough to move around quickly. Its head was long and low and its jaws held small, sharp, needle-like teeth with jagged edges.

PERFECTLY PRESERVED

So many skeletons were found at Ghost Ranch that scientists had to be careful not to muddle up the bones of each *Coelophysis*. Many of the jumbled bones were eventually covered up so that two perfect examples of *Coelophysis* stood out from the rest. Copies of these skeletons can be seen today in many dinosaur museums throughout the world.

Is it true that some modern-day animals eat their young?

Although it seems cruel, some of today's animals kill their young. They do this because they have to. If there are too many mouths to feed and not enough food, the youngest and weakest in the animal group will be killed and eaten to save the adults, which can go on to breed again. When a new male takes over control of a pride of lions, it sometimes kills the young so that it can mate with a female and produce its own young. Golden hamsters, when kept in cages, may eat their young if they are disturbed.

HOMALOCEPHALE

When the mating season came round, *Homalocephale* had head-to-head pushing contests to see which was the strongest in the herd.

Scientists have a good picture of what this dinosaur looked like as much of its skeleton has been found. *Homalocephale* was about as long as a large male lion and would have stood just above the waist height of a human. It walked on two legs, ate plants and lived in small herds, like modern sheep.

MONSTER FACTS

- **NAME:** *Homalocephale* (hom-al-oh-sef-a-lee) means 'flat head'
- **SIZE:** 3m long and about 1m high
- **FOOD:** low-growing plants
- **LIVED:** 72 million years ago in the Late Cretaceous Period in China and Mongolia

LEVEL-HEADED

Homalocephale is a member of a family of flat-headed dinosaurs. Its broad, thick skull had an important use. When two *Homalocephale* met, they pushed their knobbly heads against each other. It was their way of deciding which of them was in charge. Their strong back and long hind legs worked like cars' shock absorbers, taking the strain of these violent contests.

WIDE HIPS

Unlike many other dinosaurs, *Homalocephale* had very wide hip bones. This led some scientists to suggest that it may not have laid eggs like other dinosaurs, but gave birth to live young instead.

SALTASAURUS

The discovery of this dinosaur was exciting – it was the first plant-eating giant known to have armour.

Longer than a bus, *Saltasaurus* lived on land, but enjoyed an occasional wallow in water like elephants today. This sauropod is known from five incomplete skeletons that were found in the late 1970s.

HUNDREDS OF STUDS

When *Saltasaurus* was found, there were hundreds of bony studs lying by it. Some were as small as a fingernail and others were bigger than a palm of an adult hand.

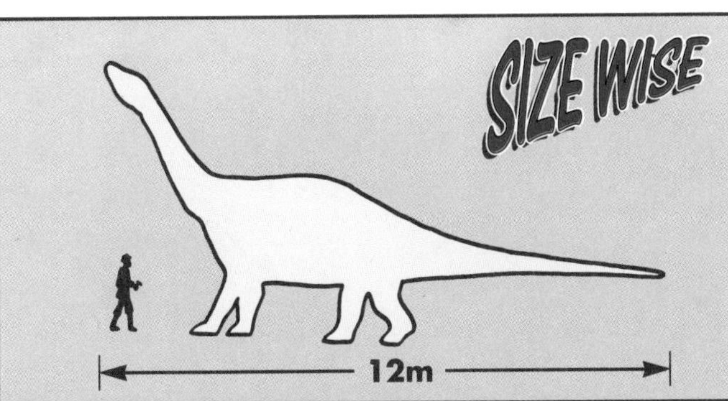

MONSTER FACTS

- **NAME:** *Saltasaurus* (salt-a-saw-rus) means 'reptile from Salta', after the place where its remains were discovered
- **SIZE:** 12m long
- **FOOD:** plants and leaves from tall trees
- **LIVED:** 70 – 66 million years ago in the Late Cretaceous in Argentina

BUMPY BODY

The studs were part of the dinosaur's armour. They showed scientists that *Saltasaurus'* body was scattered with round, bony plates. In between these were hundreds of small, knobbly studs for added protection.

TOUGH TAIL

Protected by its armour, *Saltasaurus* browsed among the tree-tops. It reared up on long hind legs to reach food, using its flexible tail for support.

Monster lizards of the deep

Clidastes

About 100 million years ago, giant lizards called mosasaurs ruled the oceans of the world.

The fierce hunters of the Late Cretaceous seas were not fish, they were lizards. Mosasaurs (mo-za-saws) evolved from *Opetiosaurus* (o-pet-ee-oh-saw-rus), a relation of today's monitor lizard, into 'monsters' like the ones on this page.

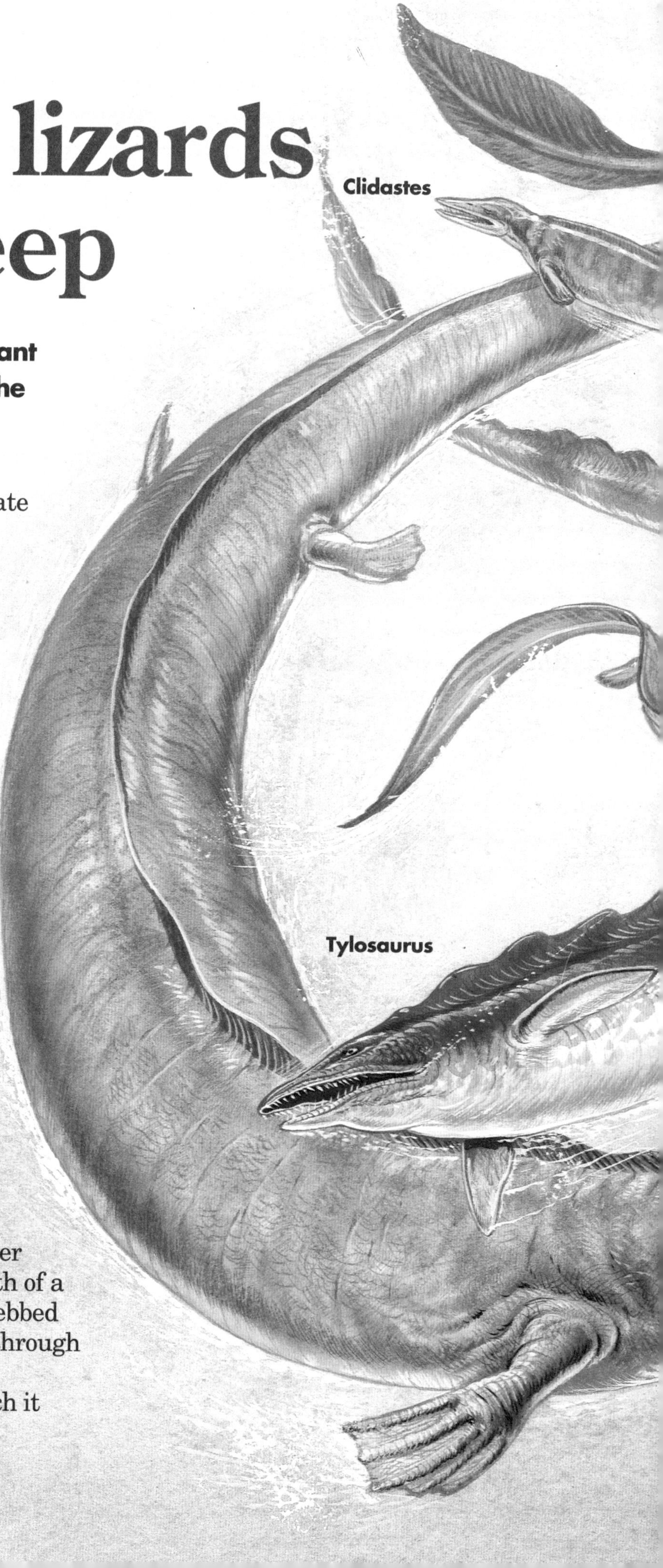

NARROW HEAD

An early mosasaur, *Clidastes* (kly-das-teez), was one of the smallest members of the family. Measuring about 3.5m long, its slim body and narrow head made it streamlined. With a slender tail ending in a broad flipper, *Clidastes* was a fast swimmer. Its flippers were only slightly webbed, so it would not have been particularly good at turning in the water.

Tylosaurus

KILLER-SIZED

Platecarpus (plat-ee-car-pus), another early mosasaur, was about the length of a killer whale (4m). Equipped with webbed flippers and a finned tail, it moved through the water in snake-like movements. *Platecarpus* ate fish and squid, which it snapped up in sharp-toothed jaws.

SPEEDY TAIL

Plotosaurus (plo-toe-saw-rus), meaning 'swimming lizard', lived in the seas that once covered modern-day California, USA. This lizard built up speed by swinging its broad tail fin from side to side in powerful sweeps. It steered a course through the water using solid flippers. *Plotosaurus'* lungs were efficient and the oxygen it breathed provided the energy it needed to sprint after any prey that strayed across its path.

Platecarpus

BIGGER THAN T REX

Hainosaurus (hane-oh-saw-rus) was probably a savage killer. It was longer than land-bound *T rex,* which grew up to 14m in length, and must have eaten lots of food to get the energy it needed. Like modern sharks, it regularly shed teeth to make way for newer, sharper ones. An extra set of teeth grew from the roof of its throat and acted like a trap for unwary fish.

Plotosaurus

MASSIVE MOUTH

Like other mosasaurs, *Tylosaurus* (tie-lo-saw-rus) had a large head and an impressive pair of jaws. Its body was 8m long, twice the length of today's killer whale, and its flippers were well developed to help *Tylosaurus* move around in the water in search of smaller prey.

The prehistoric oceans would have been a dangerous place for a diver. Massive *Hainosaurus* was almost 10 times as long as an adult woman.

Finding Mosasaurus

The first mosasaur was found over 200 years ago by some men digging by candlelight in a chalk quarry.

What they found was the fossil of a huge jaw. It was discovered in the valley of the River Meuse, in Holland. Because of this, the animal was called 'Meuse lizard', or *Mosasaurus,* and gave its name to the family group.

A NEW THOUGHT

It was a French scientist named Georges Cuvier who decided that the jaw belonged to a sea creature that was no longer alive. Cuvier was one of the first people to suggest that species die out. We now know that different kinds of animals die out all the time, but in those days some scientists thought that this was nonsense.

A WORLD-WIDE SUCCESS

Since the discovery in Holland all those years ago, many other mosasaur fossils have been found across the world. It now seems likely that mosasaurs ruled the Late Cretaceous seas of modern-day North America, Africa and New Zealand, as well as Europe. These world-wide finds have meant that experts have been able to put together a detailed picture of how mosasaurs lived.

BENDY BACKBONE

Mosasaurus had about 100 backbones – four times as many as a human. Each vertebra was joined to the next by a flexible ball-and-socket joint, allowing *Mosasaurus* to move in the water like eels.

Mosasaurus **was built to hunt fish and glide through the water. It had a flat head, short neck, long teeth and a special jointed jaw to help it swallow big fish.**

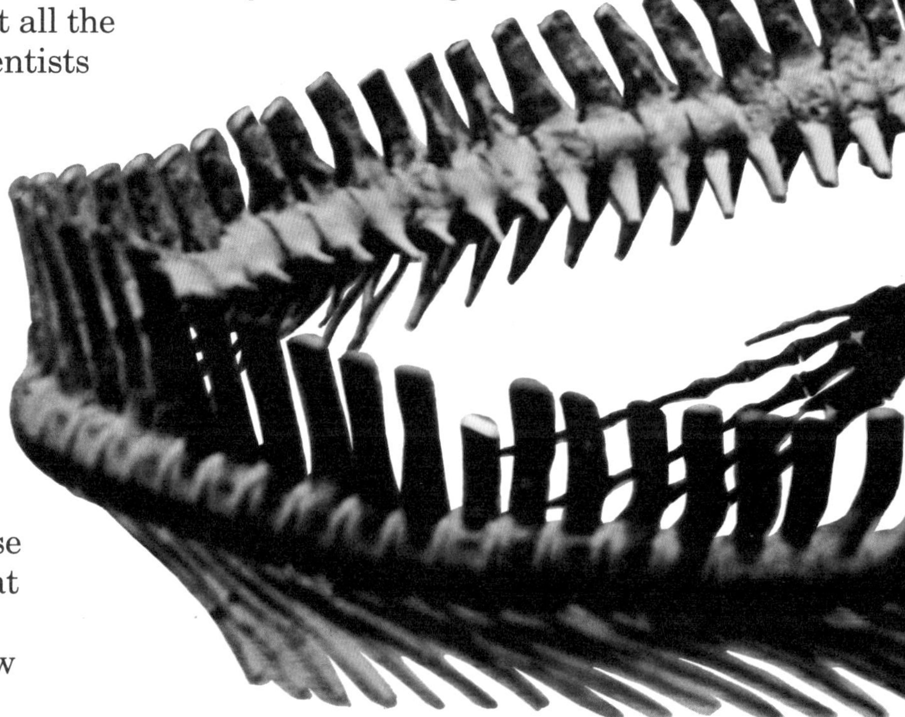

Baron Cuvier (left) 'invented' the idea of extinct animals and has since become known as the father of modern palaeontology. In spite of modern technology, many of his methods are still used. Today, we know that changing conditions cause animals to become extinct all the time.

***Mosasaurus* skeleton**

OPEN WIDER

Like other mosasaurs, *Mosasaurus* had special jaws. Half way along its lower jaw was an extra joint. This let it expand its jaws to cope with big mouthfuls of food. Its lower jaw not only dropped lower, but moved out sideways too. This meant that *Mosasaurus* rarely bit off more than it could chew. Monitor lizards and snakes still have this special jaw hinge. Snakes can swallow mice and rats in one go.

CURVED FANGS

Bedded into these special jaws were rows of teeth that curved backwards. They were sharp enough to cut through any fish that *Mosasaurus* caught. As one tooth wore down another grew in its place, just like sharks' teeth today.

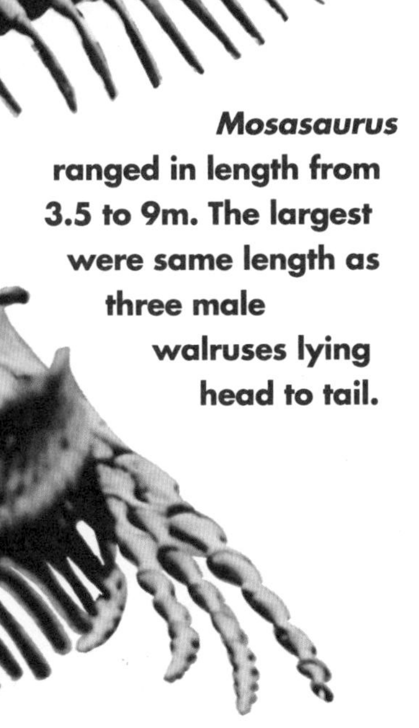

***Mosasaurus* ranged in length from 3.5 to 9m. The largest were same length as three male walruses lying head to tail.**

Is it true that a schoolboy on holiday once found the living fossil of a mosasaur?

In 1983, a schoolboy from Britain found the carcass of a sea creature while on holiday in Gambia, Africa. He described it like this: 'Its body was large, with no blow-hole and no distinct neck, and there were two flippers behind its head and two in the pelvic region.' Unfortunately, he did not take any photographs of the animal, so experts cannot tell what it might have been. However, some think it was a living fossil of a mosasaur. The mystery monster will probably never be identified.

A herd of *Coelophysis* scuttle through the dense Triassic undergrowth. They leap nimbly over fallen logs and plants on their slender, muscular legs. Some members of the group glance around, keeping a look out for predators, or a tasty insect to snap up.

COELOPHYSIS

3-D Gallery 23

PROTOCERATOPS

- **Four-legged dinosaur with bony frill**
- **Lived about 80 million years ago in China and Mongolia**
- **Measured 1.8m long**
- **Ate plants**

A hip discovery

Dinosaurs are divided into two major groups because of the difference in the shape of their hip bones.

Until about 100 years ago, scientists thought that one dinosaur was much like the next. That is, until 1887, when Professor Harry Govier Seeley made an important discovery. He saw that there were two basic groups of dinosaur. And the difference between them was – their hips!

A GIANT LEAP

The hip bones of one group of dinosaurs were a different shape from the hip bones of the other. This really was a big discovery. It meant that scientists could arrange all the different types of dinosaurs into two groups, or 'orders'. An order is one of the names that scientists give to a specific group of animal.

NAMING THE GROUPS

It is important for scientists to classify (arrange) animals in different groups so that they can study them more easily. Modern-day animals are put into groups, too. The orders that Seeley discovered are known as 'saurischia', which means lizard-hipped, and 'ornithischia', which means bird-hipped.

Stegosaurus **was an ornithischian, or bird-hipped dinosaur.**

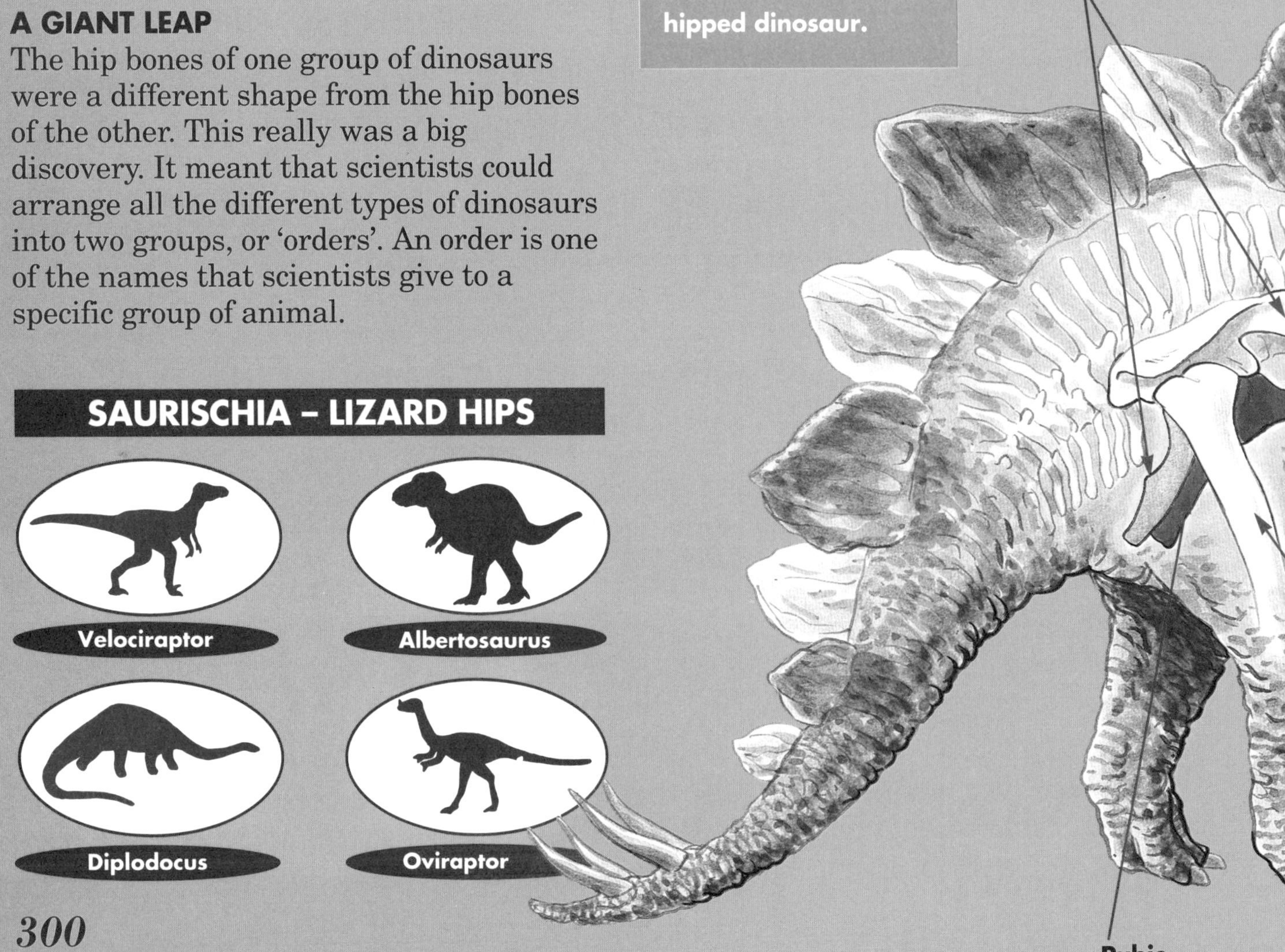

LIZARD HIPS
The saurischia (saw-riss-kee-a) were named because their hip bones were similar to those of lizards. Their front hip bone, or pubis, pointed forward.

BIRD HIPS
The ornithischia (or-ni-thiss-kee-a) were given their name because their hip bones were more like those of birds. The pubis pointed backward.

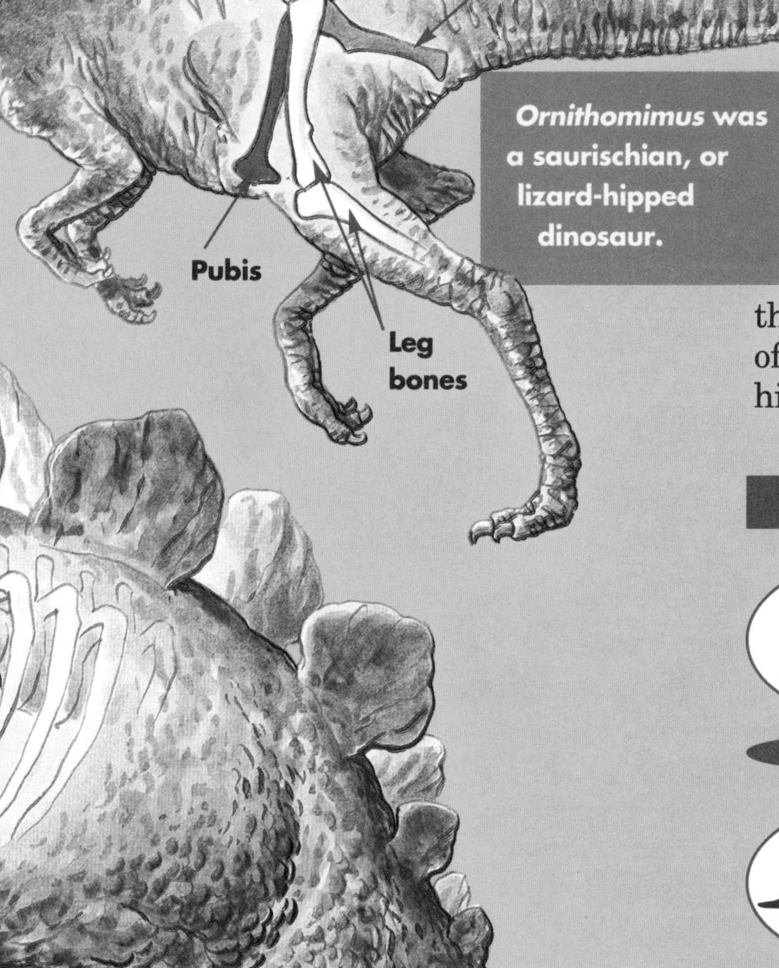

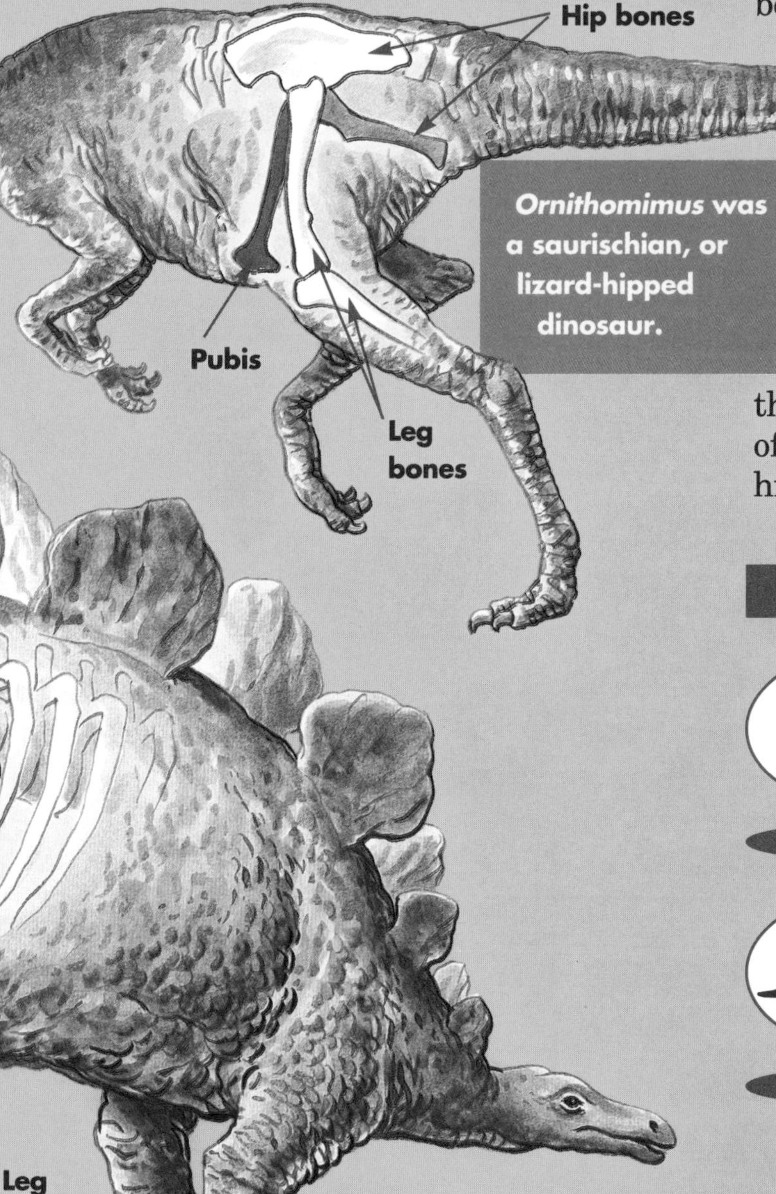

Ornithomimus was a saurischian, or lizard-hipped dinosaur.

NOT ALL THE SAME
The dinosaurs in each of the two orders did not look alike – they did not even walk on the same number of legs. The lizard-hipped group were either two-footed meat-eaters (theropods) like *Tyrannosaurus rex* and *Albertosaurus,* or huge four-footed plant-eaters such as *Diplodocus.*

SUCCESSFUL BIRD HIPS
The bird-hipped dinosaurs all had horny beaks. Some, such as *Hypsilophodon*, walked on two legs and were lightly built so that they could run fast. Others, like *Triceratops,* were much heavier and walked on four legs. They were different from the lizard hips in other ways, too. Ornithischians were herbivores, which meant that they ate only plants. At the end of the Age of the Dinosaurs, there were more bird-hipped than lizard-hipped dinosaurs.

ORNITHISCHIA – BIRD HIPS

Stegosaurus

Stygimoloch

Triceratops

Edmontonia

Iguanodon

The joined-together reptiles

Heavily armoured from head to tail, the ankylosaurs ('joined-together reptiles') were the tanks of the dinosaur world.

These fearsome-looking dinosaurs had bones in their skin that fitted together like a suit of armour. So they were called ankylosaurs (an-ky-loh-saws), which means 'joined-together reptiles'.

TWO FAMILIES

There were two families of ankylosaurs: the nodosaurids (no-do-saw-rids) and the ankylosaurids (an-ky-loh-saw-rids). All the dinosaurs pictured here belong to the nodosaurid family.

FIRST ON THE SCENE

The first nodosaurid lived 180 million years ago, during the Middle Jurassic Period. The first ankylosaurid did not arrive on the Earth until 85 million years later.

Nodosaurus

Hylaeosaurus

Polacanthus

NODOSAURID CHECK LIST
- **Walked on all four feet**
- **Armoured body**
- **Narrow head**
- **Ate plants**

NODOSAURID DATES

Polacanthus lived in the Early Cretaceous, 120 million years ago. *Sauropelta* (saw-roh-pelt-ah) appeared about 10 million years later. *Nodosaurus* (no-do-saw-rus), *Struthiosaurus* (strooth-ee-oh-saw-rus) and *Panoplosaurus* (pan-o-plo-saw-rus) all lived in the Late Cretaceous Period. *Panoplosaurus* was the last known nodosaurid. It was alive right at the end of the Age of the Dinosaurs.

LUMPS AND BUMPS

Very few nodosaurid fossils have been found, but experts think these dinosaurs looked a bit like giant armadillos. They probably had low, barrel-like bodies and short, powerful legs. *Nodosaurus,* which gave its name to the family, means 'knobbly reptile'. All the nodosaurids were covered with knobbly armour. Some were also studded with long, sharp spikes.

IT'S A FACT

DWARF DINOSAURS

Three other types of dinosaur were found in the same area as the nodosaurid *Struthiosaurus* and they were all much smaller than normal dinosaurs. Experts believe these tiny types of dinosaur might all have lived on a small island and over millions of years gradually shrunk to fit their habitat better.

LONG AND SHORT

Sauropelta was the biggest nodosaurid. It was about as tall as a hippopotamus and up to 8m long, about the same length as a 24-seater bus. *Struthiosaurus* was the baby of the family. It was a dwarf dinosaur, no taller than a medium-sized dog and about 1.8m long. That's almost the same length as a man lying down.

BATTLE PLANS

Nodosaurids were peaceful plant-eaters. They were not very big and their bony armour was their only protection against giant meat-eating dinosaurs. When attacked, they might have behaved a bit like the modern-day tortoise, which protects its head and legs by pulling them inside its shell. Nodosaurids did not have shells, but they probably defended themselves by crouching down and huddling under the thick shield of their armour plating. Nodosaurids were heavy and it would have been difficult to tip them over. Most attackers probably gave up and went off in search of easier prey.

All about ankylosaurids

The dinosaurs pictured here are ankylosaurids. Like nodosaurids, they were covered in bony armour, but they also had clubbed tails.

Ankylosaurids had broader heads and fewer spikes than nodosaurids. Most important, they had a powerful weapon – a mighty, club-ended tail. Their tail clubs were huge and heavy, and were made out of chunks of bone joined together into one great lump. An ankylosaurid protected itself by swinging its tail at an attacker. A well-aimed blow could have toppled *T rex*.

IN AT THE END

Ankylosaurids roamed the Earth towards the end of the Age of the Dinosaurs, in the Late Cretaceous. However, they did not all live at the same time. *Euoplocephalus* (you-oh-plo-seff-a-lus) and *Pinacosaurus* (pine-ak-oh-saw-rus) lived 5 million years before *Saichania* (say-kha-nee-ah). *Ankylosaurus* (an-ky-loh-saw-rus) survived until all of the dinosaurs became extinct.

Saichania

HIGH AND LOW
Ankylosaurus was the last and largest ankylosaurid. It was about as tall as an elephant and up to 10m long, about the same as the wing-span of a small plane. *Saichania* grew up to 7m long. *Euoplocephalus* measured 6m long and *Pinacosaurus* was slightly shorter at 5m.

BONE HEADS
Ankylosaurids had incredibly thick head armour made out of huge slabs of bone. *Euoplocephalus* even had bony eyelids. They must have snapped shut a bit like steel shutters to protect its eyes from the claws of an attacker.

Is it true that the ankylosaurids were slow movers?

Probably not. Ankylosaurids were built like tanks, but they did not crawl along. Scientists believe that these dinosaurs were quite quick on their feet. They probably moved more like a modern rhinoceros and could charge at a frightening speed.

WHERE IN THE WORLD?
So far, fossils of ankylosaurids have only been found in Mongolia, China and western North America. However, the nodosaurids lived in many more places. A nodosaurid has even been found in Australia and few dinosaurs have been found in Australia up to now.

But, wherever they lived, all the ankylosaurids ate plants. One of them, *Pinacosaurus,* had such small, weak teeth that it must have survived by eating only the very softest parts of plants.

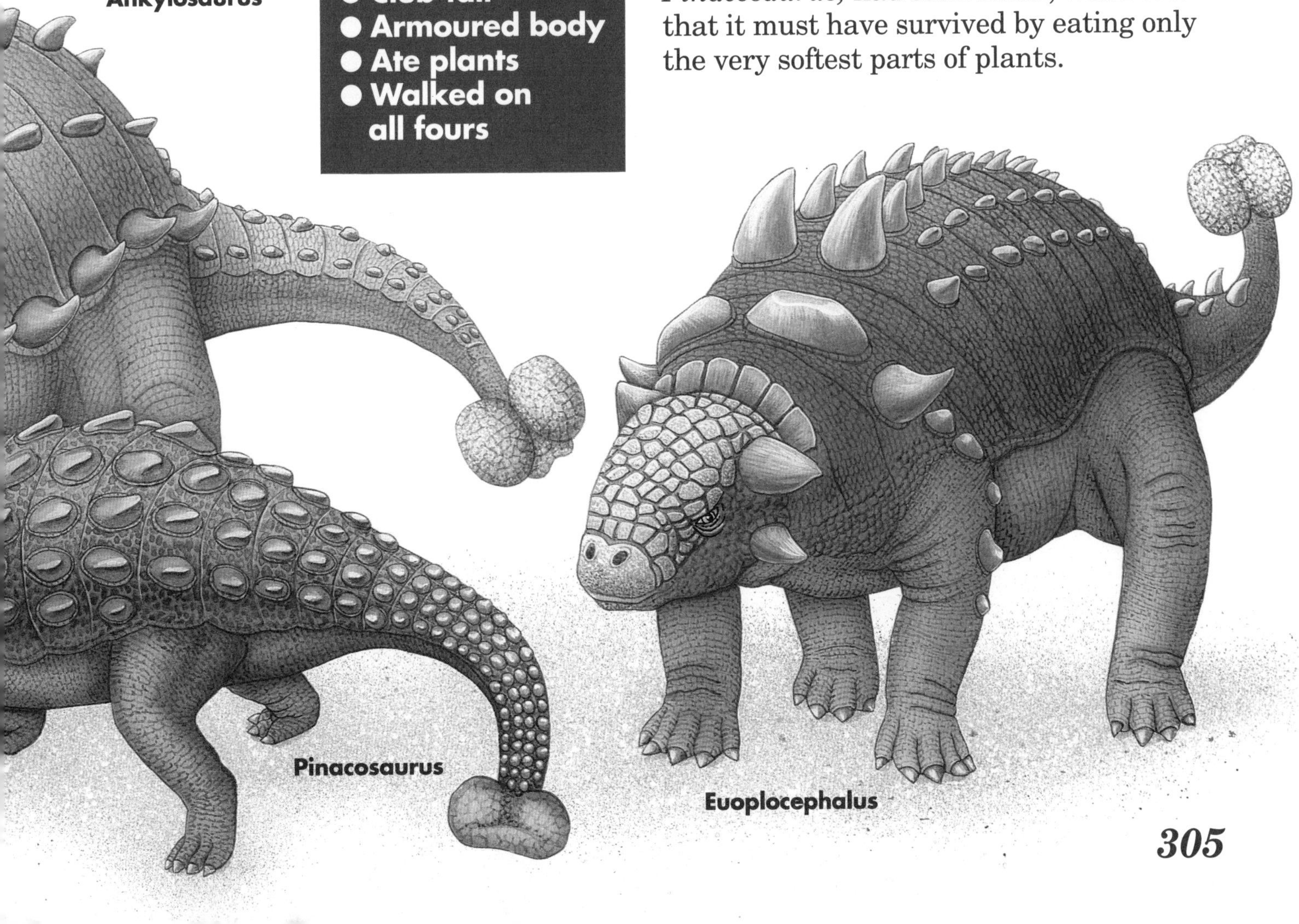

ANKYLOSAURID CHECK LIST
- Broad head
- Club-tail
- Armoured body
- Ate plants
- Walked on all fours

Ankylosaurus

Pinacosaurus

Euoplocephalus

3-D Gallery
43
STEGOSAURUS V CERATOSAURUS

The silence of a North American plain is shattered as two ravenous *Ceratosaurus* pounce for the kill. Once they get their sharp claws and massive teeth into *Stegosaurus'* flesh, the peaceful plant-eater won't stand a chance .

ASK THE EXPERT
Dr. David Norman of Cambridge University answers your dinosaur questions

How did dinosaurs cope with very cold weather?

Quite simply – they did not! When dinosaurs lived, there were no ice-covered North and South Poles and the weather was quite mild. In fact, by today's standards, it was probably uncomfortably hot throughout the world. It would have been cooler nearer the poles and so dinosaurs migrated to these areas to feed in the summer, but travelled back toward the equator during the winter.

Did any dinosaurs eat mammals?

Fast meat-eating dinosaurs, such as *Troodon*, may well have fed on little furry mammals. These dinosaurs had long, agile hands for catching scampering animals. Small mammals did most of their hunting at dusk, so dinosaurs like *Troodon* had eyes as large as saucers for spotting their prey in the failing light.

Could T rex swim?

Although we cannot be absolutely sure, my guess would be yes – *T rex* probably could swim. Despite its huge size, *T rex* was relatively light. It had lots of air-filled spaces in its bones, which would have helped it to float in water, and with its long, powerful back legs it may have been a good swimmer.

What sort of dinosaur had the most bones in its skeleton?

Most dinosaurs had roughly the same number of bones – about 300. This means that tiny *Compsognathus* and massive *Seismosaurus* had about the same number of bones. But the ankylosaurs were the boniest of all the dinosaurs. Some had hundreds of bones welded to their bodies or forming studs on their skin. Spiky *Sauropelta,* for example, may have had as many as 1000 bones.

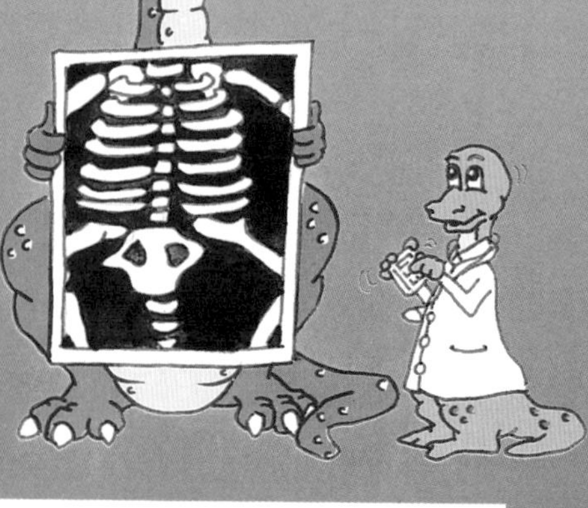

DINOSAURS!
DISCOVER THE GIANTS OF THE PREHISTORIC WORLD

ANATOTITAN

With no claws, spikes or big teeth to protect it from predators, *Anatotitan* probably escaped into deep water.

ecause *Anatotitan* lived in fertile lowland areas, it had lots of juicy shrubs to feed on. Swamps and rivers were dotted about the land, but *Anatotitan* preferred to look for food on solid ground.

PADDLE HANDS

Anatotitan was longer than three cars and as heavy as a rhinoceros. Its size made it too slow to outrun fast meat-eaters. So *Anatotitan* probably plunged into deep water to make a get-away. The bones of its hands were covered with skin that joined its fingers together. *Anatotitan* looked as if it was wearing mittens and used its hands like paddles in the water. A wide tail, lashing from side to side, helped it swim even faster.

BROAD BEAK

With its wide, toothless, duck-like bill, *Anatotitan* could scoop up big mouthfuls of plants. Tough twigs were neatly nipped off by the edge of its beak, which was sharp and horny like a turtle's. Further back in its mouth, up to 1000 strong teeth helped *Anatotitan* munch the twigs and cones until they were soft enough to swallow. Unlike some hadrosaurs, this dinosaur did not have a head crest. Its snout took up half the length of its low, flat head.

DIAMOND TEETH

Anatotitan had small, diamond-shaped teeth. On their own they look weak and feeble. But inside *Anatotitan's* cheeks, hundreds of these little teeth were fused together by a sort of bony cement. This created an immensely strong grinding surface, which worked like a millstone to crush tough conifer twigs and seeds.

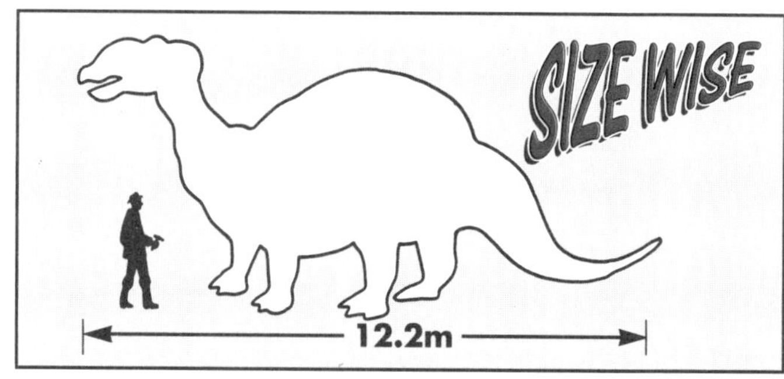

Today's ducks use their bills to nip at plants, too. The skull (below) shows how *Anatotitan* got its name – 'giant duck'.

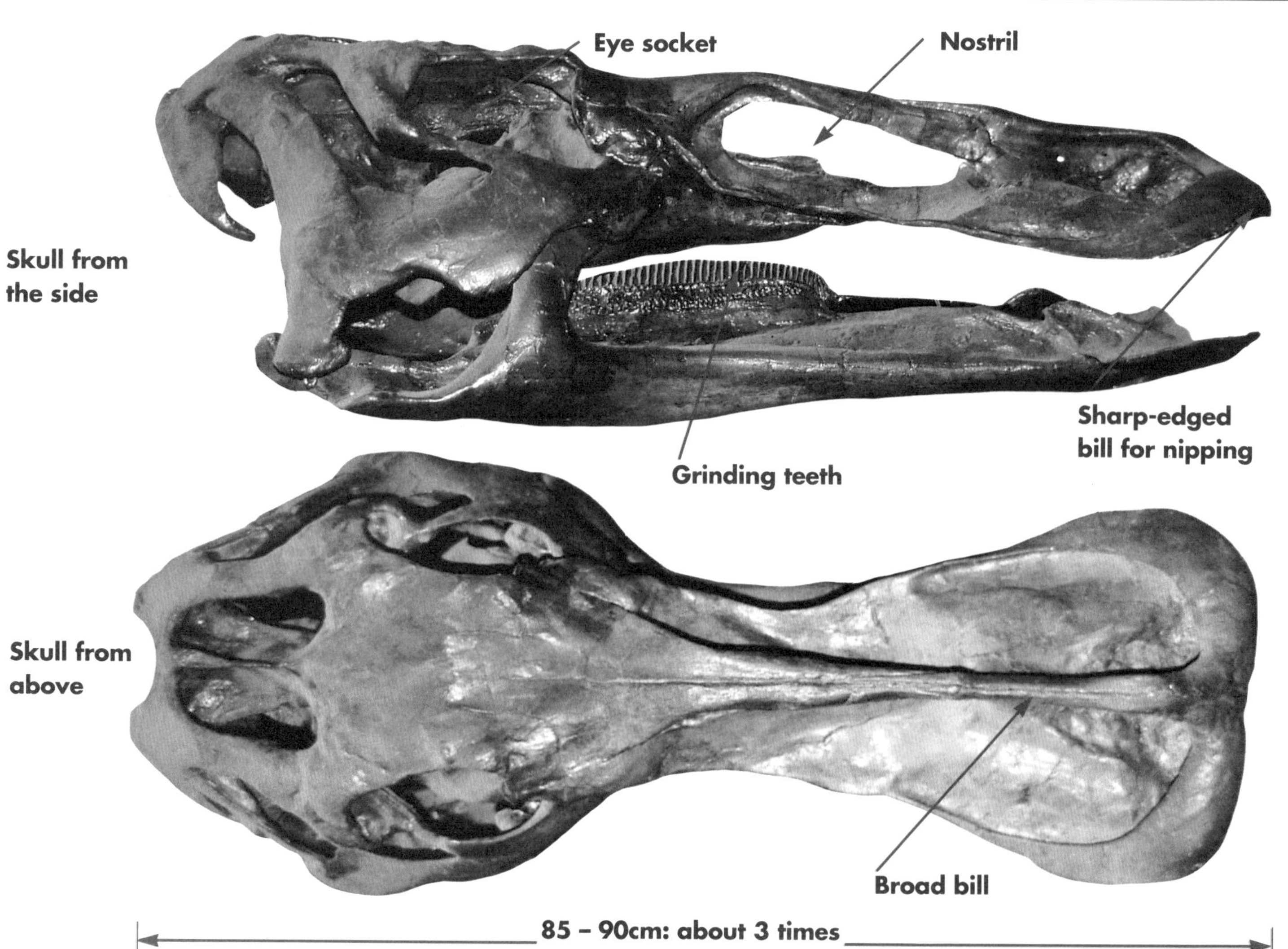

MONSTER FACTS

- **NAME:** *Anatotitan* (a-nat-oh-tite-an) means 'giant duck'
- **SIZE:** up to 12.2m long
- **FOOD:** plants, leaves, twigs and cones
- **LIVED:** about 75 million years ago in the Late Cretaceous Period in North America

Eye socket

Nostril

Skull from the side

Sharp-edged bill for nipping

Grinding teeth

Skull from above

Broad bill

85 – 90cm: about 3 times the height of this page

PUFFED UP
Like the hadrosaur *Saurolophus*, *Anatotitan* did not have a tubular head crest. Instead, it had shallow dents in the sides of its face. It is possible that *Anatotitan* was able to puff up these pouches, like an elephant seal inflates its snout. The result was probably a loud noise to warn off intruders.

Is it true that hadrosaurs 'talked' to each other?

Some hadrosaurs had flaps of skin that could be blown up like a balloon. Others had crests like hollow tubes. Usually, these were attached to nostrils and so the dinosaurs could make amplified noises or calls. They could use the sound to scare off rivals. Or it may have been the dinosaurs' way of saying 'hello'!

STRONG SENSES
Anatotitan spent most of the time on land and could not always rely on plunging into water to escape predators. It was an intelligent creature and used its well-developed senses to stay alert to danger. *Anatotitan* had large eyes and could probably spot a stalking predator some distance away. It also used its good sense of hearing as another early warning device. Some scientists believe that hadrosaurs had an acute sense of smell, too.

TRACK CLUES
Anatotitan may have found safety in numbers. There is evidence to suggest that hadrosaurs moved in groups or herds. By looking at footprints and the direction of tracks, scientists have found that large numbers of the same family of dinosaur moved together at the same time. *Anatotitan* probably lived and travelled across land in the safety of a herd.

TUOJIANGOSAURUS

With pointed plates and a spiked tail, peaceful *Tuojiangosaurus* looked much fiercer than it really was.

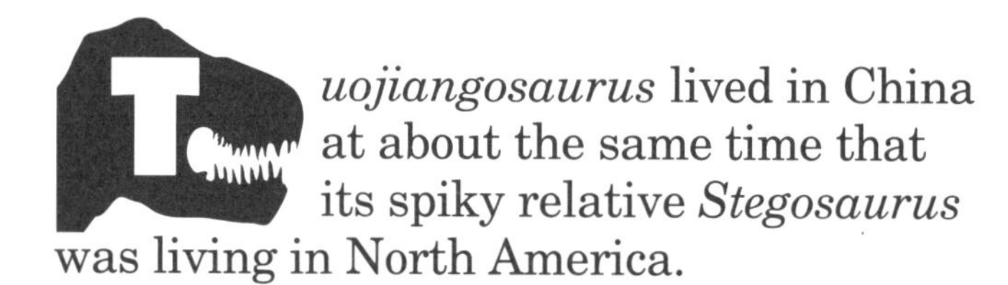

uojiangosaurus lived in China at about the same time that its spiky relative *Stegosaurus* was living in North America.

MONSTER FACTS

- **NAME:** *Tuojiangosaurus* (too-oh-yang-oh-saw-rus) means 'Tuojiang reptile'
- **SIZE:** 7m long and about 2m high
- **FOOD:** low-lying plants
- **LIVED:** about 150 – 140 million years ago in the Late Jurassic Period in China

POINTED PLATES AND TAIL SPIKES

Along its neck, back and tail, *Tuojiangosaurus* had 15 pairs of cone-shaped plates. Spikier than *Stegosaurus'* plates, they were used to fend off *Tuojiangosaurus'* enemies. At the end of its short, muscular tail, it also had two pairs of sharp spikes that pointed upwards. This dinosaur used its tail to swipe any meat-eater that came too near.

SOAKING UP THE SUN

Can you imagine a dinosaur sunbathing? *Tuojiangosaurus'* spines were used to soak up the sun. They worked like solar panels, absorbing heat. Between the spines there were grooves that contained blood. As the blood warmed up, the heat passed into the dinosaur's body like water in a radiator.

STOMACH STONES

Tuojiangosaurus had weak teeth that were no good for grinding tough food. So it probably swallowed stones along with the plants it ate. The stones mashed the food in its belly.

DASPLETOSAURUS

This fearsome two-legged meat-eater opened its huge jaws and killed its prey in one deadly rush.

Daspletosaurus was longer than a coach and had a massive head. Like *Tyrannosaurus,* its arms were tiny compared with the rest of its body. *Daspletosaurus* walked on its strong back legs. It took long strides, so it moved quite fast in spite of its size.

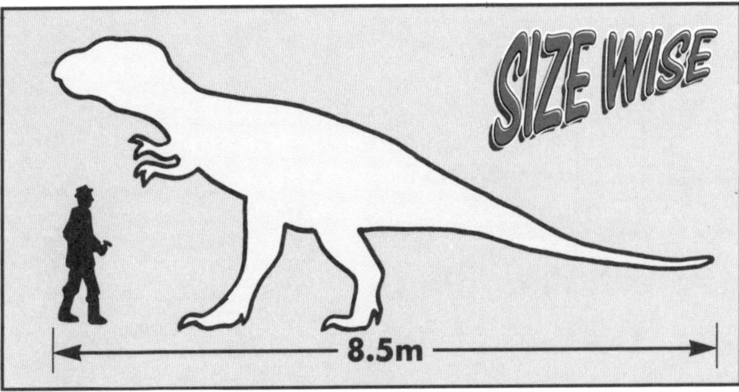

MONSTER FACTS

- **NAME:** *Daspletosaurus* (da-spleet-oh-saw-rus) means 'frightful reptile'
- **SIZE:** 8.5m long
- **FOOD:** meat, especially other dinosaurs
- **LIVED:** about 80 million years ago in the Late Cretaceous Period in Alberta, North America

SURPRISE ATTACK

As its body was so heavy, *Daspletosaurus* used its speed in short bursts and relied on surprise to catch prey. It lurked about in the shadows of trees until it spotted a likely victim, such as the horned dinosaur *Styracosaurus*. Then *Daspletosaurus* leapt out and ambushed its prey.

HEADING THE SHOCK

Daspletosaurus rushed at its prey with wide-open jaws. The dinosaurs collided with a colossal thump. *Daspletosaurus'* gigantic head had to take the shock of the impact. Special hinges inside its jaws gave it extra flexibility and protected the bones in its skull from damage.

OUT FOR THE COUNT

Once the victim was stunned, *Daspletosaurus* sank its teeth into the soft flesh. The tight grip of the attacker's jaws made escape impossible. It was only a matter of time before the victor was enjoying the spoils.

Last of the pterosaurs

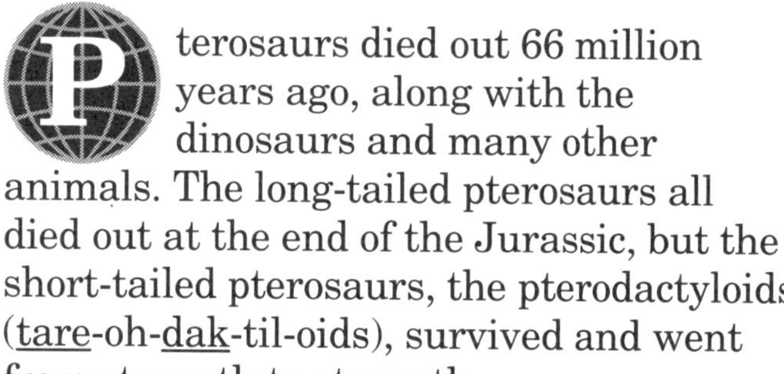

Before they died out, pterosaurs had evolved into the strangest and biggest flying creatures ever to live on Earth.

Pterosaurs died out 66 million years ago, along with the dinosaurs and many other animals. The long-tailed pterosaurs all died out at the end of the Jurassic, but the short-tailed pterosaurs, the pterodactyloids (tare-oh-dak-til-oids), survived and went from strength to strength.

THE CHANGING WORLD

After the Jurassic came the Cretaceous Period. It was warmer and sea levels rose to cover much of the land. Continents slowly drifted across the globe, crashed into each other and gradually formed huge mountain ranges.

SHORT TAILS' SUCCESS

The pterodactyloids ('wing-fingered pterosaurs') made the most of these new conditions. There were many different kinds of pterodactyloid pterosaur, but they all had two things in common – short tails and long, narrow wings. From far away, they must have looked like soaring seabirds such as gulls and albatrosses. In fact, during the Cretaceous Period, birds were becoming more common. For a time, they shared the skies with the pterosaurs.

BIGGER AND BETTER

Pterodactyloids grew larger during the Cretaceous Period. They also became better at flying and gliding. To save energy, they glided huge distances without flapping their wings. Warm air currents blowing up hillsides and mountains carried some pterodactyls along, just like hangliders today. Others glided over the vast oceans and developed strange beaks for feeding on plankton (minute sea creatures), fish or seashore shellfish.

Is it true that pterosaurs had warm blood?

Most reptiles are cold-blooded. They have to wait for the sun to warm their bodies, so that their muscles can work. Birds and mammals are warm-blooded. Their bodies make their own warmth by using energy in the food they eat, so they can always be active. Two clues indicate that pterosaurs were warm-blooded. They must have carried out complicated flying manoeuvres. These needed active muscles and a big brain, which work best only when warm. Also, many fossils clearly show that pterosaurs were furry. Fur has few other uses, except to keep its owner warm!

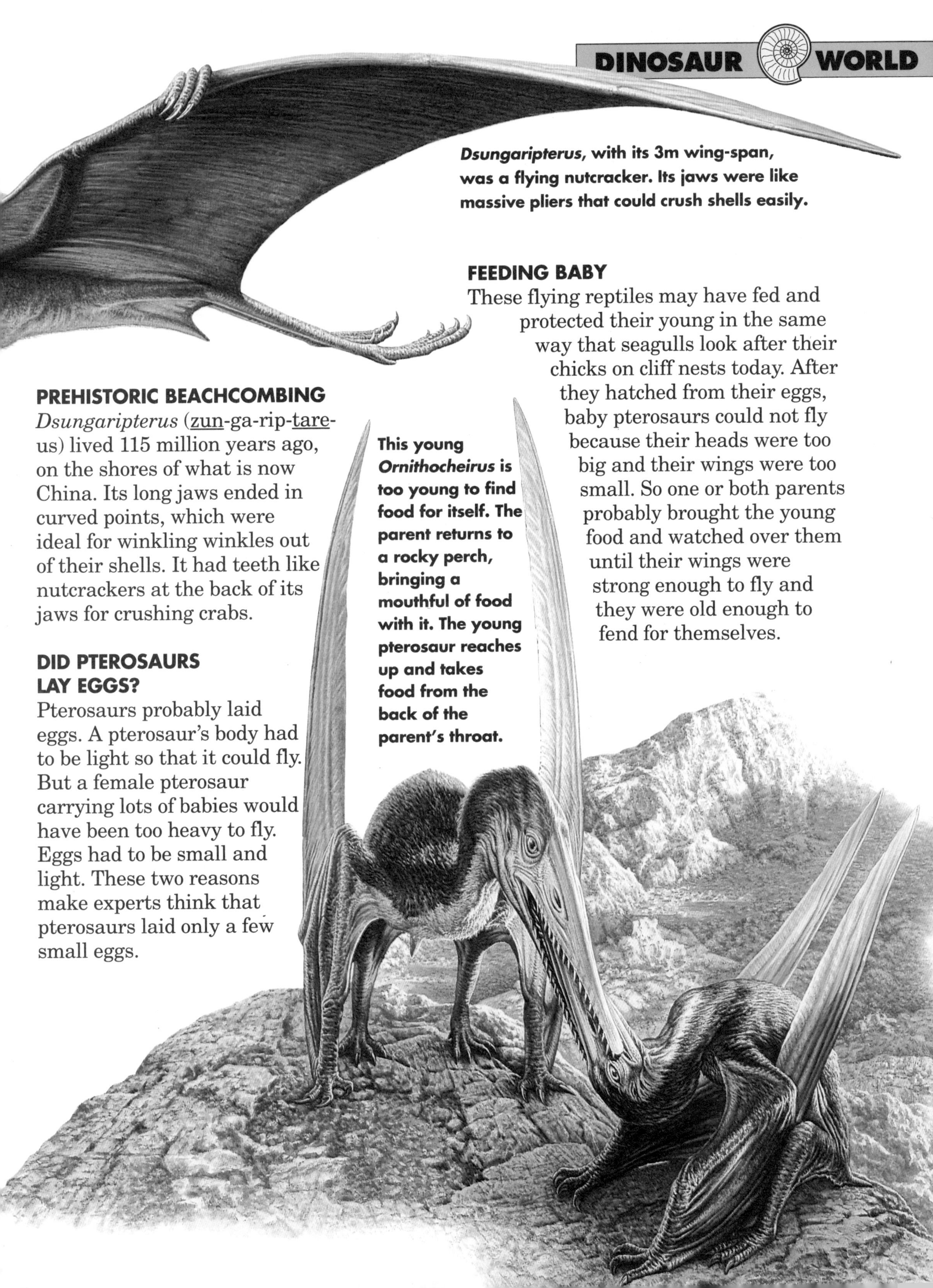

Dsungaripterus, with its 3m wing-span, was a flying nutcracker. Its jaws were like massive pliers that could crush shells easily.

FEEDING BABY

These flying reptiles may have fed and protected their young in the same way that seagulls look after their chicks on cliff nests today. After they hatched from their eggs, baby pterosaurs could not fly because their heads were too big and their wings were too small. So one or both parents probably brought the young food and watched over them until their wings were strong enough to fly and they were old enough to fend for themselves.

PREHISTORIC BEACHCOMBING

Dsungaripterus (zun-ga-rip-tare-us) lived 115 million years ago, on the shores of what is now China. Its long jaws ended in curved points, which were ideal for winkling winkles out of their shells. It had teeth like nutcrackers at the back of its jaws for crushing crabs.

This young *Ornithocheirus* is too young to find food for itself. The parent returns to a rocky perch, bringing a mouthful of food with it. The young pterosaur reaches up and takes food from the back of the parent's throat.

DID PTEROSAURS LAY EGGS?

Pterosaurs probably laid eggs. A pterosaur's body had to be light so that it could fly. But a female pterosaur carrying lots of babies would have been too heavy to fly. Eggs had to be small and light. These two reasons make experts think that pterosaurs laid only a few small eggs.

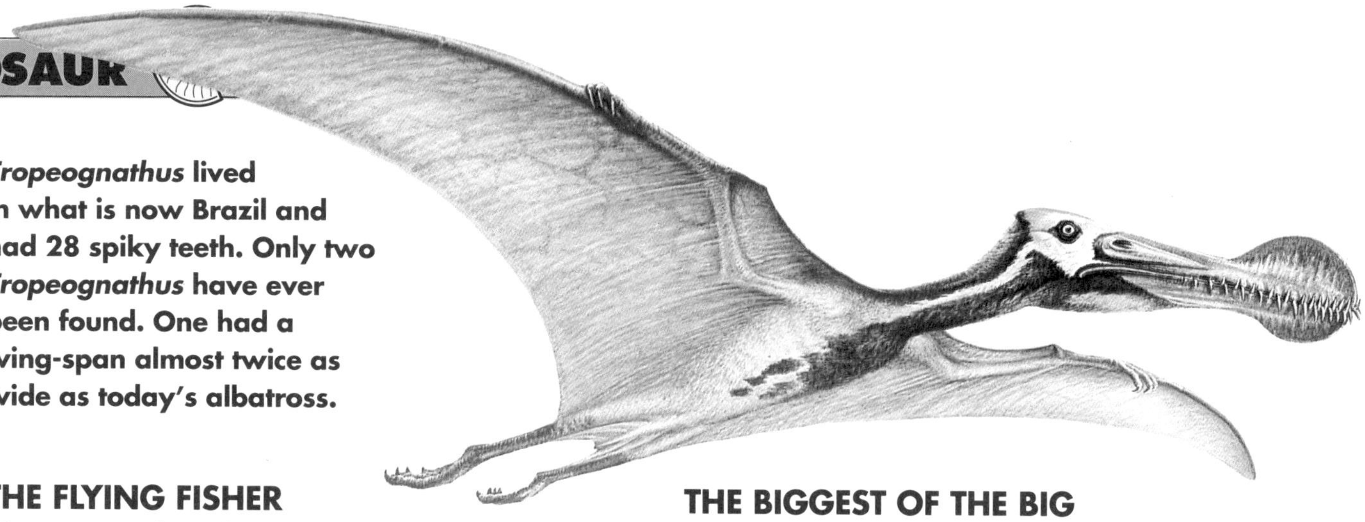

***Tropeognathus* lived in what is now Brazil and had 28 spiky teeth. Only two *Tropeognathus* have ever been found. One had a wing-span almost twice as wide as today's albatross.**

THE FLYING FISHER

Tropeognathus (trop-ee-og-nath-us) was one of the strangest pterosaurs. It was big, too, with a 6.2m wing-span. Its name means 'keel-jaw', and it was called this because its beak was made up of two parts, each like the keel of a yacht, one on the top, the other on the bottom. Sharp teeth stuck out from the sides. This weird design probably helped *Tropeognathus* to snap up food. The keels on its beak helped it cut through the water, just as the keel of a yacht helps it move fast. The pterosaur would fly low over the waves, cutting through the surface of the water with its beak to catch fish and squid.

IT'S A FACT

PTEROSAURS AROUND THE WORLD

After a slow start, fossil-hunters began to find pterosaur fossils on every continent, except Antarctica. So these winged reptiles must have lived all over the world. Lots of the fossils are beautifully preserved. This is because many pterosaurs flew along coasts and over the sea. When they died, their bodies were quickly buried in the mud and sand, and gradually turned to rock.

THE BIGGEST OF THE BIG

One of the last pterosaurs was the spectacular *Quetzalcoatlus* (kwet-zal-coat-lus), named after the traditional Mexican feathered snake-god Quetzalcoatl. This huge creature, its head longer than a man, was probably as big as a flying animal could ever be. It adapted to the place in which it lived. *Quetzalcoatlus* was so big that it could not have taken off without help from the winds whistling through the mountains and canyons of Texas, USA. Once in the air, it could glide on the air currents for a long time.

Three *Quetzalcoatlus* soar above the canyons and rocks of what is now western Texas, USA.

THE END OF THE PTEROSAURS

No one knows why the pterosaurs died out. Perhaps a vast meteorite collided with the Earth, throwing huge dust clouds into the air which blotted out the sun. Gliding in the cold air, choked with dust and unable to see clearly, these fantastic reptilian fliers soon disappeared from the world.

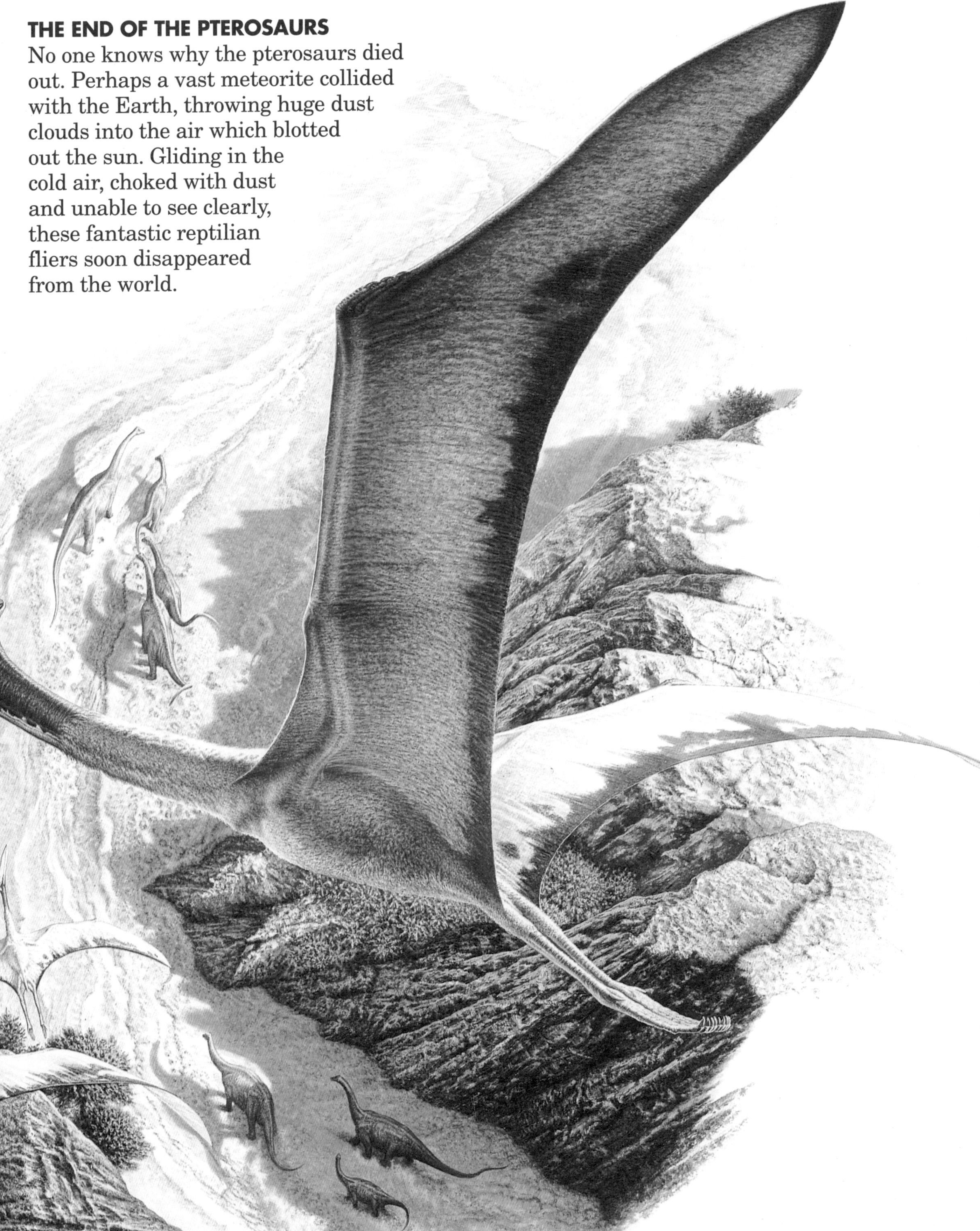

GIANTS OF THE PAST

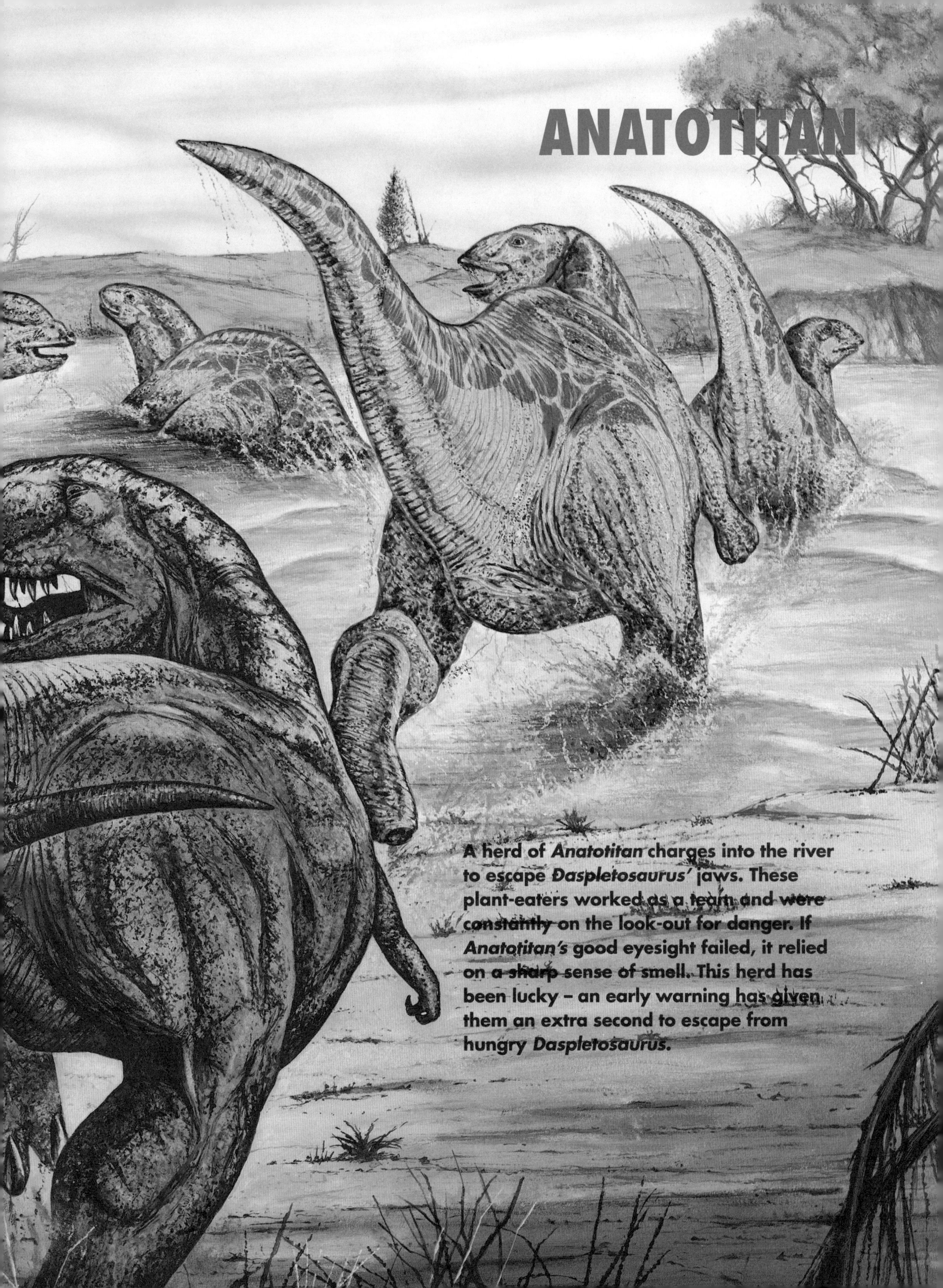

ANATOTITAN

A herd of *Anatotitan* charges into the river to escape *Daspletosaurus'* jaws. These plant-eaters worked as a team and were constantly on the look-out for danger. If *Anatotitan's* good eyesight failed, it relied on a sharp sense of smell. This herd has been lucky – an early warning has given them an extra second to escape from hungry *Daspletosaurus*.

3-D Gallery

GALLIMIMUS

- Tall, ostrich-like dinosaur
- Lived 70 – 66 million years ago in southern Mongolia
- Measured 4m long
- Ate eggs, plants, insects, lizards

24

Neck and neck

Long, short, thick or thin, the shape of a dinosaur's neck depended on the job it had to do.

Dromiceiomimus

READY TO SPRING

One problem that faced small theropods, such as *Dromiceiomimus*, was the speed with which their prey could escape. Lizards and insects were very quick to get away. Theropods had long necks, which they could straighten in a second – ready to seize prey. This action was like the sudden unwinding of a spring.

STICKING ITS NECK OUT

Mamenchisaurus' neck was 9m longer than a giraffe's. It had 19 neck bones. Experts used to think that it held its neck stretched out straight, like *Diplodocus*. Scientists now think that *Mamenchisaurus* held its head up high to eat the juiciest leaves in the trees. To lower its head, *Mamenchisaurus'* long neck worked rather like a huge crane on a building site.

Is it true that all dinosaurs had the same number of neck bones, just like mammals do?

It is true that all mammals have the same number of neck bones. For example, both humans and giraffes have seven bones in their necks. This is not true of dinosaurs. Short-necked dinosaurs had fewer neck bones than long-necked ones. *Psittacosaurus*, for instance, had only six.

S-SHAPED NECK

Duckbilled dinosaurs, such as *Corythosaurus*, had necks rather like modern bisons'. Their backbones sloped down steeply from their shoulders and their necks were very curved. This meant that their heads were always close to the ground – in a perfect position for a quick nibble at low-lying shrubs.

Corythosaurus

Dinosaurs' necks helped the animals to wrench raw meat off the bone, reach up for the juiciest leaves on a tree-top, fight a rival or stop an enemy attack.

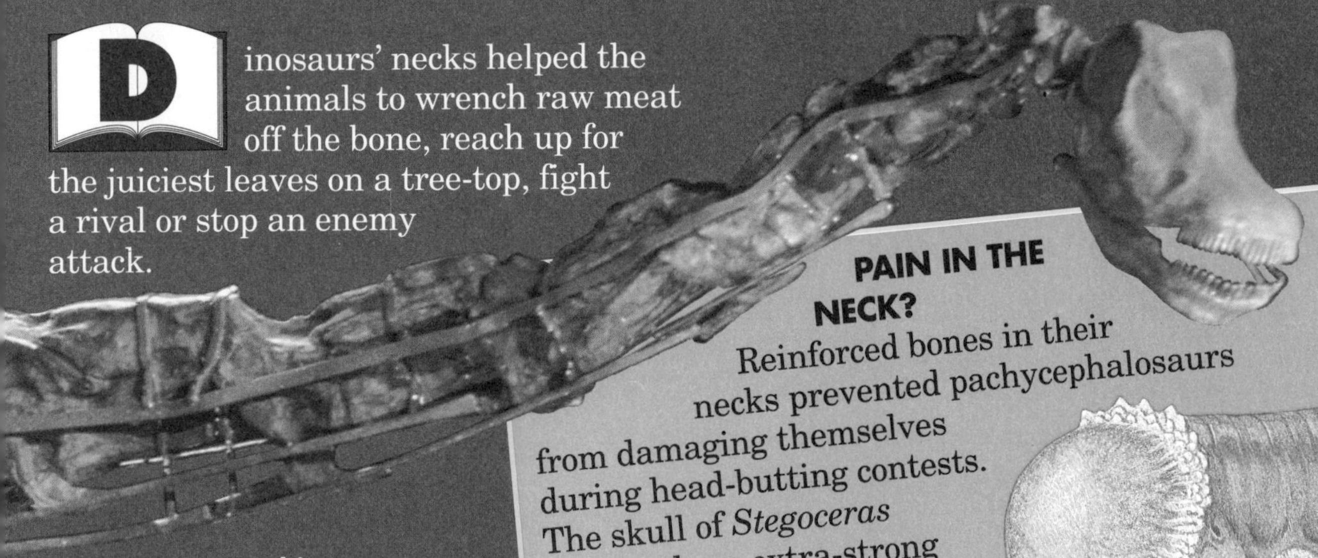

Mamenchisaurus

PAIN IN THE NECK?

Reinforced bones in their necks prevented pachycephalosaurs from damaging themselves during head-butting contests. The skull of *Stegoceras* shows where extra-strong muscles joined its head to its neck. The neck acted like a shock absorber.

Stegoceras

The veins in *Albertosaurus'* neck (below) stand out as the predator uses its neck muscles to twist and pull flesh from *Edmontonia*. The solid collar of bony plates around *Edmontonia's* neck meant that a predator had to flip the armoured dinosaur over to reach the fleshy underneath of its neck.

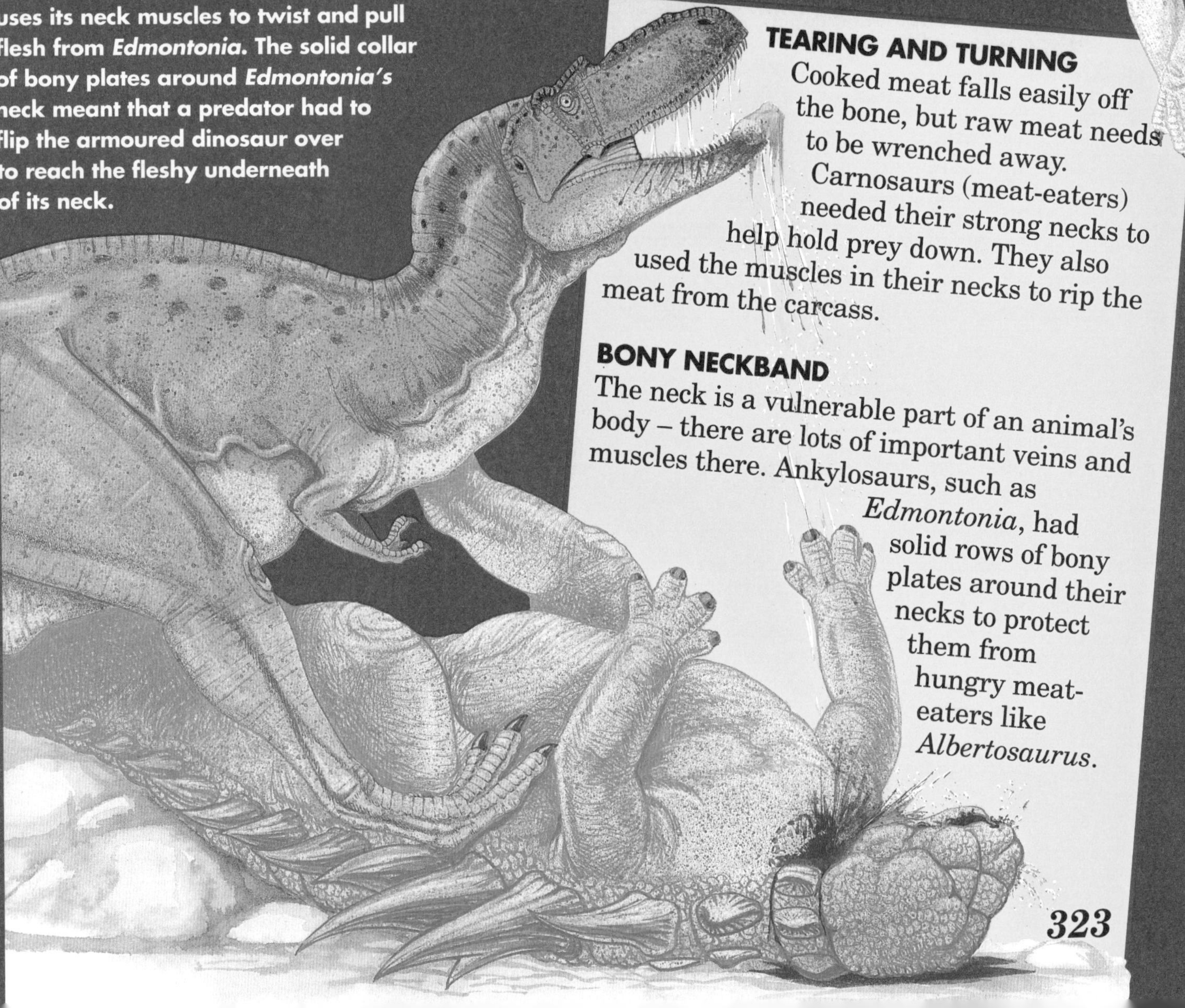

TEARING AND TURNING

Cooked meat falls easily off the bone, but raw meat needs to be wrenched away.

Carnosaurs (meat-eaters) needed their strong necks to help hold prey down. They also used the muscles in their necks to rip the meat from the carcass.

BONY NECKBAND

The neck is a vulnerable part of an animal's body – there are lots of important veins and muscles there. Ankylosaurs, such as *Edmontonia*, had solid rows of bony plates around their necks to protect them from hungry meat-eaters like *Albertosaurus*.

A dinosaur walked here

We can see where dinosaurs walked millions of years ago because they left footprints behind. Footprints give scientists important clues about how dinosaurs lived.

Dinosaur footprints made in mud or sand sometimes dried out and then fossilized. They are called 'trace fossils' because they are not part of an actual animal. Just as detectives can discover a lot from footprints left at the scene of a crime, palaeontologists can tell a great deal about dinosaurs from the footprints they left.

WE KNOW WHAT YOU'RE DOING!

From the different sizes and shapes of the footprints, experts can usually work out which kind of dinosaur made them. They can tell whether a dinosaur was walking or running. Sometimes they can even work out how fast a dinosaur ran. It is also possible to tell when a dinosaur was swimming. Big, heavy dinosaurs left large, deep footprints. Footprints of meat-eating dinosaurs were usually different from those of plant-eaters. Lots of tracks of the same kind in the same place often meant that a whole herd of dinosaurs had passed that way.

FIRST FOOTPRINTS

Three-toed footprints like the huge one on this page were discovered almost 200 years ago. They were among the first dinosaur fossils found in the USA. Scientists then thought they were made by gigantic, ancient birds.

Some dinosaur footprints are so big that a six-year-old could use one as a paddling pool.

BABY FOOT
This is the footprint (left) made by *Iguanodon's* hind foot. It is almost life-size, but it is small for *Iguanodon*. Experts think it was probably made by a youngster weighing about half a tonne. Adult footprints have been found which are three times bigger.

BACK TRACK
Iguanodon's three-toed hind foot had to be strong enough to support the dinosaur's great weight. An adult could weigh up to two tonnes. It probably walked on its toes, just like modern cats and dogs.

The foot that made the print: *Iguanodon's* footprint is between 120 and 110 million years old. These dinosaurs left their tracks in several places, including England.

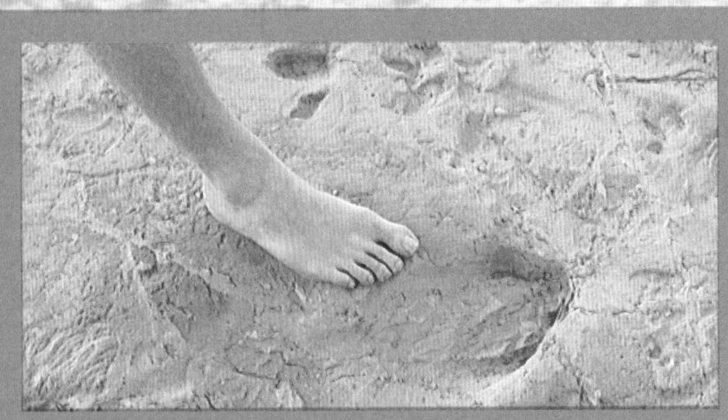

Footprints (above) scattered over rocks in Queensland, Australia. They were made by a big meat-eater chasing small plant-eaters across a river bed.

***Iguanodon* walked here (right). It left its footprints in soft mud which eventually became stone.**

Making tracks

Follow these footprints and become a dinosaur detective. Find out which dinosaur left which tracks.

CLUE 3

These footprints look a bit like the ones in Clue 2. They have the same bird-like track, but they are spaced much further apart. Were they made by a dinosaur with very long legs or was this dinosaur running somewhere?

This dinosaur walked on its hind feet and left a bird-like track. Meat-eaters, such as *Allosaurus*, walked on two legs and made this kind of track. Did *Allosaurus* walk here leaving these footprints?

CLUE 1

These fossil footprints are as deep as a washing machine. They were made by a very heavy dinosaur that walked on all fours and had toes like a modern elephant. Did a giant sauropod, such as *Brachiosaurus*, walk this way 150 million years ago?

Some of these footprints are the same as those in Clue 1. But where are the footprints of its hind feet? Was the dinosaur doing handstands or was it in water, pulling itself along on its front legs?

CLUE 5

Here are some large footprints like those in Clue 1. In between them are some smaller footprints of the same kind. What is going on? Are the owners of the big footprints attacking the owners of the little ones or are they looking after them?

GOT IT!

(1) The first footprints belonged to the four-footed sauropod *Brachiosaurus*. It left them as it walked alone.

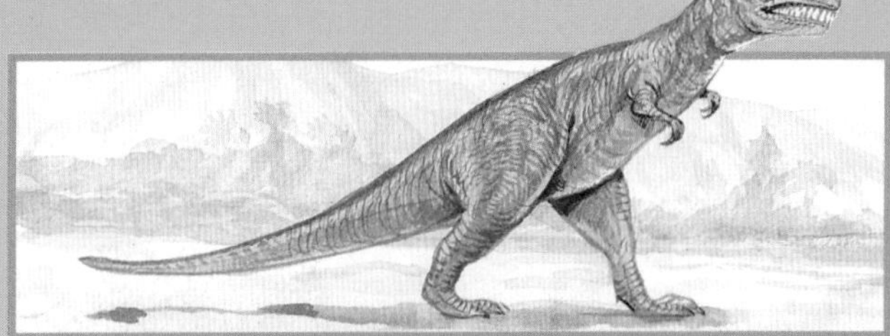

(2) The second footprints belonged to a two-legged dinosaur. These ones were made by a meat-eater like *Allosaurus*.

(3) The third tracks were left by speedy *Gallimimus* as it ran flat out.

(4) *Brachiosaurus* made the fourth set. It used its front legs to pull itself through water, its back feet trailed behind.

(5) The last tracks were made by a herd of *Brachiosaurus*. Large adult tracks are on the outside, small tracks made by babies are on the inside. The young were safe in the middle.

A family of *Protoceratops* is disturbed by a marauding gang of *Velociraptors*. *Protoceratops* can put up a tough defense, especially when its young are threatened. But the hooked hind toe of *Velociraptor* slashes cruelly into the plant-eater's soft underbelly and the huge jaws will clamp on to its victim's throat with fatal results.

3-D Gallery 44

VELOCIRAPTOR V PROTOCERATOPS

Dr. David Norman of Cambridge University answers your dinosaur questions
ASK THE EXPERT

How much water did dinosaurs drink?

Dinosaurs did not need to drink very much. Like most reptiles, they lost very little water from their bodies. This was because they did not sweat (their skin was tough and waterproof) and they did not pass water as urine but as a paste, like bird droppings. They got most of their water from the things they ate, such as plants or other animals.

How much food did Apatosaurus eat in one day?

There is no way of knowing how much food *Apatosaurus* may have eaten. We can compare this huge dinosaur with today's elephant. This is not very helpful, though. For example, a two-tonne elephant eats over 100kg of food a day. *Apatosaurus*, which may have weighed as much as 10 elephants, may have eaten the same amount as an elephant – or much more. The real answer, of course, is that we don't know for sure.

Could any dinosaurs re-grow their tails, like lizards?

No, they could not. Lizards have a special breakage zone in the middle of their tail bones. There is no proof that dinosaurs had a breakage zone like this. They definitely did not shed and re-grow their tails.

Did dinosaurs' claws ever get in the way, like budgies'?

Budgies that are kept in cages need to have their claws clipped because they do not wear them down naturally. Dinosaurs would not have had this problem, they would have naturally worn their claws down in the wild.

DINOSAURS!
DISCOVER THE GIANTS OF THE PREHISTORIC WORLD

OVIRAPTOR

Speedy *Oviraptor* was only the same size as a wolf, but it was cheeky enough to steal eggs from under the nose of bigger dinosaurs.

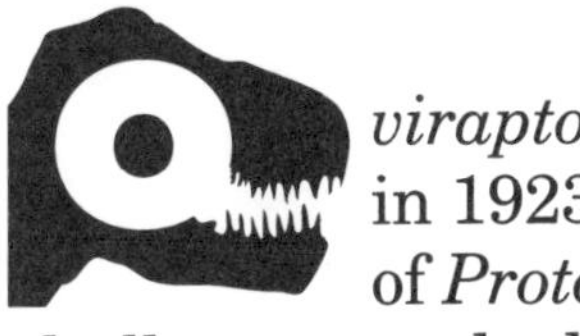*viraptor's* skeleton was found in 1923, just next to a nest full of *Protoceratops'* eggs. The skull was smashed. Scientists think *Oviraptor* may have died in the middle of a daring act of theft. Imagine *Protoceratops* returning to its nest to discover *Oviraptor* attempting to steal its eggs. In a rage, the parent probably stamped on the thief's head.

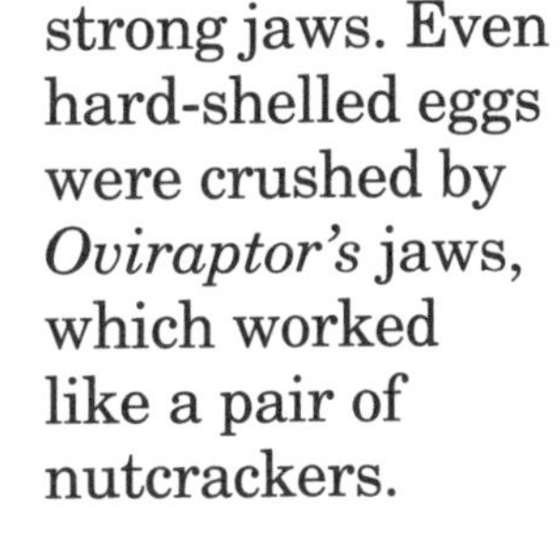

DAGGER BITE

Dinosaur eggs had thick shells. Unlike hens' eggs, they were hard to crack. Instead of teeth, *Oviraptor* had two sharp prongs pointing down from the roof of its mouth. These could pierce an egg like daggers.

CURVED BEAK

Being toothless was not a problem for *Oviraptor*. The eggs it looked for were easily dealt with by its curved beak and strong jaws. Even hard-shelled eggs were crushed by *Oviraptor's* jaws, which worked like a pair of nutcrackers.

What gave *Oviraptor* a bump on its nose? Scientist do not really know. Although several skulls have been found, the nose bumps on them are all different. Maybe the bump grew as the dinosaur got older. Some *Oviraptor* skulls have fancy crests, others do not. Perhaps it was only the male dinosaurs that had crests.

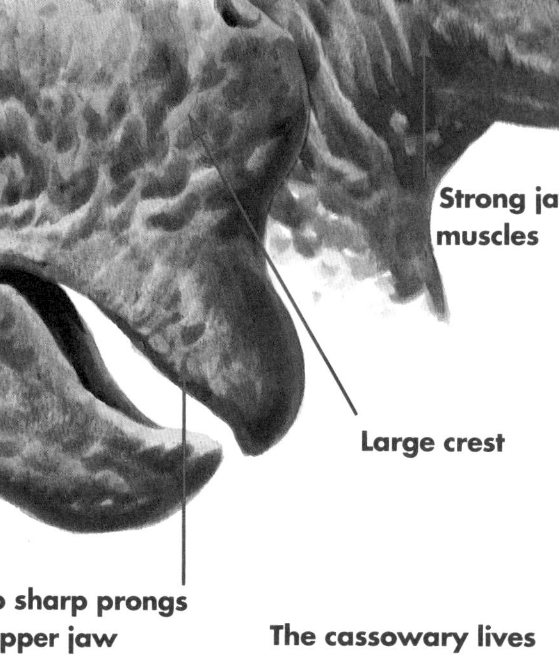

The cassowary lives in the rainforests of Australia and Papua New Guinea today. Like *Oviraptor,* it has a toothless beak, a splendid crest and long, fast legs.

NOSE BUMP

Not all *Oviraptor* skulls look the same. Some have a small, bony bump above the nostrils. Others have a large crest. With its short skull and big eyes, *Oviraptor* looked rather like a cassowary, a big, flightless bird that lives in Australia today.

WISHBONES

Scientists have discovered that *Oviraptor* had a very unusual bone in its shoulder. Most dinosaurs have a pair of shoulder bones, one on each side. However, *Oviraptor* had two bones that joined together to form one curved collar bone. It looked a bit like the chicken's wishbone that some people pull for good luck today.

Is it true that some dinosaurs made it quite simple for *Oviraptor* to find their eggs?

Some hadrosaurs returned to the same nesting site year after year. Herds of these dinosaurs nested together. Each nest could contain as many as 30 eggs. By returning to the same place every year, these hadrosaurs probably made life very easy for *Oviraptor* – at nesting times it would have known exactly where to go to get its next meal.

MONSTER FACTS

- **NAME:** *Oviraptor* (ove-ih-rap-tor) means 'egg thief'
- **SIZE:** between 1.5m and 2m long
- **FOOD:** meat and other dinosaurs' eggs
- **LIVED:** about 80 million years ago in the Late Cretaceous Period in southern Mongolia

GRASPING HANDS

Oviraptor had three fingers on each hand with sharp, curved claws. The first finger was quite a bit shorter than the other two. *Oviraptor* used it like a thumb, curving it round towards the other fingers to grip prey tightly. These slender hands helped *Oviraptor* snatch its favourite snack – fresh dinosaur egg – and hold on to it tightly until the contents were sucked dry.

FAST GETAWAY

Such an agile and keen hunter was a great nuisance to other dinosaurs. After one of its smash-and-grab raids, *Oviraptor* made a quick exit. It escaped on two long legs powered by strong muscles. As it ran, these muscles helped *Oviraptor* to swing its legs rapidly and work up to a fast speed. On each foot there were three strong, clawed toes.

***Oviraptor* did not need a fast getaway car! After raiding a nest, this thief took off at top speed on its two long legs. With no sharp teeth to defend itself, *Oviraptor* needed to be quick.**

POLACANTHUS

Longer than a rhinoceros, spiky *Polacanthus* was saved from the sea.

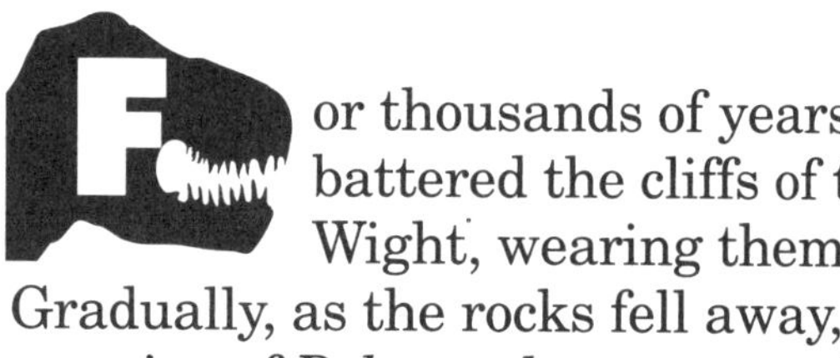

For thousands of years, waves battered the cliffs of the Isle of Wight, wearing them down. Gradually, as the rocks fell away, the remains of *Polacanthus* appeared. Before the skeleton was found, by the Reverend William Fox in 1865, much of it had already been washed away into the sea.

UNDER ATTACK

The ferns that covered southern England 120 million years ago were munched by sturdy *Polacanthus*. Plodding along on its stout legs, it kept a look out for preying carnosaurs. If danger threatened, *Polacanthus* crouched close to the ground to protect its belly. The sight of its bony studs and spikes stopped many predators in their tracks. They wandered off to find a more tempting meal.

MONSTER FACTS

- **NAME:** *Polacanthus* (poh-lah-can-thus) means 'many spikes'
- **SIZE:** 4m long and about 1m high
- **FOOD:** low-growing plants and ferns
- **LIVED:** about 120 million years ago in the Cretaceous on the Isle of Wight, England

SHARP FRILL

Polacanthus probably wore its impressive spikes like a frill down the sides of its body and long, heavy tail. Inside its small mouth, leaf-shaped teeth stripped leaves from plants.

OPISTHOCOELICAUDIA

Opisthocoelicaudia **was as long as two large crocodiles and slightly taller than a fully grown giraffe.**

In the dry, windswept landscape of the Gobi Desert in Mongolia, scientists discovered the headless skeleton of *Opisthocoelicaudia* from the Cretaceous. This was a great surprise because most sauropods lived millions of years before, in the Jurassic.

MONSTER FACTS

- **NAME:** *Opisthocoelicaudia* (oh-pis-thoe-seel-ih-kow-dee-a) means 'tail bones hollow at the back'
- **SIZE:** 12m long
- **FOOD:** plants and leaves from trees
- **LIVED:** 75 million years ago in the Late Cretaceous Period in Mongolia

DAMAGED DINOSAUR

Teeth marks were found on the fossilized leg of *Opisthocoelicaudia*. It had been gnawed by some other animal. Perhaps a passing dinosaur found its dead body and made a meal of its head and neck. Or they may have been bitten off in a fight. Experts have tried to guess what the dinosaur's head looked like. Some think the heads of *Camarasaurus* or *Nemegtosaurus* fitted quite well with the rest of the body.

BULKY BODY

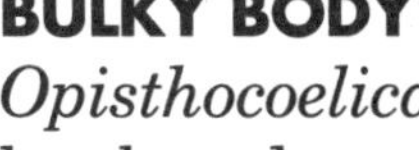

Opisthocoelicaudia lumbered about on thick, chunky legs with its short, stiff tail held above the ground. Now and again, it stopped to browse among the tree-tops. When it reared up to reach the juiciest leaves, the dinosaur used its strong tail as a support.

Rulers before the dinosaurs

Imagine the shock if 3m-long *Paracyclotosaurus* climbed out of a garden pond. It's huge compared with today's amphibians, like newts.

Dinosaurs were not the first animals to rule the land. Amphibians did – 150 million years before!

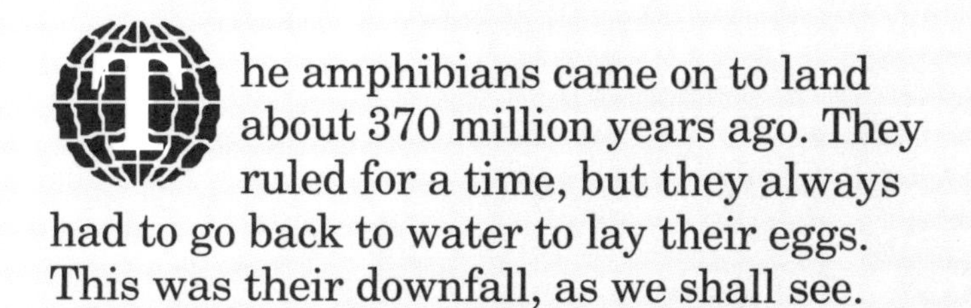

The amphibians came on to land about 370 million years ago. They ruled for a time, but they always had to go back to water to lay their eggs. This was their downfall, as we shall see.

THE AMPHIBIANS' RISE ...

Amphibians were the first four-legged animals to live on land. They evolved from lungfishes. These strange fish could breathe air when the water dried up, and haul themselves over the mud on their fleshy fins to find a new pond. During the Age of the Amphibians (345 – 280 MYA), all shapes and sizes of amphibians stalked the land and splashed about in the swamps of the warm, steamy fern forests.

... AND THEIR FALL

By 300 million years ago, some of the first reptiles appeared. In dry areas, these early reptiles grew in number. They were much better equipped to survive, with their waterproof skin and shelled eggs. Amphibians had trouble, because their damp, slimy skin needed moisture, and their jelly-covered eggs needed water. So the reptiles gradually took over the land.

WATER OR DRY LAND?

Only a few amphibians were left to live alongside the dinosaurs. Among them were the ancestors of today's amphibians – frogs, toads, newts and salamanders. When dinosaurs took over, amphibians had two choices to survive. They could return to the water full-time, or they could evolve to cope with dry land.

As long as a large car, *Cyclotosaurus* was bigger than its Australian relative *Paracyclotosaurus*.

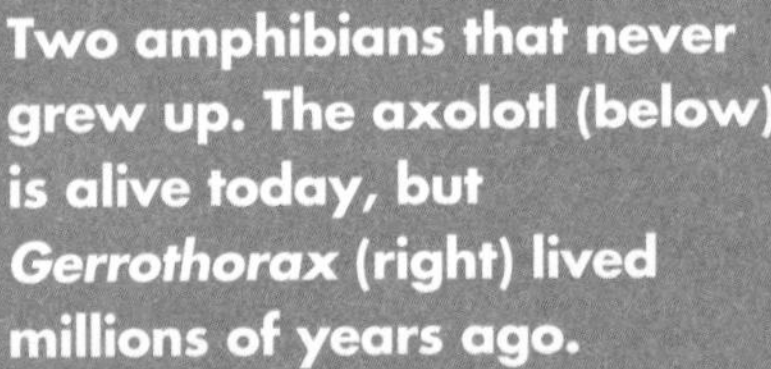
Two amphibians that never grew up. The axolotl (below) is alive today, but *Gerrothorax* (right) lived millions of years ago.

'PETER PAN' AMPHIBIANS

Today, a few amphibians never really grow up. They keep their tadpole-features, such as gills for underwater breathing, even when they are adults. The strange-looking creature, axolotl, is one of these 'Peter Pan' amphibians. *Gerrothorax* was another. It lived 200 million years ago and looked very like a huge axolotl with armour. Its body measured about 1m long.

BACK TO THE WATER

Amphibians that went back in the water no longer needed their large walking legs, so they developed swimming legs instead. One of these back-to-water amphibians was *Paracyclotosaurus*, from what is now Australia. It was nearly 3m long and probably lived on the beds of lakes and rivers. Its cousin, *Cyclotosaurus*, from Europe, was even bigger at 4m! Another relative was *Mastodonsaurus*, whose head alone was over 1m long.

What is? AN AMPHIBIAN

The word amphibian means 'two lives' – part in water, part on land. Typical amphibians begin their life as eggs in the water. The eggs hatch into tadpoles, which breathe through gills, like fish. The tadpoles then develop into adult amphibians. They live on land, breathing with lungs, and through their moist, slimy skin. So for two good reasons – eggs and breathing – most amphibians are tied to water.

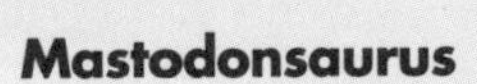
Mastodonsaurus

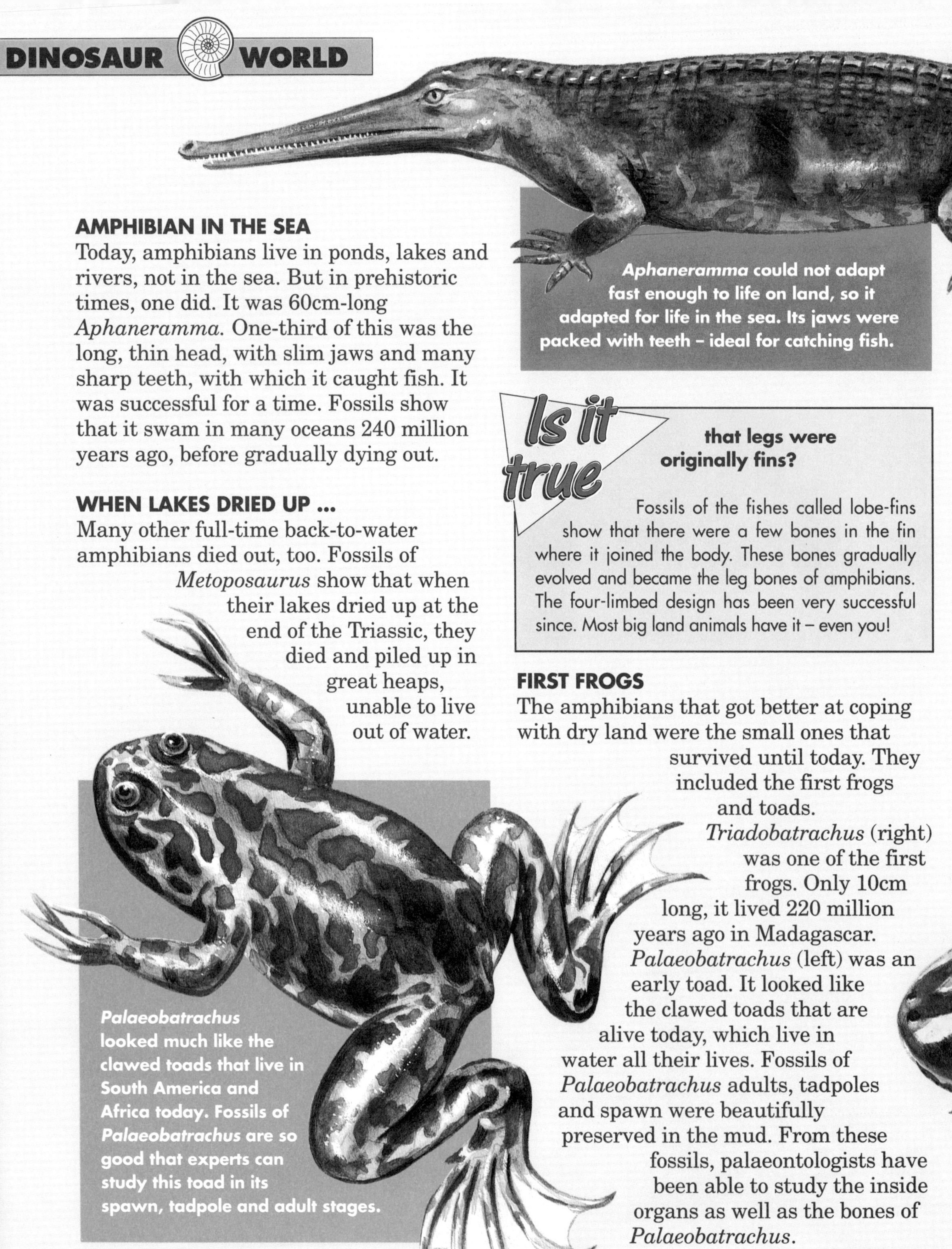

Aphaneramma could not adapt fast enough to life on land, so it adapted for life in the sea. Its jaws were packed with teeth – ideal for catching fish.

AMPHIBIAN IN THE SEA

Today, amphibians live in ponds, lakes and rivers, not in the sea. But in prehistoric times, one did. It was 60cm-long *Aphaneramma*. One-third of this was the long, thin head, with slim jaws and many sharp teeth, with which it caught fish. It was successful for a time. Fossils show that it swam in many oceans 240 million years ago, before gradually dying out.

WHEN LAKES DRIED UP ...

Many other full-time back-to-water amphibians died out, too. Fossils of *Metoposaurus* show that when their lakes dried up at the end of the Triassic, they died and piled up in great heaps, unable to live out of water.

Is it true that legs were originally fins?

Fossils of the fishes called lobe-fins show that there were a few bones in the fin where it joined the body. These bones gradually evolved and became the leg bones of amphibians. The four-limbed design has been very successful since. Most big land animals have it – even you!

FIRST FROGS

The amphibians that got better at coping with dry land were the small ones that survived until today. They included the first frogs and toads. *Triadobatrachus* (right) was one of the first frogs. Only 10cm long, it lived 220 million years ago in Madagascar. *Palaeobatrachus* (left) was an early toad. It looked like the clawed toads that are alive today, which live in water all their lives. Fossils of *Palaeobatrachus* adults, tadpoles and spawn were beautifully preserved in the mud. From these fossils, palaeontologists have been able to study the inside organs as well as the bones of *Palaeobatrachus*.

Palaeobatrachus looked much like the clawed toads that live in South America and Africa today. Fossils of *Palaeobatrachus* are so good that experts can study this toad in its spawn, tadpole and adult stages.

FOOTPRINT NURSERY

Karaurus (below right) was one of the first of the group of amphibians that includes newts and salamanders. *Karaurus* was only 20cm long and lived 150 million years ago in Kazakhstan, Asia. It could have hatched from spawn and grown up in the puddle-filled footprint left by a giant dinosaur!

NEWTS ALIVE

Newts that are alive today still look like their prehistoric cousins. However, their skin is more leathery than slimy. This helps them to live in dry places. They are all hungry hunters, catching worms, small fish and other little creatures.

LEGLESS AMPHIBIANS

Besides frogs and toads, newts and salamanders, there is another group of amphibians alive today. These are caecilians – strange creatures with no legs that look like big worms or small snakes. They burrow in the soil in tropical places, fiercely chasing worms and insects. One fossil dates back to dinosaur times. It is a single backbone of the caecilian *Apodops*, 65 million years old.

LONG LIVE THE AMPHIBIANS

By the end of the Age of the Dinosaurs, amphibians were much less common. In terms of numbers, they are not very common today, either. But amphibians were crawling around the Earth a long time before the dinosaurs. And they have survived a long time after, too!

Today's newts and salamanders have drier skin than *Karaurus* (left). This amphibian needed to keep moist all the time to survive.

In real life, *Triadobatrachus* was a little bit smaller than it is on this page. Only about 5 million years after the first dinosaurs appeared, *Triadobatrachus* was hopping around Madagascar, a large island off the south-east coast of Africa.

Cunning *Oviraptor* has egg on its face! The 'egg thief' has been caught red-handed. *Oviraptor* leaps away in surprise as a female *Protoceratops* tries to grab its tail. Normally a peaceful animal, *Protoceratops* lashes out in anger when she sees her eggs crushed into fragments of shell. *Oviraptor* is not equipped to fight back. The only way out is to escape – and fast!

OVIRAPTOR

3-D Gallery

SCELIDOSAURUS

25
• Armoured dinosaur studded with bony nodules
• Lived 195 – 180 million years ago in China, the USA and England
• Measured 4m long
• Ate plants

Body guards

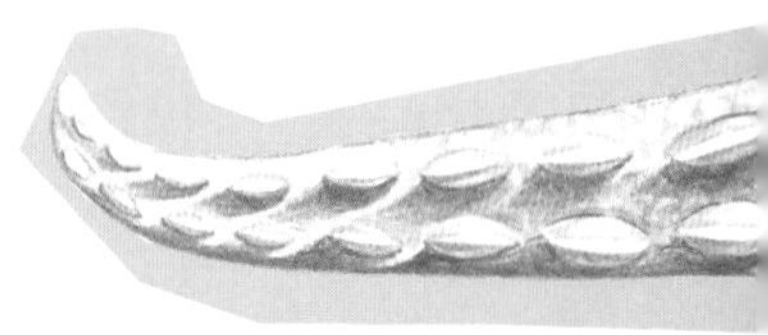

If you think suits of armour were only worn by medieval knights, then take a look at these armoured dinosaurs.

Some dinosaurs developed their own suits of armour to protect themselves from danger. Welded to their skin were hundreds of bony plates. Some dinosaurs, such as *Sauropelta*, are thought to have had as many as 1000!

BUILT LIKE A TANK

Ankylosaurus was the largest ever armoured animal. At well over 11m, it was the size of a tank and almost as strongly protected. It had a large club at the end of its tail, which it swung out at approaching enemies. But *Ankylosaurus* did have a weak spot – its belly.

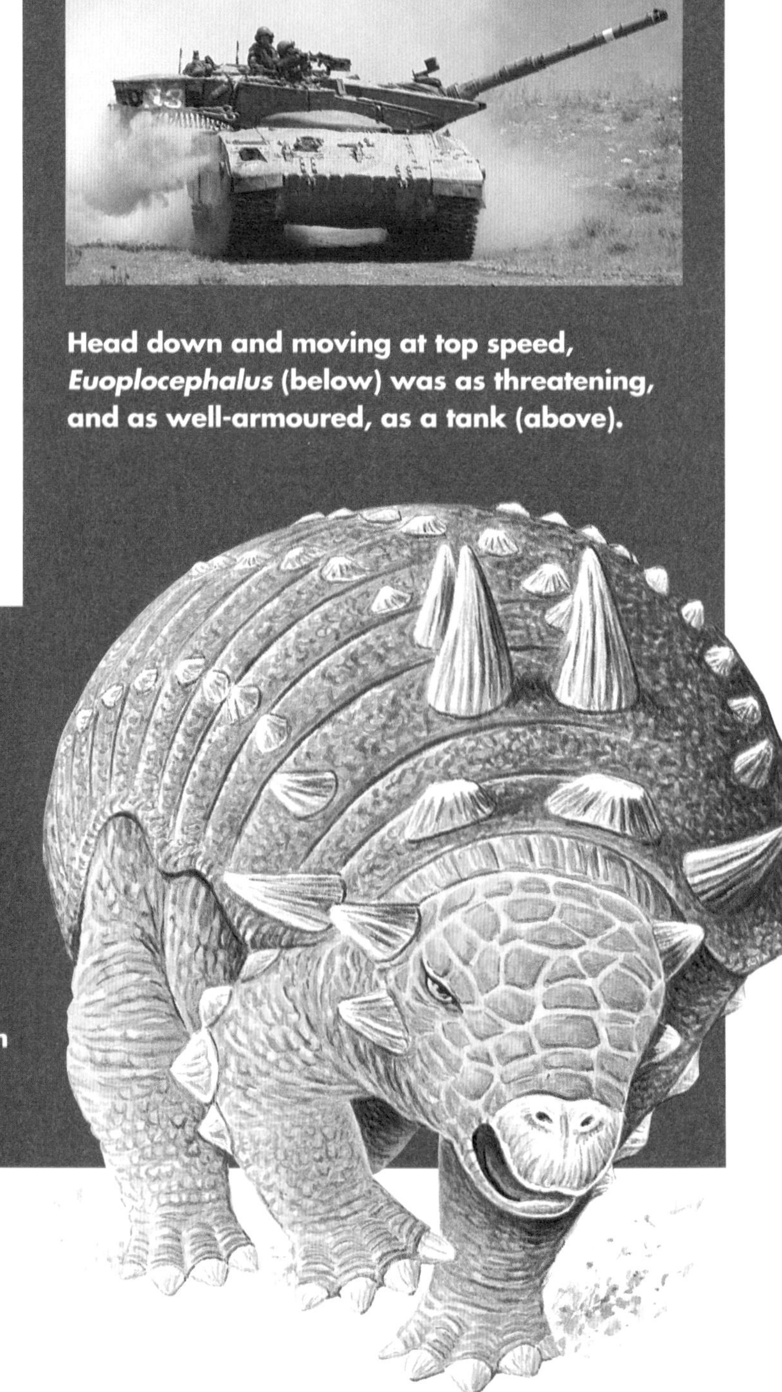

Head down and moving at top speed, *Euoplocephalus* (below) was as threatening, and as well-armoured, as a tank (above).

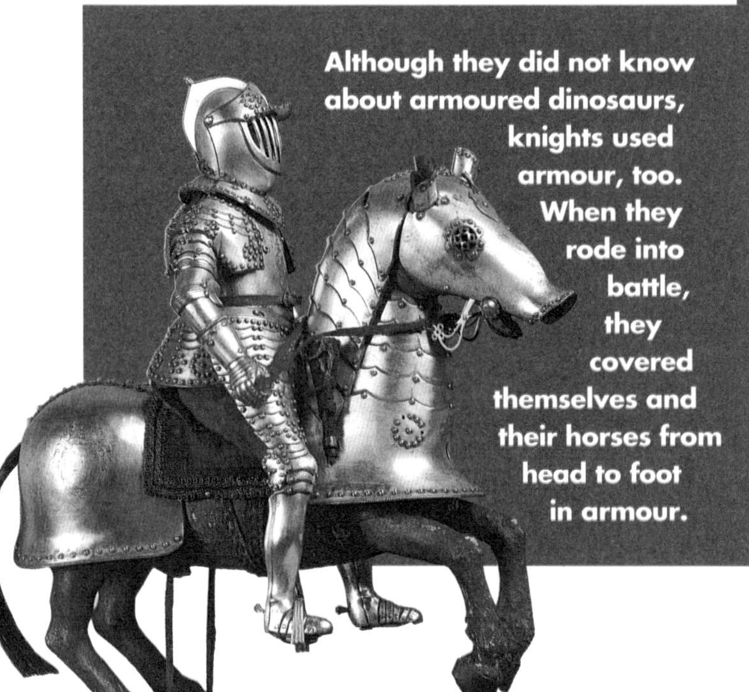

Although they did not know about armoured dinosaurs, knights used armour, too. When they rode into battle, they covered themselves and their horses from head to foot in armour.

The spikes on its neck and body protected *Polacanthus* (left) from attack from the side. Across its lower back, *Polacanthus* may have had extra bony lumps under its skin for added protection.

Bony plates were welded under *Euoplocephalus'* skin. The oval plate on the right of this picture is the size of an egg.

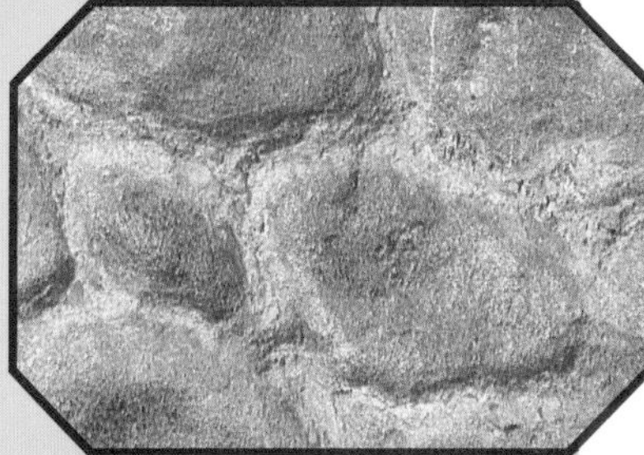

***Polacanthus* was covered in bony nodules, as this fossil impression of skin shows.**

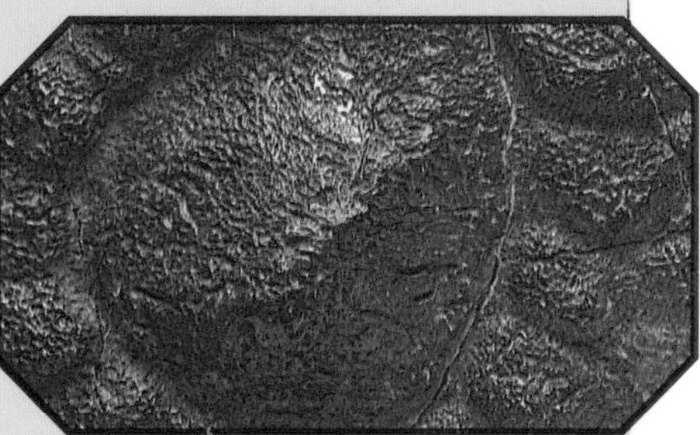

WEAK SPOT

Scientists have found fossils of *Ankylosaurus* lying on its back. This may have been because it fell into a river and drowned, but it is possible that a carnosaur rolled the ankylosaur over and attacked its unprotected belly.

DUCKING FROM DANGER

If there was no hope of escape, an ankylosaur would crouch down and tuck its legs underneath its body. Any hungry meat-eater trying to get a grip on its tough body was likely to come away with a few broken or blunted claws.

STRANGE SAUROPOD

Experts used to think that only dinosaurs like those on this page had armour. But, in 1980, they changed their minds when an armour-plated sauropod, called *Saltasaurus*, was found.

Although much smaller, today's armadillo (above) is the nearest animal we have to the ankylosaurs. If a predator threatens, it lies still on the ground, protected by its armour.

***Hylaeosaurus* (right) avoided any blows from predators by crouching down and turning itself into a mobile bomb shelter.**

Footprints across time

Strings of dinosaur footprints are called trackways. Trackways can tell a story. Be a dinosaur detective, follow the clues to solve a trackway mystery.

The mysterious dinosaur trackway (right) shows two sets of prints. One is bird-like, the other is larger and rounded.

One of the most mysterious trackways was found in Texas, USA. There are two very different sets of footprints side by side. What made them and what were they doing?

CLUE 1 The small, bird-like tracks shown in the picture above belonged to a fierce meat-eating theropod. The footprints are beside and slightly behind the bigger, rounded tracks. Palaeontologists think the bird-like tracks were made by *Allosaurus*, which grew up to 12m long.

CLUE 2 These footprints were made by a plant-eating sauropod as it plodded across a mud-flat about 160 MYA. It was probably *Apatosaurus*. This dinosaur was huge – as long as a tennis court and as heavy as seven elephants. Its footprints were also gigantic, measuring about 1m wide.

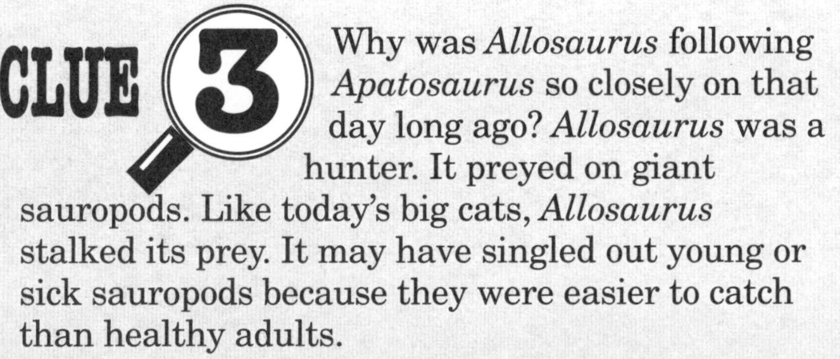

Why was *Allosaurus* following *Apatosaurus* so closely on that day long ago? *Allosaurus* was a hunter. It preyed on giant sauropods. Like today's big cats, *Allosaurus* stalked its prey. It may have singled out young or sick sauropods because they were easier to catch than healthy adults.

On the African plains today, cheetahs stalk a lunch of wildebeest just as some dinosaurs stalked their food millions of years ago.

The clearest fossil footprints are often those first made in sand. Will the sharp tracks left by a modern heron (below) become fossils of the future?

GOT IT!

Was *Allosaurus* stalking *Apatosaurus*? Yes, scientists think that it was. When the tracks were discovered, they were the first clue that some meat-eating dinosaurs hunted their prey, rather than waiting for it to drop dead.

HAPPY ENDING?

Did *Allosaurus* kill *Apatosaurus*? Perhaps the giant was too much for one *Allosaurus* and it may have escaped. The trackway ends suddenly, so we will never know.

IT'S A FACT

LONGEST TRACKWAY

The longest trackway discovered so far is in Colorado, USA. It was made by four *Apatosaurus* walking side by side. The trackway is over 215 metres long.

On the speed track

By studying trackways experts can find out just how speedily some dinosaurs were able to run.

The fastest dinosaurs looked like modern ostriches, and are known as ostrich dinosaurs. They dashed about on their hind legs, using their long toes to grip the ground.

GALLOPING GALLIMIMUS

Gallimimus, which lived at the end of the Age of the Dinosaurs, was an ostrich dinosaur – and one of the speediest. Its long legs were powered by strong muscles and its body was well-balanced by its neck and tail. By studying its footprints carefully, palaeontologists have estimated that *Gallimimus* could probably run flat out at a speed of about 56 km/h.

If you could put *Gallimimus,* a galloping horse and a cyclist in a race against each other, they would probably cross the finishing line in a dead heat. Palaeontologists have carefully measured the distance between *Gallimimus'* fossilized footprints. From these measurements they calculate that this dinosaur could have run at speeds of 56 km/h – which is about as fast as a cyclist or a galloping horse.

High in the La Sal Mountains in Utah, USA, an expert (above) studies the distance between the fossilized footprints of a giant meat-eater. The study may help tell how fast the dinosaur was travelling.

IT'S A FACT

FASTEST DINOSAUR

The fastest dinosaur was *Dromiceiomimus*. It could run more quickly than an ostrich, which has a top speed of 65 km/h. *Dromiceiomimus* had an extra-long shin bone and that helped it dash along.

SPEED CHECKS

Experts can tell how fast dinosaurs could move from their trackways. To find out, they measure the distance between two prints made by the same foot. That distance is called a stride length. The faster a dinosaur moved, the further apart its footprints were. So a long stride means a dinosaur was moving fast.

PRINT YOUR SPEED

Next time you are in a place where you can leave footprints, such as on the beach or a muddy path, you can do your own speed check experiment. Try walking first, then go back and run for the same distance. You will see how much further apart your footprints are when you are moving fast.

The tracks above were left by one of the fastest animals alive today. They were made by an ostrich (below) as it sped across an African desert. The flick marks show that it was running flat out – about 65 km/h.

45 3-D Gallery

BRACHIOSAURUS & ALLOSAURUS

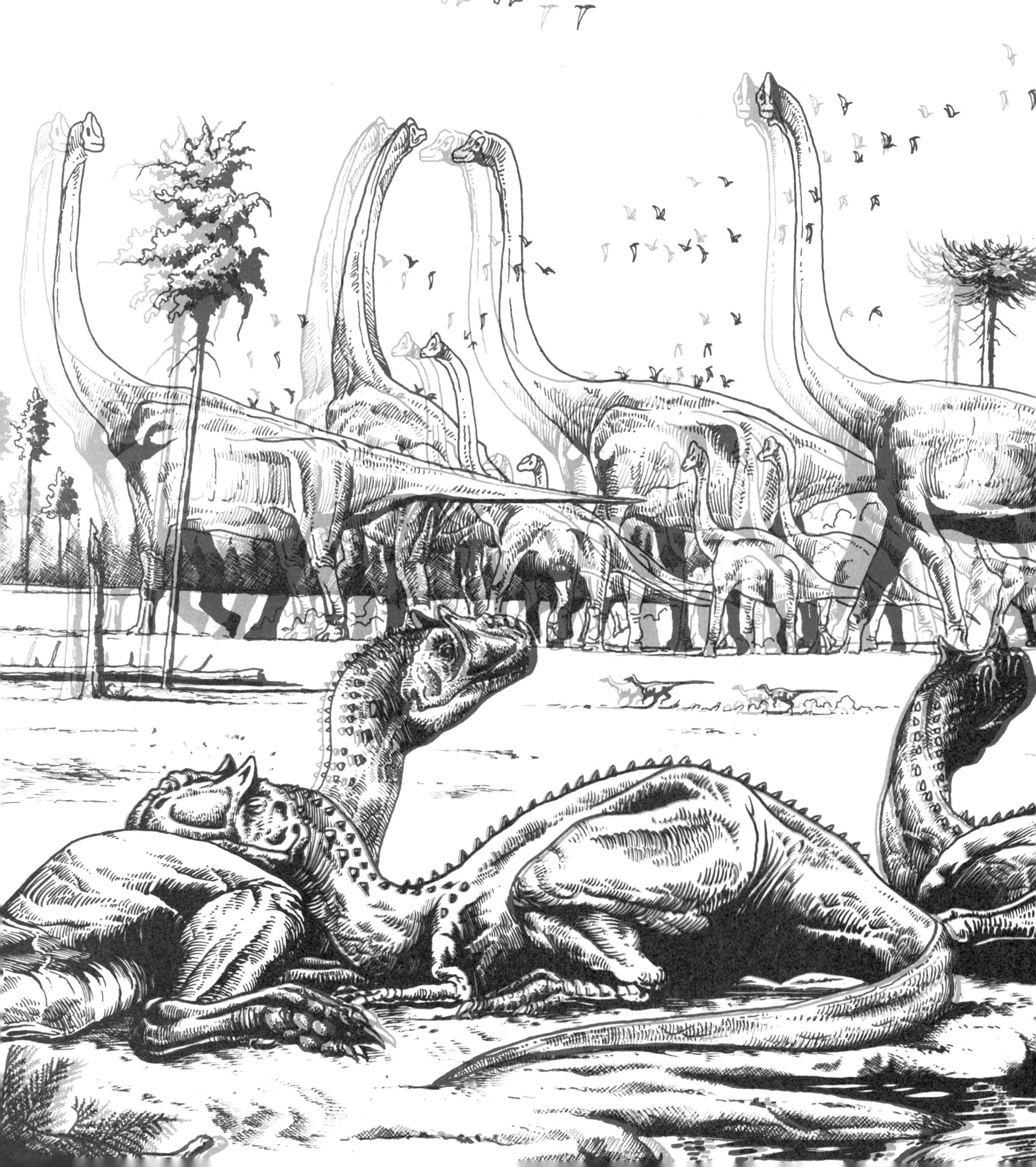

A herd of *Brachiosaurus* disturbs a group of *Allosaurus* relaxing next to a swamp. If they are hungry the carnivores will attack. But they must take care, a terrified herd of sauropods could stampede and crush the predators underfoot.

Dr. David Norman of Cambridge University answers your dinosaur questions
ASK THE EXPERT

Why did dinosaurs grow so big?

Not all dinosaurs were huge – there were lots of medium-sized and small ones, too. Some had plates or spikes that made their bodies look a lot larger than they actually were. Long-necked dinosaurs needed long tails to balance the weight of their tails. Some dinosaurs did have large bodies, but many were no larger than more recent animals – such as mammoths and rhinos. Dinosaurs often seem larger-than-life, but in reality they came in all different shapes and sizes.

How did baby sauropods feed?

Baby sauropods probably fed on low-growing plants. In areas where these dinosaurs lived, the ground was covered with ferns and young shoots of larger plants. This soft vegetation provided young sauropods with a nutritious diet. Only when they were older and larger would they have graduated to the tougher leaves and twigs of trees.

Did any dinosaurs eat fish?

This is a difficult question. I have to admit that I do not know whether dinosaurs ate fish. It has been suggested that a new dinosaur from Surrey, England, named *Baryonyx* was a fish-eater. It had smooth, conical teeth in the back part of its jaws – much like those of a fish-eating creature. Fish scales were found near to the animal, which looked as though they might have come from *Baryonyx's* stomach.

Which dinosaur laid the most eggs in one nest?

We do not know for sure, but I think that *Protoceratops* holds the record. Its nests contain about 30 eggs. Whether they were all laid by a single female, at one time, is unclear. Some scientists suspect that several females may have shared a nest. This would certainly explain the large number of eggs.

DINOSAURS!
DISCOVER THE GIANTS OF THE PREHISTORIC WORLD

PLATEOSAURUS

Plant-eating *Plateosaurus* was the first large dinosaur to live on Earth.

Before *Plateosaurus* lived, the biggest plant-eater was about the size of a large pig. *Plateosaurus* was much bigger – about as long as a bus. Sometimes it walked on four legs and fed on plants that grew on the ground. At other times, it reared up on strong back legs and looked for another place to feed. *Plateosaurus* might spot a cluster of tree ferns in the distance and head in that direction for the next meal. For, unlike any dinosaur that had existed before it, *Plateosaurus* could reach up to the tops of the highest trees.

NO COMPETITION

Many skeletons of *Plateosaurus* have been found. This dinosaur lived all over Europe and its fossils have been found in 50 different places. Perhaps the reason that *Plateosaurus* survived so well was because it did not have to compete for its food with other dinosaurs. None of the dinosaurs that lived at the same time as *Plateosaurus* was big enough to reach the tops of trees.

LEAF SHREDDER

Plateosaurus had leaf-shaped teeth with jagged edges. It used them to strip leaves from branches and shred tough shoots. Some scientists think that it ate meat as well as plants because its teeth were jagged like those of meat-eating theropods. But *Plateosaurus* had larger, coarser teeth than most meat-eaters.

***Plateosaurus'* skull has a set of teeth that look vicious enough to cut through meat, but they were actually designed for shredding leaves.**

MASHED FOOD

Plateosaurus' teeth and jaws were not well designed for chewing. It probably swallowed stones that lay in its stomach and worked like a grinder, mashing food to a pulp.

OFF BALANCE

Although it tilted back easily onto its hind legs to feed, *Plateosaurus* found walking upright quite difficult. Its long, flexible neck made it too top-heavy to walk on two legs all of the time. *Plateosaurus* was much more comfortable walking on all fours.

MONSTER FACTS

- **NAME:** *Plateosaurus* (plat-ee-oh-saw-rus) means 'flat reptile'
- **SIZE:** between 6 and 8m long
- **FOOD:** plants and leaves from trees
- **LIVED:** about 210 million years ago in the Late Triassic Period in France, Switzerland and Germany

Is it true that when dinosaurs first appeared on Earth all the continents were joined?

Yes! There were no seas dividing the land 225 million years ago. Early dinosaurs could wander all over the place. About 20 million years later, at the end of the Early Jurassic Period, two continents had formed. They were called Laurasia and Gondwanaland.

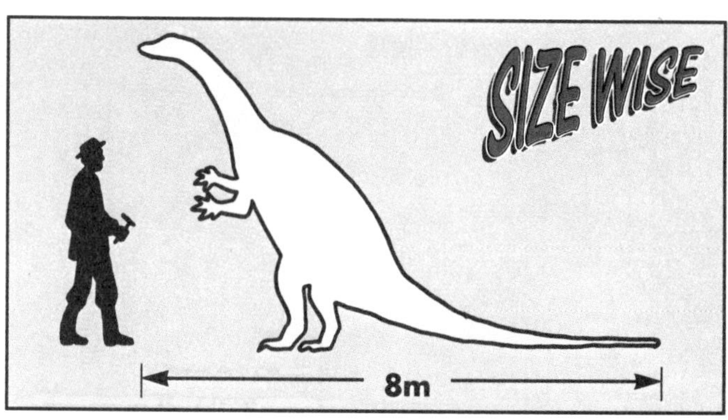

FLEXIBLE FINGERS

If you try to bend your fingers back you will probably find that they hardly move at all. Your bones are arranged in a way that makes this movement almost impossible. *Plateosaurus* could bend its fingers back quite easily. Its fingers were remarkable. The dinosaur rested them on the ground like toes, but if *Plateosaurus* wanted to grasp something, it bent its five clawed fingers forward in a tight grip.

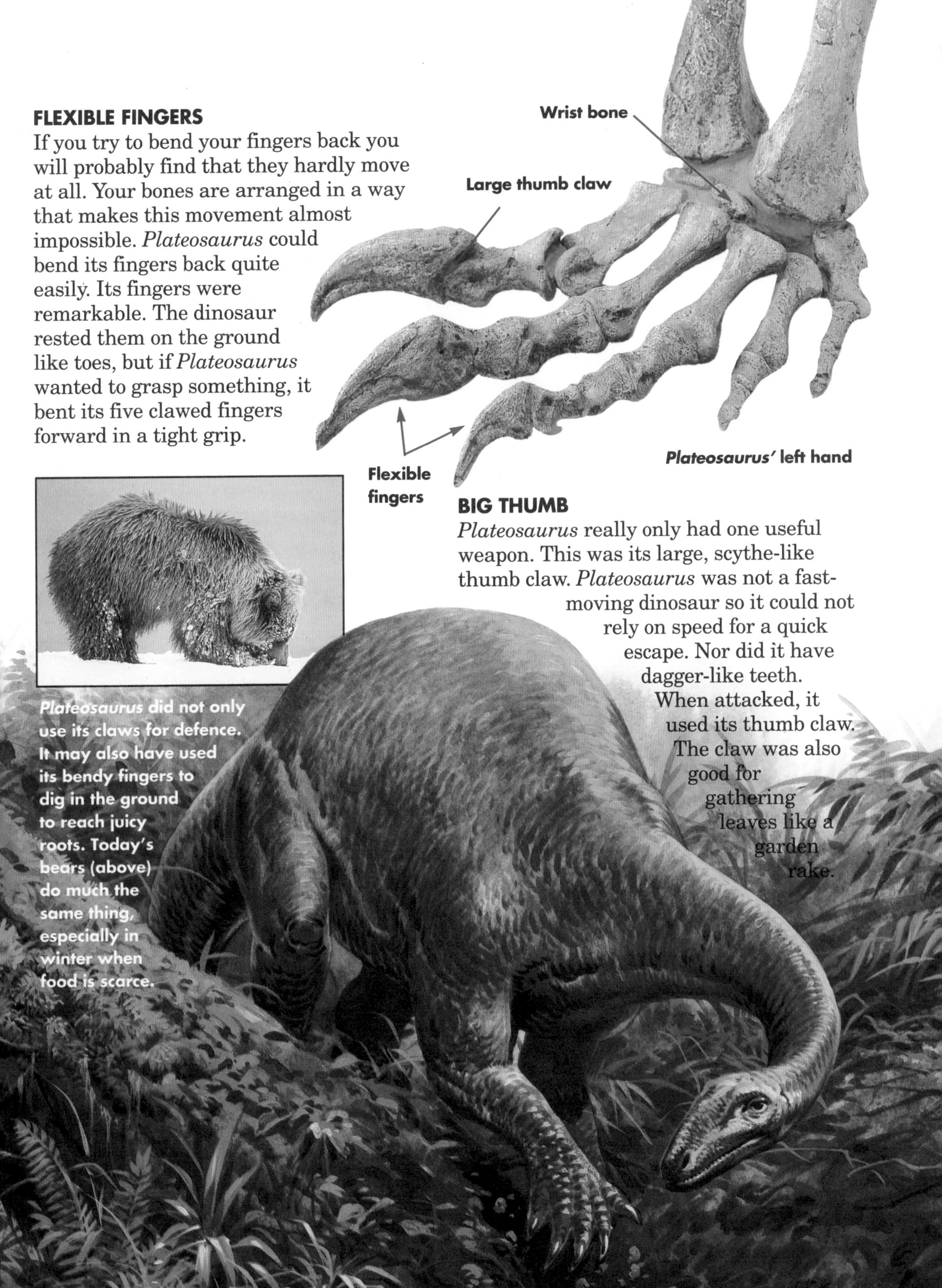

***Plateosaurus'* left hand**

BIG THUMB

Plateosaurus really only had one useful weapon. This was its large, scythe-like thumb claw. *Plateosaurus* was not a fast-moving dinosaur so it could not rely on speed for a quick escape. Nor did it have dagger-like teeth. When attacked, it used its thumb claw. The claw was also good for gathering leaves like a garden rake.

Plateosaurus **did not only use its claws for defence. It may also have used its bendy fingers to dig in the ground to reach juicy roots. Today's bears (above) do much the same thing, especially in winter when food is scarce.**

ORNITHOMIMUS

Ornithomimus was a sprint runner of the dinosaur world.

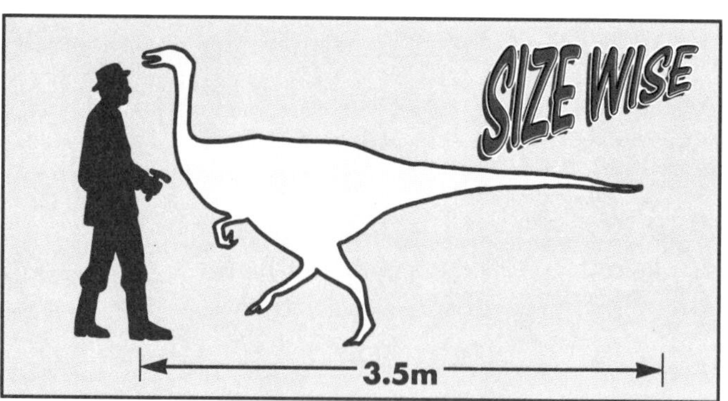

Intelligent *Ornithomimus* was one of the most graceful and lively of all dinosaurs. About the size of a pony and as long as a car, *Ornithomimus* is part of a group known as 'ostrich dinosaurs'. It had a lot in common with those big, flightless birds of today. Its long, muscular legs were built for speed and agility. *Ornithomimus* had a small skull at the end of its long, slender neck and its bones were very light.

MONSTER FACTS

- **NAME:** *Ornithomimus* (or-nith-oh-mime-us) means 'bird mimic'
- **SIZE:** 3.5m long
- **FOOD:** anything small enough to swallow – insects, lizards, mammals and fruit
- **LIVED:** 70 million years ago in the Late Cretaceous Period in North America and Tibet

VARIED DIET

Nimble *Ornithomimus* had a wide choice of things to eat. It was probably omnivorous, which means that it ate both meat and plants. *Ornithomimus* used its long arms and clawed hands to pull down branches. It could reach the choicest buds and berries. With its keen eyes and great speed, *Ornithomimus* could chase small lizards or pluck flying insects from the air. It chomped them up in its horny, toothless beak and swallowed them in chunks.

THREE FINGERS

Ornithomimus had flat, narrow claws on its feet. These gripped the ground like spikes on running shoes, stopping the dinosaur's feet from slipping as it sprinted after its prey.

LONG TAIL

Unlike an ostrich, *Ornithomimus* had a long tail. At almost 2m, it took up more than half of *Ornithomimus'* total length. Its tail was much less flexible than its bendy neck. *Ornithomimus* held its tail out stiffly behind itself when it ran. If it was running quickly over rough ground, *Ornithomimus'* tail helped to keep the dinosaur's balance.

ABELISAURUS

Abelisaurus had knife-like teeth and a skull as long as a cricket bat.

Everything we know about *Abelisaurus* is based only on one skull. It was discovered in Argentina in the 1980s. No bones from the dinosaur's body were found, but scientists have built up a good picture of what meat-eating *Abelisaurus* looked like.

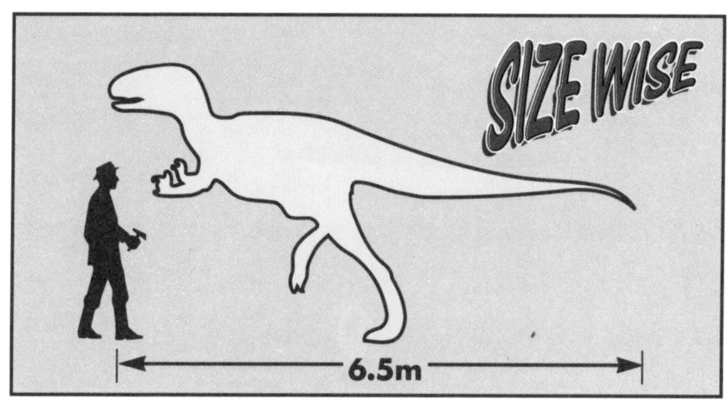

MONSTER FACTS

- **NAME:** *Abelisaurus* (ah-bell-ih-saw-rus) means 'Abel's reptile'
- **SIZE:** about 6.5m long
- **FOOD:** meat
- **LIVED:** about 80 million years ago in the Late Cretaceous Period in Patagonia, Argentina

TWO LEGGED

Abelisaurus was longer than a Nile crocodile and weighed about as much as a rhinoceros. It was taller than the goal-posts on a football pitch and walked on two muscular legs. It was able to move quickly in short attacking bursts of speed. Like *Tyrannosaurus* (to which it may have been distantly related), its front legs were tiny and high up on its body. Its clawed hands were used for slashing the flesh of its prey.

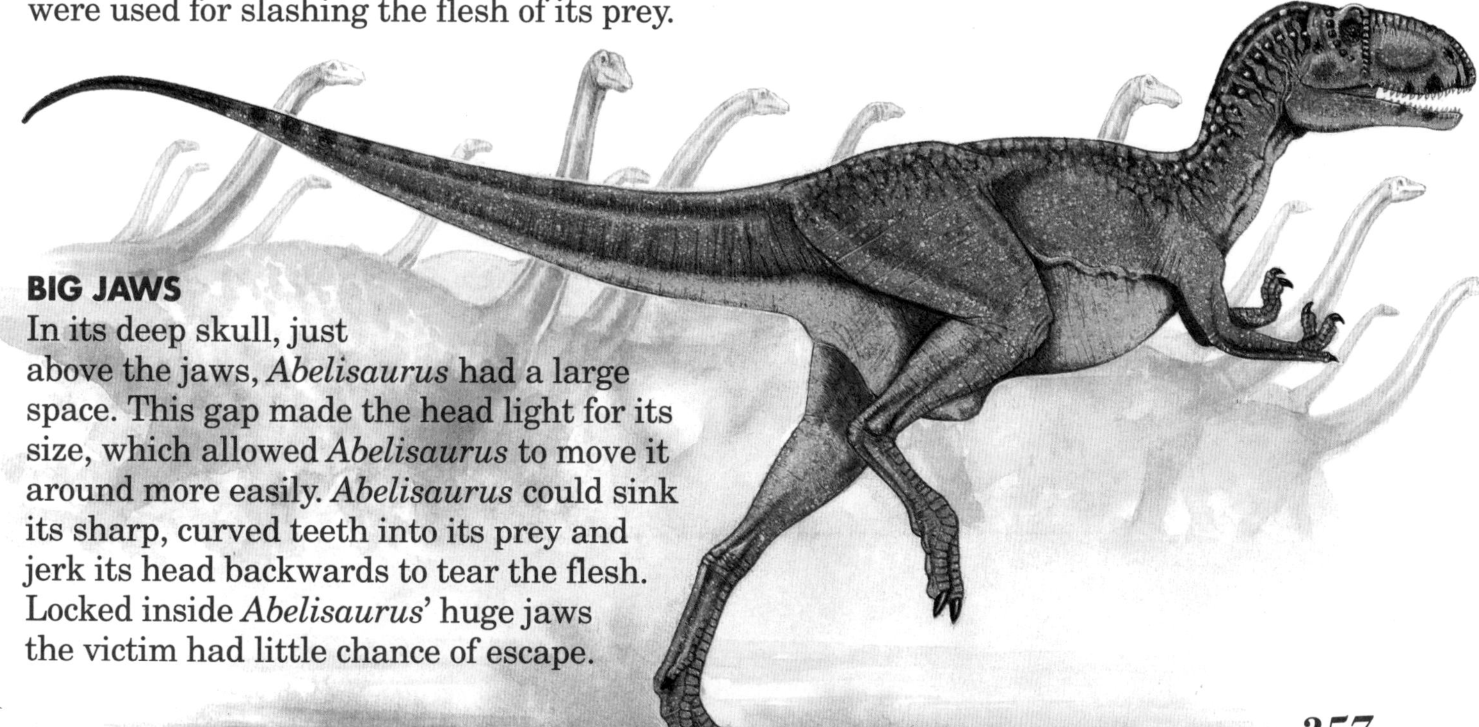

BIG JAWS

In its deep skull, just above the jaws, *Abelisaurus* had a large space. This gap made the head light for its size, which allowed *Abelisaurus* to move it around more easily. *Abelisaurus* could sink its sharp, curved teeth into its prey and jerk its head backwards to tear the flesh. Locked inside *Abelisaurus*' huge jaws the victim had little chance of escape.

The other 'Jaws'

Crocodiles appeared on Earth at about the same time as dinosaurs. These successful reptiles lived in the sea.

Dinosaurs did not live in the seas. Instead, the oceans were crowded with many other kinds of reptiles.

MONSTERS FROM THE DEEP

There was one group of fearsome prehistoric hunters, whose freshwater cousins still live today. If you swam in the prehistoric sea, they would swallow you for lunch. These were the sea-crocodiles.

Just like the prehistoric sea-crocs, the modern saltwater crocodile (above and top) can travel long distances in the sea, but usually stays near the coast. Many saltwater crocodiles are killed by people, so they are now protected by law.

Take a look at dangerous *Teleosaurus* (below) and see how crocodiles adapted to a life at sea.

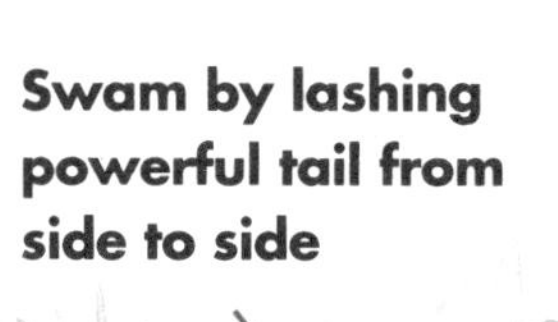

Swam by lashing powerful tail from side to side

Bony plates of armour became smaller and lighter

Strong tail and webbed feet made this animal a powerful swimmer

IT'S A FACT

ONLY ONE SEA-CROC

There are 22 kinds of crocodiles alive today. Only one of these lives in the sea. It is the estuarine or saltwater crocodile. It is not a descendant of the prehistoric sea-crocs, but a freshwater crocodile that has recently taken to the sea.

CLOSE COUSINS

Crocodiles are closely related to dinosaurs and at one time they lived alongside each other. Somehow, crocodiles survived the catastrophe that spelled **THE END** for the dinosaurs. Today, crocodiles remain almost unchanged.

FROM LAND TO THE SEA

Early in their evolution, crocodiles went back into the water, away from the dinosaurs on land. Their body shapes changed so that they were more suited to life in the water. Most early crocodiles lurked in rivers and swamps, feeding on fish and grabbing animals that came to drink. A few crocodiles went further – out to sea. They looked like a modern crocodile called a gharial (ga-ree-al).

STREAMLINED CROCS

One gharial-like sea-croc was *Teleosaurus* (tel-ee-oh-saw-rus), the 'end reptile', another was *Steneosaurus* (sten-ee-oh-saw-rus). These deadly beasts had streamlined bodies that were the length of a family car. Rows of needle teeth helped them to catch flapping fish and squirming squid. In time, their skin became less bumpy and they spent most of their lives in the water. Like modern turtles, they only had to come ashore for one thing – to lay their eggs.

Eyes at the top of the head. This meant the crocodile could lie low, with just its eyes above the water so it could still see

Nostrils on top of the snout allowed the crocodile to breathe while lying low in the water

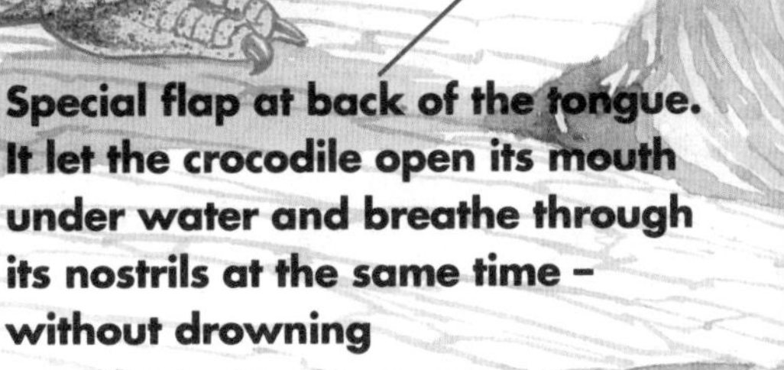

Special flap at back of the tongue. It let the crocodile open its mouth under water and breathe through its nostrils at the same time – without drowning

Gharials (below) live in Indian rivers today, not in the sea. They look like *Teleosaurus* (left) – they even have the same thin snout – but they are not closely related.

MORE LIKE A FISH

Some sea-crocs became even more suited to an ocean-going life. They even started to look more like fishes. They lost the heavy, bony armour and their skin became smooth and slippery. Legs evolved into flippers. Tails became tall and thin, more like fins. But they were still reptiles and they had lungs, not gills. They had to come to the water's surface for a breath of fresh air, as whales do today.

Scientists are not sure whether prehistoric sea-crocs crawled onto land to lay their eggs like the sea-dwelling green turtle (above) does today.

LONG SNOUT

One of these sea-crocs was *Metriorhynchus* (met-ree-or-rin-kuss). The name means 'long snout' – which it certainly had! This 3m-long hunter lived during the late Jurassic Period. Its tail tipped down near the end, with a fin sticking up.

Metriorhynchus **(above) was a big eater. It ate squid and pterosaurs, but it also went for fish that were 6m long – twice its own length!**

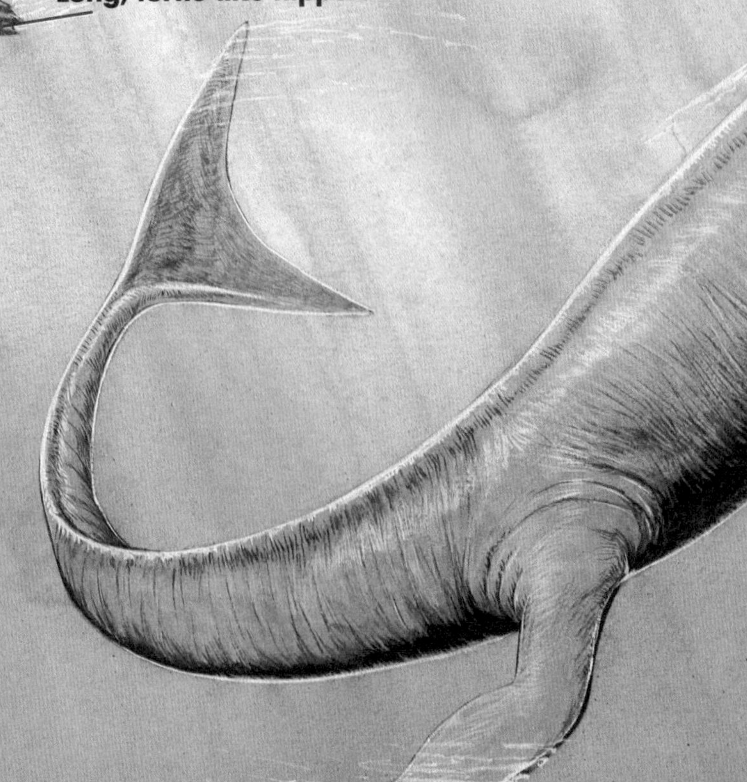

TERROR IN THE WAVES

Sea-crocs were just as fierce as their freshwater cousins. Fossils show that *Metriorhynchus* ate many types of fish. It also grabbed squid – and even the occasional pterosaur!

How did it breed? Perhaps the females pulled themselves onto the beach using their long flippers, as sea turtles do nowadays, and laid their eggs in the sand.

TAIL TALE

Towards the end of the Jurassic Period, sea-crocs became even better suited to life in the ocean waves. *Geosaurus* (gee-oh-saw-rus), which means 'rock reptile', had a tail fin very similar to that of a fish or ichthyosaur. It must have been a very fast swimmer, thrashing its tail from side to side and using its wide paddles for steering. *Geosaurus'* flippers would have been useless on land. So it may have had some way of producing its babies in the water. Like ichthyosaurs, the female probably carried the eggs inside her body until they hatched. The babies would float or swim straight to the surface to breathe, perhaps helped by their mother.

Is it true that some eggs hatch inside the mother?

Yes. The female keeps her eggs safe and warm inside her body until they hatch. The babies come out of the eggshells and then out of the mother's birth opening fully formed and ready to swim, breathe and feed. Today, sea-snakes, several kinds of fishes, some amphibians and some sharks have babies this way. The are all called ovo-viviparous. 'Ovo' means egg, 'vivi' means alive, and 'parous' is to do with birth. In prehistoric times, ichthyosaurs and some sea-crocodiles, such as *Geosaurus*, were probably ovo-viviparous.

TOO-FAST FOOD

The whole sea-croc group did not last much longer after the Jurassic Period. During the Cretaceous Period, they were replaced by the pliosaurs and mosasaurs. Also, more advanced bony fishes were replacing the older, slower types of fishes that many sea-crocs ate. Faced with this changing world, the sea-crocodiles died out well before the last of the dinosaurs.

***Geosaurus* (left) helps her babies to the surface for their first gulps of air. She probably gave birth to her babies in the sea, just like the lemon shark (below).**

A baby lemon shark is born. It is already fully formed. The baby shark hatched out of its egg before it came out of its mother's body. Perhaps this is how *Geosaurus* was born.

GIANTS OF THE PAST

PLATEOSAURUS

A massive storm caused a sudden flood to flash through a valley and overcome a herd of *Plateosaurus*. The roaring flood water swept the dinosaurs before it. Hundreds of *Plateosaurus* desperately tried to reach dry land, but were sucked under the water and drowned. When the flood waters receded, the dinosaurs' bodies formed a huge graveyard, which was discovered in Germany millions of years later.

3-D Gallery 26

HETERODONTOSAURUS

- Early plant-eater with three different kinds of teeth
- Lived 190 – 180 million years ago in southern Africa
- Measured 1.2m long
- Ate tough plants

A peek at beaks

Nearly all dinosaurs had teeth. So why did some of them need beaks?

Not all dinosaurs had beaks of course; *T rex* had so many teeth that it did not need a beak. But a beak was an essential tool for those dinosaurs that ate a lot of tough leaves and branches.

CUTTING EDGE

Ferns, cycads, palms and oak trees grew very successfully during the Cretaceous Period. Although these plants had quite soft leaves, their stalks were tough and woody. Just as gardeners use sharp cutters to prune bushes, some dinosaurs were equipped with a sharp, nipping beak to slice through stems.

PARROT DINOSAUR

Psittacosaurus is thought to be the first member of the ceratopian family. Its teeth were not as well-developed as later ceratopians, such as *Triceratops*, but like the rest of its family, it had a sharp, curved beak. The shape of its snout was so bird-like that the experts who discovered it called it 'parrot lizard'.

Its curved beak lets this macaw crack the hardest nut. *Psittacosaurus*' beak (far left) was strong, too.

***Triceratops* (left) used its beak to chop plants into manageable bite-sized pieces.**

BIGGER AND BETTER

As time went by, horned dinosaurs developed even better beaks. By the Late Cretaceous, ceratopians' beaks were perfectly designed for their purpose. *Triceratops* was one of the last known dinosaurs to walk the Earth. Its beak cut through large, tough plants like a pair of wire cutters.

BITE-SIZE PIECES

Once the leaves and stems were nipped off the bush, a horned dinosaur could store them in its cheeks. The food was then moved to the back of the mouth where rows of teeth sliced it up before the dinosaur swallowed.

EATING ALL DAY

Rather like our hair and nails, dinosaurs' beaks were always growing. If dinosaurs' beaks had not re-grown, a lifetime of munching on leaves and branches would eventually have worn them right down.

***Dryosaurus* (left) lived during the Jurassic, the age of the conifers. Its narrow beak was perfect for nipping off pieces of tough fir.**

BONY BEAK

The inside of a dinosaur's beak was made of bone. This bone was covered in a horny coating. Like dinosaurs' claws and skin, this did not fossilize well. We know about this horny coating because palaeontologists have found some rare skulls with the horny covering still on the beak.

***Tenontosaurus* (right) daintily nips a small shoot from a tree.**

PICKING AT THEIR FOOD

Some experts think that beaked dinosaurs were quite choosy with their food. Dinosaurs with narrow beaks, such as *Hypsilophodon,* may have nipped shoots and buds that looked particularly good. Duckbills were probably less fussy. They may have used their broad bills to pick up mixed mouthfuls of vegetation.

***Hypsilophodon* had a narrow beak that let it choose single leaves and stems to eat.**

Is it true that some modern reptiles have beaks?

Beaked dinosaurs had tremendous biting power. This has survived in some present-day animals. Turtles, like this loggerhead turtle (below), have been known to inflict a nasty bite with their beaks. During World War II, a loggerhead turtle attacked an inflatable life-raft full of British airmen with its curved beak. Like beaked dinosaurs, turtles are not naturally aggressive, but they are short-sighted – maybe the loggerhead turtle saw the lifeboat as a threat!

Running with the herd

Some of the most exciting trackway discoveries prove that dinosaurs roamed the land in herds.

In North America, huge areas of mudstone have been found covered in a mass of dinosaur footprints. Many of the footprints are going the same way. Experts believe this means that the dinosaurs must have been travelling in large groups, or herds.

PROTECTING THE YOUNG

These trackways provide important clues about the way dinosaurs in herds behaved. Some sauropod trackways show big footprints on the outside and smaller ones in between. Experts believe that this was because the herd moved in a special way to protect its young. Adult dinosaurs stayed on the outside to frighten off predators, while the babies stayed safely in the middle.

Five massive sauropods left these tracks as they plodded along together millions of years ago.

A herd of *Brachiosaurus* travels across the country in search of food. They strip the trees and push them over, eating everything. As they go, their footprints churn up the land.

MODERN HERDS

Today, many animals, such as wildebeest, that live in herds on the great African plains migrate (move) to fresh feeding grounds at different times of the year. They travel hundreds of miles in great herds across the plains to find enough food to feed themselves.

Huge herds of animals still roam our planet, millions of years after the last dinosaur died. These wildebeest (right) can sense rain 50 km away. Several thousand of them move together to find the rain and fresh grass. Like dinosaurs, they leave trackways as they pass.

POLE TO POLE

Dinosaur herds behaved in much the same way millions of years ago. Fossil bones of plant-eating dinosaurs have been found amazingly close to both the Arctic and Antarctic Circles. There would have been plenty of food there in the summer but almost none in the winter. So it seems likely that the herds were just summer visitors, travelling north and south in search of food.

IT'S A FACT

TOO COLD FOR COMFORT

Winters in the Arctic and the Antarctic were cool and dark in the Age of the Dinosaurs. Dinosaurs would have needed warm coats to survive.

But there is no evidence that they grew any fur to keep the cold out. Scientists believe that this is another good reason to think that herds migrated away from the Poles when winter came.

Changing the landscape

What happened to the countryside when herds of massive dinosaurs ate their way across the land?

Dinosaurs needed lots of food to keep going. Herds of the biggest plant-eaters must have been on the move almost all the time searching for fresh feeding grounds.

STRIPPING THE FORESTS

Giant sauropods were specially adapted to make feeding as easy as possible. They all had extra-long necks which they either used to munch on low-growing ferns or to tear leaves off high branches. Just one *Brachiosaurus* may have eaten 1,500kg of food in a day. So a herd of sauropods could have stripped a forest almost bare.

When *Brachiosaurus* (below) pushed trees over to reach the leaves, light reached plants growing on the forest floor and gave them a chance to grow. Elephants can do this, too.

Just like today's elephants (above), *Brachiosaurus* must have stripped the countryside of its vegetation. But this was not always a disaster for the land ...

FAST FOOD

Plant-eating dinosaurs devoured almost everything, from pine cones to palm leaves. They were built to eat a huge range of plants. Sauropods like *Brachiosaurus* simply swallowed everything up. Ceratopians like *Triceratops* used their horny beaks and the scissor-like teeth at the back of their mouths to rip off the toughest leaves.

The havoc below, made by elephants, must be like the damage *Brachiosaurus* left behind. Scientists think dinoturbation (disturbing the land) helped to create the right conditions for the first flowering plants to grow.

HELPING PLANTS TO GROW

The largest modern plant-eater is an elephant. A feeding herd can cause so much damage to woodland that they sometimes have to be shot to reduce their numbers. But experts now believe elephants can also help the countryside by creating more open places. New plants can grow there on which other animals can feed. Elephants also produce a lot of dung. Dung makes the soil more fertile. It also contains seeds from the trees the elephants have eaten, which grow into new trees. Herds of dinosaurs may have helped their environment in the same way.

DID DINOSAURS INVENT FLOWERS?

Herds of giant plant-eating dinosaurs must have left vast areas of stripped trees and trampled earth behind them. Experts think that sauropods might have helped the first flowering plants to flourish in the Cretaceous Period. Flowering plants, like the magnolia below, spread quickly in the areas that had been cleared, just as weeds spring up in a freshly dug garden.

THE PLANTS FIGHT BACK

No other group of plant-eaters since the dinosaurs has been able to eat so many different sorts of vegetation. Many of today's plant-eaters eat grass, and there was no grass at the time of the dinosaurs.

Few plants survived the Age of the Dinosaurs but the ones that continue to grow today still have the special defences they must have developed millions of years ago to try to stop the dinosaurs eating them. They include ferns which contain special chemicals that can poison animals that try to feed on them, and some prickly-leaved plants and leathery-leaved trees like the monkey puzzle tree.

46
3-D Gallery

IGUANODON V BECKLESPINAX

A ravenous *Becklespinax* tries to get his claws into what he hopes will be his next snack, a baby *Iguanodon*. But its spectacular spines do not manage to frighten away adult *Iguanodon* who rush to protect their baby. This time it looks as if *Becklespinax* is going to be defeated by *Iguanodon*.

Dr. David Norman of Cambridge University answers your dinosaur questions
ASK THE EXPERT

Why did some dinosaurs have head crests?

A crest or ridge on the head is something very noticeable – in the same way that you would immediately spot someone in the street wearing a funny hat, or a bright green wig. This is precisely the idea. Dinosaurs with crests wanted to be noticed. They wanted to scare predators away, to attract other dinosaurs or just to let others know that they were there. Nearly all the crests were different so that dinosaurs could tell one from another.

Could dinosaurs catch and eat pterosaurs?

We have no evidence that dinosaurs regularly ate pterosaurs, but if a small hunting dinosaur caught a pterosaur on the ground, it would have eaten it. However, they were probably rather bony to eat. A few giant sea-going reptiles (plesiosaurs) may have eaten pterosaurs that had crash-landed into the sea.

Did any dinosaurs eat shellfish?

To eat shellfish, animals usually need broad, flat teeth. They use these hammer-like teeth to crack open the hard shells. There is no evidence that any dinosaurs had teeth like this. Experts agree that it is unlikely that dinosaurs ate shellfish.

How can experts tell when a dinosaur lived?

This is the work of geologists – scientists who study rocks. There is a variety of techniques which geologists use to date rocks. The most important one is called 'radiometric dating'. First, geologists find out if a rock is radioactive, and then they can tell how old it is. For example, they can find out if it is from the Triassic, Jurassic or Cretaceous and from what part of the period. Any dinosaur fossils that are found in the rock will be the same age.

DINOSAURS!
DISCOVER THE GIANTS OF THE PREHISTORIC WORLD

CENTROSAURUS

***Centrosaurus* was a sociable dinosaur. Living in great herds, it usually had plenty of company.**

Hundreds of fossils of this horned dinosaur were found in the Red Deer Valley area of Alberta, Canada. Scientists were able to work out not only what *Centrosaurus* looked like, but how it lived. It was about as long as an elephant and as tall as an adult human. With a single horn on its snout and a chunky body, *Centrosaurus* looked like a big rhinoceros.

UNDER ATTACK

When attacked by giant tyrannosaurids (two-legged meat-eaters), a herd of *Centrosaurus* had a clever way of keeping safe. The males formed a ring around the young and female dinosaurs and faced outwards with their sharp horns at the ready. Just like a ring of wagons in the old Wild West, this circle of dinosaurs was difficult for the attackers to break through.

TRAMPLED BONES

The scientists who found the fossilized herd of *Centrosaurus* noticed that some of the bones were broken. The bones looked as if they had been trampled on. It is possible that the damage was done as the herd stampeded when trying to cross a fast-flowing river.

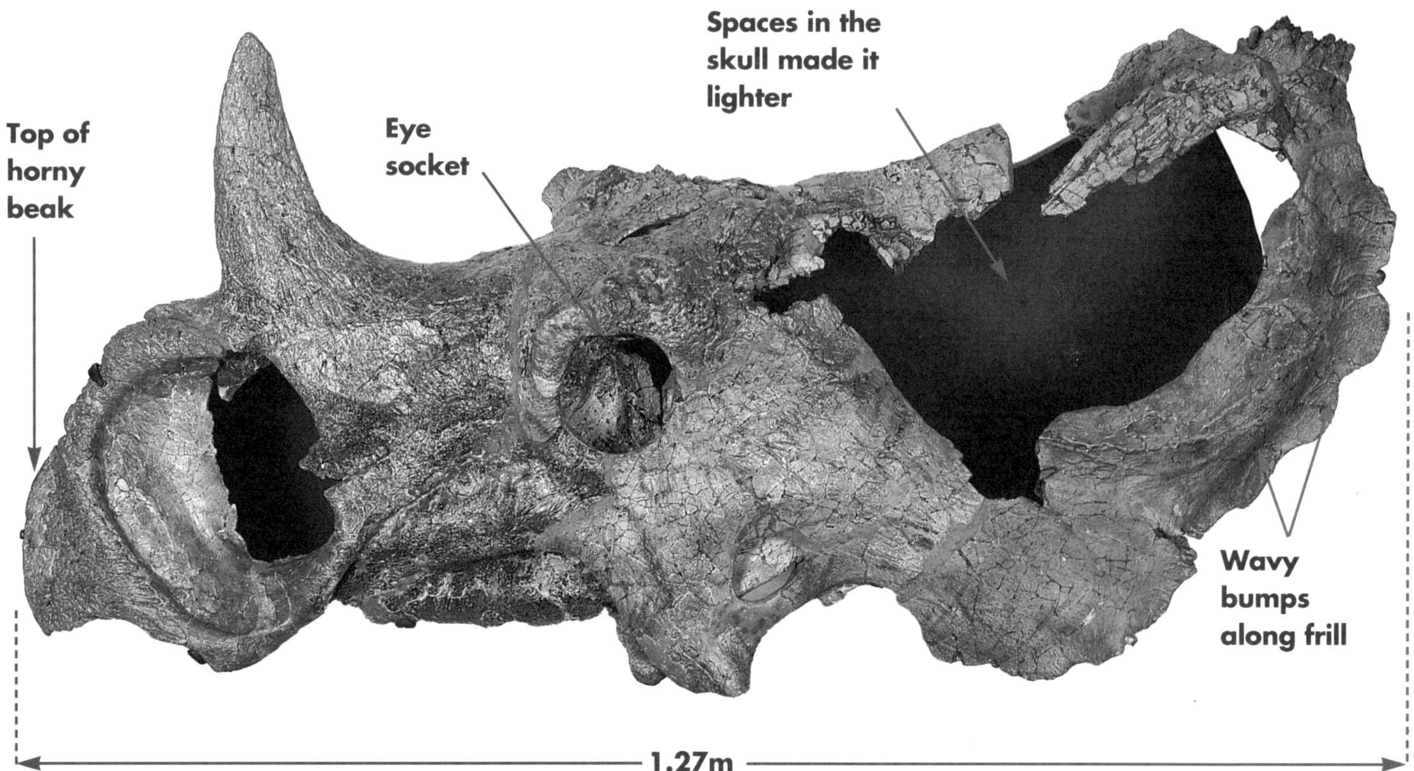

***Centrosaurus'* skull is so big that it could just fit on a two-seater sofa. The bumps along the frill may have just been for decoration.**

MONSTER FACTS

- **NAME:** *Centrosaurus* (sen-troh-saw-rus) means 'sharp pointed reptile'
- **SIZE:** about 6m long and 1.8m high
- **FOOD:** low-growing plants
- **LIVED:** about 80 million years ago in the Late Cretaceous Period in Alberta, Canada

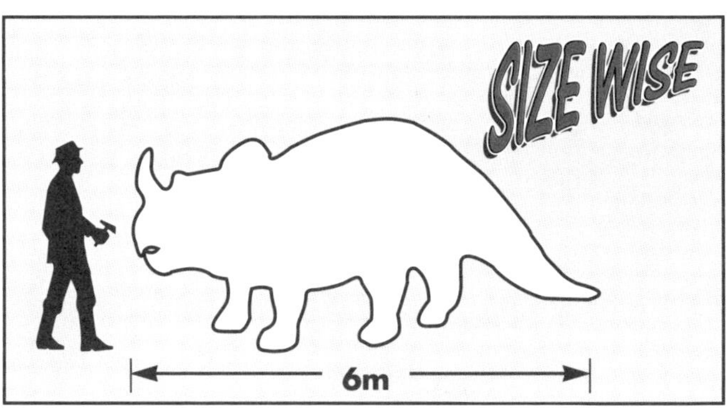

FIGHT NOT FLIGHT

Centrosaurus was not built for speed. With its heavy body and pillar-like legs, it had to stand its ground against predators. *Centrosaurus* did not always stay with its herd. When it went off alone to look for food, it became a tempting target for meat-eaters like *Albertosaurus.* But predators had to move fast. If *Centrosaurus* caught sight of its attacker, it crouched low, spreading its legs apart ready to charge like a rhinoceros. Imagine that sharp, pointed horn coming straight at you. Even the biggest dinosaur could be hurt – or killed – when speared by *Centrosaurus.*

HEAVY HEADED

Because its head and frill were so big compared with the rest of its body, *Centrosaurus* needed a very strong neck and shoulders. Even a small shake of the head put a lot of pressure on *Centrosaurus'* bones. Some of its neck bones were welded together for extra strength.

TIP TOES

Centrosaurus had broad feet with splayed toes. This provided a large surface so that its great weight was evenly spread. As it walked, *Centrosaurus* probably put its hoofed toes to the ground rather than its whole foot. Its front legs were very strong. Shorter than the hind legs, they bore much of the weight of the massive head and body.

SLICING THROUGH

Snipping off shoots with its beak, *Centrosaurus* browsed among low-lying plants. Its teeth had sharp edges that sliced through plants like a guillotine. New teeth grew as the old ones wore out.

A BIG FRILL

Attached to *Centrosaurus'* neck was a bony frill with little, wavy bumps along the edge. Scientists believe that the frill was probably a sort of dinosaur status symbol. It may have been brightly coloured to help *Centrosaurus* to stand out from the crowd, or attract a mate.

IT'S A FACT

FAMOUS SITE

About 500 dinosaur skeletons have been found in the Red Deer Valley in Canada. Known as the 'Badlands', this area is one of the most important dinosaur sites in the world. It contains fossils of hadrosaurs, ankylosaurs, *Albertosaurus* and a whole herd of horned *Centrosaurus.*

***Centrosaurus'* frill would have been almost useless for defence. It is far more likely that it was used to make an impression. A male *Centrosaurus* may have coloured his frill at mating time, in the hope of standing out from the crowd.**

TARBOSAURUS

For its size, *Tarbosaurus* had the smallest arms of any predatory dinosaur. They were not even long enough to reach its mouth.

Some scientists think that *Tarbosaurus* is so like *Tyrannosaurus* that they must be the same animal. But *Tarbosaurus* was found in Mongolia – thousands of miles from Canada where *Tyrannosaurus* lived. *Tarbosaurus* also had a larger head and a lighter body than its Canadian relative.

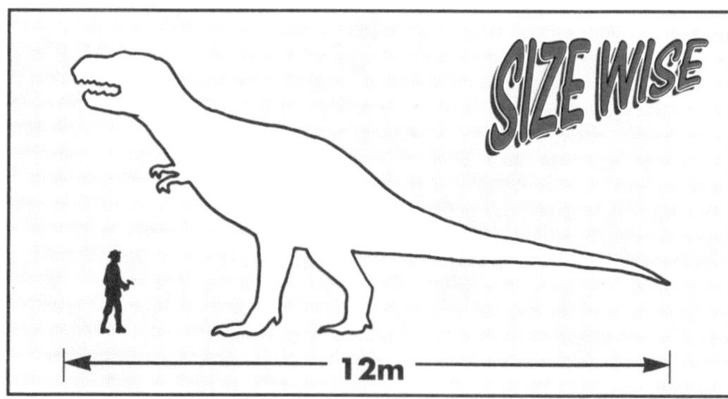

MONSTER FACTS

- **NAME:** *Tarbosaurus* (tar-boh-saw-rus) means 'alarming dinosaur'
- **SIZE:** about 12m long
- **FOOD:** meat, especially other dinosaurs
- **LIVED:** about 70 million years ago in the Late Cretaceous Period in Mongolia

TERRIBLE TEETH

The sight of *Tarbosaurus* with its mouth gaping wide must have been terrifying – its skull alone was as long as a leopard! Its whole body was longer than three cars. Inside its upper jaw, 27 long, curved teeth were poised ready to sink into the flesh of another dinosaur.

FEEBLE HANDS

Tarbosaurus had tiny arms and hands. These were no good for fighting, but each finger had a strong claw that the dinosaur used to push against the ground as it stood upright. *Tarbosaurus* had much stronger feet and three large, clawed toes. Its long ankle bones meant that it could move fast enough to give another dinosaur a nasty surprise.

RHABDODON

Dainty *Rhabdodon* was as fleet-footed as a gazelle as it sprinted along on long, slender legs.

About as long as a family-sized car, *Rhabdodon* was bigger and heavier than its relative *Hypsilophodon*. Both these animals belong to a group nicknamed 'gazelle dinosaurs'. *Rhabdodon* moved with the same grace and strength as an agile gazelle. It was so speedy that it could outrun most predators.

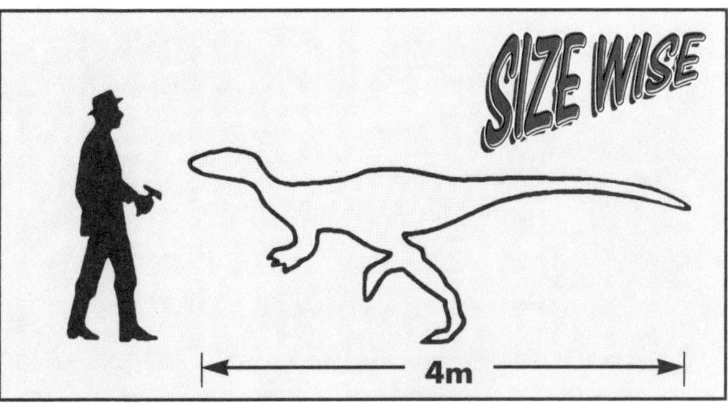

MONSTER FACTS

- **NAME:** *Rhabdodon* (rab-doh-don) means 'rod tooth'
- **SIZE:** about 4m long
- **FOOD:** leaves from plants, trees and shrubs
- **LIVED:** about 80 million years ago in the Late Cretaceous Period in France, Austria and Romania

WELL CHEWED

Rhabdodon did not have to be reminded to chew its food well! It had an efficient way of eating its favourite plants and shoots. First, it nipped off a branch with the sharp edge of its horny beak. Inside its strong jaws, *Rhabdodon* had rows of teeth that overlapped to form a keen cutting blade. Its fleshy cheeks pushed food back towards the blade to be chewed over and over again. Even the toughest plants were soon minced into a soft mush.

FINGERS AND TOES

Rhabdodon probably had five fingers on each hand, which helped it grasp branches and pull them down as it browsed among trees and shrubs. All of the four toes on its feet were tipped with claws. These gave *Rhabdodon* a firm grip as it sprinted along the ground.

The great survivors

There are creatures stalking the Earth today whose ancestors hunted dinosaurs – they are the crocodiles.

There's something sinister about a crocodile. With its sprawling legs, slinky tail and rows of pointed teeth, it lurks in the timeless swamp, waiting to grab a victim. Crocodiles seem to be from another time, before people lived on Earth – in fact they are!

CROCODILE KINDS

There are 22 kinds of crocs alive today. They include the crocodiles themselves, alligators, caimans from Central and South America and gharials from India. Together they are known as crocodilians. They are survivors of a group that has flourished for millions of years during and after the Age of the Dinosaurs.

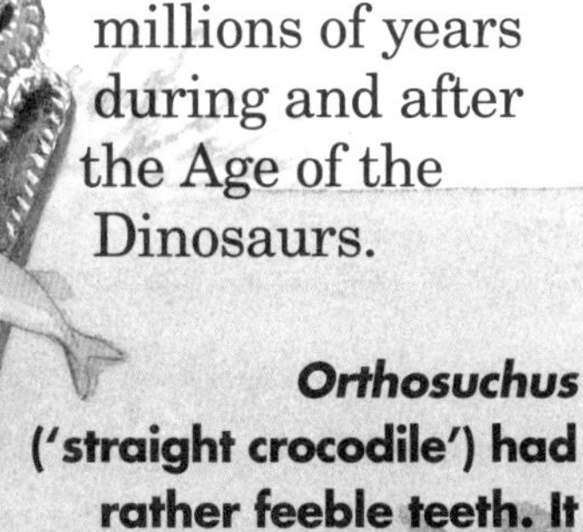

***Orthosuchus* ('straight crocodile') had rather feeble teeth. It probably fed on fish that it snapped up in the swamp.**

CROCODILE KIN

Where did crocodiles come from? About 250 million years ago, a new group of reptiles appeared – the 'ruling reptiles' (archosaurs). Three important groups of animals evolved from the early archosaurs: the pterosaurs in the air, the dinosaurs on land and the crocodiles in rivers and swamps. This means crocodilians are the closest living cousins of the dinosaurs.

WAY OF LIFE

In some terrible catastrophe at the end of the Cretaceous, dinosaurs and pterosaurs died out. The crocodiles were the only survivors and they have hardly changed for almost 200 million years. So we can look at them today and work out how the prehistoric crocodiles lived.

CROCODILE DESIGN

Crocodiles have ankle joints that let them walk with their legs sticking out at the sides of their bodies. They can also trot along with their legs almost straight beneath them. With their eyes and nose sticking above the water, crocodiles look like old logs as they lie in wait for prey. A special flap separates crocodiles' breathing and eating tubes, so these animals can open their mouths to bite victims under water.

Orthosuchus

***Protosuchus* was one of the earliest crocodiles. This long-legged animals was also one of the smallest. It was named by the famous fossil hunter Barnum Brown.**

Living alligators (above), caimans (left) and crocodiles (below) are still masters of their environments. Today, their only enemies are humans.

FIRST CROCS

Protosuchus (pro-toh-soo-kuss), 'first crocodile', lived about 200 million years ago. Looking at the picture of *Protosuchus* (above), you might not think that it looks much like a crocodile. At about 1m long, it lived on dry land and had a wide head, a light body and long legs. Like a crocodile, it had sharp teeth and an armour-plated back. *Orthosuchus* (or-tho-soo-kuss) lived at about the same time as *Protosuchus*. With a short snout, it looked more like the crocodiles we know today. *Orthosuchus* had shorter legs than *Protosuchus,* with long fingers and toes.

What is? THE SECRET OF CROCODILE SURVIVAL

Scientists think that crocodiles have survived for so long because they can cope with change. They eat whatever is available, alive or dead. They can move on land or in water. They are good parents, and give their babies a sure start in life. If things get too uncomfortable, they sleep in the mud or even at the bottom of a river! Crocodiles have survived because they are not fussy – they can eat anything or live more or less anywhere.

SUNBATHING

The ancient crocodiles were almost certainly cold-blooded animals, like the crocodiles of today. They would sunbathe to get warm, ready for a burst of action. If a croc was too hot, it would open its mouth and let the breeze cool its tongue and the lining inside its mouth. Being cold-blooded meant the crocs used little energy and they could survive for several weeks on one big meal.

This crocodile (below) is not laughing, it is cooling down. Breezes waft across the inside of its mouth and cool the blood that is just under the skin's surface. Ancient crocodiles probably gaped like this as well.

LIVING WITH IGUANODON

The fossils of two crocodiles were found down the mine at Bernissart, Belgium, where 39 *Iguanodon* were discovered. One was called *Goniopholis* (gon-ee-oh-fo-lis). It was 3m long and had 23 pairs of teeth. The other, *Bernissartia* (ber-ni-sar-tia), was only 1m long and is named after the coal-mining village. There were plenty of other fossils found down the mine, too, including reptiles, fish and plants.

TYPICAL!

Experts are not sure whether *Goniopholis* and *Bernissartia* were feeding on fish or dead *Iguanodon* when they died. But they are sure that these animals were typical crocodiles. *Bernissartia* had sharp teeth at the front of its mouth and flat teeth at the back – possibly for crushing bones.

Is it true that crocs can't chew?

A crocodile has no cutting or chewing teeth. Its cone-shaped teeth are designed simply for grabbing. So if it catches an animal that is too big to swallow whole, it wedges the animal under the water, against a log or stone. Then it takes hold of the flesh, spins round and breaks off the flesh. Sometimes the croc leaves the body to rot, then tears off bite-sized chunks.

Deinosuchus

A modern caiman (left) swims with just its eyes above the water.

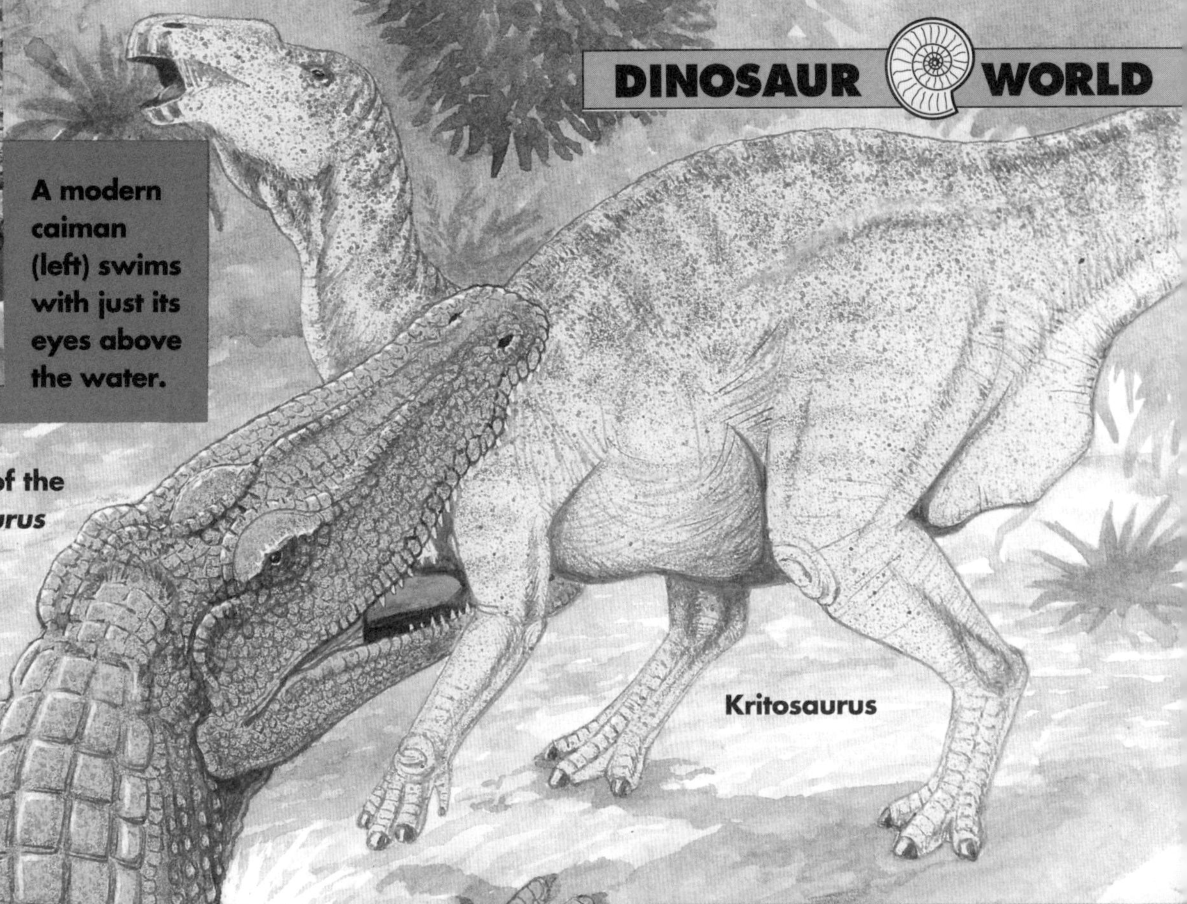

Deinosuchus leaps out of the river and gives *Kritosaurus* the shock of its life as it comes to drink! The crocodile's skull was 1.8m long, so its body may have been about 14m long – that's as long as *T rex*!

Kritosaurus

This fierce-looking Nile crocodile (right) guards her eggs.

TERRIBLE GIANT

During the Cretaceous, crocs were large and successful. *Deinosuchus* (die-no-soo-kus), 'terrible crocodile', was a 14m-long giant – four times the size of today's crocodiles. It hid in the water and grabbed dinosaurs and other creatures that came to drink. Not all the ancient crocs were the size of *Deinosuchus*. Some were tiny lizard-like crocodiles called atoposaurids, which lived in the Late Jurassic and Early Cretaceous. One of the biggest of these, *Alligatorium* (al-ig-a-tor-ee-um), was only 40cm long.

DINOSAUR CLUES

Despite being fearsome hunters, today's crocodilians make excellent parents. The mothers lay eggs in nests made of sand or rotting compost, and carefully look after their babies until they squeak and begin to hatch. Then she carries them to a nursery pool, where she guards them until they can feed themselves.

Crocodiles and dinosaurs are close relatives. By watching crocodiles today – as they keep their bodies warm, catch and eat their food, and carefully look after their babies – we can get an idea of how dinosaurs may have lived in the past.

GIANTS OF THE PAST

CENTROSAURUS

A herd of *Centrosaurus* tries to dash across a wide river. Perhaps a large predator has made this group scatter in all directions. As they try to run, the water slows them down. Their fear makes them careless in their escape and they move into fast-flowing water. The weaker members of the herd drown. Eighty million years later, these *Centrosaurus* resurface as fossils in the rocks of Alberta, Canada.

3-D Gallery

PROTOCERATOPS BABIES

- Two newly born dinosaurs with bony frills
- Lived about 80 million years ago in China and Mongolia
- Measured about 30cm
- Ate plants

Brains

Scientists know a lot about dinosaurs, but are they smart enough to know how clever dinosaurs were?

Dinosaurs are often seen as rather dim, slow creatures but scientific detective work has changed this old idea.

BRAIN WAVES

The brain is the control centre of any animal. It sends orders along pathways (nerves). Without these messages from the brain, dinosaurs would not have been able to eat, move, smell, scratch or see!

Alert *Saurornithoides* has just caught its dinner with its gripping claws, and is already on the look out for pudding. When it hears a tasty insect buzz past, *Saurornithoides* spins around and snatches it.

Saurornithoides

Scientists make models of dinosaurs' brains so that they can study them. They fill the space in the centre of a dinosaur skull with a liquid plastic, which hardens into a solid mould in the shape of the brain. This mould (right) shows the shape of *Iguanodon's* brain.

BRAIN POWER

It is likely that some dinosaurs were cleverer than others. To find out how bright a dinosaur was, experts need to know how big its brain was in comparison with its body. Experts look at the model of a dinosaur's brain (above), and work out how much it weighed. Then they calculate the weight of the dinosaur's body. Once they know these two things, scientists do a simple sum to work out what percentage of the animal's entire weight is 'brain-weight'.

Messages from *Saurornithoides'* brain moved with lightning speed round its body. This meat-eater had quite a well-developed brain. This meant that it was:

- **Quick-witted with a good sense of smell, excellent eyesight and sharp hearing**
- **Speedy – good at hunting and running away from danger**
- **Nimble, with quick reactions**

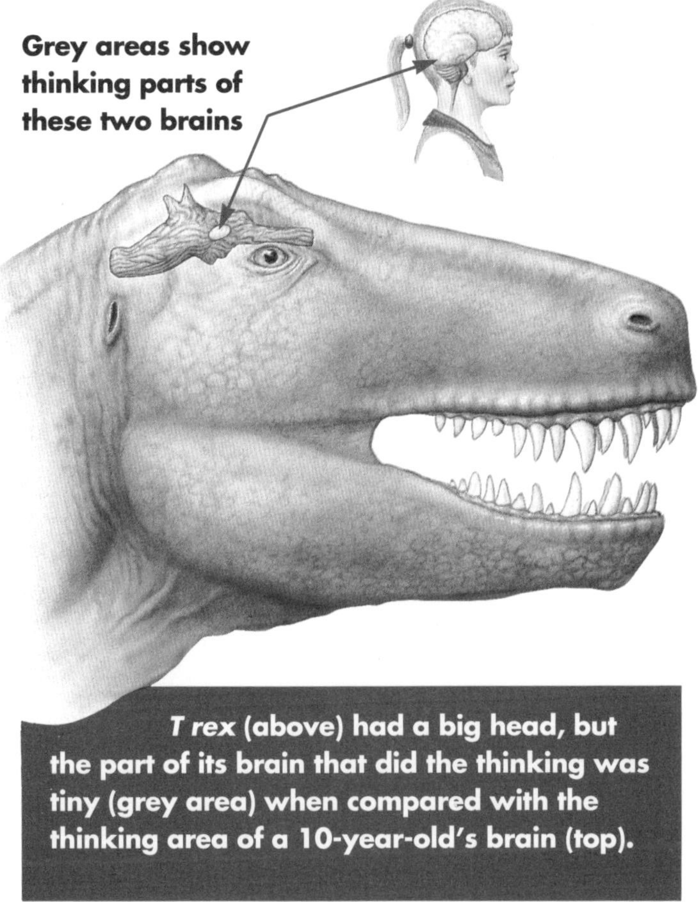

T rex (above) had a big head, but the part of its brain that did the thinking was tiny (grey area) when compared with the thinking area of a 10-year-old's brain (top).

TOP OF THE CLASS

A dinosaur with a relatively heavy brain, compared with its body weight, was probably brighter than a dinosaur with a relatively light brain.

DINOSAUR MASTERMIND

Small meat-eaters, such as *Saurornithoides* (left), had better brains than many other dinosaurs. This meant that they were faster and smarter than slow, lumbering sauropods, with relatively small brains.

SMARTER THAN US?

Among the last dinosaurs to walk the Earth were the clever, turkey-sized predators. Imagine if dinosaurs had not died out. Their brains may have continued to improve and evolve over the millions of years before humans arrived. With such a huge headstart on us, dinosaurs might have become cleverer than humans.

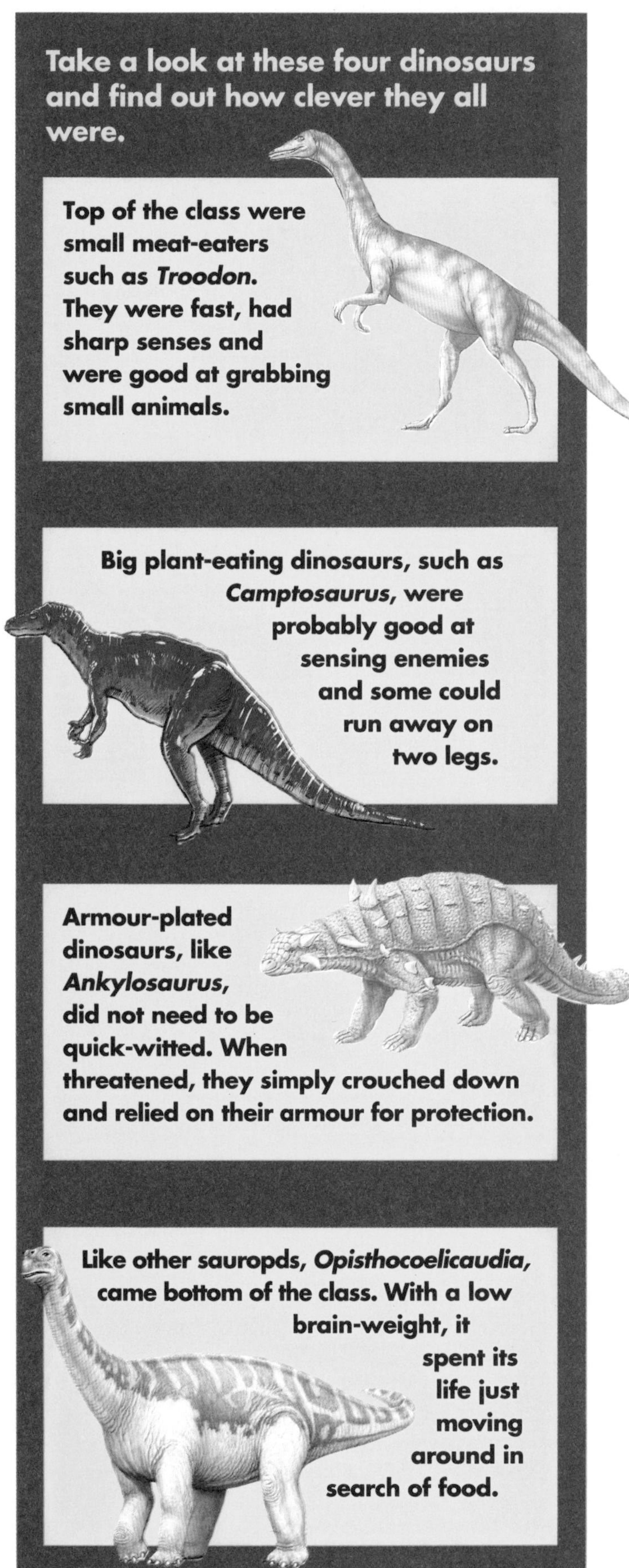

Take a look at these four dinosaurs and find out how clever they all were.

Top of the class were small meat-eaters such as *Troodon*. They were fast, had sharp senses and were good at grabbing small animals.

Big plant-eating dinosaurs, such as *Camptosaurus*, were probably good at sensing enemies and some could run away on two legs.

Armour-plated dinosaurs, like *Ankylosaurus*, did not need to be quick-witted. When threatened, they simply crouched down and relied on their armour for protection.

Like other sauropods, *Opisthocoelicaudia*, came bottom of the class. With a low brain-weight, it spent its life just moving around in search of food.

Fight to the death

In 1971, experts discovered one of the most amazing fossil finds yet – two dinosaurs locked in a weird embrace.

What were the dinosaurs doing and why did they die together? Follow the clues and see if you can solve a dinosaur mystery.

UNCOVERING A CRIME
This palaeontologist (right) is carefully clearing dust away from the bones of two dinosaurs. He is uncovering an ancient mystery. See if you can work it out.

IT'S A FACT

RARE FIND
Only two fossils of dinosaurs fighting each other have been found. The fossils of dinosaurs that died alone tell us a lot about the animal, for example where it lived and what it looked like. But a fossil of two dinosaurs fighting each other provides important clues about how they attacked an enemy and defended themselves.

CLUE 1

The long, flat-nosed head suggests that this was meat-eating *Velociraptor*.

CLUE 2

This triangular-shaped head might have belonged to a plant-eating *Protoceratops*. This dinosaur had a bony, shield-like neck frill.

CLUE 3

Velociraptor's hooked hind toe claw has plunged into the stomach of *Protoceratops*.

CLUE 7

It looks as if *Protoceratops* has used its armoured head to smash into *Velociraptor's* chest.

CLUE 6

Protoceratops has caught hold of *Velociraptor's* arm in its sharp beak.

CLUE 5

With its arms and claws, *Velociraptor* has gripped hold of *Protoceratops'* neck frill.

CLUE 4

Velociraptor's other hind toe has grabbed at the throat of *Protoceratops.*

GOT IT!

Did both *Velociraptor* and *Protoceratops* die during a fierce struggle? Yes, they were fighting each other. They were so badly wounded that they both died during the battle.

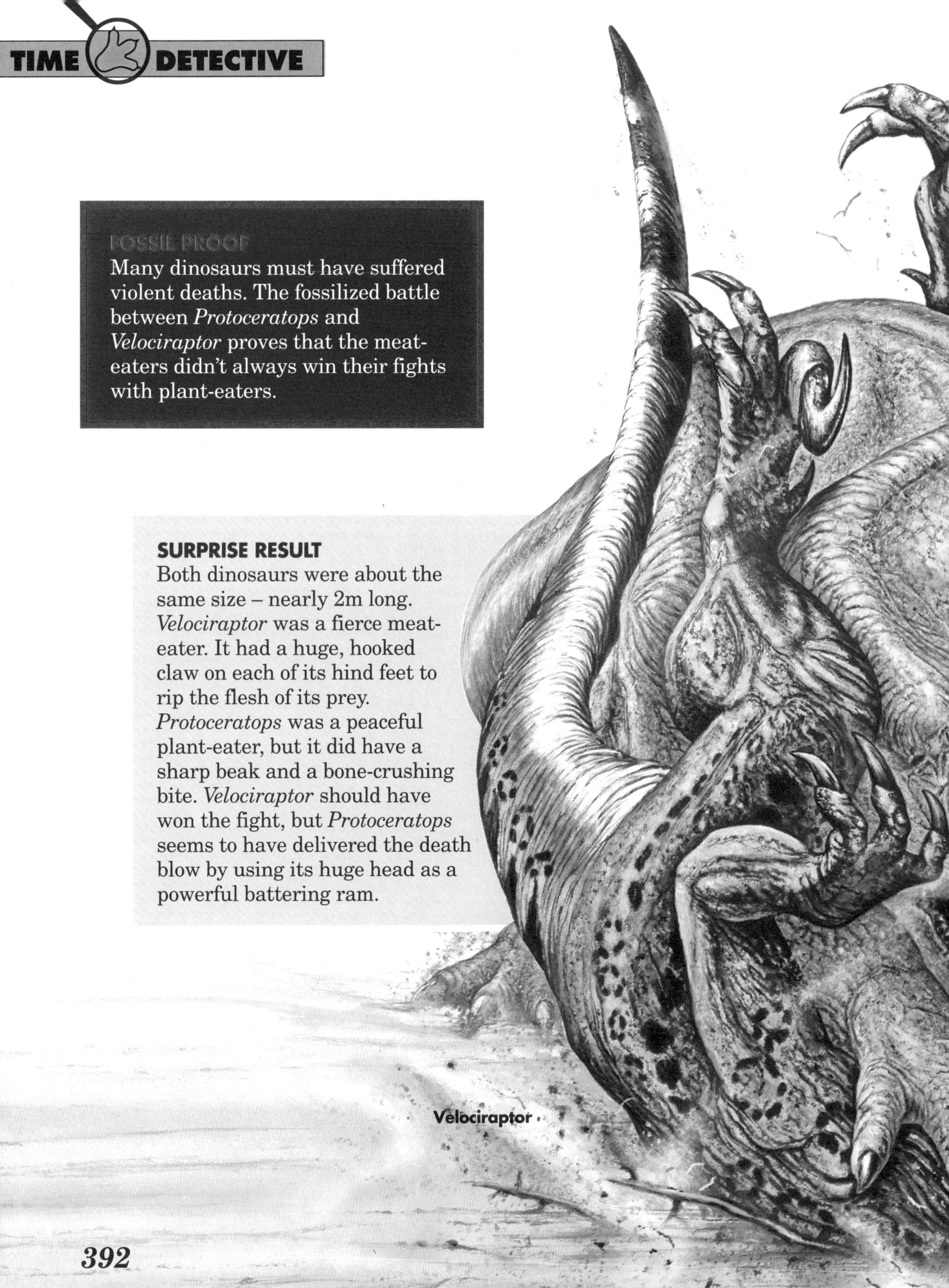

FOSSIL PROOF

Many dinosaurs must have suffered violent deaths. The fossilized battle between *Protoceratops* and *Velociraptor* proves that the meat-eaters didn't always win their fights with plant-eaters.

SURPRISE RESULT

Both dinosaurs were about the same size – nearly 2m long. *Velociraptor* was a fierce meat-eater. It had a huge, hooked claw on each of its hind feet to rip the flesh of its prey. *Protoceratops* was a peaceful plant-eater, but it did have a sharp beak and a bone-crushing bite. *Velociraptor* should have won the fight, but *Protoceratops* seems to have delivered the death blow by using its huge head as a powerful battering ram.

DESERT DEATH

The two fighting dinosaurs died about 80 million years ago. But the fossil skeletons were complete and they were still in almost the same positions in which they died. They were found in the Gobi Desert, Mongolia.

CAUSE OF DEATH

Experts are puzzled by the ferocious fight that peaceful *Protoceratops* put up. Some think the dinosaur fought back extra hard because it was defending its nest. Others believe the two dinosaurs might have been buried alive by a sudden, violent sandstorm during their battle.

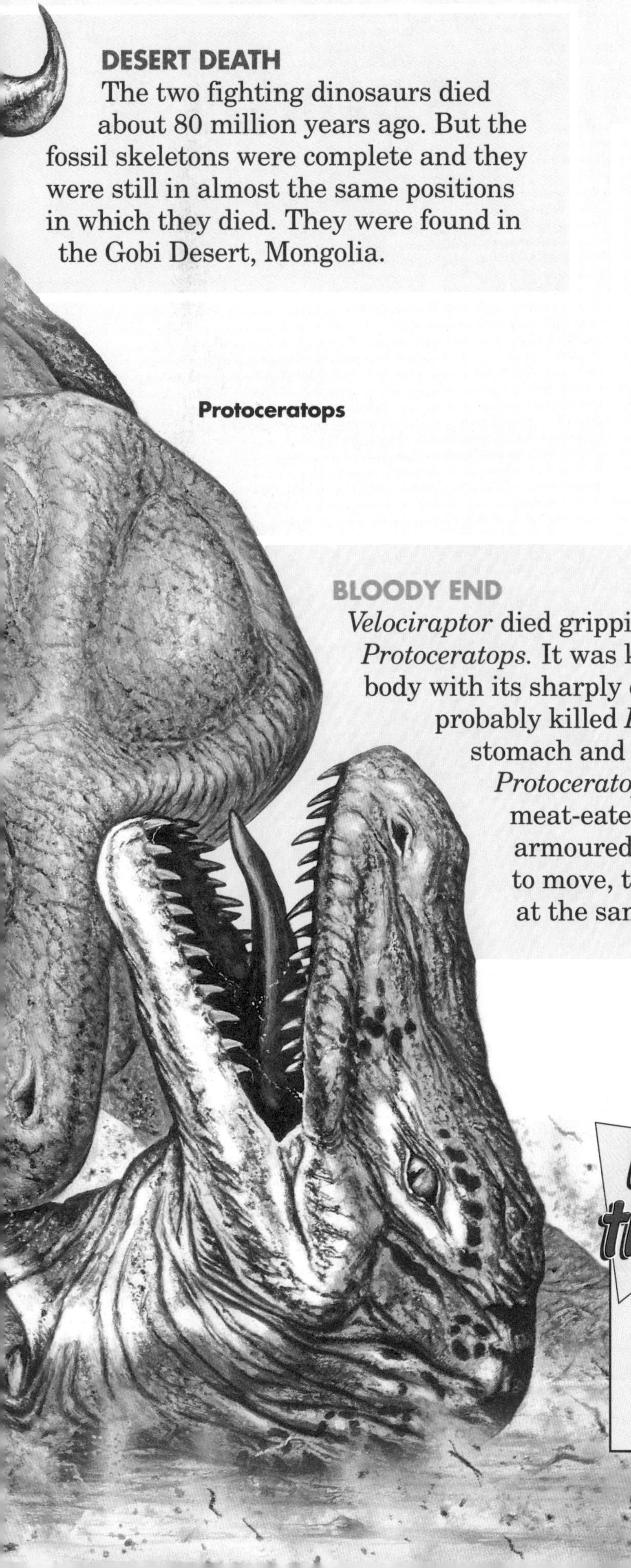

Protoceratops

BLOODY END

Velociraptor died gripping the head shield of *Protoceratops.* It was kicking out at the plant-eater's body with its sharply clawed hind feet. *Velociraptor* probably killed *Protoceratops* by slashing its stomach and ripping out its insides. But *Protoceratops* had managed to smash the meat-eater's chest with its powerful armoured head. Locked together, too weak to move, the two dinosaurs must have died at the same time.

Is it true that *Protoceratops* killed an egg-eating *Oviraptor*?

Oviraptor was found lying on top of a nest filled with eggs belonging to *Protoceratops.* Some experts think that the 'egg thief' was caught in the act of raiding the plant-eater's nest, and killed by an angry *Protoceratops* parent.

47 3-D Gallery

ALLOSAURUS V. DRYOSAURUS

Starving flesh-eating *Allosaurus* are on the rampage again! Plant-eating *Dryosaurus* don't have a chance. Desperately they try to splash across the lake to safety. They know that if it comes to a fight they have no defense against *Allosaurus*' gaping tooth-lined jaws.

ASK THE EXPERT

Dr. David Norman of Cambridge University answers your dinosaur questions

Can dinosaurs be small?

Yes, they can! I have held a complete dinosaur in the palm of my hand. It was a tiny South American dinosaur named *Mussaurus* (which means 'mouse reptile') – but it was probably a baby dinosaur. Its skull was the size of a small matchbox.

How many enemies did dinosaurs have?

This is a very tricky question. I am afraid I cannot tell you the answer because I do not know. All dinosaurs had enemies – some more than others. Little plant-eaters had lots of enemies, while some of the big meat-eaters had hardly any – they were much too fierce!

If a very important bone from a dinosaur's skeleton broke, how would an expert fix it?

If an important bone broke, we would simply glue it together again! There is no knack to it, but we do have to use a special sort of glue. Palaeontologists don't just mend bones, they break them, too! But we only deliberately break a bone if we need to learn more about it. We obviously have to do this very carefully.

Which was the strongest dinosaur?

Seismosaurus was probably the strongest dinosaur because it would have needed huge muscles to move around. It may have weighed 40 or 50 tonnes. That's about as heavy as 10 elephants. Imagine carrying that enormous weight around with you all day!

DINOSAURS!
DISCOVER THE GIANTS OF THE PREHISTORIC WORLD

CORYTHOSAURUS

***Corythosaurus* had a unique head crest. It looked as if it had half a dinner plate standing up from its head.**

Longer than a bus, *Corythosaurus* browsed among the conifers and shrubs of the Late Cretaceous. Standing on its back legs, it was tall enough to peer through the top windows of a modern two-storey house.

GOOD SENSE

Gentle *Corythosaurus* was not a born fighter. It had no armour, spikes or sharp claws. To keep out of trouble, it relied on its strong senses of sight and hearing.

SHOW OFF

Corythosaurus made quite a spectacle of itself, showing off its head crest and making its own special noises. It probably made such an impression on its rivals that they had second thoughts about starting a fight.

BIG NOISE

Imagine the quiet of a spring evening in the Late Cretaceous. Suddenly, the peace is disturbed by the most amazing bellowing and honking. A chorus of duckbilled dinosaurs is making its call. With their different shaped head crests, this family of dinosaurs made a variety of sounds. It may have sounded like a primitive brass band!

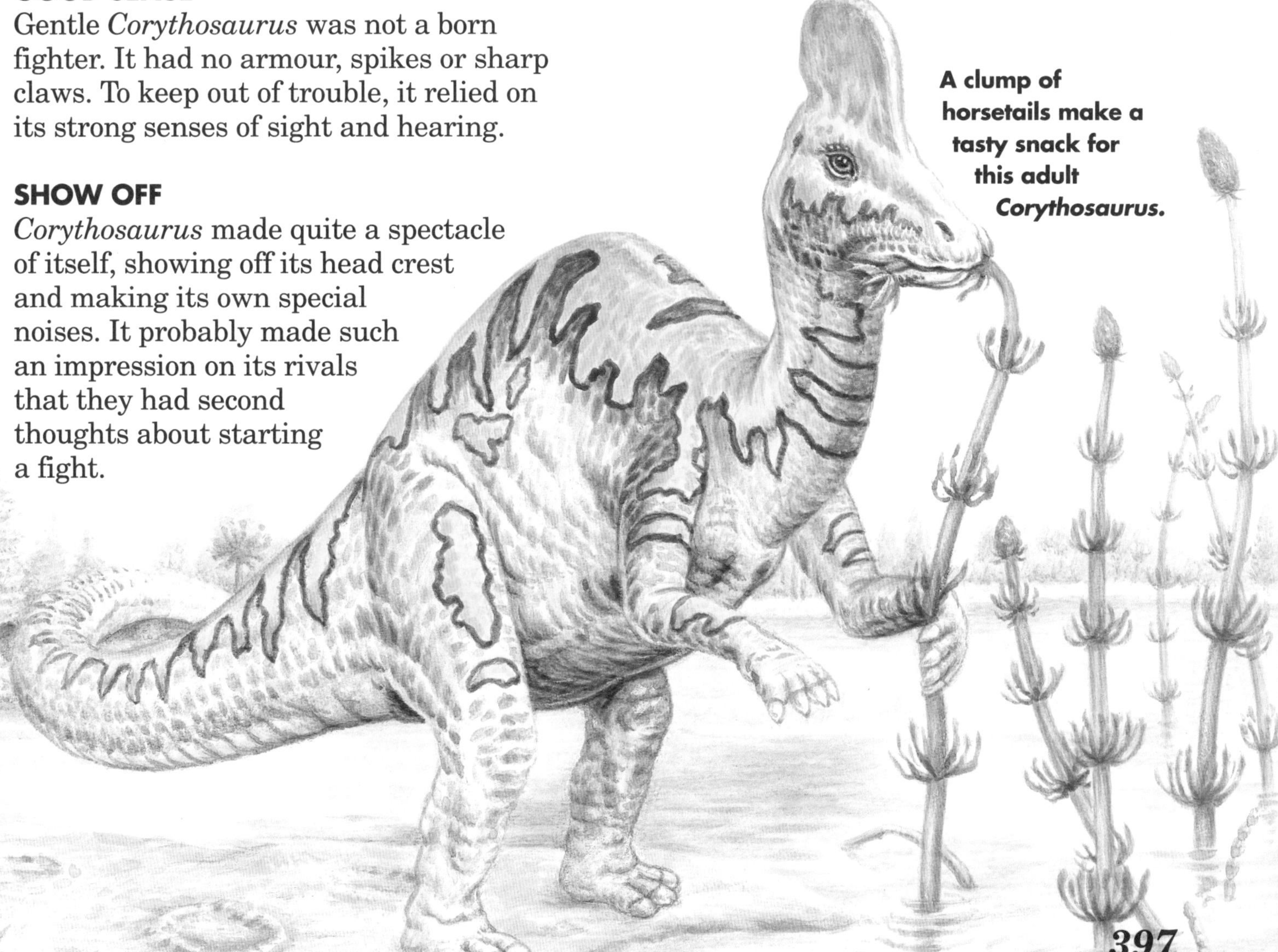

A clump of horsetails make a tasty snack for this adult *Corythosaurus*.

Skull probably belonged to a young adult *Corythosaurus*. Its crest is quite large

Flattened bill

Eye socket

Rows of teeth

79CM – MORE THAN TWICE THE HEIGHT OF THIS PAGE

GREEK HELMET

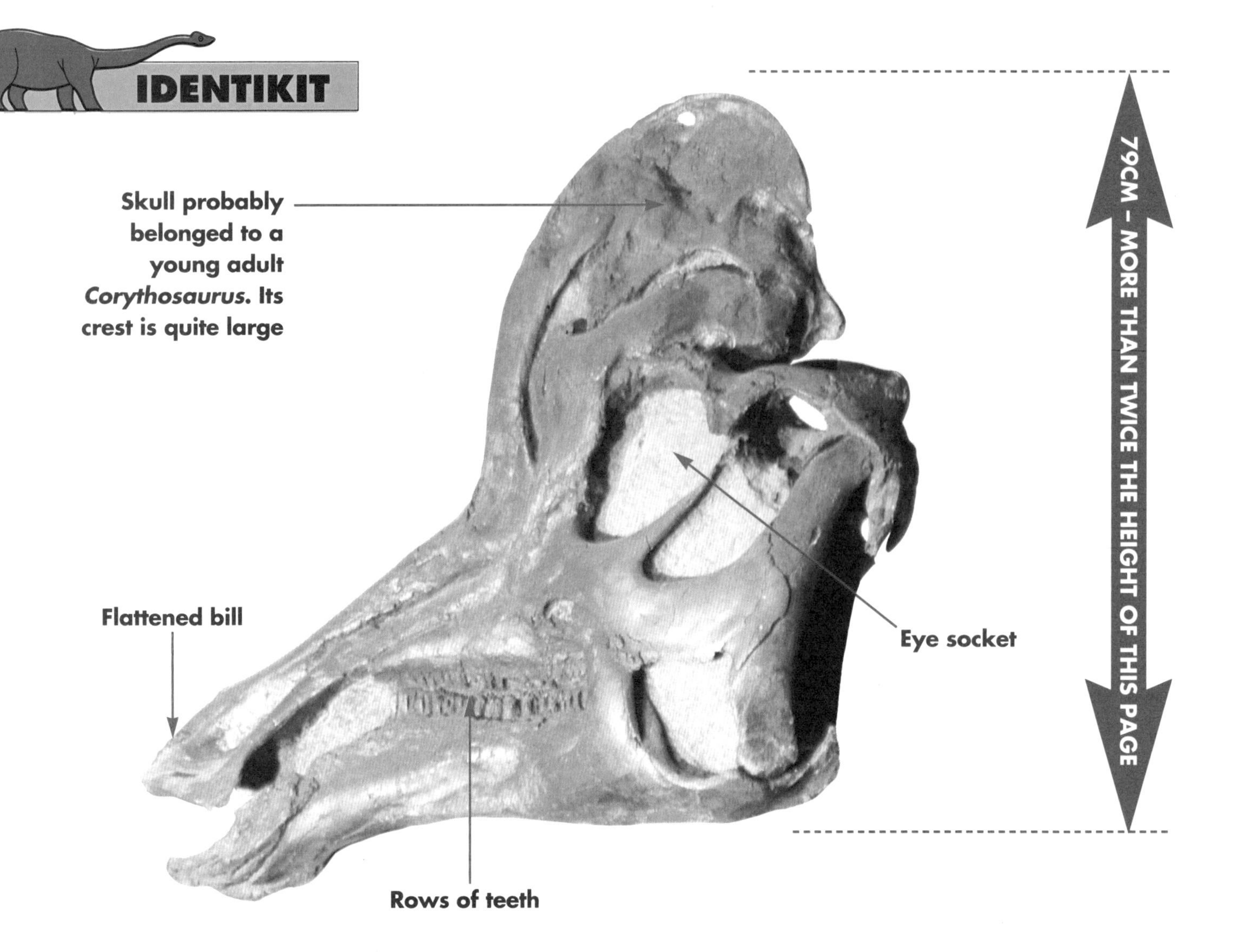

Corythosaurus had a high, narrow crest, shaped a little bit like an ancient Greek soldier's helmet. Breathing tubes ran from the dinosaur's nostrils to the back of its throat and passed through the large crest. Using its great lung power, *Corythosaurus* could bellow by sending gusts of air though the crest. Although duckbills had similar body shapes, their crests were not the same. This meant that they all looked different from one another and made different sounds.

SIZE WISE

The discovery of *Corythosaurus* crests of varying sizes once confused scientists. Now they believe that smaller crests belonged to young or female *Corythosaurus*. A young animal had virtually no crest at all, just a little bump above its eyes.

MONSTER FACTS

- **NAME:** *Corythosaurus* (co-rith-oh-saw-rus) means 'Corinthian (of Corinth, in Greece) helmet reptile'
- **SIZE:** up to 10m long and 7m high
- **FOOD:** plants, twigs, roots and cones
- **LIVED:** about 75 million years ago in the Late Cretaceous Period in Alberta, Canada

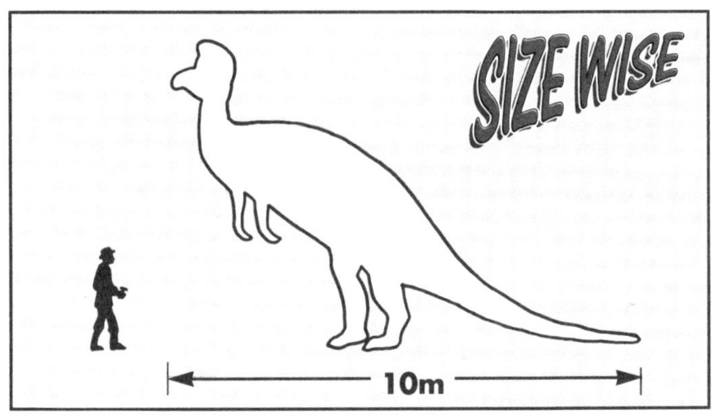

SLOW SWIMMER

Although *Corythosaurus* was probably capable of swimming, it did not break any speed records. With its clumsy, heavy body, it did not have the agility to escape a predator on foot. However, it may have plunged into a river or lake and paddled slowly to the other side to outwit a non-swimming dinosaur.

TOUGH DIET

Corythosaurus enjoyed eating twigs and roots, as well as cones of conifers (a type of tree including firs and pines) and seeds. These were tough to eat, but *Corythosaurus* had teeth that could cope with the chewiest food.
With its long, narrow snout *Corythosaurus* could reach the tasty plants that other dinosaurs could not reach.

Is it true that plants are harder to digest than meat?

Plant-eating dinosaurs had longer and larger digestive systems than meat-eaters. The reason for this is simple: the tough plants that made up the plant-eaters' diet were harder to chew up and digest than the meat that the meat-eaters devoured. Plant-eaters broke up their food thoroughly so that their bodies could absorb the nutritious parts.

NEW TEETH FOR OLD

When *Corythosaurus* lost a tooth, another one grew to replace it. It had hundreds of teeth packed tightly together in rows. They made a surface as rough as a vegetable grater. *Corythosaurus* nipped off shoots with its sharp, horny beak as easily as a pastry cutter slicing through dough.

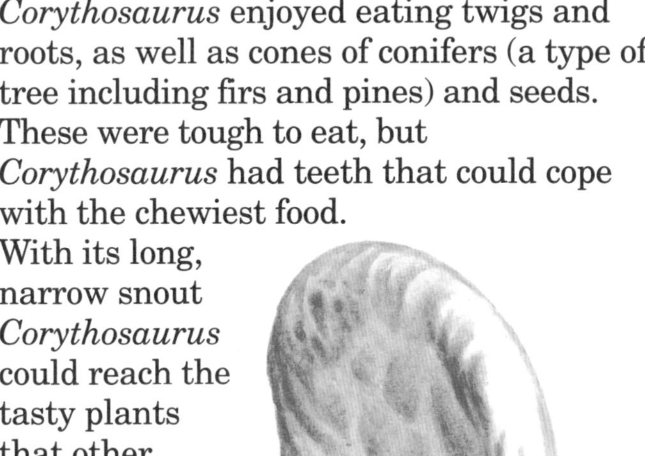

A family meal! Adults had tall crests and babies only had small bumps on their heads. Just as our bones grow when we are young, *Corythosaurus'* crest got bigger as it grew older.

ORNITHOLESTES

***Ornitholestes* seized small, ground-dwelling animals and crushed them with its powerful bite.**

Ornitholestes lived among larger meat-eaters, such as huge *Allosaurus,* and relied on the speed and strength of its long, slender legs to keep it out of danger.

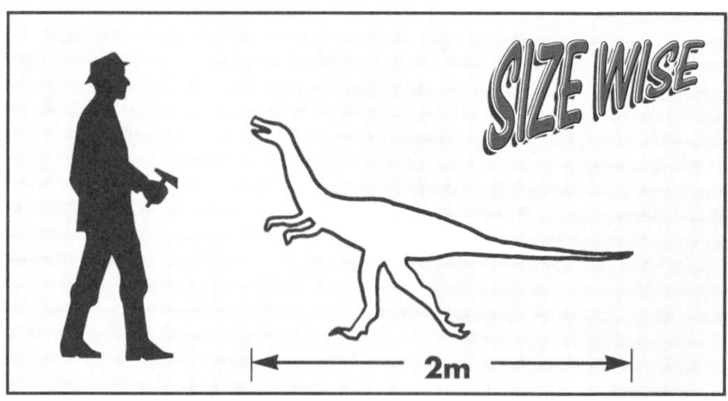

SOLE SKELETON
Only one complete skeleton of *Ornitholestes* has been found so far. It was one of the smaller dinosaurs, about the length of a small pony. As it ran after prey, this dinosaur used its long tail to help it balance.

MONSTER FACTS

- **NAME:** *Ornitholestes* (or-nith-oh-less-teez) means 'bird robber'
- **SIZE:** 2m long
- **FOOD:** small animals such as lizards, frogs and early mammals
- **LIVED:** about 150 million years ago in the Late Jurassic Period in North America

GRIPPING HANDS
The other two fingers were especially long and well-designed for gripping prey. In spite of its name, no one is quite sure if *Ornitholestes* caught birds.

EAGLE EYES
Ornitholestes had good eyesight, which helped it spot lizards and small mammals as they raced to hide under ferns and rocks. If the unlucky animals were caught, *Ornitholestes* made short work of them with its sharp, curving teeth.

CURLING THUMB
When we pick something up, our thumbs curl inward. *Ornitholestes* probably used its small third finger like a thumb to help it grip its wriggling prey.

STYRACOSAURUS

***Styracosaurus* was a magnificent dinosaur. A crown of long spikes stood out from its broad frill.**

Even from a distance, rivals could not mistake *Styracosaurus* for another dinosaur. Like the huge antlers of a red deer stag, its extraordinary spikes attracted mates and frightened enemies. *Styracosaurus* did not have to risk a fight. A mere wave of the head did the trick!

MONSTER FACTS

- **NAME:** *Styracosaurus* (sty-rak-oh-saw-rus) means 'spiked reptile'
- **SIZE:** 5.5m long and about 2.5m high
- **FOOD:** low-growing plants
- **LIVED:** about 80 million years ago in the Late Cretaceous Period in Alberta, Canada, and Montana, USA

DEADLY WEAPON

The spikes were too weak to be useful for fighting, but *Styracosaurus* had another fearsome weapon – a huge nose horn.

HORN SPEAR

With a flick of its nose, *Styracosaurus* inflicted deadly damage on the biggest predators. Its horn pierced their unprotected flesh to leave a gaping wound. *Styracosaurus'* neck bones were very strong and helped it carry the weight of its massive head.

FIRM FOOTING

Longer than two small cars, *Styracosaurus* walked on four sturdy legs. Its toes were splayed out to give it firm footing and to support its body weight. Roaming over the plains of North America, it fed on low-growing plants using its curved, parrot-like beak to snip off shoots.

Swarming in the seas

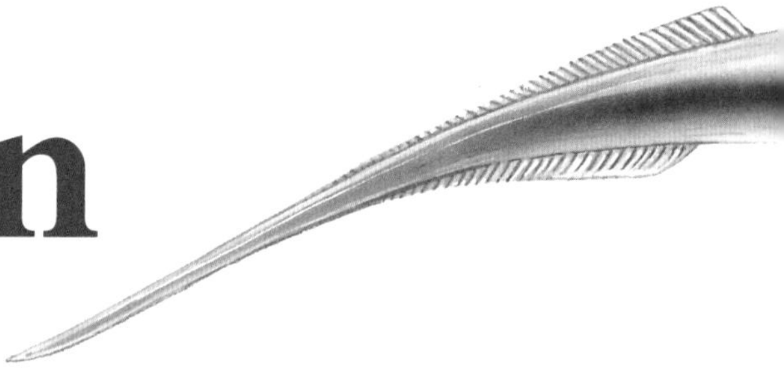

The prehistoric underwater world was jam-packed with animal life.

Many of the creatures that swam beneath the prehistoric waves look familiar. Some of them, such as sharks, horseshoe crabs, shellfish and jellyfish, have descendants that are still alive today. Other animals, like the curly-shelled ammonites and the squid-like belemnites, are only known from their fossils.

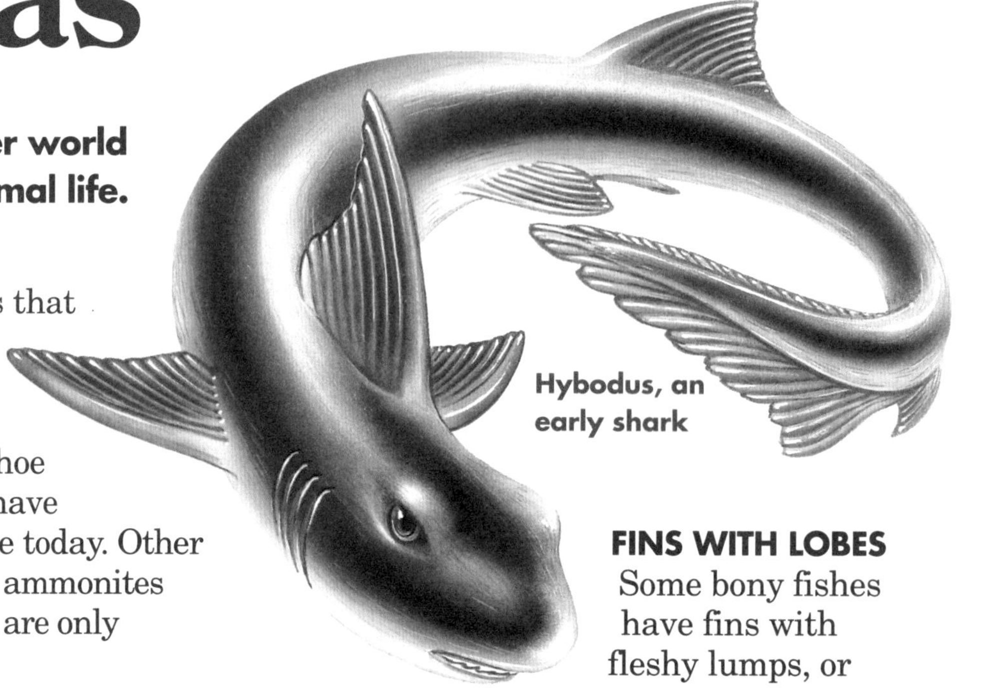

Hybodus, an early shark

SOME FISH NEVER CHANGE

Fishes appeared 400 million years ago, long before the dinosaurs. There were two main kinds: those with gristle (cartilage) skeletons and those with bony skeletons. Sharks and rays have gristle skeletons. At the beginning of the Dinosaur Age, sharks such as 2m-long *Hybodus*, a hunter, were already masters of the seas. The winged-ray *Aellopos* and the rat-fish *Ischyodus* swam alongside it. These fishes have hardly changed since.

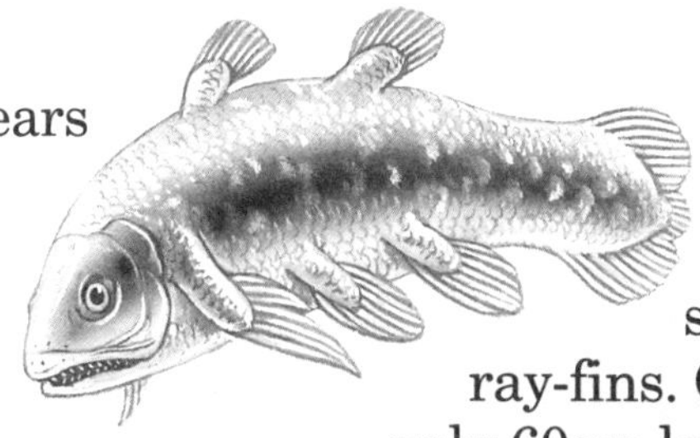

Macropoma

FINS WITH LOBES

Some bony fishes have fins with fleshy lumps, or lobes, where they join the body. They are lobe-fins. They evolved before the main fish group, the ray-fins. They were never as successful in the water as the ray-fins. One lobe-fin was *Macropoma*, only 60cm long, but with a deep body. It belonged to the same group as today's 'living fossil', the coelacanth, and it lived near the end of the Dinosaur Age.

Aellopos, a winged ray

Sea-lilies

Ischyodus, a rat-fish

What is? A MOLLUSC

Shellfish, squids, octopuses and snails are all molluscs. None of them has a backbone, so their bodies are soft. Some molluscs live in the sea, others in rivers or on land. They get about on a muscular 'foot' that is under their bodies. Some molluscs, like snails, have shells. Others, like slugs, do not. Most molluscs are herbivorous, but some eat meat.

A squid

FINS WITH RAYS

Ray-fins exist today. They have stiff spines, or rays, that can open the fin like a fan. The ray-fins are an ancient group, but they only began to flourish at the same time as the dinosaurs. They had thick, heavy scales and a top-heavy tail. *Lepidotes* looked like a modern cod and lived during the Jurassic Period in seas all over the world.

Lepidotes

ESCAPE FROM DEATH

As time went on, the ray-fins improved their design. Their scales became lighter and their tails better balanced. All sorts of shapes and sizes appeared. *Leptolepis* was about 20cm long and looked like a herring. Compared with earlier fishes, it was swift and agile, and able to stay out of the jaws of the great hunting reptiles. The seas have teemed with ray-fins ever since, from mackerel to marlin, bass to barracuda.

Leptolepis

ALL ARMS

Octopuses and squids are modern molluscs. Their cousins in the Dinosaur Age were ammonites and belemnites, which left many fossils behind. *Gonioteuthis* was a belemnite. It was a squid-like creature with a long, bullet-shaped shell inside its body. Although they were little, these sea creatures were fierce hunters.

CURLY-WURLY SHELLS

Stephanoceras was one of many thousands of kinds of ammonites. Although they lasted for millions of years, the belemnites and ammonites died out with the dinosaurs.

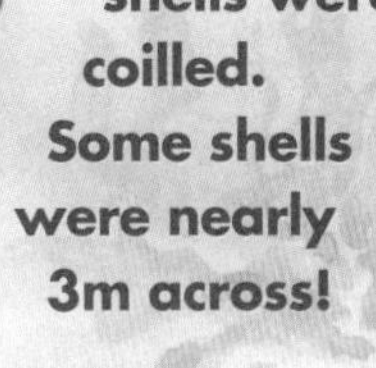

Ammonite shells were coilled. Some shells were nearly 3m across!

Gonioteuthis, a belemnite

A CORAL REEF IN THE AGE OF THE DINOSAURS

STINGERS AND BUILDERS

Fossils of soft-bodied jellyfish and sea anemones are rare. They tell us that these floppy animals were poisoning prey with their stinging tentacles long before life had began on land. Closely related are corals, tiny animals that make their own stony cups to sit in.

CRABS AND COUSINS

On the prehistoric sea bed, crabs and their crawling cousins looked much the same as today. Crabs like *Eryon* and shrimps such as *Aeger* crept over and cleaned the coral, picking up bits of left-over food. The horseshoe crab is a weird beast that is not a true crab, but a closer cousin of spiders and scorpions. It appeared long before the dinosaurs and is still around today.

STATELY STARFISH

Starfish and their relatives, sea-urchins and sea-lilies, have survived for more than 400 million years. The chalky plates in their skin make good fossils. A dinosaur wading through shallow water may have seen the starfish *Calliderma* hunting mussels, the brittle star *Geocoma* and the sea-urchin *Acrosalenia,* with its soft body protected by long, pencil-like spines.

Calliderma, a starfish

Coeloptychium, a sponge

The strange horseshoe crab is one of the longest surviving. It still lives in the seas off south-east Asia and North America.

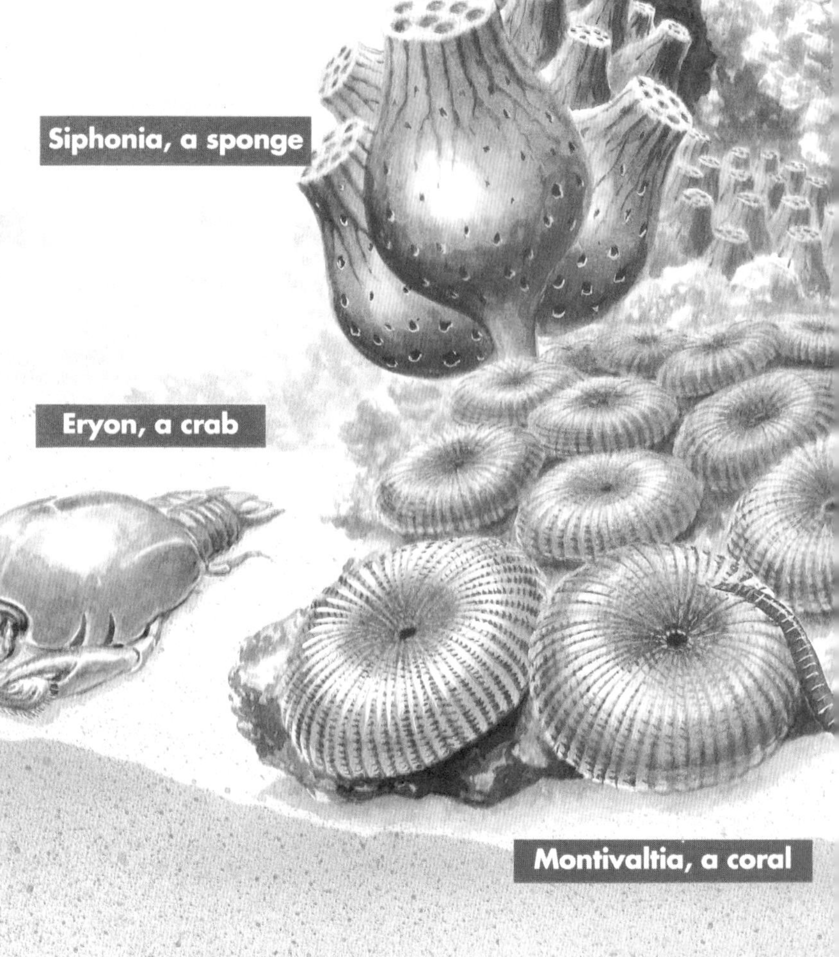

Siphonia, a sponge

Eryon, a crab

Acrosalenia, a sea-urchin

Montivaltia, a coral

LIVING FOSSILS

Lampshells (also called brachiopods) are some of the best examples of 'living fossils' – animals that have barely changed over millions of years. Outside, lampshells look like molluscs, but they evolved separately from molluscs. *Lingula* is a lampshell, which is known from fossils that are about 200 million years old, the same time as the first dinosaurs waded into water – and found the sea wasn't for them!

SHELLED FOR SUCCESS

Thousands of molluscs lived during the Dinosaur Age. *Pleurotomaria* was a sea snail, *Dentalium* had a tusk-shaped shell and burrowed in mud, picking up food with its tentacles. *Mytilus* is a great survivor. It is the common mussel we know so well today.

This coral reef is a huge pile of skeletons left by coral polyps, animals which look like minute jellyfish. When they die, new polyps grow on top (right). Thousands of years later, a reef forms and then an island. Corals have shaped the land since the Dinosaur Age.

Present-day mussels feed in the same way their ancestors did. They suck in sea water and filter food from it.

Rudists, a mollusc

Polytholosia, a sponge

Aeger, a shrimp

Actinastrea, a coral

Pleurotomaria, a sea snail

Geocoma, a brittle star

Mytilus, the common mussel

Dentalium, a mollusc

Lingula, a lampshell

GIANTS OF THE PAST

CORYTHOSAURUS

As the sun sets, pterosaurs soar through the pink mist and strange noises float through the air. The fading light has made it difficult for *Corythosaurus* parents to see their young. A small group of younger dinosaurs has become separated from the adults. The leader of the herd raises its head and calls the youngsters back to the safety of the herd.

3-D Gallery 28

APATOSAURUS FAMILY

- A family of browsing sauropods
- Lived about 150 million years ago in North America
- Measured 21m long when fully grown
- Ate plants

RECORD BREAKERS

The largest and smallest

The largest and smallest dinosaurs that ever walked the Earth are featured on these pages.

Dinosaurs were not the mightiest animals that ever lived. Today there is a monster that is bigger than any known dinosaur – the blue whale (the longest is 33.5m long). You would have to line up 56 of the smallest dinosaurs head-to-tail, just to span the length of this huge sea monster.

BUILT LIKE A HOUSE

Some dinosaurs were as tall as a house, others were the height of a chicken. When we think about dinosaurs, the big record breakers come to mind, but many dinosaurs were quite small.

FRAGILE – HANDLE WITH CARE!

Fossils of tiny dinosaurs are rare finds. Small, fragile bones are either overlooked or they get broken before they are found.

SMALL IS SUPER

Being small was good news for some dinosaurs. *Saltopus* (60cm long) and *Lesothosaurus* (90cm long) were light enough to run after lively lizards and buzzing insects. They could also run away and hide from larger predators.

BIG IS BEST

There were advantages to being large. A predator would look twice at a big plant-eater before it attacked. Size was not only off-putting, it also let huge sauropods reach the juiciest leaves in the trees.

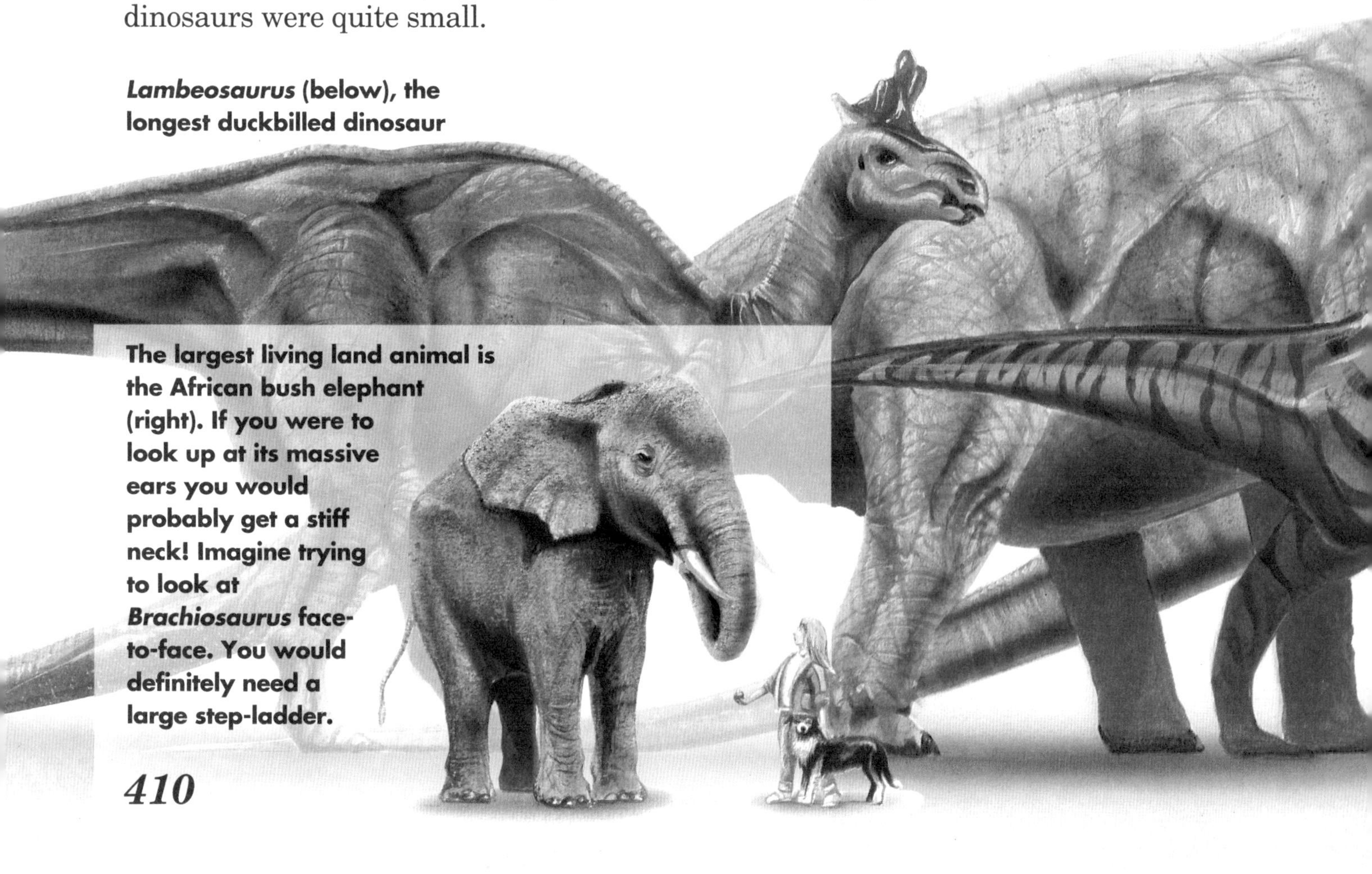

***Lambeosaurus* (below), the longest duckbilled dinosaur**

The largest living land animal is the African bush elephant (right). If you were to look up at its massive ears you would probably get a stiff neck! Imagine trying to look at *Brachiosaurus* face-to-face. You would definitely need a large step-ladder.

THE LONGEST

DINOSAUR: Although we do not yet have complete skeletons, *'Supersaurus'* and *'Ultrasaurus'* probably measured 25 – 30m long. *Seismosaurus* measured an earth-shaking 30m.
HADROSAUR: *Lambeosaurus* (15m long).
ARMOURED DINOSAUR: *Ankylosaurus* (11m).
MEAT-EATER: *Spinosaurus* (15m).
HORNED DINOSAUR: *Triceratops* (9m).
ARMS: *Deinocheirus* had 2.6m long arms. Its body has not been found yet, but it could have measured 7.8m long.
NECK: *Mamenchisaurus'* neck was 11m long.
TAIL: *Diplodocus'* tail was 15.4m long.
TRACKWAY: In 1983, a trail of *Apatosaurus* footprints was found. It was 215m long.

THE LARGEST

DINOSAUR: *Seismosaurus* was 30m long and weighed 80 tonnes. Although *Ultrasaurus* weighed more (100 – 130 tonnes), it was slightly shorter.
COMPLETE DINOSAUR: The biggest complete dinosaur skeleton in a museum is *Brachiosaurus*.
FOOTPRINTS: The biggest footprints found so far were made by a duckbilled dinosaur. Each footprint measured 1.36m long and was 81cm wide. The biggest sauropod footprint so far is 1m wide.
CLAWS: *Therizinosaurus* had massive, sickle-shaped claws – they were 80cm long.
SKULL: *Torosaurus'* skull was huge and measured 3m long. This included its enormous frill.
EYES: *Dromiceiomimus* had the biggest eyes – and brilliant eyesight to match!
EGG: *Hypselosaurus* laid eggs that were 30cm long.

THE HEAVIEST

DINOSAUR: *Seismosaurus* may have weighed 51 tonnes – heavier than nine African elephants.
MEAT-EATER: *T rex* weighed about 5.7 tonnes, that's heavier than two Rolls Royces!

THE SMALLEST

DINOSAUR: A baby *Troodon* was found which measured just 7 – 8cm. A baby *Mussaurus*, smaller than a man's thumb, has also been found. If they had lived, these dinosaurs would have grown much bigger.
ADULT DINOSAUR: *Saltopus:* 60cm long; *Compsognathus:* 60 – 80cm long.
EGG: An egg found near *Mussaurus* measured 2 – 3cm long.

***Diplodocus* had the longest tail**

***Brachiosaurus* (left), the largest complete dinosaur**

***T rex* was the heaviest meat-eater**

***Compsognathus* (magnified)**

***Compsognathus* was tiny, about the size of a large chicken**

Huge herds

Fossil clues show that some dinosaurs probably lived in herds. Experts now think some of those herds might have contained hundreds, or even thousands, of dinosaurs.

One important clue that dinosaur herds may have been big are trackways with many footprints all going in the same direction. Another good clue was the discovery of huge numbers of bones belonging to the same sort of dinosaur buried together. One of the largest burial grounds, or 'bone beds', contained 10,000 duckbilled *Maiasaura*!

BABY BOOM

Many nests made by *Maiasaura* have also been found in one place. Experts think they were part of a mass nesting site. So large herds of *Maiasaura* probably returned to the same nests to lay their eggs, again and again. They did this to help protect their babies. Many dinosaurs nesting together might have stopped predators from stealing the eggs.

SAFETY IN NUMBERS

Dinosaurs probably herded together for safety, just as many animals do today. Like modern herds, dinosaur herds probably had an order in which every animal, from the leader down to the youngest dinosaur, knew its place in the herd. The weaker members, like the young or the sick, were protected by the strongest.

LEADER OF THE PACK

In modern herds, adult males fight to find out which is the strongest. The winner leads the herd and mates with the females. This helps the herd to have strong babies. Dinosaurs probably behaved in the same way.

POUNDING THE PLAINS

Maiasaura and *Chasmosaurus* are just two types of plant-eating dinosaur that herded together to protect themselves from fierce meat-eating dinosaurs. Modern grass-eaters, like wildebeest and gazelles, do the same.

HUNTING IN HERDS

Not only plant-eating dinosaurs formed herds. Some of the smaller meat-eaters did, too. Trackways show that *Coelophysis* travelled about in large, fast-moving herds. They hunted on land and might have even fished in shallow water, like modern water birds.

A gazelle herd (above) gallops across the African plains. Dinosaurs lived in herds, too. A herd of nervous zebra (below) scatter when a lion stalks them for lunch. Some meat-eating dinosaurs stalked plant-eaters like this.

DINOSAUR 'LIONS'

Big meat-eating dinosaurs like *Albertosaurus* were probably the 'lions' of the dinosaur world. They would have formed small packs rather than huge herds. Packs of *Albertosaurus* might have stalked large herds of plant-eating dinosaurs. They waited to pounce in much the same way that lions do when they stalk game on the African plains today.

Two hungry *Albertosaurus* stalk their prey. Has the herd of *Chasmosaurus*, quietly feeding in the morning sunlight, spotted the danger that lurks near them? Turn the page to find out.

BODY GUARDS

When danger threatened plant-eating dinosaurs, they probably behaved like any modern grass-eating herd under attack. They banded together to protect weaker members. Stronger members, usually large males, guarded the outside of the herd. They acted as look-outs and watched carefully for signs of possible attackers. If they saw anything suspicious, they alerted the rest of the herd.

EASY PREY

Hungry modern hunters, like lions, cheetahs and wolves, stalk herds of grass-eaters for their next meal. They kill the weakest and slowest members of the herd, such as the young or sick. Meat-eating dinosaurs must have done the same.

***Albertosaurus* closes in for the kill. It will try to pick off a weak member of the herd.**

NOSE FOR TROUBLE

Animal look-outs use their noses as well as their eyes to sense danger. If the wind is in the right direction, they can pick up the smell of a predator hiding nearby, then they warn the rest of the herd.

KEEPING THEIR EYES PEELED

Dinosaurs probably kept their eyes peeled at all times. Experts believe some dinosaurs were camouflaged to keep hidden while they stalked prey. So a keen sense of smell and excellent eyesight were needed to discover a hidden enemy dinosaur – before it was too late.

The herd of *Chasmosaurus* has spotted the enemy. The adults form a circle round the young to protect them from danger.

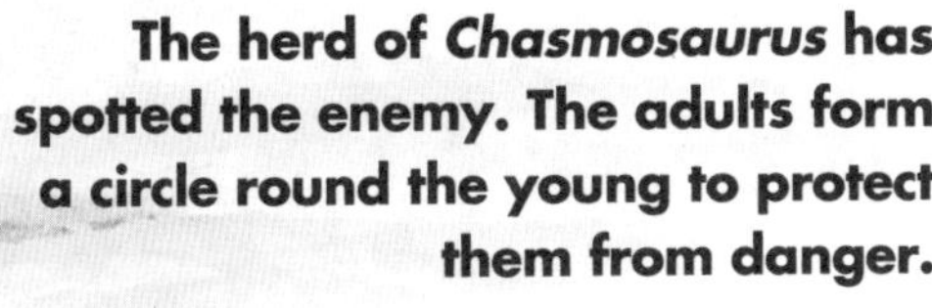

IT'S A FACT

SPEED KILLS

Large meat-eating dinosaurs could sprint at speeds of up to 40 km/h for short periods. Big plant-eating sauropods could only reach about 8 km/h. So they had no chance of outrunning their enemies.

SHOW OF STRENGTH

When danger threatens, big modern plant-eaters, such as African elephants and musk oxen, form a protective wall around their young. A herd of *Chasmosaurus* might have stood its ground in a similar way, forming a circle around weaker herd members. Facing outward with their heads down and their shield-like neck frills and bristling horns up, they must have been a very frightening sight.

Musk oxen (left) encircle their young if they are attacked by wolves. Pioneers of the Wild West (above) made a ring of wagons to protect themselves from attack by Indians.

48 3-D Gallery

UTAHRAPTOR V DEINONYCHUS

A *Deinonychus* pack has brought down and killed a young sauropod, but there are unwelcome guests at the feast! Two *Utahraptors* have seized the chance of a free meal, chasing off or toppling their smaller, fleet-footed rivals.

Dr. David Norman of Cambridge University answers your dinosaur questions
ASK THE EXPERT

What sort of habitats did dinosaurs live in?

To answer this question about dinosaurs and habitats is quite difficult. But put simply, it is true that dinosaurs had habitats in which they preferred to live. However, these were not all the same. Some, such as *Triceratops*, seem to have preferred mixed woodland areas, while others, such as huge herds of hadrosaurs, seem to have lived in open areas such as plains. Other dinosaurs were happiest in fairly dense forested areas, while the pachycephalosaurs usually made their homes in upland areas, rather like mountain goats do today.

Could dinosaurs jump or make a reasonable leap?

Large dinosaurs were not designed for jumping. However, some of the small dinosaurs like *Ornitholestes* and *Compsognathus* were much more agile and would no doubt have been able to jump well.

What dinosaur lived the longest time?

We do not yet have enough clues to tell how long dinosaurs lived, so we cannot discover which might have lived longest of all. I don't think that many dinosaurs would have lived longer than about 100 years. Most would have died at a much younger age, either through disease or by being attacked by their enemies which killed them for food.

How would you recognise a fossil on the beach?

Fossils are very difficult to spot, your eyes have to be ready to see them. Lots of experience and luck helps. Sometimes experts walk right past them thinking that they are just pebbles. I have just been given such a 'pebble' which turned out to be the skull of an armoured dinosaur – a find of some importance.

DILOPHOSAURUS

Dilophosaurus may have been a scavenger, feeding on the remains of dead dinosaurs that it found.

One of the oldest, large, meat-eating dinosaurs, *Dilophosaurus* was about as long as an elephant. An almost complete skeleton was discovered in 1942 by a team of scientists in Arizona. At first *Dilophosaurus* was mistaken for the English dinosaur, *Megalosaurus*. But 22 years later, when its skull was found, *Dilophosaurus* was revealed as a different and rather odd-looking dinosaur.

TWO RIDGES

Dilophosaurus had a strange crest on its head. It was made from two thin, curved ridges of bone. Standing side by side, they looked like two halves of a plate, standing in a plate rack. *Dilophosaurus* did not use its curious crest to fight its enemies, it was far too delicate.

SIGHT SIGNAL

Another dinosaur could recognise *Dilophosaurus* quite easily by its crest. With such an odd-shaped head it must have stood out from its surroundings, even from a long way away. Perhaps it used its mysterious crest as a special signal, telling friends and warning enemies that *Dilophosaurus* was on the move.

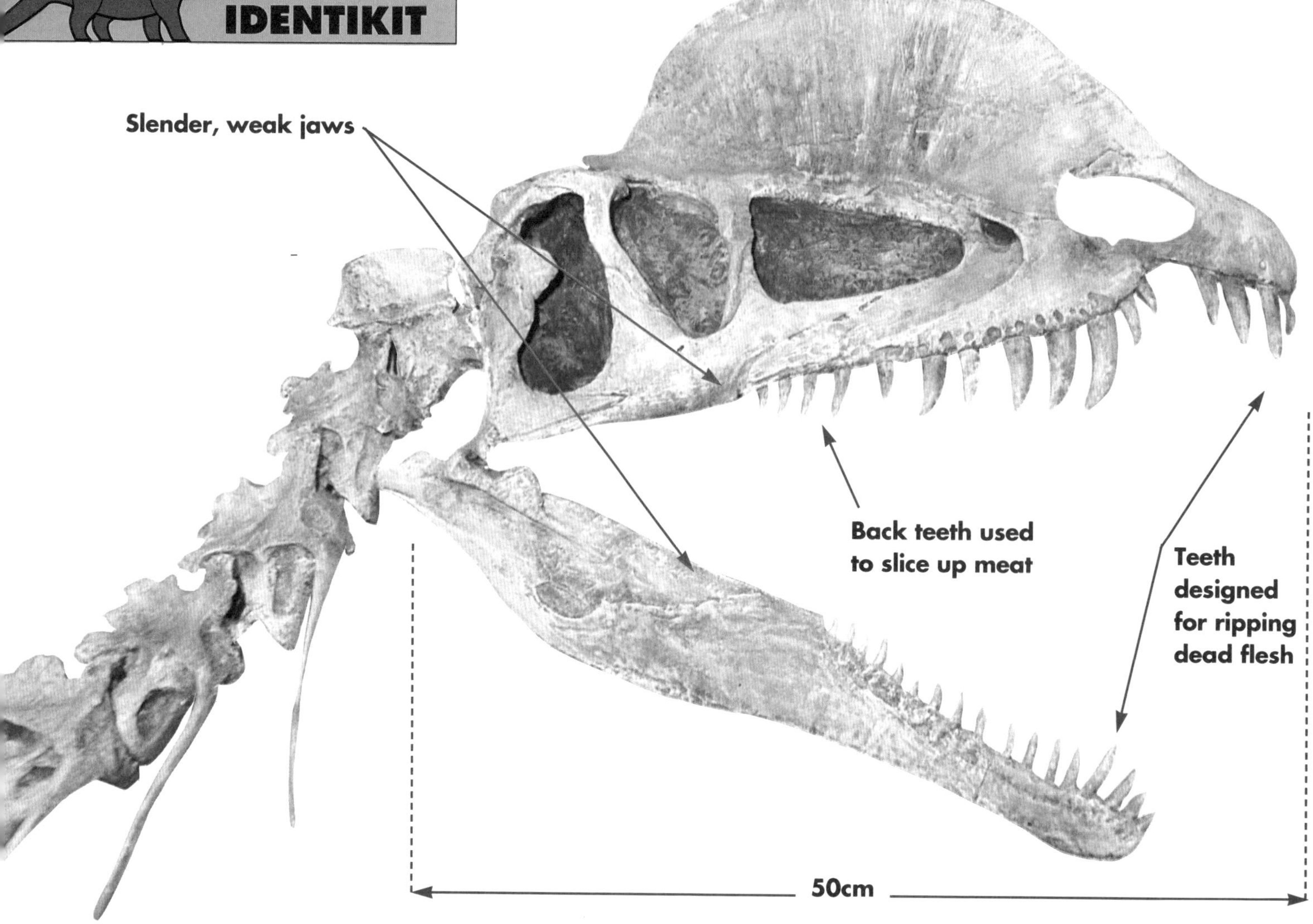

Slender, weak jaws

Back teeth used to slice up meat

Teeth designed for ripping dead flesh

50cm

MONSTER FACTS

- **NAME:** *Dilophosaurus* (die-loaf-oh-saw-rus) means 'two-ridged reptile'
- **SIZE:** 6m long
- **FOOD:** meat, possibly dead animals
- **LIVED:** 190 million years ago in the Early Jurassic Period in Arizona, USA

WEAK JAWS

Unlike the carnivorous dinosaurs that lived 40 million years later, *Dilophosaurus* had weak, slender jaws. It may have chased after smaller, plant-eating dinosaurs. But without a powerful bite *Dilophosaurus* was probably not a deadly killer like some of its relatives.

TEARING TEETH

Dilophosaurus had a lazy way of finding its dinner. Rather than using its precious energy to gallop after prey, it probably made a meal of the remains of dead dinosaurs. Long, slim teeth at the front of its jaw were perfect for tearing and plucking at carrion (dead animals). *Dilophosaurus* used its back teeth to slice and cut the meat.

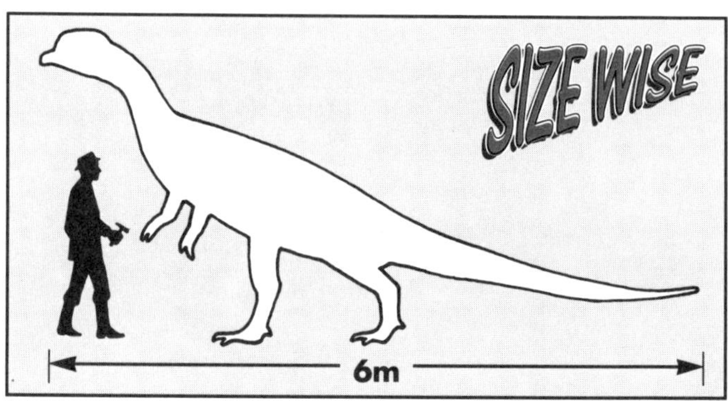

FOUR FINGERS

Dilophosaurus had short, strong arms which were quite high up on its body. On its hand were four fingers. Three of these fingers had sharp claws which were good for ripping the flesh from the bones of its already-dead prey. *Dilophosaurus* used its claws like a pair of small garden rakes to strip away meat from a carcass.

Is it true that North America has the most dinosaur exhibits?

Yes. North American museums have more dinosaur exhibits than anywhere else. For example, many of the best known dinosaurs such as *Tyrannosaurus rex*, *Stegosaurus* and *Diplodocus* were found in North America. Even today, many new, exciting finds are still discovered in the fossil beds of Canada and USA.

STRONG NECK

Dilophosaurus had many similar features to its carnosaur relatives. Its head was big in comparison to its body. Strong muscles controlled its long, flexible neck. *Dilophosaurus* was quite agile and ran along on its back legs and bird-like feet. Its tail was held above the ground to balance the weight of its body.

WATER WADER

As it wandered along through the ferns and conifers, *Dilophosaurus* left bird-like footprints. When it wanted to swim, *Dilophosaurus* probably waggled its tail and kicked with its back legs to propel itself along. Claw prints show how it gave its large body a bit of a push by touching the bottom now and again with the tip of its toes. You may have done the same when you first tried to swim!

SCELIDOSAURUS

It took a lot of detective work to discover what we know of strange, armoured *Scelidosaurus.*

In 1985 new skeletons of *Scelidosaurus* were discovered on the coast of Dorset, southern England. Added to those found in the last century, these fossils gave scientists a good idea what *Scelidosaurus* really looked like.

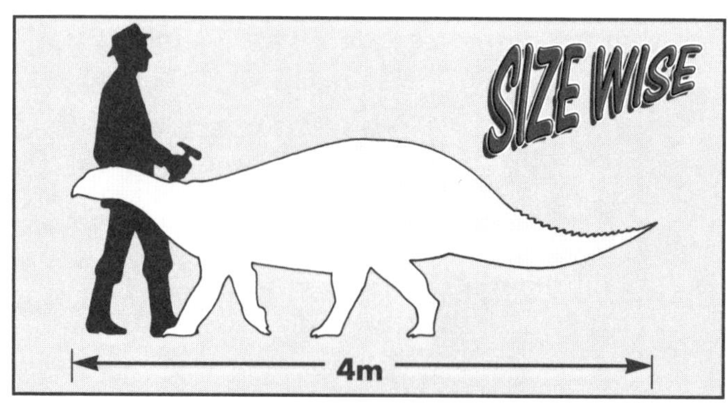

MONSTER FACTS

- **NAME:** *Scelidosaurus* (skel-ide-oh-saw-rus) means 'limb reptile'
- **SIZE:** about 4m long
- **FOOD:** plants
- **LIVED:** about 190 million years ago in the Jurassic in Arizona, USA, England and Tibet

CONES AND BUMPS

Just behind its ears *Scelidosaurus* had a cluster of three bony studs. They looked rather like fancy earrings! All along its body the dinosaur's thick skin was covered by a mosaic of rounded scales. Spaced along its back and sides, cone-shaped studs stood out to give *Scelidosaurus* extra protection from predators. If threatened, *Scelidosaurus* probably crouched down low or ran off in a rare burst of speed.

FOUR FOOTED

Scelidosaurus stomped along on four heavy legs. A short tail stuck out stiffly behind for balance. It nosed among ferns and low-lying shrubs and snipped shoots with its sharp leaf-shaped teeth.

SHUNOSAURUS

***Shunosaurus* was the first sauropod with a tail club to be discovered.**

Since 1979 more than 10 skeletons of this huge, Chinese dinosaur have been discovered.

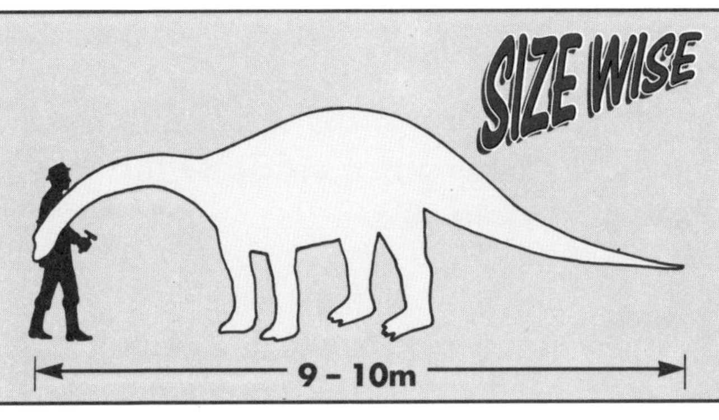

LEAF RAKER

For *Shunosaurus,* life was one long lunch. It had large, spoon-shaped teeth that it used like a curved rake. It could not reach as high as some of its larger relatives, so *Shunosaurus* probably fed on leaves from smaller trees.

MONSTER FACTS

- **NAME:** *Shunosaurus* (shoo-no-saw-rus) means 'Shu (Sichuan) reptile'
- **SIZE:** 9 – 10m long
- **FOOD:** plants
- **LIVED:** about 190 million years ago in the Jurassic Period in Sichuan Province, China

SPECIAL WEAPON

Even though they were so big, plant-eaters like *Shunosaurus* were in constant danger from predators. They had heavy bodies and moved quite slowly on pillar-like legs. However, lucky *Shunosaurus* may have had a special weapon. At the end of its long, muscular tail was a bony club. This solid lump was not in the same league as the massive tail clubs of big armour-plated dinosaurs like *Ankylosaurus.* But this powerful weapon must have dealt a nasty blow when swung from the end of *Shunosaurus'* long tail.

Fur and whiskers

Small, furry mammals waited in the wings to take centre stage when the dinosaurs died out.

Many people think that mammals suddenly appeared when the dinosaurs died out 66 million years ago. In fact, there were mammals all through the Age of the Dinosaurs.

AMONG EARLY MAMMAL GROUPS WERE:–

- **Triconodonts, (TCDs) whose teeth had three cusps (points).**

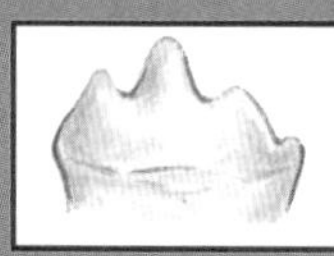

- **Multituberculates, (MTBs) whose teeth had lots of cusps.**

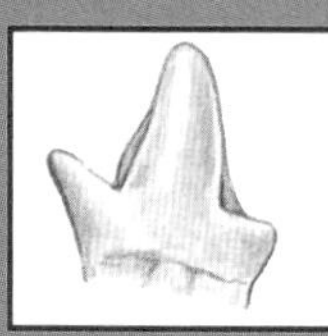

- **Pantotheres, who had teeth of different shapes and sizes.**
- **Monotremes, who sometimes had no teeth, and who are the only survivors today.**

TEETH GALORE

Early mammals had fragile bones, which left few fossils. But their hard teeth made much better fossils. Most of what we know about them comes from their teeth. Scientists even group them by their teeth!

***Morganucodon* scurried about at night catching insects. It was smaller than today's house mouse (right).**

Morganucodon

TWO SETS OF TEETH

The earliest true mammals, the triconodonts or TCDs lived over 200 million years ago. *Morganucodon* was one of them. Tiny holes in its nose bones suggest that it had whiskers. If so, it probably had fur, too. Its teeth were designed for eating insects. TCDs were mostly tiny, shrew-like animals that hid among plants catching insects and other small creatures. With fur to keep them warm, they may have been active at night, when most dinosaurs were too cold to hunt.

MTBS

During the Age of the Dinosaurs the most common mammals were the multituberculates, or MTBs. They lived on Earth for about 130 million years and only died out around 30 million years ago. This means they survived long after the dinosaurs had gone.

IT'S A FACT

THAT MAMMAL TEETH ARE COMPLICATED!

Reptiles have simple teeth. New ones grow when old ones wear out. Mammal teeth have many different patterns of cusps (points). These patterns help fossil experts identify the rare fossils of early mammals. Baby mammals suck their mother's milk, so they do not need teeth. They grow their first set of teeth just before they eat solid foods. These first teeth are replaced by adult teeth, which must last a lifetime. (So look after yours!).

Many MTBs lived in trees, like today's squirrels (left). *Kamptobaatar* (right) could run up and down tree trunks and anchor itself with its tail. It kept its young in a pouch.

SQUIRRELS AND BEAVERS

The first plant-eating mammals were MTBs. *Kamptobaatar*'s long tail could grasp branches. Some MTBs became quite large. *Taeniolabis* was beaver-sized and lived just when the dinosaurs died out.

CHISELS AND CRUSHERS

MTBs had teeth like today's rats and mice. There were long chisel-shaped teeth called incisors at the front of the mouth to gnaw tough food, then a gap, and molars with rows of points at the back of the mouth to crush food. Their jaws moved easily so they could crush leafy food well.

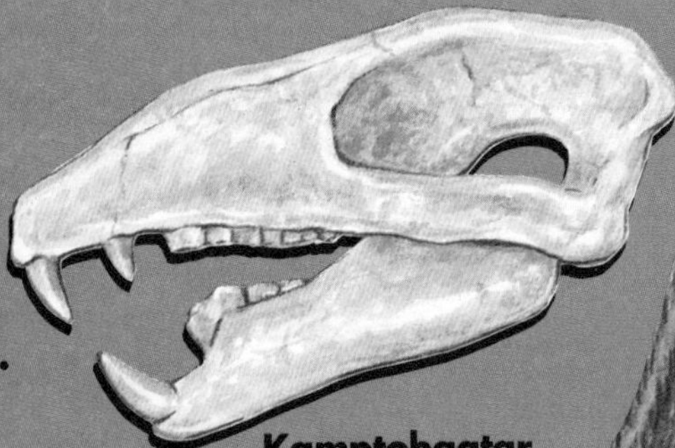

Kamptobaatar skull

Kamptobaatar

Taeniolabis

SHORTAGE OF FOSSILS

We have tonnes of fossils of the huge mammals that appeared after the dinosaurs. But fossils of mammals that lived during the Age of the Dinosaurs are scarce. This may be because the creatures themselves were rare. Or they lived and died in places where fossils did not form. Or their bones were so small and delicate that they are lost forever. Or all three.

***Crusafontia* has a modern look-alike: the tree-shrew (right) lives in South East Asia.**

Crusafontia

IN-BETWEEN ANIMALS

The strange monotremes, or egg-laying mammals, were also around in the dinosaur days. Monotremes give a glimpse of an in-between stage of evolution, because they have features of both reptiles and mammals.

FURRY EGG-LAYERS

Monotremes have fur like mammals, and the mothers make milk to feed their babies. But monotremes lay eggs like reptiles. They are not very good at keeping their blood warm. And their skeleton has many reptile-like bones. The first monotremes appeared 120 million years ago.

The echidna (left) is rare, its monotreme relatives lived 120 million years ago.

The duck-billed platypus has fur and lays eggs like its prehistoric relatives.

SOLE SURVIVORS

Today, only two types of monotreme survive on Earth. They are the duck-billed platypus and the echidna, or spiny anteater, that live in Australia.

LOW PROFILE

Another group of mammals, the pantotheres, kept a low profile during the Age of the Dinosaurs. One example is *Crusafontia*. Palaeontologists have found fossil skeletons of this small, furry animal which are almost complete – amazing for an early mammal!

FOUND DOWN A COAL MINE

These fossils are in pieces of coal from the Guimarota Mine in Portugal. They show that *Crusafontia* lived during the Late Jurassic Period, about 150 million years ago. It looked like a tree-shrew today, with large eyes and long tail, and a body about 20cm in length.

What is? A NOCTURNAL ANIMAL?

Most reptiles are diurnal, or active in the daylight. They rely on the Sun to keep them warm. In the cool of the night, they become too cold to run about, so they hide and rest. The first mammals were probably easy prey for speedy, fierce, hunting dinosaurs. So it is very likely that they were nocturnal, which means that they were active in darkness. To be nocturnal they needed several features.

- Warm blood – there was no heat from the Sun.
- Fur (hair) to keep in the body warmth.
- Extra-large hairs, called whiskers, to feel the way in the dark.
- Big eyes and sensitive ears, also to find the way in the dark.
- A relatively big brain, to cope with these new sensations and way of life.

TOWARDS MODERN MAMMALS

During the Dinosaur Age, some pantotheres quietly evolved into the small ancestors of all the modern mammals. Soon they began to flourish. *Didelphodon* was a marsupial, very like today's opossums. *Protungulatum* had hoof-like claws and lived on the ground, eating plants. *Erythrotherium* was a tree-dweller, and possibly an ancestor of monkeys, apes – and even of humans, too.

Two *Erythrotherium* cling to a tree. Although they look nothing like us they may be our ancestors.

Marsupials are animals that keep their young in a pouch. The opossum (left) lives in North America today. It has a pouch just like *Didelphodon* (bottom), one of the ancestors of modern marsupials.

Erythrotherium

Protungulatum

Didelphodon

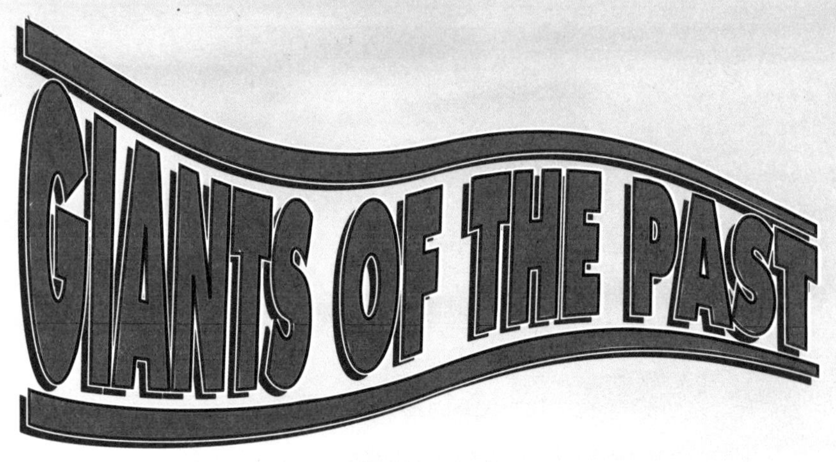

DILOPHOSAURUS

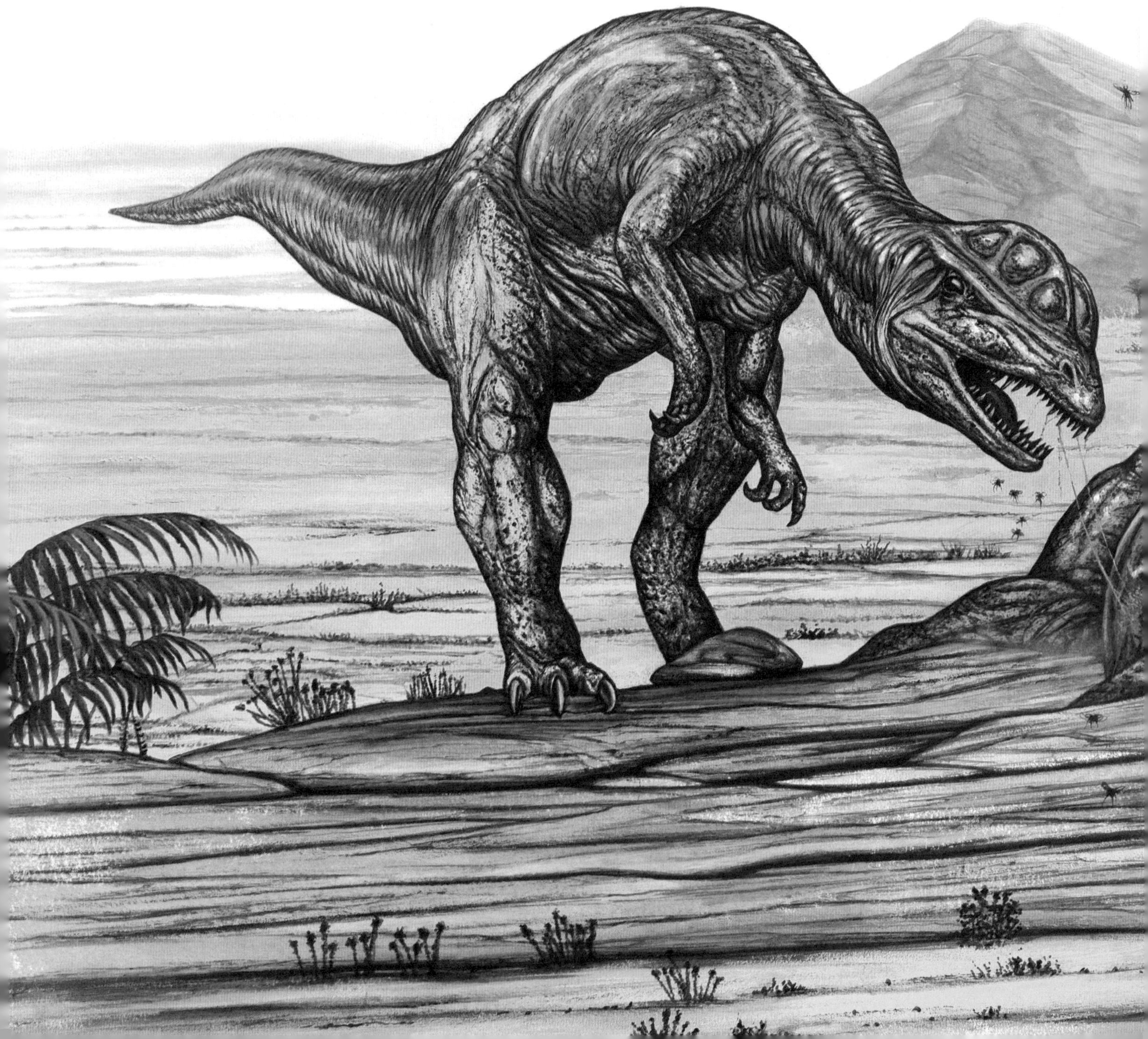

Two scavenging *Dilophosaurus* enjoy a tasty meal of leftovers. They are not natural killers, they prefer to let other dinosaurs do the hard work. A more skilled hunter has killed a huge herbivore, eaten as much as it could, then moved away. The two *Dilophosaurus* have come to feast on the carcass and pick the bones clean.

3-D Gallery

BARYONYX

• A meat-eater, named after its 'heavy-claws'
• Lived 130 million years ago in England, UK and Africa
• Measured 9.5m long
• Ate meat, possibly fish

RECORD BREAKERS

The fastest and the slowest

Imagine a dinosaur race. Which dinosaur do you think would win? Here are the fastest and slowest.

Like animals in the modern world, dinosaurs probably only went fast when they needed to. If a meat-eater spotted a likely meal it dashed off in hot pursuit. A plant-eater only needed to hurry if a predator was hot on its heels.

RUNNING AFTER DINNER

Today's animals behave in a similar way. Lions lie around for most of the day, saving their energy. But when they have to chase their dinner they sprint at top speed.

SPACED OUT

When palaeontologists find footprints they can work out roughly what speed the dinosaur was travelling. If the tracks are close together the dinosaur was probably walking along quite slowly. If the footprints are widely spaced, it is likely that the dinosaur was running.

A medium-sized theropod's top speed was 45 km/h. It walked at a much slower pace.

Struthiomimus **(centre) could run at 50 km/h.**

In 1988, Olympic sprinter Carl Lewis, ran at 43.37 km/h.

Brachiosaurus **(4 – 6 km/h walking), last across the finishing line.**

Human (5 – 6 km/h walking)

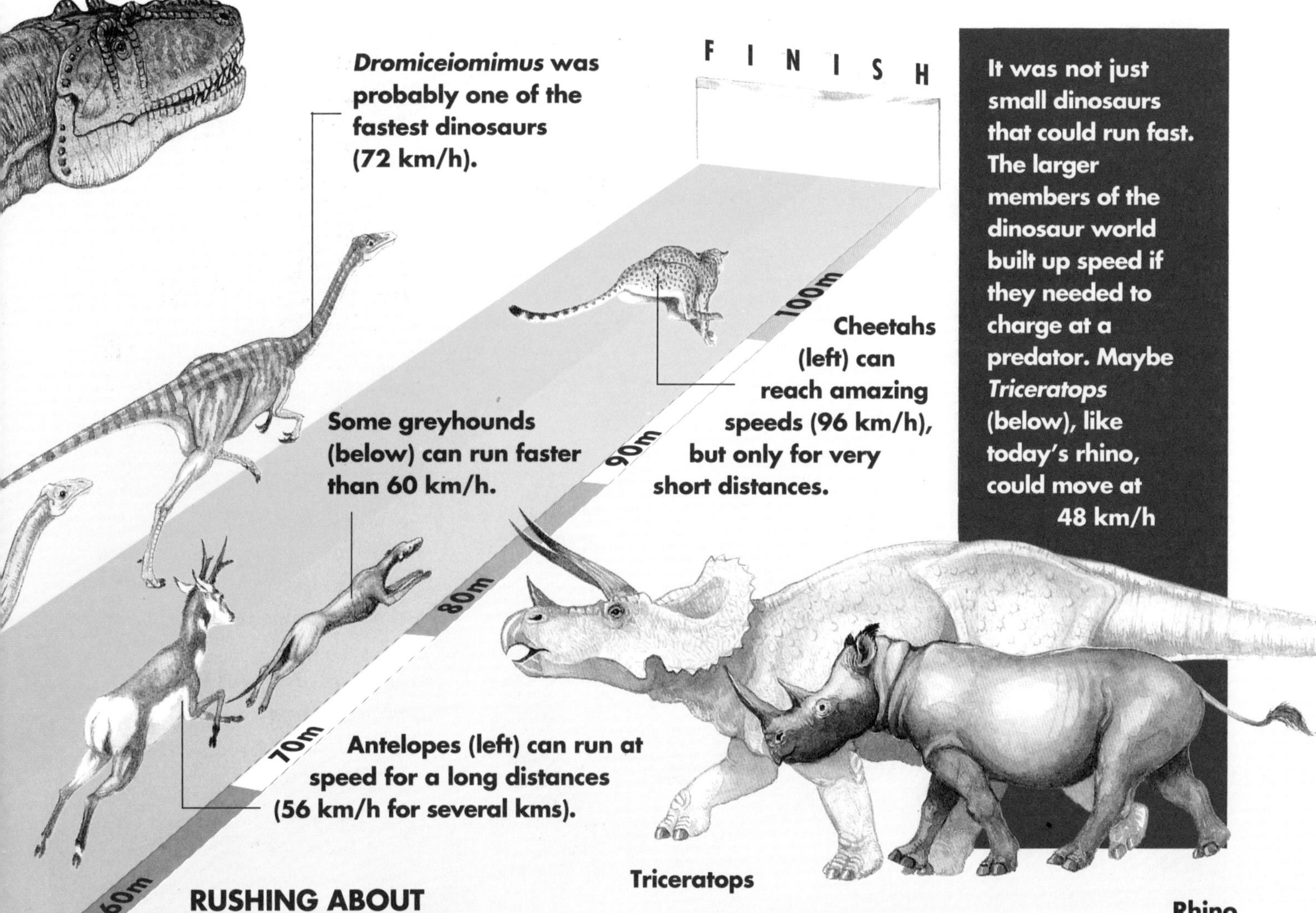

Dromiceiomimus **was probably one of the fastest dinosaurs (72 km/h).**

Cheetahs (left) can reach amazing speeds (96 km/h), but only for very short distances.

Some greyhounds (below) can run faster than 60 km/h.

Antelopes (left) can run at speed for a long distances (56 km/h for several kms).

It was not just small dinosaurs that could run fast. The larger members of the dinosaur world built up speed if they needed to charge at a predator. Maybe *Triceratops* (below), like today's rhino, could move at 48 km/h

Triceratops

Rhino

RUSHING ABOUT

Once they have worked out the dinosaur's speed, scientists are faced with a tricky problem. Was the dinosaur moving at an average speed or was it going at full pelt? *Dromiceiomimus* is known to have gone at a lightning 72 km/h sometimes, but it is very unlikely that it dashed about at this speed all day! Its walking pace must have been much slower.

Large cats, like a lioness (left), dash after their prey. A medium-sized theropod, such as *Ceratosaurus*, may have done the same, but for most of the time it moved at a much slower pace.

I SAY, I SAY, I SAY!

What's the difference between an ostrich and a greyhound? Obviously, one's a bird and one's a dog, but they do have some things in common too. They both have quite light bodies, relatively long legs and they are excellent runners. *Struthiomimius*, one of the fastest dinosaurs, also had long, muscular legs and a light body.

LARGE, BUT LIVELY

Triceratops certainly did not have a streamlined, agile body. But with its good acceleration it could suddenly speed up to charge at its enemies. Unlike sauropods, whose straight pillar-like legs had to support their massive weight, horned dinosaurs had quite flexible legs that allowed them to charge.

Dinosaur descendants

Which of today's animals can claim to be the dinosaurs' closest living relatives?

How do you tell which kind of modern animal is related to a dinosaur? It's not easy. Some creatures may look a bit like dinosaurs, but that is not enough. To be a real relative, their bones have to be similar and they have to behave in the same sort of way as well.

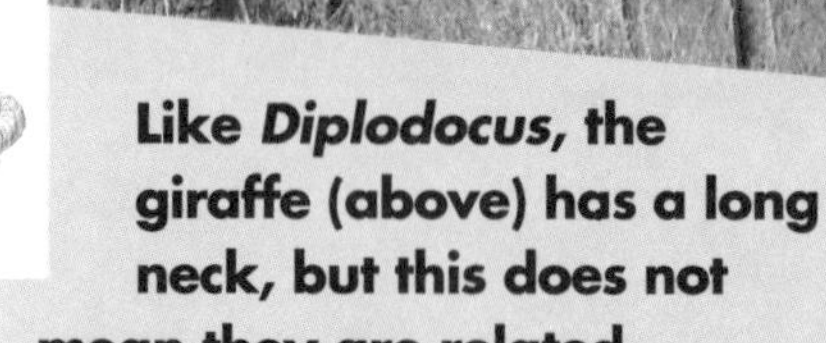

Like *Diplodocus*, the giraffe (above) has a long neck, but this does not mean they are related.

***Ankylosaurus* and today's armadillo have armour-plating, but aren't cousins.**

LOOK-ALIKES

Each of these three animals looks, or behaves in the same way as certain dinosaurs.

- A giraffe uses its long neck to eat from tree tops, like *Diplodocus*.
- An armadillo is protected by bony armour in the same way as *Ankylosaurus*.
- A rhinoceros looks like *Triceratops*, with its big stocky body and nose horn. Could they be related? None of these animals is related to dinosaurs. Giraffes, rhinos and armadillos are mammals. They are warm-blooded and they give birth to live babies. They come from a completely different animal family. Dinosaurs were reptiles. They were probably 'cold-blooded' and they laid eggs. So are today's reptiles the descendants of dinosaurs?

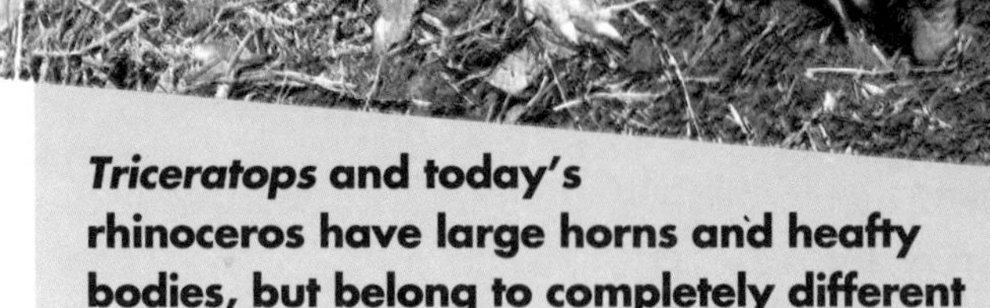

***Triceratops* and today's rhinoceros have large horns and heafty bodies, but belong to completely different animal families.**

NAMESAKE

Lizards are reptiles, but although the dinosaur *Iguanodon* was named after a modern lizard, the iguana, these reptiles are not descended from dinosaurs.

Iguana

ALL ALONE

The strange-looking tuatara from New Zealand is the only surviving member of one group of reptiles from the Age of the Dinosaurs. Tuataras have looked like this for 130 million years. They look a bit like mini-dinosaurs, but their bodies are different. They are not the dinosaurs' closest living relative.

Tuatara

Leopard tortoise

RULING REPTILES

The dinosaurs belonged to a major group of reptiles known as the archosaurs or 'ruling reptiles'. Crocodiles lived in the Age of the Dinosaurs. They were also descended from the archosaurs but they formed a different group from the dinosaurs. At one time, crocodiles were thought to be the dinosaurs' closest living relatives. But experts now think a much more unlikely creature is the true descendant of the dinosaurs........

Crocodiles have scaly skin like dinosaurs, but they are only very distant relatives.

TURTLES, TORTOISES AND TERRAPINS

These hard-shelled creatures are all members of another group of reptiles. Their groups survived when the dinosaurs died out. These reptiles still look more or less the same as they did 150 million years ago, when the dinosaurs were still alive. But they are not closely related to dinosaurs, they are a different branch of the family tree.

COO-ER! IS THIS WHAT THE DINOSAURS HAVE BECOME?

It is hard to believe that a fluffy pigeon could have anything in common with a dinosaur. But it does. Many scientists believe that birds are the closest living relatives of the dinosaurs. The bones in the legs of a modern pigeon are arranged in a very similar way to those in the legs of meat-eating dinosaurs, such as *Deinonychus* and *Compsognathus.* Because of this, experts think the pigeon could have evolved from those dinosaurs.

BIRDS AND BEASTS

Birds may look very different from reptiles. But they do have some very important things in common. Birds have scales on their legs. They also lay shelled eggs like reptiles. Because of these things, experts think birds and reptiles must be related.

BIRD MIMICS

Certain types of dinosaurs, such as *Struthiomimus,* looked so much like birds, they are called 'bird mimics'. *Struthiomimus* means 'ostrich mimic' because it looked rather like, and probably ran as fast as, today's ostriches.

EARLY BIRD

Archaeopteryx is the earliest known bird. It lived 150 million years ago and could be the link between dinosaurs and today's birds. It looked very like a reptile with pointed teeth, claws and long bony tail. More importantly, its hip bones, arms and leg bones were almost identical to those of *Compsognathus.* So dinosaurs might have evolved through *Archaeopteryx* into birds.

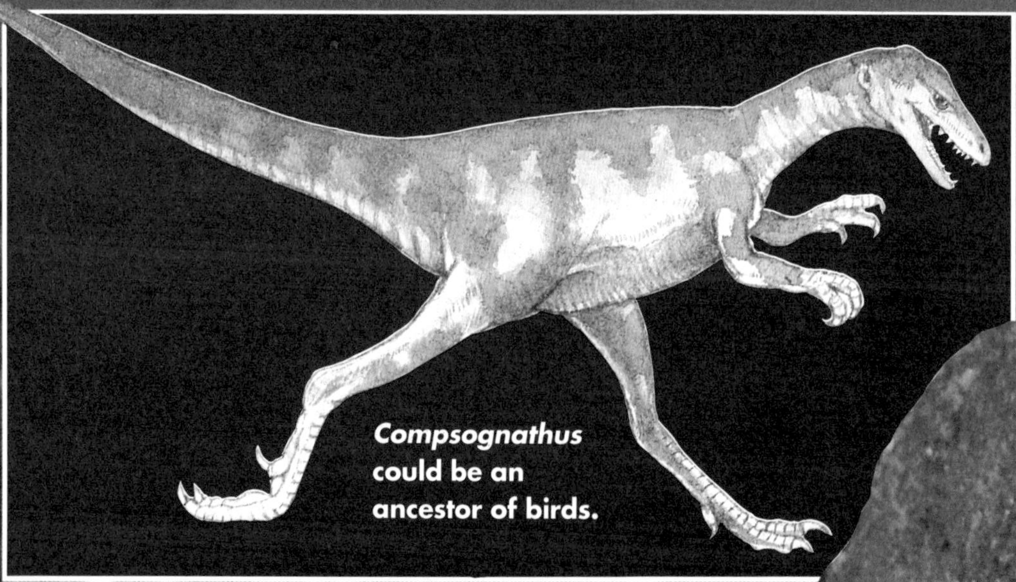

Compsognathus **could be an ancestor of birds.**

CLAW WINGS

This hoatzin bird (left) looks rather like *Archaeopteryx*. The hoatzin bird lives in the forests of South America today. Young hoatzin birds have claws on their wings, like *Archaeopteryx* did. They use them to climb up trees.

The hoatzin bird (above) and the pigeon (left) are probably true dinosaur descendants. They are related to ancient *Archaeopteryx* (right) which scientists believe to be descended from the dinosaurs.

The pigeon that you feed in the park is probably one of the dinosaurs' closest living relatives.

IT'S A FACT

THIS BIRD COULD NOT FLY

Archaeopteryx could not fly very well. It probably used its feathered arms, or 'wings', to make short, fluttering jumps upwards to catch insects.

49
3-D Gallery
MAIASAURA

A peaceful evening in the Late Cretaceous Period is disrupted by a sudden volcanic eruption. Gripped by fear, a *Maiasaura* herd stampedes through its nesting site, desperate to escape the spew of burning, molten lava.

Why did Brachiosaurus have such large nostrils?

At one time, scientists thought that *Brachiosaurus* may have spent some time in water and used its nostrils like a snorkel. But *Brachiosaurus* probably spent most of its time on land and used its huge nostrils to control its body temperature. *Brachiosaurus* would puff air in and out through its nostrils which would have helped to cool the blood in its head very effectively.

How did Stegosaurus protect itself from its enemies?

Stegosaurus protected itself with its tail. It swung its very spiky tail at its enemies. The swinging, spiked tail must have made it very difficult for an enemy to get near to *Stegosaurus*. If it did the spikes would have given it terrible injuries!

What subjects do I need to study at school to become a palaeontologist?

To be a palaeontologist you will need to study science at school. At university you will need to study biology or geology (or both together if that is possible). Choose a department that has a person who teaches palaeontology. From then on it is a matter of getting a good degree in your subject. After that you'll need to apply to a university to do research in an area of palaeontology that interests you. You could do this part of your study in your home country or go abroad.

Did baby dinosaurs bite?

Yes, most definitely! Even baby dinosaurs, like *Tyrannosaurus rex* young, had very sharp teeth and would not hesitate to bite anything.

Picture Credits:
American Museum of Natural History: 346(L),
Ardea: 349(TL), 368(BL)
Argentine Museum of Natural Sciences: 222(B).
Sue Baker: 60-63,
Robert Harding Picture Library: 344(T, L)
Institut Royal des Sciences Naturelles, Brussels: 217(T), 237(T)
Mirror Syndication: 294(B)
Natural History Museum London: 2(T), 7, 9(7), 18(T), 19, 24(T), 46(T), 68, 82(T), 83, 84, 85, 90(T), 112(T), 113(T), 134(T), 170(T,BL), 171, 178(T), 184(T), 190(T), 191(T), 192(T), 193, 202(B), 203(B), 204(T), 213(T), 214(BR, BL), 215, 217(B), 225(B), 229(T), 234(background) 236, 238/239, 244, 252/253, 256, 266(T), 271(B), 278, 283(insets), 289, 295(T), 322(T), 324(bkg), 325, 345(R, 1 & 2), 347(BR), 354(T), 355(TR), 358(C), 371(BR), 376(T), 388(T),
NHPA: 8(2), 17(T), 25(T), 135, 148, 149(T), 150, 151(B), 157(T), 170(BR), 183(B), 194(T), 237(B), 257, 272(T, BL), 273(C), 279(TR), 332(B), 337(CL), 349(CR), 358(T), 359(BR), 360(T), 366(TC), 367(BR), 369(TR), 381(TL, CL, B), 383(CR), 403(T), 405(TR, CR, BR), 413(TR, CR), 415(B), 424©, 425(TC), 426(TR, B), 427(CL), 434(R1, R6), 435(TL, TR, CL), 436Æ, 437(TL).
Dr. David Norman: 200(T), 201(T), 214(T), 310(B),
Oxford Scientific Films: 195(B), 271(T), 238(B), 347(TR), 355(CL), 371(CL),.404(L).
Oxford University Museum: 16 (R)
Pinsharp 3-D Graphics: 10/11, 20/21, 34/35, 42,/43, 56/57, 64/65, 76/77, 86/87, 100/101, 108/109, 122/123, 130/131, 144/145, 152/153, 166/167, 174/175, 188/189, 196/197, 210/211, 218/219, 232/233, 240/241, 254/255, 276/277, 298/299, 320/321, 342/343, 364/365, 386/387, 408/409, 430/431,.
Planet Earth: 283(CR), 349(BR), 361(BL), 370(T,BL), 435(BR).
Museum of the Rockies: 172(B), 194(B)
Royal Ontario Museum, Toronto: 398(T).
Royal Tyrell Museum/Alberta Community Development:
Science Photo Library/John Mead: 47(T)
W. Szarynski/Institute of Paleobiology, Warsaw: 282(B), 390.
Zefa: 8(1), 15(CR), 16(BL), 345(R, 3), 434(R3)

Artwork:
Hamesh Alles: 38/39, 40/41
Graham Berry: 344(BR), 345 (T, B), 375, 377, 384/385, 424(BL), 425(B), 426(CR), 427.
Black Hat: 222(T), 268(T), 288(T), 290(T), 291(T), 301(L), 310(T), 312(T), 313(T), 333(T), 334(T), 335(T), 336, 337(T, B), 338/339, 354(B), 356(T), 378(T), 389(R2),398(B), 400(T), 401(T).
Black Hat /Paul Mitchell: 48(T), 180(T), 181(T),
Black Hat/ Richard Prideaux: 50/51,
Black Hat/ Jane Spenser 52/53
Robin Carter: 402, 403, 404, 405415(CR).
Chris Christoferou: 269,
Mike Dorey: 102/103, 124/125, 146/147, 168/169, 190, 212, 213(B), 235, 300, 324(B),
John Frances: 331, 332(T), 333(B), 340/341, 355(B), 362/363,
Una Fricker: 378
Lee Gibbons: 406/407, 410/411.
Tony Gibbons: 45, 47(B), 54/55, 89, 91(B), 98/99, 104/105, 106/107, 111, 113(B), 120/121, 149(B), 151(T),
Grisewood & Dempsey/Garden Studio: 229(B)
Ryz Hajdul: 397, 399.
Kingfisher: 2(B), 3, 4(T), 5(T), 8(3), 9, 14, 15, 17(B), 24,(B), 25(B), 26(T), 27(T), 44, 28, 29, 30, 31, 36, 37, 49(T), 58/59, 68(B), 70(T), 71(T), 80, 91(T), 92(T), 93(t), 112(B), 114/115, 134(B), 136, 137(T), 156(B), 158, 159(T), 160(C,B), 161, 178(B), 179, 184(B), 195(T), 202(T), 203(T), 204(B), 205, 213(C), 224(B), 225(T), 245(B), 246(T), 247(T), 266(B), 268(B), 389(R1, R3), 420(B), 422(T), 423(T), 434(R2, R3), 436(BL)437Æ.
Neil Lloyd: 1, 4(B), 5(B), 12, 23, 26(B), 27(B), 32/33, 67, 69, 78/79, 126/127, 128/129, 133, 135(B), 142/143, 160(T), 162/163, 177, 186/187, 199, 201(B), 208/209, 221, 223, 230/231, 243, 279(BL), 287, 288(B), 296/297, 309, 311, 318/319, 392/393, 421, 423(B), 428/429, 434(R5).
Deidre McHale: 22, 44, 66, 88, 110, 132, 154, 176, 198, 220, 242, 264, 286, 308, 330, 352, 374, 396, 418, 440.
Deborah Mansfield: 156(T), 192(B), 270, 272(BR), 273(T), 304/305,
Robert Morton: 290(B), 334(B),
Natural History Museum, London/John Sibbick: 234(L), 247(B), 248/249, 250/251, 259, 265, 267(B), 274/275, 280/281, 291(R), 302/303, 312(B), 313(B), 314-317, 353, 356(B), 366(TL, BL), 367(TL, CL, CR), 400(B), 401(B), 419, 422(B),
Russel Pearman: 6
Clive Prtichard: 412, 413, 414.
Andrew Robinson: 159(B), 258, 260/261, 279(BR),
Graham Rosewarne: 48(B), 49(B), 70(B), 71(B), 81, 82(B), 92(B), 93(B), 137(B), 155, 157(B), 164/165, 172(T), 173, 180(B), 181(B), 182, 185, 234,(R), 246(B), 267(L), 322(B), 323, 357(B), 358(B), 360(B), 380, 381(T), 382, 432/433.
Bernard Thornton Artists/ Tim Hayward: 72-75, 94-97, 116-119, 138-141, 206/207, 226/227, 228(B), 292/293, 294(T), 326/327, 346(R), 348, 368, 370(CR), 371(T),.
Steve Weston: 335(B), 379(B), 388, 389(TR, R4),.
Steve White: 262/263, 284/285, 306/307, 328/329, 350/351, 372/373, 394/395, 416/417, 438/439.